Democracy and the Rule of Law in Classical Athens

This volume brings together essays on Athenian Law by Edward M. Harris, who challenges much of the recent scholarship on this topic. Presenting a balanced analysis of the legal system in ancient Athens, Harris stresses the importance of substantive issues and their contribution to our understanding of different types of legal procedures. He combines careful philological analysis with close attention to the political and social contexts of individual statutes. Collectively, the essays in this volume examine the relationship between law and politics, the nature of the economy, the position of women, and the role of the legal system in Athenian society. They also show that the Athenians were more sophisticated in their approach to legal issues than has been assumed in the modern scholarship on this topic. At the same time, several of the studies warn against importing anachronistic ideas into the analysis of Athenian Law.

Edward M. Harris is Professor of Classics and Ancient History at the University of Durham. A scholar of Athenian Law, economy, and social history, he is the author of *Aeschines and Athenian Politics* and coeditor (with Lene Rubinstein) of *The Law and the Courts in Ancient Greece.*

DEMOCRACY AND THE RULE OF LAW IN CLASSICAL ATHENS

Essays on Law, Society, and Politics

Edward M. Harris
UNIVERSITY OF DURHAM

CAMBRIDGE
UNIVERSITY PRESS

CAMBRIDGE UNIVERSITY PRESS
Cambridge, New York, Melbourne, Madrid, Cape Town, Singapore, São Paulo, Delhi

Cambridge University Press
32 Avenue of the Americas, New York, NY 10013-2473, USA

www.cambridge.org
Information on this title:www.cambridge.org/9780521852791

First published 2006
Reprinted 2007

Printed in the United States of America

A catalog record for this book is available from the British Library.

Library of Congress Cataloging in Publication Data

Harris, Edward Monroe.
Democracy and the rule of law in classical Athens : essays on law, society, and politics / Edward M. Harris.
p. cm.
Includes bibliographical references and index.
ISBN 0-521-85279-x (hardback)
1. Constitutional history – Greece – Athens. 2. Rule of law – Greece – Athens – History.
3. Democracy – Greece – Athens – History. 4. Law, Greek. I. Title.
KL4361.32.A75H37 2006
340.5′38 – dc22 2005029329

ISBN 978-0-521-85279-1 hardback

To Arielle

Contents

Preface

SEVERAL YEARS AGO COREY BRENNAN SUGGESTED THAT I COLLECT A NUMBER OF my essays on Athenian Law and publish them in a single volume. With his encouragement, I submitted a proposal to Cambridge University Press, which agreed to publish this volume. I have not included every article that I have published on the subject of Athenian Law, but only those that fall into one of four general categories: Constitutional Law, Law and Economy, Law and the Family, and Aspects of Procedure. In general, these essays focus on specific laws and legal procedures and attempt to place them in their political, social, and economic contexts. They therefore pay less attention to the ways in which the Athenians interpreted, applied, and enforced the law in their courts. This topic will be the subject of another book on *The Rule of Law in Action: The Nature of Litigation in Classical Athens.* Aside from a few minor stylistic changes, I have not revised the essays. I have tried to take account of recent work on Athenian Law in the sections entitled "Afterthoughts" that follow most of the essays.

I am writing these words at the University of Durham in the United Kingdom, but the work on these essays was done while I was a member of the Department of Classics at Brooklyn College and the Graduate School of the City University of New York. I could never have done this work without the encouragement and support of my former colleagues in New York, for which I am deeply grateful. I wish to express my thanks to Dee Clayman, Roger Dunkle, Hardy Hansen, Ellen Koven, Gail Smith, Philip Thibodeau, John van Sickle, Craig Williams, Donna Wilson, Howard Wolman, and Peter Zaneteas.

Several scholars who helped me by reading over drafts of these essays and offering advice are thanked in the notes, but I would like to single out two people who were especially supportive during the past decade: Fred Naiden and Lene Rubinstein.

I have been very fortunate to work with Beatrice Rehl at Cambridge University Press, Katie Greczylo at TechBooks, and Brian Bowles. I deeply appreciate their kindness, efficiency, and patience. This volume has also benefited from the perceptive comments of the two anonymous readers for the Press.

The work on this book was completed while I was an NEH Fellow at the American School of Classical Studies in Athens. I would like to thank the NEH for its support and Steven Tracy, the Director of the School, and his staff for making my stay in Athens both productive and enjoyable.

I would also like to express my gratitude to my family for their support and understanding over the past two decades.

My interest in law has been part of a family tradition: my great-grandfather and grandfather on my mother's side were lawyers, and my father was General Counsel at Pitney Bowes until his retirement in 1988. I think there was an expectation that I too would go to law school, but something seems to have gone wrong, and I ended up teaching Classics and Ancient History. But the family tradition persists: my daughter is now studying to become a lawyer. This book is dedicated to her.

Durham, November 2005

Acknowledgments

I.1) "Solon and the Spirit of the Law in Archaic and Classical Greece" was originally published in J. Blok and A. Lardinois, eds. *Solon of Athens: New Historical and Philological Approaches*. Leiden: Brill, 2006.

I.2) "Pericles' Praise of Athenian Democracy" was originally published in *Harvard Studies in Classical Philology* 94 (1992) 57–67.

I.3) "Antigone the Lawyer, or the Ambiguities of *Nomos*" was originally published in E. M. Harris and L. Rubinstein, eds. *The Law and the Courts in Ancient Greece*. London: Duckworth, 2004: 19–56.

I.4) "How Often Did the Athenian Assembly Meet?" was originally published in *Classical Quarterly* 36 (1986) 363–77.

I.5) "When Did the Athenian Assembly Meet? Some New Evidence" was originally published in *American Journal of Philology* 112 (1991) 329–45.

I.6) "Demosthenes and the Theoric Fund" was originally published in R. Wallace and E. M. Harris, eds. *Transitions to Empire: Essays in Greco-Roman History, 360–146 B.C. in Honor of E. Badian*. University of Oklahoma Press: Norman, OK, and London, 1996: 57–76.

II.1) "Law and Economy in Classical Athens: [Demosthenes] *Against Dionysodorus*" was originally published at the Web site www.stoa.org/projects/demos/home.

II.2) "When Is a Sale Not a Sale? The Riddle of Athenian Terminology for Real Security Revisited" was originally published in *Classical Quarterly* 38 (1988) 351–81.

II.3) "*Apotimema*: Athenian Terminology for Real Security in Leases and Dowry Arrangements" was originally published in *Classical Quarterly* 43 (1993) 73–95.

II.4) "The Liability of Business Partners in Athenian Law" was originally published in *Classical Quarterly* 39 (1989) 339–43.

II.5) "Did Solon Abolish Debt-Bondage?" was originally published in *Classical Quarterly* 52 (2002) 415–30.

II.6) "Notes on a Lead Letter from the Athenian Agora" is to be published in *Harvard Studies in Classical Philology* 102 (forthcoming).

III.1) "Did the Athenians Regard Seduction as a Worse Crime than Rape?" was originally published in *Classical Quarterly* 40 (1990) 370–7.

III.2) "Did Rape Exist in Classical Athens? Further Reflections on the Laws about Sexual Violence" was originally published in *DIKE* 7 (2004) 41–83.

III.3A) "Women and Lending in Athenian Society: A *Horos* Re-Examined" was originally published in *Phoenix* 4 (1992) 309–21.

III.3B) "Notes on a *Horos* from the Athenian Agora" was originally published in *Zeitschrift für Papyrologie und Epigraphik* 131 (2000) 101–5.

III.4) "The Date of Apollodorus' Speech against Timotheus and Its Implications for Athenian History and Legal Procedure" was originally published in *American Journal of Philology* 109 (1988) 44–52.

III.5) "A Note on Adoption and Deme Registration" was originally published in *Tyche* 11 (1996) 123–7.

IV.1) "'In the Act' or 'Red-Handed'? *Apagoge* to the Eleven and *Furtum Manifestum*" was originally published in G. Thür, ed. *Symposion 1993: Vorträge zur griechischen und hellenistischen Rechtsgeschichte.* Boehlau: Cologne, Weimar, and Vienna, 1994: 129–46.

IV.2) "How to Kill in Attic Greek: The Semantics of the Verb (ἀπο)κτείνειν and Their Implications for Athenian Homicide Law" was originally published in E. Cantarella and G. Thür, eds. *Symposion 1997: Vorträge zur griechischen und hellenistischen Rechtsgeschichte.* Boehlau: Cologne, Weimar, and Vienna, 2001: 75–88.

IV.3) "The Penalty for Frivolous Prosecution in Athenian Law" was originally published in *DIKE* 2 (1999) 123–42.

V.1) "Pheidippides the Legislator: A Note on Aristophanes' *Clouds*" was originally published in *Zeitschrift für Papyrologie und Epigraphik* 140 (2002) 3–5.

I would like to thank the publishers of these books and journals for permission to reprint these essays in the present volume.

Abbreviations

AESCHIN.	Aeschines
AESCHYLUS	Aeschylus
EUM.	*Eumenides*
PR.	*Prometheus Bound*
SUPPL.	*Supplices*
AND.	Andocides
AR.	Aristophanes
ACH.	*Acharnenses*
AV.	*Aves*
EC.	*Ecclesiazousai*
EQ.	*Equites*
LYS.	*Lysistrata*
NUB.	*Nubes*
PL.	*Ploutos*
RAN.	*Ranae*
TH.	*Thesmophoriazousai*
VESP.	*Vespae*
ARIST.	Aristotle
ATH. POL.	*Constitution of the Athenians*
NE	*Nicomachean Ethics*
RHET.	*Rhetoric*
POL.	*Politics*
DEM.	Demosthenes
DIN.	Dinarchus
D. H.	Dionysius of Halicarnassus
AMM.	*Letter to Ammaeus*
D. S.	Diodorus Siculus
EUR.	Euripides
HIPP.	*Hippolytus*
IT	*Iphigenia among the Taurians*
HARP.	Harpocration

HDT.	Herodotus
HOM.	Homer
IL.	*Iliad*
OD.	*Odyssey*
HYP.	Hyperides
ATH.	*Against Athenogenes*
DEM.	*Against Demosthenes*
EUX.	*Against Euxenippus*
IS.	Isaeus
ISOCR.	Isocrates
LYCURGUS	Lycurgus
LEOCR.	*Against Leocrates*
LYS.	Lysias
MEN.	Menander
PAUS.	Pausanias
PL.	Plato
AP.	*Apology of Socrates*
LG.	*Laws*
POL.	*Politicus*
R.	*Republic*
PLB.	Polybius
PLU.	Plutarch
DEM.	*Demosthenes*
MOR.	*Moralia*
TH.	Thucydides
XEN.	Xenophon
ATH. POL.	*Constitution of the Athenians*
CYR.	*Cyropaedia*
HELL.	*Hellenica*
LAC. POL.	*Constitution of the Spartans*
MEM.	*Memorabilia*
BGU	*Aegyptische Urkunden aus den königlichen Museen zu Berlin. Griechische Urkunden*. Berlin 1895–.
FGRHIST	F. Jacoby, *Die Fragmente der griechischen Historiker*. Leiden 1957–.
ICRET	M. Guarducci, *Inscriptiones Creticae* I–IV. Rome 1935–50.

IERYTHRAI	H. Engelmann and R. Merkelbach, *Die Inschriften von Erythrai und Klazomenai*. Bonn 1972.
IG i[3]	D. M. Lewis, L. Jeffery, and E. Erxleben, *Inscriptiones Atticae Euclidis anno anteriores.*[3] Berlin 1981–98.
IG	*Inscriptiones Graecae*. For bibliographical details see L-S-J p. xlii.
LIMC	*Lexicon Iconographicum Mythologiae Classicae*, Zürich and Munich 1981–99.
L-S-J	Liddell/Scott/Jones, *A Greek-English Lexicon.*[9] Oxford 1940.
P. OXY.	*Oxyrhynchus Papyri*. London 1898–.
SEG	*Supplementum Epigraphicum Graecum.*
SIG[3]	W. Dittenberger, *Sylloge Inscriptionum Graecarum*. Leipzig 1915.

Introduction

THIS VOLUME BRINGS TOGETHER ESSAYS THAT I HAVE PUBLISHED ON ATHENIAN LAW over the past two decades. As a whole, I believe the essays contribute not only to our understanding of Athenian Law, but also to the study of the constitutional history of democratic Athens, the nature of the Athenian economy, and the position of women in Athenian society. The essays are also unified in terms of their method. In contrast to much recent work that emphasizes questions of procedure, these essays turn our attention to the substantive aspects of Athenian Law. This approach places greater stress on careful philological analysis of key terms in statutes as well as a more sophisticated awareness of legal issues. Many modern scholars give the Athenian legal system low marks and compare it unfavorably with Roman Law. These essays aim in part to show that the Athenians were more sophisticated in legal matters than many have assumed. On the other hand, one should not exaggerate the level of development attained by Athenian Law. Several of the essays therefore warn against importing anachronistic ideas (e.g., Roman ideas about real security, the notion of corporation, the concept of rape, and the modern distinction between larceny and embezzlement) into the study of Athenian Law.

But these essays do not concentrate exclusively on the minutiae of individual statutes or on narrow technical questions. Many of the essays attempt to place Athenian laws in their broader political, economic, and social context. The essays in the first section on "Law and Constitutional History" examine the laws of Athens in the light of Athenian ideas about the role of law in preventing tyranny and about the relationship between the rule of law and democracy. The essays in the second section on "Law and Economy" show how the Athenians developed the legal infrastructure needed to support the growth of formal credit relations, which formed the basis of a rudimentary market economy. As a whole, the essays of this section question assumptions held by several scholars about the "primitive" nature of the Athenian economy. Several of the essays in the third section concerning "Law and the Family" deal with the question of women's agency in Athenian society. The first two essays examine not only the legal procedures that could be used in cases of sexual violence, but also how social attitudes about women shaped these statutes and the way that they were enforced. Another pair of essays in this section look at the restrictions on women's financial activities and to what extent they actually limited women's role in economic decisions. The essays in the fourth section on "Aspects of Procedure" challenge a recent view that the Athenian legal system did not aim to provide a set of substantive norms but only to provide an arena for citizens (primarily rich and powerful ones) to pursue private feuds. The first two essays demonstrate the importance of analyzing the substantive aspect of Athenian laws and show how the substantive differences shape their procedural aspect. The last essay in this section shows that the Athenians had serious reservations about citizens who abused the legal system to pursue private vendettas and established severe penalties for those who did so.

I. LAW AND CONSTITUTIONAL HISTORY

Several scholars have assumed that the Greeks in general and the Athenians in particular considered popular rule incompatible with *eunomia* or "the rule of law." For instance, Ostwald (1986) and Hansen (1974) argue that the Athenians upheld the doctrine of popular sovereignty in the fifth century BCE, but after the Peloponnesian War they abandoned this ideal and upheld the sovereignty of law. Ober (1989), on the other hand, thinks that the rule of law was an oligarchic slogan promoted by conservative philosophers like Aristotle and was contrary to democratic ideology. Yet Sealey (1987) claims that the Athenians never aimed at achieving democracy, but instead tried to achieve a republic ruled by law.

Several of the essays in this section question the assumption held by these scholars that the Athenians found democracy and the rule of law antithetical. They show in part that the Athenians believed that the two ideals went hand in hand, with each supporting the aims of the other. The first two essays show how the Athenians sought to achieve the rule of law by dividing the functions of government and by creating a system of checks and balances. The essay on *Antigone* turns to the question of the sources of legitimacy and the relationship between law and religion in democratic Athens and studies the figure of the tyrant, the man who is the antithesis of the rule of law. The final essay shows how the Athenians used the laws about ownership and the distribution of public funds to balance the differing interests of the rich and the poor and promoted a democratic ideal of social harmony between classes.

The first essay on "Solon and the Spirit of the Law in Archaic and Classical Greece" analyzes the Greek conception of the rule of law found in Solon's poetry and in the laws of Archaic and Classical Athens, and falls into two parts. The first part examines the way the Near Eastern lawgivers such as Hammurabi envisioned their role as lawgivers and their relationship to the law and contrasts it with the different approach of Solon and other Greek lawgivers. Such a comparison helps to illustrate what is distinctive and original about Solon's view of his task. Hammurabi and other Near Eastern lawgivers were monarchs; establishing laws for their kingdoms was just one of their tasks. They did not hand down their laws to the people for them to administer. The laws they created were their laws and demonstrated their justice and right to hold power. They were accountable to the gods alone, not to other mortals. Solon, by contrast, viewed monarchy as tyranny, the very opposite of the rule of law. Solon did not impose his laws from an impregnable position as ruler, but portrayed himself as a neutral arbiter who stands between competing factions. Instead of using the law to gain power or justify his position, Solon distributed power to various parts of the community to administer his laws, then departed for exile. Other Greek lawgivers were often outsiders who did not, or could not, hold power in the *poleis* for which they created their laws.

The second part of the essay shows how an understanding of the different approach taken by the Greek lawgivers helps to explain why Greek laws took on a different shape and form from those of the Near Eastern kings. The laws of the latter do not generally indicate who has the power to punish various offenses because the laws belong to the king and are his to administer. By contrast, the laws of Solon and of other early Greek *poleis* often go into detail about which bodies or officials have the power to enforce the laws. To prevent tyranny, the laws of Solon and of other Archaic *poleis* often impose term limits or divide powers among different magistrates to prevent anyone from accumulating too much power. To curb abuses of power and the failure to uphold the law, the statutes of Greek *poleis* often contain penalties for magistrates. These two features are absent from the laws of the Near Eastern kings. Finally, several early Greek laws contain entrenchment clauses to ensure that the laws remain stable and are not overturned by those in power; such clauses are not found in the laws of Hammurabi and other Near Eastern kings. These types of clauses are found not only in laws from democratic communities, but also from aristocratic *poleis*. Despite their political differences, therefore, the Greeks were united by a common belief in the rule of law, which is reflected in the shape of their statutes.

Modern political thought divides government into three parts: executive, legislative, and judiciary. Each part performs different tasks and to some extent operates on different principles. All three parts form a system of checks and balances, which ensures political stability. The next essay in this section, "Pericles' Praise of Athenian Democracy," analyzes a passage from Thucydides (2.37) to show how the Athenians also divided their government into three parts, but in a different way. According to Aristotle and other authors, these parts were the deliberative (the Council and Assembly), the magistracies, and the courts. The deliberative combined some of the functions of the modern legislative (e.g., passing laws) and executive branches: it decided all major questions regarding public administration and held elections for office. It operated on the principle that the vote of the majority was binding on the entire community. The courts dispensed justice for individuals and followed the principle that all men are equal before the law. In Athenian democracy there were two methods of appointing magistrates: election and appointment by lot. When electing officials, the Athenians did not consider social class, but the candidate's ability. Offices filled by lot were a way of allowing less wealthy citizens to participate in public administration. This essay shows that Aristotle's division was not a philosophical idea, but was developed by the Athenians themselves as early as the fifth century BCE. It shows in greater detail how the Athenians implemented the Solonian ideal of distributing power to parts of the community and avoiding the concentration of power, which helped to promote political stability.

The third essay in this section, "Antigone the Lawyer, or the Ambiguities of *Nomos*," examines the problem of legitimacy (what makes a given rule a law [*nomos*]?) and the relationship between democracy and the rule of law in Classical Athens through a study of Sophocles' *Antigone*. The essay starts with a review of the basic features of a law, then studies the sources of legitimacy in Greek thought. It shows there was no conflict between divine and human law in Classical Athens: the laws of the gods were the laws of the *polis* and vice versa. The conflict between Antigone and Creon in Sophocles' play is therefore not between two types of law, but two conceptions of law. Antigone and her fiancé Haemon believe that a *nomos* requires the approval of the gods and the consent of the community. For them there is no conflict between the rule of law and popular sovereignty; on the contrary, the two go hand in hand. Since Creon's order forbidding the burial of Polynices lacks the support of both the gods and the community, it is only the order of a magistrate and does not supersede the universal law that requires burial for all free persons. Creon, on the other hand, thinks a *nomos* is whatever the ruling power decides. His view is close to that of the Near Eastern monarchs, who are discussed in the first essay. But toward the end of the play, Creon recognizes that he must follow the "established laws," those that fulfill all the criteria of legitimacy.

The following pair of essays, "How Often Did the Athenian Assembly Meet?" and "When Did the Athenian Assembly Meet? Some New Evidence," deal with a central issue in constitutional law, namely, the number of meetings held by the Assembly, where all major decisions were made. M. H. Hansen has argued that in the fifth century the Athenians based their constitution on the idea of popular sovereignty and made the Assembly the supreme body. In the fourth century, by contrast, they subordinated the Assembly to the law courts and upheld instead the ideal of the rule of law. One of Hansen's main arguments for this view is that around 350 the Athenians limited the number of times the Assembly could meet to four times a prytany. Since they could not call extra meetings, they tended to save one or two meetings for late in the prytany in case an emergency arose. This reform was part of a movement to limit the power of the Assembly in comparison with that of the lawcourts. Hansen also argued that the ancient scholia that defined the term *ekklesia synkletos* as an extra, emergency meeting of the Assembly were not reliable. In his view such a meeting was one of the four regular meetings called on short notice. The first essay analyzes the evidence for the term *ekklesia synkletos* and shows that there is no reason to doubt the meaning found in the scholia. The second essay examines one of these scholia that states the Assembly normally met on the eleventh, around the twentieth, and around the thirtieth of every month. A study of all the preserved prescripts in Athenian decrees in the Classical and Hellenistic periods proves this information to be roughly correct. Taken together, these essays support the conclusion of "Antigone the Lawyer" that there was no shift from popular sovereignty to the rule of law around 400 BCE. On the contrary, the Athenians considered the two ideals to be perfectly compatible with one another. In fact, the Athenians believed that democracy was the only form of government where the rule of law could exist.

The final essay in this section, "Demosthenes and the Theoric Fund," studies the laws about the distribution of public funds in the fourth century and the way the laws balanced the interests of the wealthy and average citizens. According to the traditional scholarly view, there was a struggle in the middle of the fourth century BCE between the supporters of Eubulus and those of Demosthenes: whereas Eubulus allegedly advocated the distribution of public wealth through the Theoric Fund to poor citizens, Demosthenes wanted to use the money in this fund to pay for military campaigns to stop Macedonian aggression. A detailed examination of the passages from Demosthenes' speeches used to support this view shows that he did not attack the Theoric Fund, but actually defended its role in promoting social harmony and was later elected to administer the fund. What Demosthenes objected to were attempts to spend money from the Military Fund to pay for festivals and other nonmilitary expenses. The traditional view of a conflict between Eubulus and Demosthenes about the use of public funds therefore rests on no solid foundation. The final part of the essay shows how the laws of Athens played a major role in reducing social tensions by protecting private property, which provided security for the wealthy against arbitrary confiscation, and by distributing public revenues through the Theoric Fund to benefit the less affluent. This essay calls into question the view that social harmony was achieved in Classical Athens by the people's control of political discourse. On the contrary, the Athenians attempted to reduce class tensions through compromises between competing interests that were worked out through legislative procedures. What united the rich and the poor was a common belief in the rule of law, which protected the agreements contained in the laws.

II. LAW AND ECONOMY

The second section examines several aspects of the connections between law and economy in Classical Athens. The first essay, "Law and Economy in Classical Athens," serves as a general introduction to the section. It starts by sketching the basic features of the Athenian economy and discusses the level of specialization of labor and its implications for the development of markets and commerce. Because the Athenian economy grew to the point where transactions moved beyond the traditional channels of family, neighbors, friends, and patronage, it created the need for market exchange and for rules to regulate that type of exchange. The first part of the essay outlines many of the laws devised to regulate commerce, promote trade, and resolve disputes between debtors and creditors. The second part is a case study of the demosthenic speech *Against Dionysodorus,* which studies how these regulations worked in practice.

The next two essays study the rules about real security, which is crucial for the development of credit relations in a market economy. When a creditor lends money to a borrower, he needs some assurance that the borrower will repay the loan. One way of providing this assurance is for the borrower to set aside some property as security for repayment. Earlier scholars believed that the Athenians, like the Romans, had at least two forms of real security, *prasis epi lysei* (where the lender acquired ownership of the security) and *hypotheke* (where the borrower retained ownership). The second essay in this section, "When Is a Sale Not a Sale? The Riddle of Athenian Terminology for Real Security Revisited," shows that the analogy from Roman Law is misleading. The Romans could distinguish between two or more forms of security because they possessed formal modes of conveyance and possessory interdicts. Because the Athenians did not have either of these legal mechanisms, they could not make such distinctions and therefore from a legal point of view had one basic form of security. The lack of formal modes of conveyance also made it impossible for the Athenians to answer the question "who owned the security?" during the life of a loan. But despite these drawbacks, the Athenians were still able to carry on complex transactions involving real security and thus provide an important part of the legal framework needed to develop market relations.

The third essay, "*Apotimema*: Athenian Terminology for Real Security in Leases and Dowry Agreements," carries forward the study of Athenian terminology for real security and modifies slightly one of the conclusions of the previous essay. Scholars have believed that *apotimema* was a different form of security from the ones normally used in loans though they have not been able to agree how and why it differed. This study demonstrates that *apotimema* is a general term for real security, which could be applied to property pledged for any kind of payment whether it be in a rental, dowry, or loan agreement. This makes it possible to understand an important law about real security preserved at Demosthenes 41.7. This law recognized the rights of creditors to property taken in lieu of repayment. It therefore served to provide a legal basis for the terms of real security and helped to support economic development of credit relations. Finley believed that the Athenian economy had reached only a primitive stage of development and as a result did not have laws about real security. The findings of this essay indicate that his view requires considerable modification.

The fourth essay in this section, "The Liability of Business Partners in Athenian Law," helps us to understand how, despite the absence of modern notions of legal personality, the Athenians were still able to develop the legal arrangements necessary to carry on overseas trade. It has long been recognized that Athenian Law, like Roman Law, did not develop the modern notion of corporation or partnership. This meant that when one lent money or made a contract, it was always to an individual or several individuals, not to an abstract legal entity in which several individuals held shares and which was represented by officers appointed by the shareholders. This created a potential obstacle in maritime loans where the lender provided money to a merchant or shipowner who sailed from Athens to purchase goods in a foreign port. Once the borrower left Athens, the lender might not be able to track him down if he defaulted on the loan. To get around this obstacle, the Athenians devised contracts where the creditor would make the loan to a pair of borrowers. One of the borrowers would sail with the ship and cargo, while the other would remain in Athens. Since the contract specified that repayment could be demanded from either or both borrowers (joint and several liability), the creditor received the assurance that he could recover his loan from the borrower who stayed behind if the other borrower never returned.

The fifth essay, "Did Solon Abolish Debt-Bondage?," challenges a long-held view that Solon abolished the practice of debt-bondage in Archaic Athens. Finley went so far as to argue that Solon's measure was actually responsible for the rise of chattel slavery in democratic Athens. The first part of this essay draws a distinction between enslavement for debt, where the defaulting debtor becomes the slave of the creditor, and debt-bondage, where the debtor remains under the creditor's control only until he pays off his debt. This distinction is then traced through the Near Eastern lawcodes down to the lawcode of Gortyn in the fifth century BCE. The second part of the essay examines the language of Solon's law and demonstrates that it must outlaw enslavement for debt, not debt-bondage. The third part collects several passages that reveal that the practice of debt-bondage continued to exist in Classical Athens, while the fourth part studies Solon's poetry to show that his reforms affected people who fell into slavery, not into debt-bondage. The final part of the essay ties in with the conclusion of "Demosthenes and the Theoric Fund" and shows how the laws of Athens balanced the interests of creditors and debtors to provide the legal framework necessary for the development of market relations. This balance of interests also contributed to preserving social peace and reducing class tensions in Classical Athens.

The final essay in this section, "Notes on a Lead Letter from the Athenian Agora," draws attention to the position of slaves in the Athenian economy. A few years ago, D. Jordan published a lead letter dating from the fourth century BCE found in the Athenian Agora. The letter was written by a man named Lesis working in a forge who complains about being mistreated and was sent to the writer's mother and a man named Xenocles, who are asked to help. Jordan believed that the writer was a free apprentice, but a careful analysis of the letter's contents shows that Lesis must be a slave entrusted by his masters to a smith. The letter thus sheds valuable light on the condition of slaves in the Athenian economy and how the law dealt with the treatment of slaves. In contrast to the protections afforded free debtors, slaves were vulnerable to exploitation and abuse. The letter thus reminds us of the limits to the rule of law and democratic ideals in Classical Athens.

III. LAW AND THE FAMILY

The essays in the third section examine how the laws of Athens regulated matters involving women and the family. The first two essays study the laws concerning rape and seduction and show that although the Athenians might punish rape with considerable severity, they tended to evaluate acts of sexual violence in terms of the intent of the aggressor and paid less attention to the consent or lack of consent of the female victim. The next essay studies the rules restricting women's ability to conduct financial transactions and how women still managed to play a role in the management of the household despite the existence of these rules. The final two essays deal with the ability of minors to give testimony and the deme registration of adopted children who returned to the household of their natural parents.

In a speech written by Lysias, a defendant states that the Athenians considered the seduction of a wife a worse crime than rape. This conclusion has startled some scholars, but none has questioned the reliability of his description of the legal remedies for these offenses. The first essay in this section, "Did the Athenians Regard Seduction as a Worse Crime than Rape?," examines the procedures and penalties for those who seduced women and for those who committed rape and shows that Lysias' account is highly misleading. First, the laws about homicide allowed the man who caught someone on top of his wife, mother, daughter, sister, or concubine to kill him without penalty – this provision applied to both rapists and seducers. Second, it was possible to bring a *graphe hybreos* (public action for outrage) against those who committed rape; the penalty on conviction for this offense might be death. The presentation of the laws by Lysias' client is therefore partial and selective, designed for the rhetorical needs of his case. This study serves as a cautionary lesson about the interpretation of statutes found in the Attic Orators.

The next essay, "Did Rape Exist in Classical Athens? Further Reflections on the Laws about Sexual Violence," takes up an issue neglected in the previous one: the differing attitudes toward sexual violence in Classical Athens. The sources for Athenian social life reveal a startling dichotomy: in some cases acts of sexual violence are severely punished, yet in others, men who commit rape are treated leniently, and gods who have sex with mortal women against their will incur little or no blame. This dichotomy is all the more striking when one contrasts the ancient Greek attitude with the modern punishments for rape, which treat the crime with the utmost severity in all cases. A first step toward understanding the difference between ancient and modern attitudes is to observe that when the Greeks condemn sexual violence, they call it *hybris*, a word that is not used when such acts receive lenient treatment. An understanding of this concept is therefore key to explaining ancient attitudes. The term *hybris* has two aspects: a subjective side (the mental state of the aggressor) and an objective side (the harm done to the victim). The person who commits *hybris* does so in a certain state of mind, which is the opposite of *sophrosyne*, the Greek virtue of self-control and moderation. The man acting with *hybris* displays an inability to control his passions and desires, which causes him to have contempt for other people and for the law. This behavior often results in acts that bring dishonor to the victim and lower his or her standing in the eyes of society. *Hybris* also causes the victim to feel angry and humiliated. Acts of sexual violence are condemned when they are committed with *hybris*, that is, out of a desire to indulge one's own pleasure and to humiliate the victim. However, a man who forces a woman to have sex out of love and desire is treated more leniently provided he is willing to marry the victim and thus remove any taint to her reputation. When gods have sex with mortal women against their will, they do not do it to cause pain and dishonor, but to give them remarkable offspring or some other honor. And in some cases sexual violence is used as a justified punishment for slaves or for the women of hostile cities. Thus, the Athenians and other Greeks did not evaluate acts of sexual violence from the point of view of the woman, but according to the male's intention. If his intention was to humiliate, he was harshly punished; if not, he was treated less severely.

The third essay, "Women and Lending in Athenian Society: A *Horos* Re-Examined," studies the restrictions placed on women's activities in the economic sphere and the impact they had on their ability to conduct financial transactions.

The Athenians had a law that forbade women to conduct transactions involving more than a *medimnus* of barley, a relatively small amount. Yet in several cases we find women making loans in excess of this amount. This essay studies two of these cases to show how women might take the initiative in financial transactions despite the limits placed on them by law. The evidence for the first case is found in an inscription on a *horos* recording the terms of an *eranos* loan. In this kind of loan several people made contributions to a *plerotes*, a person who collected these amounts, turned the loan over to the borrower, and then administered the terms of the loan. On the *horos* in question the person who collected the contributions of 500 drachmas and made the loan was a woman (*plerotria*), but the person who received the security from the man acting as surety for the lender was a man. The *horos* illustrates how a woman could and did handle financial transactions involving substantial amounts, but from the legal point of view it was always a man who contracted the loan and had the right to enforce its provisions. This helps us understand a loan made by a woman attested in Demosthenes 42, which has puzzled several scholars. The speech indicates that a loan of two thousand drachmas was made by the wife of Polyeuctus, but a careful reading of the text also reveals that the loan was made from her husband's property and formed part of his estate at his death, not hers. These two transactions enable us to understand how the law restricting women to small transactions worked in practice: it did not stop them from participating in financial matters, but it required that they do so with the consent of men. I have also included a brief article published with Kenneth Tuite, "Notes on a *Horos* from the Athenian Agora." This article provides a new reading of one line of the *horos* (based on autopsy of the stone), which confirms one of the points in the previous essay, and a revised interpretation of one phrase in the *horos* based on some evidence I overlooked in the original publication.

The fourth essay, "The Date of Apollodorus' Speech against Timotheus and Its Implications for Athenian History and Legal Procedure," examines the rights of male minors in Athenian courts. In the past scholars have assumed that Athenian males could not testify in court until they reached the age of majority at eighteen. On the basis of this assumption, Arnold Schaefer dated Apollodorus' *Against Timotheus* ([Dem.] 49) to the year 362/61 because Apollodorus' brother Pasicles, who testified at the trial, did not become eighteen until that year. But there is no evidence that males under the age of eighteen were barred from testifying. On the other hand, Apollodorus could not have delivered his speech against Timotheus to recover loans made from his father's bank after Pasicles became eighteen because he relinquished his interest in the bank at that time. Finally, Apollodorus could not have brought a suit against Timotheus in 362/61 because the general was away from Athens at the time. The speech must therefore have been delivered before 366/65 or earlier when Pasicles was younger than eighteen. A correct dating of the speech shows that male minors could testify in court and that there was no connection between the right to testify and citizen status. Indeed, we know that foreigners were also allowed to appear as witnesses.

The section concludes with a "A Note on Adoption and Deme Registration." The laws of Athens allowed a man without legitimate offspring to adopt a son to provide himself with an heir who could take over his property at his death. The adopted son then relinquished all rights of inheritance in the household of his natural father. If the adopted son married and left an heir in the household of his adoptive father, however, he could return to the household of his natural father and regain his rights as heir. The laws of Athens also required that a father register his son in his deme as soon as he reached the age of majority. But in what deme was an adopted son who returned to his father's household registered, that of his adoptive father or that of his natural father? This essay studies the evidence found in Demosthenes 44 to show that the adopted son was registered in the deme of his adoptive father and remained registered there even if he returned to the household of his natural father. This enables us to explain how Clearchus, the son of Nausicles (*IG* ii^2 1629, lines 707–9), could become his father's heir yet be registered in a different deme from that of his father.

IV. ASPECTS OF PROCEDURE

The essays in the fourth section address various aspects of legal procedure. The first two stress the importance of examining substantive issues when trying to explain varying legal procedures for different offenses. To explain the different procedures for theft, one must first analyze the term *ep'autophoro* ("red-handed" or "obviously guilty"), which is found in the law for one of these procedures. In similar fashion, to understand how the Athenians dealt with those who plotted to commit murder, it is necessary to study the meaning of the term *apokteinein* (to kill) and its substantive implications. The final essay looks at the general intent of the procedures established to punish offenses against the community. Some recent scholars have argued that these procedures were used mainly to pursue private feuds and had little to do with enforcing the law. This essay shows that the Athenians considered it wrong to employ public actions in this way and that severe penalties were laid down for those who attempted to abuse public procedures to harass private enemies.

The first essay in this section, "'In the Act' or 'Red-Handed?' *Apagoge* to the Eleven and *Furtum Manifestum*," analyzes the two procedures for punishing theft in Athenian law. The first was the *dike klopes*, a private action for a payment of damages twice the value of the stolen object. The second was *apagoge* to the Eleven, a public action. The owner of the stolen object could arrest the thief and bring him to officials called the Eleven. If the thief confessed or initially denied his guilt but was convicted in court, he was put to death. Why was there such a difference between the penalties for the two procedures? This essay shows that the key to the solution lies in the requirement that in *apagoge* to the Eleven the thief must be caught *ep'autophoro*. This term is glossed in the *Digest* as *furtum manifestum* in Roman Law, an offense that also was harshly punished. An analysis of the terms *ep'autophoro* and *furtum manifestum* shows that they both covered cases where a person was caught with stolen goods in circumstances that made it virtually certain that he was the actual thief. This was different from the situation covered by the *dike klopes* in Athenian Law and *furtum nec manifestum* in Roman Law, where one did not have to prove that the person holding the stolen goods was the actual thief. The substantive difference thus explains the difference in penalties for the different types of procedures. Like the essays on real security, this essay also discusses the issue of using analogies drawn from Roman Law for understanding Athenian legal procedures. In the case of real security, the analogy with Roman Law is misleading, but in studying theft the analogy turns out to be fruitful. All three essays taken together illustrate the potential and the drawbacks of these analogies and thus have methodological implications for the study of Athenian Law.

The laws of Athens distinguished among three basic types of homicide: deliberate (*ek pronoias*), unwilling (*akousios*), and just or legitimate homicide (*dikaios* or *kata tous nomous*). There is some disagreement, however, how the law treated men who plotted a murder carried out by someone else. MacDowell believes that men who plotted were tried by the *dike bouleuseos* (private action for planning murder), whereas Gagarin argues that the person who plotted a murder was subject to the same procedure as one who killed with one's own hands and denies the existence of an action for plotting of homicide (despite the explicit statement of *Ath.*

Pol. 57.3). The second essay in this section, "How to Kill in Attic Greek," shows that the controversy can be resolved by examining a substantive issue neither of these scholars has addressed: the meaning of the term *apokteinein* (to kill), which occurs in all the statutes about homicide. A study of the verb in Attic prose shows that it describes the action of a person who causes death in any way. The term therefore covered both the action of a person who kills with a weapon (direct causality) and the person who arranges to have someone else commit murder (indirect causality). In one case a defendant was convicted on a charge of homicide in an Athenian court simply for encouraging an assailant to strike. Since his words caused the death of the victim, he was considered guilty of murder. On the other hand, several passages show that the *dike bouleuseos* was available against those who planned to kill but did not actually do so and was thus similar to the modern crime of attempted homicide. This essay also illustrates the importance of studying substantive issues when analyzing the differences between various legal procedures in Athenian Law.

According to Lycurgus (*Against Leocrates* 6), the aim of the Athenian courts was to uphold the laws and to punish those who broke them. Some recent scholars, however, have questioned this view of the courts and have claimed that the Athenians used them not to enforce the rule of law but to pursue private feuds and to harass personal enemies. The final essay in this section, "The Penalty for Frivolous Prosecution in Athenian Law," reveals that the Athenians were hostile to litigants who used the courts for this purpose. The traditional view of these penalties is that the person who did not follow through a public case after initiating it or failing to gain one-fifth of the votes at a trial was punished only with a fine of 1,000 drachmas and the loss of the right to bring the same kind of public suit in the future. M. Hansen has argued that this penalty was not strictly enforced and has also claimed that many litigants dropped suits without incurring a penalty. A careful study of the evidence demonstrates that the penalty for frivolous prosecutions was the loss of the right to bring any type of public action. An analysis of the cases cited by Hansen shows that "not following through (*epexelthein*)" meant not showing up at the preliminary hearing (*anakrisis*) after initiating a prosecution or at the trial. Prosecutors were allowed to drop cases provided they did not attempt to deprive the Treasury of fines. Compared with the procedures against malicious prosecutions in British Law during the eighteenth century, the penalties for frivolous prosecution in Athenian Law were far more harsh. Nothing could better demonstrate Athenian hostility toward those who abused the courts to pursue private feuds.

V. ENVOI

The final essay, "Pheidippides the Legislator: A Note on Aristophanes' *Clouds,*" serves as a comic envoi and is a close study of the legal language in a passage from Aristophanes' *Clouds.* After receiving an education in Socrates' Thinkery, Pheidippides returns to show his father Strepsiades what he has learned. Pheidippides says that he has formulated a new law allowing sons to beat their fathers, but grants an exemption for all the blows received prior to the passage of the law. The language the young man uses carefully imitates the phraseology of several Attic laws and decrees. This essay shows that Aristophanes expected his audience to recognize this language and thus assumed that average citizens had a working knowledge of Athenian Law and legal terminology. The laws of Athens were accessible not merely to the educated few; they were the common possession of the entire citizen body.

The essays in this volume have not been revised aside from correcting minor errors and changing the style of citation for ancient sources and modern works to make it uniform throughout. In some of the original versions of the earlier essays, I translated the Greek term *dikastes* as "juror" but have now corrected this to "judge" throughout – for my reasons see Harris (1994a). After some of the essays, I have added a brief section of "Afterthoughts" to take note of criticisms and replies made by other scholars.

I have included in this collection essays that look mainly at particular statutes or at broad questions of law and examine the substantive side of Athenian Law. I have therefore not included several essays (Harris [2000a], Harris [2004b], Harris [2004c], Harris [2005], and Harris [forthcoming c]) that deal primarily with the ways in which the Athenians interpreted and applied their laws. Those who want more "theory" than they find here and wish to know why I do not believe that the Athenians used their courts to pursue feuds should read those essays, especially Harris (2000a) and Harris (2005). I plan to revise these essays in the near future and use them as the basis of another book, tentatively entitled *The Rule of Law in Action: The Nature of Litigation in Classical Athens.*

I hope that many of the essays in this volume will appeal not only to specialists in Greek Law, but also to the "general Classicist" or to anyone interested in legal history. Although some of the essays analyze specialized topics such as real security and the number of meetings held by the Athenian Assembly, others were written for undergraduate audiences and are aimed at the general public. For the nonspecialist I would recommend especially chapters I.1, I.3, I.6, II.1, II.5, II.6, III.1–III.3, IV.2, and the comic envoi. For those with more advanced knowledge of Classics and Athenian Law, I would suggest all of the other essays with the exception of I.4 and I.5, which are aimed mainly at specialists in Athenian history and Greek epigraphy.

I

Law and Constitutional History

1.1 Solon and the Spirit of the Law in Archaic and Classical Greece

The scattered remains of the laws enacted by the Greek *poleis* (city-states) during the Archaic and Classical periods hardly appear to form a unified body of law.[1] Most of our evidence for Greek Law in this period comes from two *poleis*, Athens and Gortyn on the island of Crete. Several statutes from the collection of laws created by Solon in 594 have been preserved, but many of these are found in late sources such as Plutarch and lexica compiled by scholars during the Roman Empire or the Byzantine period, and it is often difficult to tell how much of the information they provide is reliable.[2] There are two main problems encountered when studying the laws attributed to Solon. On the one hand, a law attributed to Solon may have been a genuine law dating from the Archaic or Classical period, but not a law that Solon himself enacted. One thinks for example of the laws about the appointment of *nomothetai* attributed to Solon by Demosthenes (20.93–4). These were actual laws that were in force at the time, but we know that these *nomothetai* were not created until after 403 BCE.[3] On the other hand, a law attributed to

[1] I would like to thank Josine Blok and André Lardinois, the organizers of the Solon conference, for inviting me to present an oral version of this essay in Soeterbeeck and for their help in revising it for publication. An earlier version of this essay was presented to the American Society of Legal History in San Diego, CA (November 2002), to the Department of Classical Studies, University of Michigan (November 2002), and to the Classics Department, Tulane University (October 2003). A slightly different French version was presented to the Centre Glotz, Université de Paris I (Panthéon-Sorbonne) in January of 2003. A shorter version was presented in Italian to a class at the Istituto di Diritto Romano at the University of Milan in October 2004. I would also like to thank several friends and colleagues who have read various versions of this essay and offered help and encouragement: Eva Cantarella, Alberto Maffi, Lorenzo Gagliardi, Lene Rubinstein, Fred Naiden, Donna Wilson, Robin Osborne, Jean-Marie Bertrand, Pauline Schmitt-Pantel, and Pierre Fröhlich. I owe a special debt of gratitude to Raymond Westbrook for his advice about the Near Eastern material and his timely gift of the two volumes of Westbrook (2003). All translations of the poems attributed to Solon are my own.

[2] The problem of determining which laws are genuinely Solonian has been discussed by Ruschenbusch (1966), but see now the essays by Blok, Gagarin, Rhodes, and Scafuro in Blok and Lardinois (2005).

[3] See Hansen (1991) 167–8.

Solon may have been a forgery completely invented by a later author. For instance, Aeschines (1.6–23) discusses several laws of Solon about schools for boys, the prosecution of *hybris*, and the penalties for male prostitutes. In the manuscripts of his speech we find inserted several documents purporting to be the texts of these laws of Solon, but it has long been recognized that these are all forgeries.[4]

For Gortyn there are two major inscriptions containing laws on property and the family. The longer inscription, often called "the Gortyn Lawcode," is hardly a code in the modern sense, that is, a complete and systematic collection of all the main laws governing the life of a community; for instance, missing from its provisions are any statutes about homicide and public crimes like treason.[5] What is more, we know nothing about the historical context that produced this collection of laws nor about the aims of the legislators at Gortyn. The evidence for laws in other Greek *poleis* comes mainly from inscriptions, many of which are preserved only in fragments or are hard to interpret. Moreover, we often know little or nothing about the circumstances surrounding the enactment of these laws. At first glance, the possibility of discerning any single living spirit in this heap of dry bones seems quite remote.

M. I. Finley once went so far as to claim that one cannot speak of "Greek Law" in any meaningful sense since Greece was divided into hundred of different *poleis*, each with its own laws and institutions.[6] Yet though there certainly existed significant differences among these *poleis*, they were all united by certain values that enabled them to share a common Greek identity. Prominent among these values was the ideal of the "rule of law."[7] Even if one cannot speak of early Greek law as a unified legal system, we can still discover several common features in the statutes of the Greek *poleis*, which, taken together, reflect a unified set of principles shared by many of these different communities in the period 650–400 BCE. As P. J. Rhodes has recently observed, "There is enough similarity between what is attested for different states (...) to suggest that, in spite of justified protests against the use of inference from one place at one time to fill gaps in our knowledge of another

[4] See Drerup (1898) 305–8.

[5] On the meaning of the term "lawcode," see Westbrook (2000) 33–4 and the essays in Lévy (2000). For objections to calling any of the collections of early Greek laws a lawcode, see Hölkeskamp (1999).

[6] Finley (1975) 134–46.

[7] For the importance of the ideal of the rule of law in Greek identity, see E. Hall (1989) 198–200. In J. Hall (2002) I can find no discussion of the role played by the ideal of the rule of law in the formation of Greek cultural identity.

place at another time, some valid generalizations can be made about Greek law and Greek judicial procedures."[8] It is this underlying set of general principles that I call "The Spirit of Greek Laws."[9]

Despite the many problems created by our sources, historians of Greek Law are fortunate in one regard: they have the poetry attributed to Solon, the most famous lawgiver of the period. We may never be able to determine who is the actual author of these verses; they may have been written by the person who created a set of laws for the Athenians in 594 or be the product of a tradition of poetry that created the persona of an ideal lawgiver.[10] What is important for legal historians is that this poetry expresses the aims and values of the Archaic Greek lawgivers and therefore helps us understand the spirit in which the Greek *poleis* created their laws. The Greeks also circulated many myths about their lawgivers, which, if used with caution, also provide valuable information about contemporary attitudes.[11] These stories, though generally worthless as evidence for actual events, can still reveal Greek views about the role of the ideal lawgiver and the aims of legislation.

The first section of this essay begins with a study in contrast. I start by examining the way in which the Near Eastern lawgivers such as Hammurabi and Lipit-Ishtar envisioned their role in society and their relationship to the laws that they created. Their attitude is then contrasted with the way in which the poems of Solon present the task of the lawgiver and also with the image of the lawgiver found in several traditional stories. This will help us understand not only what is distinctive about the Greek attitude toward the role of the lawgiver, but also what is original about the persona of the lawgiver found in the poems attributed to Solon. The second part of the essay studies how these contrasting views about

[8] Rhodes with Lewis (1997) 529–30 note 2. In a careful study of territorial claims in Classical and Hellenistic Greece, Chaniotis (2004) has demonstrated that the Greeks attempted to follow a set of common principles when settling territorial disputes between *poleis*. Despite the differences between their legal systems, the Greeks appear to have recognized the validity of basic modes of conveyance in determining the ownership of land belonging to a *polis*. Three of these modes of conveyance find parallels in the private law of the Greek *poleis*. On the "established laws" recognized and followed by the Greek *poleis*, see Harris (2004a) 26–33.

[9] When I use the word "spirit," I do not mean to contrast the "spirit of the law" with the "letter of the law." Nor do I wish to promote the idea that there existed a transcendent *Geist* that united all the Greeks and pervaded their institutions.

[10] On this issue see the essays of Blaise, Lardinois, and Stehle in Blok and Lardinois (2005).

[11] On these legends see Szegedy-Maszak (1978).

the role of the lawgiver and the place of law in society affected the shape and form of laws in the Greek *poleis* of the Archaic and Classical periods.

I. THE IMAGE OF THE LAWGIVER IN THE ANCIENT NEAR EAST AND ARCHAIC GREECE

Perhaps the best way to appreciate what is original about the Greek view of the lawgiver and his role in society is to contrast it with the manner in which the lawgivers of the Ancient Near East viewed their relationship to law and justice. Although the collections of laws discovered in the Near East and those of the Greek *poleis* treat many of the same topics (e.g., adoption, theft, slavery and debt-bondage, leases, homicide), the Near Eastern kings had a very different conception of their position in the community from that of the early Greek lawgivers.[12] Monarchs like Hammurabi acted both as lawgiver and as the supreme judge in their kingdom at the same time. They did not just lay down laws but also administered these laws either directly or through their subordinates. As we will see, they did not grant permanent powers to magistrates, who had the right to administer the law by virtue of holding an office. This had a profound impact on their view of the law and its role in society and set them apart from the image of the Greek lawgivers.

The preface that Hammurabi (ca. 175 BCE) placed at the beginning of his laws provides the best evidence for his view of his role.[13] Hammurabi does not tell us that he had his laws inscribed on a stele in response to a request by his people; he claims to have been appointed king by the gods Anu and Enlil to bring justice to his subjects:

> The gods Anu and Enlil, for the enhancement of the well-being of the people, named me by name Hammurabi: the pious prince, who venerates the gods, to make justice prevail in the land, to abolish the wicked and the evil,

[12] For instance, both the law collections of Hammurabi and Lipit-Ishtar as well as the laws of several Greek *poleis* contained regulations about slavery and debt-bondage. See Harris (2002a) with the literature cited there.

[13] For the laws of Hammurabi and Lipit-Ishtar, I have used the translations and system of reference found in Roth (1995). This is not the place to enter into the debate about the extent to which Hammurabi's laws were actually followed in practice. Bottéro (1992) 156–84 argues that his "lawcode" is "a work of science devoted to the exercise of justice," not a set of actual laws. Finkelstein (1961) 102 calls them "pious hopes and moral resolve rather than effective law," but see now Westbrook (2000) and especially Lafont (2000). For a brief summary of the debate see Roth (1995) 4–7, who analyzes several cases where subjects appealed to the provisions in Hammurabi's laws and clearly expected them to be followed.

> to prevent the strong from oppressing the weak, to rise like the sun-god Shamash over all humankind, to illuminate the land.
>
> (i 27–49)

In a similar way, Lipit-Ishtar (ca. 1930 BCE) says Anu and Enlil called upon him to bring justice and order to his kingdom:

> At that time, the gods Anu and Enlil called Lipit-Ishtar to the princeship of the land, Lipit-Ishtar – the wise shepherd, whose name has been pronounced by the god Nunamnir – in order to establish justice in the land, to eliminate cries for justice, to eradicate enmity and armed violence, to bring well-being to the lands of Sumer and Akkad.
>
> (i 20–37)

Rendering justice is only one of Hammurabi's many roles: he is a king (ii 22–31), a military leader who defeats his enemies in battle (ii 68-iii 16; cf. iii 70), and a religious leader who builds temples and offers prayers and sacrifices to every god in the pantheon (ii 22–31, iii 55–64, iv 7–22, 32–52, etc.). Hammurabi is thus not an outsider who comes from abroad merely to resolve disputes as an impartial arbitrator. He is an absolute monarch who rules all aspects of his subjects' lives. Like Lipit-Ishtar, he compares himself to a shepherd who takes good care of his flock (i 50–62; xlvii 9–58): "I am indeed the shepherd who brings peace, whose scepter is just." Hammurabi does not concern himself with the details of administering justice; in his laws he does not assign different kinds of cases to various magistrates or grant specific powers to individual officials. The laws on his stele are *his* laws, and they demonstrate that the verdicts he renders as king are just:

> Let any wronged man who has a lawsuit come before the statue of me, the king of justice, and let him have my inscribed stele read aloud to him, thus may he hear my precious pronouncements and let my stele reveal the lawsuit for him; may he examine his case, may he calm his (troubled) heart, (and may he praise me) saying: Hammurabi, the lord, who is like a father and begetter to his people, submitted himself to the command of the god Marduk, his lord, and achieved victory for the god Marduk everywhere. He gladdened the heart of the god Marduk, his lord, and he secured the eternal well-being of the people, and provided just ways for the land.
>
> (xlviii 3–38)

Hammurabi does not place his laws in the hands of his people for them to administer their own affairs. Although Hammurabi delegated tasks to his officials, "(a)ll these officials were appointed by the central administration and reported ultimately to the king. Hammurabi's correspondence with his high officials shows him intervening directly in day-to-day administration, frequently giving instructions on individual cases." In the judicial sphere, Hammurabi "had jurisdiction both at first instance and on appeal."[14] The only other person who can administer his laws is his successor, who will assume his multiple duties as king and judge (xlviii 59ff.). If another king does not abide by Hammurabi's rules, the only ones who can punish him are the gods; Hammurabi's laws contain no measures that would enable his human subjects to hold their rulers accountable. In answer to the question "quis custodiet custodes?" (who will guard the guardians?), Hammurabi has no other answer than "the gods."

> But should that man not heed my pronouncements, which I have inscribed on my stela, and should he slight my curses and not fear the curses of the gods, and thus overturn the judgments that I rendered, change my pronouncements, alter my engraved image, erase my inscribed name and inscribe his own name (in its place) – or should he, because, out of fear of these curses, have someone else do so – that man, whether he is a king, a lord, or a governor, or any person at all, may the great god Anu, father of the gods, who has proclaimed my reign smash his scepter and curse his destiny.
>
> (xlix 18–52)

Of course, if Hammurabi were to give others the power to discipline the king, this would undermine his entire conception of monarchy. After all, one cannot have the sheep telling the shepherd he is wrong.[15]

[14] Westbrook in Westbrook (2003) 365–6. Cf. Bottéro (1992) 165: "We know that in Mesopotamia the rendering of justice was a royal prerogative. The ruler often delegated the duty to his representatives, even to professional judges, but it belonged to him in his own right. The procedural accounts, as well as the royal correspondence, that have survived, show more than once how lower authorities refer certain difficult or unusual cases to the royal tribunal." The situation was similar in Pharaonic Egypt during the New Kingdom – see Jasnow in Westbrook (2003) 289, 295. In *Exodus* Moses also serves as chief judge and lawgiver, but the books of *Judges* and *Kings* are more critical of kings – see Frymer-Kenski in Westbrook (2003) 981–3 and 991–2.

[15] As Josine Blok points out to me, the prophets of the Hebrew Scriptures often criticize the kings of Israel for not upholding the law in the same way as Greek *manteis* could object when a king or other powerful men did not obey *themis* and *dike*. But the laws in *Exodus* and *Deuteronomy* do not provide

The Greeks saw the justice of the Near Eastern kings in a more sinister light. The story told by Herodotus (1.96–100) about the rise of Deioces to power among the Medes reveals their suspicions about such an approach to law.[16] According to Herodotus, the Medes lived independently (*autonomon*) in scattered villages after they won their freedom from the Assyrians. Ambitious to unite the Medes under his rule, Deioces set about gaining a reputation for honesty. The men in his village grew to trust him and invited him to settle their disputes. As his reputation grew, more and more people submitted their disputes to him until he finally declared he had had enough and would judge no more lawsuits. His withdrawal plunged the country into lawlessness (*anomia*) and forced the Medes to make him king. Once in office, Deioces demanded that his subjects build him a vast palace at Ecbatana. When the palace was complete, Deioces remained inside to keep himself safe from plots and communicated with his people through messengers. He continued to judge lawsuits, but all cases were now submitted to him in writing so that he could keep his distance from the people.

In Herodotus' story about Deioces, there is a contrast between independence and lawlessness, on the one hand, and monarchy (*basileia*), which brings law and order (*eunomia*), on the other. But the Greeks considered kingship tyranny (*tyrannis*), the absolute power of one man who is not accountable to the people whom he rules. Deioces' constitutional position is symbolized by his physical distance from the people: he rules from his palace, hidden behind seven high walls. Deioces does not view the achievement of law and order as an end in itself, but as a means to gain power. And just as law and order is associated with tyranny, lawlessness is associated with the independence of the villages before Deioces' accession to power.

In the eyes of the Greeks, the *tyrannis* of Deioces was the very antithesis of the rule of law. According to the Herodotus (7.104), the Spartan exile Demaratus told the Persian monarch Xerxes that their countries were very different from each

legal procedures for bringing formal charges against the king, and the Hebrew Scriptures do not record any trial of a king of Israel similar to the trials of the Spartan kings in the Archaic and Classical periods. On the trial of the Spartan kings, see David (1985).

[16] On the historicity of the story of Deioces, see Briant (2002) 26: "The institutions set up by Deioces (capital, personal guard, audience ritual, Eyes and Ears of the king) are strangely similar to Achaemenid institutions frequently described in Greek authors, so much so that we are tempted to think that Herodotus (...) applied, or could have applied what he knew of the Persian court practices of his own day as a veneer over an entirely imaginary Media." The story therefore tells us more about Greek attitudes toward the Near Eastern kings than about actual historical events.

other. Whereas the Persians feared their king as their master (*despotes*, the word for one who owns slaves) and did his commands, the Spartans had the law alone as their master. When violence and disorder gave the Athenian lawgiver Solon the chance to seize power for himself, he acted in a very different way from the Near Eastern kings. To begin with, Solon (or the persona of the lawgiver presented in Solon's poetry) refused to accept the position of tyrant:

> If I spared the land of my country,
> and did not grasp after tyranny and violence, which
> would have defiled and dishonored my reputation,
> I am not ashamed. Thus I think my fame will surpass that of all men.
>
> Solon fr. 32 [West]

For Solon monarchy does not bring about law and order, but is associated with violence and is equivalent to slavery:

> From a cloud come the might of snow and hail,
> Thunder from shining lightning,
> By the powerful men a city is destroyed, and into the slavery
> Of a single ruler (*monarchou*) the people falls through its folly.
> Once you raise a man up too high, it is not easy to restrain
> Him later; right now you must heed this advice.
>
> Solon fr. 9 [West]

Unlike Hammurabi, Solon does not hand down his laws and judgment to the people from his position as ruler or as a member of the ruling class. He never compares himself to a shepherd guarding over his flock or a father looking after his children.[17] Solon stands apart from both the people and its leaders and acts as an impartial arbiter. In one poem Solon compares himself to a boundary stone: "I

[17] The image of the leader as the shepherd of his people is frequent in Homer (e.g., *Il.* 1.263; 2.85, 105, 243, 254, 772; 4.296, 413) – see, however, Haubold (2000) 28–32, who argues that in Homer "The shepherd is a failed ideal, exposing to scrutiny a social world without effective social structures." In democratic Athens by contrast we never find a politician who describes his role in this way. The image of the shepherd is replaced by the image of the watchdog, who looks after the interests of his master and obeys his commands, or of the captain, who steers the passengers on his ship to safety. For the image of the watchdog, see Dem. 25.40; 26.22 and the parody of the image by Aristophanes (*Eq.* 1017–35). By contrast, the image of the shepherd appears to have acquired negative associations. In Plato's *Republic* (1.343b-c) Thrasymachus compares the ruler to a herdsman who keeps sheep and cattle with a view only to his own profit and that of his master. When Socrates discusses the character of the Guardians

stood between them, like a boundary stone in the middle ground" (fr. 37.9–10 [West]). He places himself on the same level as the Athenians but in an impartial position, apart from each side. In another poem he compares himself to a wolf surrounded by dogs that threaten him on all sides. Had Solon favored one side or another, the result would have brought destruction for the city (fr. 36.22–7 [West]).

Solon does not hand down just decisions from an impregnable position of authority as Hammurabi and Lipit-Ishtar did. Justice is achieved when there is a proper balance of power between the people and their leaders. To create this balance, Solon distributes power to each group while protecting both from injustice.

> To the people I gave as much privilege as was sufficient
> Neither removing nor granting more honor.
> As for those who have power and excel in wealth,
> I saw to it they suffered no harm.
> I stood casting a mighty shield over both sides,
> I allowed neither group to win an unjust victory.
>
> Solon fr. 5 [West]

> The best way would be for the people to follow its leaders,
> Neither too unrestrained nor forced by violence.
>
> Solon fr. 6.1–2 [West]

In contrast to Deioces, Solon did not use his position as lawgiver to gain a position as absolute ruler. Nor did he attempt to combine the roles of king and judge. According to legend, once Solon finished setting down his laws, he made the Athenians swear to abide by his laws, then left Athens for ten years (Hdt. 1.29). In similar fashion, the Spartan lawgiver Lycurgus was not one of the kings, but served merely as guardian and regent for his nephew King Leobotas during his youth (Hdt. 1.65). Several of the lawgivers mentioned by Aristotle in the *Politics* (2.9.5–7.1274a) were complete outsiders in the communities to which they gave laws. Philolaus, who formulated many laws for the Thebans, was an exile from Corinth. Charondas gave laws to his native Catana, but also to other colonies of Chalcis

in Callipolis, he compares them to watchdogs (*R.* 2.375e–376b). For the imagery of political leadership, I am indebted to a forthcoming essay by Roger Brock.

in Sicily and Southern Italy. The Chalcidians in Thrace brought Androdamas all the way from Rhegium in Southern Italy to provide them with laws. When the people of Cyrene in North Africa were unhappy with the monarchy of Battus and wished to improve their government, Herodotus (4.161) informs us they consulted the priestess of Apollo at Delphi. She told them to consult the Mantineans on the Greek mainland. In response the people of Mantinea sent their most distinguished citizen Demonax to Cyrene. Demonax took some powers away from the king and distributed them to the people, but did not create an office for himself. Once his work was done, he appears to have departed.[18] For Hammurabi the roles of judge, who administered the law, and king went hand in hand; the Greek *poleis* often preferred to assign the position of lawgiver to someone who did not, or could not, hold political power. In Hammurabi's eyes the laws and the will of the king were inseparable; in fact, Herodotus (3.31.4) believed that there was a law among the Persians that allowed the king to do whatever he wanted. By handing their laws over to the people to administer and remaining outsiders, Solon and Demonax made it possible for legislation to become detached from the legislator.[19]

Instead of using the law to create a position for himself and justify his power, Solon envisions law as a way of creating the right relationship between leaders and the people. The resulting balance ensures justice and order. In the tale of Deioces, law and order were associated with monarchy and contrasted with disorder and lawlessness (*anomia*). Solon does not see law and order (*eunomia*) as one part of a simple opposition between authority and chaos, but as a mean between the extremes of anarchy and tyranny (cf. Aeschylus *Eum.* 526–30). Obedience to leaders will not necessarily bring justice since they are prone to *hybris*, insolence that leads to greed and violence. This in turn can lead to anarchy, which brings slavery for the poor.

> There is no justice in the leaders of the people, who are about
> To suffer much anguish for their great arrogance.
> For they do not know how to restrain their insolence or keep
> Order and the pleasures they have now in peaceful feasts.
> * * *

[18] A similar figure is Epimenides, who according to Plutarch (*Solon* 12.4–5) came from Crete to change Athenian religious practices and thus paved the way for Solon's legislation. On this story see the contributions of De Blois and Blok in Blok and Lardinois (2005).

[19] I owe this point to Westbrook (2000) 42: "legislation became detached from the legislator."

They grow rich by trusting in unjust deeds
* * *
Nor do they spare the goods of gods and men,
But one loots and steals from one, another from another,
And they do not respect the firm foundation of Justice,
Who watches in silence all deeds done in the past and present,
And will come in time to bring retribution for all.
This inescapable wound comes to the entire community,
And it has fallen quickly into slavery,
Which stirs up civil strife and arouses war from its sleep,
Which destroys the splendid youth of many men.
Our beloved city is swiftly ground down by enemies
In conspiracies where friends harm friends.
These evils range among the people; many of the poor
Come to the land of foreigners,
Sold into slavery, bound in degrading chains.

Solon fr. 4.7–25 [West]

Solon's laws bring not only order and justice but also freedom and deliverance from slavery in two senses, figurative and literal: first, the land is no longer enslaved by those who oppressed it during the preceding *stasis*, and second, peace has made it possible to free those men who had been carried off as slaves. When describing his achievements, Solon boasts that he has removed division from Attica and made the land free again (fr. 36.4–7 [West]). The end of *stasis* has also brought freedom to those who had been seized and sold abroad (fr. 36.8–12 [West]) and those who were being held as slaves in Attica (fr. 36.13–15 [West]).[20] For Hammurabi, obedience to the king and respect for law go together. There is not a word in

[20] On the interpretation of these lines, see Blaise (1994) 31–2 and Harris (1997) 107–10. Mülke (2002) 378 claims that since Earth is invoked in Solon's prayer, it must be treated as a real substance ("tatsächlich die attische Erde als Substanz betroffen war"); he thereby seriously misrepresents my arguments, and thus his objections carry no weight. I do not claim that the earth is here used as a symbol, but that the expression "remove boundary-markers from the earth" is a metaphorical way of saying "removing strife from the land." My analysis depends on the view that these verses are about the actual land of Attica, which was afflicted by *stasis*. For additional evidence and arguments that strengthen my interpretation of this passage, see Harris (2002a). For a modernizing approach to the issue of the *horoi*, see the contribution of Ober in Blok and Lardinois (2005). On Ober's modernizing approach, see the trenchant criticisms of Rhodes (2003) 72–6, 80, 82–3, 88.

his laws about preserving the freedom of his subjects. Solon sees the rule of law as an alternative to the rule of one man and does not use the law to seize power as a tyrant. In his opinion, the rule of law should serve to liberate the community as well as to bring order. The greatest threat to freedom is the greed of those in power. To preserve freedom, therefore, the lawgiver should restrain the leaders of the people. The way to prevent disorder is not to require that all obey one leader, but to allocate power to various groups to achieve the correct balance. The lawgiver may create the laws, but he must then turn them over to the people of Attica for them to run their affairs on their own. Then he must depart.

II. THE RULE OF LAW IN ACTION IN THE GREEK *POLEIS*

In the first section we discovered how the views expressed in Solon's poetry about the role of the lawgiver and the function of law in society differed profoundly from those of the Near Eastern monarchs. But how did the lawgivers of the Greek *poleis* attempt to put their ideals into practice? How did their views about law in general affect the shape of specific laws passed during the Archaic and Classical periods?

One of Solon's main concerns was to prevent tyranny, the concentration of power in the hands of one person. For the laws to rule, the power to enforce them should not be entrusted to a single man, but distributed widely throughout the community. Solon's concern about tyranny was not a fear of an imaginary threat: a few decades before Solon's archonship, Cylon had seized the acropolis and attempted to take control of the city (Hdt. 5.71; Th. 1.126). And less than fifty years after Solon established his laws, Peisistratus succeeded in making himself tyrant of Athens (Hdt. 1.59–64; [Arist.] *Ath. Pol.* 14–17). According to Thucydides (1.18), many of the Greek *poleis* endured a period of tyranny. Solon created penalties for those who attempted to set up a tyranny ([Arist.] *Ath. Pol.* 8.4), but his main strategy for avoiding the concentration of power was to distribute it among various boards of officials or political bodies.[21] To assign rights and duties to different parts of the community, Solon created four property classes and specified

[21] On the reliability of the sources for Solon's constitution, I am in general agreement with the excellent essay by Peter Rhodes in Blok and Lardinois (2005). See also Rhodes (1981) 136–62.

the property qualifications needed for various offices ([Arist.] *Ath. Pol.* 7.3–4). Those who fell beneath a certain minimum were classified as Thetes and allowed only to attend the Assembly and judge cases in the law courts. He also created a Council of Four Hundred and distributed different powers to the Areopagus and to the Assembly ([Arist.] *Ath. Pol.* 8.4). To keep all leaders accountable, he made their conduct in office subject to review by the people. To some extent Solon was only continuing a process that had begun before him. The attempt to divide power among various officials can already be seen in the duties of the nine archons: the Polemarch led the army, the six Thesmothetai judged trials, and the King Archon had religious duties ([Arist.] *Ath. Pol.* 3.1–5). Already in the law of Draco about homicide from about 620 BCE, the task of judging cases is not assigned to one official, but to two boards of magistrates: the Basileis are to pronounce judgment while the Ephetai are to decide the verdict.[22]

The contrast with the laws of Hammurabi and Lipit-Ishtar could not be more stark. The laws of Hammurabi and Lipit-Ishtar never specify which magistrates are to enforce the laws nor grant judicial powers to different officers. Nor do they provide measures to make magistrates accountable. Take for example the following provisions on adoption from the laws of Hammurabi (paras. 185–90):

> If a man takes in adoption a young child at birth and then rears him, that rearling will not be reclaimed.
>
> If a man takes in adoption a young child, and when he takes him, he is seeking his father and mother, that rearling shall return to his father's house.
>
> A child of (i.e., reared by) a courtier who is a palace attendant or a child of (i.e., reared by) a *sekretu* will not be reclaimed.
>
> If a craftsman takes a young child to rear and then teaches him his craft, he will not be reclaimed.
>
> If he should not teach him his craft, that rearling shall return to his father's house.
>
> If a man should not reckon the young child whom he took and raised in adoption as equal with his children, that rearling shall return to his father's house.

[22] Meiggs and Lewis (1969) #86 = Koerner (1993) #11, lines 11–13. For a summary of the debate about the different tasks performed by these two sets of officials, see now M. Gagarin (2000).

The laws found in the Jewish Scriptures also do not generally state which official is assigned to each type of case (e.g., *Exodus* 21–3; *Leviticus* 18–27). The laws of Athens were quite different and could be very specific about the precise jurisdiction of magistrates. By the fifth century the laws and decrees of Athens often went into considerable detail about the duties of various magistrates. For instance, a decree passed by Callias and dated to 434/3 gives a very detailed job description for the new office of Treasurers of the Other Gods (*IG* i³ 52). The new treasurers are to be selected by lot at the same time as other officials (lines 13–15); they are to perform their duties on the Acropolis in the Opisthodomos (lines 15–18); they will count out and weigh in the presence of the Council the money they receive from the present treasurers, Epistatai, and Hieropoioi in the temples (lines 18–21); they will record the amounts they receive and the total but list silver and gold separately (lines 24); in the future they will write up the amounts they receive and spend on a stele and submit this to the Logistai and submit to an examination (*euthynai*) when they leave office (lines 21–7); their term of office is to last from Panathenaea to Panathenaea (lines 27–9). The decree goes into such detail that it even grants them the power to open and shut the doors of the Opisthodomos (lines 16–17)! Here the Assembly carefully delineates the duties of different officials and clarifies the relationships among them in a way that is unparalleled in the laws of the Near Eastern kings.

This careful division of duties among different officials is characteristic not only of the Athenian laws in the period of Solon and later, but also of laws in many Greek *poleis* during the Archaic and Classical periods. This feature sets them apart from the laws of Hammurabi and Lipit-Ishtar. One of the earliest Greek laws is the Rhetra from Sparta. There is still considerable debate among scholars about the precise meaning of its provisions, but the document distinguishes Kings, Council of Elders, and the People and allots different powers to each body (D. S. 7.12.6; Plu. *Lycurgus* 6.1–10).[23] The text of a law from Chios dated to the early sixth century is fragmentary and difficult to decipher but grants different responsibilities to various bodies and magistrates (Koerner [1993] #61 = *Nomima* I 62). There appear

[23] Cf. Maffi (2002) 196: "È l'opinione largamente condivisa che il testo della G. R. (= Grande Rhetra) enunci la struttura costituzionale della Sparta arcaica, articolata su tre organi: i due re, la *gerousia* e il *damos*." Maffi's essay contains a helpful review of past scholarship on the Rhetra and offers an interesting new interpretation of the relationship among these three bodies.

to be laws passed by the people (A, line 1). The Demarchs may have had the power to levy fines (A, lines 3–6), and the Council hears appeals and can inflict fines (C, lines 1–15).

By distributing powers to different officials, these laws made it possible for one set of officials to act as a check on other officials. In an early fifth-century law from Athens, the Treasurers of the sanctuary on the Acropolis are to open the temple not less than three times a month. If they fail to do their duty, the Prytaneis will fine them two drachmas (Koerner [1993] # 5 = *IG* i³ 4B). Another law from Athens in the late fifth century sets out regulations for the captains of triremes and gives the Overseers of the Navy-yard the power to fine them for any infractions (Koerner [1993] #15 = *IG* i³ 153). A law from Olympia dated to the early fifth century imposes penalties on those holding the highest office and the Basileis who do not enforce its provisions, then instructs the Hellanodikas to collect a fine from them (Koerner [1993] #37). A law from Chios dated to the late fifth century requires the Boundary Guards to make sure no one moves boundary stones; if they do not impose legal penalties, the Fifteen are to fine them [Koerner [1993] #62A, lines 9–19). A law from Lyttos in Crete dated to around 500 forbids the Kosmoi to receive foreigners except in certain cases. When they violate this rule, they are to be tried before judges (Koerner [1993] #87). A fifth-century law from Erythrai forbids anyone to serve as secretary to the same magistrate more than once and instructs the Exetastai to inflict fines on those magistrates who violate this ban (Koerner [1993] #74 = *I Erythrai* 1). A sixth-century law from Olympia grants certain guarantees to the Theokolos ("one who cares for the god"), a religious official, but forbids him to appropriate goods belonging to others. Cases involving violations are to be heard by the Iaromaos (Koerner [1993] #39). In a similar fashion, the Ephors of Sparta had the power to depose other magistrates who did not obey the laws (Xen. *Lac. Pol.* 8.4). The laws of the Greek *poleis* thus illustrate in concrete terms how these communities put into practice the idea, found both in Solon's poetry and in the story of Demonax, that one of the chief tasks of the legislator was not just to lay down rules for individuals to follow but also to distribute power to various bodies and to avoid the concentration of power.

Solon and the early Greek lawgivers are also credited with devising four other ways of preventing tyranny and promoting the rule of law. These were: 1) establishing term-limits for magistrates, 2) imposing penalties for magistrates who did not uphold the law, 3) assigning powers not to a single magistrate but to a board of officials, and 4) adding entrenchment clauses to ensure that those in power did not overturn the laws.

1) An important means of avoiding the accumulation of power in the hands of one person was to forbid magistrates to hold office for more than a year at a time and to prevent them from holding the same office ever again (or only after a certain interval). Already before Solon the Areopagus had appointed men to serve as Archon for only a year at a time ([Arist.] *Ath. Pol.* 8.2). This rule was extended to cover all offices except military ones, which required training and experience ([Arist.] *Ath. Pol.* 62.3).[24] One of the earliest Greek laws comes from the Cretan city of Dreros (650–600 BCE) and states that if a man holds the office of Kosmos, he should not be Kosmos again for ten years (Koerner [1993] #90 = *Nomima* I #81). A sixth-century law from Gortyn stipulates that the same man must not hold the office of Kosmos again within three years, the office of Gnomon within ten years, and the office of Kosmos for foreigners within five years (Koerner [1993] #121 = *ICret* IV 14, G-P). In a decree from Erythrai dated to the fifth century BCE, citizens are forbidden to serve as one of the Heleorontes again within ten years. Those who defy this ban must pay ten staters (Koerner [1993] #77 = *I Erythrai* 17). Another decree from Erythrai, dated to the middle of the fifth century, makes it illegal to be a member of the Council again within four years (Koerner [1993] #76 [= *I Erythrai* 4], line 12; cf. Koerner [1993] #74 = *I Erythrai* 1). In Sparta the most important office aside from the kingship was that of the Ephors, who held wide powers to police the activities of all citizens. But the position was so powerful that the Spartans did not entrust it to one man alone, but to a board of five men, each of whom were elected by the Assembly and could serve for only one year (Plu. *Agesilaus* 4 with Richer [1998] 304–9). The same was true for the navarchy at Sparta (Xen. *Hell.* 2.17; D. S. 13.100.18; Plu. *Lysander* 7.3).

2) One of the most striking features of early Greek laws is the number of penalties that are laid down for officials who do not uphold the law. As van Effenterre and Ruzé observe, "la legislation archaïque paraît aller bien au-delà de cet aspect dissuasif ou répressif. Elle traduit une méfiance systématique à l'égard

[24] For discussion see Rhodes (1981) 696. The only exception was the Council, where citizens were allowed to serve twice. For the link between the prohibition of *iteratio* and preventing tyranny, see the third-century law from Ilion against tyranny in Dareste, Haussoullier, and Reinach (1891–1904) #22.II.32–42 (ἐὰν δέ τις τὸ δεύτερον [σ]τρατηγήσηι ἢ ἄλλην ἀρ[χὴν] ἄρξηι).

des pouvoirs."[25] This is another feature of early Greek laws that set them apart from the laws of Lipit-Ishtar, Hammurabi, or the Jewish Scriptures: the latter rarely, if ever, stipulate what is to be done if the magistrate responsible for enforcing a law fails to do his duty.[26] Solon was not so trusting of those in power. He saw the greed and arrogance of leaders as a potential threat to order in the *polis* (fr. 4.7–25 [West]) and made conduct of officials subject to review by the Areopagus ([Arist.] *Ath. Pol.* 8.4). The laws were to apply to leaders as well as subjects. This included the lawgiver himself. In fact, there are several myths where the lawgiver breaks his own law and willingly submits to punishment. For instance, Charondas made it illegal to carry weapons in the Assembly under penalty of death (D. S. 12.19.1–2; Valerius Maximus 6.5 ext. 4). One day he armed himself with a dagger to protect himself from brigands in the countryside, but forgot he was still carrying it when he entered the Assembly. When someone criticized him for breaking his own law, he took out his dagger and killed himself.[27] Such myths have no value as historical evidence but show that the Greeks believed no one was above the law and that officials were not exempt from the law's provisions.[28] Hammurabi or any other Near Eastern monarch would hardly tell such a story about himself or one of his predecessors.

The same distrust of magistrates is evident in the laws from many *poleis*. Penalties for magistrates that do not carry out the law are attested in laws from many *poleis* throughout the Greek world. One of the most striking features of early Greek laws are the numerous penalties for magistrates who fail to perform their duties. One of the earliest Greek laws, dated to the seventh century BCE, comes from Tiryns near Argos in the Peloponnese (Koerner [1993] # 31). The law instructs magistrates called the Platiwoinarchoi to fine the Platiwoinoi thirty *medimnoi* (a large amount of

[25] van Effenterre and Ruzé (1994–95) I.393.

[26] In the actual text of his laws Hammurabi does provide one provision about the punishment of corrupt judges (para. 5) and another about corrupt military officers (para. 34). See also Laws of Eshnunna para. 50. The idea that the king should be subject to the law appears in an embryonic form in *Deuteronomy* 17:14–20, but the passage provides no legal mechanism to make the king accountable. I owe this point to Raymond Westbrooke.

[27] For similar examples see Szegedy-Maszak (1978) 206, note 37.

[28] As M. H. Hansen (1998) 118, has noted, "The Renaissance and Baroque concept of the sovereign as supreme legislator who himself stands above the laws is foreign to the ancient Greeks who invariably emphasized the supremacy of the laws and held that a *polis* ruled by a monarch who set himself above the law was a tyranny, a perverted form of community, which, in its extreme form, had ceased to be a *polis*."

grain) for some violation, which is not preserved, then threatens Platiwoinarchoi with a double penalty if they do not levy this fine. A fragment of a fifth-century law or decree from Argos contains two penalties for magistrates. The initial part of the inscription, which probably contained the substantive provision of the measure, is missing but the extant part threatens an official (ἀϝρεύο[ν]) with the same penalty inflicted on traitors (πολεμί[ον]ς ἐπάγον – "the one who introduces enemies").[29] Another early law from Arcadia, dated to the sixth or fifth century, forbids women to wear fine clothes at a festival for Demeter and orders the Demiorgos to fine them thirty drachmas if they do not dedicate such clothing to Demeter (Koerner [1993] # 35). If they do not collect this fine, they are subject to punishment, possibly a curse for ten years. An amusing regulation from Olympia inscribed around 500 forbids sex in the temple and requires those who violate the ban to sacrifice a cow and perform purificatory rites (Koerner [1993] # 41 = *IvOl* #7). This penalty applies not only to the offender but also to the Thearos ("one who watches") in charge of the temple, probably for allowing the offense to take place – or perhaps (as his title implies) for watching it happen. Another provision from the same inscription declares that if anyone passes a judgment contrary to the written law, his decision is null and void (Koerner [1993] #42 = *IvOl* 7). Although no magistrate is named, the provision clearly applies to those who have the authority to judge legal disputes. A law from Naupactus from the same period forbids the Demiorgoi to make a greater profit than what is written in the law – if they violate this, they must dedicate a statue to Apollo (Koerner [1993] #48).

A law from the Aegean island of Thasos inscribed during the fifth century sets forth a penalty for some violation, then imposes a double fine on magistrates who allow violators to escape scot-free (Koerner [1993] #67, lines 9–10). A law from Eretria of the late sixth century appears to impose a penalty on the Archos who does not follow the law in collecting fines (Koerner [1993] #73). An inscription from Miletus dated to between 470 and 440 pronounces banishment on several individuals and offers a reward to those who kill them. The city assigns the task of paying the reward to the Epimenioi. If they do not pay the reward, they will owe the money themselves. If the city seizes the banished men, the Epimenioi have the responsibility for executing them. Should they fail to do so, each will owe a penalty of fifty staters (Koerner [1993] #81 = *Nomima* #103). A recently

[29] For the text see Mitsos (1983) 245 with the translation in van Effenterre and Ruzé (1994–95) #110.

discovered inscription from Thasos dated to the early fifth century contains several regulations about keeping public roads clean and assigns their enforcement to the Archoi and the Epistatai. If these officials do not impose the required fines, they are themselves to owe double this amount (Duchêne [1992] 19–20, lines 11–13, 48–9).

These provisions find several parallels in Athenian decrees from the fifth century. The Standards Decree orders the generals to send off heralds to announce its new rules to the cities under Athenian control; if they do not perform their duty, each is to be fined 10,000 drachmas (Meiggs and Lewis [1969] #45 §9). A decree about the citizens of Phaselis grants them the privilege of having their cases heard before the Polemarch; if any other magistracy tries their cases, the judgment is to be null and void and the magistrate shall owe a fine of 10,000 drachmas to Athena (Meiggs and Lewis [1969] #31, lines 15–22). A decree of tribute payment orders the Prytaneis to bring cases about its provisions into the Council and threatens them with a penalty (the amount is not preserved) if they fail to do so (Meiggs and Lewis [1969] #46, lines 35–7). A decree about the collection of first fruits (ἀπαρχαί) for the sanctuary at Eleusis requires the Hieropoioi to receive within five days any grain offered to them from the Greek cities; if they do not receive it, they are subject to a penalty of 1,000 drachmas (Meiggs and Lewis [1969] #73, lines 18–21). A decree proposed by Thoudippos in 425/24 threatens the Prytaneis with severe penalties, one of 1,000 drachmas for failure to introduce a discussion about tribute to the Assembly (Meiggs and Lewis [1969] #69, lines 28–33), another of 10,000 drachmas, a huge sum, for not completing work concerning the tribute before the end of their term of office and for preventing the collection of the tribute (lines 36–8).

This distrust of those in power is another feature that is found not only in democratic constitutions such as that of Athens but also in aristocratic constitutions such as that of the Spartans. The Spartans too believed that no person, no matter how powerful, was above the law, and did not hesitate to bring even their kings to trial for overstepping their powers.[30]

3) Another means of avoiding the concentration of power was to assign functions not to a single individual assisted by several subordinates, but to a group of officials, each of whom was on the same footing as his peers. This feature is perhaps best seen in Athenian democracy. The Aristotelian *Constitution of the*

[30] On the trials of the Spartan kings see note 15.

Athenians, dated to the 320s, gives the names of many boards of officials, but the following list includes only those boards attested in the period 600–400 BCE:

Archons – [Arist.] *Ath. Pol.* 3.2–3 with Develin (1989) 2–3
Basileis – *IG* i³ 104, line 11 with Gagarin (2000)
Eleven – [Arist.] *Ath. Pol.* 7.3; 52.1
Generals – [Arist.] *Ath. Pol.* 22.1 with Rhodes (1981) 264–5
Hellanotamiai – Th. 1.96.2
Hieropoioi of Eleusis – *IG* i³ 391, lines 10–11
Kolakretai – [Arist.] *Ath. Pol.* 7.3; *IG* i³ 7, line 9; 11, line 13; 36, line 8; 73, lines 26, 28 with Rhodes (1981) 139–40
Logistai – [Arist.] *Ath. Pol.* 54.2 with Rhodes (1972) 111
Naukraroi – [Arist.] *Ath. Pol.* 8.3 with Rhodes (1981) 151–3
Poletai – [Arist.] *Ath. Pol.* 7.3; 47.2–3 with Rhodes (1981) 552–5
Supervisors of Eleusis – *IG* i³ 32
Supervisors of the Mint – *IG* i³ 1453, lines 8, 12
Treasurers of Athena – [Arist.] *Ath. Pol.* 4.1; 7.3; 8.1; *IG* i³ 590
Treasurers of the Other Gods – *IG* i³ 52, lines 13–31 with Linders (1975)

Athens is perhaps unusual in the number of boards attested in this period, but several other *poleis* in this period are known to have one or more boards of magistrates. Even though the literary and epigraphical evidence is not as plentiful for these *poleis* as it is for Athens, Argos has nine boards attested, Thasos six, and Olympia five. Even small communities have several boards: Dreros has at least three, Gortyn five. (See the Appendix.) The tendency to entrust powers to a board of officials rather than to a single magistrate is thus characteristic not only of democratic *poleis* like Athens and Argos, but also of *poleis* without democratic constitutions like Gortyn and Sparta.

4) For the law to rule over everyone in the community, there must be safeguards to prevent the powerful from altering the law to suit their wishes. In the famous Constitutional Debate among the Persian nobles, Herodotus (3.80.5) has Otanes say that two of the worst vices of tyrants were that they violate women and disrupt the ancestral laws. Demosthenes (24.139–43) praised the Locrians because they had a law that the person who proposed a new law had to make his proposal with a noose around his neck; if the proposal did not pass, the noose was tightened and the proposer strangled. Not surprisingly, the Locrians for many years passed only

one new law. The Greeks saw changes in the law not as a sign of legal progress or as a healthy adaptation to new realities, but as a symptom of disorder.[31] Thucydides (1.18.1) reports that the Spartans had had the same laws for over four hundred years. For him this was not the mark of mindless adherence to tradition, but an indication of their *eunomia* and their freedom from tyranny. According to Herodotus (1.29), Solon, after laying down his laws, made the Athenians swear an oath that they would not alter his laws for ten years. The reason why he left Athens to go abroad was because he did not want to be forced to change any of his laws. According to Plutarch (*Solon* 25), the Athenians agreed not to change his laws for a hundred years.

The early laws of the Greek *poleis* show their concern for the stability of their laws by adding entrenchment clauses that punish those who propose changes with harsh penalties. For instance, Demosthenes (23.62) quotes a provision from Draco's law on homicide, which reads: "let any magistrate or private citizen who is responsible for annulling this law or changing it be outlawed and his children and his property." We find an equally harsh entrenchment clause in a law about property from Halicarnassus around 465–50: "If anyone wishes to destroy this law or propose a vote to annul it, let his property be sold and dedicated to Apollo and let him go into exile. If it (i.e., his property) is not worth ten staters, let him be sold into slavery abroad and let there be no (possibility of) return to Halicarnassus" (Koerner (1993) #84 [= *Nomima* I #19], lines 32–41). There is a similar clause in a fragment of a fifth-century law or decree from Argos: "If anyone annuls the provision written on the stele, the proposer and the presiding magistrate will suffer the same penalty as the one who brings in enemies" (*Nomima* I #110, lines 5–9). In a law dated around 525–500 the Locrians appear to divide a plain among citizens and grant rights to owners. To ensure that this division remains unchanged, the law threatens those who propose any change with severe punishment: "Unless the Assembly, under pressure of war, so decides, whoever proposes a division or puts the matter to a vote in the council of elders or in

[31] For frequent changes in laws as a sign of chaos, see, for example, Dem. 20.90–2. Aristotle (*Pol.* 2.5.12–14.1269a) presents a different rationale for not changing the laws. He recognizes that the laws must sometimes change to adapt to new circumstances, but if it becomes too easy to change the laws, men will acquire the habit of disobeying the government. Since he believes the role of the *polis* is to make men virtuous, he explains the need to preserve established laws in terms of their effect on the character of the citizens rather than as a means of restraining those in power.

the city or in the chosen men, let him and his family be accursed forever and his property be confiscated and his house destroyed as in the law about homicide" (Meiggs and Lewis [1969] #13, lines 7–14).

There are several examples of entrenchment clauses in decrees from fifth-century Athens.[32] A decree passed by Callias probably in 434/33 appears to order officials to spend money for construction on the Acropolis and for no other purpose without the Assembly's approval (Meiggs and Lewis [1969] #58B, lines 15–17). If anyone proposes spending money for any other purpose or puts such a motion to the vote without obtaining immunity from the Assembly, he is subject to the same penalties as those who propose an *eisphora* (property tax) (lines 17–19). The Standards Decree contains a similar provision that inflicts a penalty on the person who proposes a motion violating its provisions or the person who puts such a motion to the vote (Meiggs and Lewis [1969] #45, clause 8). These two Athenian decrees share one important feature with those from Argos and Locris: each one threatens not only the proposer but also the official who puts the illegal motion to a vote. At the beginning of the Peloponnesian War, the Athenians voted to set aside 1,000 talents as a reserve fund to be used only in the event of a naval invasion. To ensure that the fund remained untouched, they laid down the death penalty for anyone who proposed to use the money or spend it for some other purpose (Th. 2.24).[33] When the Athenians were debating how to change their constitution in 411, they could not proceed without first removing the restrictions about making proposals to alter the laws (Th. 8.67.2; [Arist.] *Ath. Pol.* 29.4).[34] The practice of appending entrenchment clauses to laws and decrees was so widespread that they "are found from Tauromenium and Issa in the west to places as far to

[32] On entrenchment clauses in Athenian statutes, see Lewis (1997) 136–49. In an essay on resistance to change in the law at Athens, Boegehold (1996) does not discuss entrenchment clauses either in Athens or in other Greek *poleis*.

[33] Before voting to use the reserve fund in 412, the Assembly first removed the penalties against such a measure (Th. 8.15.1).

[34] For other examples of entrenchment clauses, see *IG* i² 58, lines 1–5; 71, lines 52–4. For later examples of entrenchment clauses, see, for instance, Rhodes and Osborne (2003) #37, lines 95–7 (decree of *genos* of the Salaminioi 363/62), #49, lines 18–25 (decree of Amphipolis, 357/56), #54, lines 28–31 (decree of Mylasa 367/66–355/54), #78, lines 26–35 (decree of Xanthians 337) #83 ii, lines 20–6 (decree of Eresus). For further examples see those cited in Rhodes with Lewis (1997) 524–5. The addition of entrenchment clauses was no longer necessary in Athens after the creation of the *nomothesia* procedure in 403 (see Hansen [1991] 165–75) and the introduction of the *graphe paranomon* in the late fifth century (see Hansen [1974]).

the east in Asia Minor as Acmonia and Termessus, and they are used also by an Antigonid king and by the Romans."[35] What is striking is that the concern with the stability of the laws was not confined to oligarchic or democratic *poleis*; it was a goal that transcended political organization.

III. CONCLUSION

The Greek *poleis* of the Archaic and Classical periods were a diverse group of communities, differing in size, in political structure, and in many other ways. But they were to a large extent united by a common faith in the rule of law and their distrust of tyranny. *Eunomia* was an ideal that both Spartans (Hdt. 1.65; Th. 1.18.1) and Athenians (Aeschin. 1.5; 3.6) pursued. It was also an ideal that set them apart in their eyes from their non-Greek neighbors and helped them to construct their cultural identity in the years leading up to the Persian Wars and afterwards. Solon's poems contain perhaps the earliest and most articulate expression of this "spirit of the laws" in early Greece. But the ideal of the rule of law was not an empty slogan, a cultural ideal that had no impact on social reality. On the contrary, the Greek *poleis* devised many strategies for putting this ideal into practice, strategies that we can study in the inscriptions that preserve their statutes and decrees.

APPENDIX. BOARDS OF MAGISTRATES ATTESTED IN THE GREEK *POLEIS* BEFORE 400 BCE

Amorgos
Archontes – *Nomima* I #90
Atrax (?) (Thessaly)
Tagoi – *Nomima* I #102, line 8
Axos (Crete)
Kosmoi – *Nomima* II #18, line 8
Arcadia
Kosmoi – *Nomima* I #22, lines B9–10
Argos
Artynai – Thuc. 5.47.9; *Nomima* I #107 (= Koerner [1993] #27), line 2 with Piérart [2000] 305

[35] Rhodes with Lewis (1997) 524–5.

Strategoi – Wörrle [1964] 89–100
Damiourgoi – *IG* IV 506, line 7; *Nomima* I #87 (nine); *Nomima* I #88 (six); *Nomima* I #101, line 1 with Piérart (2000) 305
Hodelonomoi – *Nomima* I #65, line 18
Iaromnamones – *Nomima* I #86, lines 3–8 (four); *Nomima* I 101, line 1; *Nomima* I #110, line 2
Twelve – *Nomima* I #65, line 1
Wikadeis – *SEG* 33:286
Platiwoinarchoi – *Nomima* I #78 Blocks 1–4, Side A; Block 6; Block 7; Block 11
Platiwoinoi – *Nomima* I #78 Blocks 1–4, Side A (= Koerner [1993] # 31)
Argoura (Thessaly)
Tagoi – Koerner (1993) #50, lines 7–8
Chaleion (Locris)
Damiorgoi – *Nomima* I #53, line B13
Xenodikai – *Nomima* I #53, line B1
Chios
Basileis – *Nomima* I 62 (= Koerner [1993] #61), lines A4, D4
Demarchoi – *Nomima* I 62 (= Koerner [1993] #61), lines A3–4
Fifteen – Koerner (1993) #62, lines A19, B1–2
Orophylakes – Koerner (1993) #62, lines A15–16
Corcyra
Agoranomoi – *Nomima* I #99
Dreros
Damioi – Koerner (1993) #90 (= *Nomima* I #81), line 5
Kosmoi – Koerner (1993) #90 (= *Nomima* I #81), lines 1–5
Ithyntai – *Nomima* I #27, line 1
Twenty – Koerner (1993) #90 (= *Nomima* I #81), line 5
Eltynia (Crete)
Kosmoi – In *Nomima* II #80 line 8, van Effenterre and Ruzé read κόσμος but Koerner (1993) #94 has κόσμον
Eretria
Archoi – *Hesperia* 33 (1964) 381–91, line 9 (= Koerner (1993) #73)
Erythrai
Exetastai – *Nomima* I #84 (= Koerner [1993] #74), line 14
Heleoreontes – *Nomima* I #85 (= Koerner [1993] #77), lines 1–2, 18–19
Prytanes – *Nomima* I #106 (= Koerner [1993] #75), lines A29, C15–16, 21–2

Gortyn
Gnomones – *Nomima* I #82 (= Koerner [1993] #121), Blocks g-p line 2
Karpodaistai – *Nomima* I #49 (= Koerner [1993] #152), line 15
Kosmoi – *ICret* IV 72, col. v, lines 5–6; *Nomima* I #82 (= Koerner [1993] #121), Blocks g-p, line 2
Orpanodikastai – *ICret* IV 72, col. xii, lines 7, 11–12
Titai – *Nomima* I #16 (= Koerner [1993] #153), line 7; *Nomima* I #30 (= Koerner [1993] #154), line 20; *Nomima* I #82 (= Koerner [1993] #121), Blocks g-p, line 2
Halicarnassus
Mnemones – Koerner (1993) #84 (= *Nomima* I #19), lines 8, 10, 11–12, 31
Lindos
Epistatai – Koerner (1993) #56, line 21
Strategoi – Koerner (1993) #56, line 41 (cf. 10–11, 48–9)
Miletus
Epimenioi – Koerner (1993) #81 (= *Nomima* I #103), lines 5, 8, 10, 11
Prytaneis – *Nomima* I #94, lines 3–4
Naupactos
Damiorgoi – Koerner (1993) # 48 (= Meiggs and Lewis [1969] #13), line 22
Olympia
Basileis – *Nomima* I #23 (Koerner [1993] # 37), line 3
Damiorgoi – *Nomima* I #23 (Koerner [1993] #37), line 6
Iaromaoi – *Nomima* I #51, lines 5–6
Mastroi – *Nomima* I #23 (= Koerner [1993] #37), lines 6–7; *Nomima* #60, line 2
Proxenoi – *Nomima* I #51, lines 4–5 [36]
Rhytte (Crete)
Kosmoi – *Nomima* #7, lines 5–6, 10–11
"Elders" – *Nomima* #7, line 11
Sparta
Agathoergoi – Herodotus 1.67 (five)
Archagetai – Plutarch *Lycurgus* 6.1, 8
Ephors – Herodotus 1.65; 6.82; 9.76; Plu. *Ag.*.1.36 (five); *Cleomenes* 7.3 with Richer (1998) 261–4

[36] See Gauthier (1972) 41–6.

Teos
Timouchoi – *Nomima* I #104 (= Koerner [1993] #78), line 29; *Nomima* I 105 (= Koerner [1993] #79), lines D22–3
Thasos
Archoi – *Nomima* II 95 (= Duchêne [1992]) lines 10–11, 27
Archontes – Koerner (1993) #70 (= Meiggs and Lewis [1969] #83), lines 6, 13–14
Demiourgoi – Koerner (1993) #69, lines 7–8
Epistatai – *Nomima* II 95 (= Duchêne [1992]) lines 25, 29, 40–1, 47
Karpologoi – Koerner (1993) #67, lines 1–2, 9
Prostatai – *IG* XII, 8, 264 (= Koerner [1993] #71), line 13

Aristotle (*Pol.* 2.7.3.1272a) states that in Crete there were ten Kosmoi, but he does not indicate which *poleis* in Crete he is discussing.

1.2 Pericles' Praise of Athenian Democracy

χρώμεθα γὰρ πολιτείᾳ οὐ ζηλούσῃ τοὺς τῶν πέλας νόμους, παράδειγμα δὲ μᾶλλον αὐτοὶ ὄντες τισὶν ἢ μιμούμενοι ἑτέρους. καὶ ὄνομα μὲν διὰ τὸ μὴ ἐς ὀλίγους ἀλλ' ἐς πλείονας οἰκεῖν δημοκρατία κέκληται· μέτεστι δὲ κατὰ μὲν τοὺς νόμους πρὸς τὰ ἴδια διάφορα πᾶσι τὸ ἴσον, κατὰ δὲ τὴν ἀξίωσιν, ὡς ἕκαστος ἔν τῳ εὐδοκιμεῖ, οὐκ ἀπὸ μέρους τὸ πλέον ἐς τὰ κοινὰ ἢ ἀπ' ἀρετῆς προτιμᾶται, οὐδ' αὖ κατὰ πενίαν, ἔχων γέ τι ἀγαθὸν δρᾶσαι τὴν πόλιν, ἀξιώματος ἀφανείᾳ κεκώλυται.

– Thucydides 2.37.1

Thucydides gives Pericles very little to say in his funeral oration about the political institutions of Athenian democracy. This is no doubt in keeping with his principle of having the speakers in his history τὰ δέοντα εἰπεῖν, that is, speak those things that were suitable for the occasion.[1] For we know that the unwritten rules of the genre required the speaker to cover a good many topics, including the glorious deeds of the ancestors, the nobility of the Athenian character, the bravery of those who fell in battle, and consolation for their grieving families.[2] Yet though the rules of the genre did not permit a full-scale discussion of political institutions, the few sentences devoted to the topic in Pericles' Funeral Oration express an entire philosophy of government. What the florid Isocrates would have taken several pages to explain, the brilliantly concise Thucydides is able to compress into a few carefully worded phrases.

Because the short passage contains a rare declaration of the principles on which Athenian democracy was built, it has attracted a considerable share of scholarly attention. In recent years, however, there has been a growing tendency to

[1] Th. 1.22.1. For a recent discussion of the passage with references to earlier treatments, see Hornblower (1987) 45–65.

[2] For a study of the *topoi* of the Funeral Oration, see Ziolkowski (1981).

misinterpret the passage. Several have argued that Pericles attempts to downplay the democratic features of the Athenian constitution. Vlastos argues that, far from praising democracy, the sentences "create the impression that the democracy is in fact an aristocracy of talent."[3] Gomme is not quite so extreme, yet he nevertheless believes that the clause beginning "κατὰ δὲ τὴν ἀξίωσιν gives the modification that for public affairs there is not complete equality (since in fact everyone is *not* as good as his neighbor), but ἀξίωσις, ἀρετή determine election to office."[4] In the opinion of Oliver, Pericles praises the Athenian constitution not as a democracy but as a mixed constitution.[5] Though these scholars and those influenced by them differ about the details of interpretation, they are in general accord that Pericles is drawing a strong contrast in this passage between the democratic and the aristocratic features of the Athenian constitution.

Such an approach misinterprets the nature of the contrasts implied by the two μέν . . . δέ . . . constructions, misunderstands the underlying structure of thought in the passage, and leads to several questionable translations of key phrases. Although many scholars have correctly translated individual parts of the passage, no one has yet, to my knowledge, correctly analyzed the logical arrangement of ideas that binds these parts together. Once this arrangement has been elucidated, we can identify the nature of the contrasts implied by the μέν . . . δέ . . . constructions and discover how the ideas expressed in the passage cohere.

Since the passage treats the different aspects of Athenian democracy, it is best to start by examining how the Greeks of the Classical period viewed the various parts of the *politeia*. Their conception of the structure of the *politeia*, though similar in some regards, differed in significant ways from our view of the parts of government. In the American constitution, for instance, government is divided into three branches: the executive, the legislative, and the judiciary. In none of these branches do the citizens have direct say in the administration of public business; instead, they elect representatives to serve in the executive and legislative branches. At the Federal level, candidates for the judiciary are nominated by the executive and confirmed by the Senate in the legislative branch. The Greeks of the Classical period did not share our notion of representative government and therefore divided up the parts of the *politeia* in a different fashion. In the fifth century,

[3] Vlastos (1964) 27–9 = Vlastos (1973) 196–8. Vlastos' analysis has been endorsed by Loraux (1986) 186–9 and, in some respects, by Rusten (1989) 144–5.

[4] Gomme (1956) 108. Gomme's views are followed by Vretska (1966) and criticized by Grant (1971).

[5] Oliver (1955).

for example, the Athenians dealt with issues that we would classify as executive and legislative in the Assembly, where all citizens had a chance to vote. Even after the creation of the board of *nomothetai* in the fourth century, the power of initiative in legislative matters still lay in the hands of the Assembly.[6] Like us, the Athenians separated the political and judicial spheres, but unlike us, they divided the political sphere into the deliberative realm and the realm that covered the activities of magistrates.

The fullest exposition of the Greek view of the structure of the *politeia* is to be found in Aristotle's *Politics* (1297b35–1298a3). According to Aristotle, the three parts (μόρια) of a *politeia* are the deliberative (τὸ βουλευόμενον περὶ τῶν κοινῶν), the magistrates (τὸ περὶ τὰς ἀρχάς), and the judiciary (τὸ δικάζον). The deliberative part was responsible for foreign policy, lawmaking, and trials involving sentences of death or exile. In a democracy all the citizens are members of the deliberative body; in an oligarchy only a few. The same holds true for the judiciary: in a democracy it is the entire citizen body that mans the courts, whereas in an oligarchy the courts are in the hands of a select few. Each type of government differs also in regard to the magistracies. In a democracy every citizen is eligible for office, and candidates are either chosen by lot or elected by a vote of all the citizens. Aristotle (*Pol.* 1300a38–b5) lists several methods of appointment (some including the use of sortition) that can be considered oligarchic or aristocratic, but in each case either the right to vote in elections or the eligibility to stand for office is restricted to a small number.

This tripartite structure of the *politeia* was a traditional idea; Aristotle only elaborated on it. The threefold division is already evident in Otanes' defence of democracy as recounted by Herodotus (3.81). Otanes defends democracy for its virtues in all three areas. When the majority rules, Otanes asserts, there is *isonomia* (judiciary), magistrates are appointed by lot and subject to audit (magistracies), and all decisions about major issues are submitted to the approval of the entire citizenry (deliberative). The word *isonomia* probably has two aspects here. On the one hand, it refers to the passive right to receive justice on equal terms (equality before the law). On the other hand, it denotes the active right to participate in the judicial process by sitting on the courts.[7]

[6] For a discussion of *nomothesia* and its implications for the powers of the Assembly, see Hansen (1978) and Hansen (1979a) (= Hansen [1983a] 161–76 and 179–205).

[7] For a lucid discussion of the meaning of *isonomia*, see Raaflaub (1985) 115–17.

In Euripides' *Supplices,* Theseus' praise of democracy follows the same pattern (403–8, 426–55). In fact, the parallels between Otanes' speech and that of Theseus are quite close. In Herodotus, Otanes says that πλῆθος...ἄρχον...ἔχει *ἰσονομίαν.* In the *Supplices* (433–4), Theseus declares that under democracy γεγραμμένων δὲ τῶν νόμων ὅ τ' ἀσθενὴς | ὁ πλούσιός τε τὴν *δίκην ἴσην* ἔχει. According to Otanes, a democratic community *βούλευματα*... πάντα ἐς *τὸ κοινὸν ἀναφέρει.* For Theseus, one of the greatest signs of freedom under democracy is the fact that public meetings begin with the question τίς θέλει πόλει | χρηστόν τι *βούλευμ' ἐς μέσον φέρειν* ἔχων? Finally, Otanes cites the use of the lot to ensure that everyone has a chance to serve in office (πάλῳ...ἀρχὰς ἄρχει). Without mentioning the use of the lot, Theseus also lauds democracy for providing all citizens with the opportunity to hold power through the rotation of office (δῆμος δ' ἀνάσσει διαδοχαῖσιν ἐν μέρει | ἐνιαυσίαισιν). In his reply to this point made by Theseus, however, the herald notes that it is the use of sortition that enables the poor to hold office (ὥσπερ ἐν πέσσοις). Just as Otanes praises the excellence of democracy in all three parts of government, so does Theseus.

We can discern this threefold division again in a Demosthenic speech (Dem. 25.20). The speaker describes the rule of law in Athens and shows how it reigns over all parts of the democracy. The laws are responsible for convening the Council, summoning the people into the Assembly (deliberative), filling up the courts (judicial), and ensuring that incumbent magistrates yield their powers to those appointed to succeed them (magistracies). Note here that the deliberative function is represented by both the Council and the Assembly. And Aristotle, or one of his pupils, used this tripartite schema to organize his account of Athenian institutions found in the *Constitution of the Athenians.* The activities of the Council and the Assembly are described first (*Ath. Pol.* 43.2–49). There follows an account of the various magistracies, beginning with the sortitive offices (*Ath. Pol.* 50–4), moving on to the archons (*Ath. Pol.* 55–9), then listing the duties of other officials (*Ath. Pol.* 60–2). The account concludes with a discussion of the courts (*Ath. Pol.* 63–9).[8]

We can now turn to Th. 2.37.1. In his encomium for Athenian democracy Pericles is obviously citing the virtues of each of the three parts of the Athenian *politeia.* First, he speaks of the deliberative part: the Athenian political system "is

[8] For an excellent discussion of the relationship between Aristotle's analysis of the three parts of the *politeia* and the structure of [Arist.] *Ath. Pol.* 43–69, see Hansen (1974) 10–12.

called a democracy because the management of affairs is not in the hands of a few but in the hands of the majority" (καὶ ὄνομα μὲν διὰ τὸ μὴ ἐς ὀλίγους ἀλλ' ἐς πλείονας οἰκεῖν δημοκρατία κέκληται). Second, Pericles points to the principle of equality before the law for all citizens, a principle the Athenian judiciary follows when resolving private legal disputes (μέτεστι δὲ κατὰ μὲν τοὺς νόμους πρὸς τὰ ἴδια διάφορα πᾶσι τὸ ἴσον). Third, Pericles asserts that when selecting magistrates (προτιμᾶται) the Athenians do not pick candidates from one section of society (ἀπὸ μέρους) but in accordance with merit (κατὰ δὲ τὴν ἀξίωσιν, ὡς ἕκαστος ἔν τῳ εὐδοκιμεῖ, οὐκ ἀπὸ μέρους τὸ πλέον ἐς τὰ κοινὰ ἢ ἀπ' ἀρετῆς προτιμᾶται). Since the Athenians do not enforce a property qualification for magistracies, a man who is able to do some good for the community is not barred from office simply because lack of wealth (κατὰ πενίαν) has prevented him from displaying his worth (οὐδ' αὖ κατὰ πενίαν, ἔχων γέ τι ἀγαθὸν δρᾶσαι τὴν πόλιν, ἀξιώματος ἀφανείᾳ κεκώλυται). Pericles praises the three parts separately because a different principle is at work in each part. In matters of deliberation, decisions are made by a vote of the majority, not by the will of a small clique. The comparative πλείονας may not be used for stylistic variation so much as to allude to the procedure followed in both the deliberative bodies, the Council and the Assembly, which passed only those measures that received a plurality of the votes cast. In matters pertaining to private legal disputes, the most important principle was equality before the law for all citizens. And when it came to elections for the magistracies, Pericles claims that the crucial consideration was merit, not membership in a narrow group.

This analysis enables us to arrive at a correct understanding of the contrasts implied by the pair of μέν... δέ... constructions. The first contrast is between the collective decision making of the deliberative part of the system (ἐς πλείονας οἰκεῖν) and the rights of all *individuals* (πᾶσι, ἕκαστος) in the judicial sphere and in regard to the magistracies. The second contrast is between the *passive* right of all citizens to equality before the law in private disputes (κατὰ μὲν τοὺς νόμους) and the active right to compete for honor by running for office (κατὰ δὲ τὴν ἀξίωσιν... προτιμᾶται). Thucydides effectively brings out both the parallel and the contrasts between the two clauses by his choice of words: whereas πᾶσι balances ἕκαστος, τὰ *ἴδια* διάφορα stands in opposition to ἐς τὰ *κοινά*, and τὸ ἴσον (equality) to προτιμᾶται (with its implications of inequality). The entire passage is bound together by the parallel between the phrase μὴ ἐς ὀλίγους in the first section and οὐκ ἀπὸ μέρους in the last.

A proper understanding of the structure of thought in the passage reveals that Pericles is not contrasting the democratic façade of Athenian government with its aristocratic reality, nor introducing a modification to the general principle of equality by pointing to the importance of merit in election to office. On the contrary, Pericles is drawing a sharp distinction between Athenian democracy and Spartan oligarchy. The context makes this certain. In the sentence before his praise of democratic institutions, Pericles contrasts the Athenians, whose *politeia* is an example to others, with communities that imitate the laws of their neighbors, an obvious allusion to Sparta, which allegedly drew its constitutional inspiration from Crete.[9] The comparison continues as Pericles contrasts not only the democratic procedure of majority rule with the oligarchic rule of the few, but also the absence of a property qualification in democratic elections with the oligarchic practice of restricting eligibility for office to one section of the citizenry.[10] In the following sentences Pericles commends the Athenians for their tolerance toward one another and may be implicitly criticizing the Spartan practice of social ostracism for those who have incurred some dishonor.[11] Pericles draws further contrasts at 2.39.1 where he recalls the differences between Athens and Sparta in regard to preparation for war. The Athenians keep their city open to foreigners and rely on their inborn courage; the Spartans drive out foreigners and trust to secrecy. The Spartans subject themselves to a toilsome regimen of training; the Athenians have a less rigorous form of training but are no less courageous in battle. Thus, an interpretation that sees in Pericles' words a contrast between Athenian democracy and Spartan oligarchy fits the context far better than one that tries to find in Pericles' words an effort to portray Athens as less than fully democratic.

Those who believe that Pericles downplays the democratic aspects of the Athenian constitution and stresses its supposedly aristocratic features often produce questionable translations of the phrase διὰ τὸ μὴ ἐς ὀλίγους ἀλλ᾽ ἐς πλείονας. Vlastos translates thus: "because it is ordered with a view to the many, not the

[9] Sparta imitates Cretan institutions: Herodotus 1.65.4. Cf. Marchant (1891/1966) 170. Gomme (1956) 107 arbitrarily denies the allusion; Rusten (1989) 144 makes no comment.

[10] For a study of the oligarchic nature of decision making at Sparta, see de Ste. Croix (1972) 124–51, 353–4. Pericles may be exaggerating the oligarchic nature of the Spartan constitution in order to make the contrast more pointed. Some thought the Spartans possessed a mixed constitution: Pl. *Lg.* 692a; Arist. *Pol.* 1294b13–35; Plb. 6.10.

[11] Herodotus 7.231; Xen. *Lac. Pol.* 9.4–6; Plu. *Agesilaus* 30.

few."[12] Ostwald gives this version: "run with a view to the interests of the majority, not of the few."[13] Rusten has something similar: "because we govern not for the few but for the many."[14] Sealey's translation is along the same lines: "since our constitution is administered not for a few but for the majority."[15] The phrase receives this treatment from C. Meier: "It is called government of the people (*demokratia*) because we live in consideration not of the few but of the majority."[16] This way of rendering the phrase has distinguished forbears: Hobbes has "We have a form of government (. . .) which, because in the administration it hath respect not to a few, but to the multitude, is called a democracy."[17] His translation may have influenced that of Crawley: "Its administration favours the many instead of the few; this is why it is called a democracy."[18]

Several considerations militate against this interpretation. To begin with, there is the pattern of thought we have analyzed in the passage. Pericles starts by praising the deliberative part of the Athenian constitution, which was in the hands of the Assembly, where all citizens had a vote. This explains why Thucydides uses the word πλείονας, an allusion to the principle of majority rule followed in the Assembly. Second, there is the meaning of the word δημοκρατία, a compound formed from the roots of the two words δῆμος and κράτος, which mean respectively "people" and "power" and ought in morphological combination to mean "power of the people," just as ὀλιγαρχία means "rule of the few." Pericles is explaining why the constitution is called a δημοκρατία: it is because the power to deliberate on major issues lies in the hands of the people who make their decisions in the Assembly in accordance with the vote of the majority. Any constitution could claim to administer public business for the benefit of all, or most, citizens. Only democracy could boast that it placed the power of decision in the hands of the majority.

That is certainly the way the term was understood by contemporaries. Both Euripides (*Supplices* 403–41) and the writer known to us as the "Old Oligarch" ([Xen.] *Ath. Pol.* 1.8) portray Athens as a community controlled by the decisions

[12] Vlastos (1964) 196.
[13] Ostwald (1986) 183.
[14] Rusten (1989) 145.
[15] Sealey (1987) 101.
[16] Meier (1990) 140.
[17] Schlatter (1975) 132.
[18] Crawley (1874/1910) 104.

of the people. In his *Knights*, Aristophanes cast the Athenian people in the role of a master and Athenian politicians as slaves who obeyed his orders. And the prescripts of Athenian decrees do not leave us in any doubt about who held the power to make public policy: all important motions that went into effect began with the phrase ἔδοξε τῷ δήμῳ.

Third, there is Thucydides' usage. When Thucydides employs the preposition ἐς in constitutional contexts, the word means "in the control of."[19] Among recent scholars, Raaflaub gets the phrase right: "the constitution is called *demokratia* (. . .) because power is not in the hands of the few but of the majority."[20] So do Warner ("Our constitution is called a democracy because power is in the hands not of a minority but of the whole people") and de Romilly ("Pour le nom, comme les choses dépendent non pas du petit nombre mais de la majorité, c'est une démocratie").[21]

Gomme's view that the phrase beginning κατὰ δὲ τὴν ἀξίωσιν introduced a qualification of the democratic principle of equality led him to argue that the phrase οὐκ ἀπὸ μέρους means "'not in rotation' (. . .) i.e. amongst other things, we do not use the lot for election to important office."[22] Many of those who have interpreted the passage in a way similar to that of Gomme have rejected this part of his analysis, but Rusten endorses it: "means 'according to turn' (. . .) and refers (. . .) to the Athenian practice of choosing most magistrates in a yearly lottery."[23] This view rests on a misunderstanding of the structure of thought in the passage. As we noted above, Pericles is contrasting democratic and oligarchic practices. In regard to elections, the distinctive feature of oligarchy is a tendency to limit eligibility to a restricted number whereas democracy places no such limitation or imposes only a very low property qualification.[24] The lot was used at Athens for many offices, but, as Aristotle reveals (*Pol.* 1300a38–b3), it was

[19] Th. 5.81.2; 8.38.3, 53.3, 97.2. See Classen/Steup (1963) 91–2. I must here confess that I myself misinterpreted the idiom in my translation of 8.97.2 in Harris (1990b) 258 and 273. Fortunately, the incorrect translation does not affect my arguments in that article.

[20] Raaflaub (1990) 60.

[21] Warner (1954/1982) 145; de Romilly (1962) 27.

[22] Gomme (1956) 108.

[23] Rusten (1989) 145–6. Cf. Rhodes (1988a) 81, 220. Vlastos (1964) 127, note 124 puts forth several reasons for rejecting Gomme's view.

[24] Property qualification for office compatible with democracy: Arist. *Pol.* 1273b35–1274a3. The system of property qualifications appears to have fallen into desuetude by the late fifth century: see Rhodes (1981) 145–6, 551.

not a distinctive feature of democracy, for it could also be found in oligarchical constitutions.

Pericles is perhaps exaggerating the importance of advancement by merit through the electoral process, passing over the widespread use of the lot for many offices. But it is possible to interpret the next phrase, in which Pericles states that poverty does not bar a man from serving the community, as alluding to the use of sortition, for it was that procedure that allowed men of modest means, who might never stand a chance of winning an election, to hold office.[25] On Gomme's interpretation, Pericles would be denying that the lot was used in Athens and thereby uttering a falsehood. Now a venial instance of *suppressio veri*, such as a failure to mention sortition, is to be expected in a Funeral Oration; an outright lie would be unpardonable. Furthermore, Gomme and Rusten are compelled to translate "in rotation." That is inconsistent with Thucydidean usage. When Thucydides wishes to express the idea of rotation in duties, he employs the phrase ἐν τῷ μέρει (4.11.3; 8.86.3, 93.2) or κατὰ μέρος (3.49.3; 4.26.3). Use of the word μέρος to mean "part of the citizenry," however, is attested elsewhere in the historian's work (6.39.1, 2). Finally, one should observe that rotation in office and sortition are not equivalent and that adherence to the former does not necessarily imply the existence of the latter. A constitution can forbid *continuatio* for elective as well as sortitive offices: witness the ephorate and navarchy at Sparta or the consulship at Rome under the *lex Villia annalis*.[26] All these reasons make it impossible to read into the phrase an allusion to the use of the lot. The phrase alludes to the oligarchic practice of restricting eligibility for office, which Pericles contrasts with the democratic practice of considering only merit when selecting men to serve as magistrates.

Pericles' encomium of Athenian democracy is similar in some regards both to that delivered by Otanes at Herodotus 3.80.2–6 as well as to the defense given by Theseus at Euripides' *Supplices* 403–8, 426–62. There is one significant exception: Otanes cites the use of the lot, and Theseus mentions the rule of rotation in office as a means of granting the people access to power, whereas Pericles appears to avoid mentioning sortition, stressing instead the absence of a property qualification and the importance of merit. The difference is not the product of any difference

[25] Sortition as a means of granting the poor access to office: Eur. *Supplices* 403–10.

[26] For rotation in the ephorate, see Th. 5.36.1. For annual rotation in the navarchy, see Th. 2.66.2, 80.2; 3.16.3; 4.11.2; 8.6.5, 20–9, 85, 99. For the *lex Villia annalis* see Astin (1957) and Astin (1958).

between the political philosophy of Theseus and Otanes, on the one hand, and Pericles, on the other, nor between those of the authors in whose works their words are reported. Rather it is due to the different contexts in which the statements are made. Otanes and Theseus are both arguing that democracy is superior to one-man rule. Under the latter regime, one man enjoys unchecked power and the people are his slaves. In a democracy the people have a share in power through the annual rotation of sortitive offices. In the Funeral Oration, however, Pericles is comparing democracy not with one-man rule but with oligarchy. Since the use of the lot and the rotation of offices could be found in both democratic and oligarchic constitutions, Pericles chooses to fasten on the topic of eligibility for office when contrasting the two forms of *politeia*. In a democracy, there is either no property qualification or only a negligible one; oligarchies often restrict candidacy to one section of the citizenry. If Pericles fails to mention the use of the lot, it is not because he views it as a sign of "vulgar democracy," incompatible with the more aristocratic version he believes exists in Athens. He omits any direct reference to sortition because it is inappropriate to the context.

Our study has shown that the praise of Athenian democracy that Thucydides composed for Pericles was no less than wholehearted. Pericles is not made to reply to the critics of democracy by alluding to its supposedly aristocratic features. In a Funeral Oration delivered for the soldiers who had given their lives to defend Athenian institutions, the democracy required no apology.[27]

Afterthoughts

I am now more inclined to believe that the final phrase in the passage (which begins οὐδ' αὖ κατὰ πενίαν) contains an allusion to the use of the lot in selecting magistrates. This would form a balance and a contrast with the previous phrase, where Pericles alludes to the absence of a property qualification for elective offices.

On Thucydides' political views, see now Leppin (1999). On the extent to which the distinction between magistrates and private citizens introduced an element of inequality into Athenian democracy, see Rubinstein (1998). On annual rotation

[27] I would like to thank Professor Kurt Raaflaub for reading an earlier version of this article and offering several brilliant suggestions for improvement. His remarks helped me to understand the nature of the two contrasts implied in the pair of μέν . . . δέ constructions. He should not be held responsible for any errors of fact or judgment in the published version.

The research for this article was supported by a Professional Staff Congress-City University of New York Research Award. The Professional Staff Congress is affiliated with the AFL-CIO.

in office as characteristic of both aristocracy and democracy, see Chapter I.1. On *xenelasia* at Sparta, which Pericles mentions at Th. 2.39.1, see now Figueira (2003).

The discussion of the passage in Hornblower (1991) 298–301 appeared too late for me to take into account. Hornblower translates "in rotation" and follows Ostwald in rendering "with a view to the interests of the many." Several objections can be made against this translation. First, it does not convey the sense of the comparative πλείονας. Second, when politicians in Athens were commended, they were praised for acting for the people (δήμῳ) as a whole, not a part of it. Third, "with a view to the interests of the many" should be expressed by the dative (πολλοῖς) or the preposition with the genitive (ὑπὲρ τῶν πολλῶν), not with ἐς followed by the accusative. Fourth, this translation makes no sense in the context. Thucydides has Pericles explain the term *demokratia,* which means power of the people, not what is in the interest of the many. My essay appears to have been unknown to Lattimore (1998) 92, who follows Hornblower in his translation of Th. 2.37.

1.3 Antigone the Lawyer, or the Ambiguities of *Nomos*

The Athenians believed that of all three forms of government only democracy measured up to the ideal of the rule of law. Aeschines (1.4–6) says that what distinguishes democracy from oligarchy and tyranny is that the Athenian type of government is ruled by the established laws, whereas the latter two are ruled by the whim of those in power.[1] In a democracy the bodies of all citizens are protected by the laws, whereas the tyrant and the oligarch rely on suspicion and armed guards to protect only themselves. Theseus in Euripides' *Supplices* (429–37) denounces tyranny because under that type of regime the law is in the hands of one man who rules by himself. Under democracy written laws are the common possession of all citizens and enable the weak to have equal justice with the rich. Not only did democracy promote the rule of law, but the rule of law also kept the democracy strong and safe. Demosthenes (25.21) holds that next to the gods the laws are responsible for protecting Athens.[2] Aeschines (3.6) states that when the Athenians observe the laws, the democracy is kept safe. Conversely, when men lost respect for the rule of law, the democracy was threatened. According to Aeschines (1.179), when the courts allow themselves to be distracted by irrelevant charges, the laws are ignored, and the democracy is undermined.

The ideal of the rule of law figures prominently in funeral orations delivered at Athens for those who died fighting for the community. Pericles in the Funeral Oration given to him by Thucydides (2.37.3) boasts that the Athenians obey both those placed in positions of power and the laws. In Lysias' *Funeral Oration* (2.19) the Athenians are praised for using the law to honor the good and punish the

[1] Ober (1989) 303 claims that "elite philosophers like Aristotle (...) considered the rule of law a good thing and something essentially different from the rule of the people." Ober cites Arist. *Pol.* 1293a3–38 to support his view, but he misrepresents Aristotle's argument, which distinguishes between forms of democracy where the laws rule and those where they do not. *Pace* Ober the passage shows that Aristotle did not consider democracy incompatible with the rule of law. Thomas (1994) 127 rightly rejects Ober's view: "appeals to the laws and the importance of upholding them (...) were often thought to reinforce the rule of the democracy, not undermine it."

[2] Cf. Dem. 24.5; Aeschin. 3.169, 196.

evil. The Athenians believe men ought to define what is just by the law, persuade by reason, be ruled by the law, and be taught by reason. We have no idea what relationship these speeches bear to the speeches actually delivered. But we know that Hyperides delivered the Funeral Oration (*Epitaphios* 25) for the soldiers who fell with Leosthenes at Lamia in 322. In his eulogy he praised them because they fought for the rule of law. Their conviction was that among men who are fortunate the voice of law, not the threats of one man, reigns supreme. Under the rule of law the safety of the citizens lay in trusting the law, not fearing those who flatter dynasts and slander the citizens.

The importance of obeying the law is also stressed in the most important oaths sworn by Athenian citizens. Those who had been selected as judges for the Athenian courts swore that they would render their verdicts in accordance with the laws.[3] And every year the new class of ephebes solemnly declared that they would obey the established laws and any laws that were established prudently in the future.[4]

Out of all the extant Attic tragedies, there is none that is more concerned with the role of law (*nomos*) than Sophocles' *Antigone*. In a famous ode, the chorus praises the man who upholds the laws and the justice of the gods (368–70). Creon declares in his first speech as king of Thebes that he will make the city greater through his laws (191), and the chorus admits that he has the power to use every law (213). When Antigone defies Creon's order not to bury the traitor Polynices, the chorus says she has disobeyed the king's laws (381–2). Yet Antigone refuses to call the king's order to leave the traitor Polynices unburied a law (21–36). In reply to Creon's charge that she broke the law (449; cf. 481), Antigone denies she has broken any law (450–1). On the contrary, she argues that Creon's orders do not take precedence over the unwritten laws of the gods (452–5). This does not stop Creon from sentencing her to execution by confinement in an underground chamber. After his angry exchange with Teiresias, however, Creon realizes he has made a mistake, rescinds his order, and says it is best to preserve the established laws (1113–14). Each character appeals to the law – which character really has the law on his or her side?

Several recent scholars believe that Creon has the law on his side and that Antigone is the one who breaks the law.[5] M. Bowra believes that Antigone is right

[3] For the importance of the judicial oath, see Harris (1994a) 133 with notes 6 and 7.

[4] Tod (1948) no. 204, lines 11–15.

[5] Since the bibliography on the play is so enormous, I have had to confine this survey of recent opinions to a few representative works. For an attempt to survey work on the play up to the late 1960s, see Hester (1971).

to insist on burying her brother Polynices, but is still disturbed by Antigone's actions. "Antigone is right but often seems to be wrong."[6] Bowra feels that although Antigone's position is correct, the Athenians would lose sympathy with her because "she is determined to break the law." He continues: "we can hardly doubt that many would think it wrong in any circumstances to break the law and would condemn Antigone because she proposes to do so."[7] Antigone may be right, but Bowra finds her self-righteous and haughty: "Antigone takes upon herself to defy the law or what is at least believed to be the law. The decision is momentous and would undoubtedly create strong prejudice against her in many of the audience.'" In Bowra's eyes, "Antigone in defiance of all this established sentiment sets herself above Creon's law and claims to know better what is right."[8]

Ostwald takes a slightly different position. He believes that the main issue in the play is the conflict "between political obligations imposed by the state's *nomoi* and religious obligations incumbent upon the family," or more briefly "between the state and the family."[9] Both sides are at fault: "the comparative disregard of kinship obligations by the state and of political obligations by the family constitutes a large part of the tragic momentum."[10] But in Ostwald's opinion "*nomos* is on the side of Creon as the legitimate ruler of Thebes,"[11] whereas "Antigone sets herself in opposition to *nomos*."[12] Goldhill, on the other hand, believes there are two kinds of laws, and that "Antigone sets the laws of the gods in opposition to the laws of the land."[13] Whitman sides with Antigone: "It is Antigone's claim that a higher

[6] Bowra (1944) 78.

[7] Bowra (1944) 79.

[8] Bowra (1944) 82–3. To be fair, Bowra elsewhere shows a more nuanced understanding of Antigone's position.

[9] Ostwald (1986) 149. Knox (1964) 76 thinks that Antigone bases her claim on "the strong indissoluble tie of blood relationship" that "had in earlier times, through the *gene*, the 'clans,' been the dominating factor in the citizen's social and political environment." This tie, Knox believes, "was a rival and even a potential danger to the newer civil institutions of the *polis*" represented by Creon. Unfortunately, Knox's ideas rely on a questionable view of the role of the *gene* that has now been demolished by Bourriot (1976). See also Parker (1996) 56–66.

[10] Ostwald (1986) 149.

[11] Ostwald (1986) 152.

[12] Knox (1964) 94 believes that Antigone opposes Creon's *nomoi*, "laws," and believes in the "*nomima* of the gods, their 'customs, ways, usages.'" This view is inconsistent with Antigone's use of language – she never calls Creon's decree a *nomos* (see Part II) and refers to the laws of the gods both as *nomima* (455) and as *nomoi* (519).

[13] Goldhill (1986) 96. Cf. Thomas (1996) 17: "There is a conflict between the laws of the state (i.e., Kreon) and the unwritten laws of the gods – here the right of burial – which have higher moral value." See, however, E. Wolf (1952) 254–5, who rightly observed: "Darum wäre es auch falsch, den Streit zwischen

law delimits the temporal authority of a king, and that if there is conflict, the king's law must yield." Whitman is not impressed by Creon's appeals to *nomos*: "rulers are called upon to justify their authority before a tribunal which represents transcendent values; in this case, Antigone is the balance in which Creon is weighed and found wanting."[14]

To understand the play, therefore, we need to understand *nomos* (the Greek word for "law") and Athenian attitudes toward the role of law in their democracy. After all, Sophocles wrote for an Athenian audience and used terms and ideas that they presumably understood. But we should not assume that the Athenian concept of *nomos* was simple and lacking in ambiguity. As we will see, there existed some uncertainty about what qualified as a *nomos*, and Sophocles exploited this uncertainty to create tragic misunderstanding. We should also not assume that Athenian attitudes to law were the same as ours. For instance, the Constitution of the United States draws a firm line between church and state, but it would be wrong to read such a distinction into a play written in Classical Athens. In the first part of this essay, I examine the Greek word *nomos*, the sources of legitimacy, the relationship between "unwritten laws" and written statutes, and the right to disobey an illegal order. In the second part, I study the debate about the law in Sophocles' *Antigone* to show that Antigone is the one who has the stronger legal arguments. Contrary to the opinion of many recent scholars, it is Creon who misunderstands the duties of a magistrate and breaks the law.

I

Before we examine the Greek word *nomos*, it is necessary to clarify what we ourselves mean by the word "law." Above all, we should avoid the Eurocentric assumption derived from modern jurisprudence that law must be enacted by a legislature and be expressed in formal, written statutes. If one adopts such an assumption, one would have to label all preliterate societies "lawless." To avoid this problem, anthropologists have identified certain attributes that are constant features of laws

Kreon und Antigone auf die Spannung 'menschlichem' und 'göttlichem' Recht hin interpretieren zu wollen; denn auch Kreon beruft sich auf göttliches Recht." Paoli (1932) believed there was a conflict between sacred and secular law in Lysias 13, but his view is rightly criticized by Todd (1993) 63. Nussbaum (1986) 51–85 does not discuss the use of the word *nomos* in the play, but still sees the play in terms of a conflict between *oikos* and *polis*.

[14] Whitman (1951) 88. Unlike many recent scholars, Whitman finds Antigone "the prototype of the perfect citizen." Others who side with Antigone against Creon are Müller (1967) and Benardete (1975).

in all societies. Such an approach works well for ancient Greece, where there was a gradual and uneven transition from unwritten laws to written statutes, which occurred over several centuries.[15] According to some sources, Classical Sparta dispensed entirely with written laws.[16] In other *poleis*, laws were transmitted orally even after the introduction of writing and in some cases handed down by singing.[17] (On the existence of unwritten laws in Greek international relations see Chaniotis [2004].)

L. Pospisil, building on the work of earlier scholars like Llewellyn and Hoebel, identifies four basic attributes of law. First, there must be an authority with the power to force litigants to accept a legal decision and to enforce the law.[18] Second, the authority who makes a decision must "intend it to be applied to all 'similar' situations in the future."[19] Third, there must be an *obligatio*, that is, a part of the law that "states the rights of one party to a dispute and the duties of the other."[20] A law can define these rights and duties negatively by naming the delict or crime that violates these rights or fails to fulfil these duties. Fourth, a law must contain a sanction.[21] The sanction is usually some form of punishment, but need not be physical. Pospisil points to the Incas, who had two forms of punishment: flogging, scourging, forced labor, and death for commoners, but non-physical sanctions for nobles. The reason for the different treatment was that the Inca "held that public ridicule and loss of office hurt a noble as much as exile or torture would a poor man and that the prestige of the nobles as a class must be upheld."[22] Pospisil notes how "Kapauku consider being shamed in public much worse than anything except capital punishment."[23] We might compare the use of *atimia*, or loss of rights, in Athenian Law or the punishment of *infamia* in Roman Law.[24]

[15] Thomas (1996). Medieval Iceland had an extensive lawcode that was preserved orally by the Lawspeaker, an elected official who recited the law to anyone who asked. See Miller (1990) 18–19.

[16] Plu. *Lycurgus* 13.1; *Mor.* 227b. See however MacDowell (1986) 1–5.

[17] For the role of Mnemones see Thomas (1996). For laws being sung see Picirilli (1981).

[18] Pospisil (1971) 44–78. Despite their interest in legal anthropology, Todd and Millett (1990) 11–18 do not examine the work of Pospisil and do not apply the analysis of "law" made by anthropologists to the term *nomos*. To my knowledge, the only attempt to apply Pospisil's analysis to Greek Law is Burchfiel (1994).

[19] Pospisil (1971) 78.

[20] Pospisil (1971) 81.

[21] Pospisil (1971) 87–95.

[22] Pospisil (1971) 91.

[23] Pospisil (1971) 89.

[24] For the use of *atimia* in Athenian Law, see Hansen (1976a). For *infamia* in Roman Law, see Crook (1967) 83–5.

Many extant laws of Athens certainly contain these four features. The standard form of a law begins with a conditional clause, which names the delict or crime, and then provides for a form of action and a penalty. Although many laws do not state which official will enforce them, by naming the action, these laws imply that the appropriate magistrate for the action will enforce whatever sentence the court imposes.[25] For instance, the law on outrage (*hybris*) begins with the phrase "if anyone outrages a child, a man, a woman, either free or a slave," and thus names the crime (Aeschin. 1.15). There follow the name of the action the victim can bring (*graphe hybreos*) and the provision for determining a penalty (*timema*).[26]

The initial phrase naming the crime or delict is invariably cast in general terms, usually in the form "if anyone . . . ," and often contains the indefinite pronoun *tis* ("someone," "anyone") to indicate that the law is intended to apply to all men. To give just a few examples:

> The law on tyranny (And. 1.96): "If *anyone* destroys the democracy at Athens or serves in any office after the democracy has been overthrown . . ."
>
> Law on Sexual Violence (Lys. 1.32): "If *anyone* brings shame upon a free man or child by violence . . ."
>
> Law on the Award of Crowns (Aeschin. 3.32): "If the Council awards a crown to *anyone* . . ."
>
> Law about Deceiving the People (Dem. 20.100): "If *anyone* deceives the Assembly, the Council, or the court by making some promise . . ."
>
> Law about Arbitrators ([Arist.] *Ath. Pol.* 53.5): "If *anyone* does not serve as arbitrator when he has reached the appropriate age . . ."
>
> Law about Claims against Inheritance (Dem. 52.17; cf. 19): "If *anyone* has a claim against a person who has died and brings an action against his heir . . ."

[25] As Hölkeskamp (1992) 95 notes, the magistrates mentioned in early laws "must obviously have a minimum degree of authority to implement, or enforce the implementation of, the norms and rules that refer to their functions."

[26] The text of the law on *hybris* found at Dem. 21.47 is a forgery; see Harris (1992c). Fisher (2001) 139–40 claims the text is genuine, but misrepresents my argument by discussing only one of the objections to its authenticity and ignoring the other objections.

Law about Mines (Dem. 37.35): "If *anyone* ejects someone from his work-area . . . "

Law about Sale of Slaves (Hyp. *Ath.* 15): "When *anyone* sells a slave, it is necessary to declare ahead if it has any disease . . . "

Law about Contracts ([Dem.] 56.2): "As many agreements as *anyone* makes with another person . . . "

Law on Qualifications of Archons (Aeschin. 1.19): "If *anyone* of the Athenians is a prostitute, he is not permitted to be one of the nine archons . . . "

In several passages Aristotle says that a law deals with general or universal rights and duties, not with particular situations. In the *Rhetoric* (1.1.1354b4–8) he distinguishes between the role of the lawgiver and that of the judge and member of the Assembly. The decision of the lawgiver is not about individual circumstances, but about future events and general matters.[27] In the *Nicomachean Ethics* (5.14.1137b11–14, 27–9) Aristotle draws attention to the fact that every law is about a general matter, and that it is not possible for the law to speak in general terms about individual cases. The very essence of fairness (*epieikeia*) is to serve as a corrective of the law in those areas where the law is deficient because it deals with general matters. Aristotle also notes that the laws cannot speak with precision since it is not easy to give general definitions about all things (*Pol.* 1282b4–6). This principle was also recognized by the orators. Demosthenes (24.159) criticizes a law proposed by Timocrates because he was proposing it for his friend, and it failed to lay down the same rule for all people. In fact, the Athenians in 403 made it illegal to pass a law that was directed at a single individual (And. 1.87).[28]

Aristotle also clearly differentiated between the sphere of the laws and that of the magistrates. In the *Politics* (1282b2) he holds that "It is proper for the laws when rightly laid down to be sovereign, while the magistrate or magistrates should have supreme powers over matters as to which the laws are quite unable to pronounce because of the difficulty of making a general rule to cover all cases." While the laws contain general provisions for all men to follow, the magistrates dealt with

[27] Cf. Pl. *Pol.* 295a: the lawgiver "makes the law for the generality of his subjects under average circumstances."

[28] Although it was possible to enact an *ad hominem* law if there was a quorum of 6,000, the Athenians appear to have rarely if ever taken advantage of this exception. See Hansen (1979a) 28–31.

the application of the laws in particular circumstances (*Pol.* 1292a33). Aristotle's ideas about the relationship of the magistrate to the law are also in keeping with the Athenian view of the relationship. When the archons and the members of the Council entered office each year, they too promised to perform their duties in accordance with the laws ([Arist.] *Ath. Pol.* 55.5; cf. 7.1; Xen. *Mem.* 1.1.18). A speaker in a speech by Lysias (16.12) reminds the court that "the laws explicitly state that neither a general nor a cavalry-commander nor anyone else is superior to them."

The Athenians created several procedures to make sure that officials obeyed their oath. The Areopagus had general oversight over all magistrates to see that they obeyed the laws (And. 1.84). Individual citizens also had the right to denounce to the Council any magistrate who did not rule in accordance with the laws. If the Council voted against the magistrate, the matter was referred to the court for trial and possible punishment ([Arist.] *Ath. Pol.* 45.2). One could also use the *eisangelia* procedure to bring a charge against a magistrate in the Assembly, which would examine the charge and if it had any merit hand the case over to a court.[29] At the end of their terms of office, all magistrates had to submit their accounts to the *logistai* to make sure they had not embezzled public funds.[30] After they passed this examination, anyone who wished could still bring a charge against them before magistrates called the *euthynoi*.[31] As if these procedures were not enough, the Assembly took a vote on the conduct of all magistrates once every prytany, that is, ten times a year; if a magistrate did not win a vote of confidence, he was deposed and stood trial ([Arist.] *Ath. Pol.* 43.4; 61.2).[32]

Our discussion so far has shown that the Athenians considered a *nomos* a general provision applicable to all people (or broad categories of people) for an unlimited amount of time. The Athenians also believed that magistrates should be subject to the laws and created several procedures to put this ideal into practice. But did the Athenians consider every general provision laid down by the authorities of a *polis* qualified to be a *nomos*? This question arises in a fascinating conversation between Pericles and Alcibiades recorded in Xenophon's *Memorabilia* (1.2.42). When Alcibiades asks Pericles what he thinks a *nomos* is, Pericles replies that laws are

[29] For the *eisangelia* procedure see Hansen (1975).

[30] For the *logistai* see [Arist.] *Ath. Pol.* 48.3; 54.2 with Rhodes (1981) 597–9.

[31] For *euthynoi* see [Arist.] *Ath. Pol.* 48.4 with Rhodes (1981) 561–2.

[32] On the *epicheirotonia* see Rhodes (1981) 523, 682–3. Timotheus was removed from the office of general by this method in 373/2 ([Dem.] 49.9–10).

provisions that the people approve and enact when they meet together, which indicate what must be done and what must not be done. Alcibiades wants to know what Pericles would call the provisions enacted when a small group meets together as happens when there is an oligarchy. Pericles revises and broadens his definition of *nomos* to include all provisions – as many as the ruling part of the community enacts when it deliberates. Alcibiades invites Pericles to apply this to the case of a tyrant; if a tyrant enacts provisions about what to do, are they also called *nomoi*? Pericles agrees that they are.

Alcibiades next asks Pericles what violence and lawlessness are. Pericles replies that these occur when the stronger party forces the weaker party to do what it decides, not by persuasion but by violence. If this is so, Alcibiades pursues, are not all the orders a tyrant forces the citizens to perform without persuading them therefore lawlessness? This forces Pericles to withdraw his claim that whatever a tyrant enacts without persuasion is a law. Alcibiades then applies this line of reasoning to oligarchy and democracy – if these forms of government enact provisions not by persuasion but by force, these cannot be called laws. At this point Pericles admits defeat and withdraws from the debate.

It is impossible to know whether Xenophon presents us with a version of an actual conversation or has invented this interchange between the two great men. But the argument reveals that the Athenians might be ambivalent about the use of the word *nomos*. One might call a general provision enacted by the ruling part of the city a *nomos*, but a provision lacked the full qualifications to be a law if it was enacted by force and not by persuasion.

We find the same ambivalence about the use of the word *nomos* in the dialogue *Greater Hippias* (283d–285b) attributed to Plato. Socrates is discussing the lessons Hippias gives in many Greek cities and asks him if he has ever made any money for his teaching in Sparta. Hippias says he cannot teach there because the Spartans require their sons to receive only their traditional education. Socrates asks Hippias if law is a harm or a benefit to a community. Hippias replies that laws are made to benefit the community. Socrates then gets Hippias to agree that when a legislator fails to implement what is good, what he produces is not a law nor lawful. Conversely, what is more beneficial is more lawful. Socrates next draws out the implications of this statement: if it is more beneficial for the Spartan youth to learn from Hippias, it must also be more lawful for them to receive his education. If the Spartans do not entrust their sons to Hippias, they will therefore be breaking the law. This leads to the paradoxical conclusion that the Spartans, who had a reputation for being the most law-abiding people in all of Greece, are in reality lawbreakers.

In both passages we find the same ambivalence about the word *nomos*. On the one hand, one can call any general command issued by a community or its rulers a law. This definition of law comes very close to that of John Austin, who argued that laws were orders of a sovereign backed by threats. On the other, only a general provision that is just or beneficial to the community deserves to be called a law. This in turn implies that any general provision that is not just or good for the community is "unlawful." This ambivalence about the words for law made it possible for Aeschylus to have the chorus in *Prometheus Bound* (150–1) claim that Zeus "rules contrary to the law (ἀθέτως) by his new laws (νόμοις)." Zeus has ordered that Prometheus be punished for stealing fire and giving it to mankind. Since Zeus is the king of gods and men, his orders have the force of law. But since the chorus finds his punishment of Prometheus unjust and his rule a tyranny (10), they at the same time declare his rule "illegal."[33]

Aeschines (3.190) reveals a similar uncertainty about what qualifies as a law. The orator recites a poem where the Thirty are described as men who "ruled the city with unjust laws" (ἀδίκοις θέσμοις). Yet Aeschines describes the same men as those who "ruled contrary to the laws" (παρὰ τοὺς νόμους ἄρξαντας). The poem says that the Thirty ruled by means of their laws, that is, they issued general commands and enforced them. But the poet calls these laws unjust. Aeschines, on the other hand, is not willing to call their actions "lawful" even if they were performed in accordance with the orders they issued. For Aeschines, all the actions of the Thirty were against the laws, and the regulations they enforced cannot be called laws. These laws Aeschines refers to are obviously not the laws passed by the Thirty themselves, but must be general principles of justice (or perhaps the laws of the democracy), which are alone just and therefore qualify to be laws.[34]

In the midst of this uncertainty about law, what were the sources of legitimacy that marked out the "true" laws? How could the ruling element in the *polis* persuade

[33] We may find a trace of this uncertainty as early as Homer (*Od.* 9.106–15), who says that the Cyclopes do not meet in the *agora* and are without *themis*, "law" (106, 112; cf. 189, 214–15), yet at the same time each administers law (*themisteuei*) to his wife and children (114).

[34] Since the Athenians believed their laws were just, Carey (1996) 41 notes the orators usually speak as if "the laws and justice are on the same side. And in many contexts the laws and justice are treated as identical."

citizens to enact a law and to obey it? A passage of Demosthenes (25.16) supplies the answer:

> The laws aim at what is just and good and advantageous. They seek this, and when this has been found, this is established as a general order, equal and similar for all, and this is a *nomos*. The law is that which all men ought to obey for many reasons, but above all because every law is an invention and gift of the gods, a tenet of wise men, a corrective of errors voluntary and involuntary, and a general covenant of the whole community, in accordance with which all men in that community regulate their lives.
>
> (trans. Vince)

What is striking about the passage is that Demosthenes does not isolate one element and privilege it above all others as the sole source of legitimacy for a true *nomos*. According to Demosthenes, the law derives its legitimacy from several sources: 1) the will of the gods, 2) human reason, 3) moral improvement, and 4) the agreement of the community. The Athenians did not differentiate between two types of law, secular and sacred, each of which drew its legitimacy from a different source and was administered and enforced by different institutions.[35] A law in the fullest sense of the word was not only passed by the Assembly, which granted the approval of the community, but also sanctioned by the gods. One should therefore not attempt to search for a distinction in Athens similar to that found in Medieval Europe between the king's law administered by the king and his courts and Canon Law administered by the Catholic Church in separate courts. The law of the democracy was the law of the gods and vice versa. Since it embodied universal principles of justice, law served to improve those it ruled.

Several texts from different genres assert that the gods are responsible for the laws men enact and follow. Heraclitus (fr. 253 Kirk-Raven; 114 Diels-Kranz) says "those whose speak with sense must rely on what is common to all, as a city must rely on its laws, and with much greater reliance. For all laws of men are nourished by one law, the divine law; for it has as much power as it wishes and is sufficient for all and is still left over" (trans. Kirk and Raven). Heraclitus sees no clash between the laws of the *polis* and the laws of the gods. In fact, the laws of the *polis* derive their strength from the laws of the gods. The *polis* does not form a

[35] Ostwald (1986) 148 is thus mistaken in seeing a conflict between religious and secular law in *Antigone*. See also note 15 and Parker (2004).

potentially rival source of legitimacy. Instead, the laws of the *polis* are subordinate to the laws of the gods and depend on them for their legitimacy. There is a similar relationship between divine law and human law in Plato's *Crito* (54c6–8). At the end of their imaginary lecture to Socrates, the laws of the *polis* (50a6–7) warn the philosopher that if he breaks his agreement with them, "our brothers in Hades will not receive you kindly, knowing that you tried to destroy us to the best of your ability" (54c6–8). Here the laws of the gods are described as the brothers of the laws of the *polis* and thereby placed on a level of equality (the text does not say who their parents are). This is slightly different from the formulation of Heraclitus, who makes the laws of the *polis* subordinate to the divine law. Despite the slight difference, both authors consider both sets of laws to be closely related and to share common interests. If Socrates breaks the laws of the *polis*, the laws of the gods who will judge him in the underworld will not ignore his crime and come to the aid of the laws of the *polis*. If the laws of the *polis* are not able to punish a crime during the lifetime of the criminal, the laws of the gods will see to it that he is punished in the afterlife. The two sets of laws do not pursue different aims, but work together to serve one end, which is to bring about justice.

The view that the gods are the authors of the laws of the *polis* occurs several times in Greek tragedy. When Athena institutes the court of the Areopagus in Aeschlylus' *Eumenides* (484), she says she "will lay down a law for all time." The chorus in Sophocles' *Oedipus the King* (863–70) pray that they may "enjoy a favorable destiny as long as they observe a pious holiness in words and deeds, respecting the laws that walk on high, born in the heavenly sky whose father is Zeus alone, and whom no mortal nature of men gave birth to." Euripides in the *Ion* (442–3) echoes the idea, but places a typically Euripidean twist on the notion. The young man Ion asks in protest, "How is it just for you gods to enact laws for men and yet yourselves act lawlessly?" Ion criticizes the gods for their conduct, their failure to abide by the laws they lay down for mortals. Yet he does not question the view that the laws men follow are handed down by the gods.[36]

The belief in divine authorship of the true laws is not merely philosophical speculation or poetic fancy. The Attic orators, who addressed the hundreds of

[36] Ion is not referring to a law about religious matters here but to the law about rape (Lys. 1.32). See also Eur. *Ion* 1312–17 (Apollo lays down law about supplication). For Zeus as the author of the laws of the *polis*, see also Pl. *Protagoras* 322c–d. I do not understand how Burkert (1985) 248 can assert "Greek gods do not give laws."

citizens who judged cases or attended trials, also appeal to the belief. Demosthenes (23.81) says it was the gods who established the courts for homicide. He is uncertain who created the procedures to be followed in trials for murder, but he says they are either gods or heroes (23.70; cf. Antiphon 1.3). Xenophon (*Lac. Pol.* 8.5) tells us that Lycurgus acquired divine approval from Delphi for his laws before he proposed them to the Spartan assembly.[37] Cleisthenes also involved the Pythia at Delphi when he introduced the new political system of ten tribes in 508/7 ([Arist.] *Ath. Pol.* 21.6). And the Athenian Assembly sought divine favor for their actions by placing the word *theoi* (gods) at the beginning of laws and decrees.[38]

Since the Council and the Assembly sought the approval of the gods when they enacted laws, the gods helped them to enforce the laws of the *polis*. At the beginning of each meeting of the Assembly, sacrifices were performed, and the herald made a prayer to the gods and uttered a curse on all those who deceived the people.[39] According to Lycurgus (*Against Leocrates* 93), Apollo acted as a sort of divine policeman for Athens. After the politician Callistratus was condemned to death by an Athenian court, he fled the city to avoid punishment. During his exile, he consulted the god of Delphi and received the response that if he returned to Athens he would receive what he deserved from the laws. Encouraged by the oracle, he returned to Athens and supplicated at the altar of the Twelve Gods. He was nevertheless put to death by the city. "Justly so," adds Lycurgus, "since for the unjust the proper treatment from the laws is punishment. The gods correctly granted the victims of his injustice the opportunity to punish the guilty man." (For the relationship between supplication and the law, see Naiden [2004].) Since the gods were concerned about the laws of the *polis*, Antiphon (6.6) tells us that an unjust verdict is an offense and an act of impiety against both gods and the laws.

The laws the gods laid down were often called "the unwritten laws" or the "common laws" of mankind. Socrates in Xenophon's *Memorabilia* (4.4.19) asks

[37] Compare the divine approval for the Great Rhetra in Tyrtaeus fr. 4 (West) lines 1–4.

[38] See, for example, Meiggs and Lewis (1969) ## 46, 64, 69, 77, 89, 90; *IG* ii^2 6, 23, 107, 108, 111, 113, 116, 119, 129, 135, 136, 140, 142. Compare the fourth-century decree of Cyrene and the original decree of Thera about its colony in Meiggs and Lewis (1969) # 5, lines 1, 24–45. Note too that Solon (fr. 31 [West]) asks for Zeus to confer fame and success on his laws.

[39] For the sacrifices see Aeschin. 1.23 with scholia. For the prayer see Din. 2.14. For the curse see Dem. 19.70; 23.97; Din. 2.16. For a parody of these prayers see Ar. *Th.* 295–311. Similar rituals were performed before each meeting of the Council – see Rhodes (1972) 36–7.

Hippias if he knows "what are the unwritten laws?" Hippias answers that they are the laws followed in every country in respect to the same situations. Since these laws have been enacted by diverse peoples speaking different languages, Hippias is forced to admit "the gods laid down these laws for men."[40] The unwritten laws of the gods and the laws enacted by men do not clash but support each other. Plato in the *Laws* (793a–b) compares the unwritten laws (ἄγραφα νόμιμα) to "bonds of every constitution, joining all laws laid down in writing and established and those to be laid down in the future." They are like supports placed by builders in houses; if they give way, the whole house falls together with them. The idea expressed by Plato is similar to that of Heraclitus: the written laws receive their strength from the unwritten laws and will collapse without their support. The unwritten laws contain the underlying principles of legitimacy on which the written laws are based.[41]

Perhaps the best way to understand the connection between the unwritten laws and the written laws of the *polis* is to examine the three most important unwritten laws and their relationship to Athenian statutes. In his discussion of the unwritten laws enacted by the gods, Xenophon singles out three: 1) honor the gods, 2) respect one's parents, and 3) repay a debt.[42] Athens had many laws to ensure that everyone honored the gods. There were dozens of regulations prescribing sacrifices for the gods and regulating the kinds of victims and other details. For instance, when Nicomachus was appointed to write up the laws of Athens, the regulations

[40] Compare Arist. *Rhet.* 1368b5ff., where the law common to all men is called the unwritten law and contrasted with the written law. Ostwald (1973) 76–7 believes that the former "contain moral and social rules which are part of a more general that cannot be reduced to writing," but see below for the relationship between the unwritten laws and the written laws.

[41] The unwritten laws mentioned by Pericles (Th. 2.37.3) are probably different from those discussed by Xenophon in the *Memorabilia* (4.4.19), which are general principles, grounded in the will of the gods or nature, which form the basis for the written laws. The unwritten laws of Pericles are customs followed by a specific community, customs enforced not by the courts, but by public opinion (αἰσχύνην ὁμολογουμένην). As Carey (1996) 35 suggests, they are thus similar to the individual, unwritten laws discussed by Arist. *Rhet.* 1.13.1373b. A prosecutor at Lys. 6.10 recalls how Pericles advised the Athenians to enforce against impious men not only the written laws but also the unwritten laws that the *exegetai* follow when they dispense advice. The speech is probably a later forgery, but the passage still raises intriguing questions. Was the speaker arguing that the interpretations of religious laws given by the *exegetai* such as that described at Dem. 47.67–71 have the force of law? For the legal status of the advice given by the *exegetai*, see Parker [2004] 64–5.

[42] Xenophon also includes the prohibition against incest, but there appears to have been no specific Athenian law against this crime. Aeschylus (*Suppl.* 698–709) lists treating strangers justly, honoring the gods, and respecting one's parents as the three basic laws.

he compiled included several concerning sacrifices (Lys. 30.17–21). The Assembly discussed religious business as a regular item on its agenda ([Arist.] *Ath. Pol.* 43.6),[43] and many of its laws and decrees dealt with sacred rites and the administration of temples.[44] To ensure that these decrees were carried out, the Assembly also appointed a number of religious officials (e.g., [Arist.] *Ath. Pol.* 54.6–7: two boards of ten men each to perform sacrifices; 57.1: Superintendents for the Mysteries). In addition to their secular duties, the Archons supervised religious matters. The Eponymous Archon arranged the procession at the Thargelia and the ones for Asclepius, Zeus the Savior, and the Dionysia ([Arist.] *Ath. Pol.* 56.4–5). The King Archon looked after the Mysteries and the Lenaea festival (57.1) and settled disputes about rights to priestly privileges (57.2). The Polemarch made sacrifices to Artemis the Huntress and Enyalius (58.1). The Council was also responsible for supervising festivals, performing sacrifices, and other religious business.[45] And magistrates of the *polis* examined the activities of all priests and priestesses about their duties.[46] (For examples of religious laws enforced by the Council and Assembly in other *poleis,* see Parker [2004].) Finally, if anyone failed to honor the gods, any citizen could bring a public action for impiety against him and have the case tried in one of the courts.[47] The written laws of Athens did not clash with the unwritten law that one should honor the gods. On the contrary, the written laws about religion served to enforce this unwritten law.

The duty to respect one's parents was enforced by the *graphe kakoseos goneon,* a public action against harming parents. The offense was considered so serious that it was open to any Athenian to bring the charge, and the penalty was complete loss of citizen rights.[48] Aeschines (1.28) says that the law on public speakers forbids the man who beats his father or mother or does not provide his parents with food and lodging from addressing the Council, Assembly, and law courts. The penalty for violating this law was also complete loss of rights.[49] When candidates for

43 There was a law requiring a meeting just to discuss the Dionysia (*IG* ii^2 780; 781; Dem. 21.9. (The law found at Dem. 21.8 is a forgery – see Harris [1992c] 76.)

44 For example, *IG* i^3 46 (= Meiggs and Lewis [1969] #49) lines 9–13; 52 (= Meiggs and Lewis [1969] #58) 64–9; 78 (= Meiggs and Lewis [1969] #71); *IG* ii^2 47; 140; 204; 216; Schwenk (1985) no. 21.

45 See Rhodes (1981) 127–34.

46 Aeschin. 3.18. Lycurgus' speech *On the Priestess* may have been delivered at a trial about the conduct of a priestess. See Conomis (1961) 107–20.

47 On prosecutions for impiety see Parker (1996) 207–9, 214–15.

48 And. 1.74; Dem. 24.60, 103, 107. On the duty to look after one's parents see Rubinstein (1993) 64–8.

49 For the penalty see Hansen (1976a) 72, 79–80.

the archonship were examined, the Council asked them whether they treated their parents well. If the Council discovered that a candidate had neglected his duty to his parents, they disqualified him ([Arist.] *Ath. Pol.* 55.3–4).[50] The unwritten law that one should repay a benefit provided the rationale behind the laws about debt.

Demosthenes (18.274–5) sees a similar relationship between the laws of the *polis* and the unwritten laws. The orator observes that men draw a distinction between unjust deeds committed deliberately, culpable errors (*hamartia*), and accidents, for which men are not held responsible. "This principle will be obvious not only in the laws, but nature herself has marked out these distinctions in the unwritten laws and human habits." Here Demosthenes has substituted nature (*physis*) for the gods as the authors of the unwritten laws of mankind, but the relationship between the written laws and the unwritten laws is the same: they do not conflict with each other, but are parallel to each other.[51] The distinction between actions committed deliberately and against one's will was well established in the Athenian lawcode. The laws of homicide considered deliberate homicide and homicide committed against one's will different types of offense and punished each with a different penalty ([Arist.] *Ath. Pol.* 57.3). The laws about damage required payment of an amount double the damage inflicted if the act was intentional, but only an equivalent amount for damage caused against the defendant's will (Dem. 21.43. Cf. *IG* i³ 6B, lines 45–9).

The relationship between the unwritten laws of the gods and the laws of the *polis* forms an important part of the larger relationship between religion and the *polis*. As C. Sourvinou-Inwood has put it, religion

> is a model articulating a cosmic order guaranteed by a divine order which also in complex ways grounds the human order, perceived to be incarnated above all in the properly ordered and pious *polis*, and providing certain rules

[50] Timarchus was convicted for breaking this law and suffered *atimia* (Dem. 19.257, 284).

[51] Note that at Eur. *Bacchae* (890–6), the chorus say one must not consider anything superior to the laws, then identify what has been lawful for a long time (τό τ᾽ ἐν χρόνῳ μακρῷ νόμιμον) with both what is divine (τὸ δαιμόνιον) and what is created by nature (ἀεὶ φύσει τε πεφυκός.). For discussion of the passage see Dodds (1960) 189–90, who believes "the Chorus anticipate in principle Plato's solution of the νόμος-φύσις antinomy, viz. that when the two terms are properly understood νόμος is seen to be founded upon φύσις" and points to Pl. *Lg.* 890d. I would interpret the phrase as providing three separate reasons for obeying the laws mentioned in the previous phrase: divine origin, long observance, nature. For long observance as a reason to respect the law, see Antiphon 6.2.

> and prescriptions of behaviour, especially toward the divine through cult, but also toward the human world – prescribing, for example, that one must not break one's oaths (e.g. Homer, *Iliad* 3.276–80; 19.259–60), or that one must respect strangers and suppliants who have the special protection of the gods, especially Zeus, precisely because they are most vulnerable.[52]

We have now seen that the Athenians recognized that there was potentially some ambiguity about the word *nomos.* On the one hand, the ruling power in a community might issue general provisions, which from one perspective might be called *nomoi* yet might still lack full legitimacy and thus might not deserve to be called *nomoi* in the true sense. The Athenians therefore made a distinction in some contexts between "laws" and "the established laws." The distinction between the two appears in the Ephebic Oath (Tod [1948] 2:204): "I will obey those who are ruling prudently and the established laws and those which they may prudently establish for themselves in the future" (καὶ εὐηκοήσω τῶν ἀεὶ κρlαινόντων ἐμφρόνως καὶ τῶν θέσμων τῶνl ἱδρυμένων καὶ οὓς ἂν τὸ λοιπὸν ἱδρύσωlνται ἐμφρόνως). The oath makes a distinction between laws that have already been established and those which "they" (i.e., the Athenians) may establish prudently in the future. In the case of the established laws, the Ephebes pledge to obey without qualification. As for orders given by magistrates and any laws enacted in the future, the Ephebes swear to obey only if they are issued "prudently" (ἐμφρόνως). The oath therefore grants priority to the established laws, which take precedence both over the orders of magistrates and over any laws that the Athenians may enact in the future. The established laws are those laws that have been established in the proper way and thus meet the criteria of legitimacy and deserve to be obeyed.

It is striking that Andocides states the Dicastic Oath required Athenian judges to swear that they would vote according to the established laws (And. 1.91: ψηφιοῦμαι δὲ κατὰ τοὺς *κειμένους νόμους*. Cf. Antiphon 5.96: καὶ ὑμεῖς περὶ ἐμοῦ κατὰ *τοὺς κειμένους νόμους* διαγνώσεσθε). Aeschines (1.6) echoes this terminology when he says that communities under a democratic constitution manage their affairs not just in accordance with the laws, but with the established laws. Aeschines adds that the Athenians are strong when they practice *eunomia* and do not allow themselves to be destroyed by lawbreakers. There are two aspects to *eunomia* – first, it is necessary to enact laws that are good and beneficial to the

[52] Sourvinou-Inwood (1990) 301–2.

community and to obey the established laws.[53] Aeschines thus appears to equate laws that are good and beneficial with the established laws. Any ruling power can enact *nomoi* – to achieve true *eunomia* one must enact laws that meet the criteria of legitimacy.

The Athenians believed the established laws deserved greater respect because the antiquity of laws was a sign that they had stood the test of time and human experience. Antiphon (5.14–15 = 6.2) singles out the laws about homicide for praise: "I think that all would agree that the laws that are established about such matters are the finest and most righteous of all the laws. They are indeed the oldest laws in this land, and furthermore they are absolutely consistent [literally 'they are the same about the same things'], which is the greatest indication that laws have been well made. For time and human experience teach men what is unsound (...) And thus the laws about homicide, which no one has ever dared to overturn, have been established in the best way." Demosthenes (24.24) also recognizes the inherent superiority of older laws. He praises the laws: "All these laws have been established for a long time, judges, and they have often passed the test and proven to be advantageous for you. No one has even denied that they are not good."

The expression "established laws" appears significantly in Thucydides' famous analysis of the civil strife at Corcyra (3.82.6). The historian observes that in times of *stasis* (civil strife) groups of men band together not with the support of the established laws but for the sake of gain in defiance of the established laws. They may form pacts of trust among themselves not in accordance with divine law but in order to break the law. Thucydides is indulging his fondness for stylistic *metabole*, but it is striking that he uses "established laws" and "divine law" interchangeably. Thucydides recognized that one faction might seize power in the community, enact *nomoi* that lacked full legitimacy, and rule in accordance with these laws. This is why he chose the expression "established laws" in this context – one of the terrible features of *stasis* was that the rival groups tended to ignore those established laws that command the respect of all citizens because they embody true justice. In a similar way Herodotus (3.80.5) states that one of the worst features of a

[53] For these two aspects of *eunomia* see also Arist. *Pol.* 4.8.1294a3–7: "Establishing good laws is not *eunomia* if they are not obeyed. For this reason we must suppose that one aspect of *eunomia* is to obey the established laws, another aspect is to establish good laws that they remain obedient to (for it is also possible to obey bad laws)." Note how Aristotle, like Aeschines, equates established laws with well formulated or good laws. Hdt. 1.65.5–66.1: Lycurgus brought about *eunomia* by changing the laws and ensuring that they were not broken.

tyrant is his tendency to upset the "ancestral laws" (*νόμαιά* τε κινέει *πάτρια*).[54] Herodotus knew that a tyrant might issue general orders to his subjects, which one might call "laws." What he found dangerous about a tyrant was his willingness to overturn those laws that men had over time found to deserve respect because they are in accord with universal notions of justice.

The Ephebic Oath not only makes a careful distinction between ordinary laws and "established laws." It also implicitly recognizes the right of citizens to disobey orders given by magistrates that are not ἐμφρόνως – not made with a sound mind or not in accordance with the laws. This right did not just exist in theory. An incident recounted by the orator Apollodorus ([Dem.] 50.46ff.) illustrates how an Athenian citizen put this right to disobey illegal orders into practice. During his service as trierarch, Apollodorus received an order from the general Timomachus to sail his ship from the island of Thasos to Macedonia. Callippus, who was apparently acting in conjunction with Timomachus, accompanied Apollodorus during the voyage. When the ship reached a trading post on the coast opposite Thasos not far from Macedon, Callicles, one of the sailors on the ship, asked if he could speak privately with Apollodorus. Callicles told Apollodorus that he had found out that Timomachus wanted him to pick up the exile Callistratus, who had been condemned twice in Athenian courts. Callicles advised him against letting the exile on board his ship "since the laws do not allow it" (οὐ γὰρ ἐῶσιν οἱ νόμοι). Armed with this information, Apollodorus confronted Callippus and asked him where they were sailing to and why. When Callippus treated him with scorn and threatened him, Apollodorus remained firm and declared he would transport no exile since the laws made it illegal to receive an exile. When his sailors returned to the ship, Apollodorus ordered the pilot to set his course for Thasos, not Macedon. Callippus objected and ordered him to sail to Macedon where the general had ordered them to sail. The pilot knew which side his bread was buttered on: he

[54] Ancestral laws are identified with unwritten laws by Pl. *Lg.* 793a. Ancestral laws (*ta patria*) appear to be equivalent to established laws at Dem. 24.139. In contrast to tyranny, Athenian democracy respected these ancestral practices: see the expression κατὰ τὰ πάτρια in *IG* i³ 7, lines 8, 13, 19 (restored), 22; 78, lines 4, 11, 26, 34; 131, line 5; And. 1.83; and Dem. 21.51, 54. Note that the hierophant Archias was convicted of impiety in court for making sacrifices contrary to ancestral laws (Dem. 59.116: παρὰ τὰ πάτρια). Cf. Dem. 19.86. According to Dinarchus (1.55), the Areopagus reported those who violated *ta patria*.

Lewis (1954) 17–21 and Ostwald (1986) 145–8 argue that in the decree about the Praxiergidai the Assembly was asserting its control over *ta patria* of the *genos*, but the wording of the decree seems rather to indicate that the Assembly recognized the authority of *ta patria*. See also Parker (1996) 124–5.

said Apollodorus was the captain of the ship and it was Apollodorus who paid his wages so he would do what Apollodorus told him to do. On his return to Thasos, Timomachus summoned Apollodorus, but Apollodorus feared arrest so he sent a messenger to find out what he wanted. From the rest of the narrative we find that Apollodorus was never prosecuted or punished for his defiance of Timomachus' orders.

The most famous example of the doctrine that it is wrong to obey an illegal order is Socrates' defiance of the Thirty. Xenophon in the *Memorabilia* (4.4.1–3) recalls how the philosopher was law-abiding and always obeyed the magistrates. Xenophon notes, however, that Socrates obeyed them only "in regard to what the laws command." He thus implies that Socrates never obeyed an illegal order. He gives two examples of Socrates' obedience to the laws, the same two that Socrates himself recounts in the *Apology* (32b–c). The first took place during the trial of the generals after the battle of Arginousai when Socrates refused to put an illegal motion to the vote. The second occurred during the reign of the Thirty, who ordered him not to speak to the young and to arrest a citizen they planned to execute. Socrates rejected both the motion proposed in the Assembly and the orders of the Thirty because they were contrary to the laws.

It may be ironic to find Apollodorus, the son of a freedman and an unscrupulous *parvenu*, compared with Socrates, the paragon of philosophical virtue. Irony aside, the two incidents show that Socrates' actions were not unconventional, an unorthodox stand on philosophical principle. Both the ambitious politician and the philosopher hostile to politics shared a common belief in the rule of law. Each man therefore placed his allegiance to the laws above his obligation to obey magistrates.

In fact, Xenophon in his *Constitution of the Spartans* (8.2) contrasted Sparta with other Greek *poleis* in their attitudes toward magistrates. "In other cities the most powerful citizens do not even wish to give the impression that they are afraid of magistrates, thinking this is illiberal, while in Sparta the leading citizens show the greatest respect for the magistrates and pride themselves on being humble and running rather than walking in answer to a summons. They think that if they set an example of exaggerated obedience the rest will follow; this is precisely what has happened" (trans. Moore). When Xenophon speaks of other Greek *poleis*, he is probably thinking of Athens, the city that he knew best. He is clearly drawing the contrast in terms most favorable to Sparta, the object of his praise in the tract. From what we know about the Athenian attitude toward the laws, however, we can see that the Athenians did not so much show less respect for magistrates, but held the laws themselves in higher esteem. Their attitude toward magistrates did not stem from disrespect but rather from their conviction that the magistrates were not the supreme authorities in the *polis,* but were subordinate to the laws. In Athenian democracy private citizens held the magistrates accountable and could prosecute them for failing to follow the laws. In Sparta the job of overseeing the magistrates was in the hands of the Ephors (Xen. *Lac. Pol.* 8.4).[55] Pericles in his Funeral Oration (Th. 2.37) boasts that the Athenians obey both those in power and the laws, but they clearly placed a higher value on obedience to the laws.[56] Evidently, the Spartans placed greater emphasis on obedience to authority. In fact, Demosthenes (22.31–2) contrasts the democratic attitude toward magistrates with the oligarchic view. In a democracy everyone has the right to criticize those who have led shameless lives; in an oligarchy no one can criticize magistrates no matter how disgraceful their conduct has been. It is thus no coincidence that when the Spartan Menelaus comes on stage in Sophocles' *Ajax* (1070–6) to forbid the burial of the Attic hero, he insists on the need for obedience and fear of authority and resents Teucer's outspoken criticisms.[57] But that was not the Athenian way.

II

We are now in a position to discuss the conflict about *nomos* in Sophocles' *Antigone.*[58]

In the prologue to the play, Antigone and Ismene come on stage to discuss recent events. Their brothers Eteocles and Polynices, the sons of Oedipus, have died fighting over control of the city of Thebes. Creon has decreed that Eteocles, who fought to defend the city against foreign invasion, be buried with full honors in return for his noble sacrifice. Polynices, who came to attack the city with foreign

[55] Compare Arist. *Pol.* 1270b6-20 on the powers of the Ephors. Note also that Aristotle complains that the Ephors do not judge cases according to the laws.

[56] Note the similar idea in Xen. *Lac. Pol.* 8.1: "we all know that at Sparta more than anywhere else they obey the magistrates (*tais archais*) and the laws (*tois nomois*)."

The different attitudes toward obedience to magistrates may explain the difference between the text of Simonides' epigram for the Spartans who died at Thermopylae found in Herodotus (7.228: "obedient to their orders [*rhemasi*]") and the one in Lycurgus (*Leocr.* 109: "obedient to their laws [*nomimois*]").

[57] Note also how Menelaus stresses the need for *sophrosyne,* another word often associated with aristocratic government (cf. Th. 3.83).

[58] The inelegant translations of Sophocles' *Antigone* in this section are my own unless otherwise indicated.

allies, is to be left unburied, his flesh devoured by birds and dogs. From the very outset of the play, Antigone makes it absolutely clear how she regards Creon's order not to bury Polynices – it is an order made in his capacity as magistrate:

> And now what order (κήρυγμα) do they say the general (στρατηγὸν) has
> recently imposed on the entire city (πανδήμῳ πόλει)?
>
> (7–8)

In her next speech she makes two important distinctions: between Creon's treatment of Eteocles and his punishment of Polynices, and between an order (*kerugma*) and a law (*nomos*).[59] In regard to the burial of Eteocles, Antigone recognizes that Creon is acting in accordance with law (*nomos*) and justice (*dike*).

> Eteocles, as they say, in accordance with justice
> (...) and law he has hidden under the earth
> With all the honors belonging to corpses placed below.
>
> (23–5)[60]

Antigone then contrasts Creon's treatment of Polynices, which she implies is not in accordance with law and justice by omitting these terms in her account of the rest of the king's order.[61] Once again, she is careful to describe his command as an order by using three verbs constructed from the same root as *kerugma* (order):

> But as for the corpse of Polynices, who suffered a miserable death,
> they say it has been forbidden for the citizens by his order (ἐκκεκηρῦχθαι)
> to cover him in burial or for anyone to lament him,
> but leave him unmourned, without burial, a pleasant

[59] For the verb ἐκκηρύττειν denoting banishment by order of magistrates, see Lys. 3.45. For κήρυγμα as order of a magistrate, see Dem. 21.179. For κηρύττειν referring to the order of magistrates, see Dem. 25.56. For κηρύττειν and κήρυγμα referring to the order of a king see Dem. 20.31 (κηρύττειν); 33.36 (κήρυγμα); *SIG*[3] 741, line 23. Foley (1995) 134 claims the term has democratic overtones, but see Griffith (1999) 122, who rightly notes that the term can be used in democratic and autocratic contexts. Griffith, however, does not observe how Antigone refuses to call Creon's order a law.

[60] There is a problem with the text of lines 23–4 (it is unlikely that both σὺν δίκῃ and δικαίᾳ stood in the text, but unlike Lloyd-Jones and Wilson, I would athetize χρησθεὶς δικαίᾳ since δίκῃ is parallel to νόμῳ and the two words are linked by καὶ), but the idea is clear. For a recent discussion see Griffith (1999) 126, who adopts the emendation of Schütz.

[61] The contrast is implicit in the opposition between the *men* in line 23 and *de* in line 26.

> store of food for birds looking for something to eat.
> Such commands they say the good Creon has issued (κηρύξαντ' ἔχειν)
> for you and me – yes, I say also for me –
> and that he is coming here to announce these clear orders (προκηρύξοντα)
> to those who do not know about them.
>
> (26–34)

Antigone has a strong legal case in viewing Creon's command not to bury Polynices as an order (*kerugma*) and nothing more. To qualify as a law (*nomos*), it would have to apply to all Thebans or a broad category of people. The order does threaten all Thebans with punishment if anyone buries Polynices, but it is directed mainly at one person. As we noted above, Athenian laws were general provisions, not orders aimed at specific individuals. Second, the order does not apply to a broad category of actions, but only one specific action – the burial of a single man named Polynices. Third, Creon's order does not extend for an indefinite period of time – it is relevant to this one occasion. Fourth, we have seen that a true law (*nomos*) draws its authority from several sources – the gods, human reason, the consent of the community – but it does not derive authority from the power of a magistrate. But Antigone stresses the fact that Creon makes this order only as a magistrate (8: *strategon*), not as a legislator. In the first scene, which follows the prologue and the entry of the chorus, it becomes clear that Creon has issued his order on no other authority than that attached to his position as ruler. Nowhere in the play do we hear that Creon has consulted the gods, employed the services of a *mantis*, asked for the approval of the Delphic oracle, or proposed a motion before the people or the Elders for a vote. Thus, Antigone has a strong case in regarding Creon's command not to bury Polynices as only an order (*kerugma*) without the force of law (*nomos*). His order does not qualify as a law and does not meet all the criteria required for an established law.

Ismene does not dispute with Antigone over this basic point, but argues that they still should not go against Creon's order:

> Yet for the two of us who have been left behind alone,
> Consider how much worse our suffering will be if against
> the law we will violate the decision and power of tyrants.
>
> (58–60)

Ismene too is careful in her use of language. She says that burying Polynices would be to violate the decision (ψῆφον) and the power (κράτη) of the rulers. Like her sister, Ismene does not call Creon's decree a law, only his decision.[62] Although Ismene does not think Creon's order is a *nomos*, she argues that to defy the order and the power of a ruler would be in defiance of the law (*nomos*). The law she has in mind is the law that one must obey those in power. She does not believe obeying Creon's order is the right thing to do since she later says that she will ask forgiveness from those below (65–8); she would only find it necessary to ask forgiveness if she thought her action was wrong. But she draws attention to the fact that they are subjects. As women, they must be obedient to men, and as subjects they must follow the orders of those in power.

> We must bear in mind this fact, namely, that both of us are women,
> and so it is not in our nature to fight against men,
> And further that since we are ruled by those stronger than us
> we must obey these orders and any still more painful than these.
>
> (61–4)

She justifies her position by saying that although it may be unjust to obey Creon's order, she does so only because she is forced to.

> So I therefore while asking those below earth
> to have forgiveness since I am compelled in these matters,
> I will obey those who have come into power.
>
> (65–7)

Already in the prologue we find an important debate about legal issues. Antigone says Creon's command is only an order and implies that in regard to Polynices' burial it is not in accordance with the law (*nomos*). Ismene is willing to admit that Creon's order does not have the force of law, but argues that it is also their legal duty to obey magistrates who are in power in terms that are reminiscent of the Ephebic Oath's requirement to obey magistrates.[63]

[62] The word *psephos* literally means "pebble." Since the Greeks used pebbles to vote, the word acquired the meaning of "vote" or "decision" – see L.-S.-J. *s.v.* II.5.c. There is no need to follow Knox (1964) 63 in finding "democratic associations" in the word or to think it "hints that Creon speaks for the whole body of the citizens" since the word is found in nondemocratic contexts (e.g., Aesch. *Suppl.* 7).

[63] Ismene's point is similar to the statement of Socrates at Pl. *R.* 339b, with which Thrasymachus agrees, that it is just to obey the rulers. It is significant that when Thrasymachus changes his position and

It is crucial to note that Antigone and Ismene agree that Creon's order is wrong. Antigone does not state this explicitly until the Second Scene (450–5), but she implies this much when she contrasts Creon's treatment of Eteocles – done in accordance with law (*nomos*) – and that of Polynices. They disagree only about the way they should respond to his order. There can be no doubt that they are correct in finding Creon's order in violation of the laws of the gods that were recognized and enforced by all *poleis*.[64] Already in the Homeric poems we find the belief that the failure to perform proper burial rites will bring down the wrath of the gods. When Achilles refuses the dying Hector's request to allow his father to recover his body for burial, Hector warns him that he may become a source of anger among the gods (*Il.* 22.358). His prediction is accurate: at the Council of the Gods after Patroclus' Funeral Games, Apollo condemns Achilles' refusal in strong terms (24.39–45). When Zeus summons Thetis, he instructs her to tell Achilles the gods are angry with him, and Zeus is more enraged than the rest of the immortals (24.112–15). Thetis repeats his message to her son almost verbatim (24.134–6), and Achilles does not doubt the truth of her report. What is striking about these passages is that they reveal that burial was not just a concern of the Chthonic deities, but also for the Olympians. The fact that Hector is an enemy and has killed many of Achilles' friends makes no difference. We find the same belief about burial in the *Odyssey*. When Odysseus goes to the Underworld, he meets Elpenor, who tells his captain how he got drunk and fell off the roof of Circe's house to his death. Just like Hector, Elpenor warns Odysseus that if he does not bury his companion, he will become a source of anger among the gods (*Od.* 11.73).

Several texts from the fifth and fourth centuries BCE state that it was a common *nomos* of the Greeks to allow the enemy to recover their dead comrades for burial.

objects to Socrates' points in this section, he does not reject this point. Griffith (1999) 133 does not observe the connection between Ismene's argument and the arguments found in the orators about obeying the law versus following the orders of magistrates.

64 The most thorough discussion I have found of the issue in English is in Hester (1971). Ostwald (1986) relies on this discussion, but Hester's analysis of the sources is unreliable. The discussion of Griffith (1999) 29–32 is unsatisfactory. His assumption that traitors executed by being thrown into the pit (*barathron*) "where their corpses would presumably be left to rot" (cf. note 92 "without likelihood of burial") is contradicted by passages stating that the bodies of traitors were cast outside the boundaries of Attica. See, for example, Aeschin. 3.252 with scholia (545 Dilts). Cf. Parker (1983) 47, note 52: "At Athens, 'throwing into the pit' was primarily a mode of execution (...) There is no evidence that recovery of the body by relatives was legally forbidden."

Thucydides (4.97–8) reports the Thebans refused to return to the Athenians their dead soldiers until they evacuated Boeotia. The Athenians objected that the Thebans were violating a common law of the Greeks and that they had no right to barter corpses for political advantage. As Pritchett notes, "The Greek convention was not that the victor had to perform funeral rites over the dead of the vanquished, but that he had to extend the right of *anairesis* (recovery of corpses) when it was requested by the vanquished."[65] The Greeks even recognized the right of their barbarian enemies to proper burial. According to Pausanias (1.32.5), the Athenians themselves claimed to have buried the Persian soldiers who died at Marathon.[66]

In fact, the burial of Polynices became a common theme in Athenian propaganda, a proof of Athenian piety and justice. Lysias (2.7–10) devotes much attention to the story in his *Funeral Oration*. The passage, ignored by most critics writing about *Antigone*, deserves to be quoted in full, but I will make only three points here.[67] First, according to Lysias the Athenians thought that the Seven who attacked Thebes had already paid the penalty for their crimes by their death and deserved no further punishment. Second, the Theban refusal to bury the dead offended both the gods below, by not giving them their due, and the gods above, by polluting their temples, a view in full agreement with the Homeric evidence. Lysias' statement is also similar to Antigone's claim that Creon's decree has the approval of neither Zeus nor the gods below (450–5). Third, the Athenians, although they had no previous quarrel with Thebes, went so far as to invade Boeotia and fight a battle against the Cadmeans to recover the bodies of the Seven for burial in Eleusis. If the Athenians felt it right to go to the extreme

[65] See Pritchett (1985) 240, with a thorough collection of testimonia on 235–41. Cf. Parker (1983) 48: "Creon's offence is the familiar one of denying an enemy the right to burial." Griffith (1999) 28–32 does not take this evidence into account.

[66] Hester (1971) points out that Pausanias says "Lysander did not allow burial of the Athenian dead at Aegospotamoi," but omits to add that this was considered one of his disreputable actions. Hester claims Herodotus 9.83 indicates the Persians who died at Plataea were not buried. This misrepresents the evidence since Herodotus never states they were left unburied. On the contrary, he states that the body of Mardonius was buried and does not suggest the treatment of his body was exceptional. At 9.86.1 Herodotus says the bodies of the men who died at Plataea were buried in this way, and there is no reason to believe he excludes the Persians.

[67] Despite its relevance to *Antigone*, I can find no discussion or reference to Lysias' account of the burial of Eteocles in Bowra (1944), Knox (1964), Ostwald (1986), or Goldhill (1986). Sourvinou-Inwood (1989) 143 attempts to dismiss this evidence by claiming that these legends postdate Sophocles' play, but Foley (1995) 140 shows that they actually predate *Antigone*.

of marching into Boeotia and risking their lives to enforce the Greek *nomos* about burial, Antigone's action must have *a fortiori* appeared reasonable and justified to the Athenian audience who watched Sophocles' play.

Lysias' story about the burial of the Seven is not unique in Athenian literature. Far otherwise; the incident appears to have been one of those defining moments in the mythological past for Athenian identity. There were some variants in the tradition: Philochorus, Aeschylus in the *Eleusinians* (Plu. *Theseus* 29.4), and Isocrates (*Panathenaicus* 168; cf. *Panegyricus* 55–6) claim the Thebans returned the bodies without a fight, whereas Herodotus (9.27.3) and Euripides in the *Suppliants* agree with Lysias about the battle.[68] But all treat the Theban refusal as a serious offense and hold that the Athenians did everything they could to recover the bodies. Several of these texts refer to the right of burial as a νόμος or as νόμιμα.

Hester and Ostwald, however, have drawn attention to the Athenian law forbidding the burial of traitors in Athenian soil.[69] Hester claims there existed "a general law requiring that the bodies of traitors be cast out unburied." But according to Xenophon (*Hell.* 1.7.22), the law only forbade the burial of traitors and temple-robbers in Attic soil. Lycurgus (*Leocr.* 113–15) reports that the Athenians dug up the bones of the traitor Phrynichus and cast them outside of Attica. They also executed his defenders Aristarchus and Alexicles and refused them burial in their territory. According to a document found in a biography in Plutarch's *Moralia* (834), a similar prohibition applied to Archeptolemos and Antiphon.[70]

There is, of course, a world of difference between these provisions and Creon's decree. All the Athenians did was to forbid burial within Attica (or territory controlled by Athens in the case of Antiphon and Archeptolemus). Creon goes much further: he forbids burial at all. The Athenians did not attempt to prevent these enemies from being buried anywhere.[71] To do so they would not have had their bodies cast out, but kept above ground in Attica, just as Creon does with

[68] Dem. 60.9 alludes to the incident without indicating which version he endorses.

[69] Hester (1971) 19–21 and Ostwald (1986) 151 with note 41. See by contrast Parker (1983) 47: "Prolonged public exposure of the corpse, as prescribed by Creon in the *Antigone*, was not the practice of any Greek state, and when mentioned is treated as shocking."

[70] Cf. note 64 above. Compare also the similar prohibition on burial in Attica for those convicted of destroying the alliance between Athens and her allies in *IG* ii^2 43, lines 61–2.

[71] The Athenians recognized that even those who had been banished from Athens still deserved burial – see Din. 2.18 with Dem. 25.54, 65, 77.

Polynices. There is no question Creon's order goes against unwritten laws or the common laws of the Greeks (Th. 4.97–8).

But what about Ismene's point that it is a law (*nomos*) to obey the magistrates in power? Here we need to return to the Ephebic Oath. In the oath the Ephebes swear to obey orders issued by magistrates, but only those which are issued prudently (*emphronos*). This implies that any order that is not prudent does not have to be obeyed, and certainly an order that violates the law qualifies as an order that violates the standard of prudence.[72] So Antigone is correct – she is right to regard Creon's order as only an order, and she is correct that she is entitled to disobey it. Antigone's defiance is similar to Socrates' refusal to obey the illegal orders of the Thirty Tyrants or (to take a less exalted parallel) Apollodorus' disobedience to Callippus' orders.

Ismene's argument that she deserves pardon since she is only following the orders of a magistrate is one that several litigants used in Athenian courts. When Lysias (12.26) prosecuted Eratosthenes and asked him whether he arrested his brother Polemarchus, he replied that he was acting under orders and out of fear, yet admits the execution of Polemarchus was unjust. But Lysias (12.29–31) rejects his argument and claims Eratosthenes was in a position to disregard these orders and should have. In another speech of Lysias (15), the prosecutor charges the younger Alcibiades with cowardice and desertion for serving in the cavalry when he was enrolled in the infantry. The generals in charge defend him by saying that he acted under their orders (Lys. 15.6), but the prosecutor argues that their order was illegal, for the laws do not give them the power to enroll someone in the cavalry who had not passed the examination for that part of the army (Lys. 15.11). In a third speech of Lysias, the speaker accuses a group of grain-sellers of violating the law against hoarding. When the grain-dealers offer the excuse that they were acting under orders, the speaker counters that one magistrate, Anytus, merely advised them to stop bidding against each other and did not order them to break the law about hoarding (Lys. 22.5–9). Even if the magistrates had commanded them to break the law, that would make no difference: "when there are laws expressly written about some matter, shouldn't both those who disobey them and those

[72] I owe this point to Siewert (1977), though I do not agree with his view that "obedience to magistrates and future laws is required until the Areopagus declares them unreasonable" (104). Apollodorus certainly did not wait to consult the Areopagus before disobeying the order of Callippus. Goldhill (1986) 95 does not understand Antigone's argument, which justifies her disobedience on the grounds that Creon's order violates the law, an acceptable view to contemporary Athenians.

who order them to do what is illegal pay the penalty?" Though Ismene's argument might have been familiar to an Athenian audience, these three passages indicate that it was not a strong one and was vulnerable to serious objections. Antigone's anger at her sister's refusal to help her bury Polynices may strike us as excessive, but from a legal point of view her arguments are very strong. They are also in keeping with Athenian views about the role of law in a democracy.

After Antigone and Ismene part ways, the chorus of Theban elders enters and sings about the defeat of Polynices and his army (100–54). For Antigone and her sister, the events of the previous day have brought renewed suffering to their accursed family. For the people of Thebes, the defeat of Polynices means freedom and safety. In the midst of this public rejoicing, Creon enters to take control of Thebes and to issue orders about Eteocles and Polynices. Creon's speech in the first scene (163–210) was quoted with approval by Demosthenes in his *False Embassy* speech (19.247) against Aeschines. This has led some scholars to infer that Creon's statements would have met with the approval of the audience. For Bowra the fact that Demosthenes quotes the speech indicates the "general acceptability" of his words.[73] Sourvinou-Inwood believes Creon "at vv. 175–90 speaks the *polis* discourse, exemplifying democratic patriotism – which is indeed how Demosthenes took the lines."[74] In the opinion of Foley, "Creon (. . .) mouths democratic ideology in his first speech."[75] But the speech, despite its apparently sound opinions, subtly indicates Creon's shortcomings.[76] Demosthenes quotes only a portion of the speech, which he commends for its stress on loyalty to the city. He contrasts the patriotic sentiments in one part of Creon's speech with Aeschines' alleged treason, his decision to prefer the friendship and hospitality of Philip to his duty to Athens. But Demosthenes does not cite Creon as an example of a good magistrate. Indeed, he says that Aeschines should know these lines since he was a *tritagonistes*, an actor who took the lesser roles, and the *tritagonistes*

[73] Bowra (1944) 68. Cf. Knox (1964) 181, note 52.

[74] Sourvinou-Inwood (1989) 135. Oudemans and Lardinois (1987) 164–5, 167, 174 tend to follow Sourvinou-Inwood in their view of Creon.

[75] Foley (1995) 144.

[76] Griffith (1999) 155–6 thinks that much of Creon's speech "would presumably be charged with positive associations" for most Athenians, but draws attention to "such undemocratic terms as *thronos* (166, 173) and *krate panta* (173, cf. 1163) and *sebontas* (166) as applied to his own status" which "strike a discordant note." One might add that Creon has gained power not by democratic election but by virtue of his kinship with the dead Eteocles (173–4).

normally played the part of tyrants.[77] Despite his admiration for a single section of his speech, Demosthenes clearly considered Creon a tyrant just as Ismene (60), Antigone (506), Teiresias (1056), and the Messenger (1169) do. Creon's behavior in the rest of the scene bears them out.

Creon's speech begins well. He thanks the gods and gives them credit for the victory over Polynices (162–3). These lines undermine the view that Creon acts as the champion of the state against religion. The first hint we get of his character and beliefs is when he praises the elders of Thebes. He commends them not for their justice, virtue, or piety, but for their loyalty and obedience to the previous rulers of Thebes.

> So now I sent for you, chosen from all,
> first that I knew constant in respect
> to Laius' royal power; and again
> when Oedipus had set the state to rights,
> and when he perished, you were faithful still
> in mind to the descendants of the dead.
>
> (164–9, trans. Wyckoff)

From the very beginning Sophocles makes Creon's priorities clear: he values obedience to the authorities above all other qualities. There are many qualities he could have singled out. It is significant that he chooses this one alone.[78] His emphasis on the need for obedience recalls Xenophon's description of the Spartan approach to the rule of law.

The rest of Creon's speech in the first scene is full of noble sentiments about patriotism (175–92) and ends with his proclamation of the decree forbidding the burial of Polynices (192–210), which he correctly labels an order (*kerugma*). He declares that the ruler must not give in to fear. In his opinion everyone should place the safety of the community at the top of their priorities. He then calls on Zeus to witness his oath to these "laws" (184). But it is clear that Creon issues these laws on no authority other than his own. To recall our discussion in Section I, Creon believes that a law is any command issued by the ruling power. His view is thus similar to Pericles' initial definition of *nomos* in his discussion with Alcibiades

[77] Dem. 19.247 (*tyrannous kai skeptra echontas*).

[78] By way of contrast, note how Oedipus compliments the chorus for their just response at *Oedipus the King* 280.

in Xenophon's *Memorabilia*: since he has succeeded to the position of king (173–4: "I have complete power and the throne"), anything he orders has the force of law. The stage is now set for his confrontation with Antigone in the second scene. Each character has a different conception of law: Antigone believes that a law must have divine approval and the consent of the community, whereas for Creon whatever the ruling power orders is the law and must be obeyed. Their differing views about *nomos* will bring about the tragedy that ensues.

What is the attitude of the chorus to his speech? Certainly they do not openly challenge him, but then again they are not in a position to do so. They are the elders of the community, and it is their job to support and advise the ruler. Yet their words indicate they harbor doubts about his decree and its legitimacy. Their response to his speech subtly reveals their attitude:

> This is your decision, son of Menoeceus, about
> how to treat the enemy and the friend of the community.
> It is in your power, I suppose, to administer every law
> about the dead and as many of us as are still alive.
>
> (211–14)

What the chorus do not say is almost more significant than what they say. They state "this is your decision" and thus dissociate themselves from Creon's edict. They deliberately do not voice their approval of his decree nor agreement with his decision and stress that his order is the result of his decision alone. What is more, Creon never asks for their approval or advice. In his authoritarian way, he presents the Elders of Thebes with a fait accompli and expects their obedience.[79] They merely recognize that Creon has the legal power to enforce his decisions and refrain from saying his decision is just or lawful. Their use of the particle που (213: "I suppose") is also significant.[80] As Denniston observes, "From που meaning 'somewhere' is developed the sense 'I suppose,' 'I think,' the particle conveying a feeling of uncertainty in the speaker."[81] Denniston goes on to note that the particle often occurs when the speaker is being ironical. The chorus' words

[79] Unlike Creon, Oedipus is ready and willing to listen to the chorus' advice at *Oedipus the King* 280–6.

[80] The majority of the manuscripts read πού τ'. The unmetrical variant ποτ', found in manuscripts K and S, is easy to explain as a mistaken omission of the upsilon. Erfurdt was clearly correct in emending to πού γ', an easy change (Τ to Γ), adopted by Griffith (1999) 163. Lloyd-Jones and Wilson accept Platt's τοῦτ', but this removes the tone of doubt and is otiose.

[81] Denniston (1954) 490–1.

are hardly a ringing endorsement of Creon's speech and edict. Their following words strengthen this impression. When Creon asks them to help enforce his orders (215), the chorus suggests he assign this task to some younger man (216). Their lack of eagerness to help Creon implement his decree is telling. Creon then says there are already men guarding Polynices' body (217) and asks them not to cooperate with those who disobey (219). To this the chorus reply that no one is so foolish that he desires to die (220). Their answer reveals that their obedience comes not from any conviction that his order is just but from fear of punishment.

The next sign of the chorus' doubts comes later in the same scene after the guard reports the mysterious burial of Polynices (278–9):

> My thought has long suggested the doubt
> that this deed may have been done by the gods.

The chorus expresses itself obliquely. They are too tactful to say the burial is an omen of divine displeasure at Creon's order. They carefully suggest the possibility the gods may have been somehow responsible without drawing out the implications for Creon's order. Despite the chorus' tact, Creon quickly recognizes the implication of their doubts. They suggest that he is mistaken and his order is wrong. He does not pause to consider whether the chorus may have a point. His language is abusive and intemperate, his reaction the response of a tyrant suspicious of plots. He tells the chorus to "shut up" (παῦσαι). If they do not, they will appear "foolish and old." His words are all the more insulting when one remembers the respect the Greeks had for their elders.[82] Creon does not appeal to *salus populi* to justify his order. Instead, he invokes the will of the gods. He cannot believe the gods would have the same regard for the man who came to burn their temples as they have for the man who defended them (282–8; cf. 199–200). Like Antigone, he also bases his position on the will of the gods. But just as he is mistaken about his duties as magistrate, he is also mistaken about the will of the gods, as the prophecies of Teiresias and his subsequent misfortunes make clear. Creon rightly suspects that he does not have the community on his side (290–2), but interprets their defiance as the result of bribery (293–301) in much the same way as he will later accuse Teiresias of taking money. Creon implicitly recognizes that the chorus have their doubts, but cannot admit the possibility that they

[82] For respect for elders, see note 48.

might disagree for sound reasons. All Creon can see is disobedience; the idea that someone might have a reason to question his orders is incomprehensible to him.

The chorus reveals its own view of the law in the choral song that follows the first scene. Their song is an elaborate priamel, which reaches its climax in lines 365–75.[83] The entire ode lists the various skills that bring men wealth and success and make them an object of admiration. Among these skills are navigation (334–7), agriculture (337–41), hunting and fishing (342–7), taming of animals (347–52), the invention of language (354–5), the ability to live together in cities (355–6), building (356–8), and medicine (363–4). But the chorus lists all these skills only to note their limitations; despite their power to transform the natural environment, these skills can bring men to good or to evil (365–7). Man's ultimate success depends not on his skill and power to subdue nature, but his moral choices (368–70): if he obeys the laws of Earth (νόμους . . . Χθονός) and the justice of the gods (θεῶν . . . δίκαν), he will meet with success (literally, "high in his city"). But if he recklessly pursues evil, he will be without a city. The chorus implicitly dissent from Creon's priorities. For the king the key to the safety of the community is loyalty and obedience. For the chorus the most important duty is to the laws and justice of the gods.

Several scholars have argued that the chorus distinguish between two types of law and authority: the laws of the land (i.e., of the *polis*) and the laws of the gods. On this reading, their message is that citizens must obey both types of laws to achieve success. Such an interpretation collides with several objections. As we saw in Section I, the laws of the city drew their legitimacy from the laws of the gods. The Greeks did not recognize different and potentially conflicting sources of authority, one religious (the gods) and another secular (the *polis*). Second, the chorus calls these laws the laws of Earth, not the laws of Thebes. In fact, the chorus in the next scene implicitly contrast these laws with the laws of Creon, which they call the laws of the king (381–2: *nomois tois basileiois*). In this play the words *Ge* (and its equivalent *Chthon*) used without qualification always refer to Earth, never to the land of Thebes.[84] Moreover, the expression for the laws of the city is the laws of the *polis* – one never finds the expression "the laws of (the) land"

[83] For a study of the conventions of the priamel, see Race (1982). Cf. Griffith (1999) 185.

[84] See, for example, 24, 65, 113, 134, 250. When the word refers to the land of Thebes, it is qualified by an adjective that limits its application (110, 199, 287, 1162). At 187 and 736 the word is used to refer to the territory of Thebes, not to a political community.

(οἱ τῆς χθονὸς νόμοι *vel sim.*) used to refer to the laws of a political community. Most significant, however, is that when the chorus use the word "earth" a few lines earlier, they refer not to the land of Thebes, but to the deified Earth (337: θεῶν τε τὰν ὑπερτάταν Γᾶν ἄφθιτον).[85]

Why does the chorus refer to the laws of the gods as the laws of Earth? The reason is that the goddess Earth is often associated with justice and law. In the *Odyssey* (19.109–14) when the good king upholds justice, it is the earth that rewards his community by bearing wheat and barley and making the trees heavy with fruit. The same link between the earth and justice is found in the *Homeric Hymn to Earth* (30.11–2). For this reason the poets call Themis, the goddess of justice, the daughter of Earth (Hesiod *Theogony* 135; Aeschylus *Eum.* 1–4; Eur. *IT* 1259–68); Aeschylus (*Pr.* 209–11) actually identifies Earth with Themis.[86] And in the next scene Antigone informs Creon that justice lives with the gods below the earth (451). Xenophon (*Oeconomicus* 5.12) claims that Earth teaches men how to be just. It is thus no accident that when Solon declares he has brought law and justice to the Athenians, he calls on Earth to be his witness (Solon fr. 36.3–6 [West]). Despite their outward loyalty to the king, the chorus does not agree that obedience to authority is the most important value for a *polis*; what saves the *polis* is its obedience to the laws of the gods.

In the next scene the Guard brings Antigone and with obvious relief reports to Creon how he caught her burying Polynices. After hearing the report, Creon turns to Antigone and asks her if she denies the Guard's allegations (441–2). Antigone admits the truth of his report (443). Creon next dismisses the Guard and asks her if she is aware she has violated his decree (446–7: ᾔδησθα). The sequence of his questions is interesting from a legal point of view. There are two aspects to every crime: first, the wrongful action, and second, the mental element. The Athenians appear to have recognized the principle that the person who unknowingly breaks the law deserves lenient treatment. In a demosthenic speech, the accuser reminds the court that one should grant pardon to those who unwillingly violate one

[85] One might object that the words *Ge* and *Chthon* have different associations, but see Aeschylus *Pr.* 205 and 210 with the comment of Griffith (1983) 126: "Chthon is here identical to Ge." For the two terms used interchangeably without any perceptible difference in meaning, see also Eur. *IT* 1262 and 1267, and the *Homeric Hymn to Earth* (30), lines 1–3.

[86] *IG* ii² 5130 reveals the existence of a priestess of Earth-Themis, who may be associated with the temples of Themis and Earth (Pausanias 1.22.1–3). On Themis in general and her links with Earth, see Stafford (1997). For worship of Earth in Athens, see also *IG* i³ 7, line 12.

of the written laws through lack of experience with public life ([Dem.] 58.24). Regulations from the temple of Athena dating to the early fifth century prohibit certain actions in the sanctuary, then establish fines if anyone performs any of these actions "knowing" (εἰδώς) they are illegal (*IG* i^3 4, lines 6, 12). A law about the Mysteries from the fourth century provides for prosecution if anyone "knowing" (εἰδώς) that he was not a member of the Eumolpidai or Kerukes conducted an initiation.[87] Creon first establishes that Antigone performed the wrongful action (the burial), then determines whether she possesses the required mental element (awareness her action was wrong). Once again, Antigone confesses she knew about Creon's decree.

Creon then goes one step further. He asks Antigone if she dared to violate these laws (449: καὶ δῆτ' ἐτόλμας τούσδ' ὑπερβαίνειν νόμους). At this point, Antigone draws the line. She admits Creon's order is a decree, that is, issued by a ruler in a position of authority. But she correctly denies Creon's order the status of a law. Her words are once again carefully chosen (450–5):

> οὐ γάρ τί μοι Ζεὺς ἦν ὁ κηρύξας τάδε,
> οὐδ' ἡ ξύνοικος τῶν κάτω θεῶν Δίκη
> τοιούσδ' ἐν ἀνθρώποισιν ὥρισεν νόμους,
> οὐδὲ σθένειν τοσοῦτον ᾠόμην τὰ σὰ
> κηρύγμαθ' ὥστ' ἄγραπτα κἀσφαλῆ θεῶν
> νόμιμα δύνασθαι θνητὸν γ' ὄνθ' ὑπερδραμεῖν.
> It was not Zeus who issued this decree,
> nor did Justice, who lives with the gods below,
> mark out such laws among men.
> Nor do I think your decrees (*kerugmath'*) are so strong
> that one who is mortal can override the unwritten and
> unshakeable laws (*nomima*) of the gods.

Creon's order is the decree of a magistrate. If Zeus had issued the decree, that would have been a different matter. But his order is not a *nomos* that has divine authority. Justice did not set forth such laws – therefore Creon's decree cannot have the force of law no matter what he calls it. She continues by pointing out that the orders of a magistrate cannot override the unwritten and unshakeable laws of the gods. Most scholars pay attention to the contrast between the authority of

[87] For the text see Clinton (1980) 263, line 27 with the commentary at 278.

the gods and the authority of a mere mortal. But Antigone's legal point is equally significant: the laws take precedence over the orders of a magistrate. Unlike the orders of a magistrate that apply only to specific occasions for a limited period of time, the laws are eternal (455–6). Far from dismissing the claims of the *polis*, Antigone understands its legal institutions better than Creon does. She appeals not only to the gods but also to the opinion of the community: when Creon claims she alone of all the Cadmeans sees the matter this way, Antigone replies that they also see it her way, but hold their tongues in his presence (508–9). From careful study of the elders' words, we see that her opinion is justified. Thus, Antigone bases her opposition to Creon not only on religious grounds, but also appeals to the opinion of the community. Because Creon has the support of neither, his orders in her opinion are not laws.

Creon as usual misses the point. He repeats his accusation that she has broken the laws (480–1). He continues to act like a tyrant at the end of the scene when he sentences Antigone to death without a trial (567–81). Despite Antigone's claim she has not broken the law, Creon does not submit her case to a court and allow her to plead her side before impartial judges. His summary judgment is contrary to Athenian democratic ideology and in particular the Athenian law that magistrates could not put citizens to death without a trial.[88] According to Herodotus (3.80.5: κτείνει τε ἀκρίτους), such behavior was characteristic of the tyrant.

Creon makes his political philosophy clearer in his speech to Haemon in the third scene. For him the worst evil is *anarchia*, the kind of disorder that results when there is no respect for authority (672). This is what destroys both communities (*poleis*) and families (*oikous*) (673–4). What saves many lives is obedience to rulers or magistrates (675–6: *peitharchia*). (It is curious how Creon speaks only of bodies, not of souls.) In the realm of the family, this means women must obey men (678–80) and sons must obey fathers (639–40). In fact, Creon is just as concerned about the family as Antigone is. In the traditional way, he reasons that the man who is a good man in his dealing with his own household (*oikeioisin*) will clearly be a just man also in the community (*kan polei*) (661–2).[89] Thus, they do not disagree about the relative importance of the family vis-à-vis the community. Their disagreement

[88] See Carawan (1984).

[89] This is a common view found in several Athenian authors. See Aeschin. 1.30; Aeschin. 3.78; Pl. *Pol.* 259b–c, Xen. *Mem.* 3.4.12; 6.14. Cf. Arist. *NE* 10.9.1180b3–5.

concerns a different issue: Antigone believes in working for justice in both the family and in the community, whereas Creon stresses obedience to authority in each sphere. Creon's preference for obedience over justice becomes apparent where he says that "whomever the *polis* places (in command), it is necessary to obey him in small matters and in just matters and in their opposites (i.e., in small and unjust matters)" (666–7: ἀλλ' ὃν πόλις στήσειε, τοῦδε χρὴ κλύειν/ καὶ σμικρὰ καὶ δίκαια καὶ τἀναντία).[90] Creon's speeches might have gone over well in Sparta. I doubt they would have found a receptive audience in Athens.

At first Haemon tactfully attempts to convince his father to change his mind (663–723). He repeats Antigone's point that the citizens sympathize with Antigone, but do not express their support openly for fear of incurring the king's anger (690–5). Although Haemon declares that he has his father's best interests in mind, Creon refuses to follow the advice of a younger man (726–7). When Haemon counters that his advice is just (728–9), Creon again stresses the need for order and obedience (730). The next lines reveal that Creon now does not care whether the *polis* supports him or not. After Haemon states the entire city of Thebes does not side with his view of Antigone (733), Creon indignantly asks, "Will the *polis* then tell us what we must order?" (734) and "Must someone besides me rule this land?" (736). Haemon disagrees: "There is not a city which belongs to one man" (737). But Creon insists that power belongs to him alone: "Is not the *polis* normally considered to belong to the ruling power?" (738). Creon next asserts his authority as a father and asks if his son is "taking him to court?" (742). Neither Creon's position in the *oikos* nor his power in the *polis* intimidate Haemon; his father is still acting unjustly (743). Once again, Creon emphasizes the need to maintain respect for authority: "Am I going wrong by honoring my office (*archas*)?" (744). Haemon replies that Creon does not honor his office by trampling on the honors due to the gods (745). Creon can see no higher source of authority than his own power; Haemon believes all rulers are subject to a higher authority.

[90] Lloyd-Jones and Wilson place brackets around these verses for no apparent reason. Griffith (1999) 239 does not doubt the authenticity of these lines and remarks they show Creon's "increasing disregard for morality." Sourvinou-Inwood (1989) 144, note 37 claims Creon's "view that a citizen must obey *polis* authority in things just and unjust was official *polis* discourse," but does not distinguish between Athenian attitudes toward obedience to the laws and those toward obedience to magistrates.

Like Antigone, Haemon does not view the *polis* and the gods as conflicting sources of authority. In their opinion, Creon's orders are wrong both because they dishonor the gods and because they do not enjoy popular support. The play does not pit *raison d'état* against the claims of religion. Haemon and Antigone both uphold the democratic view that rulers must obey the laws, which embody divine will and have the consent of the people.

Once the argument between Creon and Haemon breaks off, the debate over legal issues ends. The action of the rest of the play unfolds the consequences of Creon's legal error and religious misjudgment. It is only when Teiresias predicts the punishment he will suffer for his mistake that Creon finally learns his lesson. When he changes his mind, his choice of words is significant (1113–14):

> I fear that it is best to live one's life until
> the end preserving the established laws (τοὺς καθεστῶτας νόμους).

Creon belatedly realizes that his orders contravened the established laws.[91] This is the only passage in the play where we find the term "established laws," and the fact that it comes at a climactic point in the action cannot be a coincidence. As a ruler, Creon could issue orders to the community. If he wished, he could even call them laws. He now grasps the fact that his so-called laws lacked the full legitimacy enjoyed by the established laws. The "laws" he issued had the backing of neither the gods nor the community. (Note how quickly the chorus endorses Teiresias' prediction at 1091–4.) In short, he has failed to live up to the Athenian ideal that granted priority to the established laws. When he finally understands his duties as magistrate, however, the damage has already been done, and he must suffer for his error. His punishment and remorse fill the remainder of the play and drive the point home.

Since Antigone suffers just as Creon does, one might be led to assume that she too must be wrong in a way. Antigone does commit suicide, but her misfortune results not from her decision to defy Creon. She dies because she loses faith in the justice of the gods and the support of the people, who seem to have abandoned her as she is led to the underground chamber (907, 919–23). In the prologue

[91] Griffith (1999) 313 does not comment on Creon's use of the term in these lines.

Antigone is confident she is right; facing death alone, she is no longer so certain.[92] Questions and doubts fill her final words:

> Why in my misfortune should I look
> to the gods? What ally should I call on? So now,
> trying to be pious, I am punished for impiety.
> If then the gods find these things good,
> Our suffering will teach us we are wrong.
> But if these men are wrong, may they suffer no greater
> Harm than the injustice they have done us.
>
> (922–8)

This is the reason she takes her life; it is despair that kills her, not arrogance or any mistake about her duties as a citizen. Had she been more confident in her position, she would have known the gods would rescue her. If she had waited just a few hours, Creon would have released her from the chamber, reunited her with Haemon, and all would have ended happily. But this is a tragedy, and Antigone is after all a woman, who (at least in the eyes of Greek males) lacks courage in the face of danger.[93] Although her view of the law is ultimately vindicated, Antigone does not have the courage to face life alone in the dark chamber and takes her life, unaware that she is about to be saved. If Antigone makes a mistake, it is not

[92] On the basis of the word *nomois* at 847, one should not go so far as to think that Antigone here admits Creon's orders have the force of law. The context of the line is crucial to its interpretation. Antigone is lamenting her punishment, which will deprive her of a proper funeral (844–9). Since she is singing about the rhythmical chants that accompany a funeral (*aklautos*), the word *nomos* here should mean "strains (of music)" or "tunes," that is, strains of mourning (see L.-S.-J. *s.v.* II.1). She takes the chorus as witnesses to "what strains of mourning do I go to this heaped up burial prison (consisting in) a strange tomb." The indirect question merely expands on the thought expressed by ἄκλαυτος. Even if one wishes to translate the term *nomois* at 847 "laws" and the entire phrase "By what laws do I go . . . ," this still does not show that Antigone recognizes that Creon's order has the force of law. The indignant question "By what sort of laws do I go?" assumes the implicit answer "These are no kind of laws at all."

[93] On the Athenian view that women lack courage see Dover (1974) 100–1. Since my main interest in this essay is the debate over the meaning of *nomos* and the relationship between democracy and the rule of law, I have not been able to do justice to the important issue of gender in the play. Although Creon is wrong about forbidding the burial of Polynices, Antigone is not entirely in the right and makes several mistakes that contribute to her own misfortunes and those of Creon. I am therefore sympathetic to some of the points made by Sourvinou-Inwood (1989), but would analyze Antigone's errors somewhat differently. I hope to explore these issues elsewhere.

because she is too bold, but because she is not bold enough to believe that the gods will ultimately protect her.

To put it in simplest terms, the clash between Antigone and Creon is about the meaning of the word *nomos*. Creon believes that whatever he as ruler commands has the force of law. Antigone and her fiancé Haemon uphold the Athenian view; for them a law must have the favor of the gods and the consent of the community. The chorus equivocates – it recognizes that ultimate success rests on obedience to the laws of gods, but is willing to call Creon's order laws. Although Creon's view of the law is similar in a way to that of Austin, it would be wrong to analyze the debate between Antigone and Creon in terms of an opposition between the positivist view of law and the doctrine of natural law. Antigone and Haemon appeal both to the gods and to the opinion of the community. Creon's decree is wrong not only in substantive terms because it goes against the justice of the gods and the rights of the dead. Creon also makes a procedural error by failing to consult with the people before making what he calls a law. He commits a further procedural mistake by not giving Antigone a trial before the people despite her denial of wrongdoing. In Creon's eyes the ruler has the authority to issue laws. For Antigone and Haemon only the people have that power. Although the men in the audience might have found Antigone harsh and too outspoken, they would have recognized that her disobedience was in keeping with the Athenian ideals of democracy and the rule of law, two ideals that in their eyes were not incompatible.

Afterthoughts

The importance of the story of the burial of Polynices found in the Funeral Orations for our understanding of *Antigone* is studied in Bennett and Tyrrell (1990). In this essay I did not discuss the idea of Ostwald (1969) that there was a difference between the term *thesmos*, which was a kind of law that was imposed from above, and the term *nomos*, which had its roots in popular custom and was a more democratic term that became current in the middle of the fifth century and gradually replaced *thesmos* as the word for "law" in the fifth century. Hölkeskamp (2002) 123–6 has now shown that the two terms are used interchangeably without any appreciable difference in meaning, thus undermining Ostwald's view that there was a shift in the Athenian conception of law after the introduction of the democracy under Cleisthenes.

1.4 How Often Did the Athenian Assembly Meet?

I

According to the Aristotelian *Constitution of the Athenians* (*Ath. Pol.* 43.4), the Assembly in Athens met four times every prytany. At each one of these meetings, certain topics had to be discussed or voted on. For instance, a vote concerning the conduct of magistrates presently in office was to be taken at the κυρία ἐκκλησία. At another meeting, anyone who wished to could request a discussion of any matter, be it private or public. Nothing is said in this passage or anywhere else in the *Constitution of the Athenians* about the possibility of holding additional meetings of the Assembly in times of emergency, but in a few passages in the Attic orators we find the term ἐκκλησία σύγκλητος used. The scholia to the passages and some entries in the ancient lexica indicate that this term refers to an extra meeting of the Assembly that could be convened at short notice in order to deal with emergencies.

On the basis of this information, scholars have in the past concluded that the Assembly normally met four times each prytany in the Classical period, but that extra meetings, called ἐκκλησίαι σύγκλητοι, could also be held if the need arose.[1] Recently, however, M. H. Hansen, whose work on many aspects of Assembly has greatly increased our understanding of Athenian democracy, has challenged the *communis opinio*.[2] Hansen argues that the evidence found in the scholia and lexica is unreliable and should be disregarded. In his view, several passages in the speeches of Aeschines and Demosthenes and some lines in *IG* ii² 212 indicate that the Assembly met a fixed number of times each prytany, no more, no less.

[1] For example, Busolt and Swoboda (1920–6) 987–8; Glotz (1928) 182–3; Jones (1960) 108–9; Ehrenberg (1965) 67; Staveley (1972) 79.

[2] Hansen first set forth this idea in Hansen (1975) 51–7. He restated his position with new arguments in Hansen (1977) and presented further arguments in (1979b). Both of these articles were reprinted with addenda in Hansen (1983a). References in this chapter will be made to this volume.

Consequently, an ἐκκλησία σύγκλητος cannot have been an additional meeting of the Assembly. Hansen then proposes a new definition of the term ἐκκλησία σύγκλητος: "one of the four meetings held during a prytany . . . summoned by the *prytaneis* at short notice or in accordance with a decree passed on a previous Assembly or by the Council." It stood in contrast to the "ordinary meeting," which was "summoned by the *prytaneis* at their own initiative and at four days' notice."[3] Hansen's arguments have been doubted by P. J. Rhodes,[4] but they have not received close scrutiny. I think that Rhodes' skepticism is well justified in this case, and in this chapter I shall attempt to show that Hansen's interpretation of the evidence should not be accepted.

Before proceeding to examine Hansen's interpretation of the passages he uses to establish his position, I would like to set out some *a priori* reasons for doubting his thesis that a limitation was placed on the number of times the Assembly could meet each prytany. As all students of Greek history know, the Athenians had what we call a "direct democracy," a form of government in which all major decisions were taken by the Assembly where all citizens were entitled to vote. Nevertheless, the Assembly tried, especially in the fourth century BCE, to conduct its business according to set rules, which were designed to promote fairness and order in its discussion of public business.[5] These rules were self-imposed and did not represent any limitation on the powers of the Assembly, but were rather an attempt by that body to discipline itself, to act in a responsible fashion and not in a way that would bring it into disrepute. Only if the Assembly were run in an orderly fashion could it function efficiently. But such a restriction as Hansen envisages on the number of times it could meet each prytany would not have advanced the goals of fairness, order, and efficiency. On the contrary, this restriction would have inhibited the ability of the Assembly to respond to emergencies. Hansen assumes that the *prytaneis* always made sure that the stipulated number of meetings was never used up before the end of the prytany and that they always saved one meeting that could be used to deal with any emergencies that might suddenly occur.[6] Yet, what would have happened if this one meeting was used to deal with an emergency early in the prytany, but then another emergency, demanding immediate attention,

[3] Hansen (1983a) 42.
[4] Rhodes (1981) 521–2.
[5] For a useful summary of the reforms of the fourth century, see Rhodes (1980).
[6] Hansen (1983a) 43. Hansen pursued this idea in Hansen (1982) (= Hansen [1983a] 83–102).

occurred at the end of the prytany, by which time the limit for that prytany had already been reached? Would the *prytaneis* have simply turned to the people and said that they could not call another meeting and that the matter would just have to wait until the beginning of the next prytany? I find it hard to believe that they would.

This is only an argument from common sense, and, like all such arguments, rests on the assumption that the Athenians were as clear-sighted and rational as we fancy ourselves to be. I would like to think that the Athenians did possess these wonderful qualities, but that is a proposition that needs to be proved, and it can only be proved by analyzing the evidence we have at our disposal. Let us, therefore, turn to look at the passages on which Hansen builds his arguments.

II

We need to look first at the evidence found in the scholia and lexica. Some of the explanations they provide for the term are obviously wrong, but others give clear and concise definitions:

Schol. Dem. 18.73: σύγκλητος ἐκκλησία λέγεται ἡ γενομένη διά τι ἐξαίφνης κατεπεῖγον. τρεῖς γὰρ ἐκκλησίαι τοῦ μηνὸς γίνονται ὡρισμέναι, ἡ δὲ σύγκλητος οὐχ ὡρισμένη.[7]

Schol. Dem. 24.20: ἰστέον γὰρ ὅτι κατὰ μῆνα τρεῖς ἐκκλησίας ἐποιοῦντο, . . . πλὴν εἰ μὴ ἄρα ἀνάγκη τις κατέλαβε πολέμου, ὥστε καὶ περὶ ἐκείνου ἄλλην ἐκκλησίαν ποιῆσαι πλέον τῶν ὡρισμένων.[8]

Harpocration s.v. σύγκλητος ἐκκλησία· τῶν ἐκκλησιῶν αἱ μὲν ἐξ ἔθους καὶ κατὰ μῆνα ἐγίνοντο. εἰ δέ τι ἐξαίφνης κατεπείξειεν ὥστε γενέσθαι ἐκκλησίαν, αὕτη ἐκαλεῖτο σύγκλητος ἐκκλησία. Δημοσθένης ἐν τῷ κατ᾽ Αἰσχίνου.[9]

Hansen (p. 41) correctly observes that "the scholiasts and lexicographers refer invariably to three *ecclesiai* every month instead of four *ecclesiai* every prytany." Originally, Hansen (p. 41) was willing to admit that "in so far as their notes are reliable they refer to the period of twelve phylae (when a prytany probably was concurrent with a month)." Later Hansen (pp. 73–80) changed his mind and decided that this information was also incorrect for the Hellenistic period.

[7] Cf. schol. Dem. 19.123.

[8] Cf. schol. Aeschin. 1.60; Photius *s. v.* κυρία ἐκκλησία; schol. Ar. *Ach.* 19.

[9] Cf. *Suda* and *Etym. Magn. s.v.* σύγκλητος and Pollux 8.116.

His main objection to the testimony of the sources of the Classical or even the Hellenistic period is that they set the ἐκκλησίαι σύγκλητοι apart from the ἐκκλησίαι νόμιμοι or ὡρισμέναι, neither of which terms, Hansen (p. 41) notes, "can be found in the sources of the Classical or even the Hellenistic period." He continues by pointing out, "On the contrary, the descriptions given by Aeschines (τεταγμέναι ἐκ τῶν νόμων, 2.72) and Demosthenes (ὅταν ἐκ τῶν νόμων καθήκῃ, 19.185) indicate that there was no technical term for what the lexicographers and scholiasts call ἐκκλησίαι νόμιμοι or ὡρισμέναι and modern historians 'ordinary meetings.'"

Are the scholiasts and lexicographers really inventing a technical term? Or are they just trying to express in their own words their idea of what an "ordinary meeting" was? It is true that the Classical sources do refer to meetings τεταγμέναι ἐκ τῶν νόμων and meetings called ὅταν ἐκ τῶν νόμων καθήκῃ, but just because the scholiasts and lexicographers used different expressions from those used by the Classical sources does not necessarily mean that they are referring to two different kinds of meetings. As Hansen himself notes, there was no technical term for an "ordinary meeting" of the Assembly in the Classical period and it was referred to by at least two different periphrases.[10] This left the scholiasts and lexicographers with no choice but to invent a term to designate this kind of meeting. Thus, the argument from terminology does nothing to impugn the testimony of the scholiasts and lexicographers.

What is striking about these sources is that they do appear to have known precisely how many times the Assembly met each month in the Hellenistic period.[11] This makes it very likely that, when commenting on the relevant passages in Aeschines and Demosthenes, the authors of the scholia and lexica consulted Hellenistic sources to find a definition of the term ἐκκλησία σύγκλητος. When they used this information to explicate the passages in the orators, either they did not realize that the number of tribes and prytanies had been changed between the Classical and Hellenistic periods, or they were aware of the change, but did not bother to adjust the information they found in their Hellenistic source to fit the conditions of the Classical period. There is consequently good reason to think that the scholiasts and lexicographers should be trusted for the Hellenistic

[10] For a possible explanation of this phenomenon, see note 17.

[11] During the period of the twelve tribes, a prytany was probably concurrent with a month (Hansen [1983a] 41; Pritchett and Neugebauer [1947] 68).

period. But what about the Classical period? I can see no reason to think that, when the Athenians decided to add two more tribes, they also decided to change the meaning of the term ἐκκλησία σύγκλητος. The switch to twelve tribes involved no more than that and did not entail a complete transformation of the entire system of prytanies and the way in which the Assembly was run. In short, I see no reason for thinking that the meaning of the term ἐκκλησία σύγκλητος must have changed between the Classical and Hellenistic periods.

The information found in the scholia and lexica is often unreliable and should never be uncritically accepted, especially when no source is cited to vouch for the information provided. Yet, even though the authors of the scholia and lexica in this case do not name any sources, it does appear that they must have had some. For this reason, their explanation of the term ἐκκλησία σύγκλητος should be taken seriously, not tossed out without further consideration. It may be that the definition they provide for this term does not work in the passages of the Classical authors where it is used. If that is the case, it should be rejected and another definition of the term will have to be formulated. On the other hand, if this definition does make sense in the passages where the term is used, we ought to consider it to be correct.

III

Hansen's most important objection to the traditional definition of the term ἐκκλησία σύγκλητος as an additional meeting of the Assembly is his argument that the Assembly met a fixed number of times each prytany, no more, no less. Let us now look at the passages on which Hansen bases his argument. The first is Dem. 19.154:

> ἐπειδὴ γὰρ ἐκκλησία μὲν οὐκέτι ἦν ὑπόλοιπος οὐδεμία τὸ προκατακεχρῆσθαι, οὗτοι δ' οὐκ ἀπῇσαν, ἀλλ' αὐτοῦ διέτριβον, γράφω ψήφισμα βουλεύων, τὴν βουλὴν ποιήσαντος τοῦ δήμου κυρίαν, ἀπιέναι τοὺς πρέσβεις τὴν ταχίστην.

To understand this passage, we must set it in context. Demosthenes is describing the period after the ratification of the Peace of Philocrates. By the terms of that treaty, Philip and Athens agreed that each one should retain only those territories that each one presently held, thereby implicitly renouncing claims to territory held by the other party.[12] However, Philip was not bound by the provisions of this treaty until he swore the oaths to the treaty. The purpose of this section of Demosthenes' speech is to prove his charge that Aeschines and the other ambassadors who were ordered by the Assembly to receive the oaths from Philip deliberately delayed their departure from Athens with the aim of giving the king more time to seize Athenian fortresses in Thrace before he had to swear the oaths to the treaty.[13] Demosthenes claims that he knew of this alleged plot and did his best to thwart it. If such a plot did exist and Demosthenes did know of it, one wonders why he did not denounce his fellow ambassadors to the Assembly at the time. For this there is a simple explanation – the entire charge is sham. The fortresses in Thrace did not lie in Athenian territory, but in the kingdom of Cersebleptes.[14] Besides, even if they did belong to Athens, the delay of the embassy would have made no difference at all, as Aeschines was quick to point out.[15] The fortresses must have fallen to Philip before 25 Elaphebolion, the date on which Cersebleptes surrendered to Philip, just about the time the Second Embassy was elected to travel to Philip.

The falsehood of Demosthenes' charge in this section is not directly relevant to Hansen's argument, but it should warn us to be wary when using Demosthenes as a source and to expect him to omit important details when it suits his purpose. We also need to keep in mind that Demosthenes is trying to place his own actions in the best possible light and to portray himself as the self-appointed guardian of Athenian interests. Consequently, the most routine actions suddenly become brilliant moves in an effort to outsmart his opponents. This is precisely what happens in this passage. It is clear that the Assembly ordered the Council to supervise the departure of the ambassadors. Acting in accordance with the wishes of the Assembly, Demosthenes passed a motion in the Council on 3 Mounichion instructing the ambassadors to proceed to Philip and to receive the oaths from him, a perfectly routine procedure.[16] But in the context of the imaginary plot to

[12] [Dem.] 7.26.

[13] Dem. 19.150–4.

[14] For the location of these fortresses, see Badian (1980) 64 and the references cited there. Demosthenes (18.27) states that at the time of their capture these fortresses were held by Thracians.

[15] Aeschin. 2.89–93.

[16] Hansen (1983a) 36 wonders "Why should the people resign some of their powers if an extraordinary assembly could be summoned at any moment?" This misrepresents the situation. The matter of supervising the departure of the embassy was routine business, which could be delegated to the Council without risk and did not necessitate the calling of another meeting of the Assembly. For delegation of powers to the Council by the Assembly, see Rhodes (1972) 82–5, 92 n. 4, 161, 182–3, 186–8,

give Philip time to overrun the Thracian fortresses, this seemingly routine action gains a deeper significance. Demosthenes describes a dire predicament: Philip is moving toward the Thracian fortresses, no more meetings of the Assembly remain, since they have already been used up, and the Athenian ambassadors are delaying. But the resourceful Demosthenes is not to be outfoxed – he takes advantage of the fact that the Assembly ordered the Council to supervise the departure of the embassy and passes a motion instructing the ambassadors to leave at once. The plot is temporarily foiled.

Why does Demosthenes fail to mention the possibility that an additional meeting of the Assembly could be held in this situation? The answer is ready to hand – to admit this possibility would have spoiled the entire point he was trying to make.[17] As a careful reader of the orators, Hansen himself is well aware of how adept Demosthenes is at suppressing inconvenient details of constitutional procedure when it suits his purpose. Hansen (p. 29) notes very shrewdly how Demosthenes (19.185) does this elsewhere:

> In this passage Demosthenes gives a detailed description of how the Athenian democracy worked. The phrase ὅταν ἐκ τῶν νόμων καθήκη indicates that the meetings of the assembly were held on fixed days or summoned at several days' notice. There is no reference to ἐκκλησίαι σύγκλητοι, but Demosthenes' silence on this point is not surprising. He wishes to emphasize the laborious and slow democratic procedure in opposition to the efficiency of an oligarchy or a tyranny.

218. Rhodes does not include Dem. 19.154 in his list of instances where the Assembly delegated powers to the Assembly.

[17] Hansen (1983a) 36 makes much of the fact that "Demosthenes says explicitly that not a single *ecclesia* was left, and his emphatic expression must comprise both regular and extraordinary meetings." But how would Demosthenes have said "there were no more 'ordinary meetings' left," when, as Hansen himself has noted, there was no technical term for an "ordinary meeting"? Yet, there was probably no need for a technical term, since the word ἐκκλησία all by itself without the addition of σύγκλητος could mean an "ordinary meeting." In the opposition between the two expressions ἐκκλησία and ἐκκλησία σύγκλητος we have an example of "semantic marking," whereby "the semantically marked lexeme is one that is more specific in sense than the corresponding semantically unmarked lexeme" and "the unmarked member of the opposition has both a more general and a more specific sense according to context" (Lyons [1977] I: 307–8.) In this case, the expression ἐκκλησία is the unmarked member of the opposition and can have a more general sense, namely, "a meeting of the Assembly," or a more specific sense, namely, "an ordinary meeting of the Assembly," whereas the expression ἐκκλησία σύγκλητος is the marked member of the opposition and carries only the specific meaning, namely, "an additional meeting of the Assembly called for an emergency."

We can easily restate this to fit Dem. 19.154: "in this passage Demosthenes wishes to emphasize the lack of opportunity he had to thwart the plans of the other ambassadors and to demonstrate to the court how brilliant he was to take advantage of the powers granted to the Council to hurry the malingering embassy on its way. Accordingly, he concentrates on the powers granted to the Council and the possibility of summoning an extra meeting of the Assembly to denounce the insidious schemes of his opponents is cunningly passed over in silence."

So much for Dem. 19.154 as evidence for a limit on the number of meetings of the Assembly that could be called each prytany. We must now look at Aeschin. 2.61. Here Aeschines maintains that Demosthenes arranged two meetings of the Assembly on the 18th and 19th of Elaphebolion in order to "snatch away in advance (προϋφαιρῶν)" the meetings of the Assembly before the envoys from the other Greek cities had arrived in Athens. Hansen (p. 37) maintains that Demosthenes could be described as "snatching away the meetings in advance," only "if a fixed number of assemblies were held every prytany, since the Athenians were now forced to discuss the peace during the meetings held on Elaph. 18 and 19 and take the vote on the peace." This misunderstands the situation described by Aeschines. We know that the Assembly had sent ambassadors to the Greek states παρακαλῶν τὰς πόλεις ὑπὲρ τῆς ἐλευθερίας τῶν Ἑλλήνων and that around the beginning of Elaphebolion 346 these ambassadors were expected to return to Athens in the near future.[18] These ambassadors were apparently sent out to invite the Greek cities to send embassies of their own to Athens where they could all confer together about how best to defend Greek freedom.[19] In the speech he delivered against Aeschines in 343, Demosthenes (19.16) stated that these ambassadors indeed arrived in Athens and listened to Aeschines speak in favor of peace and alliance with Philip and urged the Assembly not to allow any of the other Greeks to share in the treaty. In his reply to this accusation in his own speech at that trial, Aeschines implicitly agreed with his opponent that the Athenians had indeed invited the Greeks to send embassies to Athens and that they were expected to arrive there in Elaphebolion 346. Aeschines (2.61–2) then went on to deny that the Greek ambassadors were able to make it to Athens in time to attend the meetings of the Assembly on 18 and 19 Elaphebolion. According to Aeschines, the culprit who saw to it that these meetings of the Assembly were

[18] Aeschin. 2.60.
[19] Aeschin. 3.68–70.

called before the Greek embassies had a chance to travel to Athens was none other than Demosthenes himself. Therefore, what Aeschines means by the participle προϋφαιρῶν is that Demosthenes snatched away from the Greek embassies the chance to attend the meetings of the Assembly that discussed the treaty with Philip by setting the dates for those meetings on days that were earlier than the soonest possible time the Greek embassies could reach Athens. It is, therefore, perfectly possible to make sense of Aeschin. 2.61 without postulating any hypothesis about a limit to the number of meetings of the Assembly that could be called in one prytany.

Hansen (p. 37) next claims to find support for his hypothesis at *Ath. Pol.* 43.3, where he quite correctly notes that it is stated that those who act as *prytaneis* convene the Assembly four times each prytany or forty times a year. He observes that no mention is made of the possibility of summoning "extraordinary meetings when required in addition to the forty ordinary meetings." Relying on an *argumentum e silentio*, Hansen infers that, since this possibility is not mentioned, the *prytaneis* could not summon extra meetings of the Assembly. There is nothing wrong per se with *argumenta e silentio*, but this part of the *Constitution of the Athenians* is not the best place to use them. The *Constitution of the Athenians* is our most informative source for the Athenian constitution, but it is not always exhaustive in its treatment of each topic.[20] In this section alone, Rhodes has observed that the list of items to be considered on the agenda of the Assembly is not complete.[21] Nor does this work mention the fact that the *prytaneis* were required to give four days' notice for a meeting of the Assembly – this is reported to us only by Photius (s.v. πρόπεμπτα).[22] The silence of the *Constitution of the Athenians* cannot be summoned to speak on behalf of Hansen's hypothesis. The only reasonable inference that can be made from *Ath. Pol.* 43.3 is that the *prytaneis* regularly held four meetings of the Assembly each prytany. On the basis of this passage taken by itself, we cannot decide whether or not exceptions were made to this rule, but given the incomplete

[20] Perhaps it is not inapposite to note that elsewhere Hansen (1983a) 203 has remarked "In Aristotle's *Constitution of the Athenians* the *nomothetai* are passed over in silence. Does this mean that *nomothesia* had been abolished after 329/8 or stopped being of any importance? Certainly not. *Argumenta e silentio* of this kind based on the *Constitution of the Athenians* are of no value whatsoever."

[21] Rhodes (1981) 523.

[22] It is curious how Hansen, who is so skeptical about the evidence of the scholia and lexica for the term ἐκκλησία σύγκλητος, confidently accepts this piece of evidence from Photius for which there is no supporting evidence from the Classical period.

nature of much of the information found in the *Constitution of the Athenians*, it would be unwise to rule out this possibility.

To sum up: None of the passages adduced by Hansen prove that there existed a limit on the number of meetings of the Assembly that could be held in each prytany. By the same token, nothing in these passages can be used as evidence to show that an ἐκκλησία σύγκλητος was not an extra meeting of the Assembly that could be summoned for special occasions in addition to the four regularly scheduled meetings.

IV

We can now consider the arguments that Hansen employs to formulate his new definition of the term ἐκκλησία σύγκλητος. First of all, he notes (p. 38) that Aeschines distinguishes between ἐκκλησίας συγκλήτους and ἐκκλησίας τεταγμύνας ἐκ τῶν νόμων but does not tell us how these differed. To determine what the difference is between the two terms, Hansen turns to a passage of Demosthenes (19.122–3) where it is clear that the term ἐκκλησία σύγκλητος "means a meeting of the assembly summoned at short notice" (p. 38). This, of course, is nothing new – the scholia and lexica include this feature as part of their definition of the term. What, then, are ἐκκλησίαι τεταγμέναι ἐκ τῶν νόμων? Hansen (p. 39) suggests that they are "meetings held on fixed days or summoned at proper notice." To justify this definition, he draws attention to another passage of Demosthenes (19.185) where the orator describes how the Council can convene meetings of the Assembly only ὅταν ἐκ τῶν νόμων καθήκῃ. What are these νόμοι referred to here? Hansen believes that they include the stipulation, reported by Photius (s.v. πρόπεμπτα), that the *prytaneis* were required to publish the agenda for a meeting of the Assembly at four days' notice.

Hansen is concerned, however, that this new definition will not cover certain meetings of the Assembly in Elaphebolion 346, which in his opinion were ἐκκλησίαι σύγκλητοι. Accordingly, he includes another category of meetings of the Assembly to be also considered ἐκκλησίαι σύγκλητοι and contrasts them with "ordinary meetings":

> If one of the four meetings held during a prytany was summoned by the *prytaneis* at short notice or in accordance with a decree passed on a previous assembly or by the Council, the meeting was an ἐκκλησία σύγκλητος. On

the other hand, if it was summoned by the *prytaneis* at their own initiative and at four days' notice, it was an "ordinary meeting."

(p. 42)

At this point Hansen adds a further argument to support his new definition. He notes that "Aristotle describes some fixed items on the agenda for all the four meetings held during a prytany" and concludes that if "the ἐκκλησίαι σύγκλητοι were included among the four meetings we must assume that the people at an ἐκκλησία σύγκλητος had to deal with routine matters prescribed for this meeting before they could debate the urgent or important matter which had occasioned the summoning at short notice or by special decree." Hansen claims that this assumption is proved correct by *IG* ii² 212, an inscription that records an honorific decree passed in the archonship of Themistocles (347/46) for three Bosporan princes. In this decree, those who will act as *proedroi* at the meetings of the Assembly scheduled for 18 Elaphebolion are instructed to see to it that the matter of the money owed to these princes is brought up for discussion (*IG* ii² 212, line 57). According to Hansen's definition, this meeting of the Assembly was an ἐκκλησία σύγκλητος "since the date of the meeting was fixed by a decree carried by Demosthenes." Hansen then draws attention to the phrase μετὰ τὰ ἱερά, which he believes refers to the discussion of τρία ἱερῶν, which the *Constitution of the Athenians* tells us formed part of the regular agenda at two of the four meetings of the Assembly held every prytany (*Ath. Pol.* 43.6). This is alleged by Hansen to prove that "an ἐκκλησία σύγκλητος was not reserved for the discussion of some urgent matter. It was not an additional meeting, but one of the forty ἐκκλησίαι described by Aristotle."

There is only one problem with this last argument, but it is a fatal one: τὰ ἱερά in the phrase μετὰ τὰ ἱερά does not refer to a discussion of the τρία ἱερῶν, mentioned at *Ath. Pol.* 43.6, but to the sacrifices that were performed at the beginning of every meeting of the Assembly.[23] In the inscription no reference is made to *a discussion* of sacred matters, but to *the* sacred matters. It is important to note the presence of the article in the phrase μετὰ τὰ ἱερά and its absence in the phrase τρία ἱερῶν. In the first phrase, the article indicates that something specific is being referred to, that is, "the (one, specific) sacred business,"[24] which consisted

[23] Aeschin. 1.22–3 with scholia; scholia to Ar. *Ach.* 44; Dem. 54.39. Cf. Jacoby on *FGrHist* 334 F 16.

[24] For the use of the article see Renehan (1976) 69–74.

of the customary sacrifices that were performed at the beginning of every meeting of the Assembly. In the second, any three points relating to sacred business that happen to be of concern are put on the agenda to be discussed. *IG* ii^2 212 does not, therefore, lend support to Hansen's argument for a new definition of the term ἐκκλησία σύγκλητος. In fact, it is not even relevant to the discussion at all.

We need to return to Aeschin. 2.72. In this passage Aeschines appears to distinguish between two different types of meetings of the Assembly: ἐκκλησίας συγκλήτους, and those τεταγμένας ἐκ τῶν νόμων. Hansen thinks Aeschines is drawing a contrast between meetings held at short notice or summoned by decree (his definition of ἐκκλησία σύγκλητος) and those summoned by the *prytaneis* in accordance with the laws, especially the one regarding publication of the agenda four days ahead. But, if Aeschines wished to contrast these two types of meetings, he would surely have expressed himself differently. The *prytaneis* are not said to τάττειν ἐκκλησίας – they are said to προγράψαι ἐκκλησίας.[25] If Aeschines were trying to say what Hansen wants him to say, he would have spoken of ἐκκλησίας προγεγραμμένας, not τεταγμένας.

On the other hand, the phrase ἐκκλησίας τεταγμένας ἐκ τῶν νόμων is a perfectly good way of describing the four "ordinary meetings" of the Assembly that the *prytaneis* were legally required to call each prytany and for which certain items of the agenda were fixed by the laws. This kind of meeting could well be referred to as one that was "arranged for by the laws." The "ordinary meetings" stood in contrast to the extra meetings of the Assembly that did not have any fixed items on the agenda, these being the ἐκκλησίαι σύγκλητοι. We should also point out that if we use these traditional definitions of these terms, the passage of Aeschines gains far more thrust. Aeschines is reminding the court of the desperate situation in which Athens found herself in early 346 – things were so bad that the number of extra meetings exceeded that of the "ordinary meetings." If we interpret the term ἐκκλησίας συγκλήτους in this passage according to the traditional definition, Aeschines is saying in effect that things were so bad in early 346 that, in addition to the four ordinary meetings, at least five ἐκκλησίαι σύγκλητοι were called every prytany for the purpose of discussing urgent business. This is far more alarming than to say merely that in early 346 most of the meetings of the Assembly were called at short notice. If Aeschines had had Hansen's definition of this term in mind when he wished to depict this dangerous state of affairs, he

[25] For example, [Arist.] *Ath. Pol.* 43.3–4; Aeschin. 2.61.

would certainly not have said that there were more ἐκκλησίαι σύγκλητοι than ordinary meetings, but rather that every meeting was an ἐκκλησία σύγκλητος, or, in other words, that circumstances were so pressing that the Athenians were never able to postpone their discussions of these urgent matters until after the normal four-day interval had elapsed.

In short, I do not find Hansen's attempt to formulate a new definition of the term convincing. Of the evidence he puts forward to justify his definition, *IG* ii² 212 is not relevant to the issue; Dem. 19.185 can be used to support either the traditional definition of the term or Hansen's new definition; and Aeschin. 2.72 is better interpreted by using the traditional definition of the term. If anything, our examination of this evidence has provided fresh support for the traditional definition of the term ἐκκλησία σύγκλητος.

V

It is time to turn to Hansen's analysis of the meetings of the Assembly in Elaphebolion 346. This is not the place to enter into a discussion of all the many issues concerning these meetings; I wish only to make two points that bear directly on the matter of the ἐκκλησία σύγκλητος.

In his revised analysis of these meetings Hansen (pp. 68–71) still has the Assembly meeting on five days, that is, 8, 16, 18, 19, and 25 Elaphebolion, in prytany viii of the archonship of Themistocles (347/6). This, of course, would appear to contradict his theory that at the maximum only four meetings of the Assembly could be convened each prytany. He attempts to circumvent this difficulty by claiming that the meetings on 18 and 19 Elaphebolion counted as one meeting, reducing the total number of meetings in this prytany to a more acceptable four. Hansen argues that such an interpretation is justified because "the two meetings on Elaph. 18 and 19 were prescribed by one decree, the agenda was the same for both meetings and the *prytaneis* issued probably only one summons." First of all, it is not true that the agenda was the same for both meetings. The matter of the money owed to the Bosporan princes was on the agenda for the meeting of 18 Elaphebolion only and not for the meeting on the following day (*IG* ii² 212, lines 65–6). Similarly, the discussion of the treaty with Philip was on the agenda for that day, whereas the vote on the treaty was on the agenda for 19 Elaphebolion and not on that for the previous day (Aeschin. 2.65–6). Hansen also misinterprets *Ath. Pol.* 43.4 when he states that this passage says "that the prytaneis were empowered to summon four meetings during their term of office." On the contrary, the passage states that the *prytaneis* convene (συνάγουσι) four meetings of the Assembly. Nothing is said of four summonses, any one of which could be used to summon two or more meetings. It is simply unacceptable to count the two meetings on 18 and 19 Elaphebolion as one meeting. Reading from the decree of Demosthenes that set the dates for the meetings, Aeschines (2.61) refers quite plainly to two meetings (δύο ἐκκλησίας).[26]

Although we must count the meetings on 18 and 19 Elaphebolion as two meetings, it is possible to eliminate the meeting on 8 Elaphebolion. In his speech of 330 against Ctesiphon, Aeschines (3.66–7) says that Demosthenes proposed (γράφει ψήφισμα) that the *prytaneis* convene a meeting of the Assembly (ἐκκλησίαν ποιεῖν) on 8 Elaphebolion. First of all, we need to note that Aeschines does not say whether or not this proposal was passed and nothing in the text allows us to give a definitive answer to this question. Thus, even if we believe what Aeschines says here, we still would not be able to say that this proposal did pass and that consequently a meeting of the Assembly did take place on 8 Elaphebolion. Second, it is uncertain whether or not Aeschines could prove his charge. At the end of this section of the speech in which he has referred to several decrees (3.62–8), Aeschines has a number of decrees read out, but does not specify which ones. The decree of Demosthenes calling for a meeting on 8 Elaphebolion may have been among them and it may not have been. It is therefore possible that Aeschines did not have any evidence to support this charge. This means that we are entitled to be skeptical about the truth of this accusation.

This skepticism increases when we note one additional fact, namely, this charge is found only in Aeschines' speech of 330 and is absent from his speech in 343, which was delivered only three years after the alleged incident. If there was any truth to this charge, why did Aeschines omit it in his earlier speech? It is more likely that the charge is baseless and that Aeschines was not confident enough to use it in 343 when the memories of the court about the events of 346 were relatively fresh. By 330 Aeschines was quite sure that the court would not remember the events of 346 in any detail and felt free to invent this charge. Indeed, there is a surprising number of unsupported charges made by Aeschines in his speech of 330 about the events of 346, none of which appears in his earlier speech. These are the following: (i) the deal between Demosthenes and Meidias (3.52), (ii) the entry of Demosthenes into

[26] Cf. Aeschin. 2.60, 65, 67; Dem. 19.13.

the Council by means of bribery (3.62), (iii) the ruse that Demosthenes employed to force the Assembly to accept the proposal of Philocrates on 19 Elaphebolion (3.71–2), (iv) the story of the exclusion of Cersebleptes (3.73–5), and (v) the providing of mulecarts for the Macedonian ambassadors (3.76).[27] There is no evidence that would allow us to prove that the first, second, and fifth charges are false, but documents and witnesses cited in Aeschines' speech of 343 demonstrate that the third and fourth are untrue.[28] Given this knowledge, it is certainly not unreasonable to conclude that the rest are equally unreliable. But what is more striking is that of all these five charges that figure in the speech of 330 and not in the speech of 343, not one is supported by any relevant evidence. This means that we can discard Aeschines' claim that Demosthenes proposed that the Assembly meet on 8 Elaphebolion and can eliminate this meeting from the calendar of events in prytany viii of 346.[29] We are now left with only four meetings of the Assembly in that prytany.

Oddly enough, our criticism of Hansen's reconstruction of the events of Elaphebolion 346 has removed a possible objection to his hypothesis that there

[27] Dinarchus (1.28) repeats the same charge against Demosthenes and, like Aeschines, fails to provide any evidence.

[28] The third charge is proved false by Aeschin. 2.65–6, where the decree regulating the procedure for the meetings on 18 and 19 Elaphebolion is read out. This decree stipulated that no speeches were to be made about the treaty on 19 Elaphebolion. Neither orator provides any evidence to prove that these orders were rescinded. The fourth charge is refuted by Aeschin. 2.83–6, where evidence is produced to show that Cersebleptes did indeed have a person in Athens who could have acted as his *synedros*, namely, Critobulus of Lampsacus, and that Aleximachus submitted a proposal to have him admitted to the Athenian Confederacy. This request was apparently turned down, and Cersebleptes' representative was unable to swear the oaths to the treaty with Philip ([Dem.] 12.8). I plan to deal with the problems relating to the first charge elsewhere.

[29] If this argument is accepted, it would eliminate one of the few exceptions to Mikalson's rule that the Assembly did not generally meet on festival days (Mikalson [1975] 187). Hansen (1983a) 85, note 4, noted that Mikalson incorrectly interpreted Dem. 24.26 as referring to a meeting of the Assembly and has questioned his interpretation of *IG* ii^2 1673, lines 9–10. If we eliminate all these examples, this would reduce the total number of exceptions to Mikalson's rule to a total of eight, five of which, as Mikalson himself has noted, can be explained in a reasonable way and do not pose any serious problem for his general thesis.

If one accepts my analysis of Aeschin. 3.66–7 and the validity of Mikalson's rule, the restoration of *IG* ii^2 359, lines 2–7 to give a meeting of the Assembly on 8 Elaphebolion should be viewed with suspicion. This restoration has been endorsed without question by several scholars, including Dinsmoor (1931) 372, Pritchett and Neugebauer (1947) 54, and Meritt (1961) 101–2. This restoration would be almost certain if the inscription were strictly *stoichedon*, but it is clear that, whereas most of the lines in the inscription appear to have contained 20 letters, line 6 must have contained 21.

was a limit to the number of meetings of the Assembly that could be called in one prytany. However, we need to be careful in spelling out the implications of this for Hansen's argument. Our analysis of Aeschin. 3.66–7 has removed one possible objection to Hansen's hypothesis, but it does not provide any evidence for it. We cannot rule out the possibility that Aeschines and Demosthenes did not report all meetings of the Assembly that took place during prytany viii of the archonship of Themistocles. After all, they were only interested in discussing the Peace of Philocrates and may well have left out of their speeches any references to other meetings of the Assembly that met during prytany viii simply because these meetings did not discuss business that was relevant to this treaty.[30] And even if this one possible objection to Hansen's hypothesis is removed, the others still stand and are not affected by our discussion of Aeschines 3.66–7. Nor can we use this reconstruction of the events in Elaphebolion 346 as evidence against the traditional view that the ἐκκλησία σύγκλητος was an extra meeting of the Assembly.

Before we proceed to look at the Hellenistic inscriptions, we should consider one additional piece of evidence from the Classical period. This is Th. 2.22.1 where we learn that in 431 Pericles, "fearing that any general discussion would result in wrong decisions, made under the influence of anger rather than reason" (trans. Warner), ἐκκλησίαν... οὐκ ἐποίει αὐτῶν – did not hold an Assembly. In an article written with F. W. Mitchel, Hansen has argued on the basis of this passage that there was no restriction on the number of meetings of the Assembly at this time.[31] This reveals that in the late fifth century extraordinary meetings of the Assembly could be called in addition to the regular meetings. What Thucydides is therefore saying is that in his attempts to curtail public discussion of the war, Pericles saw to it that no extra meetings of the Assembly were held in addition to the regularly scheduled meetings. This is how Gomme interpreted the passage, and I see no reason to disagree with him.[32] What is interesting about this conclusion is

[30] It is true that Demosthenes (19.154) states that by the time he passed his decree instructing the ambassadors to depart for Macedon (this was on 3 Munichion – see Aeschin. 2.91–2), there were no more regular meetings of the Assembly left in the prytany, but it is quite possible that another meeting of the Assembly might have been called between 25 Elaphebolion and 2 Munichion, or that Demosthenes is being less than honest here and tailoring the fact to fit the design of his presentation of the events in question.

[31] Hansen and Mitchel (1984). I am not convinced by the argument of Hansen and Mitchel that in the 350s the Assembly met only three times each prytany. See Rhodes (1985) 55, note 4.

[32] Gomme (1956) 76.

that it reveals that the practice of the late fifth century was the same as the practice of the fourth century according to the evidence of the scholia and lexica, evidence that, I have argued, ought to be trusted. Although some of the rules governing the procedure in the Assembly were altered in the fourth century, much remained the same and such continuity in procedure should come as no surprise.

Hansen and Mitchel believe, however, that there was a change in the period 362–55, when "the number of business meetings of the *ecclesia* was fixed at three, probably one ἐκκλησία κυρία and two other meetings." This measure was part of the same reform by which "the hearing of all political actions was transferred from the *ecclesia* to the *dicasteria*" and was undertaken "to reduce political pay, because the Athenians state was near bankruptcy."[33] Yet even if the Athenians were in the habit of holding as many as two or three trials in the Assembly each prytany (despite their almost pathological distrust of those in power, the Athenians were surely not this suspicious!), a measure that fixed the number of meetings of the Assembly at three per prytany would not have resulted in any substantial reduction in the payment of the *ekklesiastikon*. As a money-saver, this hypothetical measure would not have been very effective. Hansen's approach also forces us to invent a hypothetical reform for which there is no direct evidence whatsoever. It would seem far more sensible and economical to conclude that there was a limit on the number of times the Assembly could meet neither in the fifth century nor in the fourth century. We might add that Th. 2.22.1 does not prove that the remarks of the scholiasts and lexicographers are correct for the fourth century, but it does make it far more likely.

VI

We must now examine the use of the term ἐκκλησία σύγκλητος in Hellenistic inscriptions. Initially, Hansen (p. 74) "did not exclude the possibility that the scholiasts and lexicographers might be right in describing ἐκκλησίαι σύγκλητοι as additional meetings if the information is applied to the period of the twelve

[33] Hansen and Mitchel (1984) 16–17. For the payment of the *ekklesiastikon*, see [Arist.] *Ath. Pol.* 41.3 with Rhodes (1981) 490–3. If the average attendance was 6,000 (Hansen [1983a] 16), then each meeting of the Assembly will have cost the state only half a talent. One wonders if the *ekklesiastikon* was also paid at the ἐκκλησίαι σύγκλητοι. Although there is no evidence on this point, I find it unlikely. We know that the *ekklesiastikon* was instituted to stimulate attendance. This was probably necessary for the ordinary meetings at which dull routine business was discussed, but not for the ἐκκλησίαι σύγκλητοι at which important issues of immediate concern to all were debated.

phylai," but he later changed his mind and argued that this information did not apply to this later period, whereas his new definition of the term did. To support his revised view, Hansen pointed to the prescripts of seventeen decrees from the Hellenistic period. We should, however, point out that the term ἐκκλησία σύγκλητος appears in only four of these, one of which is heavily restored. In the other thirteen the term is absent, a phenomenon that Hansen (p. 78) explains with the assumption that "the indication of whether or not an ἐκκλησία was σύγκλητος or not was optional." He contends (p. 77) that the two meetings mentioned in *IG* ii² 554 and 857 must have been, on the one hand, because they were summoned in accordance with a decree of the Assembly and, on the other hand, because all meetings of the Assembly summoned by a decree of the Assembly qualified as ἐκκλησίαι σύγκλητοι in his opinion. This is a valid argument for calling these meetings if and only if we can accept Hansen's definition of this term.

In the case of *IG* ii² 644, 672, 775, and 1006 and *Hesperia* 5 (1936), 419–28, n. 15, Hansen assumes that these meetings must have been because they were summoned on festival days. I see nothing that compels us to accept such an assumption and to rule out *a priori* the possibility that these would have been ordinary meetings of the Assembly, whether the term "ordinary" is used in the traditional sense or in the sense that Hansen prefers. The same is true for *Hesperia* 5 (1936), 414–16, n. 12, *IG* ii ² 649 and 896. If we can take for granted Hansen's definition of the term ἐκκλησία σύγκλητος as "*inter alia* an emergency meeting summoned at short notice whereas an ordinary meeting had to be summoned at four days' notice" and accept the further assumption that in the Hellenistic period "the *prytaneis* had to preside over the meetings they had summoned and could not pass on the presidency over an assembly summoned by them to the subsequent board of *prytaneis*,"[34] we can conclude that these inscriptions record decrees passed at ἐκκλησίαι σύγκλητοι, but here again nothing forces us to accept Hansen's definition.

In *SEG* XXI 440, *IG* ii ² 897 and 954 we run into the term βουλὴ σύγκλητος. It is clear from these inscriptions that in these cases a meeting of the Council was called first on these days, followed immediately by a meeting of the Assembly. Hansen points out (p. 76) that there is only one other known instance of this, which occurred in the autumn of 339 after Philip's seizure of Elateia (Dem. 18.168ff.). At this time, "a meeting of the *boule* was followed immediately by an emergency

[34] Hansen (1983a) 77, note 22. It should be noted that Hansen's only evidence for the Hellenistic rule governing the procedure of the *prytaneis* is a passage from Demosthenes (23.92).

meeting of the *ecclesia,* undoubtedly an ἐκκλησία σύγκλητος." I think Hansen is probably correct to call this particular meeting of the Assembly in 339 an ἐκκλησία σύγκλητος, but it does not follow that all meetings of the Assembly that immediately followed meetings of the Council on the same day were ἐκκλησίαι σύγκλητοι. To generalize on the basis of one isolated example is always a risky move.

Looking at the matter from another angle, one could argue that the meetings of the Assembly referred to in these inscriptions had already been scheduled by the *prytaneis* several days earlier and that the *prytaneis* had posted the agenda for each of these meetings well in advance. At the last moment, however, a new concern arose, one that the generals wished to be dealt with immediately; but to be placed on the agenda for this meeting it needed to be approved first by the Council. To clear this hurdle, an emergency meeting of the Council was called at the request of the generals. At this meeting of the Council the new item was introduced, passed, and placed on the agenda of the previously scheduled meeting of the Assembly, which was then convened immediately afterwards. This explanation certainly makes more sense than Hansen's when one takes into consideration the fact that, although the meeting of the Council is designated as σύγκλητος, the meeting of the Assembly is not labeled an ἐκκλησία σύγκλητος. It may be possible, as Hansen (p. 78) argues, that "the indication of whether an ἐκκλησία was σύγκλητος or not was optional" and that the practice varied from one decree to the next, but I find it hard to believe that the practice should be inconsistent in one and the same decree. For these reasons, I find it preferable to categorize the meetings at which the decrees recorded in *SEG* XXI, 440, *IG* ii^2 897 and 954 were passed as "ordinary."

This leaves us with the only inscriptions that actually use the term ἐκκλησία σύγκλητος. In each of these it is perfectly possible to use Hansen's definition of the term, but it is equally possible to use the traditional definition of the term without encountering any difficulties in understanding the rest of the contents of each decree. In sum, an examination of these decrees does not advance Hansen's case one iota.

As a final argument, Hansen notes (p. 79) that the contents of these decrees passed in ἐκκλησίαι σύγκλητοι were honorific. He finds it "remarkable that such decisions were regularly on the agenda of an ἐκκλησία σύγκλητος" and concludes that "an ἐκκλησία σύγκλητος was not an assembly reserved for some urgent matter." But on the traditional definition of the term, an ἐκκλησία σύγκλητος was not just an additional meeting of the Assembly called in case of emergency. It was also a meeting for which there was no previously set agenda, as opposed to the "ordinary" meetings for which the agenda contained certain items that had to be discussed. Now the honorary decrees *IG* ii² 838 and 945 were not just passed for some minor *proxenoi* from small towns in Thrace. They were for close friends of Ptolemy III and Eumenes II. These men merited special treatment, and what could be more flattering than to call an entire meeting of the Assembly just to confer honors on them? If their honors were to be voted on at a regular meeting of the Assembly, these men would have had to wait several hours and to listen to much dull routine business, such as how many *drachmai* had been spent to pay for pigs at minor sacrifices, until their turn came up. Besides, the passing of such an honorary decree may well have been preceded by several laudatory speeches of a kind that is all too common whenever awards are distributed. These tedious speeches might have consumed several hours and have thus justified the calling of a special session. One might ask, didn't the Athenians have better things to do at their meetings in this period? The unfortunate answer is "probably not." But there is another way of looking at the matter. In the Hellenistic period the security of Athens depended not so much on her own army and fleet as on the favor of monarchs such as Ptolemy and Eumenes. Good relations with these kings were of the utmost importance, and those who could win and maintain their friendship for Athens were highly valued and merited special treatment.[35] Because of these factors, the notion of what constituted "urgent and important" business altered. The ἐκκλησία σύγκλητος was still summoned to discuss "urgent and important business," but what constituted "urgent and important business" had changed considerably from the Classical period.

Our examination of the Hellenistic inscriptions has yielded no decisive arguments against or in favor of Hansen's views. Nonetheless, the objections we have formulated still stand, and nothing in our study of the Hellenistic inscriptions has caused us to abandon them.

VII

We can now summarize our conclusions:

1) There is no reason to think that there ever was a limit to the number of times the Assembly could meet in one prytany.

[35] For the role of these friends of the Hellenistic monarchs, see Herman (1980–81).

2) We have no reason to disbelieve the traditional definition of the term ἐκκλησία σύγκλητος. As we have seen, we have no grounds for doubting the evidence provided for this term in the scholia and lexica; the definition they give for this term fits the context in each passage where it is used. Although the results of this study have been largely negative, consisting primarily of refutations of several of Hansen's arguments, I hope to have placed the traditional definition of the term ἐκκλησία σύγκλητος on a firmer basis.

Afterthoughts

The main points of this chapter have been accepted by several scholars: Rhodes with Lewis (1997) 15, note 24; Rhodes and Osborne (2003) 323; Stockton (1990) 71; Pritchett (2001) 192–201; Gauthier (1987) 314 ("Harris plaide avec de bons arguments en faveur de la thèse traditionelle"); and MacDowell (2000) 266–7 (though with slightly different arguments). Errington (1994) 137, note 6 finds the debate "inconclusive" but at 159, note 87 supplies an alternative reason for rejecting Hansen's interpretation, which he finds "in my view, in any case not very convincing."

Hansen replied to this essay in Hansen (1987a). I replied to his arguments in Harris (1991b) [= Chapter I.5].

On the method for using the information found in the Attic orators as historical evidence, see Harris (1995) 7–16. On the controversy about the embassies sent by the Greek *poleis* to Athens before the Peace of Philocrates, see Harris (1995) 158–61. On Demosthenes' charge that Aeschines and the other ambassadors on the Second Embassy deliberately delayed their departure for Macedon in Elaphebolion of 346, see now Harris (1995) 79–80, 165. The study promised in note 28 was published in Harris (1989). On the *philoi* of Hellenistic monarchs, see now Savalli-Lestrade (1998).

1.5 When Did the Athenian Assembly Meet? Some New Evidence

For ancient historians prospecting for facts about their period, the scholia found in the medieval manuscripts of Classical authors furnish much ore of varying quality. As those who have explored these regions can attest, the scholia contain many auriferous seams and, for the unwary, much fool's gold. Some entries in the scholia bear the imprint of an ancient authority and clearly consist of precious material. Yet others, which seem initially to flash with the gleam of authenticity, are, when more closely examined, found to have little value, often composed of one part reasonable inference, the rest irresponsible guesswork. The process of extraction can be difficult, and one must be careful not to mistake the spurious for the genuine. But we should also not be too quick to discard information contained in a scholium simply because its author neglected to stamp it with the citation of an ancient source. Such haste impoverishes the study of ancient history.

The purpose of this chapter is to rescue from the rubbish heap a nugget of information about the Athenian assembly found in a scholium to Dem. 24.20. The first part of this scholium informs us that the Athenians used to hold three meetings of the Assembly each month, but if some military emergency suddenly arose, an extra meeting might be summoned. The second part tells us at what times of the month meetings of the Assembly were normally held.

> κατὰ μῆνα τρεῖς ἐκκλησίας ἐποιοῦντο, βουλευόμενοι περὶ τῶν ἐν τῇ πόλει πραγμάτων, πλὴν εἰ μὴ ἄρα ἀνάγκη τις κατέλαβε πολέμου, ὥστε καὶ περὶ ἐκείνου ἄλλην ἐκκλησίαν ποιῆσαι πλέον τῶν ὡρισμένων. καὶ ἐγίνετο ἡ πρώτη ἑνδεκάτῃ τοῦ μηνός, ἡ δὲ δευτέρα περὶ τὴν εἰκάδα, ἡ δὲ τρίτη περὶ τὴν τριακοστήν.[1]

[1] Cf. schol. Aeschin. 1.60; Harp. *s.v.* κυρία ἐκκλησία; *Suda* K 2670; Photius *s.v.* κυρία ἐκκλησία; schol. Ar. *Ach.* 19 (to be associated with *Suda* E 470). All my citations of the demosthenic scholia are from the superb new edition of Dilts (1983–86).

The information found in the first part of this scholium is similar to that found in a scholium on Dem. 19.123 and in an entry in the lexicon of Harpocration (σύγκλητος ἐκκλησία), both of which add that an extra meeting called during an emergency was called an ἐκκλησία σύγκλητος.[2] Until recently, scholars accepted this information without question and concluded that the Assembly met a fixed number of times each prytany – four times a prytany during the period of the ten tribes ([Arist.] *Ath. Pol.* 43.4), but probably three times a prytany during the period of the twelve tribes – but that extra meetings called ἐκκλησίαι σύγκλητοι could be summoned if the need arose.[3] In recent years, however, the information found in these passages has become the subject of a scholarly dispute.[4] I do not wish here to continue that dispute; in the pursuit of truth, some polemic is inevitable, but when protracted, it becomes tiresome and fruitless. Rather, I will examine the evidence about the information contained in the second half of the scholium on Dem. 24.20 about the dates of Assembly meetings.

Usually when we come upon an interesting piece of information in the scholia that is not vouched for by the citation of an ancient source, we have no means of checking its veracity. In this case, however, we have a large amount of evidence that confirms its reliability. The evidence comes from the prescripts of Attic inscriptions that preserve decrees enacted by the Assembly.[5] These prescripts

[2] The first part of the scholium to Dem. 19.123 is found in Codex A, the second in F[2] and Y. Similar information to that contained in Harpocration *s.v.* σύγκλητος ἐκκλησία is found in *Suda* Σ 1292; *Etym. Magn.* 733.15; Pollux 8.116. The scholium for Dem. 18.73 quoted by Hansen (1979b) 149 and by Hansen (1987a) 38 is not ancient evidence but probably derives from schol. Dem. 19.123 (see Dilts [1985] 257–9).

[3] For example, Busolt and Swoboda (1920–26) 987–8; Glotz (1928) 182–3; Jones (1960) 180–9; Ehrenberg (1965) 67; Staveley (1972) 79.

[4] Hansen first challenged the reliability of the evidence found in the scholia and lexica in Hansen (1975) 51–7. He restated his position with new arguments in Hansen (1977) and presented further arguments in Hansen (1979b). Both of these articles were reprinted with addenda in Hansen (1983a). I defended the evidence of the scholia and lexica in Harris (1986) (= the previous chapter of this volume). Hansen defended his position in Hansen (1987a). Hansen's defense of his position has convinced neither me nor Rhodes (1988b).

[5] Since the inscriptions recording decrees of the Assembly dating before 341/40 do not indicate the day of the month in their prescripts, there is no epigraphical evidence for the date of meetings before that year. See Henry (1977) 37. For the one exception, see note 47. All the rest of the evidence comes from the speeches of Apollodorus, Aeschines, and Demosthenes. Mikalson (1975) 129 observes that the terms of the truce of 423 (Th. 4.118.11–13) were to go into effect on Elaphebolion 14 and concludes that this "in all probability indicates that a meeting of the Ekklesia occurred on this day." The inference is improbable. The terms of a treaty between two Greek communities went into effect not after it was ratified by their respective Assemblies (or other representative bodies), but when those designated by

often record the dates on which decrees were passed and thus indicate on what days of the month the Assembly met. The evidence provided by the inscriptions, along with some information in the literary sources, is substantial enough to enable us to draw some conclusions about the normal schedule of meetings of the Assembly and thereby to test the reliability of the information contained in the second part of the scholium on Dem. 24.20.[6]

Since the scholium appears to describe procedure during the period of the twelve tribes when a prytany was generally a month long, we will consider first the evidence for that period.[7] The following list gives the day of the month and the meetings known to have taken place on that day. For the sake of completeness, I have included the few known decrees from the period of the thirteen tribes, but have marked them with an asterisk.

EVIDENCE FOR THE DATES OF MEETINGS OF THE ASSEMBLY IN THE PERIOD OF THE TWELVE TRIBES

1st: There is no indisputable evidence for a meeting on this day.
2nd: There is no indisputable evidence for a meeting on this day.
3rd: There is no indisputable evidence for a meeting on this day.
4th: There is no indisputable evidence for a meeting on this day.

each community swore the oaths to the treaty. See Kußmaul (1969) 18–19. The stipulation that the truce of 423 was to go into effect on Elaphebolion 14 indicates only that the oaths were to be sworn on that day. The decree instructing the Athenian representatives was in all likelihood passed several days before Elaphebolion 14.

[6] The task of assembling the evidence for the dates of meetings has been greatly facilitated by Mikalson's excellent work on the sacred and civil calendar. Like Mikalson (1975) 10, I have adopted a conservative approach, accepting as evidence "only those restorations which are demonstrably correct." Since Mikalson was primarily interested in finding out whether the Assembly met on festival days, he did not include decrees passed by the Assembly for which the day of the month, but not the name of the month, is known. My list includes such decrees as well as all those published after Mikalson completed the work for his study.

[7] Harris (1986) 365 (= page 83 of previous chapter). Cf. Pollux 8.115:

> πρυτανεία δέ ἐστι ὁ χρόνος ὃν ἑκάστη φυλὴ πρυτανεύει. καὶ ὅτε μὲν δέκα ἦσαν πλείους ἑκάστῃ φυλῇ αἱ ἡμέραι, ἐπεὶ δώδεκα ἐγένοντο, ἑκάστη φυλὴ μηνὸς πρυτανείαν ἔχει.

The statement is roughly correct but does not represent a strict rule consistently followed in every year. See Meritt (1961) 135–6; Raubitschek (1958) 84–6 has suggested Pollux drew on Philochorus' *Atthis* and Theophrastus' *Nomoi*.

5th: Mikalson believes that there are two meetings of the Assembly attested for this day,[8] but his interpretations of the decrees he cites as evidence are unlikely. One of the inscriptions records a meetings on Posideon 5, 220/19 (*Hesperia* 38 [1969] 425–31, no. 2 [Traill] lines 1–4). The prescript describes the decrees as βουλῆς ψηφίσματα, but Mikalson prefers to follow Traill, the editor of the inscription, who drew attention to line 13, which indicates the measure was a decree of the Assembly and argues that the phrase in line 4 is an error. Habicht *per litteras* suggests a more plausible explanation: "the date refers, in fact, to the meeting of the Council, when the probouleuma was drafted." Mikalson believes that *IG* ii² 656 records a decree of the Assembly passed on Elaphebolion 5, 284/83, but the inscription seems rather to reproduce a decree passed by a tribe.[9]

6th: There is no indisputable evidence for a meeting on this day.

7th: There is no indisputable evidence for a meeting on this day.

8th. There is no indisputable evidence for a meeting on this day.

9th: Metageitnion 9, 271/70 (*Hesperia* 23 [1954] 287–96 [Dinsmoor] lines 2–6).
Metageitnion 9, 268/67 (*IG* ii² 687, lines 2–5).[10]
Boedromion 9, 119/18 (*Hesperia* 47 [1978] 286, no. 15 [Traill] lines 1–4).
Boedromion 9 101/00 (*IG* ii² 1028, lines 1–3).[11]
Pyanopsion 9, 178/77 (*Hesperia* 51 [1982] 60–2, no. 3 [Tracy] lines 1–3).
Posideon 9, 116/15 (*IG* ii² 1009, lines 28–30).
Gamelion 9, 282/81 (*Hesperia* 7 [1938] 100–9, no. 18 [Meritt] lines 2–6).
Elaphebolion 9, 295/94 (*IG* ii² 647, lines 1–7).
Elaphebolion 9, 241/40 or 240/39 (*Hesperia* 17 [1948] 3–4, no. 3 [Meritt] lines 2–5).[12]
Elaphebolion 9, 171/70 (*Hesperia* 3 [1934] 14–18, no. 17 [Meritt] lines 43–6; see also *Hesperia* 15 [1946] 198–201).
Elaphebolion 9, 118/17 (*IG* ii² 1008, lines 49–50).
Skirophorion 9, before 240/39, possibly 254/53 (*IG* ii² 784, lines 1–4).[13]
(Month not preserved) 9, late second century BCE (*IG* ii² 1019, lines 1–2).

[8] Mikalson (1975) 88, 122.

[9] See Wilhelm (1914) 179; *IG* 656 *addenda*; Henry (1977) 74.

[10] For the archon-year, see Heinen (1972) 115–17; Habicht (1979) 116, note 11.

[11] Lines 66–8 of this inscription mistakenly give the day as ἕκτῃ.

[12] For the archon-year, see Habicht (1979) 133–41 (241/40); Osborne (1989) 225 (240/39).

[13] For the archon-year, see Habicht (1979) 137–41 (before 240/39 in a year of the Greater Panathenaia); Osborne (1989) 237 (254/53).

10th: Boedromion 10, 118/17 (*IG* ii^2 1008, lines 1–3).
*Thargelion 218/17 (?) (*IG* ii^2 843, lines 1–5).

11th: Hekatombaion 11, 286/85 (*IG* ii^2 650, lines 1–5).
Hekatombaion 11, soon after 261, possibly 255/54 (*Hesperia* 38 [1969] 418–25, no. 1 [Traill] lines 1–4).[14]
Metageitnion 11, 247/46 or 246/45 (*Hesperia* 52 [1983] 52 [Dontas] lines 1–5).
*Metageitnion 11, 204/03 (*IG* ii^2 973, lines 2–6).
Pyanopsion 11, 122/21 (*IG* ii^2 1006, lines 50–1).
Poseideon 11, 282/81 (*IG* ii^2 666, lines 1–4).
Poseideon 11, 104/03 (*IG* ii^2 989 as reedited with new fragments by M. L. Lethen, *Hesperia* 26 [1957] 25–8, no. 1 lines 1–4 and 40–2).
Gamelion 11, 107/06 (*IG* ii^2 1011, lines 63–5).
Gamelion 11, 103/02 (*IG* ii^2 1034, lines 1–3).[15]
Mounichion 11, 187/86 (Pritchett and Meritt ([1940] 117–18, lines 2–5).
Mounichion 11, 185/84 (*IG* ii^2 897, lines 1–6).[16]
Mounichion 11, mid second century BCE (*IG* ii^2 996, lines 1–3).
Mounichion 11, 106/05 (Josephus *AJ* 14.8.5).
Thargelion 11, 262/61 or 251/50 (*IG* ii^2 770, lines 1–4).[17]
Thargelion 11, early second century BCE (*Hesperia* 33 [1964] 183–4, no. 34 [Meritt] lines 2–7).
Skirophorion 11, 272/71 (*Hesperia* 26 [1957] 54–5, no. 11 [Meritt] lines 2–7).

12th: Metageitnion 12, 247/46 (*IG* ii^2 778, lines 1–5).[18]
Mounichion 12, 190/89 (*IG* ii^2 947, lines 9–12).[19]

13th: Elaphebolion 13, 184/83 (*Hesperia* 5 [1936] 419–28, no. 15 [Meritt] lines 1–4).[20]

[14] For the archon-year, see Habicht (1979) 126–8 (soon after 261); Osborne (1989) 237 (255/54).

[15] For the archon-year, see Meritt (1977) 161–91.

[16] Hansen (1983a) 152–3 classified this meeting as an *ekklesia synkletos*, but I questioned his position in Harris (1986) 375 (= page 99 of this volume). Hansen (1987a) 47 quotes most of my argument but, strangely enough, leaves out the last sentence, which contains what I think is the strongest objection to his view. However, Hansen (1987a) 48 rightly notes: "We must bear in mind, however, that the reconstructions advanced by Harris and myself only apply if the rules affecting sessions of the *boule* and *ekklesia* were basically the same as in the fourth century, and this is certainly a far-reaching assumption." With that statement, I am in full agreement.

[17] For the archon-year, see Habicht (1979) 126 (262/61); Osborne (1989) 237 (253/52 or 251/50, more likely the latter).

[18] For the archon-year, see Habicht (1979) 133–41.

[19] For the archon-year, see Tracy (1984) 43–7.

[20] For the archon-year, see Lewis (1988) 19–20.

14th: Boedromion 14, 106/05 (*IG* ii² 1011, lines 2–3).
Thargelion 14, 235/34 (*IG* ii² 790, lines 2–5).

15th: There is no indisputable evidence for a meeting on this day.

16th: Pyanopsion 16, 242/41 or 241/40 (*IG* ii² 795, lines 1–4; cf. *Hesperia* 4 [1935] 551).[21]
Pyanopsion 16, 106/05 (*IG* ii² 1011, lines 31–2).
Mounichion 16, 296/95 (*IG* ii² 644, lines 1–6).
Thargelion 16, 107/06 (*IG* ii² 1011, lines 73–4).
Skirophorion 16, 188/87 (*IG* ii² 893, lines 2–6; see also *AJP* 78 [1957] 375–81).
Skirophorion 16, 165/64 (*IG* ii² 949, lines 1–4).

17th: (Month not preserved) 17, 303/02 (*IG* ii² 734, lines 3–7).[22]

18th: Boedromion 18, 283/82 (*IG* ii² 657, lines 1–5).
Boedromion 18, 268/67 (*Hesperia* 5 [1936] 418–19, no. 14 [Meritt] lines 2–5; cf. *Hesperia* 38 [1969] 110–12).[23]
Boedromion 18, 247/46 or 246/45 (*Hesperia* 7 [1938] 121–3, no. 24 [Meritt] lines 2–4).[24]
Boedromion 18, 236/35 (*IG* ii² 787, lines 1–4).
Pyanopsion 18, 304/03 (*IG* ii² 481, lines 1–5).
Pyanopsion 18, 116/15 (*Hesperia* 16 [1947] 170–2, no. 67 [Meritt] lines 2–4).
Poseideon 18, 270/69 (*Hesperia* Suppl. 17 [1978] 2–4, lines 5–8; cf. *SEG* 28 [1978] no. 60).
Anthesterion 18, 235/34 (*IG* ii² 788, lines 1–5).
Anthesterion 18, 163/62 (*Hesperia* 3 [1934] 27–31, no. 20 [Meritt] lines 2–5; cf. *Hesperia* 13 [1944] 266).
Thargelion 18, 302/01 (*IG* ii² 503, lines 1–5).
Skirophorion 18, 181/80 (*Hesperia* 53 [1984] 370–4, no. 3 [Tracy] lines 1–4).
(Month not preserved) 18, 194/93 (*IG* ii² 888, lines 1–3).[25]

19th: Posideon 19, 146/45 (Roussel and Launey [1937] no. 1504, lines 50–1).
Anthesterion 19, 286/85 (*IG* ii² 651, lines 3–8).
Anthesterion 19, 189/88 (*IG* ii² 978 as restored by Meritt, *Hesperia* 26 [1957] 65, lines 2–7).

[21] For the archon-year, see Habicht (1979) 133, 143 (242/41); Osborne (1989) 225 (241/40).
[22] For the archon-year, see Karapa (1974) 159–63.
[23] For the archon-year, see note 10.
[24] For the archon-year, see Habicht (1979) 133–41.
[25] For the archon-year, see Habicht (1982) 165.

Elaphebolion 19, 164/63 (*Hesperia* 26 [1957] 72–7, no. 22 [Meritt] lines 1–4).
Mounichion 19, 279/78 (*IG* ii^2 672, lines 1–3).
Mounichion 19, before 247/46 or 243/42 (*IG* ii^2 775, lines 28–31; see also *Hesperia* 7 [1938] 145 and *Hesperia* 28 [1959] 174–8).[26]

20th: (Month not preserved) 20, before 224/23 (*IG* ii^2 857, lines 1–3).

21st: Metageitnion 21, 305/04 (*IG* ii^2 796, lines 1–4; see also *Hesperia* 5 [1936] 203).
Metageitnion 21, 299/98 (*IG* ii^2 641, lines 1–7).
Maimakterion 21, 289/88 (*IG* ii^2 669, lines 1–5).
Maimakterion 21, 262/61 or 261/60 (Diogenes Laertius 7.10).[27]
Anthesterion 21, 20/19 (*SEG* 30 [1980] no. 93, lines 1–5).
Elaphebolion 21, 249/48 or 248/47 (*IG* ii^2 780, lines 2–4).[28]
Elaphebolion 21, 247/46 (*IG* ii^2 781, lines 2–5).[29]
Elaphebolion 21, 186/85 (*IG* ii^2 896, lines 2–5).
Elaphebolion 21, 128/27 (*Hesperia* 4 [1935] 71–81, no. 37 [Dow] as reedited with new fragments by Meritt, *Hesperia* 15 [1946] 201–13, no. 41, lines 101–4).
Mounichion 21, 273/72 (*Hesperia* 51 [1982] 53–4, no. 10 [Walbank] lines 2–5).
Skirophorion 21, 303/02 (*IG* ii^2 493, lines 2–8, and 494, lines 2–8).
Skirophorion 21, 302/01 (*IG* ii^2 505, lines 1–4).
Skirophorion 21, 273/72 (*IG* ii^2 676, lines 2–6).
(Month not preserved) 21, soon after 261 or 255/54 (*IG* ii^2 697, lines 1–5, as restored by Dow, *Hesperia* 32 [1963] 352–6. See also Meritt, *Hesperia* 38 [1969] 433–4).[30]
(Month not preserved) 21, 195/94 (*IG* ii^2 702, lines 2–5).[31]

22nd: Pyanopsion 22, 178/77 (Dow, *Hesperia* Suppl. 1 [1937] 120–4, no. 64, lines 1–3).
Elaphebolion 22, 247/46 or 246/45 (*IG* ii^2 680, lines 1–5).[32]
Elaphebolion 22, 145/44 (?) (*IG* ii^2 967, lines 1–5).[33]

[26] For the archon-year, see Habicht (1979) 133–41 (before 247/46); Osborne (1989) 224 (243/42).

[27] For the archon-year, see Habicht (1979) 114.

[28] For the archon-year, see Habicht (1979) 139–41, 143–5 (249/48); Osborne (1989) 237, 241 (249/49 or 248/47).

[29] For the archon-year, see note 18.

[30] For the archon-year, see note 14.

[31] For the archon-year, see Tracy (1978) 257–8.

[32] For the archon-year, see note 24.

[33] For the archon-year, see Habicht (1988).

Mounichion 22, 109/08 (*BCH* 59 [1935] 64–70 [Béquignon] lines 1–7).
(Month not preserved) 22, 299/98 (*IG* ii² 642, lines 2–9).

23rd: Metageitnion 23, 301/00 (*IG* ii² 640, lines 2–7; see also *Hesperia* 4 [1935] 547).
Elaphebolion 23, 190/88 (Pritchett and Meritt [1940] 121–3, lines 1–4).[34]
Thargelion 23, 184/83 (*Hesperia* 10 [1941] 275–7, no. 73 [Pritchett] lines 1–4).[35]
Skirophorion 23, after 262 or 260/59–256/55 (*IG* ii² 772, lines 1–5).[36]
Skirophorion 23, 181/80 (*IG* ii² 889, lines 1–4; see also Meritt [1961] 197).
Skirophorion 23, 140/39 (*IG* ii² 971, lines 9–10).

24th: There is no indisputable evidence for a meeting on this day.

25th: Boedromion 25, 266/65 (*IG* ii² 665, lines 1–4).
Boedromion 25, 227/26 (*IG* ii² 837, lines 2–6).
Pyanopsion 25, 302/01 (*Hesperia* 9 [1940] 104–11, no. 20 [Pritchett] lines 2–7).
Pyanopsion 25, 252/51 or 251/50 (*IG* ii² 769, lines 1–6).[37]
Posideon 25, 188/87 (*IG* ii² 890, lines 1–4).
Gamelion 25, 169/68 (*IG* ii² 910 as reedited by Dow, *Hesperia* Suppl. 1 [1937] no. 71, lines 1–4).
Skirophorion 25, 285/84 (*IG* ii² 654, lines 1–7).

26th: There is no indisputable evidence for a meeting on this day.

27th: Boedromion 27, 127/26 (*Hesperia* 4 [1935] 71–81, no. 37 [Dow] as reedited by Meritt, *Hesperia* 15 [1946] 201–13, no. 41, lines 76–8).
*Gamelion 27, 208/07 (*IG* ii² 849, lines 1–4).[38]

28th: Anthesterion 28, 302/01 (*IG* ii² 500, lines 2–6).
(Month not preserved) 28, 137/36 (*IG* ii² 974, lines 1–4).

29th: Metageitnion 29, 302/01 (*Hesperia* 1 [1932] 45–6 [Broneer] lines 1–5).
Metageitnion 29, 281/80 (*Hesperia* 4 [1935] 562–5, no. 40 [Meritt] lines 1–5).
Metageitnion 29, 226/25 (*Hesperia* 4 [1935] 525–30, no. 39 [Meritt] lines 2–7).
Pyanopsion 29, 273/72 (*IG* ii² 674, lines 1–2).

[34] For the archon-year, see Habicht (1982) 170, 177.

[35] For the archon-year, see note 20.

[36] For the archon-year, see Habicht (1979) 116 (after 262); Osborne (1989) 241 (260/59–256/55).

[37] For the archon-year, see Habicht (1979) 128 (251/50); Osborne (1989) 237, 241 (252/51 or 251/50, more likely the former).

[38] For the archon-year, see Habicht (1982) 169.

Posideon 29, 302/01 (*Hesperia* 3 [1934] 6–7, no. 7 [Meritt] as reedited with new fragments by Meritt, *Hesperia* 5 [1936] 414–16, no. 12, lines 2–7).
Posideon 29, 160/59 (*IG* ii^2 953, lines 1–4).
Gamelion 29, 304/03 (*IG* ii^2 483, lines 1–8).
Gamelion 29, 135/34 (Dow, *Hesperia* Suppl. 1 [1937] no. 56 as reedited with new fragments by Pritchett, *Hesperia* 9 [1940] 126–33, no. 26, lines 1–4).
Elaphebolion 29, 194/93 (*IG* ii^2 850, lines 1–3).[39]
Mounichion 29, 188/87 (*IG* ii^2 892, lines 1–2).
Thargelion 29, 300/299 (*IG* ii^2 585 as restored by Meritt, *Hesperia* 32 [1963] 4–5, lines 1–7).
Thargelion 29, 147/46 (Roussel and Launey [1937] no. 1505, lines 41–3).
(Month not preserved) 29, before 159 (*IG* ii^2 954, lines 1–4).[40]
(Month not preserved) 29, *circa* 50 (*IG* ii^2 1040, lines 20–2).

30th: Boedromion 30, soon after 261 or 260/59–256/55 (*IG* ii^2 700, lines 1–4; cf. *Hesperia* 7 [1938] 110–14, no. 20).[41]
*Boedromion 30, 214/13 (*Hesperia* 48 [1979] 174–8, no. 1 [Tracy] lines 1–4).
Gamelion 30, 285/84 (*IG* ii^2 653, lines 1–5).
Anthesterion 30, 267/66 (*IG* ii^2 661, lines 1–5).
Anthesterion 30, 229/28 (*IG* ii^2 832, lines 1–5).
Elaphebolion 30, 286/85 (*IG* ii^2 662 as reedited with a new fragment by Lethen, *Hesperia* 26 [1957] 29–30, no. 2, lines 1–3).
Mounichion 30, 293/92 (*IG* ii^2 649 as reedited with a new fragment by Dinsmoor [1931] 3–15, lines 1–4).
Skirophorion 30, 304/03 (*IG* ii^2 486, lines 3–8; *Hesperia* 7 [1938] 297, no. 22 [Schweigert] lines 3–8).
Skirophorion 30, 303/02 (*IG* ii^2 495, lines 1–6; 496, lines 1–7; 497, lines 1–7).
Skirophorion 30, 283/82 (*IG* ii^2 659, lines 2–7).
Skirophorion 30, 276/75 (*IG* ii^2 685, lines 1–6).
Skirophorion 30, 275/74 (*Hesperia* 2 [1933] 156–8, no. 5 [Meritt] lines 1–4).
Skirophorion 30, 271/70 (Meritt [1961] 192–4, lines 1–5).
Skirophorion 30, 192/91 (*IG* ii^2 916, lines 8–11; see also Pritchett and Meritt [1940] 115–16).

[39] For the archon-year, see Habicht (1982) 165.
[40] For the archon-year, see Habicht (1988) 238.
[41] For the archon-year, see Habicht (1979) 144 (soon after 261); Osborne (1989) 241 (260/59–256/55).

Skirophorion 30, 169/68 (*SEG* 25.118, lines 2–7; *IG* ii² 911, lines 1–5).
Skirophorion 30, 168/67 (*IG* ii² 945, lines 2–5).
(Month not preserved) 30, 306/05 (*IG* ii² 472, lines 2–6).
(Month not preserved) 30, 305/4 (*IG* ii² 797, lines 3–6).
(Month not preserved) 30, 285/84 (*IG* ii² 660, lines 25–7).

This evidence gives the following totals for meetings of the Assembly during the period of the twelve tribes:

Day of Month	Number of Meetings	Day of Month	Number of Meetings
1st	0	16th	6
2nd	0	17th	1
3rd	0	18th	12
4th	0	19th	6
5th	0	20th	1
6th	0	21st	15
7th	0	22nd	5
8th	0	23rd	6
9th	13	24th	0
10th	1	25th	7
11th	15	26th	0
12th	2	27th	1
13th	1	28th	2
14th	2	29th	14
15th	0	30th	18

These figures reveal that the information found in the scholium to Dem. 24.20 is roughly correct: out of the 126 regular meetings for which we know the day of the month, 90 (or 71 percent) fell on the 11th (ἐνδεκάτη), on the 18th, 19th, 20th, 21st, 22nd, or 23rd (περὶ τὴν εἰκάδα), or on the 29th or 30th (περὶ τὴν τριακοστήν).[42] Remarkable also is the fact that none of the days for which no meetings are attested is in the immediate temporal vicinity of the dates listed in the scholium. The only day that has a sizeable number of meetings attested and falls outside these days is the 9th. Yet we should note that of the thirteen

[42] I have omitted from these totals the meetings on Skirophorion 30, 169/68 (*IG* ii² 911, lines 1–7) and Skirophorion 30, 168/67 (*IG* ii² 945, lines 2–5) since they were *synkletoi ekklesiai*. The reason for calling these special extra meetings on the last day of the year was probably a large amount of business that had to be completed before the end of the year. I imagine that in these cases a regular meeting had been held the day before, but the Assembly had been unable to get through everything that had to be done before the end of the year, necessitating an extra meeting on the following day.

meetings attested for that day, four occurred in Elaphebolion, a month in which the Assembly could not meet on the 11th because of the Dionysia.[43]

There is another possible way of explaining the high number of meetings on the 9th. The scholium indicates that there was some flexibility in the scheduling of the second and third meetings, which respectively occurred "around the twentieth" and "around the thirtieth." The inscriptions show that such flexibility did indeed exist. The inscriptions also suggest that the same flexibility existed in the scheduling of the first meeting, for it often fell on the 9th. Note that if we include the meetings "around the eleventh" along with the meetings around the twentieth and thirtieth, we arrive at a total of 106 meetings out of all those attested, or 84 percent. I suspect that the author of the scholium was misled here by the text he was commenting on. He read in Dem. 24.20 that the Athenians regularly held a meeting of the Assembly on Hekatombaion 11 to discuss laws, and apparently concluded that the first meeting of the Assembly in the following months occurred on that day instead of "on or around the eleventh," as was actually the case. Whatever the true explanation, it is clear that the information about the normal meeting days of the Assembly found in the scholium is roughly correct. Where its author found this information remains something of a mystery, but there can be no doubt about its reliability. That in turn makes it probable that the rest of the information found in the scholium on Dem. 24.20 is also reliable for the period of the twelve tribes.

But what about the period of the ten tribes when a prytany was longer than a month and when there must have been four months in which there were more than three regular meetings? There is no evidence for the period before 360, but the literary sources and inscriptions provide us with dates of forty meetings for the last fifty years of the period of the ten tribes.[44] One might expect the schedule to have been different during this period, but the evidence, which I present below, suggests otherwise:

EVIDENCE FOR DATES OF MEETINGS OF THE ASSEMBLY IN THE PERIOD OF THE TEN TRIBES

1st: There is no indisputable evidence for a meeting on this day.
2nd: There is no indisputable evidence for a meeting on this day.
3rd: There is no indisputable evidence for a meeting on this day.

[43] Mikalson (1975) 185.
[44] See note 5.

4th: There is no indisputable evidence for a meeting on this day.
5th: There is no indisputable evidence for a meeting on this day.
6th: There is no indisputable evidence for a meeting on this day.
7th: There is no indisputable evidence for a meeting on this day.
8th: Elaphebolion (?) 8, 326/25 (*IG* ii² 359, lines 2–7).[45]
Aeschines (3.66–7) alleges that in 347/46 Demosthenes drafted a motion to have the Assembly meet on Elaphebolion 8 of that year, but he does not reveal whether or not the proposal secured approval. Hansen claims that the phrase ἐνταῦθ' ἕτερον νικᾷ ψήφισμα Δημοσθένους in the next section shows that Demosthenes "proposed *and carried* both decrees," that is, both the proposal mentioned in this section and the previous one to have the Assembly meet on Elaphebolion 8. Hansen's point rests on an inference from Aeschines' use of the word ἕτερον, but the inference is unwarranted. The adjective merely distinguishes the second decree from the first. There is no implication about the fate of the first decree.[46]
9th: Metageitnion 9, 333/32 (*IG* ii² 338, lines 1–5).
10th: Skirophorion 10, 331/30 (*IG* ii² 349, lines 3–7).
11th: Hekatombaion 11, 356/55 (*IG* ii² 127, lines 4–7).[47]
Hekatombaion 11, 352 (Dem. 24.26).
Hekatombaion 11, 323/22 (*IG* ii² 365, lines 1–4).
Boedromion 11, 320/19 (*IG* ii² 380, lines 2–6).
Maimakterion 11, 319/18 (*Hesperia* 9 [1940] 345–8, no. 44 [Schweigert] lines 4–8).
Gamelion 11, 314/13 (*IG* ii² 450, lines 1–6).
Thargelion 11, 332/31 (*IG* vii 4235, lines 2–7, and 4253, lines 2–7).

[45] In Harris (1986) 373, note 29 (see note 29 of this volume's previous chapter), I cast doubt on the traditional restoration of *IG* ii² 359 to give a meeting on Elaphebolion 8. Thanks to Professor Habicht, I was able to examine a squeeze of this inscription in the epigraphical Library at the Institute for Advanced Study in Princeton. Autopsy obliges me to admit that the letter after ὀγδόῃ in line 5 appears to be an iota, making the restoration ἱ[σταμένου] hard to avoid. For a full discussion of this inscription, see Schwenk (1985) 308–13.

[46] Compare the use of the word at Aeschin. 3.252. Here ἕτερος is used to refer to another person who was prosecuted for deserting Athens during the crisis after Chaeronea, but was acquitted by one vote. One cannot infer from the use of ἕτερος the fate of the previous person mentioned, since that person was in fact convicted and executed. In similar fashion, one cannot infer the fate of Demosthenes' first proposal at Aeschin. 3.66–7 from the use of the word ἕτερον when referring to the second proposal.

[47] The month and day of the month are not given, but the date must be Hekatombaion 11 since the decree was passed on the eleventh day of the first prytany.

Thargelion 11, 330/29 (*IG* ii² 351, addenda, lines 2–7).
(Month not preserved) 11, 333/32 (*IG* ii² 340, lines 1–7).

12th: Elaphebolion 12, 319/18 (*Hesperia* 7 [1938] 476–79, no. 31 [Crosby] lines 1–7; see also Meritt [1961] 122).
Mikalson (1975) 28 believes that Dem. 24.26 refers to a meeting of the Assembly on Hekatombaion 12, 352, but Hansen (1982) 332, note 5 correctly observes that the passage refers to a meeting of the *nomothetai*, not of the Assembly.

13th: There is no indisputable evidence for a meeting on this day.

14th: Thargelion 14, 330/29 (*IG* ii² 352, lines 2–10).
Posideon 14, 320/19 (*IG* ii² 381, lines 2–8, and 382, lines 2–7).

15th: There is no indisputable evidence for a meeting on this day.

16th: Pyanopsion 16, 329/28 (*IG* vii 4254, lines 2–7).
Skirophorion 16, 347/46 (Dem. 19.58).

17th: There is no indisputable evidence for a meeting on this day.

18th: Elaphebolion 18, 347/46 (Aeschin. 2.61; 3.68; *IG* ii² 212 lines 55–7).
Skirophorion 18, 335/34 (*SEG* 21.272, lines 2–7).

19th: Elaphebolion 19, 347/46 (Aeschin. 2.61; 3.68).[48]
Elaphebolion 19, 332/31 (*IG* ii² 345, lines 2–7. Cf. *IG* ii² 346 and 347).
Mounichion 19, 319/18 (Plu. *Phocion* 34.1–37.1).

20th: There is no indisputable evidence for a meeting on this day.

21st: There is no indisputable evidence for a meeting on this day.

22nd: There is no indisputable evidence for a meeting on this day.

23rd: Thargelion 23, *circa* 327/26 (*IG* ii² ii 1673, lines 9–10).

24th: Metageitnion 24, 362/61 ([Dem.] 50.4).

25th: Elaphebolion 25, 347/46 (Aeschin. 2.90; Aeschin. 3.73).
(Month not preserved) 25, 334/33 (*IG* ii² 335, lines 1–7).

26th: There is no indisputable evidence for a meeting on this day.

27th: Skirophorion 27, 347/46 (Dem. 19.60).
(Month not preserved) 27, 336/35 (*IG* ii² 328, lines 1–6).

[48] Hansen (1987a) 43–4 draws attention to Aeschin. 2.53 and argues that the meetings of Elaphebolion 18 and 19, 347/46 constituted one double meeting, not two meetings. But Aeschines is inconsistent when referring to these meetings: in other places he refers to these meetings with the plural (Aeschin. 2.60, 65, 67; cf. Dem. 19.13). This means that Aeschines' language is not a reliable guide and is thus a poor support for Hansen's view. What should not be trusted is the official language of the decree of Demosthenes that set the dates for these meetings. Quoting from this decree, Aeschines (2.61) quite plainly refers to two meetings (δύο ἐκκλησίας).

28th: There is no indisputable evidence for a meeting on this day.
29th: Thargelion 29, 338/37 (Aeschin. 3.27).
(Month not preserved) 29, 338/37 (*IG* ii² 356, lines 1–8).
30th: Maimakterion 30, 321/20 (*Hesperia* 30 [1961] 289–91, no. 184 [Meritt] lines 3–7).
Gamelion 30, 318/17 (*Hesperia* 4 [1935] 35–7; no. 5 [Oliver] lines 1–2).
Elaphebolion 30, 328/27 (*IG* ii² 354, lines 2–7).
Elaphebolion 30, 320/19 (*IG* ii² 336b, lines 5–7).
Skirophorion 30, *circa* 330/29 (*IG* ii² 415, lines 7–11).
Skirophorion 30, 322/21 (*IG* ii² 375, lines 1–7).[49]
(Month not preserved) 30, 341/40 (*IG* ii² 229, lines 2–7).
(Month not preserved) 30, 337/36 (*IG* ii² 242, lines 2–5).
(Month not preserved) 30, 336/35 (*IG* ii² 330, lines 47–9).
(Month not preserved) 30, 335/34 (*IG* ii² 330, lines 1–4).
(Month not preserved) 30, 327/26 (*IG* ii² 357, lines 2–6).

This evidence gives us the following totals for meetings of the Assembly during the last fifty years of the period of the ten tribes:

Day of Month	Number of Meetings	Day of Month	Number of Meetings
1st	0	16th	2
2nd	0	17th	0
3rd	0	18th	2
4th	0	19th	3
5th	0	20th	0
6th	0	21st	0
7th	0	22nd	0
8th	1	23rd	1
9th	1	24th	1
10th	1	25th	2
11th	9	26th	0
12th	1	27th	2
13th	0	28th	0
14th	2	29th	2
15th	0	30th	11

49 The inscription gives Thargelion as the month, but this must be an error for Skirophorion. See Schwenk (1985) 449–51.

Although the sample for this period is smaller than that for the period of the twelve tribes, the totals for the 11th and the 30th stand out: these two days alone account for almost half of the meetings attested in this period. If we combine the totals for the days indicated in the scholium, we find that they make up 28 out of 41 attested meetings, or 68 percent, a figure that is strikingly close to the 71 percent for the period of the twelve tribes. The circumstances surrounding the meetings of Metageitnion 24, 362/61, Elaphebolion 19, 347/46, and Skirophorion 16, 347/46 indicate that they were probably σύγκλητοι ἐκκλησίαι.[50] If we deduct them from the total number of regular meetings in this period, we arrive at a figure of 27 out of 37 attested meetings, or 73 percent, a figure that is even closer to the one obtained for the period of the twelve tribes. And if we add the meetings "around the eleventh," the figure rises to 30 out of 37 meetings, or 81 percent, as compared with 84 percent for the period of the twelve tribes. These figures make it certain that the information contained in the scholium to Dem. 24.20 is reliable for the last fifty years of the ten tribes.

The normal schedule of regular meetings of the Assembly was obviously dictated in both periods by the festival calendar. Out of the first eight days of each month, seven were monthly festival days.[51] Even though the fifth was not a festival day in any month except for Boedromion, it appears that the *prytaneis* usually waited until the eleventh to summon a meeting of the Assembly, though in the period of the twelve tribes a meeting might sometimes occur on the ninth. Since the Assembly had to hold forty regular meetings during the year in the period of the twelve tribes, there had to be a meeting about once every ten days. That necessitated a meeting at the very end of the month, since the Assembly did not meet again until the ninth or eleventh of the following month. The remaining meeting then had to fall on a date roughly midway between the other two, that is, "around the twentieth."[52]

[50] The meeting of Metageitnion 24, 362/61 was called in response to news about dangerous developments in several areas. The meetings of Elaphebolion 19 and 25 were obviously additional meetings called to deal with extra business arising from the negotiations for the Peace of Philocrates. The meeting of Skirophorion 16, 347/46 was summoned to deal with the proposals brought back by the second embassy from Philip, which demanded immediate action.

[51] Mikalson (1975) 13–20.

[52] This reveals that Hansen's claim that in the period of the ten tribes what mattered in the scheduling of meetings of the Assembly was "the day of the prytany, and not the day of the month" is mistaken (Hansen [1982] 331–50 = Hansen [1983a] 83–102).

We can now return to our point of origin. Our examination of the evidence, both epigraphical and literary, has revealed that the information about the normal schedule of Assembly meetings found in the scholium on Dem. 24.20 is accurate for the period of the ten tribes beginning (at the latest around 360) and also for the period of the twelve tribes. Where the author of this scholium found this information we do not know; Theophrastus' *Nomoi* and Philochorus' *Atthis* are possible candidates. Whatever his source, his information is clearly reliable. And that ought to apply also to his statement that the Athenians normally held three meetings of the Assembly each month, but might in emergency situations hold an extra meeting. As the scholium on Dem. 19.123 tells us, these extra meetings were called σύγκλητοι ἐκκλησίαι.[53]

Afterthoughts

Errington (1994) 136–7, note 4 accepts my conclusions about the reliability of the information contained in the scholion on Dem. 24.20 for the Hellenistic period but finds the evidence for the period of the ten tribes less compelling. On this see below.

Not long after I published this essay, Professor Lewis sent me a hand-written note telling me "you are basically correct." Unfortunately, Professor Lewis passed away soon afterwards so I was never able to ask him what he meant by "basically."

Hansen (1993) is a reply to this essay. In the first part of the essay Hansen (1993) 101 alleges that my conclusion was that "the *ekklesia* was summoned according to the festival calendar." He then claims that this "conclusion does not tally with Arist. *Ath. Pol.* 43.3," where "we are told that the *prytaneis* have to summon the people four times in a prytany (and not three times in a month)." In support of his objection, he rightly points out that many decrees before ca. 340 BCE were

[53] I would like to thank Professor J. Mikalson for supplying me with references to the relevant inscriptions published since the completion of *Sacred and Civil Calendar*. I would also like to express my gratitude to Professor C. Habicht for his generous help and encouragement. Professor Habicht read over an earlier draft of this article and provided me with information about Hellenistic chronology. He also enabled me to make use of the resources of the Epigraphical Library at the Institute for Advance Study at Princeton. In addition, I would like to thank Professor M. Dilts and Professor S. V. Tracy, who were kind enough to answer my inquiries about the demosthenic scholia and Attic inscriptions, respectively. Finally, thanks are due to the anonymous referee of *American Journal of Philology*, where this piece originally appeared, who made several useful suggestions. None of these persons is to be held responsible for any remaining errors.

dated only by "prytany without referring to the day of the month." In the second part, Hansen (1993) 109–12 admits that the evidence found in the scholion to Dem. 24.20 is reliable for the period of the twelve tribes, but he does not draw out the implications of his admission for the meaning of the term σύγκλητος ἐκκλησία. But he then argues that the information found in the scholion does not apply to the period of the ten tribes because "there is no conspicuous concentration of meetings around the 20th."

In response to the first point, I would simply note that I do not claim that "the *ekklesia* was summoned according to the festival calendar." What I wrote was that the "normal schedule of regular meetings of the Assembly was obviously dictated in both periods by the festival calendar." That is very different. I then pointed out that when scheduling meetings the *prytaneis* had to pay attention to the festival calendar and that this influenced their choice of days. Nor is there a discrepancy between the information found in the scholion to Dem. 24.20 and that found at *Ath. Pol.* 43.3. The author of the scholion was interested in the number of meetings per month and the dates of meetings; the author of the *Ath. Pol.* was interested in the number of meetings per prytany. There is no contradiction here since each author approaches the same question from a different perspective. When viewed from the perspective of the festival calendar, the *prytaneis* summoned three regular meetings per month in the Hellenistic period and roughly the same number during most months in the Classical period. When viewed from the perspective of the bouleutic calendar, the *prytaneis* summoned four meetings every prytany in the period of the ten tribes. Hansen's list of decrees that are dated by the day of the prytany but not by the day of the month is very useful, but it is not relevant to my argument. This disposes of Hansen's first objection.

In response to the second point, I would draw attention to the additional evidence Hansen helpfully provides in footnote 25, which, when combined with my evidence for the period of the ten tribes, proves exactly the opposite of what he claims. In this footnote Hansen refers to six prescripts where the dates of the month can be restored with reasonable certainty, dates I did not place in my list of evidence and should have included. *IG* ii^2 454, lines 3–4 is too fragmentary to allow us to determine the precise date, but the five other prescripts do appear to give us days of the month. These are: 1) *IG* ii^2 335, lines 5–6 (25th day of the month); 2) *IG* ii^2 368, lines 4–6 (9th day of the month); 3) *IG* ii^2 382, lines 5–6 (14th day of the month); 4) *IG* ii^2 546, line 3 (21st day of the month); 5) *SEG* 21:324

(18th day of the month). This alters the totals for the period of the ten tribes given in my essay:

Day of Month	Number of Meetings	Day of Month	Number of Meetings
1st	0	16th	2
2nd	0	17th	0
3rd	0	18th	3
4th	0	19th	3
5th	0	20th	0
6th	0	21st	1
7th	0	22nd	0
8th	1	23rd	1
9th	2	24th	1
10th	1	25th	3
11th	9	26th	0
12th	1	27th	2
13th	0	28th	0
14th	3	29th	2
15th	0	30th	11

This, however, gives us a noticeable cluster of seven meetings on the 18th, 19th, and 21st, an amount that is larger than any other four-day period except for the periods around the eleventh and around the thirtieth. This rather undermines Hansen's assertion that "there is no conspicuous concentration of meetings around the 20th." This takes care of his second objection. One should also note that if we deduct the meetings of Metageitnion 24, 362/61, Elaphebolion 19, 347/46, and Skirophorion 16, 347/46, which were probably σύγκλητοι ἐκκλησίαι, the percentage of meetings falling around the 11th, 20th, and 30th was 32 out of 42, or about 76 percent in the period of the ten tribes, very close to the 84 percent attested for the period of the twelve tribes. This makes it very difficult to avoid the conclusion that the information found in the scholion to Dem. 24.20 is reliable both for the period of the ten tribes and for the period of the twelve tribes.

1.6 Demosthenes and the Theoric Fund

THE ROAD TO HISTORICAL ERROR IS OFTEN PAVED WITH GOOD INTENTIONS. Certainly no one had better intentions than the scholar Libanius when he wrote his hypothesis to Demosthenes' *First Olynthiac.* Observing that Demosthenes makes a proposal about Athenian finances in the speech, Libanius realized that contemporary readers might find the orator's discussion of the topic unclear. He therefore ventured to offer an account of the Theoric Fund and the Athenian law regulating its disbursement to help readers understand Demosthenes' proposal. Once upon a time, Libanius explains, there were no seats made of stone in the Theater of Dionysus, only wooden benches. Nor was there any charge for admission. As a result, scuffles and brawls often broke out as everyone rushed to grab a seat. To prevent this mayhem, the leaders of the community decided to charge a fee of two obols for seats. They also began to distribute public funds to the poor so that they would be able to afford the price of admission. This practice gradually developed to the point that all public funds were distributed. Instead of receiving a wage for service in the army, citizens preferred to remain at home to attend religious festivals.

Libanius states that this led to a situation in which the Athenians no longer wished to serve on military campaigns and endure the dangers of warfare. They therefore passed a law making it a capital offense to propose that the money in the Theoric Fund, from which the distributions were made, be paid for military purposes. This explains why Demosthenes, in response to the hypothetical question "Do you propose that the money be spent on military purposes?" replies "No, by Zeus, not I." Afraid of the penalty for such a measure, the orator declines to propose that the Theoric Fund be employed for military purposes.

One would like to know where Libanius found this information. Perhaps that is the wrong question: after all, how can we be sure that his source was not his own imagination? Certain details in the story are suspect. Libanius says that the Athenians used to receive a wage for military service, but we know that Athenian hoplites served without pay. His statement that there came a point where all public funds were distributed to citizens is a wild exaggeration and is contradicted by everything we learn about Athenian finances from the Aristotelian *Constitution of the Athenians*.[1]

The law about the Theoric Fund also invites skepticism. Libanius says that the Athenians made it a capital offense to propose that the fund be used for military purposes, but this clashes with evidence from contemporary sources. One piece of evidence comes from Demosthene's account of the debate about the Peace of Philocrates.[2] During this debate, which took place a mere two years after the delivery of Demosthenes' *First Olynthiac*, Eubulus made a forceful argument in favor of accepting peace and alliance with Philip. He warned the Assembly that if they did not ratify the treaty, they would have to go down to the Piraeus and man the fleet, to impose the *eisphora* (a tax on the wealthy to finance the fleet), and to convert the money in the Theoric Fund to military purposes. The argument outlines the alternatives that lay before the Athenians: they must either make peace with Philip or be prepared to shoulder the burden of continued warfare. For his argument to be cogent, these must be realistic possibilities, not fantasies. There was nothing unrealistic or illegal about manning the fleet or about raising money through the *eisphora*. By the same token, the possibility of converting the Theoric Fund to military use must have been perfectly realistic and in accordance with the laws.

Another piece of evidence that casts doubt on Libanius' law concerning the Theoric Fund is found in a fragment of Philochorus (*FGrHist* 328 fr. 54) preserved by Dionysius of Halicarnassus (*Amm.* 1.11). Philochorus records under the archonship of Lysimachides (339/38) that the Athenians voted on Demosthenes' proposal to devote all their money to military purposes. This must have included the money in the Theoric Fund since Philochorus states also that the Athenians decided also to postpone work on ship sheds and the arsenal, projects that were paid for by money from the fund (Aeschin. 3.25).

Despite the problems in his account of the Theoric Fund, modern scholars have generally trusted in the good intentions of Libanius. His statement that it was illegal to convert the Theoric Fund to military use is widely accepted, and Demosthenes' argument in the *First Olynthiac* is accordingly interpreted as a veiled

[1] For the *merismos*, see *Ath. Pol.* 48.1–2. For a concise account of public finances in the period, see Hansen (1991) 260–4.

[2] Dem. 19.291.

attack on the fund.[3] To explain how money from the fund was used for the war against Philip in 339/38, scholars have assumed that Demosthenes was able to abolish the law sometime in the late 340s. But if Demosthenes was so hostile to the Theoric Fund, why did he later not only praise it in his *Fourth Philippic* (10.35–42) but also become supervisor of the fund sometime early in the next decade? One might try to escape the awkward implications of the evidence by denouncing the *Fourth Philippic* as a forgery and Demosthenes as a hypocrite and an opportunist. Or one might avoid these temptations and take a fresh look at the evidence.

The aim of this essay is to reexamine Demosthenes' statements about the Theoric Fund without the spurious assistance of Libanius' suspect explication. Libanius may have had good intentions, but that is no guarantee that he constructed his account of the Theoric Fund from reliable sources. My discussion will begin with an analysis of the two passages in the *First Olynthiac* where Demosthenes makes suggestions about military finances. Once the meaning of these passages is clear, it will be possible to interpret what Demosthenes has to say about Athenian military finances in the *First Olynthiac* without Libanius' assistance. The second section will examine the proposal Apollodorus made about the Theoric Fund in 348, which he describes in his speech *Against Neaira* ([Dem.] 59.4–8). Several scholars who accept Libanius' statements about the Theoric Fund have seen a contradiction between the evidence found in the *First Olynthiac* and the information found in the *Against Neaira*. A careful study of the relevant passages will reveal no contradiction exists. The third and final section will analyze Demosthenes' remarks about the Theoric Fund in the *Fourth Philippic* and the role the fund played in maintaining the fragile consensus that ensured social harmony in fourth-century Athens.

I

Demosthenes discusses military finances twice in his *Third Olynthiac*. The first passage (3.10–13) begins with a hypothetical question: Demosthenes imagines one of the citizens in the Assembly admitting that an expedition must be sent to Olynthus and expressing his determination to help the city resist Philip, but

[3] For previous treatments of the Theoric Fund, see H. Francotte (1913); Kahrstedt (1929); Glotz (1932); van Ooteghem (1932); Schwan (1934); Buchanan (1962); de Ste. Croix (1964); Cawkwell (1962); Cawkwell (1963); Rhodes (1972) 235–40; Hansen (1976b); Carey (1992) 152–6. Trevett (1992) 145 follows Hansen (1976b) and has nothing original to add to the discussion.

asking how this should be done. Demosthenes prefaces his reply with a warning that his proposal may strike them as odd, then advises the Assembly to appoint Nomothetai. These Nomothetai should not frame any new law. Instead, they should repeal those laws that are now harming Athenian interests.

Demosthenes has two kinds of laws in mind: those that grant exemption from military service (οἱ δὲ τοὺς ἀθῴους ἀτακτοῦντας καθιστᾶσι) and have an adverse effect on the morale of citizens who are willing to perform their duty (τοὺς δὲ δέοντα ποιεῖν βουλομένους ἀθυμοτέρους),[4] and those that distribute (διανέμουσι) money from the Military Fund (τὰ στρατιωτικά) to citizens who remain at home (τοῖς οἴκοι μένουσι) for the purpose of attending dramatic festivals (θεωρικά). The crucial feature to note is the use of the article τά before στρατιωτικά and its absence before θεωρικά. Demosthenes is here discussing the Military Fund, which was controlled by military officials and was normally drawn on for expenses incurred by the army and navy.[5] At the end of their terms of office, all generals and other military officials were required to provide an account of their payments from the fund to the Logistai ([Dem.] 49.12; Aeschin. 3.13–15). Demosthenes is thus objecting to the laws that allow the Athenians to distribute money from the Military Fund to citizens so they can purchase theater tickets.

Contemporary evidence shows that the Assembly could direct officials to spend money from the Military Fund for nonmilitary purposes and thus provides parallels for the practice attacked by Demosthenes in this passage. The evidence comes from four inscriptions. The first records a decree passed in 346 to grant privileges to the Bosporan rulers Spartocus II and Pairisades I and their brother Apollonius (*IG* ii^2 212). Androtion, who moved the main decree, proposed that the two rulers each receive a gold crown worth one thousand drachmai at every celebration of the Great Panathenaea, that is, once every four years. The money from these crowns was to be paid by the Apodektai from the Military Fund (lines 42–4). This was not a trivial sum: it was enough to purchase a theater ticket costing two obols for each of six thousand Athenians.

4 For the laws granting exemption to those participating in festivals, see Dem. 21.15; 39.16–17. See also MacDowell (1989b) 70–2.

5 Note the comment of the scholion to Dem. 3.11 (Dilts 91): εἰ τὰ θεωρικὰ τῇ θεωρίᾳ ἐδίδοσαν, οἰστὸν ἂν ἦν. νῦν δὲ τὰ τῶν στρατιωτῶν τοῖς θεωροῦσι νέμουσι. On the Military Fund, see Brun (1983) 143–81.

The practice is attested again in a decree of the Assembly passed in the year 331 (*IG* VII 4252).[6] The author of the decree is Phanodemus, who proposed that the god Amphiaraus be honored with a crown for taking good care of all Athenians and other people who came to his temple in search of health and protection. The decree instructs the treasurer of the Military Fund to provide a sum of ten drachmai for the making of the crown and orders him to present it to the caretakers of the temple after it is ready for dedication in the shrine (lines 15–25). The accounts of the supervisors (Epistatai) of Eleusis and the treasurers of Demeter and Kore provide a third example of the practice (*IG* II^2 1672). These accounts record that in the second prytany of the year 329/28 the supervisors had a sum of two talents, 1,775 drachmai, and three fourths of an obol, which had been lent to them for construction of a cross-wall by the treasurer of the Military Fund, the Apodektai, and an unnamed banker (lines 39–40). This disbursement from the Military Fund differs from the previous two in being a loan and not an outright payment, but it is similar in that it was also made for nonmilitary purposes.

The final inscription contains the accounts of the treasurers of Athena from the year 334/33 (*IG* II^2 1493).[7] This inscription is not so well preserved as the preceding ones, but it appears to list payments made by the treasurer of the Military Fund for Nikai, or Victory statues, and processional vessels. In the fifth prytany the treasurers apparently received more than three talents from the military treasurer (lines 9–13).[8] If the restorations provided by Koehler and accepted by Kirchner are correct, they received two more payments made by the treasurer of the Military Fund in subsequent prytanies (lines 14–20).

Returning to the *Third Olynthiac*, we can now see that Demosthenes is not attacking the Theoric Fund for depriving Athens of money for military expeditions. Rather, he is criticizing the Assembly for drawing on the Military Fund to defray nonmilitary activities, a practice well attested in the epigraphic record. Demosthenes claims that this practice and the exemption from military service granted to those running festivals are demoralizing to those citizens who wish to do their duty and serve on campaigns. Both the practice of drawing on the Military Fund

6 For a full discussion of this inscription with references to recent scholarship, see Schwenk (1985) 198–201.

7 For a discussion of this inscription, see Mitchel (1962). Mitchel presents strong arguments for restoring the names of Demades as Treasurer of the Military Fund.

8 After 307 the Treasurer of the Military Fund became one of the principal financial officers at Athens. See Rhodes (1972) 108–10.

for nonmilitary expenditures and these exemptions were established and protected by laws (νόμοι) that Demosthenes wants to abolish, something that can be done only by appointing Nomothetai. Only when the Athenians rescind these laws and provide speakers with a safe way to say what policy is best for Athens, Demosthenes argues, should they look for someone who will propose measures that everyone realizes are for the collective interest. Until that time, they should not expect any speaker to risk destruction by proposing what is best for the Athenians. Demosthenes is slightly vague, a quality that Aeschines (2.34: σκοτεινόν) later criticized him for, but his point appears to be that the present laws make it impossible to make proposals (ψηφίσματα) needed in the present crisis, namely, to require that money from the Military Fund be spent only for military purposes and that the exemptions enjoyed by those managing the festivals be abolished. As matters now stand, anyone who makes such a proposal (ψήφισμα) will be attacked for transgressing the laws (13: τοὺς νόμους παραβάντα) and thus be subject to legal penalties (δοῦναι δίκην). What Demosthenes means is that the speaker who moves these measures will risk prosecution by a *graphe paranomon*, a charge that carried stiff penalties upon conviction.

In the next section Demosthenes talks about the need for everyone to back up words with actions and to take responsibility for the predicament they are now in (14–17). In his usual vein, he lectures the Assembly about the importance of making difficult decisions, especially choosing what is best over what is pleasant if it is not possible to pursue a policy that combines both. In response to this point, Demosthenes poses another hypothetical question (19): What if someone has a way to leave the Theoric Fund (τὰ θεωρικά) untouched and can identify other sources of revenue for military expeditions? Is not this person a better adviser than those who argue that what is best cannot be combined in the same policy with what is pleasant? His argument appears to equate what is pleasant with the possibility of leaving the Theoric Fund intact and what is best with finding money for military expenditures. The imaginary speaker rejects the assumption that what is best and what is pleasant cannot be incorporated into a single policy. Demosthenes does not disagree with this argument. On the contrary, he says, "I agree, since it is possible to combine the two" (φημ' ἔγωγε, εἴπερ ἔστιν). The Greek verb φημί standing alone without an object in indirect discourse means "I agree" or "I say yes" in the same way as οὐ φημί by itself means "I say no" or "I deny."[9] The conjunction εἴπερ when followed by a verb in the present

[9] For this meaning of the verb, see L-S-J, *s.v.* φημί III.

tense and employed in conjunction with a verb in the present tense in the main clause means "since" and loses its conditional force.[10] J. H. Vince, the translator of the Loeb edition of the speech, renders the sentence in misleading fashion: "I grant you, men of Athens – if the thing were possible."[11] This translation strongly suggests that the possibility of leaving the Theoric Fund untouched and finding money elsewhere for military needs may not be feasible, precisely the opposite of Demosthenes' meaning.

The particle ἀλλά, which begins the next sentence, marks a strong shift and introduces a new point. Demosthenes is once again rather cryptic, but his words can be interpreted in a way that harmonizes with our interpretation of the previous passage. Demosthenes introduces a paradox, which, though framed in general terms, is directly related to the situation at hand. "How has it ever been, or will it ever be, possible for someone who spends his present funds [τὰ παρόντ'] on things he should not [spend them on] to be well supplied for things that he should [i.e., spend them on]?" This general statement applies directly to the argument Demosthenes made earlier about the Military Fund. "Spending funds on things one should not" alludes to the practice of spending money from the Military Fund for nonmilitary purposes such as dramatic performances. This produces a lack of money for military activities, the purpose of the fund. The reason Demosthenes rephrases his argument in general terms is to show the Assembly how absurd their management of finances has been. Note that the general statement does not apply to the management of the Theoric Fund. After all, that fund was created to pay for tickets to dramatic performances; using the money in that fund for that purpose does not fit the description "spending funds on things one should not." The mention of the Theoric Fund a few lines above makes it tempting to apply the general statement to it, but the particle ἀλλά clearly dissociates the general statement from the previous argument.

Demosthenes also criticizes the practice of raiding the Military Fund to pay for dramatic festivals in the *First Olynthiac* (Dem. 1.19–20). In this speech, Demosthenes discusses the need to send not one but two military forces to Olynthus. One force must help defend the Olynthians and their allies; the other should raid

[10] For the use of εἴπερ see L-S-J, *s.v.* II; Smyth (1956) 504–5. For other examples in Demosthenes, see 1.2; 8.10; 9.10; 11.13; 19.244; 20.129; 21.6, 37; 23.101. Note that Vince translates as "since" at Dem. 20.129 and "seeing that" at Dem. 23.101. MacDowell (1990) translates εἴπερ as "if" at Dem 21.6, 37, and 212, but in each case the clause following the word expresses an idea the speaker strongly believes to be true. One should compare the use of εἰ to introduce a fact as a ground of argument; see L-S-J, *s.v.* εἰ B VI.

[11] Vince (1930) 1: 53.

Macedonian territory and put Philip on the defensive (16–18). An effort of this scale will require money, but Demosthenes asserts that the Athenians have enough to finance the two expeditions. In fact, he claims, they have more money than any other people (19). The significant point here is that Demosthenes is speaking about money assigned for military operations (στρατιωτικά), not money earmarked for festivals (θεωρικά). The problem with the Athenians, Demosthenes argues, is that they use this money assigned for military operations not as they should but as they wish (ὡς βούλεσθε). As the scholion on the passage remarks, "use as they wish" means "use for dramatic festivals." Demosthenes predicts that if the Athenians give this money back to those serving in the military, they will need no new source of revenue to pay for expeditions (οὐδενὸς ὑμῖν προσδεῖ πόρου). If they do not, they will need additional revenue to make up for the money spent on dramatic festivals, or worse still, they will not have any revenue at all (ἅπαντος ἐνδεῖ τοῦ πόρου). Here again, Demosthenes must be assailing the practice of drawing on the Military Fund for nonmilitary purposes. He cannot be talking about taking money from the Theoric Fund to pay for the war since he says the Athenians should "give back" the money in question to the soldiers. He is referring to money in the Military Fund that was originally put there to pay for soldiers' expenses but was taken away to pay for dramatic festivals and must therefore now be "given back" to the fund.

Demosthenes next poses another hypothetical question for the purpose of clarifying his point. He imagines someone in the Assembly asking him whether he is moving a proposal that this money be devoted to military activities (σὺ γράφεις ταῦτ' εἶναι στρατιωτικά). Demosthenes replies that he is not moving a decree (μὰ Δί' οὐκ ἔγωγε). This makes sense, for Demosthenes is advising the Athenians to renounce their destructive habit of draining the Military Fund to pay for theater tickets, something they now do without a thought (ἄνευ πράγματων). That does not require a formal motion, which the Proedroi would submit to the Assembly for approval. All it requires is that Athenians stop doing what they have previously done and thereby allow the money in the Military Fund to be spent as it was intended. Demosthenes makes this point clear in the next sentence. In his opinion (ἐγὼ μὲν γὰρ ἡγοῦμαι), the soldiers must have supplies (στρατιώτας δεῖν κατασκευσθῆναι) and this money (i.e., the money in the Military Fund) has already been earmarked for military purposes (ταῦτ' εἶναι στρατιωτικά). If the money is used as it should be, there will be a uniform system whereby the money is spent (λαμβάνειν) and the Athenians do what needs to be done (ποιεῖν τὰ δέοντα). "What needs to be done" is, of course, to send expeditions to defend Olynthus against Philip (cf. the use of the same verb at Dem. 3.19). As matters now stand, the Athenians spend money from the Military Fund for festivals (εἰς τὰς ἑορτάς). If this practice does not stop, the Athenians will have to resort to raising money by means of the *eisphora* to pay for their war against Philip.

This analysis of the passages about Athenian finances in the *First Olynthiac* and the *Third Olynthiac* reveals that Demosthenes nowhere criticizes the Theoric Fund. His concern is with the Military Fund, which is being frittered away on activities that do not help to support the war against Philip. Nor do we need to accept the existence of Libanius' law concerning the Theoric Fund to understand these passages; the contemporary evidence provided by inscriptions affords much better guidance in our attempt to understand Demosthenes' arguments. We can now see that Demosthenes did not regard the Theoric Fund as a dangerous welfare program that was corrupting the Athenian character and robbing the army of the funds it needed to halt Philip's aggression. On the contrary, he claims that as long as the Athenians use the Military Fund for its stated purpose, they can leave the Theoric Fund untouched. The Athenians do not have to choose between guns and butter; they can have both if they manage their finances in a sensible fashion.

II

The next item to examine is the proposal about Athenian finances made by Apollodorus in 349/48. Our source of information for his proposal is the prologue of the speech he wrote for the prosecution of Neaira brought by his kinsman Theomnestus ([Dem.] 59.3–8).[12] Theomnestus, who delivered the prologue of the speech before allowing Apollodorus to present the rest of the case, recounts how in 349/48 Apollodorus passed a motion in the Council calling on the Assembly to vote whether the surplus in the Athenian budget should be devoted to military purposes (στρατιωτικά) or paid out for festivals (θεωρικά). In other words, Apollodorus' motion invited the Assembly to decide whether the surplus should be paid into the Military Fund or into the Theoric Fund. Theomnestus states that the proposal was in accordance with the laws. Yet Apollodorus was nevertheless prosecuted and convicted on a charge of passing an illegal decree.

[12] On Theomnestus and his family, see Davies (1971) 437–8.

Since Apollodorus made his proposal in the same year as Demosthenes delivered his *Olynthiacs*, scholars have naturally attempted to interpret Apollodorus' proposal in the light of their interpretation of Demosthenes' contemporaneous remarks about Athenian finances. The fact that Apollodorus was prosecuted for passing a decree about money for the Theoric Fund indeed appears to confirm the authenticity of the law reported by Libanius that forbade proposals to use money from the Theoric Fund for military purposes. But Libanius says the penalty for proposing such a measure was death; Apollodorus was only fined a talent. Another difficulty is that Theomnestus explicitly states that the content of Apollodorus' decree was fully in accordance with the laws. As we discovered earlier, Libanius' law, which seems at first glance to provide the clue to elucidating Apollodorus' proposal and conviction, turns out to be an obstacle to understanding.[13] Once again, it is necessary to examine the text without Libanius' guidance.

Theomnestus recounts how Apollodorus became a member of the Council when Athens was at war with Philip. The stakes in the conflict were high: victory meant becoming the greatest power in Greece, recovering lost territory, and triumph over Philip; defeat would bring the loss of valuable allies, the loss of Athenian reputation abroad, and dangerous threats to their possessions in northern Greece. At this critical juncture, Apollodorus passed a decree in the Council calling on the Assembly to decide whether the surplus in the budget should be paid into the Military Fund or the Theoric Fund. One significant feature of Apollodorus' proposal is that is deals exclusively with the surplus in the budget. It thus concerned a different issue from the one discussed by Demosthenes in the *Olynthiacs*, in which the management of the Military Fund was the focus of attention. There Demosthenes argued that the money in the Military Fund would be sufficient to finance the campaign to defend Olynthus provided that the Athenians did not draw on it to pay for attendance at festivals. Apollodorus evidently thought that the predicament had become more serious; in his estimation the normal sources of revenue for the Military Fund were not sufficient for the war. He therefore proposed that the Assembly supplement them with the annual surplus from the budget. Or Apollodorus may have made his proposal sometime later than Demosthenes' *Olynthiacs*, at a time when the situation had deteriorated to the point where more money was required to meet the increased danger to Athenian

[13] Hansen (1976b) 235, note 10 believes that Libanius' law is genuine but represents a paraphrase of a penalty clause for attempting to reverse laws about the Theoric Fund.

security. We should bear in mind that in the *Olynthiacs* Demosthenes discusses only how to fund expeditions to aid Olynthus. When Apollodorus made his proposal, Theomnestus claims that Athens was not only assisting Olynthus but also defending her possessions in Lemnos, Imbros, Skyros, and the Chersonnese as well as her interests in Euboea (3–4).

Theomnestus contends that Apollodorus' proposal was made in accordance with the law, but the provision he cites has not been correctly understood. The traditional way to render the clause that gives the provision is to translate the phrase κελευόντων... τῶν νόμων as "the laws prescribed." For instance, A. T. Murray in the Loeb translation of the *Against Neaira* gives: "For the laws prescribed that when there was war, the funds remaining over from the state expenditures should be devoted to military purposes."[14] C. Carey in the most recent edition of the speech renders it thus: "For the laws prescribed that in time of war the surplus of the administration should be used for military purposes."[15] Such a translation makes little sense. If the laws ordered that the surplus should be given to the Military Fund in time of war, why did the Assembly need to vote on the question? And if the law commanded this, how could the Assembly then have the power to order that the surplus be paid into the Theoric Fund if it so voted?

There is no flaw in the Greek text; the fault lies with the translators. In Attic Greek the verb normally means "to order" or "to command." In contexts where the subject of the verb is "the law" or "the laws," however, D. M. MacDowell has observed that it "is virtually a synonym of ἐᾶν; a law is said to κελεύειν if it merely permits it."[16] This translation of the verb makes much better sense in the context of Theomnestus' account of Apollodorus' proposal. One should therefore interpret his words to say that the laws of Athens allowed only for the surplus to be used for military purposes. Since the Assembly was permitted to do this, Apollodorus passed a *probouleuma* in the Council instructing the Assembly to vote on the question. When the Assembly met, the vote was held, and the decision was made to pay the surplus from the budget into the Military Fund.

[14] Murray (1939) 6: 353.

[15] Carey (1992) 31. Cf. Cawkwell (1963) 60: "the laws actually required that in time of war these surpluses should be used for the former" (i.e., military purposes). Cawkwell believes that Apollodorus misrepresents the law, but his desperate remedy is unnecessary; see below.

[16] MacDowell (1989c) 259–61. MacDowell cites [Xen.] *Ath. Pol.* 2.18; Lys. 1.49; and Dem. 48.10, but does not include [Dem.] 59.4.

After its ratification, however, the decree was attacked as illegal by his enemy Stephanus, and Apollodorus was convicted and fined a sum of one talent (5–8). What was illegal about Apollodorus' proposal?[17] As Theomnestus makes clear, the laws permitted the Assembly to decide how to use the surplus in time of war. The trouble is that Theomnestus is not an impartial witness. As a relative of Apollodorus, who wrote the speech, he naturally stresses the part of his proposal that was legal and neglects to specify what elements in it may have contravened the laws. Instead, he alleges that Stephanus won his case by suborning perjury and misleading the court with irrelevant slander (5).[18]

In the absence of Stephanus' reply or any other source favorable to him, it is impossible to evaluate Theomnestus' unsupported charge. Yet even if the allegation is false, Stephanus' charge could have related to procedural irregularities in the manner the decree was formulated or passed. Or there may have been some other aspect of the decree's contents, left unmentioned by the partisan Theomnestus, that violated the law. But there is no reason to doubt the authenticity of the law cited by Theomnestus permitting the surplus to be allocated to the Military Fund in time of war. If Eubulus could in 346 propose to spend the money in the Theoric Fund for military purposes, it is reasonable to expect that the surplus could have been employed in the same fashion two years earlier.

Two observations are in order. First, it is important to distinguish between the proposal made by Apollodorus in 348 and the more drastic measure passed by Demosthenes in 339. Apollodorus moved that the Assembly consider only the question of the distribution of the budget surplus. He did not propose to touch the Theoric Fund directly. The decree Demosthenes passed after the outbreak of war with Philip was far more comprehensive, directing all money to be devoted to military use. The difference between the two proposals is clearly to be explained in terms of the changed circumstances Athens faced in 339. In

17 Hansen (1974) 34 misinterprets the reasons for the prosecution and the law cited by Theomnestus when he holds that "the decree is attacked for being at variance with the law providing that in times of war the surplus shall be used as *stratiotika*."

18 W. Rennie in the Oxford Classical Text of the speech follows Sauppe's bold transposition and moves the phrase ὡς ὦφλε τῷ δημοσίῳ ἐκ πέντε καὶ εἴκοσιν ἐτῶν from 8 and places it after the phrase μάρτυρας παρασχόμενος in 6. Hansen (1976b) 238–45 accepts the transposition and argues that Apollodorus did not break Libanius' law since his proposal concerned only the surplus in the budget, not the normal revenues paid into the Theoric Fund. This is an important point, but nothing compels us to accept the transposition.

348 Philip's attack on Olynthus and its allies was not perceived as a dire threat to Athenian interests. Demosthenes may have thought that Philip's aggression was a major danger to Athens, but his three *Olynthiacs* suggest that he had an uphill struggle in convincing the Assembly to see things his way. Hence the more modest proposals of Demosthenes and Apollodorus in 348. The situation in 339 was far more alarming. In that year Philip seized Elateia in Phocis near the Boeotian border. Although Demosthenes was able to forge an alliance between Athens and Thebes, the danger was far closer and much more serious.[19] For this reason, Demosthenes apparently had no trouble in persuading the Assembly to convert all public funds to military use in the face of the clear and present danger.

Second, nothing compels us to view the feud between Apollodorus and Stephanus as part of an ongoing battle over the Theoric Fund between a "peace party" led by Eubulus and a "war party" headed by Demosthenes. Apollodorus' measure was not designed as an attack on the Theoric Fund, but only as a temporary expedient aimed at providing the funds necessary to meet an immediate crisis. Apollodorus may have been an associate of Demosthenes, but Demosthenes, as we have seen, was not hostile to the existence of the Theoric Fund.[20] Nor are there grounds to believe that Stephanus' prosecution was motivated by a desire to protect the Theoric Fund, then under the control of Eubulus.[21] On the contrary, Eubulus came forward at the trial of Neaira to testify as a witness for Apollodorus, not for Stephanus ([Dem.] 59.48). And to portray Eubulus as a "dove" who fought against spending public funds on military preparedness would be to misrepresent his political activity. Far from being a pacificist, Eubulus is reported by Aeschines (3.25–6) to have used his control over the Theoric Fund to build an arsenal. Dinarchus (1.96) appears to credit him with the construction of ship sheds and with strengthening the navy in general. In fact, Dinarchus rated Eubulus' contribution to Athenian military resources higher than that of Demosthenes.[22]

Although the authors of the scholia to Demosthenes' orations assume that Eubulus was often the target of his attacks, there is very little evidence in the

[19] The panic in Athens after the capture of Elateia is well described in Dem. 18.169–79.

[20] Aeschin. 2.165 suggests close ties between Apollodorus and Demosthenes, but it is difficult to determine how much trust to place in the words of an enemy of Demosthenes.

[21] Eubulus controls Theoric Fund: Aeschin. 3.25. For the nature of Eubulus' control over the fund, see Cawkwell (1963) 54–8.

[22] On Din. 1.96, see Worthington (1992) 266–8. On Eubulus' contribution to military preparedness, see the good discussion of Cawkwell (1963) 65–6 with *IG* ii^2 1627, lines 353–4.

speeches themselves for a major conflict between the two men over public policy.[23] In his speech *Against Meidias*, Demosthenes (21.206–7) merely attempts to discourage Eubulus from testifying on behalf of the defendant. He points out that Eubulus did not rise to defend Meidias when the Assembly passed its vote against him for his insulting behavior at the Dionysia. It would therefore be inconsistent for him to testify on Meidias' behalf at his trial. Since Eubulus clearly does not believe in Meidias' innocence, Demosthenes speculates that he may testify for his opponent simply out of a desire to retaliate against him. But Demosthenes parenthetically adds that he does not know what he may have done to offend Eubulus. To judge from this passage, the differences between the two men were hardly serious.

One gains a similar impression from Demosthenes' remarks about Eubulus in the speech he delivered against Aeschines in 343 (19.289–93). Here again, he criticizes Eubulus for testifying on behalf of the defendant at the trial. He recalls how Eubulus did not ask for clemency for his cousin Hegesilaus or for Thrasybulus until after the court had cast its vote to convict them. If Eubulus declined to plead on behalf of his own relatives before the court's first vote, how can he now do so for Aeschines? He further points out how Aeschines lent support to Eubulus' enemy, Aristophon, when the latter prosecuted Philonicus. Finally, he reminds the court how Eubulus recently called down curses on Philip and swore that he wished to see Philip destroyed. Given his hostility to Philip, how could Eubulus possibly defend Aeschines? How can Philip be destroyed if Eubulus comes to the defense of men like Aeschines who take the king's bribes? Just as in the speech *Against Meidias*, Demosthenes does not attack Eubulus for his policies but rather attempts to dissuade him from testifying on behalf of his opponents. In neither passage does Demosthenes speak as if there existed any major dispute about public issues such as the Theoric Fund.

III

With the misconceptions about his attitude toward the Theoric Fund swept away, Demosthenes' defense of the fund in his *Fourth Philippic* is no longer perplexing. Earlier scholars, who believed that Demosthenes makes veiled criticisms of the

[23] For Eubulus identified in the scholia as the target of Demosthenes' attacks, see the scholia to Dem. 1.19 (128a Dilts); 2.28 (190 Dilts); 2.30 (198ab Dilts); 2.31 (204 Dilts); 3.11 (67 Dilts); 3.27 (126 Dilts); 3.29 (136, 138a, 139c Dilts); 13 (163, 167 Dilts).

fund in his *Olynthiacs,* thought that his remarks in the *Fourth Philippic* clash with his former opposition to it. To explain away his alleged inconsistency of attitude, Schaefer and others went so far as to contend that the *Fourth Philippic* is a forgery.[24] Careful study of the *Olynthiacs,* however, reveals no clash between the remarks about the fund in the earlier speeches and those in the *Fourth Philippic.* As a result, there is no longer any reason to question the authenticity of his defense of the fund in the *Fourth Philippic* or to accuse the orator of political inconsistency.[25] This is a welcome finding since Demosthenes' argument in favor of the fund is an important document for our understanding of class relations in the Athenian democracy. It describes the nature of the consensus that promoted the fragile stability Athenian society enjoyed during the rise of Macedonian power under Philip II.

Demosthenes, like a true statesman, prefaces his defense of the Theoric Fund with a declaration of impartiality. He proposes to speak on behalf of the poor in response to the complaints of the wealthy as well as to defend the rich against the accusations brought by the needy. This impartiality is the mark of the good *rhetor,* who places the good of the *polis* as a whole ahead of the interest of any single class. The rhetorical pose of acting as a neutral arbiter between rich and poor is a traditional one and can be traced back as far as Solon's poetry ([Arist.] *Ath. Pol.* 12.1, 5). His defense of the poor was undertaken not just to protect their interests but also to strengthen the common welfare of the entire *polis* (Dem. 10.35–6).

Demosthenes deals first with the criticism leveled by the wealthy at the Theoric Fund. He recalls how not long ago public revenues never rose above 130 talents a year, yet the wealthy did not shirk their duty as trierarchs or refuse to pay the *eisphora.*[26] Since then, revenues have risen to four hundred talents a year under the influence of good fortune, and the rich have thus been relieved of much of their responsibility to contribute to the defense of Athens. If the rich have gained from

[24] Schaefer (1858) 94–103, esp. 100; Blass (1887–98) IIIB, 1: 382–4. Milns (1989).

[25] McCabe (1981) 196 has shown that there are no stylistic grounds for denying authenticity to Dem. 10. For the charge of inconsistency, see Cawkwell (1963) 63: "but the truth is that he was less a model of constancy to his contemporaries than to his latter-day admirers, and ἡ τύχη ποιοῦσα had changed his opinion along with the city's finances."

[26] Didymus (*Commentary on Demosthenes* 8.49) believes that Demosthenes is referring to the period after Aegospotamoi. Cawkwell (1963) 61, note 85 argues persuasively against his view. Demosthenes is more likely referring to the recent past, most probably to the period after the Social War.

Athens' good fortune, why should the poor not also profit from the increase in public revenues (37–9)?

To justify payments to the poor out of public funds, Demosthenes introduces an analogy. He compares the citizens of a community to parents and reminds the Assembly how the laws require young men to support their parents in old age.[27] Should young men fail to meet their duty, they would render themselves vulnerable to a suit for ill-treatment (40–1). Just as younger men are bound by nature and by law to look after their parents' welfare, so too should the community ensure that none of its citizens have their needs neglected. In other words, Demosthenes argues that the poor have a natural right to receive distributions of public revenue. To this argument from natural justice, Demosthenes adds one based on practical considerations: if the community does not provide for the needs of the poor, they will look elsewhere for assistance. To deprive them of their necessities would run the risk of alienating them.

Here Demosthenes implicitly raises the spectre of *stasis* and the concomitant threat of a a violent redistribution of property (41–2).[28] To get an idea of what the Athenian élite had to fear, one need only recall the massacre of the wealthy at Argos in 370 (D. S. 15.57.3–58.4; see also Plu. *Mor.* 814b). The violence arose from bitter class warfare: popular leaders had stirred up the masses against certain members of the upper class, who then plotted to overthrow the democracy. The plot was evidently discovered, at which point almost all of the conspirators, fearing they would confess under torture, killed themselves. But one man was tortured before he could commit suicide and turned informer, denouncing thirty prominent citizens. All thirty were executed without a proper investigation of the charges, and their property was confiscated. With popular suspicions now confirmed, the democratic leaders had an easy time convicting other wealthy citizens on false charges. The judicial carnage continued until over 1,200 Argives were put to death.

A recent author has argued that "communication was the tool the political equals used to exert their ideological hegemony over both social and political elites" and that "the masses controlled the upper classes through ideological

[27] On the importance of γηροτροφία and the charge of ill-treatment of parents, see Rubinstein (1993) 64–8 and Millett (1991) 129–35.

[28] On the revolutionary threat of *anadasmos ges*, see de Ste. Croix (1981) 298, 608–9.

means."[29] This naive approach to the issue of social stability in Athens ignores Demosthenes' shrewd observation that the wealthy acceded to the demands of the mass of citizens partly out of fear that a refusal might result in bloodshed. The late Chairman Mao was more than a bit cynical when he declared that all political power comes out of the barrel of a gun. The Athenian upper class would certainly have understood what he meant.

Having established the moral right and the practical necessity of distributions to the poor, Demosthenes turns to defend the wealthy (43–5). He optimistically asserts that no one – or at least no Athenian – is so savage and inhumane as to grow angry when he sees the needy receiving public funds. Yet though the poor have the right to receive a share of public revenues, this right does not extend so far as to give them power over the private possessions of the wealthy. Demosthenes makes a sharp distinction between the principle that applies to public property and that pertaining to private property. Although all Athenians share the privileges of citizenship fairly and equally, the wealthy also have the right to lead their lives in safety and in freedom from fear (μὴ δεδοικότας). Though the wealthy must be willing to make contributions from their private resources in time of war, the people must at the same time respect the rights of ownership.

Once again Demosthenes speaks in vague, general terms, but he appears to urge the people not to abuse their power in the courts to confiscate the property of the wealthy as a means of increasing public revenues.[30] Demosthenes is not the only author to warn of this abuse: several litigants in Lysias' speeches express their fear that the court may allow considerations of public finance to dictate its verdict. One speaker complains how unscrupulous prosecutors try to frighten the courts into condemning innocent men by claiming that there will be no funds to pay them unless they confiscate the defendant's property (Lys. 27.1). Another says that defendants normally receive a fair trial when there is enough money for public activities, but when there is not, the Council is compelled to condemn citizens and politicians on baseless charges in order to balance the budget by seizing their possessions (Lys. 30.22).

[29] Ober (1989) 338–9. In his unsatisfactory account of class relations, Ober nowhere so much as mentions the role of the Theoric Fund. For similar criticisms of Ober, see the trenchant remarks of Lane Fox (1994) 143.

[30] Hyperides (3.33–6) lists instances in which the courts resisted the temptation, but the fact that he felt a need to defend the courts against the charge suggests it was a serious issue. Cf. Isoc. 15.159–60.

Two incidents that took place in other democracies illustrate the dangers of this abuse. In Corcyra in 427, the democratic leader Peithias used the courts to retaliate against five wealthy citizens who were sympathetic to Sparta. The fine they were condemned to pay was so steep that they set themselves up as suppliants and begged to be allowed to pay the fine in installments. When Peithias refused to relent, they broke into the Council and murdered him and many of his followers (Th. 3.70.3). Euphron of Sikyon also took advantage of the courts to rob the wealthy of their property. As soon as he was elected general after setting up a democracy, he proceeded to send many rich men into exile for supporting Spartan interests and seized their goods (Xen. *Hell.* 7.1.46).

Demosthenes' perceptive analysis is valuable for the light it sheds on the nature of the social contract that maintained social peace in democratic Athens. His analysis shows that stability was not the product of a uniform ideology held by all Athenians. In fact, his remarks reveal the presence of radical differences of opinion about the distribution of wealth. The poor insisted on their rights as citizens to benefit from public revenues; the wealthy considered themselves entitled to protection of their private property from arbitrary confiscation. This constitutes his view of the social contract, which prescribes the duties of each class (45: ἃ παρ᾽ ἑκατέρων εἶναι δεῖ). To ensure compliance, there must be legal procedures in place to enforce these duties and to punish those who neglect them (ἐν νόμῳ διορθώσασθαι δεῖ). Demosthenes may have in mind the legal protections for private property in the Dicastic Oath, which pledged not to carry out a cancellation of debts or a redistribution of property. Demosthenes' remarks make it clear that the rich and the poor evaluated the democratic order to a large extent in terms of its impact on their material interests, and their conflicting interests gave rise to differing views about the way to manage public funds. Rich and poor were not united by a common ideology, or by the "mediating and integrative power of communication between citizens," but by what J. Rawls has called an "overlapping consensus." In this type of consensus groups may hold different convictions about major issues, but they share an allegiance to certain principles, such as the basic rules of political and legal procedure. It is this area where their views overlap that provides for the consensus that ensures political stability.

In democratic Athens, the rich and the poor might quarrel over the distribution of material wealth, but each could find some advantage in upholding the legal and political order. The poor looked to the public treasury to help meet their needs. Distributions from the Theoric Fund were so crucial to maintaining social peace that Demades called them the "glue of the democracy."[31] Demosthenes shared this view of their importance, and in the period after Chaironea he sought and gained election to the post of supervisor of the Theoric Fund.[32] He knew that the poor remained loyal to the democracy because it bestowed material benefits, not because it had the nebulous "power to assign meaning to symbols," which could not put bread in their mouths.[33] The rich trusted in the guarantees for ownership of private property contained in the oath sworn by the archons upon entering office ([Arist.] *Ath. Pol.* 56.2). What united them was their common interest in maintaining Athenian power abroad and their allegiance to the rule of law, which provided stability at home.

Afterthoughts

On the authenticity of Dem. 10, see now Hajdu (2002) 44–9.

[31] [Plut.] *Mor.* 1011b.

[32] Aeschin. 3.24. Cawkwell (1963) 58 believes that Aeschin. 3.159 alludes to Demosthenes' tenure in this office, but see Harris (1994b).

[33] Ober (1989) 339.

II

Law and Economy

II.1 Law and Economy in Classical Athens: [Demosthenes] *Against Dionysodorus*

SOMETIME AROUND 322 BCE, A MAN NAMED DAREIUS BROUGHT A PRIVATE ACTION in an Athenian court against a merchant called Dionysodorus. Dareius and his business partner Parmeniscus had made a loan to Dionysodorus and his partner Pamphilus for a trading voyage to Egypt and back. In his opening words of his speech to the court, Dareius describes the risks confronting men who made maritime loans.

> We who decide to engage in maritime trade and to entrust our property to other men are clearly aware of this fact: the borrower has an advantage over us in every respect. The borrower receives a clearly agreed upon sum of money, but all he leaves behind is just his promise to perform his legal duties in a small tablet bought for two obols and written on a tiny scrap of paper. We on the other hand do not promise to give the money, but immediately turn it over to the borrower. What do we place our trust in and what assurance do we receive when we part with our money? You and your laws which order that all agreements one makes willingly will be binding.

In his closing words, Dareius discusses the close connection between the role of the courts in enforcing contracts and the volume of trade in the marketplace of Athens.

> Do not ignore the fact that by resolving one dispute you are passing a law for the entire port of Athens. Many of the men who have chosen to engage in overseas trade are watching you to see how you will decide this case. If you think that written contracts and agreements between partners should be binding and if you will not take the side of those who break them, those

> involved in lending will more readily make their assets available. As a result, the port will thrive, and you will benefit. But if shipowners are allowed to enter into written contracts requiring them to sail to Athens but then sail their ships to other ports, claiming that their ship was wrecked and providing such excuses such as the ones this Dionysodorus here is using, and are allowed to pay only a share of the interest for the length of the journey they have sailed and not the interest under the terms of the contract, nothing will stand in the way of the cancellation of all contracts. For who will be willing to risk his own money when he sees that written contracts are not enforced, that arguments such as these carry more weight, and that the demands of wrongdoers prevail over justice? No one at all, judges; this is not in your collective interest nor in the interest of those who have chosen to work in commerce, the very men who are most useful both for all of you in common and individually for the person who deals with them.

Dareius' words reveal a keen awareness of the relationship between law and the economy. In his eyes, a healthy economy depends on the willingness of the courts to enforce contracts and assure lenders that their money will be repaid. This essay will take its cue from Dareius' words and study how the laws of Athens supported the growth of market relations in Attica and overseas trade between the Piraeus and other Greek *poleis*. Part I begins by examining the nature of the Athenian economy, then sketches some of the laws and legal mechanisms the Athenians developed to regulate market transactions and promote commerce and trade. Part II studies the speech *Against Dionysodorus* found in the demosthenic corpus and analyzes the dispute between Dareius and Dionysodorus to discover what it reveals about the nature of the legal relationship between lenders and merchants involved in overseas trade.

I

The economy of any given community is shaped to a large extent by the nature of its technology and the degree of the specialization of labor. In a society where technology has not progressed beyond subsistence agriculture, households will have little surplus to exchange with each other, and the community will not produce enough food to support a large workforce engaged in nonagricultural crafts. The economy of such a society will have no need for a permanent marketplace, and the relative infrequency of commodity exchange will produce few commercial disputes. The predominant forms of exchange will be gift-giving and the payment of tribute to local lords in exchange for protection.

Classical Athens had progressed far beyond this primitive level of development. The most important technical developments were in the field of metallurgy, which enabled the Athenians to produce an array of iron tools and other products. Smiths made helmets, greaves, breastplates, and spears for soldiers; scythes, pruning-hooks, and ploughs for farmers; and knives for everyday use. Potters marketed a wide variety of vases for dining and *symposia* as well as amphoras and other jars for storage and transport. Many were engaged in making varous types of clothing: there were fullers, dyers, sewers, weavers, tanners, shoemakers, and dye-makers. There were also numerous men employed in the building trades: carpenters, lead-cutters, lathe-workers, stone-cutters, sawyers, brickmakers, shipwrights, and muleteers for hauling heavy materials. And there were dozens, if not hundreds, who provided various services: doctors, barbers, hairdressers, wetnurses, inn-keepers, clothes-cleaners, bankers, money-changers, bath-house keepers, prostitutes, musicians, and various kinds of teachers. In fact, a recent study has found more than a hundred and seventy different occupations in Classical Athens. This was not a primitive economy based solely on subsistence agriculture.

To exchange the goods and services produced by these craftsmen, there was a need for a permanent marketplace and numerous retail merchants, both men (*kapeloi*) and women (*kapelides*). Our sources mention many people selling various sorts of commodities: salt-sellers, sausage-sellers, sellers of olive-oil, fishmongers, butchers, sellers of cumin, sellers of honey, wine-sellers, sellers of cheese, sellers of charcoal, needle-sellers, booksellers, clothes-sellers, lamp-sellers, sellers of flax, and sellers of cloaks. The market in Athens was so large that it was divided into several different sections. Parts of the *agora* were named after the goods sold there. Pollux (9.47–8) mentions how Eupolis singled out the place "where books are for sale" and has one of his characters recall how "I went around to the garlic and the onions and the incense and straight to the perfume, and around to the trinkets (*gelge*)." If one were looking for wine, one went to the area around the city gate in the Kerameikos or Potter's Quarter (Is. 7.2). Alexis in his *Kalasiris* tells about a quarter known as the "rings" where utensils were sold (Pollux 10.18–19). A separate part of the market was called the women's *agora*. The number of people working in nonagricultural occupations was so large that it was probably more than half of the population of Attica.

In the *Republic* (370e–371b), Plato observes that a *polis* with many *technai* (trades or occupations) cannot exist without imports from abroad. Although some scholars believe that the Greek *polis* aimed at self-sufficiency, the ability to produce everything it needed on its own soil without resorting to trade, the Athenians appear to have had no qualms about importing many goods from abroad. In his Funeral Oration, Pericles boasts that "the greatness of our city brings it about that all the good things from the world flow in to us, so that it seems just as natural to enjoy foreign goods as our own local produce" (Th. 2.38. Cf. Isocr. 4.42). The Old Oligarch ([Xen.] *Ath. Pol.* 2.7) observes how the Athenians trade with many different areas and import exotic delicacies from abroad; Sicily, Italy, Cyprus, Egypt, Lydia, Pontus, the Peloponnese, and other regions ship their distinctive products to Athens. In his *Acharnians* Aristophanes has his comic hero Dikaiopolis establish a personal marketplace so he can trade with Athens' enemies, Thebes and Megara. From Thebes there come "marjoram, pennyroyal rush-mats, lampwicks, ducks, jackdaws, francolins, coots, wrens, and dabchicks" (874–6), and Megara supplies salt and garlic (760–1). Even in 401 when Athenians were still recovering from a devastating siege followed by a bloody civil war, their imports appear to have been worth almost 2,000 talents a year (Andocides 1.133–5). The most important import was grain. Demosthenes (20.31–2) states that the Athenians imported 400,000 *medimnoi* a year from the Black Sea region alone, but Sicily and Egypt were also major suppliers.

The extensive marketplace in the *agora* and the large volume of overseas trade did not arise in a legal and political vacuum. In a small-scale economy where most transactions occur among family, friends, and neighbors, there may be little need for legal regulation; social pressure and the ties of friendship (*philia*) suffice to create the necessary amount of trust needed to exchange goods and services. By contrast, in a large market like the *agora*, which served all of Attica and where most exchange took place between strangers, it was necessary to have magistrates and courts to provide merchants and their customers with the assurance that all transactions would be fair and that all contracts would be enforced. The main officials in the *agora* were the *Agoranomoi* or Market-Controllers. There were five in the city and five in the Piraeus. According to the Aristotelian *Constitution of the Athenians* (*Ath. Pol.* 50.1), they were responsible for supervising all items bought and sold so that they were in an acceptable condition. Grain was the main source of food for most Athenians, and there were special officials called *Sitophylakes*, or Grain-Wardens, to supervise the sale of grain, flour, and bread (*Ath. Pol.* 51.3). The position was so important that the number of Sitophylakes was increased from five to twenty in the city and from five to fifteen for the Piraeus. These officials regulated the price of grain, then checked to see that millers did not charge too large a markup for barley-flour and the bakers sold bread at a price that was not too far above the cost of grain. The *Astynomoi*, or City-Controllers, on the other hand, maintained order and enforced regulations for the entire city of Athens (*Ath. Pol.* 50.2). One of their duties was to supervise the hiring of women who played the flute, harp, or lyre and to keep their fees to no more than two drachmas. They also enforced building regulations to stop construction that encroached on public roads or created drainage problems.

To ensure that sellers used the correct weights and measures, there were ten *Metronomoi* or Controllers of Measures. The *Constitution of the Athenians* (51.1) describes the duties of the Metronomoi in very general terms, but an inscription dated to the second century contains a law about the use of weights and measures (*IG* ii^2 1013). It is unlikely that the duties of the Metronomoi changed very much over time so that many of its provisions are probably tralatician with minor changes to take account of modifications in coinage standards. The magistrates responsible for implementing this law are to make sample measures for wet and dry goods and weights and to compel all those who buy and sell to use them (lines 7–9). The law is comprehensive: it applies to sellers in the *agora*, in workshops, in retail shops, in wine shops, and storehouses (line 9). Magistrates cannot make weights larger or smaller than these prescribed weights (lines 10–11). If the magistrates do not comply, they are to owe 1,000 drachmas to Demeter and Kore (lines 10–13). Private citizens have the right to report the property of those officials who incur the fine (lines 13–14), but the task of checking to see that everyone uses these weights is placed in the hands of officials (lines 14–15). The Council of 600 has the job of making sure no one is using counterfeit weights and measures (lines 16–18). There follow detailed regulations about how to measure various items such as nuts and beans for sale (lines 19–26). If merchants do employ containers smaller than the required size, the magistrate should sell the contents at public auction, deposit the price at the public bank, and destroy the container (lines 27–9). To keep the official weights and measures in permanent use, the law instructs a certain Diodorus, the son of Theophilus from the deme of Halieus, to hand them over to three public slaves stationed in various places. These slaves are to make them available to any magistrates who request them (lines 37–42). The final clause in the law makes those who commit offenses in regard to these weights and measures subject to the law about *kakourgoi* – this may be the same law mentioned in the *Constitution of the Athenians* (52.1) about thieves, enslavers, and clothes-snatchers, which gave private citizens the right to arrest these offenders – and instructs the Areopagus to mete out punishment to those who violate its provisions (lines 56–60).

Plato (*R.* 371b; cf. Arist. *Pol.* 1.3.13.1257a) observes that a *polis* with a high volume of trade required coinage to facilitate exchange. It is possible to sustain a high volume of commodity exchange with just weighed silver bullion, but coins contain certain advantages that facilitate exchange. Since coins have fixed values and contain precious metal that has already been weighed and checked for purity, they enable merchants and customers to conduct transactions with greater efficiency, to increase the speed of exchange, and to make exchange subject to the law. To facilitate market transactions, the Athenians minted several denominations of silver and bronze coin. The largest denomination in the fourth century BCE was the tetradrachm, and smallest denominations were the quarter-obol (some in silver, but later large numbers in bronze) and the eighth-obol or *chalkous* (small numbers in silver, but large numbers in bronze after 350 BCE). This range of denominations shows that coinage was not designed just for infrequent purchases of expensive goods or for payments of taxes and fines, but for everyday buying and selling of small items in the *agora*.

The law of Nicophon passed in 375/74 gives us specific information about how the Athenians enforced regulations about silver coinage (*Hesperia* 43 [1974] 157–61; for an English translation see P. Harding, *Translated Documents of Greece and Rome 2: From the End of the Peloponnesian War to the Battle of Ipsus* #45). The main official responsible for implementing the law is a public slave called the *Dokimastes*, or Tester, who sat near the tables, that is, where the bankers conducted their business in the *agora*. The Tester was ordered to evaluate any coins given to him for examination. After testing them, he was to return the genuine ones, but to keep the counterfeit coins, cut them in two, and turn them over to the Mother of the Gods (lines 8–13). If the Tester does not perform his duties, the *Syllogeis* (Convenors) of the People are to give him fifty lashes (lines 13–16). In the event that someone refuses to accept silver coins approved by the Tester, all his goods on display that day are to be confiscated (lines 16–18). The law then specifies where charges are to be brought and empowers magistrates to decide cases involving fewer than ten drachmas (lines 18–23). For larger sums, they must bring the case before the court. If the various officials assigned to carry out the law do not perform their duties, a private citizen can report them to the Council, which has the power to impose a fine up to 500 drachmas and to remove the offender from office.

Some scholars believe that the enforcement of the law in Classical Athens lay primarily in the hands of private citizens, but it is hard to square this view with the ancient evidence for the administration of law in the *agora*. In the law of Nicophon the primary responsibility for enforcing the law lies in the hands of a public slave, the Tester, the Syllogeis who supervise him, the Sitophylakes, and the Council, which supervises all these officials. Private individuals can provide information to these officials and receive rewards, but it is the officials who confiscate counterfeit coins and the goods of merchants who do not accept good coins. In the law about weights and measures, there is also some role for private initiative in reporting offenses, but the most important tasks in overseeing these regulations lie in the hands of the Metronomoi, public slaves, and the Areopagus. The growth of market transactions in the Athenian *agora* grew to the extent that strict regulations were needed to ensure fairness and order, and the enforcement of these regulations was primarily in the hands of public officials.

Extensive specialization of labor and the development of market-relations also created a need for several types of contracts. The laws of Athens contained a general provision that all agreements that the parties entered into willingly and that did not violate the law were binding, that is, the courts would enforce them if one party refused to abide by the terms of the contract (e.g., [Dem.] 56.1–2). There was also a rule against fraud, which invalidated contracts where one party acted deceitfully (Hyp. *Ath.* 14). There were various types of contracts for hire (*misthosis*); like the Roman contract of *locatio-conductio,* Athenian contracts for hire covered agreements where one hired the labor of another person, where one leased some land, a building, or some movable item (e.g., [Dem.] 56.24), and where one hired a craftsman to produce a certain item or perform a task (e.g., Dem. 53.21). There is some controversy about the nature of contracts for sale in Athenian Law, but it is clear that the Athenians recognized that a sale created rights and duties for both parties. In particular the seller was required to "warrant" (*bebaioun* is the Greek term) the sale, that is, he had to guarantee that he was the actual owner of the object he was selling. This protected the buyer against a third party who might later come forward, claim to be the actual owner, and demand that the buyer return it to him. In the case of slaves, there was also a warranty against latent defects; if one sold a slave who turned out to have a disease, the buyer could return the slave and demand repayment of the sale price (Hyp. *Ath.* 15). This warranty may have extended to sales of other commodities (Lys. 8.10–12).

The Athenians also knew the practice of providing earnest money (*arrhabon*). When two parties agreed to a sale, but the buyer could not pay the full purchase price, he could give the seller earnest money until he could come up with the rest of the cash. If he failed to make the full payment, the seller could keep the earnest money as a penalty. On the other hand, if the seller refused to accept full payment and convey the item to be sold, the law allowed the buyer to sue him for a certain amount. Theophrastus (*On Laws* fr. 21.5 [Szegedy-Maszak]) states that the laws of Thurii permitted the buyer to bring an action for the full amount of the sale price, and the laws of Athens may have contained a similar provision. There were also contracts for deposit (*parakatatheke*), which were similar to the Roman contract of *depositum* (Dem. 36.5–6), and suits that enabled lenders to sue borrowers when they defaulted. If the lender made his loan at an interest rate of 1 percent per month (12 percent per year) or to provide capital for starting an enterprise, he could bring his case as a "monthly suit." This meant his case received privileged treatment and was accepted every month, thus avoiding long delays that might causes financial losses ([Arist.] *Ath. Pol.* 52.2).

Two contracts that are important for an understanding of the dispute between Dareius and Dionysodorus are partnership (*koinonia*) and real security (*apotimema*). One of the most striking features of Athenian laws regulating commercial activities is the absence of any concept akin to the modern legal notion of corporation. Despite the presence in Athenian society of numerous *koinoniai*, groups of individuals cooperating for some purpose, be it commercial or otherwise, Athenian Law concerned itself solely with individual persons and did not recognize the separate legal existence of collective entities. And just as Athenian Law did not recognize the legal existence of corporations or collective enterprises, it also did not possess the notion of corporate liability. This meant that if someone entered into an agreement with a group of individuals and one of those individuals violated the terms of the agreement, the plaintiff proceeded only against the individual who acted contrary to the agreement, not against the group as a whole. If the plaintiff won his suit, he had a right to receive compensation only from the defendant's private property; he did not have a claim on all the funds held in common by the group. Instead of forming a corporation, business partners would enter into an agreement called a *koinonia* (partnership) or *koinopraxia*, which was similar to the Roman contract of *societas* (Justinian *Institutes* 2.25). This arrangement set forth what each party would contribute to the joint enterprise and what share in the profits each was entitled to receive. Suits arising from these agreements received special treatment as "monthly suits" in the Athenian courts, which would indicate that they were sufficiently numerous to merit separate attention ([Arist.] *Ath. Pol.* 52.2).

The practice of providing security was an effective way of providing lenders with some assurance that they could recover their money in the event of the borrower's default. The Athenians had two basic contracts for security, personal security (*engye*) and real security (*apotimema*). In personal security for a loan, the borrower arranges for a third party to come forward and to promise the lender that he will fulfill the borrower's obligations in the event that the borrower does not make interest payments or repay the principal. In real security, the borrower pledges some of his property, either movable or immovable, as security to the creditor. If the borrower defaults, the creditor has the right to seize the property pledged as security and, if he wishes, to sell it for cash in lieu of repayment. Some scholars have claimed that the Athenians had no laws about real security and that this reflected the primitive nature of the economy. The sources for Athenian Law, however, provide at least three examples of laws about real security. One protected the ownership of the lender who seized property pledged as security as a result of default (Is. 10.24). If someone challenged another person's ownership of property, the laws allowed the latter to defend his ownership by proving that he had received it as security. A second law protected the lender who acquired a security in this way from further claims by the borrower (Dem. 41.10). A third law provided the lender with an action against the borrower if he defaulted and refused to turn over goods pledged as security (Is. 6.31; [Dem.] 56.3, 38, 40, 45). These laws show that lenders did not rely just on social attitudes about reciprocity when making loans. As Dareius says in the speech *Against Dionysodorus*, lenders trusted in the protections afforded by the legal system.

The courts of Athens enforced contracts made not only by citizens but also by metics and foreigners. In modern terminology, the laws of Athens recognized the principle of "supranationality" in commercial disputes. This meant that even if one was not a citizen of Athens, one could still bring a private action against another party no matter what his citizenship. Some scholars claim that the Athenian courts served primarily as an arena for competition among élite citizens, but the preserved court speeches show that foreign merchants were also active in bringing suits. For instance, Demosthenes (21.176) recalls how Evander of Thespiae brought a commercial suit against Menippus of Caria and won a judgment of two talents. Granting foreigners access to the courts and enforcing their contracts was an important way of promoting overseas trade. In fact, all four of the individuals involved in the case described in *Against Dionysodorus* appear to have been metics. Athens was not the only community to recognize supranationality in commercial disputes: Dareius imagines the possibility of Athenians getting involved in legal cases in Rhodes (Dem. 56.47; cf. Dem. 32.18; 45.64).

Since the import of grain was so vital for the food supply of Attica, the laws of Athens contained several measures aimed at maintaining an adequate supply of grain and keeping prices low. First, there was a ban on all exports of grain from Attica (Dem. 34.37; 35.50–1; 58.8–9). Second, there was a law that made it illegal for any Athenian or metic to engage in transporting grain to any port besides Athens or to make a loan for such a trading voyage (Dem. 35.50). Third, there was a law that prohibited purchases of more than fifty *phormoi* of grain (Lys. 22.5–6). There is some debate as to whether this law aimed at preventing hoarding or the formation of cartels, but the intent was clearly to prevent the manipulation of grain prices. Fourth, there were laws fixing the amount of profit that millers could make on ground barley and that bakers could make on loaves of bread ([Arist.] *Ath. Pol.* 51.3). Fifth, a recently discovered law of Agyrrhius passed in 374/73 BCE orders the Assembly to sell the grain collected from two taxes – the *pentekoste* or 2 percent tax on grain and the *dodekate* or 8 1/3 percent tax collected in the islands of Lemnos, Scyros, and Imbros – not before the month of Anthesterion at a price fixed by the Assembly (*Hesperia* Supplement 29 [1998] 4–9). The *pentekoste* was collected on all grain imports and the *dodekate* was a transit tax collected on all grain that merchants brought to the islands and then shipped to other ports. The month of Anthesterion was right before the harvest and during the time when the seas were closed to shipping. Since shortages of grain might occur at this time, the law therefore instructed the Assembly to sell the grain collected from the two taxes during this month in order to keep prices low (lines 36–44). Sixth, the Assembly often voted honors to foreign kings who granted special privileges to men shipping grain to Athens (Dem. 20.29–40; *IG* ii^2 212).

This brief survey reveals that the Athenians not only developed a market economy and carried on extensive overseas trade but also established numerous officials for supervising their marketplace and created the laws needed to regulate market transactions and resolve commercial disputes. The next section examines how some of these laws worked in practice in a dispute between two lenders and two borrowers involved in overseas trade.

II

When reading a court speech by an Attic orator, one must always bear in mind that the speech presents only one side of a case where there was at least one other side of the story. For this reason, a reader must always be careful to notice which statements made by a litigant are supported by the evidence of documents or the testimony of witnesses and which are not. Even if the statements made by one speaker appear to be reliable, it is still possible that he may have omitted key facts or relevant information. In some places litigants report what they believe their opponents will say, but in the absence of their actual statements, it is impossible to know how accurately the speaker presents the views of his opponent. With these caveats in mind, let us turn to the speech given by Dareius, *Against Dionysodorus*.

Dareius begins his narrative by recounting the terms of the contract he and his partner concluded with Dionysodorus and Pamphilus. About a year before, in the month of Metageitnion, Dionysodorus and Pamphilus asked Dareius to lend them money on the security of their ship for a voyage to Egypt with either Athens or Rhodes as the final destination (5). They also promised to pay interest for the duration of the voyage to either port. The date of their request is significant: the month of Metageitnion roughly corresponds to our month of August. Hesiod in the *Works and Days* (663–5) recommends sailing only during the fifty days after the summer solstice, that is, from the end of June to about the middle of August. Vegetius (*De re militari* 4.39) writes that the best period for sailing extends from May 27 to September 14. From September 14 to November 10 sailing is risky, and after that it is too dangerous. This meant that Pamphilus was starting very late in the season and might encounter rough weather on his return trip from Egypt. Dareius does not lay any emphasis on the date of the contract, but it will become significant when looking at Dionysodorus' reply to Dareius' charges.

Dareius and Parmeniscus replied that they would not lend unless the contract required a return voyage to Athens (6). They obviously insisted on this condition because they did not wish to break the law forbidding Athenians and metics from lending money to merchants to ship grain to ports besides Athens. When Dionysodorus and Pamphilus agreed to this condition, Dareius and Parmeniscus lent them 3,000 drachmas on the security of their ship, and a written contract was drawn up (6). Dareius and his partner thus chose to accept a pledge of real security, which was standard in loans for large amounts. To support his account of these facts, Dareius has the contract read out to the court. It is crucial to observe what this piece of evidence proves and what it does not prove. All the document confirms is that the four men concluded an agreement on certain terms. It does not show that Dionysodorus and Pamphilus initially asked to borrow money for a voyage to Rhodes and not to Athens. Dareius could easily have invented this part of the narrative to demonstrate that Pamphilus at first did not wish to promise that he would return to Athens and was already thinking about sailing back only as far as Rhodes even before he set out.

According to the terms of the contract, Dionysodorus and Pamphilus received the money and sent their ship to Egypt, the latter sailing on board and the former staying behind (7). These details are also significant, for they reveal another one of the terms of the contract and help us to understand why the lenders made their loan to two borrowers and not to one. In the beginning of his speech, Dareius describes the enormous risks taken by those who lend money for overseas trade: the borrower takes the money and the ship, which serves as security for the loan, and sails away, leaving the lender behind with only a scrap of paper containing his promise. As the narrative unfolds, however, Dareius shows that his position was not quite so vulnerable as he makes it out ot be. Although Pamphilus had departed with the money and the security for the loan (his ship), the contract required that Dionysodorus stay in Athens. The purpose of this arrangement was to enable Dareius and Parmeniscus to bring an action against Dionysodorus in case Pamphilus did not return. Later on in the speech, Dareius discloses another key aspect of the contract: if the borrowers concealed their ship, they would owe double, and the lenders had the right to demand the interest and principal from either one or both of the borrowers (45). The absence of modern notions of legal personality made such a clause necessary. A modern lender can make a loan to a shipping company made up of several owners and employees. If someone in the company absconds with money and disappears, the lender can still recover his money from the company. As we noted above, in Athenian Law someone could not lend to a company but only to individuals. As a result, Dareius and his partner made their loan to two men, required that one remain in Athens, and added the stipulation that each of them (or both) was responsible for repayment of the loan (in modern legal terminology this is known as "joint and several liability"). If Pamphilus did not return, Dareius and his partner could then sue Dionysodorus. If the court awarded them damages, Dionysodorus would have to pay, then attempt to recover a share of his losses from his partner Pamphilus. If Pamphilus refused to pay, Dionysodorus could sue his partner for violating their contract of *koinonia.* One should therefore not be deceived by Dareius' rhetoric in his opening words to the court: Pamphilus may have departed with both the money and his ship, but he had to leave behind his partner Dionysodorus as a hostage for his good behavior. Dareius was not quite so vulnerable as he wanted the court to believe.

In the next part of his narrative, Dareius presents a scandalous account of Pamphilus' activities once he reached Egypt (7–9). He accuses his opponent's partner of conspiring with Cleomenes, the ruler of Egypt installed by Alexander the Great (Arrian *Anabasis* 3.5.2–5; Curtius Rufus 4.8.5), and helping him to raise the price of grain. He describes how these men had stationed their agents in various cities; these agents wrote to them indicating where the price of grain was highest and then sent their cargoes where they could reap the greatest profits. When Pamphilus left Athens, the price of grain was high. But after he left, the arrival of a large shipment from Sicily caused the price to fall. According to Dareius, it was this turn of events that caused Pamphilus to ignore the terms of the contract and sail to Rhodes where he unloaded his cargo of grain and sold it (10).

Needless to say, there was another side to the story. Further on in the speech, Dareius predicts Dionysodorus will say that the ship suffered damage on its voyage back from Alexandria and was forced to put in at Rhodes (21). To prove that he was telling the truth, Dionysodorus would state that he hired some ships in Rhodes to transport some of his cargo to Athens. There were also other creditors who were willing to accept payment of interest only as far as Rhodes (22). Dareius claims that his opponents made up this excuse and that their true reason for unloading their cargo in Rhodes was to make a larger profit. Since we do not have Dionysodorus' speech, it is hard to judge between the two accounts. But it is crucial to recall that Pamphilus had started his voyage to Egypt late in the sailing season, so he might well have encountered rough weather on his return trip to Athens.

When Dareius and Pamphilus discovered what had happened, they confronted Dionysodorus and complained about his partner's failure to return to Athens as they had promised (11). What was more, they were now open to the charge that they had broken the law by lending money to transport grain to a port other than Athens. These protests got them nowhere, so they began to request payment of the interest and principal of the loan (12). Dionysodorus expressed his willingness to comply with their demand but would pay the interest only on the voyage to Rhodes. Dareius and Pamphilus replied that they could not accept this offer.

Dionysodorus then gathered a crowd of witnesses and repeated this offer in front of them (13). This was an attempt to intimidate his opponents and also to demonstrate his own willingness to be reasonable and compromise. Some Athenians who happened to be present suggested a temporary solution: Dareius and Parmeniscus should accept the amount offered to them and take their dispute about the remaining amount to court (14). Since they did not want to appear litigious, they declared their intention to follow this solution. This put Dionysodorus on the defensive, so he stated that he would comply provided that in exchange they destroy the document containing the agreement. Dareius and Parmeniscus could naturally not accede to this condition since it would rob them of the evidence they needed to prove their case in court (15–16).

Dareius' next move was to issue a challenge (*proklesis*) (18). This was another attempt to bring social pressure to bear on his opponents and to force them to settle the dispute out of court. A challenge could take many forms. One of the best known is the challenge made to an opponent asking him to hand over his slaves for examination under torture about some key issue. The person who received the challenge might accept it (especially if he felt confident about the outcome), decline it, or propose a settlement as an alternative to further conflict. If the person who received the challenge declined it, he laid himself open to the suspicion that he lacked confidence in his own case, and his opponent might later use his refusal to accept as an argument against him. This form of dispute resolution had a long history and is found already in the account of the funeral games for Patroclus in the *Iliad* (23.261–611). In the chariot race held by Achilles to honor his dead comrade, Antilochus uses cunning to force Menelaus to fall behind him and to gain an advantage that enables him to come in second after the winner Diomedes. Angry at this ruse, Menelaus challenges him to swear an oath to Poseidon that he did not prevail by guile (581–5). This maneuver puts Antilochus in an awkward position: he can swear the oath and commit perjury in front of his companions or decline the challenge and tacitly admit that Menelaus is right. If he chooses the former option, he gains a reputation for swearing false oaths, and in the future his companions will never trust him. As a way out of his dilemma, Antilochus offers Menelaus the mare he won (586–95), and this solution satisfies his opponent and ends the conflict (596–611).

Dareius presented Dionysodorus with another kind of challenge by inviting him to submit their case to a private arbitrator (18). Private arbitration was a popular form of dispute resolution, which avoided many of the pitfalls of going to court. By using an arbitrator, both parties could avoid the delays in waiting for officials to schedule a trial and get around paying court fees. The procedure before an arbitrator was also simpler and informal. Instead of making formal speeches before hundreds of judges, the litigants presented the case to an arbitrator who could ask questions and clarify the issues. The arbitrator also had more flexibility than the judges in an Athenian court, who could either vote to accept or reject the plaintiff's request: an arbitrator could attempt to reconcile the parties, suggest a compromise solution, or render a judgment. If one of the parties then did not abide by the arbitrator's decision, the other party could bring an action in court for breach of the agreement. Dareius does not say why Dionysodorus rejected his challenge. His opponent may not have found the terms of the challenge acceptable, or the two parties may not have been able to find an arbitrator whom both could trust. Despite the failure of the challenge to settle the dispute, the tactic employed by Dareius was not a complete waste of effort: once in court Dareius drew attention to Dionysodorus' refusal to accept the challenge as a way of attacking his credibility and portraying him as difficult and unreasonable.

The preliminary skirmishes between Dareius and Dionysodorus serve to remind students of Athenian Law that a trial in court was often only the last step in a long series of maneuvers between litigants. Whatever their true intentions, each one attempted to act as if he did not wish to bring their case to court; both men strove to win over public opinion by offering compromises and avoiding the appearance of being litigious. This led to a series of proposals and counterproposals, each aimed ostensibly at reaching a settlement. Given the nature of the sources for Athenian Law, it is impossible know how often attempts at out-of-court settlements succeeded, but it would appear that Greek attitudes favored settlement over trial. The Athenians admired a bold warrior on the battlefield and a determined competitor in an athletic contest, but in the *agora* they expected citizens and metics to refrain from aggressive behavior and to demonstrate their willingness to compromise and cooperate. But social attitudes against litigiousness and the possibility of compromise were not strong enough in this instance to achieve a settlement, and Dareius was forced (or preferred) to bring his case against Dionysodorus to court.

After presenting his version of the facts in the case (5–18), Dareius turns to his legal arguments (19–44). Some scholars claim that the Athenians were amateurs in legal matters, but even the structure of Dareius' speech reveals a certain level of legal sophistication. Dareius does not throw together factual and legal arguments, but keeps the two kinds of arguments strictly separate. This separation reveals his awareness that the two kinds of arguments are different and require different methods of reasoning. The narrative of the speech recounts a series of events and carefully attempts to create causal links among these events by analyzing the motives of his opponents and showing them acting consistently in accordance with these motives. The section containing the legal arguments is very different. Here Dareius focuses more closely on the terms of the contract and contrasts how the actions of his opponents violated the contract, then refutes the arguments his opponents will present. Narrative gives way to analysis, and the different modes of presentation show that Dareius clearly understood the distinction between factual and legal arguments.

As Dareius stresses in his opening words, he relies primarily on the Athenian law stating that all agreements entered into willingly are binding. He therefore places great weight on the actual wording of the contract. He predicts that Dionysodorus will make three main arguments in his defense. First, he will claim that their ship was "wrecked" or "damaged" on its return from Egypt and forced to put in at Rhodes. To prove this assertion, Dareius will show that he hired ships at Rhodes to transport some of his cargo to Athens. Second, he will point out how several other creditors were willing to accept payment of interest only as far as Rhodes. Third, he will rely on a clause in the contract that obligated him to repay the loan only in the event that "the ship was safe." Since the ship could not arrive safely in the Piraeus, Dionysodorus was not obligated to repay the loan. This section of the speech is valuable for giving some indication of the points Dionysodorus may have made. On the other hand, one cannot be certain that Dareius does not misrepresent his opponent's arguments or fails to do them full justice.

In answer to the first argument, Dareius questions his opponent's claim that the ship suffered serious damage. If this was so, why did the ship later sail back to Egypt, and why is it now visiting every port in the sea except Athens? He brushes aside Dionysodorus' story that his partner shipped some of his cargo to Athens; he claims that they transported only the items that were selling at high prices in Athens but sold their grain in Rhodes because the price for grain was higher there. Dareius' objection rests in part on the unproven fact that the ship is now sailing again. Dareius provides no evidence for his assertion, and Dionysodorus might well have denied that the ship could have been repaired. Dareius also assumes that Dionysodorus could have shipped the grain from Rhodes to Athens, but he does not countenance the possibility that officials in Rhodes may have forced him and his partner to sell their grain there. As noted in Section I, the Athenians had a law that forbade citizens and metics from transporting grain outside of Attica and established a board of ten superintendents of the port to enforce this law ([Arist.] *Ath. Pol.* 51.4). The people of Rhodes could have had a similar law, and the officials at Rhodes might have prevented Pamphilus from shipping the grain (cf. [Arist.] *Oeconomica* 1348b33f). Such a scenario is all the more likely when one recalls that Dareius himself insists that the price of grain was much higher in Rhodes than it was in Athens. Faced with a severe shortage, officials in Rhodes are unlikely to have allowed Parmeniscus to remove the grain from their market. In fact, several sources indicate that *poleis* might detain ships carrying grain to other ports and force them to sell their cargoes (e.g., [Dem.] 50.6).

Dareius next addresses Dionysodorus' second argument that his other creditors accepted his proposal to receive the payment of interest only as far as Rhodes. He dismisses this argument on the grounds that the settlements reached with the other creditors are irrelevant to his own case (26). He insists on the terms of their agreement: either they show that the contract is not binding or abide by its terms (27). Dionysodorus probably intended to contrast the willingness of the other creditors to settle for a smaller amount of interest with Dareius' own intransigence as a way of making him look greedy and stubborn. To counter this strategy, Dareius claims that these creditors did not yield part of their gains, but actually profited from their settlement since they immediately recovered their loans at Rhodes and were then able to lend out the principal again to the two men and receive interest from their subsequent trip to Egypt and back (28–9). Dareius' counterattack not only accuses the other creditors of acting solely out of a desire for profit, but also charges them with lending money to ship grain to another port besides Athens. In reality, it may have been Dareius who was the greedy one. Whatever amount of interest the other creditors may have been earning, Dareius and his partner would have gained far more if they won their case since they were asking for double the principal or 6,000 drachmas.

Dareius devotes the longest reply to Dionysodorus' argument based on the clause that required repayment only in the case that the ship arrived safely. Dareius interprets this clause narrowly and claims it only applied in the case where the ship actually sank. Dionysodorus appears to have interpreted the clause differently (38). To judge from Dareius' brief summary of his argument, Dionysodorus was prepared to stress the clause in the contract that called for the ship to return safely to Athens. Since the ship suffered serious damage, it could not continue safely on its voyage and arrive safely in the Piraeus. In other words, Dionysodorus gave a broad interpretation of this clause, which he argued gave exemption to himself and to his partner not only if the ship sank, but also in the eventuality that it suffered damage and was unable to continue safely on its journey. Dareius' reply to this argument is that Dionysodorus could have repaired the ship and continued on his voyage to the Piraeus. But Dareius' reply may ignore the possibility that Pamphilus may first have been forced to sell the grain in Rhodes.

Whatever the actual circumstances, the different interpretations of the phrase "if the ship arrives safely" illustrate what the philosopher of law H. L. A. Hart has called "the open texture of law." Hart notes that laws and contracts usually contain general terms or cover large categories of persons or actions. Although these terms and categories provide clear guidance in most situations, it may on occasion be difficult to know how to apply a general rule to a specific situation. In this case, the phrase "if the ship arrives safely" contains a potential ambiguity. The phrase obviously exempted the borrower from repayment if the ship sunk but left it unclear how to apportion losses if the ship was only damaged and forced to seek a harbor short of its final destination. Should the borrower have to pay additional interest, or was it unfair for the borrower to shoulder all the losses caused by the unforeseen circumstances? The Athenians were certainly familiar with the practice of allocating risk; for instance, in the law of Agyrrhius discussed in Part I, one clause stipulates that the men who collected the *dodekate* had to take the entire risk of loss during transport of the grain to Athens (lines 11–15). In the private contract drawn up by Dareius and Dionysodorus, however, this question was not addressed. As a result, the dispute ended up in court. It would be fascinating to know how the court decided the legal issue involved in the case and how it arrived at its decision, but the sources are silent.

The speech *Against Dionysodorus* provides valuable information about the legal relationship between lenders and merchants in overseas trade. Although lenders took considerable risks in making loans to merchants, the law provided them with several ways of minimizing these risks. Taking advantage of *praxis*-clauses and the practice of real security and relying on the courts to enforce contracts, lenders could increase the odds of recovering their principal and earning interest.

As Dareius observes in the closing words of his speech, the laws and the courts of Athens played a major role in promoting the overseas trade that made the *agora* of Athens a thriving marketplace.

Afterthoughts

This essay was originally written for a Web site containing a series of introductory essays on Athenian Law aimed at a general audience. I have chosen to reprint it here to serve as a general introduction to the essays in Part II. Since the original publication did not have footnotes with references to modern works and did not provide a bibliography, I have added some bibliographical notes here.

For the general view of the Athenian economy adopted here, see Harris (2002a). This essay contains a preliminary list of the occupations attested in Classical Athens and provides some evidence for each of these occupations. For a good survey of the economy of fourth-century Athens, see Isager and Hansen (1975). For a good brief introduction to the Greek economy, see Migeotte (2002); an English translation of this work is a *desideratum*. For the view that most exchange in Classical Athens was gift-giving based on reciprocity among kin, friends, and neighbors and that market-exchange was marginal (not followed here), see Millett (1990). On trade in the Greek city in general, see the stimulating book of Bresson (2000) with my review in Harris (2001b). For evidence about the extent and organization of the *agora* in Classical Athens, see Wycherley (1957). For market regulations in Athens, see in general Stanley (1976). On the *agoranomoi* in the Greek cities, see Migeotte (2005). On the *sitophylakes* see Gauthier (1981). On the *astynomoi* see [Arist.] *Ath. Pol.* 51.1 with Rhodes (1981) 573–5; on the *metronomoi* see [Arist.] *Ath. Pol.* 51.2 with Rhodes (1981) 576–7.

There has been much recent interest in the nature of coinage and its role in ancient Greece. See in particular Seaford (2004) and Schaps (2004). On the "cultural" approach of Kurke, see the remarks of Kroll (2000).

For the view (not followed here) that the enforcement of law in Classical Athens lay primarily in the hands of private citizens, see Hunter (1994) 120–53. I hope to discuss this topic at greater length in the future.

The nature of Greek contracts has been the subject of considerable controversy among legal historians. Pringsheim (1950) 14–56 argued that the Greeks did not have "consensual" contracts; his view was developed by Wolff (1957), who argued that consent did not form the basis of a binding agreement for the Greeks, but rather the transfer of an object for a certain stated use (*Zweckverfügung*). This view has been criticized by several scholars and is not widely accepted: see Gernet (1955) and more recently Millett (1990) and Vélissaropoulos (1994). On the contract of *misthosis,* see Behrend (1979) with the criticisms of Biscardi (2000) 103–16. On warranty of title see Pringsheim (1950) 429–72; on warranty against latent defects see Pringsheim (1950) 472–97. On the *arrhabon* see Pringsheim (1950) 333–428.

On monthly suits see Cohen (1973) 9–30. On maritime courts in general, see Cohen (1973) and Vélissaropoulos (1980). On the absence of the notion of corporate liability, see Chapter II.4 and the literature cited there. On personal security the only extensive treatment remains Partsch (1909), which is almost a century old. The topic needs a fresh study in the light of inscriptions published since Partsch's work appeared. On real security see Chapters II.2 and II.3. On supranationality in Athenian law, see Cohen (1973) 59–65. On the grain trade of Classical Athens, one can consult Garnsey (1988) 89–164, but his conclusions require modification after the publication of the new grain-tax law of Agyrrhius – see Stroud (1998). Stroud thinks that the *dodekate* mentioned in this law was a tax on grain grown on the islands of Lemnos, Imbros, and Skyros; for doubts about Stroud's view and an alternative proposal, see Harris (1999b). On the law prohibiting the purchase of more than fifty *phormoi* of grain, see Figueira (1986).

On the speech [Demosthenes] *Against Dionysodorus* (56), see the excellent commentary in Carey and Reid (1986). On the oath-challenge as a means of dispute resolution, one can consult Mirhady (1991), but Mirhady does not analyze the social dynamics that made the practice effective. On open texture in Athenian Law, see Harris (2000a) and Harris (2004c).

II.2 When Is a Sale Not a Sale? The Riddle of Athenian Terminology for Real Security Revisited

IN ATHENS DURING THE LATE CLASSICAL AND HELLENISTIC PERIODS, IT WAS CUS-tomary for a man who was borrowing a large sum of money to pledge some property as security for the repayment of his loan. To show that his property was legally encumbered, a flat slab of stone, called a *horos*, was set up, and an inscription, indicating the nature of the lien on the property, was inscribed on the *horos*.[1] These *horoi* served to warn third parties that the man who pledged the property as security was not free to sell it or otherwise alienate it until the loan was repaid.[2] The terminology that is used on these *horoi* to indicate that the property has been pledged as security varies. On a relatively small number of *horoi*, only seven, the property is described as "lying under (an obligation)" (ὑποκειμένου, -ης, ων) for a debt, the amount of which may or may not be specified.[3] The texts found on a far greater number of *horoi*, some 128 in all, use a different type of expression.[4] On these *horoi*, the property is said to have been "sold on condition of

[1] For a description of the physical characteristics of the *horoi*, see Fine (1951) 4–6.

[2] For the purpose of this kind of *horos*, see Fine (1951) 42–3; Finley (1952), 10–21. Finley's work was reprinted by Rutgers University Press in 1985 with a new introduction by P. Millett, which contains the texts of all the *horoi* published since the appearance of Finley's work. All references in this chapter will be to the 1985 edition, which will be cited by the author's name only. Millett's introduction to this edition will be cited as "Millett in Finley (1985)." When citing the texts of the *horoi*, I will follow the system devised by Finley and followed by Millett (e.g., *horos* no. 34; *horoi* nos. 6, 8, 10).

[3] *Horoi* nos. 1, 2, 2A, 4, 5, 6, 7. The term is restored on *horos* no. 3A. Since *horos* no. 3 does not actually contain the actual term ὑποκειμένης, I have excluded it from this category, although Finley placed it under the rubric *hypotheke*. Nor have I included *horoi* nos. 80A and 81A – on these, see the discussion in Section II. The term is also found on a *horos* from Amorgos (*horos* no. 8) and on another from Lemnos (*horos* no. 10).

[4] This sum includes all those texts in which the formula is found or reasonably restored. Following the lead of Finley and Millett, I have also included those that omit the phrase ἐπὶ λύσει. There are 92 in

release" (πεπραμένου, -ης, -ων ἐπὶ λύσει).[5] The terminology used on the *horoi* to describe this kind of lien presents a striking contrast with that employed by the Attic orators: in their speeches we find the verbs ὑποκεῖσθαι and ὑποτιθέναι when it is a question of pledging security for a loan, but never πέπρασθαι with the addition of the prepositional phrase ἐπὶ λύσει.[6] In other words, the type of expression that is found on the vast majority of *horoi* does not figure even once in the works of the Attic orators. And the terminology that the orators prefer when talking of this kind of lien on property is hardly used at all on the *horoi*.

Although there has been much dispute about the precise nature of the transactions referred to by these two expressions, scholars have assumed by and large that each one denotes a different and distinct form of security transaction, one called *hypotheke*, the other *prasis epi lysei*. Despite their unanimity on this one central issue, they have been unable to agree about how these two forms of security differed from one another. Several theories have been put forward. Some, for instance, have held that *prasis epi lysei* was a "real sale" ("rein Verkauf"), whereas *hypotheke* was not.[7] Others have put forward the view that *hypotheke* represented a collateral form of security and that this set it apart from *prasis epi lysei*, which was substitutive in nature.[8] Neither of these two theories – nor any of the other alternative proposals – has been able to win general acceptance. As a result, the issue still remains unresolved.

A new approach is clearly required. In this chapter I hope to show that we can arrive at a solution to the problem by questioning the basic assumption that has been shared by all previous treatments of this topic – namely, that the two types of expression encountered on the *horoi* refer to two different forms of security. In my opinion, it has been this assumption that has prevented scholars from arriving at a satisfactory answer to the riddle of Athenian terminology for real security.

Appendix I of Finley, 22 in Appendix III of Finley, and 14 in Millett in Finley. Unlike Millett, I have excluded *horoi* nos. 80A and 81A. For discussion of these see Section II.

5 For the translation, see Finley (1985) 31.

6 Though it is true that various forms of the verb πέπρασθαι are used to describe transactions involving real security in Dem. 37, they are nowhere in that speech coupled with the phrase ἐπὶ λύσει. For a discussion of the terminology in this speech, see Section IV.

7 The main proponent of this view was Günter (1914) 16–25 (see 17 note 3, and 18 note 1 for references to earlier views on the subject).

8 This view was fully presented by Pappulias (1909) Part I. Pappulias' view was thoroughly criticized by Raape (1912) 1–48 and by Manigk (1914) 205–13.

But the problem is not just one of terminology; it involves important questions about the nature of Athenian Law and the evolution of credit and real security during the Archaic and Classical periods.

It would be impossible within the space of this chapter to review all of the numerous theories about the alleged differences between *hypotheke* and *prasis epi lysei*, much less to undertake detailed criticisms of each of them. Instead, I will begin in Section I by examining the two theories that have been most influential in recent decades, those of J. V. A. Fine and M. I. Finley, respectively. In Section II reasons for adopting a new approach will be put forward. Section III will be devoted to an analysis of the terminology used by the Attic orators and in some inscriptions to describe transactions involving hypothecation. The most extensive piece of evidence for the use of this terminology, Demosthenes' speech *Against Pantaenetus* (37), will be dealt with in Section IV. In Section V a new solution will be proposed to answer the question of why the terminology on the *horoi* differs from that used by the Attic orators. The final part, Section VI, will contain some reflections on the "origins" of real security in Classical Athens.

I

In our examination of recent views, we will take those of Fine first. Fine's views about *hypotheke* and *prasis epi lysei* are in part derived from the work of previous scholars, in part his own original contribution. He does not restrict himself to the narrow question of the differences between the two forms of security but elaborates an ambitious theory about the evolution of credit in ancient Athens. Though several general objections can be brought against his overall theory, I think it is more fair to examine his argument in detail and to see whether or not the evidence he cites can be used to support his theory.[9]

Building on the traditional assumption that in *hypotheke* "the debtor retained possession and ownership of the security," Fine argued (54) that "he was able

[9] Millett in Finley (1985) xiii delivers some telling criticisms of Fine's theory but does not refute it in detail. Cf. Gernet (1955) 345–53 ("Il semble vraiment difficile d'accepter une interprétation aussi compliqué, aussi conjecturale, qui postule un concept de la vente singulièrement affiné, et qui utilise d'un bout à l'autre une notion aussi suspecte, pour une époque très ancienne, que celle de fiction juridique"). In my review of recent opinions, I have not treated the views of Germain (1975) 333–46 and (1968). These are well criticized by Millett in Finley (1985) xix–xxi.

to borrow further on the ὅσῳ πλείονος ἄξιον."[10] The only text he cites to support this contention is [Dem.] 53.10, where the speaker Apollodorus relates how Nicostratus had borrowed money from Arethusius on the security of his farm. When Nicostratus wished to contract an additional loan on the same security or to sell it to obtain more cash, no one could be found to buy it or accept it as security for a loan (οὐδεὶς ἐθέλοι οὔτε πρίασθαι οὔτε θέσθαι) since Arethusius would not permit it. If anything, this passage would appear to indicate that the debtor did not have a right to contract additional loans on a property once it had already been pledged as security and that the debtor's ability to do so depended entirely on the consent of the creditor, not on any right implicit in this type of security. Nevertheless, Fine pressed on with his argument and claimed that "the very fact that the debtor was allowed to give a second mortgage on the ὅσῳ πλείονος ἄξιον implies that the rights of the original mortgage over the security extended only to the amount of the loan. The natural inference, then, is that if there were no secondary creditors, the 'excess' still belonged to the debtor – i.e., had to be restored to the debtor." This inference rests on the dubious assumption that the rights of the debtor vis-à-vis the creditor can be inferred from what is known about the right of one creditor vis-à-vis other creditors. But the relationship between the debtor and his creditor and that between one creditor and another are of a completely different order, and it is unjustifiable to use the information we have about one relationship to fill in the gaps in our knowledge about the other relationship.

Fine then adds an argument from an analogy with dotal *apotimema*. Since "under that contract the 'excess' was returned to the debtor," and "the *apotimema* was very similar to the hypothec, it is logical to assume that the same procedure was followed in the case of the latter institution." Unfortunately, Fine's view of dotal *apotimema* (139–40) is derived from a strained interpretation of Dem. 31.6. His explication of this passage needs to be quoted in full:

> Demosthenes, it will be remembered, had been hindered in collecting from his guardian Aphobos the damages awarded by the court, because Onetor claimed that the land had been assigned to him as *apotimema* to guarantee the restitution of his sister's dowry, which amounted to one talent. Demosthenes

[10] The view that in *hypotheke* the debtor retained both possession and ownership goes back to Hitzig (1895) 1 and was endorsed by Beauchet (1897) 2: 176–80; Lipsius (1905–15) 690–2; and Harrison (1968) 258.

> indignantly says to the court· Σκέψασθε τοίνυν τὴν ἀναίδειαν, ὅς γ' ὑμῖν ἐτόλμησεν εἰπεῖν, ὡς οὐκ ἀποστερεῖ μ' ὅσῳ πλείονος ἄξιόν ἐστι ταλάντον, καὶ ταῦτ' αὐτὸς τιμήσας οὐκ ἄξιον εἶναι πλείονος. Demosthenes' anger, of course, is caused by his insistence that in reality the land had not been given as *apotimema* and that it was not worth more than a talent. It is clear from this sentence, then, if the land serving as *apotimema* had been worth over a talent, Demosthenes would have been entitled to its value beyond that sum. Since Demosthenes here can be equated with the dotal debtor (for by court decision he was authorized to seize Aphobos's property), this passage can only mean that the value of the *apotimema* over the amount of the dowry was to be restored to the dotal debtor.

This analysis is correct in all respects save one: it misrepresents Demosthenes' position in the matter. As Fine himself observes, Demosthenes had a claim on the property of Aphobos as the result of a legal decision and the subsequent failure of Aphobos to pay the damages awarded to him by the court. He and Onetor were thus both creditors and had rival claims to the property of Aphobos. But it is Aphobos who is the dotal debtor in his relationship with Onetor – nothing in the speech suggests that by virtue of his claim to Aphobos' property Demosthenes "could be equated with the dotal debtor." After all, it was Aphobos who had married Onetor's sister, not Demosthenes.

We should also note that in dotal *apotimema* there could be no "excess." When the dowry was agreed on by the suitor and the *kyrios* of the woman to be married, the suitor marked off a portion of his property, the value of which was assessed (ἐτιμᾶτο) by the parties to be equivalent to the value of the dowry.[11] This was what Onetor appears to have done (Dem. 31.5). Once this assessment was made, it could not later be challenged in court.[12] In the event of divorce, therefore, the husband had to turn over the entire security since it had been evaluated as exactly equivalent to the dowry. If the security was in fact worth more than its assessed value, there was nothing the ex-husband could do about it – he had agreed to the original assessment, and the law required him to stand by it. After the assessment

[11] Harpocration *s.v.* ἀποτιμηματαὶ καὶ ἀποτίμημα καὶ ἀποτιμᾶν καὶ τὰ ἀπ' αὐτῶν: (...) εἰώθεσαν δὲ καὶ οἱ τότε, εἰ γυναικὶ γαμουμένῃ προῖκα διδοῖεν οἱ προσήκοντες, αἰτεῖν παρὰ τοῦ ἀνδρὸς ὥσπερ ἐνέχυρον τι τῆς προικὸς ἄξιον, οἷον οἰκίαν ἢ χωρίον.

[12] See Dem. 41.7 with Finley (1985) 53 and 245 note 61. Finley's account of dotal *apotimema* is superior to that of Fine.

had been agreed on, the price that the assessed property might fetch on the market was strictly irrelevant. If there turned out to be any difference between the assessed value of the security and the amount for which it was subsequently sold, the ex-husband had no right to any "excess." And if there was a shortage, the woman's *kyrios* did not have the right to demand that the ex-husband make up the difference. Thus, Fine's view of dotal *apotimema* rests not only on a questionable interpretation of Dem. 31.6, but also on a misunderstanding of the very nature of the institution. Since there is no reason to believe that in dotal *apotimema* the husband had a right to the "excess," Fine cannot use an analogy with this institution to prove that *hypotheke* gave the debtor a right to the "excess."

There are also problems with Fine's conception of *prasis epi lysei.* Fine holds (143) that in this form of security "since the debtor immediately lost title to the ownership of the security, he could not contract a second mortgage on it." (Cf. Fine [1951] 93–4, 155.) This would lead us to expect to discover multiple creditors listed on *horoi* set up to indicate the presence of a *hypotheke,* not on those advertising the existence of a *prasis epi lysei.* Multiple creditors do appear on several *horoi,* but never on stones that employ the terminology of *hypotheke,* only on those that use the language of *prasis epi lysei.*[13] Fine's way around this objection (154) was to claim that when several different debts are listed on a single *horos,* they must be "constituent parts of the same loan." The evidence of another inscription, however, cannot be explained away in this fashion. This inscription records the sale of a house owned by Theosebes, the son of Theophilus.[14] Despite his pious name, Theosebes had been accused of impiety and had fled Attica before his case came to trial. He was condemned in absentia, and his property confiscated and sold by the *poletai* in the year 367/66. But before his property was sold, several creditors came forward with claims against Theosebes' property. The first one was made by Smicythus of Teithras, to whom the house had been pledged as security (ὑπόκειται) for a loan of 150 drachmas (lines 14–15). The second lien was held by Kichonides from Gargettos, the son of Diogeiton, and the *koinon* of the Medontidai *phrateres* to whom the house had been "sold on condition of release" (ἀποδομένο [line 23]) by Theosebes' father Theophilus for a loan of

[13] *Horoi* nos. 11, 13, 19, 22, 32, 35, 41, 46, 97, 72A, 73A, 95A. This was pointed out by Millett in Finley (1985) xiii.

[14] The inscription was published by M. Crosby (1941) 14 no. 1.

100 drachmas (lines 17–25).[15] The third was held by Aeschines of Melite and a *koinon* of *orgeones* who had also "bought the house on condition of release" (πριαμένων . . . ἡμῶν [lines 33–4]) from Theophilus for a loan of 24 drachmas (lines 30–5). Fine (151) tried to parry the threat this inscription posed to his theory by adopting the suggestion of M. Crosby, who published the inscription, that the *koinon* of the *orgeones* must have belonged to the phratry of the Medontidai.[16] Finley called this assumption "gratuitous."[17] Not only is it gratuitous; it is also impossible. We know that *phrateres* were not subdivided into groups of *orgeones*, but into *thiasoi*.[18] The *orgeones* and the *phrateres* listed in this inscription must, therefore, have formed two separate associations that made two separate loans to Theophilus, each one secured by means of a *prasis epi lysei*. The evidence of this inscription provides an unassailable refutation of Fine's view of *prasis epi lysei*.[19]

On such a foundation Fine erected a theory about the evolution of real security in ancient Athens. Proceeding from the observation that in "the early stages of any legal system the regulations or laws concerning loans favor the creditor rather than the debtor," Fine concluded (90–1) that *prasis epi lysei* must have been the earlier institution, since according to this view it favored the creditor, and must have antedated *hypotheke*, which was more advantageous to the debtor. Fine placed the origin of *hypotheke* in the fourth century BCE and attributed its rise to two factors: first, the increasing complexity of economic life, and second, the evolution of Athenian legal ideas. "As Athenian legal ideas matured and as the distinction between ownership and possession became better defined, objections must have arisen – at least among the debtor class – against πρᾶσις ἐπὶ λύσει, because in that transaction ownership of the security, with or without actual possession, was transferred to the creditor."[20] But the evidence we have does not support such a sequence of development. If anything, it suggests that *hypotheke* came first, since the terminology associated with that form of security is found as early as 378/77, whereas the earliest dated *horoi* using the language of *prasis epi lysei* come from

[15] The phrase ἐπὶ λύσει is omitted in the text of the inscription, but for the sake of argument I have followed previous scholars who have interpreted the claim as arising from a *prasis epi lysei*.

[16] Crosby (1941) 22.

[17] Finley (1953) 491 note 45.

[18] See Ferguson (1944) 70 (for his criticism of Crosby's suggestion, see 83).

[19] For further criticisms of Fine's interpretation of this inscription, see Finley (1953).

[20] Fine (1951) 93. Fine did not offer any evidence to back up these assertions, both of which are questionable.

the archonship of Praxibulus (315/14).[21] However, this did not deter Fine, who asserted (62, cf. 92) that "it is certainly hazardous to claim without question as a hypothec every contract referred to by the verbs ὑποτιθέναι or ὑποκεῖσθαι. The possibility must not be excluded that these verbs might have had merely a general meaning, signifying any type of contract in which real security was involved." Yet if this were so, how can Fine determine when these verbs refer to *hypotheke* and when they do not? Any criterion for determining how these verbs are used, in a general sense ("any type of contract in which real security was used") or in the specific sense, must be established on the basis of the information found in the orators; however, Fine tells us that their use of terminology is unreliable as a guide. Yet without the assistance of this evidence, how are we to formulate a definition of *hypotheke* in the first place? In short, Fine's attempt to explain away troublesome evidence creates more problems than it solves. It is clear that our sources present insurmountable obstacles to his theory, obstacles that cannot be removed by special pleading nor by forced interpretations of the evidence.[22]

We can now turn to Finley's views. Following the lead of A. Manigk, Finley holds that real security in Classical and Hellenistic Athens was substitutive in nature.[23] Despite his disagreement with Fine over this issue, Finley is in perfect accord with him on one point of cardinal importance, namely, that the Athenians had two different forms of security. When it came to identifying the differences between *hypotheke* and *prasis epi lysei*, however, Finley is at something of a loss. In his analysis of Dem. 37, which he thought contained an account of a series of transactions involving *prasis epi lysei*, Finley (33–4) states:

> Essentially, then, the speech deals with a series of manoeuvers and deals in the field of security, not genuine sale. Though conveyance of the property occurs and recurs over his head, Pantainetos remains in continuous

[21] The verb is used to describe hypothecation in *IG* ii² 43, line 40 (378/77) and is used by Isocrates (21.2) when describing how a certain Nicias hypothecated his house during the reign of the Thirty. Herodotus (2.136) also uses the verb ὑποτιθέναι when describing the Egyptian practice of pledging the corpse of one's father as security for a loan. On the other hand, the earliest dated *horoi* that use the language of *prasis epi lysei* come from the archonship of Praxibulus (315/14): *horoi* nos. 11, 14, 27, 76, 85. Kirchner (*IG* ii² 2724) restored the name of the archon in *horos* no. 13 as Apollodorus (319/18). Dow and Travis (1943) 162–3 proposed Nicodorus.

[22] Although Fine's own theory is not convincing, his work does contain valuable criticisms of the views of Paoli and Meletopoulos.

[23] Manigk (1916) cols. 292–321.

> possession and control so long as he meets the interest payments and the mysterious unidentified terms of the agreement. When he defaults, the creditors take the security as forfeit; this they would have done whether the transaction was called *prasis epi lysei* or *hypotheke* or *apotimema*.

These considerations lead Finley to conclude (35) that "*prasis epi lysei* was not a genuine, complete sale" and that "its outward form, then, is sale, the essence hypothecation." That does not get us very far. We are told that *hypotheke* and *prasis epi lysei* are both types of hypothecation, differing in form: but how did these differences in form affect the creditor and the borrower? Were these differences in form accompanied by differences in substance, or do we just have two dissimilar names for one and the same procedure? And if *prasis epi lysei* was in essence hypothecation, why did the Athenians call it sale? To these questions, Finley offers no answers.

On the basis of the fact that "five out of the ten stones marking *hypotheke* obligations mention a contract, but only 8 out of 102 in the *prasis epi lysei* group refer to such an instrument,"[24] Finley (24) tentatively suggests that "the *hypotheke* was somehow more flexible than the *prasis epi lysei* and lent itself more readily to special terms and conditions, hence the more frequent need to commit the agreement to writing." Finley appears to assume that when an inscription on a *horos* records the existence of a loan made on real security, but does not mention any συνθῆκαι, no συνθῆκαι existed.[25] That is a risky assumption: the *horoi* often omit much information, such as the name of the creditor or the amount of the loan.[26] Would Finley have asserted that the absence of the name of the creditor from a *horos* must be explained by the fact that the creditor had no name? And what was it about *hypotheke* that made it more flexible than *prasis epi lysei*? Nor does Finley account for the discrepancy between the orators, who almost invariably use the terminology associated with *hypotheke*, and the *horoi*, which employ the vocabulary of *prasis epi lysei* in all but a handful of cases.[27]

[24] Finley's observation was based on the *horoi* known to him at the time. The discovery of new *horoi* has not affected it. See Millett in Finley (1985) xiii.

[25] Finley's translation of συνθῆκαι as "written contract" is, strictly speaking, incorrect. The word συνθῆκαι refers only to a document that recorded the terms of an agreement and could be used to prove the existence of an agreement. For an analysis of the term, see Kussmaul (1969) 15–20.

[26] For example, *horoi* nos. 1, 23, 45, 51, 52, 61, 62, 72, 75, 78.

[27] Although he was aware of the problem, Finley (1985) 30–1 did not offer a solution to it. Millett in Finley (1985) xiv tries to explain "the puzzling divergence between the *horoi* and the Orators

Although he does not speculate about the introduction of *hypotheke* as Fine does, Finley (35) does hazard a guess about the origin of *prasis epi lysei*:

> The reasons for the creation of such a mixed institution (...) will be found historically in the rise of security transactions in the period where free alienability of landed property was difficult and socially as well as legally restricted, juristically in the problems of execution after default and in the need for a device that would strengthen the creditor's right to evict the debtor and that would protect the new owner's claim to the property.

Finley's argument rests in part on the assumption that at some time before the fourth century BCE "the free alienability of landed property (...) was legally restricted." There is certainly no evidence for the existence of such legislation in Athens during the Archaic and Classical periods. Nor can one maintain that there must have been rules restricting alienability in Athens at this time by arguing that elsewhere in Greece land was inalienable, for, as Finley himself accurately noted, the few pieces of evidence we do have for these periods all "presuppose

on the phraseology of security obligations" with a theory about the use, or rather misuse, of terminology for hypothecation. He begins by citing Finley's observation (Finley [1985] 8) about the lack of precision in Athenian legal terminology and then goes on to claim that the "Orators were not primarily concerned with the technical accuracy of their language; instead they were intent on giving a plausible (though possibly misleading) argument." Finley's observation is sound, but it is irrelevant to Millett's point here. Finley was talking about lack of precision in Athenian legal terminology, which did not possess an elaborate set of subtle distinctions. Millett wishes to make a point about lack of accuracy, a very different matter (one can be imprecise without being inaccurate).

Millett continues by asserting that the desire of the orators to produce a persuasive argument "would naturally lead them to avoid the ambiguous terminology of *prasis epi lysei* with its implications of sale rather than security in favour of the more straightforward vocabulary of hypothecation (though possibly misleading) argument." This is implausible – if the orators "were intent on giving a plausible and persuasive (though possibly misleading) argument," one would expect them to have opted for "the ambiguous terminology of *prasis epi lysei*" with its greater potential for obfuscation in preference to "the more straightforward language of hypothecation." Millett next turns to consider the *horoi* and states that there is "no reason to expect the *horos* inscriptions to reflect with any great precision the nature of the transactions that lay behind them." Drawing attention to the fact that "the prime function of the *horoi* was to warn third parties that the property was somehow encumbered," Millett came to the rather startling conclusion that it "mattered little whether the stone said *hypotheke*, *prasis epi lysei*, or even *apotimema*." This is not plausible either. As Finley (1985) 19 correctly states, "Whatever information the stones did give had to be accurate and up-to-date if the function of public notice were to be properly served."

alienability."[28] Besides, Finley does not say how *prasis epi lysei* would have helped the creditor to overcome these hypothetical restrictions placed on the alienation of property. And, finally, his explanation of the origin of *prasis epi lysei* still does not answer the question of how this form of security differed from *hypotheke*.

Our examination of the respective views of Fine and Finley has revealed shortcomings in each one. Fine's theory is the more ambitious of the two, but it encounters serious difficulties and relies excessively on questionable interpretations of key texts. Finley is far more cautious in his treatment of the evidence. Yet, cautious as he is, Finley is unable to discern any concrete differences between *prasis epi lysei* and *hypotheke* and can do no better than to offer some vague speculation about how *hypotheke* "was somehow more flexible." Their disagreements notwithstanding, both scholars nevertheless believe that a solution to the problem can be sought by going back to the origins of real security in Athens and that *prasis epi lysei* must have been the earlier institution. The question of the "origins" of real security in ancient Athens is an interesting one, but our discussion of it must be postponed. What we need to do first is to understand what the Athenians meant by the terms that they used to express security transactions. Only after we have analyzed how the institution functioned in Classical Athens will we be in a position to investigate the factors that led to its rise.

II

The problem posed by Athenian terminology for real security clearly requires a fresh approach. In my opinion, we should begin by discarding the traditional assumption that we are dealing with two different types of security and consider the possibility that what we have is essentially one form of security that is referred to by two or more kinds of expressions. Such an approach is far from arbitrary. Indeed, it is one that is suggested by the very nature of the evidence we have at our disposal, for, as we have just seen, neither Fine nor Finley has been successful in his attempts to pinpoint any essential differences between the kinds of transactions referred to by the two types of expressions we encounter on the *horoi*.

[28] Finley (1968). Cf. Finley (1957), where it is maintained that in the Homeric poems the property regime is "one of private ownership" and that there was "free untrammeled right to dispose of all movable wealth." By pointing out that land was regularly transferred by inheritance, Finley implies that this held true also for immovable wealth.

There are other considerations that favor such an approach. As Finley (8) has justly stated, the Athenians "lacked the juristic formalism and dogmatism, and the professional jurists necessary to define and preserve the subtle lines of distinction and classification, the *elegantia iuris,* characteristic of Roman and modern law." This absence of subtle legal distinctions can best be illustrated by contrasting Athenian terminology and practice in regard to real security with that of Roman Law.[29] In Roman Law there were essentially two types of real security, *fiducia cum creditore* and *pignus.* In the former, the creditor gained ownership of the security; in the latter, the debtor retained ownership. *Pignus* could take either one of two forms. The first was the earlier form of *pignus* and was referred to by that term.[30] It granted possession, but not ownership, to the creditor. In the second form, known as *hypotheca,* the creditor gained neither ownership nor possession. We know that the Athenians were also familiar with the type of arrangement whereby the creditor took possession of the security (e.g., [Dem.] 49.51–2) and that whereby the debtor remained in possession (e.g., [Dem.] 56.3). When it came to terminology, however, the Athenians made no distinction between the two transactions. In both the same verb, ὑποτιθέναι, is used to describe the act of pledging the security ([Dem.] 49.12, 53)[31] and the pledged object is referred to as τὸ ἐνέχυρον ([Dem.] 49.52; 56.3). In the same fashion, the verb employed to indicate that an object has been pledged as security is the same verb in both arrangements (Dem. 27.9: ὑποκειμένους [creditor in possession]; [Dem.] 49.11: ὑπέκειτο [debtor in possession]). Our example clearly illustrates that the Athenians did not develop a specialized legal vocabulary to distinguish between these two kinds of arrangements. On the contrary, they lumped together what the Romans regarded as different forms of security and described them both with one rough-and-ready set of terms.

Conversely, we find the Athenians were also in the habit of using more than one type of expression to refer to a certain procedure. For instance, in the inscription recording the sale of Theosebes' house by the *poletai,* which we discussed above, two different terms (ἀμφισβητεῖ, ἐνεπεσκήψαντο) are used to express the act of bringing a claim.[32] A recently published *horos* would appear to indicate that this

[29] The following summary of Roman practices in regard to real security derives from Schulz (1951) 406–10.

[30] This is an example of "semantic marking." For a discussion of this phenomenon, see Lyons (1977) 307–8.

[31] In this case it is clear the debtor Timotheus remained in possession. See Fine (1951) 67–9.

[32] The use of these two different terms cannot be explained on the assumption that one arose from a security obligation, whereas the other did not. See Finley (1953) 474 note 4.

was true also in the case of expressions for real security. On this *horos* there are two inscriptions (*horoi* nos. 80A and 81A), the text of each being almost identical with that of the other. In both of these inscriptions we do not find ὑποκειμένης *tout court*, nor πεπραμένης ἐπὶ λύσει, but something of a hybrid: ὑποκειμένης ἐπὶ λύσει. Now we have two choices: we must either arbitrarily force these texts into the category of *hypotheke* or that of *prasis epi lysei*, or invent a third category (call it *hypotheke epi lysei*) to accommodate this recalcitrant inscription. If we adopt the first alternative, we are then compelled to admit that the Athenians could refer to one type of security with two different expressions. But once we admit this, what prevents us from ruling out the possibility that the Athenians could use three different types of expressions to refer to the same kind of transaction? If the expressions ὑποκείμενης ἐπὶ λύσει and πεπραμέμένης ἐπὶ λύσει can refer to the same form of security, why cannot ὑποκειμένης also? On the other hand, we could strictly apply the principle that dictates that for each type of expression there must exist a different form of security. Rigorous adherence to this principle would compel us to create a third form of security to stand alongside the other two. At this point, I think it is better to reach for Ockham's razor and to countenance the possibility that we have not three forms of security, each referred to by one type of expression, but rather one basic form of security referred to by several kinds of expressions.

The reason why modern scholars have readily assumed that the Athenians had two or more forms of real security is not hard to discern: observing that the Romans distinguished between various forms of security, they were led to infer that the Athenians must have done likewise.[33] Such an inference is incorrect, for in this case the analogy with Roman Law is misleading.[34] The Romans were able to differentiate between various forms of security because they possessed formal procedures for the transfer of property (*mancipatio* and *cessio in iure*) and because their laws recognized a sharp distinction between *dominium* and *possessio*.[35] This allowed them to distinguish between *fiducia cum creditore*, in which the borrower transferred

[33] For example, Hitzig (1895) 1–3 (*prasis epi lysei* equated with *fiducia cum creditore*); E. Szanto (1897) 279; Fine (1951) 61 note 3.

[34] For a recent critique of attempts to explain Greek laws in terms of concepts drawn from Roman Law, see Cohen (1983) 5–7.

[35] For *mancipatio* and *cessio in iure*, see Schulz (1951) 344–9. Formal procedures for conveyance also allowed Roman Law to distinguish between two forms of loan, the *mutuum* and the *commodatum* (Schulz [1951] 508). Such a distinction did not exist in Athenian Law: see Wolff (1957) 49–50.

ownership of the security to the creditor by means of mancipatio, and *pignus*, where there was no conveyance. In *fiducia cum creditore* the creditor gained *dominium* and was entitled to protect his right to the security by *vindicatio* and *actiones in rem*, whereas in *pignus* he only gained *possessio* and had to protect his right by means of a possessory interdict.[36] The Athenians, of course, knew nothing of such formal procedures for the transfer of property. For them the principle of the cash sale prevailed.[37] In the absence of anything resembling the *mancipatio*, they considered that ownership was transferred once the price was paid. Thus, in transactions of sale the Athenians had a simple means of determining when, and if, ownership was transferred. But without any formal procedures for conveyance, the Athenians had no way of differentiating between a form of security in which ownership was transferred to the creditor and another in which it was retained by the debtor. Nor could they distinguish between an arrangement whereby the creditor gained ownership (*dominium*) and one whereby he gained only the right of possession (*possessio*). The Athenians were well aware of the difference between ownership and possession, but their laws made no use of this distinction by granting one set of remedies to those who had ownership and another to those who merely enjoyed possession.[38] Put simply, the Athenians had nothing that resembled the possessory interdicts of Roman Law. Even had they wanted to, the Athenians just did not have the legal mechanisms that would have enabled them to create, and distinguish among, various forms of security.

Our discussion in this section has revealed that there are three considerations that tell in favor of an approach that starts from the assumption that the Athenians had essentially one form of security, which they referred to by various different terms. These considerations are: 1) the failure of attempts by previous scholars to unearth any concrete distinctions between the security transactions referred to by the different forms of expression used to refer to hypothecation; 2) the fact that the Athenians did on occasion use more than one term to refer to a single type of legal procedure; and 3) the absence in Classical Athens of any formal modes for conveyance that would have enabled them to differentiate between forms of security. We now need to examine the evidence.

[36] Schulz (1951) 406–7. *Pignus* was later protected by the *actio Serviana*.

[37] For the principle of the cash sale, see Pringsheim (1950) 179–219.

[38] Awareness of the distinction can be seen in various texts (e.g., [Dem.] 7.26). See Pringsheim (1950) 9–13; M. Kaser (1944) 136–7.

III

Our next task is to examine the terms that the Athenians used to describe transactions involving loans and real security and to determine what these terms implied by examining the contexts in which they are found. That is the only valid way of discovering what these terms mean. What we must not do is to assume *a priori* that the Athenians had formal legal definitions for the words they used to describe this kind of transaction and then try to make the evidence conform to these definitions. That kind of approach takes for granted the existence in Athens of a body of legislation that regulated transactions involving real security. Unfortunately, there is no evidence at all for this kind of legislation in Athens during the Classical and Hellenistic periods.[39] On the contrary, the meanings and implications of terms like ὑποκεῖσθαι and ὑποτιθέναι were established by common usage, not by legislative or judicial fiat.[40] Naturally, the best place to find how these terms were employed in common usage is in the works of the Attic orators, who not only use the terminology in several passages, but, more importantly, give us some information about the nature of the transactions that are referred to by these terms. The same cannot be said about the *horoi*. Despite the Attic provenance, the *horoi* are quite laconic about the details of the transactions that led to their creation. They are therefore of little assistance at this stage of our investigation.

We will begin by examining the more straightforward terms and leave aside for the moment the more problematic terms that employ the vocabulary of sale. The verb that is most commonly used in the orations to signify the act of lending is δανείζειν.[41] The loan is called a δάνεισμα.[42] "To lend on security" is expressed by the verb δανείζειν with the addition of the preposition ἐπί; the

[39] Finley (1985) 113, 296–7.

[40] My approach is similar to that of Cohen (1983) 6–7. Cohen, however, fails to appreciate the difference between ordinary language and legal language and in places appears to assume that words in common usage are used with the same precision and consistency as they are in statutes, which often begin with legal definitions of the terms they employ. For instance, his attempt to draw a clear-cut distinction between the verbs κλέπτειν and ἀποστερεῖν breaks down in the face of passages that refer to the embezzlement of public funds, as Cohen (1983) 30–3 himself recognizes. For a shrewd assessment of the differences between ordinary language and legal language, see Austin (1961) 132–7.

[41] For example, Dem. 37.4; [Dem.] 56.3 and the passages listed in note 43. The same verb is used in its middle form with the meaning "to borrow from": [Dem.] 56.3, 6.

[42] [Dem.] 49.12; 56.1; Dem. 35.9.

object pledged as security follows the preposition in the dative.[43] The debtor who pledges something as security is said to ὑποτιθέναι the security, while the creditor is said to ὑποτίθεσθαι (middle).[44] The security itself is called τὸ ἐνέχυρον.[45] As we observed above, this term can be used of a security that is held either by the debtor or by the creditor; the use of this word to describe a security implies nothing about the actual possession of the security. The security is said to ὑποκεῖσθαι or ὑποτίθεσθαι (passive) – the name of the creditor may follow in the dative and the amount of the loan in the genitive.[46] The debtor who defaulted was called ὑπερήμερος.[47] The verbs used to describe the taking of possession by the creditor after default are ἐμβατεύειν various forms of λαμβάνεσθαι (middle).[48]

Certain passages indicate that the creditor could be regarded as the owner of the security. For instance, in his second speech against Aphobus, Demosthenes (28.18) told the court that he would be reduced to an awful plight if their vote went against him since an adverse verdict would leave him with no property; much of what he did own had been pledged as security for a loan that he had taken to perform a trierarchy. The hypothecated property was no longer his, but belonged to this creditors (ἀλλὰ τῶν ὑποθεμένων ἐστίν).[49] More evidence for this view can be found in the inscription that recorded the charter of the Second Athenian League. In this document (*IG* ii² 43, lines 37–40), we learn of the guarantees granted by the Athenians to the cities that joined the league. Among them is a provision making it illegal for any Athenian to "acquire a house or land in the

[43] Dem. 32.12, 14; 36.6, 18; 37.50; [Dem.] 49.53. For the term ἐπιδανείζειν, which appears to have had the same meaning in certain cases, see Finley (1985) 297.

[44] For the active, see Dem. 28.17–18; [Dem.] 49.12, 52; Isoc. 21.2; Lys. 19.25. For the middle, see Dem. 28.18; [Dem.] 49.51 (the verb is mistranslated by A. T. Murray in his Loeb edition of the speech); 50.55; *IG* ii² 43, line 40. Sometimes the simplex takes the place of the compound: [Dem.] 53.10, 12, 13; Is. 5.21; *horos* no. 102, line 12. In *IG* ii² 43, lines 40–2 we find the compound followed by the simplex in the next line. This is an example of a syntactic phenomenon that has been noted by several scholars. See Watkins (1967).

[45] Dem. 33.10; [Dem.] 49.2, 52, 53; 56.3.

[46] [Dem.] 49.11; *horoi* 1, 2, 4, 5, 6, 7.

[47] Dem. 21.11; 33.6; 45.70. Cf. Pollux 3.85.

[48] Dem. 27.26; 37.7; [Dem.] 35.25. Note also the verb ἐνεχυράζειν at Ar. *Nub.* 241; *Ec.* 567 with Finley (1985) 222–3 note 6.

[49] For the genitive denoting ownership as opposed to mere possession, see Kaser (1944) 136–7. Note also that Nicobulus calls the property that was pledged by Pantaenetus to Evergus and himself "ours" (Dem. 37.7, 9, 29).

territory of the allies" (ἐγκτήσασθαι ἐν ταῖς συμμάχων χώραις μήτε οἰκίαν μήτε χωρίον), either by "buying" (πριαμένῳ) or by "receiving as a security" (ὑποθεμένῳ). The verb ἐγκτήσασθαι clearly means "to acquire ownership," for it is applied to the person who buys property.[50] What is notable in this decree is that the person who buys property is put on exactly the same footing as the one who accepts it as security, and both are described as gaining ownership. One should not attempt to evade the implications of this passage by claiming "Most probably it is an elliptical way of saying that the Athenians shall not be permitted to accept real property as security because the potential consequence is foreclosure and thereby the acquisition of property."[51] Such an interpretation certainly reads too much into the text, the meaning of which is clear as it stands. The ineluctable conclusion that follows from this passage is that the creditor could be considered the owner of the security.

Further evidence for this observation can be found in Demosthenes' account (Dem. 27.9–11) of his father's estate. Among the items listed there are twenty slaves engaged in manufacturing couches, from which his father received an annual revenue of twelve *mnai*. These slaves had been received as security for a debt of forty *mnai* owed him by a certain Moerades.[52] Now we would make a distinction between his possession of these slaves and his ownership of the thirty-two or thirty-three engaged in making knives, who are also included in Demosthenes' inventory. But the orator makes no such distinction, listing them alongside each other and making them both objects of the same verb κατέλιπε. This is strange to our way of thinking – we would regard the slaves pledged as security to be the property of the debtor Moerades; in drawing up an inventory of the estate of Demosthenes *père*, we would list Moerades' debt of forty *mnai* as owing to the estate and indicate that the twenty slaves were pledged as security for this debt. In calculating the total value of the estate, we would not add in the capital value of the slaves pledged as security, but only the amount of the debt owed by Moerades. This is in fact what modern commentators do, but it is not what Demosthenes *fils* appears to have done.[53] Demosthenes says that the slaves in the cutlery shop were

[50] Note also that the noun ἔγκτησις, which is formed from the same root, means "the right to own land." For a study of this term see Peçirka (1966).

[51] Finley (1985) 263. If the author of the decree had meant to refer to the acquisition of property by means of foreclosure, he would surely have used one of the verbs normally used for that procedure.

[52] For the name of the debtor, see Dem. 27.27.

[53] For the traditional analysis of the problem posed by this passage, see Davies (1971) 129–30.

worth "'five or six, and not less than three *mnai*." This seems to point toward an average value of about five *mnai*, a figure that would give us a total of about two talents, forty or forty-five *mnai* for all thirty-two or thirty-three slaves in the cutlery shop. Further on, Demosthenes tells us that the total value of the slaves in the cutlery shop, those engaged in making couches, and one talent lent out at interest came to a sum of four talents, fifty *mnai*. If we assume that Demosthenes assumed a value of forty *mnai* (the amount of the loan for which they were hypothecated) for the slaves in the furniture shop, we are forced to conclude that his arithmetic is "hopelessly inaccurate."[54] Such an unsatisfactory explanation should cause us to question the method by which it was arrived at. It is true that Demosthenes does tend to round off sums in his calculations elsewhere in this speech, but he does not make serious errors (e.g., Dem. 27.11,17, 37). Luckily, there is another method of approach: we can assume that Demosthenes used the capital value of the slaves in the furniture shop in assessing the value of this part of his father's estate. By simple arithmetic, we then arrive at a figure of about sixty-five or seventy *mnai* as the capital value of these slaves.[55] This is well within the limits of probability, for we know that it was not unusual for the value of the security to be as much as double the amount of the loan.[56]

One might try to discredit this evidence by arguing that Demosthenes is being dishonest and misrepresenting the situation (it would not be the only time). But if the Athenians thought that all encumbered property belonged to the debtor and that the creditor could not claim to be the owner of the security, Demosthenes, when attempting to misrepresent the extent of his father's estate, would not have admitted that the slaves in the cutlery shop had been pledged as security.

[54] Finley (1985) 116 ("Yet Demosthenes (...) does not think of re-calculating the value of the slaves in market-terms"). Finley curiously ignores the additional loan of 500 *drachmai* made on the security of the slaves (Dem. 27.27). That Moerades was able to contract this additional loan on the slaves from Aphobus indicates that foreclosure had not taken place before the death of Demosthenes' father. One cannot, therefore, argue that Demosthenes regards Moerades' slaves as part of his father's property because he had obtained them through foreclosure.

[55] If we calculate the market value of the slaves in the furniture shop at about 65–70 *mnai*, the annual income of 12 *mnai* would represent an annual return on investment of about 18 percent, which is comparable to that received from the slaves in the cutlery shop (30 *mnai* a year on an investment of about 160–5 *mnai*). I do not think that the Athenians actually calculated such things with any precision. Nevertheless, we would expect the price of slaves to be proportional to the value of the goods they were able to produce. For the prices of slaves varying in relation to the value of their skills, see Meiggs and Lewis (1969) 247.

[56] For securities worth twice as much at the amount of the loan, see [Dem.] 34.6; 35.18; Dem. 37.4, 31.

Quite the opposite, he would have simply said that these slaves formed part of the estate and suppressed any mention of the fact that they were being held as security, for that would have immediately given away his deceit. The only way to make sense of the passage is to assume that Demosthenes considered his father the owner of these slaves and that when assessing the value of his father's property, he accordingly used their capital value, not the amount of the loan for which they had been hypothecated. Evidently the court saw nothing amiss in Demosthenes' method of bookkeeping, for they awarded him the amount he claimed.[57]

Athens was apparently not the only Greek city during this period where the creditor might consider himself to be the owner of the security. In an inscription dated to about 300 from the island of Amorgos (*horos* no. 102), we read that a certain Niceratus along with Hegecrate and her *kyrios* Telenicus had pledged three properties as security (ἀπέδοτο... ἐπὶ λύσει) to a man named Ctesiphon in return for a loan of 5,000 *drachmai*. To show that he was the legitimate owner of these properties pledged as security, Niceratus specified how he had acquired each of them. The first he had received as the result of a division of an inheritance with his brother (lines 7–9); the second was bought from a man named Ischyrion (lines 9–11). It is the third that interests us; this property, we are informed, Niceratus had received from someone called Exacestus (lines 11–14: ἔχει θέμενος).[58] In much the same way as Demosthenes did in describing his father's estate, the inscription lists the hypothecated property alongside the two other properties that are owned outright. Despite the fact that he has received it only as security, Niceratus treats the property of Exacestus as if it were his own and uses it as security for a loan from Ctesiphon. The implication should be clear – Niceratus regards the security as his own property, just as Demosthenes *fils* considered Moerades' slaves to form part of his father's estate. The inscription from Amorgos cannot of course be used as evidence for practices in Attica. Amorgos was probably influenced by Athenian

[57] For Demosthenes' victory see Dem. 30.2. To judge from Demosthenes' reply to Aphobos' defense (Dem. 28), it does not appear that Aphobos disputed this part of Demosthenes' calculation of the amount owed to him.

[58] ἔχει θέμενος is a perfect periphrastic and means "has received as security." ἔχει is only an auxiliary verb and has no independent meaning. For the construction, see Aerts (1965) 128–60. Paoli (1930) 153–4, did not recognize the construction and misconstrued the force of ἔχει, which he took to imply that the creditor had possession. Finley (1985) 205 made the same mistake and asserted incorrectly that the inscription indicated "that there had been default."

customs in regard to the use of *horoi*, but this should not be taken to indicate that the practices of both states were completely similar in other respects.[59] Nonetheless, it does reveal that elsewhere in the Greek world the creditor might regard himself as the owner of the security, and thereby provides some support, albeit indirect, for our analysis of Demosthenes' account of his father's estate.

Since the creditor could be considered the owner of the security, the act of pledging a security could be regarded as a sale. We find evidence for this in the speech *Against Apaturius* ([Dem.] 33). In the part of the speech that concerns us, the defendant recounts how Apaturius had failed to make payment on a loan and was being pressed by his creditors, who were about to seize his ship (6: ἐνεβάτευον εἰς τὴν ναῦν, εἰληφότες τῇ ὑπερημερίᾳ). Parmeno, a friend of Apaturius, agreed to give him ten *mnai* and asked the defendant to contribute thirty *mnai*. The defendant had no cash on hand, but was able to convince the banker Heracleides to lend Parmeno the necessary sum and to accept him as guarantor of the loan. Shortly thereafter, Parmeno had a falling-out with Apaturius and requested that the defendant assume responsibility for the loan. Parmeno had already given Apaturius three *mnai*; the defendant came up with the balance, which he handed over to Apaturius, and then drew up an agreement in which he listed himself as the creditor for the entire loan of ten *mnai*. According to the terms of the agreement, Apaturius pledged his ship as security for the money owed both to the defendant and to the bank. Later on in the speech, after describing how the money was finally repaid, the defendant refers to the entire transaction as a loan (ἐδανείσθη), which it undoubtedly was. Yet, when the agreement was drawn up by which the ship was pledged as security, the transaction is called a sale (8: ὠνὴν ποιοῦμαι τῆς νεὼς καὶ τῶν παίδων). The text also makes it clear that the defendant was to remain owner only until Apaturius repaid the loan (ἕως ἀποδοίη). Just the same, the transaction is labeled a sale.

Such a conception of lending on security seems terribly mistaken to our way of thinking. We do not interpret a secured loan as a form of sale; in our eyes, as for the Romans, the pledge of security has a purely accessory character, serving only to ensure repayment of the loan in case of default.[60] We do not view hypothecation as a form of sale whereby the creditor "pays" the loan and receives a right to the

[59] For a decisive refutation of the view that the legal practices of the Greek city-states were roughly similar, see M. I. Finley (1966) (= Finley [1975] 134–52).

[60] For the accessory character of real security, see Schulz (1951) 420–2.

security in exchange for cash, since the aim of the transaction is not an exchange of goods for cash as it is in sale. The creditor enters into the agreement to reap interest, not to gain ownership of the security. Similarly, the debtor consents to the agreement with the intention of making temporary use of the cash provided by the loan, not of parting with the security in return for the cash. But we should not let our own conception of the transaction stand in the way of our attempt to understand how the Athenians construed it.

The habit of regarding the creditor as the owner of the security and the act of hypothecation as a form of sale had one curious side effect – it led to confusion about the proper label to attach to the repayment made by the debtor to the creditor. Since the transaction was in essence a loan, the monthly payments could be called interest (τόκος) and the final payment of the total sum given to the creditor as the repayment of the principal (κεφάλαιον). Yet, since the security was thought of as having been sold to the creditor, the debtor who remained in possession of the security, which consisted of a house or a workshop, was in a position analogous to that of the lessee who had rented the property of another (μίσθωσις).[61] As a result, the repayment of the principal could also be regarded as a sale whereby the debtor bought back his security by paying its price (τιμή) to the creditor. We find an example of this phenomenon in a passage from Isaeus' speech *On the Estate of Dicaeogenes* (5.21). Here we are told by the speaker Menexenus how Dicaeogenes had consented to renounce two-thirds of the estate he had inherited from his father (also called Dicaeogenes), then reneged on this agreement. It is also pointed out that at the time of the agreement Dicaeogenes was no longer in possession of the entire estate; instead, it was held by those who had bought it from him or had received it as security (21: οἱ παρὰ τούτου πριάμενοι καὶ θέμενοι). Menexenus insists that Dicaeogenes should have handed over this land unencumbered, that is, that he should have bought it back from those to whom he had sold it and have paid off the loans to show who had received it as security. We would think of these two transactions as fundamentally different. In one transaction property is bought back by means of sale, whereas in the other a loan is paid off and the security is thereby redeemed. Yet that is not how Menexenus saw it. He says that Dicaeogenes should have handed over property after having

[61] For the custom of calling the agreement between the creditor and the debtor who remained in possession of the security a lease, see Section IV. Note also the use of the word μίσθωσις on *horos* no. 102, line 15, where we would expect to find the word τόκος.

"given back the price" (ἀποδόντα τὴν τιμήν) both to those who had bought the property and to those who had received his property as security. No difference is made between buying back one set of properties and removing the lien on another set. The latter transaction is viewed as analogous to the former, and the same expression is employed to describe both. We would say that Dicaeogenes should have repaid the principal on the loan in order to redeem the hypothecated properties. Being an Athenian who could consider the creditor to be the owner of the security, however, Menexenus says that he should buy them back from the creditors by paying them the price.

All the evidence we have examined thus far appears to indicate that the Athenians regarded the creditor as the owner of the security and interpreted hypothecation as a form of sale. Yet other evidence seems to reveal exactly the opposite. Take, for instance, the inscription recording the sale of Theosebes' house by the *poletai*, which we examined in Section I. From that inscription we learn that the house of Theosebes had been pledged as security for several loans, two contracted by his father Theophilus, another by himself. If the creditors could be regarded as the owners of the security, the house of Theosebes should have belonged to those who had received it as security and the *poletai* would not have been entitled to confiscate it. But that is exactly what did happen – the house is consistently called "the house of Theosebes" and the *poletai* seized it as part of their confiscation of Theosebes' property and sold it to a certain Lysanias (lines 35–6). Evidently, the *poletai* regarded the security as still belonging to the debtor.[62]

We should also note that three successive loans were made on the same security in this case. Yet, if the security was thought to pass into the ownership of the creditor, how could Theophilus have then pledged it as security for another loan? And how could Theosebes have inherited it and pledged it as security for a loan if it had already passed into the hands of his father's creditors? It is clear that not only the *poletai*, but Theophilus and Theosebes as well, were operating on the assumption that the security belonged to the debtor.

[62] I do not understand how Finley (1953) 481 can state that this inscription "offers the first unequivocal instance of collateral security in Athens." To provide an "unequivocal instance of collateral security," we would have to come upon a case where the creditor foreclosed on a defaulting debtor and was required either by law or by contract to sell the security and to return to the debtor the difference between the sale price and the amount of the loan. But all the inscription tells us is that the *poletai* confiscated the house, paid off the debts owed by Theosebes, and then sold the house. It deals with confiscation, not foreclosure, and is thus not relevant to the issue of the existence of collateral security.

The same implication emerges from a passage in the demosthenic speech *Against Lacritus* ([Dem.] 35.21–2). According to the speaker Androcles, he and Nausicrates lent to Artemo and Apollodorus three thousand *drachmai* on the security of a cargo of three thousand jars of wine. As part of the agreement, Artemo and Apollodorus promised not to make any further loans on this security (cf. 10–11). If the creditors Androcles and Nausicrates could be regarded as the owners of the security, it would not have been possible for Artemo and Apollodorus to contract further loans on the cargo since they no longer owned it; in the event that they tried to, Androcles could have argued that the claims of these additional creditors were invalid because Artemo and Apollodorus owned the cargo and were thus not entitled to hypothecate it to anyone else. But that is not the argument that Androcles employs. Instead, he attacks Artemon and Apollodorus for contravening the terms of the agreement and never questions the validity of the claim made by the other creditor to whom his opponents hypothecated the cargo.

At this point, one might be tempted to ask, "What is going on here? Who owns the security, the creditor or the debtor?" To answer this question, we need first to recall the observations we made in Section II where we noted that the Athenians had no formal procedures for conveyance and thus lacked a means of answering the question "Who owned the security?" Because there was no legally prescribed method of resolving the question, each person naturally tended to answer it in the way that was most advantageous to himself. And so the creditor regarded himself as the owner of the security, and the debtor acted as if it belonged to him. For instance, it was obviously in Demosthenes' interest to represent the slaves that had been pledged by Moerades as security to his father as part of his father's estate. That way he could use the capital value (about sixty-five or seventy *mnai*) rather than the amount of the loan (forty *mnai*) when reckoning the losses he had suffered at the hands of his guardians. The same is true of Niceratus, the citizen of Amorgos who hypothecated to Ctesiphon the property he had received as security from Exacestus. He too found it advantageous to regard himself as the owner of the property Exacestus had hypothecated to him since it enabled him in turn to pledge it as security to Ctesiphon.[63]

[63] The creditor who delivered the speech *Against Apaturius* was also of the same opinion ([Dem.] 33.8). For other creditors who regarded themselves as the owners of the security, see Dem. 37 with the discussion in Section IV.

In similar fashion, it was in the interest of the debtor to regard the security as remaining in his ownership. The main attraction of such an interpretation was that it allowed him to contract further loans on the same security. When Theosebes pledged the house that his father already had hypothecated to the *koinon* of the Medontidai *phrateres* and to the *koinon* of *orgeones* as security for a loan to Smicythus, he obviously considered it his own property, not that of his father's creditors. So did the *poletai* and Theomnestus, the man who filed the *apographe* with them. For all these men, it was advantageous to regard the security as the property of the debtor. For Theosebes it meant that he could contract additional loans on the house; for the *poletai* it meant that they could confiscate the house and sell it; for Theomnestus it meant that he could receive his reward from the proceeds of the sale.

A debtor might, however, wish for rhetorical reasons to represent the security as belonging to his creditors. Take, for example, the passage where Demosthenes (28.18) describes to the court the dire straits to which he had been reduced by the trierarchy that he had been compelled to undertake as a result of the challenge made by Thrasylochus. To show how desperate his situation was, Demosthenes points out that he had no further resources to draw on – he could not use his own property since τῶν ὑποθεμένων ἐστίν. The fact of the matter is that he could probably have contracted further loans on his property. But mention of this possibility would have been contrary to his rhetorical aim in this passage, where he is trying to stress his helplessness in an effort to win the sympathy of the court.[64]

The confusion that reigned in the field of hypothecation about the ownership of the security is not without parallel in other areas of Athenian Law. The suit that Dareius brought against Dionysodorus ([Dem.] 56) affords an example of the sort of confusion that could arise in the area of maritime loans as a result of the absence of legislation regulating the language of maritime contracts. The dispute in this case concerned a loan of 3,000 *drachmai*, which Darieus and his associate Pamphilus had lent to Dionysodorus and Parmeniscus on the security of their ship (3). The terms of the loan recorded in the *syngraphe* specified the money was lent for a voyage from Athens to Egypt and back; if the borrowers used the money

[64] The law recorded on *IG* ii² 43 considers the creditors the owners of the security for the sake of completeness; it is trying to cover all possible ways of acquiring ownership.

for a voyage to any other port, they were to pay double the amount of the principal as a penalty (5–6, 10–11, 20). As was customary in maritime loans, the *syngraphe* included a clause that stated that the lenders had to pay only in the event that the ship returned safely to the Piraeus (22, 31). Parmeniscus sailed the ship to Egypt and upon his arrival there bought wheat and other goods. According to Dionysodorus, the ship was damaged on the return voyage and forced to put in at Rhodes, where its cargo was unloaded (20–1). When Dareius and Pamphilus learned of this, they confronted Dionysodorus, who offered to pay them the principal and the interest that had accrued as far as Rhodes (12–13, 33–4, 38, 41), an offer that several other creditors had accepted (22). Still insisting that they were entitled to the full payment agreed to in the *syngraphe*, Dareius and Pamphilus expressed their willingness to follow the suggestion of some bystanders who advised them to take what Dionysodorus had offered and to submit the dispute about the remaining interest to the court (13–14). Dionysodorus responded by asking them to destroy the *syngraphe* in return for his consent to this compromise (14–16). This request was naturally turned down by Dareius and Pamphilus, who knew that the *syngraphe* was their only means of proving their claim to the disputed interest (14–16). Unable to reach a settlement out of court, Dareius brought a suit against Dionysodorus. In the speech he delivered at the trial, Dareius indicated that Dionsyodorus would defend himself in part by claiming that he did not have to repay the loan since his ship was damaged and could not have returned safely to the Piraeus, thereby releasing him from the terms of the loan, which specified that he had to repay only in the event that the ship returned safely (31–2, 35, 41). In other words, Dionysodorus gave a broad interpretation of this clause, which he argued gave exemption to himself and to his partner not only if the ship sank, but also in the eventuality that it suffered damage and was unable to continue safely on its journey. Dareius not unexpectedly ridiculed this interpretation and offered a narrower one of his own. In his view the condition σωθείσης τῆς νεὼς had indeed been fulfilled since the ship had not sunk and was at present plying the seas. Dionysodorus, therefore, owed him and his partner the entire amount he had agreed to pay in the *syngraphe*. Once again, we have a case where there are two possible interpretations of a key phrase and each litigant selects the one that suits his position.[65] What is interesting about this case is that neither Dareius nor

[65] My interpretation of this speech owes much to the fine analysis of Meyer-Laurin (1965) 12–15.

Dionysodorus (at least as far as we can tell from his opponent's speech) appealed to any laws to justify his interpretation of the disputed phrase. Their failure to do so strongly suggests that there was no relevant legislation to guide them in this matter and consequently each man was left free to interpret the clause as he wished. The situation was much the same in the field of real security where in the absence of any legal regulations there was no way of resolving the question of who owned the hypothecated property.

We must be careful not to draw the wrong conclusions from our discussion and attempt to explain Athenian practices regarding real security in terms of a conception of ownership that differs from our own and that of the Romans. The concepts of ownership and of the transfer of ownership are well-nigh universal, shared by all civilizations. What sets one civilization apart from another is the way in which each one goes about protecting ownership and resolving disputes about ownership. One society may also have ways of determining how and when ownership is transferred that differ from those of another society. The Romans had formal modes of conveyance and a large body of legal doctrine about *traditio* to guide their judges in cases arising out of disagreements about ownership. When two Roman citizens quarreled about who owned a piece of land, they had recourse to a legal system that possessed a set of criteria that judges could use to clarify the issues at stake and perhaps even to resolve the dispute. The Athenians were very different and tended to rely more on commonsense notions such as the principle of the cash sale. When asked at what point ownership is transferred, they replied with the answer that seemed most obvious to them, namely, when the buyer pays the price to the seller. Such an approach worked adequately in most of the situations they encountered. But not in all. In the field of hypothecation their commonsense notions were insufficient, and the upshot was uncertainty about the ownership of property pledged as security. So everyone interpreted the transaction in the way that suited him best.

When using the vocabulary of sale and ownership, the Athenians of the Classical period were very much like Socrates' interlocutors in the earlier dialogues of Plato. Socrates' companions always know how to use words like "courage," "piety," and "justice" and can tell in most cases when these terms are used correctly and when they are not. What they cannot do is produce satisfactory definitions of them. Their inability to formulate satisfactory definitions does not imply that they do not understand what these terms signify; it simply means that they are incapable of formulating criteria that can explain why one usage of a given term is correct while another is not. One does not need to have a satisfactory definition of a word in mind to be able to employ that word correctly in conversation. The need for a satisfactory definition becomes pressing only when there is a disagreement about how to use a word; for instance, when one person calls an action just while another deems it unjust. To resolve this kind of dispute, it is necessary to have definite criteria that can be applied to determine which usage is the correct one.[66] The average Athenian found himself in an analogous position with regard to the terminology of ownership and the transfer of ownership. He knew how to use words like πέπρασθαι, ἀποδίδοσθαι, and ὠνεῖσθαι, and employed them in conversation to communicate with others in the *agora* and elsewhere. He knew what a sale was when he saw one and understood that when Nicodemus paid Astyphilus a sum of money for a plot of land, the former gained ownership and the latter lost it. The absence of any formal procedures for the transfer of property such as the *mancipatio* did not prevent the Athenians from transferring property, nor did it render them incapable of comprehending the implications of the transaction. The absence of any formal modes of conveyance or legal doctrines about the transfer of ownership became a problem only when the Athenians encountered an ambiguous situation, such as pledging some property as security for a loan. In hypothecation the creditor loaned money to the borrower, who in return pledged some of his property as security. By hypothecating this piece of property, the borrower temporarily lost his right to alienate it and the creditor gained the right to seize it if the borrower defaulted. But who owned it? The Romans had an easy way of answering the question: they simply asked whether *mancipatio* or *in iure cessio* had been performed. If either one had been performed, the borrower lost ownership; if neither had been, the borrower was still the owner. Without such procedures as these the Athenians, like Socrates' interlocutors, were not capable of giving a definitive answer to this question. For them the ownership of the security remained in a legal limbo in which there reigned a sort of free-for-all with everyone guided only by his own self-interest, not by juristic precepts.

Previously it was believed that the Athenians had at least two forms of hypothecation, one in which the borrower retained ownership of the security, the other where the creditor gained ownership. A rather different picture has emerged from

[66] Of course, Socrates and Plato viewed the problem somewhat differently. See Robinson (1953) 49–53.

our review of the evidence. We can now see that the Athenians did not have two or more forms of real security, but essentially one type of security where the borrower and the creditor each considered himself the owner of the security. Our next step will be to apply this conclusion to that piece of evidence that has so far proven to be the most difficult to make sense of.

IV

We are at last in a position to examine the relevant parts of the oration that Demosthenes composed for Nicobulus to be delivered in his *paragraphe* against his former debtor Pantaenetus (Dem. 37). This speech contains an extensive account of a complex series of transactions involving real security. Besides shedding much light on the topic of security transactions in Classical Athens, the speech also affords a rare glimpse into the practices of Athenian businessmen.[67] Most important, it reveals how different sets of creditors viewed their relationship with one another and what informal procedures they employed to resolve disputes involving two separate loans made on the same security. Because of the complexity of the case, it will be best to analyze in chronological order the events that are narrated by Nicobulus and to digress where appropriate.[68]

After a short introduction stating the nature of the case and containing the customary appeal to the good will of the court, Nicobulus begins his narration with a

[67] I do not consider it anachronistic to speak of "businessmen" and "entrepreneurs" in Classical Athens. For the presence of "economic activities of a capitalist kind" in the Ancient World, see the sensible comments of Goody (1986) 177–84. For Athens in particular, see Thompson (1982) 53–85.

[68] There have been several discussions of this speech. Among the more recent are Harrison (1968) 274–9; Finley (1985) 32–5; Fine (1951) 146–50. Carey and Reid (1985) 105–59 provide a very detailed and generally helpful commentary on the speech, but make no original contribution to the discussion of problems involving real security. On most issues they tend to follow Finley. Finley's analysis of the speech is flawed by his refusal to accept the implications of Nicobulus' use of the language of sale. Finley (1985) 224 note 11 tries to justify his interpretation of the use of the language of sale in contexts dealing with hypothecation by appealing to a passage from Pollux, *Onomasticon* 8.142 (= Hyp. fr. 193 Blass): Ὑπερείδης δὲ ἐν τῷ πρὸς Χάρητα ἔφη ἀποδόμενος ἀντὶ τοῦ ὑποθείς. Finley claims that in this entry Pollux "had noted the use of ἀποδόμενος without the appended ἐπὶ λύσει, and indicated that in that passage it meant 'hypothecate', not 'sell.' " That is not what Pollux indicates at all. The lexicographer merely indicates that in the passage in question Hyperides used the word ἀποδόμενος instead of (ἀντὶ) the word ὑποθείς. All this means is that in this passage the word is a virtual synonym of ὑποθείς. Nowhere in the entry does Pollux deny that the verb means "sell" or that it carries the implications associated with ownership. (I owe this observation to Professor M. Dilts.)

straightforward description of his relationship with the defendant Pantaenetus; we are told that Nicobulus and his friend Evergus lent 105 *mnai* to Pantaenetus on the security of a workshop in Maroneia and the thirty slaves in it (ἐδανείσαμεν πέντε καὶ ἑκατὸν μνᾶς ἐγὼ καὶ Εὔεργος... Πανταινέτῳ... ἐπ' ἐργαστηρίῳ... καὶ τριάκοντ' ἀνδραπόδοις). Of this sum, Nicobulus had contributed 45 *mnai*, Evergus a talent (4).[69] Next we learn that Pantaenetus had previously owed an exactly identical sum to another set of creditors, Mnesicles, Phileas, and Pleistor, and that Mnesicles was the one who sold (πρατὴρ ἡμῖν γίγνεται) the workshop to Nicobulus and Evergus (5).[70] This appears confusing at first; if Mnesicles sold the workshop to Nicobulus and Evergus, it would belong to them, and Pantaenetus would not have been capable of offering it as security for a loan. Yet we have just learned shortly before that Pantaenetus did indeed pledge the workshop as security for a loan from Nicobulus and Evergus. If we keep in mind our previous discussion about the ownership of the security, it becomes possible to make sense of the transaction that Nicobulus is attempting to describe in this passage. What appears to have happened is that Mnesicles and his associates had lent their 105 *mnai* to Pantaenetus on the security of the workshop and slaves, thereby becoming (at least in their own eyes) the owners of this property in precisely the same way that all creditors regarded themselves as the owners of the securities that had been pledged to them. Mnesicles then invited Nicobulus and Evergus to take over this loan by paying him and his associates the 105 *mnai* Pantaenetus owed them. By paying Mnesicles, Nicobulus and Evergus became Pantaenetus' new creditors, and the workshop was now hypothecated to them. As creditors, they naturally considered themselves the owners of the security (7, 9, 29). From the creditors'

[69] Carey and Reid (1985) 114–17 fail to realize that the Athenians, like the Romans, did not share our modern notion of legal personality and thus had nothing akin to the modern juristic concept of the corporation. (On this topic, see Finley [1985] 275 note 5, with the literature cited there.) As a result, their discussion of the relationship between Evergus and Nicobulus is confused and misleading.

[70] The position of Telemachus (5) can be explained in either of two ways. The first, that of Fine (1951) 147, is that Telemachus had been the owner in the sense that he had lent money to Pantaenetus and had accepted the workshop and slaves as security. He then "sold" them to Mnesicles and his associates in the sense that Mnesicles and his asociates had paid Telemachus the amount owed by Pantaenetus and thereby became Pantaenetus' creditors and the owners (at least in their own eyes) of the security. The other view, maintained by Finley (1985) 32 and Harrison (1968) 275, is that Telemachus was the actual owner of the workshop and slaves and sold them to Pantaenetus. "Presumably to pay for his purchase, he borrowed 10,500 drachmas (...) The mill and the slaves were to serve as security for the loan and this was accomplished by having Telemachus, the original owner, 'sell' directly to Mnesikles, the principal creditor" (Finley [1985] 32).

point of view, the entire transaction could be interpreted as a sale since Mnesicles and his associates were transferring their ownership of the security to Nicobulus and Evergus in return for a cash payment. The language of sale used by Nicobulus in this passage to describe how he and Evergus took over Mnesicles' loan to Pantaenetus is readily comprehensible once we realize that these creditors thought of themselves as the owners of the security.

After paying Mnesicles, Nicobulus and Evergus drew up an agreement with Pantaenetus (5). In this agreement Pantaenetus is described as "leasing" (μισθοῦται) the workshop from Nicobulus and Evergus in return for payment of interest (τόκου). The agreement itself is called a lease (μίσθωσις. Cf. 6). And later on when Pantaenetus fails to make a payment (7), the payment is not referred to as rent, but interest (τόκους). Here again, we find one of our previous points confirmed. We have already noted how Athenian creditors tended to treat a loan on security as a single transaction, not as a combination of two separate transactions with one (the pledge of security) accessory to the other (the loan). This habit led to confusion about the proper name to apply to the resulting relationship between the creditor and the borrower in regard to the security. In the mind of the creditor, the debtor who remained on a piece of land pledged as security was exactly like a lessee who had rented property from its owner. Just as the lessee paid rent at fixed intervals, the debtor paid interest every month. If the lessee failed to make a payment, he could be evicted from the leased property. The situation of the debtor was similar: in the event of default, that is, failure to make a payment, the creditor would foreclose on the property and evict the debtor. When the period of the lease expired, the lessee had to leave the leased property unless the lease was extended or he could buy the property from its owners. In similar fashion, when it came time to pay the principal on the loan, the debtor had either to "buy back" the encumbered property or to allow the creditor to take it over. Obviously, there was one essential difference: if the lessee offered to buy the property he was renting when his lease came to an end, the lessor was under no obligation to sell it to him. The debtor who borrowed on security was in a very different position: if he wanted to "buy back" the encumbered property by paying off the loan, the creditor had no right to refuse his offer. This constituted the debtor's right of redemption (λύσις), which was contained in the agreement that Nicobulus and Evergus concluded with Pantaenetus (5). By including this provision in their agreement, they made it clear how this lease differed from normal leases.

We can now return to Nicobulus' story. Soon after the agreement with Pantaenetus was drawn up, Nicobulus set off on a voyage to Pontus while Evergus remained in Athens. Sometime later, Nicobulus returned to discover that trouble had erupted during his absence. Not surprisingly, there were two versions of what had taken place. Pantaenetus claimed that Evergus had used force to eject him from the workshop contrary to the terms of the agreement. Prevented from carrying on his business, Pantaenetus was unable to make payments on the mine he had leased from the state and became a public debtor (6). Evergus' account was somewhat different. He assured Nicobulus that he had seized the workshop only after Pantaenetus had failed to make several interest payments and denied the accusation that he had used force when taking over the workshop (7). The trouble did not end there. After Evergus took possession, Pantaenetus went away and returned with another set of creditors who said the workshop had also been hypothecated to them. We should not be skeptical about the existence of this other loan; although Mnesicles derided the claims of the other creditors, Nicobulus and Evergus dealt with them in the subsequent negotiations as if their declaration was trustworthy (13–15).

Our hypothesis is once more corroborated. We have just seen how the creditors Nicobulus and Evergus considered themselves to be the owners of the security; here we see that Pantaenetus acted as if the workshop still belonged to him even after he had hypothecated it to the first set of creditors, for he went ahead and proceeded to pledge it again as security for another loan to a separate set of creditors.

With his partner Evergus in possession of the workshop, Nicobulus found himself compelled to make a choice between two alternatives, neither of which pleased him. Either he could join with Evergus in running and managing the workshop, or he could become Evergus' creditor and draw up a new lease (μίσθωσιν) and a new agreement with his former partner. Once more we come upon the word μίσθωσις being used to describe the relationship between the creditor and the debtor who remains in possession of the security. Nicobulus obviously thought that if he were to become Evergus' creditor, the workshop would stand as security for the loan and would therefore belong to him as sole creditor. For that reason, he uses the word μίσθωσις to describe the agreement that would have been drawn up between himself and Evergus were he to decide to become Evergus' creditor.

Before we move on to the last part of the speech that is relevant to our discussion, some preliminary observations about the Athenian procedure for resolving disputes about ownership and the implications of the word πρατήρ are necessary. It is widely recognized that the Athenians did not have a public land registry.[71] In the absence of such an institution, the only way an Athenian could prove that he was the rightful owner of a piece of property was to provide evidence to show that he had acquired it in a legitimate fashion. If the property had been acquired by sale, the buyer, when challenged to prove title, would have to summon the man who sold him the property and have him testify about the sale. The seller (πρατήρ) who did respond to the summons and testified was said to "warrant" the sale (βεβαιοῦν) and to become a codefendant in the case (συνίστασθαι τὴν δίκην).[72] If the seller refused to obey the summons and the buyer lost his case, the buyer could bring an action against him. By granting this action, Athenian Law in effect required every πρατήρ to act as the warrantor of each sale he made.[73] That is not to say that in any given passage the word can mean "warrantor" without any implications of sale. The word means "seller"; it carries the implications of warranty only because all sellers were required by Athenian Law to act as warrantors.[74]

Back to Nicobulus' story. When we left him, Nicobulus had returned to discover Evergus in possession of the workshop as well as to learn that Pantaenetus had another set of creditors who also had a claim on the workshop. Curiously enough, Nicobulus did not go to Pantaenetus at this point and question him about the other creditors, nor did he seek them out and challenge them to prove the validity of their claims. He went instead to Mnesicles, the man who had sold him his loan to Pantaenetus in return for a payment of 105 *mnai*. Why did Nicobulus complain to Mnesicles? Mnesicles no longer had any contractual relationship with the various parties in the dispute. Moreover, Evergus' and Nicobulus' claims against Pantaetetus derived solely from the μίσθωσις they had agreed to earlier,

[71] For the absence of a public land registry in Classical and Hellenistic Athens, see Finley (1985) 13–15.

[72] For procedure, see Kaser (1944) 159–78. For a convenient summary of the evidence in English, see Wyse (1904/1979), 435–7.

[73] Harpocration *s.v.* mentions a δίκη βεβαιώσεως, but there is no contemporary evidence for the action. Even if it did not exist, the buyer whose claim was not supported by the seller could still have proceeded against him with a δίκη βλάβης for failing to testify on his behalf ([Dem.] 49.19–20).

[74] *Pace* Finley (1985) 228–9 note 33.

an agreement in which Mnesicles had no part. But rather than regarding him as *hors d'affaire*, Nicobulus appears to have held Mnesicles responsible for supporting his claim against that of the other creditors. In the light of our remarks about the word πρατήρ, that should come as no surprise. As creditors, Nicobulus and Evergus considered the transaction whereby they bought the loan that Mnesicles had made to Pantaenetus on the security of the workshop to be a sale that conferred ownership of the workshop on them. They accordingly viewed Mnesicles as the πρατήρ, who in Athenian Law was required to act as the warrantor of the purchase. When troubles arose about the ownership of the workshop after the discovery of the other creditors, Nicobulus went to Mnesicles and expected him to fulfill his duty as warrantor by supporting the claim of Evergus and himself. Mnesicles, evidently an honest and reliable businessman, did not shirk his duty and took on the responsibility of backing up their claim (11). When all the parties met together, Mnesicles confirmed (βεβαιοῦντος) the claims of Nicobulus and Evergus in the very way a πρατήρ was expected to.[75]

Seeing that Evergus and Nicobulus were not about to abandon the case without a fight, the other creditors presented them with a formal challenge: either Nicobulus and Evergus take the money owed them and depart, or they pay them the amount that Pantaenetus owed them and thereby become sole creditors. To assure them that they would not lose if they were to accept the latter alternative, the other creditors stated that the combined amounts of both loans did not exceed the total value of Pantaenetus' workshop. Nicobulus' immediate and spontaneous response was to accept the money offered by the other creditors (13). He quite understandably wanted to wash his hands of the whole business and was able to convince Evergus of the wisdom of his choice.

It is important to understand the exact nature of the proposal that Nicobulus wanted to accept. What the other creditors had offered was either to conclude a ὁμολογία or to grant a release.[76] In return for a payment equivalent to the

[75] Carey and Reid (1985) 126 misunderstand the nature of Mnesicles' declaration when they state "Mnesicles confirmed that when he 'sold' it the property did not stand as security for these other debts." The text reads Μνησικλέους βεβαιοῦντος; Mnesicles supported the claims of Evergus and Nicobulus. The text does not indicate that Mnesicles said anything about the claims of the other creditors.

[76] The words διαλῦσαι (12) and συνεχώρησα (13) used by Nicobulus to describe the proposals of the other creditors and his response to them make it clear that they were offering a ὁμολογία or a release. For other examples of these verbs employed in connection with either of these two types of agreements,

amount of their loan to Pantaenetus, they would agree to renounce all claims to the workshop. The attraction of such an agreement for Nicobulus should be readily apparent: it would enable him to get all his money back and to cut all his ties with Pantaenetus, who had so far caused him nothing but headaches.

None of this escaped the creditors, who all of a sudden realized that they had acted hastily when making their challenge. They now saw that the agreement Nicobulus was so eager to accept contained one rather serious risk for them. They had seen how Pantaenetus had already made another loan on the security of the workshop without informing then; if Pantaenetus had done this once, might he not do it again? And was it not possible that in addition to these two loans there might be still another that Pantaenetus had borrowed from a third set of creditors? If a third set of creditors were to come forward and press their claim, the creditors who made the agreement with Nicobulus and Evergus would have to reach some sort of compromise with these new creditors. But what if the combined amounts of the loan held by these two groups came to more than the total value of the workshop? Who would take the loss in the event that Pantaenetus defaulted? With these thoughts in mind, they decided to alter their original proposal to Nicobulus and Evergus. Instead of offering to conclude a ὁμολογία or to grant a release, they now insisted that they buy the workshop from Nicobulus and Evergus, who would thereby become πρατῆρες, in the same way as the latter had bought it from Mnesicles (16, 30). In other words, the other creditors were proposing that Nicobulus and Evergus, as creditors and owners of the workshop, sell it to them for the amount that Pantaenetus owed to them. The difference between the original proposal offered by the other creditors and the revised one appears at first to be only an insignificant change of name; in place of a ὁμολογία or a release, they wanted to substitute a sale. But the change in name was accompanied by an important difference in the legal implications of the two agreements. If the other creditors were to conclude a ὁμολογία or to grant a release, all the risks of doing business with the unscrupulous Pantaenetus would be theirs. Should a third set of creditors appear, they alone would be in danger of losing money. On the other hand, if the agreement were to take the form of a sale and then subsequently a third set of creditors were to come upon the scene, Nicobulus and Evergus would

see Dem. 21.122, 216; 38.24; [Dem.] 41.14; 42.10–14; Lys. 4.1. For the ὁμολογία see Kussmaul (1969) 30–7, esp. 34: "Die ὁμολογίαι (. . .) sind wahrscheinlich *pacta*, welche ein bestehendes Rechtsverhältnis abändern oder einen Streit darüber beenden, nicht *contractus*, welche eine neue Obligation begründen." For releases see Dem. 36.10, 24–5.

be responsible as πρατῆρες for supporting the claim of the creditors they had sold to and would be forced to share their risk.[77] Well aware of its implications for him, Nicobulus hesitated to accept the revised form of the proposal.

With the negotiations at an impasse, Pantaenetus intervened and begged Nicobulus to consent to the new form of the proposal. One can easily understand why Pantaenetus was in favor of Nicobulus and Evergus selling to the other creditors: the latter did not wish to foreclose on the workshop and were content to allow him to continue to carry on his business, whereas Evergus had already seized control of the workshop and showed no sign of letting it go. Pantaenetus' entreaties failed to stir up any compassion in Nicobulus, who was by this point infuriated by his unprincipled behavior. At the same time, Nicobulus must have realized that the new proposal presented by the other creditors provided the easiest way of resolving the dispute. Guided by these considerations, Nicobulus declared he was willing to sell to the other creditors provided that Pantaenetus would grant him a release from all claims (16–17). Although he could not avoid sharing some risk with the other creditors, he could at least protect himself from the unreliable Pantaenetus. Pantaenetus did not object to his condition, and a three-sided agreement was worked out that satisfied all the parties. Nicobulus' insistence on obtaining a release later proved to have been a wise move, for sometime later Pantaenetus brought an action for damages against him. Armed with his release, Nicobulus was able to thwart the charge by bringing a παραγραφή against Pantaenetus.[78]

[77] None of the recent discussions of the speech analyzes the difference between the two proposals offered by the other creditors. Finley (1985) 34 misses the point of the revised proposal. According to him, the other creditors wanted Nicobulus and Evergus to become πρατῆρες because "Should the creditors [i.e., the other creditors] be compelled to accept the property, the question of title would become important." But Nicobulus supplies a very plausible motive for the new proposal: ἑώρων γὰρ ἡμᾶς οἷ ἐσυκοφαντούμεθ' ὑπὸ τούτου. They were worried that the same ruse that Pantaenetus had used against Nicobulus and Evergus would be used against them. This sentence does not refer to Pantaenetus' case against Evergus, nor does it imply "that the case against Evergus was at least under way at the time of the transaction with the claimaints" (Carey and Reid [1985] 129). The verb ἐσυκοφαντούμεθ' is plural, referring to both Nicobulus and Evergus. It plainly refers to Pantaenetus' deceitful maneuvers, especially his concealing the presence of the other creditors to Nicobulus and Evergus and his bringing them forward when it was advantageous for him to do so. The verb can be used of any attempt to extort concessions from another person and need not imply legal proceedings (e.g., Lys. 26.24).

[78] I imagine that it was Nicobulus alone who became πρατήρ, that is, the seller who would be required to warrant the sale, and was the only one who gained the release from Pantaenetus. It appears that when there were several sellers, one could be designated as responsible to warrant the sale; this seems to have been the case with Mnesicles (5). Such a hypothesis would explain why Evergus was not able to fend off Pantaenetus' prosecution with a παραγραφή (8–9) in the way in which Nicobulus attempted to.

Though difficult to disentangle, the complex negotiations that are narrated by Nicobulus are invaluable for the information they provide about the way in which different sets of creditors envisaged their relationship with one another. The most fascinating aspect of the dispute between the creditors is their use of procedures drawn from property law to resolve their differences. Nicobulus, who has bought the loan that Mnesicles had made to Pantaenetus on the security of the workshop, regards Mnesicles as πρατήρ and expects him to perform all the duties attached to that role. In similar fashion, the other creditors want Nicobulus and Evergus to sell to them and to undertake the responsibilities of πρατῆρες. Nicobulus' reluctance to accept the revised proposal of the other creditors can be explained only by his unwillingness to accept the responsibilities inherent in being a πρατήρ. Our discussion of the speech not only lends support to our view that the Athenian creditor regarded himself as the owner of the security, but it also reveals that in the absence of any statutes regulating security transactions, creditors had to resort to procedures borrowed from property law to resolve disputes among themselves.

Of equal importance is the "negative" evidence furnished by the speech. What is especially striking is the failure to invoke the Roman principle of *prior tempore, prior iure*. When the two sets of creditors confronted each other, no one asks who was the first to make a loan on the security of the workshop. The dispute would have been handled very differently in Roman Law. If both sets of creditors claimed that the workshop had been pledged to them by *fiducia cum creditore*, all that was necessary was to determine whose *mancipatio* or *cessio in iure* had occurred first. The first group to whom the debtor had pledged his property would be ruled the owners of the security, whereas the others would find their claim invalidated since the debtor could not transfer by *mancipatio* something that he no longer owned. Although the second group had no right to the security that they thought had been pledged to them, they could nevertheless proceed against the debtor with an *actio de dolo malo*.[79] In the case where there were two creditors, each holding a *hypotheca* on the same security, the rules were different. If the first creditor foreclosed and sold the security by virtue of a *pactum de vendendo*, he had to restore to the debtor the amount by which the sale price exceeded the amount of the loan (surplus). The second creditor had no right to take possession of the security and could not

[79] For the *actio de dolo malo*, see Schulz (1951) 605–7.

demand repayment from the first creditor who sold the security. He could demand repayment from the debtor only out of the surplus that was returned by the first creditor. If there was no surplus, the second creditor lost out.[80] Nothing even faintly resembling these Roman procedures is found in the negotiations described by Nicobulus.

Although the failure of Athenian Law to provide guidelines in the field of real security created a certain amount of confusion, it did not prevent Athenian businessmen like Mnesicles, Nicobulus, and Pantaenetus from conducting complex security transactions. Businessmen do not fear to tread where the laws have not charted the territory. Far from showing any timidity, Athenian entrepreneurs rushed ahead, relying on their own ingenuity to devise arrangements that were suited to meet the demand for credit. Of course, we must not exaggerate the role that credit played in the economy of the Classical and Hellenistic periods, nor the complexity of the financial transactions conducted at this time. Paper money, double-entry bookkeeping, commercial banks, and joint stock companies still lay far in the future. But we should not underestimate the role of credit either, nor interpret the absence of any law about real security as an indication that credit played a negligible role in the Athenian economy.[81]

V

After our lengthy tour of the evidence found in the orations, it is time to return to the *horoi* and to the question posed at the beginning of this study: why does the terminology employed by the orators differ so markedly from that seen on the *horoi*? For previous scholars who believed that the two forms of expression found on the *horoi* referred to two different kinds of security, the divergence between the vocabulary used in the orations and that encountered on the *horoi* was very perplexing. Why, they asked, did the form of security that was most frequently discussed in the speeches of the orators hardly figure at all on the *horoi*? We can now see that they were asking the wrong question. This is not surprising given

[80] For the procedure used in *hypotheca,* see Schulz (1951) 423–5.

[81] *Pace* Finley (1985) ch. 8. Cf. the criticism made in Pringsheim (1953b) 224. Even P. Millett, who takes a primitivist view of the Athenian economy, admits that "The easy availability of credit was essential to the smooth functioning of Athenian society; loan transactions of one type or another are a pervasive feature at all levels of Athenian life" (Millett [1983] 42).

that they were working on an incorrect assumption. The question we should be asking is not "Why did those who set up the *horoi* generally prefer to use *one type of security* as opposed to another?" but "Why did those who set up the *horoi* generally prefer to employ *one type of expression* rather than another?" When the question is recast in this form, an answer to it can be found.

We need to begin by recalling what the function of the *horoi* was and who set them up. Despite their chronic disagreements, scholars have generally assented to the view that the *horoi* were set up by, or at the insistence of, the creditor, who obviously desired to warn others that the property to which they were affixed was not unencumbered.[82] Since the creditor was the one who had the *horoi* set up, we should expect the inscriptions on them to serve his needs and to reflect his view of the transaction. What were the needs of the creditor? To warn third parties that the hypothecated property could not be sold, to discourage others from accepting it as security for another loan, and to express his claim in the strongest possible language. All of these needs were well served by the expression πεπραμένου (-ης, ων) ἐπὶ λύσει or simply πεπραμένου. Both expressions send a clear message to the third party who is contemplating buying or accepting as security the property on which the *horos* is placed. They warn him in unambiguous terms that he cannot buy the property since it has already been "sold" to someone else. This form of expression was also preferred because it accurately reflected the views of the creditor, who, as we have seen, interpreted the transaction as a sale that conferred ownership on himself.

Although some creditors found the expression ὑποκειμένου satisfactory, it is obvious that it is not as forceful as πεπραμένου ἐπὶ λύσει. It does not reveal how the creditor viewed the transaction and does not indicate clearly that he considered himself the owner of the security. In fact, on several of the *horoi* that employ this term the creditor felt it necessary to add a clause to show that he was not the owner of the hypothecated property. On *horos* no. 1 there is added after ὑποκειμένου (line 2) the words ὥστε ἔχειν καὶ κρατεῖν τὸν θέμενον (lines 3–4). On *horos* no. 2 a similar clause is found after (lines 4–5): ἐφ' ὧ[ι]τε ἔχειν καὶ κρατ[εῖν τὸν] ὑποθέμενον (lines 5–7). The clause should be translated "on the condition that he who has received the security is the owner."[83] The creditors

[82] There is some evidence for this assumption: see *IG* ii² 1183, lines 28–9.

[83] Finley (1985) 204 note 11 denied that the expression indicates ownership and translated it "to have and to have power." He attempted to justify his translation by arguing that "κρατεῖν does not necessarily

who set up these *horoi* obviously thought that the term ὑποκειμένων by itself was not sufficient to get their message across and decided that it would be a good idea to spell out in plain language what he thought his rights to the property were.

Other evidence lends support to this explanation. In the *poletai* inscription recording the sale of Theosebes' house, we read that when Theomnestus denounced it for confiscation, he stated that the house was pledged as security to Smicythus and used the verb ὑπόκειται. On the other hand, when the creditors came forward, they used the language of sale to express their claims to the house (line 23: ἀποδομένο; line 33: πριαμένων). The third party, Theomnestus, used the weaker term to express the claims of a creditor, whereas the creditors themselves preferred to use the stronger language of sale to show that they considered themselves to be the owners of the security, whose claims could not be brushed aside. Something similar occurs in the inscription from Amorgos, *horos* no. 102, which was put up by the creditor Ctesiphon, who was undoubtedly responsible for the language used on it. When speaking of the property pledged to himself, Ctesiphon stated that his debtor Niceratus sold it to him (line 3: ἀπέδοτο). Yet, when describing the property that Niceratus had received from Exacestus as security, he used the words ἔχει θέμενος (lines 11–12). When Niceratus is the creditor in the transaction, he calls it a sale; when he is just a third party, he uses the expression ἔχει θέμενος.

mean 'to own,' " and cited several texts in support of his assertion. In two of these passages, [Dem.] 35.25 and 49.11, the verb is used to describe the rights of creditors to a security, but nothing in the surrounding context would enable us to decide whether these rights included ownership or not. At Is. 8.2 the speaker uses the words ἔχουσι . . . καὶ κρατοῦσι when describing how his opponents were enjoying ownership of Ciron's estate. He is not disputing the fact that they own it, but readily admits it; his charge is that they obtained ownership through force and that they, therefore, were not entitled to retain ownership. In the passage from Herodotus (2.136), an old Egyptian custom that originated during the reign of King Asychis is described. At this time, we are told, a son was allowed to pledge the corpse of his father as security for a loan. It was also laid down that the creditor ἁπάσης κρατέειν τῆς τοῦ λαμβάνοντος θήκης. Once again, nothing in the surrounding context allows us to determine whether or not the rights expressed by the verb included ownership or not. Finley makes no mention of the use of the verb to denote ownership in the law of inheritance preserved at [Dem.] 43.51 (the authenticity of the wording of this part of the statute is guaranteed by the quotation at Is. 7.20), where it occurs as a synonym for κυρίους εἶναι and μοίραν λαγχάνειν. Nor does he cite [Arist.] *Ath. Pol.* 56.2, where the phrase obviously means "to own." It is found in a description of the oath that the archon swore upon entering office and is clearly a promise not to deprive citizens of the property they own. This promise is equivalent to the assurance found in the Heliastic oath not to carry out a redistribution of land or a cancellation of debts (Dem. 24.149).

One final question remains: why do the Attic orators never add the prepositional phrase ἐπὶ λύσει after the verb when they are using the language of sale to describe hypothecation? The best way to find the reason why the orators omit the phrase is to begin by considering what reason the creditors who set up the *horoi* had for adding it. The reason is not hard to discover: they probably added the phrase to indicate the conditions on which the sale had been made. The prepositional phrase tacked on after the perfect participle is put there to show that although the property belongs to the creditor, the borrower can redeem it once the loan is paid off. In the speeches of the orators that is not necessary when the language of sale is employed since the narrative in which the language is found makes it abundantly clear that the sale is taking place as part of a loan agreement. There was consequently no need to add the prepositional phrase since the judges who heard the narrative would have been aware of what the conditions of sale were. That is not true of the *horoi*, which told those who passed them little or nothing about the nature of the transactions that had led to their erection.[84]

In the final analysis, the riddle of Athenian terminology for real security turns out to be nothing more than a problem of terminology, one to be approached from a study of the ways in which Athenians used words. Previous scholars who dealt with this problem erred in part because they did not allow for the possibility of explaining the language found on the *horoi* in this fashion. For them the occurrence of two types of expression for real security had to be explained on the assumption that the Athenians possessed two different forms of security. As I hope to have shown, that assumption is incorrect for several reasons. A much better way to attack the problem is to examine how the Athenians chose to express themselves in different contexts and why they selected the words they did to communicate what was on their minds.

[84] If we adopt such an explanation to account for the language of the *horoi*, we can view the expression ὑποκειμένης ἐπὶ λύσει (*horoi* 80A and 81A – both inscriptions are on the same stone) as an idiosyncratic combination of elements from both of the standard formulas for real security. For those who maintain the traditional position that there were two forms of security, this unusual expression poses insoluble difficulties. One might suggest that the creditor who set up the *horos* made a mistake, but that is unlikely. If these were two forms of security, each of which was referred to by a different expression and bore different legal implications, such an error would have been quite serious, and serious mistakes do not go unnoticed. Yet on this *horos* the expression not only remained uncorrected, but was actually repeated!

VI

Before bringing the discussion to a close, I would like to return for a moment to the question of "the origin" of the system of credit and security found in Classical and Hellenistic Athens. As we have just seen, the search for "the origin" of real security in the Archaic period does not help us to understand how the system functioned several centuries later. That task can be addressed only by analyzing the evidence we have for Athens in the Classical and Hellenistic periods, not by speculating how the system came into existence in an earlier one. In my opinion, the search for a single origin is not only unenlightening, but it is also misguided. Lending on security in Athens of the fourth century BCE was a complex transaction, consisting of several distinct components. The loan was made in cash and its value and the interest to be paid reckoned in Athenian coinage. The creditor's right to the security and the debtor's right to redeem it formed part of a legally enforceable agreement, the terms of which were often recorded in writing. And once the borrower received the loan of cash from the creditor, he might use it to buy goods or services to obtain cash to make interest payments and finally to pay off the principal. There were thus several factors that were essential to the functioning of the system: 1) coinage, 2) writing, 3) formal legal and political institutions, and 4) an economy in which there was a regular exchange of commodities for cash by means of sale, that is, an established marketplace. Without coinage, the precise amount of the debt could not be reckoned, nor interest payments calculated. If both parties were illiterate, it would be impossible to draw up a written document containing the terms of the agreement.[85] And there would not have been any sense in putting up *horoi* unless rudimentary literacy was widespread in Attica.[86] The loan agreement itself would have meant very little had there been no formal legal institutions to enforce its provisions in the event that one of the parties failed to abide by the agreement. Finally, the debtor would have found it difficult to make cash payments to his creditor in the absence of a marketplace where he could exchange his goods and services for coinage.[87] It is impossible to isolate any one of these elements and call it the primary one that was mainly responsible for the system of credit and security found in Athens during the Classical period. Far otherwise: the system was the

[85] For written documents in loan transactions, see [Dem.] 33.15; 34.6; 35.1–13; 56.6; *horoi* nos. 1, 2, 2A, 6, 11, 13, 17, 27, 32, 39, 65.

[86] For widespread literacy in Classical Athens, see Harvey (1966).

[87] For exchange of services, see Fuks (1951).

offspring of several different factors coalescing, none of which can claim for itself the sole honor of paternity.

All of these factors were absent in Homeric society, that is, in the Greece of the eighth century BCE,[88] where coinage was as yet unknown,[89] alphabetic writing in its infancy,[90] formal legal and political institutions nonexistent,[91] and the *agora* only an informal meeting place, not a marketplace.[92] That is not to say that the Greeks of the Homeric period did not have some concept of debt and did not recognize that the creditor was entitled to seize some object as compensation if the debtor failed to repay him.[93] What they lacked was coinage that could be used to determine with some precision the amount of the debt and the amount of interest to be paid at fixed intervals. They were also without courts that could enforce the rights of the creditor and debtor. If the debtor failed to repay, the creditor had no other recourse than to resort to self-help, or to seek the assistance of some powerful figure or pillar of the community. But there were no laws that bound them to go to his assistance. In general, the creditor had to depend primarily on the honesty of the man who borrowed from him.[94]

During the Archaic period, this informal system gave way to the formal system of credit and security that flourished in Classical Athens. The transition from the one system to the other probably occurred long before 400 BCE; what the different steps were in the transition, and when they occurred, however, are unknown to us. All we can know for certain is what the economy was like before the transition and what it was like after. Yet, although our sources tell us nothing about the steps in the transition, we can identify the cause of the transition. This was the development of formal legal and political institutions, in short, the *polis*. Despite scholarly disagreements about the original reasons for the creation of coinage in Greece, it

[88] For the Homeric poems as evidence for social conditions in the eighth century BCE, see Morris (1986).

[89] Scholars are divided over the question whether coinage was introduced in the first or second half of the seventh century, but there is a general consensus that there was no coinage before 700 BCE. For the earlier dating, see Weidauer (1975) 72–109; Cahn (1977) 279–87; Kagan (1982). For the later dating, see Cook (1946) 90–1; Robinson (1951); Price (1976) 274–5; Kroll and Waggoner (1984).

[90] For the date of the introduction of the Greek alphabet, see Jeffery (1961) 12–21.

[91] Finley (1978) 74–107.

[92] For example, *Il.* 1.490; 2.93; 7.382, 414; 11.139; *Od.* 2.10, 37, 150; 8.109; 16.361; 24.420. See also Finley (1978) 78.

[93] For the notion of debt, see Hesiod *Op.* 404, 647; Hom. *Od.* 8.353. For seizure of body of the debtor resulting from default, see [Arist.] *Ath. Pol.* 2.2; 6.1.

[94] Gernet (1968) 15–16.

is clear that its use was encouraged and furthered by the rise of the *polis,* which minted the coins, regulated their value, and guaranteed their worth.[95] The rise of a formal legal system, with its magistrates, law codes, and courts, transformed what had been informal loans into the legally enforceable agreements we call contracts.[96] The terms of the agreement were written down in documents that often specified what objects would be subject to seizure in the event of default. The creditor no longer had to rely on self-help, the trustworthiness of the debtor, or the good will of the community, but could now summon the aid of the laws and those designated to enforce them.[97] The *agora* now became sacred ground and received the protection of the magistrates of the *polis.*[98] It could thus serve as a place where exchanges of commodities could safely be made, thus encouraging their growth. We should not exaggerate the role of commodity exchange in Classical Athens; to deny its presence, however, would be to falsify our conception of the Athenian economy in this period.[99] Nor should we forget the role of the Greek alphabet, which permitted widespread literacy. After all, why would a creditor bother to put up a *horos* with an inscription on it if only a restricted few could read it?[100]

Thus, it was the rise of the *polis,* with its formal legal and political institutions, that created the conditions that led to the rise of the system of credit and security found in Classical and Hellenistic Athens.[101] If there is a general conclusion to be drawn from our discussion, it is that economic institutions do not follow an autonomous line of development. Quite the opposite: they are to a large extent

95 For the role of the *polis* in the creation of coinage, see Kraay (1964) and Wallace (1987).

96 The legal status of contracts in Classical Athens is complicated by the fact that the Athenians did not distinguish between actions *ex delicto* and actions *ex contractu.* The analysis of Pringsheim (1950) 13–85 is vitiated by his assumption that the Athenians did make such a distinction. On the topic of contracts in Athenian law, one can consult Wolff (1957), but more remains to be done.

97 For the role of the demarch in seizing the property of defaulting debtors, see Ar. *Nub.* 37.

98 For the *agora* as a sacred area, see de Ste. Croix (1972) 271–2, 397–8, 399.

99 The volume of commodity exchange was significant enough to merit treatment by no less a person than the philosopher Aristotle; see Meikle (1978).

100 For a general discussion of the effects of literacy on economic life, see Goody (1986) 45–86.

101 My position is similar to that of Finley (1968) 31–2 except in regard to the rise of chattel slavery, where I think he is mistaken. Despite my numerous disagreements with the late M. I. Finley, I must confess that I have learned a great deal from his writings. Of all the works on real security in ancient Athens, I have found his to be the most useful. I would like to thank *Classical Quarterly's* anonymous referee for judicious criticisms of this piece, which caused me to rethink several of my arguments. Gratitude is also due Victoria F. Harris, who read an earlier draft of the introductory section and strongly recommended that I revise it.

the product of conditions created by the legal and political institutions. It was the advent of the *polis*, with its magistrates, law codes, marketplaces, and coinage, that brought about the transformation of the economy of the eighth century BCE into that of the Classical period. Not the other way around.

Afterthoughts

The main points of this essay have been accepted by Youni (1996), Rhodes and Osborne (2003) 179, Todd (1993) 254–5, and Gauthier (1989) 396–7.

For an analysis of the reasons why Pantaenetus won his suit against Evergus, see Harris (2004c) 253–6.

In Section I of this essay I followed Finley's view of *apotimema* and in Section III accepted his assumption that the Athenians had no laws about real security. In Harris (1993) (= the next chapter of this volume) I give reasons for rejecting both these views, but my new position does not affect my arguments in this essay. In Section IV I accepted Finley's view that the Athenians did not have a land registry. Even though the Athenians did not have a land registry in the modern sense, they and other Greek *poleis* did maintain extensive records of land sales, which could be used to prove title. See now Faraguna (1997) and (2000). In note 59 I accepted Finley's position against any concept of the unity of Greek Law. I would now modify my position on this issue – see Chapter I.1 of this volume.

On ownership as a universal concept and the incidents of ownership in Athenian Law, see now Chapter II.5, Section I.

II.3 *Apotimema*: Athenian Terminology for Real Security in Leases and Dowry Agreements

When entering into a legal agreement, it is not unusual for one of the parties to ask the other to provide some security so as to ensure that the latter's obligations under the agreement will be fulfilled. There are two basic forms of security, personal and real. In personal security for a loan, the borrower arranges for a third party to come forward and to promise the lender that he will fulfill the borrower's obligations in the event that the borrower does not make interest payments or repay the principal. In real security, the borrower pledges some of his property, either movable or immovable, as security to the creditor. If the borrower defaults, the creditor has the right to seize the property pledged as security and, if he wishes, to sell it for cash in lieu of repayment.

During the Classical and Hellenistic periods, the Athenians used both personal and real security in their legal agreements. Real security appears to have been used primarily in three types of agreements: loans, dowries, and leases. Our information about the use of real security at this time comes from two main sources: one literary, the other epigraphical. First, there are the speeches of the Attic orators written for delivery in private suits. Second, there are the many Attic inscriptions that deal with financial matters, especially the *horoi*. The *horoi* are flat slabs of stone that were placed on properties that had been pledged as security.[1] The purpose of the *horoi* was to warn third parties that there was a lien on the property.[2] The amount of

I would like to thank Dr. Paul Millett for reading over a draft of this article and offering several good suggestions for improvement. He is not to be held responsible for any remaining errors or for the length of Part I.

[1] For a description of the physical characteristics of the *horoi*, see Fine (1951) 44–6.

[2] For the purpose of this kind of *horos*, see Fine (1951) 42–3; Finley (1952) 10–21. Finley's work was reprinted by Rutgers University Press in 1985 as a volume in its *Transactions* series. The reprinted edition contains

information inscribed on the *horoi* varies. All we find on some is a short statement that the property had been pledged as security.[3] Others are more forthcoming, giving the name of the creditor and the amount of the debt or obligation.[4]

In loan agreements, several terms or expressions are employed to express the idea of real security. The property or object that is provided as security is often called ἐνέχυρον.[5] On a handful of *horoi*, only seven, the property pledged as security is described as "lying under (an obligation)" for a debt (e.g., *horos* no. 5: ὅρος οἰκίας ὑποκειμένης Ἁλαιεῦσι HH).[6] On the vast majority of *horoi*, however, we encounter the expression "sold on condition of release" (e.g., *horos* no. 16: ὅρος χωρί[ο]| καὶ οἰκίας πε|πραμένων ἐπὶ λύσει IXXXX).[7] In the orators, we frequently come upon the verbs ὑποκεῖσθαι and ὑποτιθέναι to express the idea of real security and, in some passages, the verbs of sale πεπράσθαι and ἀποδίδοσθαι, though neither verb is ever followed by the prepositional phrase ἐπὶ λύσει.[8]

Until recently, scholars believed that each type of expression found on the *horoi* was used to denote the presence of a different form of real security, one called *hypotheke*, the other *prasis epi lysei*.[9] In the previous chapter, I argued that this view

a valuable introduction by P. Millett, which provides a critical review of recent scholarship about the *horoi*. Millett's introduction also provides the texts of all *horoi* published since the appearance of Finley's original work. All references in this article will be to the 1985 edition. Millett's introduction to this edition will be cited "Millett in Finley (1985)." When citing the texts of the *horoi*, I use the numbers assigned by Finley and Millett (e.g., *horos* no. 34, *horoi* nos. 6, 8, 10).

3 For example, *horos* no. 61.

4 For example, *horoi* nos. 14, 17, 18, etc.

5 Dem. 33.10; [Dem.] 49.5, 52, 53; 56.3.

6 *Horoi* nos. 1, 2, 2A, 4, 5, 6, 7. The term is restored on *horos* no. 3A. Since *horos* no. 3 does not actually contain the word, I have excluded it from this category, although Finley *placed* it under the rubric *hypotheke*. Nor have I included *horoi* nos. 80A and 81A. For a discussion of the idiosyncratic formula found on these *horoi*, see Harris (1988b) [= Chapter II.2 in this volume] esp. 359 and 379, note 84.

7 This formula is found or reasonably restored in a total of 125 texts. There are 92 in Appendix I of Finley (1985), 22 in Appendix III of Finley (1985), and 14 in Millett in Finley (1985). Pringsheim (1953a) argued that *horoi* nos. 112, 113, 114, and 114A publicized sales, not real security. Cf. Pringsheim (1950) 163–5. For trenchant criticisms of Pringsheim's arguments, see Millett in Finley (1985) xv–xviii. For an explanation of the omission of the phrase ἐπὶ λύσει on these *horoi*, see Harris (1992b) [= Chapter III.3a in this volume]. The phrase may also be missing from *horos* no. 18A. See W. K. Pritchett (1952) 338.

8 For the terminology employed by the orators, see Harris (1988b) [= Chapter II.2 in this volume] 361–77.

9 The view that the Athenians had three types of real security goes back at least as far as Hitzig (1895), and is accepted by both Finley and Fine.

is based on an invalid analogy from Roman Law. Despite the claims of many scholars, there is no discernible difference between the forms of real security denoted by the two types of expression seen on the *horoi*. Athenian Law, unlike Roman Law, did not possess formal procedures for conveyance that would have enabled people to distinguish between a form of real security where ownership was passed to the creditor and another where it was not. The absence of these formal procedures meant that the Athenians were unable to answer the question "Who owned the security, the creditor or the debtor?" That is why we come upon situations recounted by the orators where the creditor describes the security as having been "sold" to him, while the borrower at the same time contracts other loans on the same security as if it had never passed out of his ownership. Since it was the creditor who customarily placed the *horoi* on the property pledged as security, it is not surprising that the information inscribed on the *horoi* tend to reflect his view of the transaction. For this reason, the vast majority of *horoi* contain the expression "sold on condition of release," which implies that the creditor is the owner of the security.[10]

What I did not discuss in the chapter "When Is a Sale Not a Sale?" is the terminology employed to denote real security in leases and dowry agreements. Here the terminology differs from the expressions normally used in the context of loans. For instance, when an orphan's guardian decided to lease his property, the law required that the Archon supervise the leasing of the orphan's property. To protect the orphan's interests, the Archon ordered the person who leased the property to furnish securities for the lease.[11] These securities are called ἀποτιμήματα. The term is also found on the *horoi* placed on the properties pledged as security for leases of orphans' property.[12] Identical terminology is found on the *horoi* placed on

[10] Harris (1988b) [= Chapter II.2 in this volume] 358–79.

[11] [Arist.] *Ath. Pol.* 56.7. H. Rackham in his Loeb translation of the passage incorrectly translates the word ἀποτιμήματα as "rents."

[12] It is generally agreed that the *horoi* containing the word ἀποτίμημα or ἀποτιμήματος followed by either παιδί or παισί with the name of the father in the genitive were set up in connection with leases of orphans' property. See Finley (1985) 38–9, and Fine (1951) 96–8. This formula is found on *horoi* nos. 117, 118, 119, 120, 121, 125, 126, 126B, 126C, 126D, 126E. The formula is reasonably restored on *horoi* nos. 123, 126A. On four *horoi* we find the genitive παιδός or παίδων: *horoi* nos. 122, 124, 129, 129A. The genitive is reasonably restored on *horos* no. 120A. The word ὀρφάνοις is found on only two *horoi*, nos. 116 and 128, which also use the perfect passive participle ἀποτετιμημένων instead of the noun ἀποτίμημα (-τος). *Horos* no. 130 from Arcesine on Amorgos also belongs in this category. For a discussion of *horos* no. 131, see Section I.

property that was pledged to secure the repayment of dowries.[13] Curiously enough, it is also seen on a few *horoi* set up on property pleged as security for a loan.

Several passages in the lexica give helpful discussions of the term ἀποτίμημα and ἀποτιμᾶν, the verb from which it is derived. Here is what Harpocration (*s.v.* ἀποτιμηταί) has to say:

> ἀποτιμηταὶ καὶ ἀποτίμημα καὶ ἀποτιμᾶν καὶ τὰ ἀπ' αὐτῶν. οἱ μισθούμενοι τοὺς τῶν ὀρφανῶν οἴκους παρὰ τοῦ ἄρχοντος ἐνέχυρα τῆς μισθώσεως παρείχοντο. ἔδει δὲ τὸν ἄρχοντα ἐπιπέμπειν τινὰς ἀποτιμησομένους τὰ ἐνέχυρα. τὰ μὲν οὖν ἐνέχυρα τὰ ἀποτιμώμενα ἐλέγοντο ἀποτιμήματα, οἱ δὲ πεμπόμενοι ἐπὶ τῷ ἀποτιμήσασθαι ἀποτιμηταὶ, τὸ δὲ πρᾶγμα ἀποτιμᾶν. εἰώθεσαν δὲ καὶ οἱ τότε, εἰ γυναικὶ γαμουμένῃ προῖκα διδοῖεν οἱ προσήκοντες, αἰτεῖν παρὰ τοῦ ἀνδρὸς ὥσπερ ἐνέχυρον τι τῆς προικὸς ἄξιον, οἷον οἰκίαν ἢ χωρίον. ὁ δ' αὐτὸς λόγος καὶ ἐπὶ τῶν ἄλλων ὀφλημάτων.[14]

Pollux *Onomasticon* 8.142 and the *Anecdota Graeca* 437.15 (Bekker) contain similar information. Both the Attic orators and the *horoi* confirm most of the statements made about *apotimema* by the lexica. Yet the lexica do not tell us the one thing we would most like to know: why did the Athenians use this terminology to denote real security in these contexts? Was the reason that *apotimema* was a distinct form of security that differed from other types of security? Or is there another explanation? The lexica do not say.

[13] For *apotimema* used in connection with dowry, see Dem. 30 *passim*. The standard formula on the *horoi* set up on property pledged to secure the return of a dowry is ἀποτίμημα with the name of the woman for whom the dowry was given in the dative. This formula is found on *horoi* nos. 133, 134, 135, 135A, 136, 137, 138, 139, 140, 142, 148, 152. The formula is reasonably restored on *horoi* nos. 144, 148, 151, 152A. On two *horoi* we find the genitive of ἀποτίμημα: *horos* no. 132 (ἀποτιμημάτων) and *horos* no. 141 (ἀποτιμήματος). On six *horoi* the noun is replaced by the perfect passive participle of the verb followed by προικός: *horoi* nos. 143, 145, 147, 148A, 153; on *horos* no. 150 there is a slight variation (ἐν προικί instead of προικός). The name of the woman is always in the dative, except on *horoi* nos. 145 and 148A, where it is in the genitive. On *horoi* nos. 146 and 146B the word is found without the word ἀποτίμημα.

[14] Translation: "*Apotimetai* and *apotimema* and *apotiman* and the things related to them. Those who leased the estates of orphans from the Archon used to furnish securities for [the payment of] rent. The Archon was required to send out some persons to receive [or evaluate] the securities. The securities that were received [or evaluated] were called *apotimemata*, those who were sent out to receive them were called *apotimetai*, and the action was called *apotiman*. Men in that period were also accustomed, if the relatives gave dowry for a woman who was being married, to demand from her husband something equivalent in value to the dowry as a security, such as a house or plot of land. The same is also true for other [kinds of] debts."

Whereas the lexica are silent about this matter, modern scholars have been rather loquacious. Various proposals have been put forward to explain the term *apotimema,* but none has been able to win general approval. Despite their manifold disagreements, scholars have by and large shared the significant assumption that *apotimema* was a distinct form of security, which was distinguished from *hypotheke* and *prasis epi lysei*. In this chapter, I will take the conclusion I reached in my previous chapter one step further. I will argue that just as there is no distinction to be made between *hypotheke* and *prasis epi lysei,* there is likewise no essential difference between *apotimema* and other types of security used by the Athenians. Instead, we need to examine why the Athenians chose to employ the term *apotimema* to denote real security primarily in certain contexts, in particular, leases and dowry agreements, and only rarely in regard to loans.

The solution offered here to the conundrum posed by the term *apotimema* will do more than resolve a scholarly dispute about a narrow issue in Athenian Law. A proper understanding of the term will enable us to decipher the meaning of the only extant Athenian statute concerning real security (Dem. 41.7–10). More important, an analysis of the term *apotimema* will help us to appreciate the legal sophistication of those Athenians who conducted transactions involving real security. Scholars have on occasion criticized the Athenians for their imprecise use of legal terminology.[15] Though the Athenians did not develop the subtle legal distinctions and sophisticated technical vocabulary of Roman Law, they did possess a rudimentary understanding of basic legal principles and were able to use their own simple terminology consistently and correctly. The confusion about Athenian terminology for real security was not created by the Athenians. It is the product of modern scholars operating on mistaken assumptions.

Section I of this article discusses the analyses of *apotimema* presented by M. I. Finley and H. J. Wolff, respectively, the two scholars whose views on the subject have been most influential in the past forty years.[16] A detailed examination

[15] Fine (1951) 62, 92, 105: "the Athenians undoubtedly on occasions employed this term, as they did other technical expressions, rather loosely"; Harrison (1968) 254: "Once more we are hampered by the absence of a developed technical terminology. This makes it difficult to mark in as sharp outline as we should like the distinctions between various kinds of security"; M. I. Finley (1951) 89. One should compare the distinction between *nomos* and *psephisma* that was strictly observed in regard to motions enacted by the Assembly and by the *nomothetai*, respectively. See Hansen (1978).

[16] Finley (1985) 38–52; Wolff (1953) 2.293–333. Millett in Finley (1985), whose review of recent scholarship is generally thorough, makes no reference to this article.

For references to earlier discussions of *apotimema,* see the works of Fine, Finley, and Wolff. Harrison (1968) 293–303 summarizes the views of these and other scholars, but makes no original contribution

of their views is necessary since they often rest on misinterpretations of texts containing valuable evidence about the term *apotimema.* Once we have reached a better understanding of these texts, we will be in a position to present a new explanation of the term in Section II. In Section III, I will apply this explanation of the term to an analysis of the law on real security found at Dem. 41.7–10.

I

Finley, like earlier scholars, assumed that the Athenians possessed three types of security: *hypotheke, prasis epi lysei,* and *apotimema.* Unlike Fine and several others who held that *hypotheke* was a collateral form of security, whereas *prasis epi lysei* was substitutive in nature, Finley (1985) 51–2, 107–17 argued persuasively that all three forms of security were substitutive.[17] This meant that when an Athenian creditor seized the security as a result of the borrower's default and sold it, he was under no obligation to refund to the borrower the difference between the sale price of the security and the amount of the obligation due to the creditor.

Finley noted that *apotimema* appeared to be used primarily, but not exclusively, in two types of agreement: leases of orphans' property (pupillary *apotimema*) and dowry agreements (dotal *apotimema*). When leasing the estates of orphans, the Archon sent out official evaluators to assess the value of the *apotimema.*[18] According to Finley (1985) 43, pupillary *apotimema* differed from other security transactions in that it guaranteed not only a sum of money (the annual rent-interest) but also the return of the leased property. The reason why almost all of the *horoi* set up in connection with this procedure do not record a sum of money is that most of the orphans' property consisted of realty rather than cash. Finley (1985) 44 observed that if "the orphan's estate consisted entirely of money (...) only a fictitious sum could be inscribed."[19]

to the debate. Germain (1982–84) offers some speculations about the use of *apotimema* in agreements other than the leases of orphans' estates and dowries. His views are criticized by Millett (1991) 223. Fine's view of *apotimema* is based on a mistaken conception of *hypotheke*; see Millett in Finley (1985) xiii–xiv; see also Harris (1988b) [= Chapter II.2 of this volume] 352–6.

[17] For criticism of Finley's analysis of the difference between *hypotheke* and *prasis epi lysei*, see Harris (1988b) [= Chapter II.2 in this volume] 356–8.

[18] Finley (1985) 44 believed that the "official evaluators" did not "operate in monetary terms." If so, in what terms did they operate?

[19] Finley adds that such "a procedure would be pointless since it was the orphan's property that was to be restored to him when he came of age, not its price." But if the orphan's property was damaged or contained movables that were stolen, then the price would have been of some concern.

Dotal *apotimema* was different from its pupillary counterpart in two ways. The dowry was normally a sum of money, and if the dowry were not in cash, it was customary to assess its monetary value. The *apotimema* for a dowry "therefore guaranteed the return of a fixed sum, which could be indicated on the horos like any other monetary debt." This accounts for the fact that most of the *horoi* set up to publicize dotal *apotimema* indicate an amount of money. Finley (45–6) was aware that the term *apotimema* and the related term *timema* appear in other contexts than dowry and leases of orphans' property, but did not discuss these exceptional cases.[20] This is a serious weakness in his analysis.

According to Finley, pupillary and dotal *apotimema* shared two common features that set them apart from other forms of security. In his opinion, "if Y needs a loan for whatever reason and offers his house as security, the potential lender will fix the size of the loan he is willing to make by his estimate of the value of the house." In secured loans, therefore, "the property comes first and the money second, so to speak," and "the property is the fixed amount, the prior item." In *apotimema*, however, the money comes first, the property second. When a man marries off his daughter, he fixes in advance the monetary value of the dowry, "so the problem becomes one of evaluating the husband's land to determine what proportion is an acceptable equivalent." The same is true of pupillary *apotimema* where "we begin with a fixed property holding, the orphan's *oikos*, and a fixed amount of money, the annual rent to be paid by the lessee as determined through the mechanism of the auction. Then comes the evaluation, the measuring off of a proportionate share of the successful lessee's holdings, proportionate to an amount of money and property that has been fixed beforehand."[21] This meant that the *apotimema* might consist not of an entire property but "only a particular share" that "has been decided upon as the proper equivalent for the debt." In this case there occurs "a kind of redefinition of the property which might now be divided into two parts, 'one unencumbered and one encumbered.' " Finley's view is that "the distinction between *apotimema* and *hypotheke* was not one of juristic substance at all, but one of practical procedure." The main distinguishing feature of *apotimema* was that "a more or less precise determination was made at the time the agreement was reached, fixing the property that would be accepted as the substitute for the debt."[22] The

[20] Fine (1951) 104–6 was at a loss for an explanation of these *horoi*.

[21] Finley (1985) 46. Finley appears to contradict himself here since earlier he seems to imply that the fixed value was not reckoned in monetary terms.

[22] Finley (1985) 51–2. Unlike Fine, Finley (1985) 47, 51 dismisses any link between *apotimema* and family matters as "irrelevant."

other common feature that lay behind the different uses of *apotimema* was "the time factor." Most loans in this period were short-term: leases of orphans' estates would last until the child reached the age of majority. No term was set on dotal *apotimema,* which would last as long as the marriage for which the dowry was given.

There are three objections to be made against Finley's analysis of *apotimema.* First, it is incorrect to state the *apotimema* in a lease guaranteed "the return of the leased property." Second, there is no reason to think that in secured loans, "the property comes first and the money second." Third, evidence from the *horoi* and the literary sources contradicts Finley's view that *apotimema* fixed the "property that would be accepted as the substitute for the debt."

Finley's view that *apotimema* guaranteed the return of the leased property clashes with the testimony of the lexica. Harpocration (*s.v.* ἀποτιμηταί) states that those who leased the property of orphans provided securities for the payment of rent (ἐνέχυρα τῆς μισθώσεως). Pollux (*Onomasticon* 8.142) informs us that the *apotimema* was like a security, but it was pledged for the payment of rent (πρὸς τὰς μισθώσεις). The testimony of the lexica, which derives from literary sources, is independently corroborated by contemporary inscriptions. A decree of the deme of Piraeus from the year 321/20 (*IG* ii^2 2498, lines 1–7) stipulates that those who lease certain deme properties for above 10 *drachmai* must provide security for the payment of rent (καθιστάναι ἀποτίμημα τῆς μ[ι]σθώσεως ἀξιοχρέων). The figure of 10 *drachmai* must represent an amount of rent to be paid, since it is far too low a sum for a property value.[23]

We should not mislead ourselves into thinking that an analogy can be drawn between the return of the principal in a loan and the return of leased property in a rental agreement. In a loan the borrower receives a sum of money to which he acquires full rights for the duration of the agreement. After receiving the money, the borrower can exchange the money for goods or services. The risk for the lender is that the borrower will spend the entire principal and then become insolvent before the time comes for him to repay the loan. The pledge of real security is designed to protect him against that risk by ensuring that the borrower does not alienate an amount of property equivalent in value to the principal. The lessor does not face the same risk as the lender. Whereas the lender relinquishes all rights to his money in return for a promise to repay, the lessor does not part with the

[23] A similar phrase is restored with a high degree of probability in *IG* ii^2 2494, lines 7–8.

ownership of the property he leases. All the lessee has a right to is the use of the property. He does not acquire the right to alienate it, or, to be more specific, to exchange it for cash. If the lessee tries to sell the property to an unsuspecting third party, the sale will not be valid. The lessee does not have title to the land, so he cannot pass title to someone else. And if the lessee refuses to vacate the property at the end of the lease, the lessor can evict him. Should the lessee resist eviction, the lessor has resort to the courts. In Athenian Law, the person who occupied a building or plot of land and refused to yield it to the rightful owner was subject to prosecution by a *dike exoules* and faced stiff penalties if he lost the case.[24] Thus, if the lessee proved to be insolvent, the only thing the lessor stood to lose was the payment of rent. To protect the lessor against this risk, the lessee was required to furnish an *apotimema*, real security. He did not need to demand security for the value of his property since the laws already protected his ownership. After all, a lessee could not abscond with a building or a plot of land, those assets that would have constituted the bulk of an orphan's property.[25]

The one piece of evidence Finley (1985) adduces to prove his claim that *apotimema* guaranteed the return of the leased property is irrelevant to the discussion (239 note 27). The text is *horos* no. 131, an inscription from the island of Naxos. I give the relevant portion of the *horos*:

[ὅ]ρος χωρίων καὶ
οἰκίας καὶ κεράμου
ἀποτετιμημέν-
ων τοῖς παιδίοις
τοῖς Ἐπίφρονος τοῦ
ἀρχαίου ΧΧΧ𐅅 καὶ
τῶν μισθωμάτων
τετρακοσίων δρα-
χμῶν τοῦ ἐνιαυ-
[το]ῦ ἑκάστου . . .

Horos of properties and
house including roof
which have been pledged as security
(*apotimema*) to the children
of Ephiphron for the
archaion of 3,500 *drachmai* and
for the *misthomata*
of four hundred *drachmai*
each year . . .

[24] For the *dike exoules*, see Harrison (1968) 217–21.

[25] If an orphan's inheritance consisted partly of slaves, which were included in the lease, his ownership would be protected by the law of theft (*dike klopes*). Cohen (1983) 10–33 claims that the term *klope* was limited to larceny and did not extend to cases of embezzlement, but his attempt to find such a distinction in Athenian Law rests on an anachronistic comparison with Common Law and is contradicted by the use of the word *klope* to refer to embezzlement by public officials (Aeschin. 1.110–11; 3.9–10; [Arist.] *Ath. Pol.* 54.3; Dem. 22.65; 24.112; 58.15). I hope to discuss the topic at length elsewhere.

Finley noted the word μισθωμάτων, which he interpreted as payment of rent, and assumed that the figure of 3,500 *drachmai* represented the value assigned to the property of Epiphron's children. But Finley appears to have overlooked the word ἀρχαίου in line 6, which means "principal of a loan."[26] Furthermore, Finley did not observe that the word μίσθωμα can refer to the payment of interest in secured loans.[27] Finley's interpretation of *horos* no. 131 must therefore be rejected. The language of the inscription indicates rather that the sons of Epiphron had received a cash inheritance of 3,500 *drachmai* and had loaned this amount for an annual payment of 400 *drachmai* (an interest rate a little over 14 percent) to a borrower who put up several properties as security for the loan.[28]

A similar arrangement appears in a speech of Isaeus (2.9, 27–8). In the speech we hear that Menecles was able to provide a dowry for his daughter because he had become joint lessee of the property of Nicias' children (μετασχὼν τοῦ οἴκου τῆς μισθώσεως τῶν παίδων τῶν Νικίου). The sentence indicates that Menecles received a sum of money as a result of entering into this "lease," suggesting that the arrangement was in fact a secured loan. This inference is confirmed later in the speech (27–9), where we are told that Menecles had to repay a sum of money (ἀργύριον, χρήματα) and that interest had accumulated for a long time (τόκοι δὲ πολλοῦ χρόνου συνερρυηκότες ἦσαν αὐτῷ). To repay the loan, Menecles attempted to sell some land, which otherwise would have been subject to seizure (κατοχώχιμον). There is only one way to explain the statement that the land would be subject to seizure if the money was not paid to the orphans: the land had been pledged as security for the money Menecles had received from the orphans.[29] The arrangement is precisely identical to that found on *horos* no. 131.

[26] Ar. *Nub.* 1156; Dem. 27.28, 38, 50, 64; 34.26; [Dem.] 56.30, 32, 33, 43. I know of no passage where the word refers to leased property. The word is mistranslated by J. H. Vince as "estates" in his Loeb translation of Dem. 1. 15. The passage compares Athenian policy to borrowing at a high rate of interest. The context indicates that the word must refer to the principal of a loan.

[27] *Horos* no. 102, line 15; Dem. 37.5–6 with the discussion in Harris (1988b) [Chapter II.2 in this volume] 365–6, 371–3.

[28] Fine (1951) 103–5 made the same mistake. The interest rate of 14 percent per annum is comparable to other interest rates attested in this period. See Millett (1991) 98–108.

[29] Wyse (1904/1979) 258–9 provides a good discussion of the passage, but does not observe how Menecles' lease differed from the standard leases of orphans' property. See Fine (1951) 109 note 60 for references to other discussions of the passage.

Since the *apotimema* in a lease was given to secure the payment of rent, Finley's explanation for the absence of an amount of money on all the Attic *horoi* marking pupillary *apotimema* cannot stand. Finley claimed that the *apotimema* was given to guarantee the return of the orphan's property; since any value assigned to the property would be a "fictitious amount," no amount was indicated on the *horoi* in these cases. But, as we have now seen, the *apotimema* in the lease of an orphan's estate was pledged for the payment of rent, and that figure was no "fictitious amount." The rent was a specific sum that was determined through the bidding supervised by the archon. Why was that amount not placed on the *horoi*?

We can now turn to Finley's explanation of the difference between *apotimema* and other types of security. In *apotimema*, whether dotal or pupillary, the amount of money is fixed in advance. That is to say, the amount of the dowry or the value of the orphan's property and the amount of the rent are determined first, and the evaluation of the property that will serve as security comes second. According to Finley, the situation is reversed in a secured loan, where the "potential lender will fix the size of the loan he is willing to make by his estimate of the value of the property" that will stand as security. In a secured loan, therefore, "the property comes first and the money second."

Does the money really come second in a secured loan? In normal circumstances, the borrower knows in advance how much he needs to borrow. If he wants to buy a house, he finds out how much the house is worth, then deducts what he can afford to give as a down payment in order to determine what he has to borrow. Or if he has fallen behind with his taxes or rent, he has a precise amount he has to pay off. The person who is willing to lend money first asks the borrower how much money he needs, then determines if the borrower has an amount of property adequate to secure the requested amount of the loan. If the borrower does not have enough property to meet this criterion, the lender may deny his request. But the same thing would presumably happen if the man who put in the highest bid for the rental of an orphan's estate turned out not to have enough property to furnish the necessary *apotimema*. In that case, the Archon would no doubt have denied his request to lease the orphan's property. Viewed from this perspective, a secured loan was no different from a lease secured by *apotimema*.

The story of Nicostratus' attempts to pay off his creditors illustrates the point ([Dem.] 53.6–13). Nicostratus was captured while pursuing his fugitive slave and sold on Aegina. His brother Deinon went to rescue him. Upon returning to Attica, Nicostratus told Apollodorus that some foreigners had loaned him 26 *mnai* to pay his ransom. Apollodorus gave him a gift of 1,000 *drachmai* to repay part of the loan, and Nicostratus then tried to raise the remainder on his own. He attempted to borrow money on the security of his farm, but his brother Arethusius, who had a claim of his own on the property, would not permit it. Nicostratus then turned to Apollodorus and asked him to lend him what he needed. His situation was growing desperate since the terms of the loan stipulated that the full amount be repaid in thirty days or his debt would be doubled, and the thirty-day period was about to end. Apollodorus, having no ready cash on hand, borrowed 16 *mnai* from Arcesas on the security of his lodging-house and handed this sum over to Nicostratus on the understanding that the debt would be repaid as soon as Nicostratus could raise an *eranos*-loan. What is significant for our purposes is that the amount Nicostratus needed to borrow remained constant throughout his negotiations with Apollodorus and others. For Nicostratus, the amount of money in the loan was fixed ahead of time by the ransom he was forced to pay. Finding some property to serve as security came second.

Finally, there is Finley's view that in *apotimema* "a more or less precise determination was made at the time the agreement was reached, fixing the property that would be accepted as the substitute for the debt." This collides with the evidence from the *Anecdota Graeca* (437.15 Bekker), which states that the property offered as *apotimema* was evaluated to ensure that it was worth not less, but more than the dowry (ἵνα μὴ ἔλαττον ᾖ, ἀλλὰ πλέον αὐτῆς). That makes sense. No person in his right mind would accept an arrangement whereby the security given to him was assigned a value that would remain constant regardless of any fluctuations in its market value. The lessor or the father who gave a dowry for his daughter would naturally check to see that the value of the property offered as security was greater than the amount of the obligation so that even if the market value of the property dropped considerably, its sale would still provide enough cash to pay off the obligation.

More evidence refuting Finley's view comes from Demosthenes' speeches against Onetor (Dem. 30 and 31). Prior to bringing his suit against Onetor, Demosthenes had won a judgment against his guardian Aphobus for defrauding him of a large part of his inheritance. To execute this judgment, Demosthenes attempted to seize a plot of land held by Aphobus, but was driven off the property by Onetor. Onetor claimed that the property had been pledge to him as *apotimema* for the dowry of his sister, who was married to Aphobus. According to Onetor, Aphobus had divorced his sister, so he had taken possession of the land in lieu of recovering the dowry (Dem. 30.8–9). The reliability of Onetor's assertions does not concern us. What is relevant for our discussion is Onetor's statement during the trial that he would not deprive Demosthenes of the difference between the value of the land and the talent Aphobus owed him for the return of the dowry (Dem. 31.6: οὐκ ἀποστερεῖ μ' ὅσῳ πλείονος ἄξιόν ἐστι ταλάντου). Yet if the value of the property was fixed at a price equivalent to the dowry, there could be no excess to give to Demosthenes.[30]

Horos no. 147 conveys a similar message. Here we read that a house has been pledged as security for a dowry of 1,000 *drachmai* given for the daughter of Antidorus. The value of the property beyond that amount has been pledged to the Gephyraioi and possibly other creditors as well. Once more, it is clear that the property furnished as *apotimema* is not assigned a value equivalent to the value of the dowry.[31]

In short, Finley's analysis of *apotimema* is unsatisfactory. The differences he claimed to detect between *apotimema* and other forms of security simply do not exist. And Finley cannot explain why on virtually every *horos* set up in connection with pupillary *apotimema* no amount of money is recorded.

Whereas Finley (1985) 52 believed that "the distinction between *apotimema* and *hypotheke* (...) was one of practical procedure," Wolff (1954) 316 thought that *apotimema* must differ from other forms of security in terms of juristic substance. Wolff's most original idea was his view that the definition of *apotimema* given by Harpocration, Pollux, and the *Anecdota Graeca* does not cover all uses of the term and thus gives an incomplete picture of the institution. Wolff's definition of the term is much wider: *apotimema* is an object that the debtor could surrender for an agreed value to protect himself from a legal action threatened by the creditor seeking a monetary judgment.[32] Other types of security ensure that the creditor will receive payment whereas *apotimema* protects the debtor from a legal action.

[30] Fine (1951) 139–40 uses Dem. 31.6 as evidence for his theory about *hypotheke*. For criticism of his theory, see Harris (1988b) [Chapter II.2 in this volume] 353–4. In that essay, I endorsed Finley's view of dotal *apotimema*. I now retract that endorsement.

[31] *Horos* no. 146 exhibits similar language, but the term ἀποτίμημα is missing. Wolff (1953) 316–17 made the same criticism of Finley.

[32] Wolff (1953) 318: "Auf das technische ἀποτίμημα angewendet, muss das heissen, daß dieses ein Gegenstand war, durch dessen Hingabe zu einem vereinbarten Wert der Schuldner eine ihm drohende, auf Geldverurteilung gerichtete klage von sich abwenden könnte."

Wolff launched his assault on the evidence of the lexica by drawing attention to a passage from Isaeus' speech on the estate of Philoctemon (Is. 6.36). The speaker describes how his opponents Androcles and Antidorus attempted to lay their hands on the property of Euctemon, who was at death's door. Their scheme was to register two young boys as the adopted sons of Euctemon's sons. Since Euctemon's sons had passed away several years before, his grandsons had become his heirs and would be entitled to his estate at his death. As part of the scheme, Androcles and Antidorus had themselves registered as the grandchildren's guardians and requested the Archon to supervise the leasing of their wards' property so they could become lessees and gain control of its revenues (μισθωταὶ δὲ αὐτοὶ γενόμενοι τὰς προσόδους λαμβάνοιεν).[33] The description of their request to the Archon contains a reference to offering *apotimema*:

> καὶ μισθοῦν ἐκέλευον τὸν ἄρχοντα τοὺς οἴκους ὡς ὀρφανῶν ὄντων ὅπως ἐπὶ τοῖς τούτων ὀνόμασι τὰ μὲν μισθωθείη τῆς οὐσίας, τὰ δὲ ἀποτιμήματα κατασταθείη καὶ ὅροι τεθεῖεν ζῶντος ἔτι τοῦ Εὐκτήμονος.

Wolff interpreted the phrase τὰ μὲν μισθωθείη τῆς οὐσίας, τὰ δὲ ἀποτιμήματα κατασταθείη to mean that part of the boys' property was to be leased and part to be provided as *apotimema*.[34] Wolff's interpretation of the passage was not original. Wyse, though perplexed by it, had interpreted the passage in the same way. The translations provided by Roussel and Forster reveal they concurred with Wyse's view of the passage.[35] Finley agreed with his predecessors' interpretation,

[33] The details of the plot are a bit murky; it appears that the conspirators planned to bid for the lease themselves. The passage thus indicates that the guardians themselves could bid for the lease of their wards' property (37: οἱ δ' ἐμισθοῦντο). Cf. Harrison (1968) 105–6. The practice raised the eyebrows of Wyse (1904/1979) 526–7, who felt it somehow violated the sacred bond between guardian and ward. His view is needlessly moralistic. The practice made good sense, for it gave the guardian an incentive to manage his ward's property efficiently. Without such a contract, the guardian could not legally profit from his management of the orphan's property and thus had no reason to increase its productivity. As lessees, they could exploit the property for their own profit (τὰς προσόδους λαμβάνοιεν) and would have a strong motive for increasing the revenues derived from it. The orphan would receive a share of these profits through the lease and have his property well maintained, if not substantially improved. Demosthenes (27.64) gives several examples of orphans who profited handsomely from the leasing of their estates.

[34] Wolff (1953) 301–3, with references to earlier discussions.

[35] Wyse (1904/1979) 525; Roussel (1922) 104; Forster (1927) 225: "part of the property might be leased and part might be used as security."

but shied away from analyzing the difficulties it presented.[36] Fine, too, accepted the traditional interpretation and shared Wyse's bewilderment: "it seems fantastic that in μίσθωσις οἴκου a part of the estate should be leased and part of the same estate should serve as security for the lessees."[37] Wolff believed that to solve the puzzle one had to go beyond Harpocration's account of *apotimema* and recognize that it was more than just a form of security.

If one translates Is. 6.36 in the traditional way, it is indeed difficult to reconcile the passage with Harpocration's explanation of *apotimema*. Harpocration says that *apotimema* was a security that lessees were required to furnish for the rent in a lease of an orphan's property, whereas the traditional interpretation of Is. 6.36 appears to indicate that the *apotimema* could come from the orphan's property, not that of the lessee. Luckily, there is another way of translating the passage that makes far better sense and removes the apparent conflict with Harpocration's discussion of *apotimema*. The key to understanding the mysterious pair of clauses is the role of the particles μέν and δέ. Previous scholars have assumed that these particles contrast two parts of the orphans' property (τὰ μὲν . . . οὐσίας, τὰ δὲ . . .). One part is the portion that was leased (μισθωθείη), the other the portion provided as security (ἀποτιμήματα κατασταθείη).[38] As H. Pelliccia has recently observed, however, the "particles can be used to contrast ideas that are not embedded in single words or phrases." The contrast may be a more general one between two actions or ideas, each one expressed by an entire clause.[39]

There is a contrast implied by the μέν and the δέ in Is. 6.36, but it is not a narrow one between two pieces of property. It is a more general one between two actions. On the one hand, there is the leasing of the orphan's property (τὰ μὲν

[36] Finley (1985) 41–2: "some of the property would be leased in the children's name and some put up as *apotimema*."

[37] Fine (1951) 100.

[38] MacDowell (1989a) 13–15 thinks that τὰ μέν means "part of the property," but that the δέ is a simple connective and does not respond to the μέν. But if the δέ does not respond to the μέν, τὰ μέν cannot mean "part of the property." MacDowell suggests that the part of the property to be leased was that which belonged to Euctemon's sons, the boys' fathers. But if Euctemon's sons left property at their death, guardians would have been appointed at that time to look after their sons, not several years later. MacDowell fails to see the outrageous part of the scheme, which caused the court to reject the conspirators' proposal. This was that they attempted to have the boys registered as orphans who had inherited their grandfather's property before they were actually orphaned by the death of their adoptive grandfather Euctemon. The words ζῶντος ἔτι τοῦ Εὐκτήμονος (with the stress on ἔτι) bring this out clearly.

[39] Pelliccia (1991) 35. Cf. Denniston (1954) 371.

μισθωθείη τῆς οὐσίας), and, on the other, there is the furnishing of securities by the lessee (τὰ δὲ ἀποτιμήματα κατασταθείη). Concomitant with the latter is the placing of *horoi* on the property pledged as security (καὶ ὅροι τεθείεν). One property, that of the orphans, is being leased, whereas the other, that of the lessees, is being provided as security. There is no clash with the information given by Harpocration. Contrary to Wolff's assertion, Is. 6.36 cannot be deduced as evidence to show that Harpocration's account of *apotimema* is deficient.

Wolff next turned to the use of *apotimema* in dowries. He noted the law cited at Is. 3.35, which stipulates that if a man gives a woman in marriage with an item that has not been included in the evaluation of the dowry (ὃ μὴ ἐν προικὶ τιμήσας ἔδωκεν), he cannot demand the return of this item in the event of divorce. This formal evaluation of property given as part of the dowry was especially important when land or valuables were given in place of money. This formal evaluation provided a means of avoiding disputes about the value of any property the husband might have alienated during the marriage when it became necessary to return the dowry. The procedure of evaluating items in the assessment of the total value of the dowry was called τιμᾶν ἐν προικί or ἐντιμᾶν. Wolff claims that there was a close connection between τιμᾶν and (ἐν)τιμᾶν. By evaluating some property given as part of a dowry (τιμᾶν ἐν προικί), one made it into an ἀποτίμημα.[40]

This inspired Wolff to advance a novel interpretation of the *horoi* publicizing dotal *apotimema*. In most of the *horoi* in this category, we find the word *horos*, followed by a noun (or nouns) denoting property in the genitive, then the term ἀποτίμημα (nom./acc. or ἀποτιμήματος gen.) followed by the word προικός (gen.). Wolff argued that the noun προικός must be taken with ἀποτίμημα to mean "an evaluated item of the dowry." On this reading, these *horoi* show that the land to which they were affixed had been given as part of the dowry and included in the legal evaluation of the entire dowry. Wolff then drew attention to three *horoi* that appear to indicate not that the husband has put up property as security for the return of the dowry, but that the land or house was itself dowry given to the husband. Only one of these is from Attica (*horos* no. 175: ὅρος χωρ[ί]ου καὶ οἰκίας προικὸς Ναυσικρίτη[ι]). The other two are from Syros (*horos* no. 179: Ἡγησοῦ τῆς Κλεομόρτου θυγατρὸ[ς] προὶξ τὸ χωρίον and *horos* no. 180 τῆς

[40] Wolff (1954) 303–5 with Dem. 41.27 and 47.57. The verb in the latter passage (εἴη . . . τετιμημένα) is mistranslated by Murray (1939) 311 ("mortgaged to secure her marriage portion").

Δεξικράτου προὶξ ἡ οἰκία).[41] In addition, Wolff noticed the phrase ἐν προικὶ ἀποττετιμημένης on *horos* no. 150 and ἀποτετιμημ[ένων . . .] ἐν προικὶ on *horos* no. 156 (Naxos), as well as a similar phrase ἀποτετιμημένων . . . εἰς τὴν προῖκα on *horos* no. 155 (Amorgos). In Wolff's opinion, these phrases indicate that the property had been given to the husband and evaluated as part of the dowry.

There are several objections to be made against Wolff's interpretation of the *horoi* set up in connection with dowry. First, no ancient source states that the term *apotimema* could refer to property that was evaluated as part of the dowry. Wolff essentially bases his argument on the common root shared by the verbs ἐντιμᾶν and ἀποτιμᾶν, but there is no reason to assume the latter is a subset of the former. Indeed, Harpocration (*s.v.* ἐνετιμᾶτο) draws a sharp distinction between the two verbs (Finley [1985] 239 note 32). When we come upon the noun or the verb in the Attic orators, they never refer to an evaluation of items in the dowry, but always to a pledge of security. Wolff claimed that his own interpretation of the *horoi* was superior from a linguistic point of view, but one does no violence to the Greek found on the *horoi* if the word in the phrase is construed as a genitive of purpose ("security for the dowry").[42] On *horoi* nos. 175, 179, and 180, it does appear that land and buildings have been given as dowry, but on none of these *horoi* do we find the term ἀποτίμημα. They are therefore irrelevant to the discussion.[43]

Wolff argued that Demosthenes' speech *Against Spudias* lends support to his interpretation of the *horoi* set up for dotal *apotimema* (Dem. 41). The case for which this speech was written concerns the property of Polyeuctus, who left two daughters as his heirs. The speaker is married to one of Polyeuctus' daughters and has brought suit against Spudias, the husband of the other daughter, in a dispute over the division of Polyeuctus' property. Polyeuctus had given his daughter in marriage to the speaker with a dowry of 40 *mnai*, of which he received 3,000 *drachmai* at the time of the wedding. The remaining 10 *mnai* were to be paid to him at Polyeuctus' death and until then constituted a debt (ὀφείλειν) against his property. Not long before Polyeuctus' death, the speaker took his father-in-law's

[41] For other examples of similar phrases, see Wolff (1953) 306 note 55.

[42] For the genitive of purpose, see Smyth (1956) 331. Compare the similar use of the genitive in the phrase τιμῆς ἐνοφειλομένης on *horos* no. 3 ("for the price owing"). Smyth (376–7) also lists passages where εἰς can be used to express purpose and ἐν can indicate cause.

[43] Finley (1985) 266 note 23 suggested that the word had been accidentally omitted on *horos* no. 175 as it appears to have been on *horos* no. 146.

house as security for the 10 *mnai* owed to him (5). This was done in accordance with the instructions of the dying Polyeuctus, who ordered that *horoi* be placed on his property (6). Wolff (307–11) followed Paoli and claimed that the house was given as a *datio in solutum*, that is, the surrender of some property evaluated at 10 *mnai* in satisfaction of the outstanding debt. In Wolff's opinion, this text confirms his view of the *horoi* set up in connection with dowry, since the verb ἀποτιμᾶν is several times used to describe the transaction.

The trouble with Wolff's view of the transaction is that the language of the speech indicates rather that the house was given as security for the debt of 10 *mnai* owed by Polyeuctus to the speaker. The speaker says he received the house as security for the 10 *mani*, that is, the debt, not as part of the dowry (5: τὴν οἰκίαν ταύτην ἀποτιμῶμαι πρὸς τὰς δέκα μνᾶς). When Polyeuctus instructs the *horoi* to be set up on the property, it is for the 1,000 *drachmai* debt he owes on the dowry (6: διέθεθ' ὅρους ἐπιστῆσαι χιλίων δραχμῶν ἐμοὶ τῆς προικὸς ἐπὶ τὴν οἰκίαν). Later in the speech, the speaker once more asserts Polyeuctus pledged the house as security for money owed (19: προσοφειλομένων ἀπετίμησέ μοι τὴν οἰκίαν Πολύευκτος). Besides, it is nowhere stated that the house was included in an evaluation of the dowry made at the beginning of the marriage. The verb is used strictly to refer to a pledge of security for a debt. The *horoi* are placed around the house to show that it stands as security for a debt, not that it was evaluated as part of the dowry. After Polyeuctus died, the speaker attempted to take possession of the house and collect the rents paid by its tenants (5: με τὰς μισθώσεις κομίζεσθαι). In this respect, the speaker acted just like a creditor who has seized a security in lieu of repayment.[44]

Our examination of the respective views of Finley and Wolff has not been entirely negative. Neither scholar presents a convincing account of the differences between *apotimema* and other forms of security, yet that in itself is significant. In each case where Finley and Wolff claimed to identify a feature of *apotimema* that set it apart from other security transactions, we have found precisely the opposite: the verb ἀποτιμᾶν appears to be used in much the same way as other verbs employed to denote a pledge of real security. As Harpocration states, ἀποτιμήματα are

[44] Finley (1985) 49 correctly noted the "dowry was irrelevant and accidental in this case, so to speak." He aptly drew attention to Libanius' interpretation of the transaction (Dem. 41, *hypoth.* 1): τὴν οἰκίαν τῆς ἄλλης οὐσίας ἐξελεῖν καὶ ταύτην εἰς τὸ *χρέος* δοῦναι.

things pledged as security (ἐνέχυρα). Like other securities, they were usually worth more than the amount of the obligation they secured. When the person who provided an ἀποτίμημα for some obligation defaulted, the creditor had the right to seize it. The question asked by previous scholars, namely, how did ἀποτίμημα differ from other forms of security, turns out to be the wrong question. We do not need a new answer to the old question. What we need is a new question.

II

The first step toward a solution to the enigma posed by the term ἀποτίμημα is to examine the contexts in which the word is used. Previous studies of the term have looked almost exclusively at its use in two contexts: dowry agreements and the leasing of orphans' property. Though the term is found primarily in these contexts, it is also found in other contexts as well. Pollux (8.142) states that the term was employed to refer to security for the payment of rent in general (πρὸς τὰς μισθώσεις), not just for the leases of orphans' property. The decree from the Piraeus noted above (*IG* ii^2 2498, lines 1–7) bears him out. Here the term is used to refer to real security in leases of the deme's property. In a document concerning the leasing of property of Apollo Lyceius (*IG* ii^2 2494, lines 7–8), the term is restored with a high degree of probability in a clause requiring lessees to provide real security. Further evidence comes from a fragment of Isaeus.[45] The speaker describes his financial straits, saying that no one will lend to him since all his resources have been spent on liturgies (κατελελητούργητο) or pledged as security (ἀποτιμηθέντων). He reveals in the next phrase that he is paying rent on leased property (ἀποδεδωκότι τὰς μισθώσεις). The obvious explanation of his predicament is that he cannot borrow further on his property since it has been pledged as security for one or more leases. Once again, the terminology is that of *apotimema*.

Harpocration (*s.v.* ἀποτιμηταί) observes that the term ἀποτίμημα was applied to real security for other obligations beyond the payment of rent or

[45] Is. fr. 29 (Thalheim). Note also Lys. fr. 52 (Thalheim) [= Harpocration *s.v.* τίμημα]· οὗτοι φάσκοντες πλείονος μισθώσασθαι καὶ τίμημα καταστήσασθαι. Note the similarities between the phraseology in this fragment and that used in Is. 6.36.

the return of a dowry (ὁ δ' αὐτὸς λόγος καὶ ἐπὶ τῶν ἄλλων ὀφλημάτων). A decree from the deme of Plotheia confirms his observation (*IG* ii² 1172, lines 19–22). The decree orders the magistrates to make loans from the deme's funds to whoever offers to pay the highest rate of interest (δανείζοντας ὅ[στι]ς ἂν πλεῖστον τόκον διδῶι). In addition, the potential borrower must persuade the magistrates that he can provide either real security or personal security (ἂν [πείθ]ηι τὸς δανείζοντας ἄρχοντα[ς τιμ]ήματι ἢ ἐγγυητῆι). The term employed to denote real security is τιμήματι, the simplex form of the noun, which obviously has the same meaning as the compound.[46]

Several *horoi* lend further support to Harpocration's observation. *Horos* no. 163A was set up on a property to indicate that it stood as security for an *eranos*-loan of one talent, and the term for security is ἀποτίμημα (line 3). *Horos* no. 32 records three debts secured by land and a house. The first is a loan of 30 *drachmai* given by a group called the *dekadistai*, and the third a loan furnished by a group of *eranistai*, that is, men who had made an *eranos*-loan.[47] The phrase πεπραμένου ἐπὶ λύσει is used to indicate that the property had been pledged as security to the first two groups, and the term ἀποτίμημα for the third group of lenders.[48]

Horos no. 163 has the term ἀποτίμημα but does not appear to have been set up in connection with either a dowry agreement or the lease of an orphan's property. There is no mention of dowry, and the words παιδί and παισί are likewise absent. Instead of the woman's name normally found on the *horoi* set up in connection with a dowry, a man's name has been inscribed (Διονύσωι). Unlike the *horoi* set up in connection with the leasing of an orphan's property, an amount of money is recorded. Finally, there is a reference to a written copy of the agreement (ἐπὶ συνθήκαις), a feature found only on *horoi* set up on property pledged as security for a loan.[49] *Horos* no. 159 is similar insofar as the word [ἀπ]οτιμήματος, restored

[46] For a thorough discussion of this inscription, see Whitehead (1986) 165–9. Cf. Finley (1985) 284 note 39. For the simplex used in place of the compound, see the previous note.

[47] For the *eranos*-loan, see Maier (1969).

[48] Finley (1985) 45–6 observed that the term ἀποτίμημα was used in loans, but gave no explanation for its use in this context. Note that these cases pose a serious problem for his analysis of the term, which relies on a strict distinction between the procedure for taking security in a loan and that followed in dowry and the leases of orphans' property.

[49] Written copy of agreement: *horoi* nos. 1, 2, 2A, 3A, 6, 11, 13, 17, 27, 39, 65. Cf. *horoi* nos. 9 (Amorgos), 10 and 104 (Lemnos). The word γραμματεῖον on *horoi* nos. 107 and 108 (Amorgos) probably refers to a written copy of the agreement. On these documents, see Finley (1985) 21–7. For the meaning of the term συνθῆκαι, see Kußmaul (1969).

with certainty, is followed by the name of a man in the dative (Ἀρχίαι). These two *horoi* must by process of elimination fall into the category of those set up on property pledged as security for a loan.

The contrast with the terms ὑποτίθεναι and ὑποκεῖσθαι and the phrase πεπρᾶσθαι ἐπὶ λύσει is noteworthy. This terminology is never seen in the context of leases.[50] And on merely three *horoi* is the phrase πεπραμένου (-ης, ων) ἐπὶ λύσει seen in connection with a dowry.[51] An unmistakable pattern emerges from this survey of the contexts in which each type of term occurs. The term ἀποτίμημα appears in all three contexts – leases, dowries, and loans. The other terms occur almost without exception only in the context of loans. This strongly suggests that ἀποτίμημα is a general term for real security, whereas the other terms are appropriate only in the restricted context of loans. This would explain why we find the term τίμημα, the simplex form of the compound, in the expression [τιμ]ήματι ἢ ἐγγυητῆι in the decree passed by the deme of Plotheia about leasing of deme property. The expression is clearly meant to cover all forms of security, both real and personal. The term chosen to designate real security in general as opposed to personal security is τίμημα, not ὑποθήκη or πρᾶσις ἐπὶ λύσει.

The next step toward solving the enigma is to look into the meaning of each type of term for real security and to determine why it is appropriate to the contexts where it occurs. As several scholars have noted, the verb ἀποτιμᾶν contains two elements, the prefix ἀπο- which means "off" or "apart," and τιμᾶν, which means "to evaluate."[52] Whether pledged for a loan, a lease, or the return of a dowry, the property offered as security is normally assessed by the person who accepts it to ensure that its value is equivalent to, if not more than, the amount of the obligation owed to him. When Pantaenetus borrowed money from two sets of creditors on the same property, it is clear from the resulting dispute that one set of creditors had made an evaluation of the property's value, since they declare it

[50] For the verbs ὑποτιθέναι, τιθέναι, and ὑποκεῖσθαι used to express the idea of security in loans, see Dem. 27.9; 28.18; 35.11; 41.11; [Dem.] 49.11, 12, 35, 50, 52, 53, 54; 50.55; 53.10, 12–13; 56.4, 38; Aeschin. 3.104; Is. 5.21–2; 6.33–4; Isocr. 21.2; Hdt. 2.136.

[51] *Horoi* nos. 21A, 49, and 82. *Horoi* 82A and 93 may also belong in this category, but are too fragmentary to allow certain restorations.

[52] Finley (1985) 233 note 1; 242 note 51; Harrison (1968) 256; MacDowell (1978) 144–5 ("property valued and set apart"). Cf. the phrase used by Libanius (Dem. 41 *hypoth.* 1): τὴν οἰκίαν τῆς ἄλλης οὐσίας ἐξελεῖν.

is sufficient to cover both debts (Dem. 37.12).[53] After its value is determined, the property offered as security is then set apart and marked as separate by placing *horoi* on it.

The two actions implied by the verb ἀποτιμᾶν – evaluating and setting apart – are performed in all three cases where security is found. In rental, the property pledged as security is evaluated and set aside on the understanding that the lessor can seize it in the event the lessee fails to keep up with the payment of rent. In a dowry agreement, land or buildings are evaluated to determine whether their value is greater than the value of the dowry given to the husband. *Horoi* are set up around the security offered by the husband, and if the husband and wife dissolve their union and the husband does not return the dowry, the *kyrios* of the woman has the right to take possession of the security. In a loan, the lender inspects the property the borrower intends to furnish as security and makes sure it is worth more than the amount of the loan. If the borrower defaults, the lender takes over the property. The verb ἀποτιμᾶν and the noun ἀποτίμημα are thus appropriate in all three contexts and can serve as general terms. What these terms do not indicate is whether the person who accepts the security has an existing claim on the property or only a contingent claim. All the terms imply is that the property has been evaluated and set apart.

If ἀποτίμημα is a general term used to denote real security in all three types of agreements, why are the expressions ὑποκειμένου (-ης, -ων) πεπραμένου (-ης, -ων) ἐπὶ λύσει used to describe property pledged in security in loans, but not in leases? Here it is necessary to examine the different structures of legal obligation in the two agreements.[54] In a loan, the lender gives the borrower a sum of money, which the latter can exchange for goods or services. After handing the money over to the borrower, the lender has no further obligations under the terms of the agreement. He has fulfilled his part of the bargain and has received in return a right to the repayment of the loan. The borrower, on the other hand, is in debt to the lender the instant he receives the loan and has no rights against the lender. The borrower, of course, does not have to repay the principal until the due date

[53] Finley (1985) 117 grudgingly admitted this. Other examples of evaluating the security: Dem. 35.18; [Dem.] 49.52. The latter passage reveals that Pasion regularly checked the value of all items given to him as security.

[54] This is not the place to enter into the debate about the existence of consensual contracts in Classical Athens. Pringsheim (1950) 14–57 denied their existence, as did Wolff (1957). Gernet (1951) rightly questions much of Pringsheim's analysis and his attempt to explain away such passages as [Dem.] 56.2.

arrives.[55] But his full obligation under the agreement remains unfulfilled until he repays the lender. There is thus an inherent asymmetry in the legal structure of the agreement: the lender has a right against the borrower and no further obligation, whereas the borrower has an obligation to the lender, but no claim against him. This asymmetry puts the lender in a vulnerable position, since he must perform his part of the agreement immediately and trust the borrower to perform his obligation to repay at some time in the future. The purpose of the security is to protect the vulnerable lender and the possibility that the borrower reneges on his promise to repay or becomes insolvent.

The structure of legal obligation in a lease is different.[56] The lessor agrees to permit the lessee to occupy and make use of his property for a certain period of time in return for the payment of rent. As long as the lessee pays his rent on time, he never falls into debt to the lessor. At the outset of the lease, therefore, the lessee is in a very different position vis-à-vis the lessor than the borrower vis-à-vis the lender. The lessee and the lessor begin the lease on equal terms: the lessor has an obligation to the lessee to allow him to use his property, and the lessee has the obligation to pay rent. The lessee may have other duties, such as a requirement to plant certain types of crops, but these are incidental and do not affect the fundamental structure of the agreement.[57] Provided that the lessee does not fall into arrears, he remains on an equal footing with the lessor. Each has both a right and an obligation toward the other, and neither is in debt to the other.[58] This makes a lease different from a loan where the borrower is in debt to the lender for the duration of the agreement.

This difference between the structures of legal obligation in the two agreements had an effect on the terminology applied to the security in each case. In a loan the debtor immediately incurs an obligation the instant he receives the money from the lender, who thereby acquires a claim on the property pledged to him as security. Since the property is immediately placed "under an obligation," it can be described as ὑποκειμένου and remains that way for the duration of the

[55] The borrower's right to redeem the security was strictly speaking not part of the loan agreement, but part of an accessory agreement. See Harris (1988b) [= Chapter II.2 in this volume] 364–5.

[56] On leases in general, see Behrend (1979).

[57] Requirement to plant certain crops: *IG* ii² 2494, lines 11–16. Restrictions on ploughing: *IG* ii² 2498, lines 17–21.

[58] For the rights of the lessee, see *IG* ii² 2492, lines 9–12 (right to use property for duration of lease), 29–31 (breach of agreement by lessors makes them liable to legal action); 2496, lines 22–4 (lessors promise to warrant lease and promise to pay penalty for failing to do so).

loan. Since the lender has given money to the borrower and received the pledge of security in return, it is natural for him to view the transaction as a sale and to describe the property as sold to him with the right of redemption (πεπραμένου, -ης, -ων ἐπὶ λύσει).[59]

In leases, however, this terminology is not appropriate for the security. Provided that the lessee makes regular payments of rent, he and the lessor remain on equal terms. Nor can the lessor contend that the security furnished by the lessee has been sold to him since at the outset of the agreement, he has not "paid" anything to the lessee. He has merely permitted the lessee the use of the property, which the lessee pays for in regular installments. Unlike the lender, the lessor's main obligation to the lessee lasts as long as the lease does. The lessee falls into debt to the lessor only if he falls behind in his payment of rent (*IG* ii^2 2496, lines 17–20). Thus, the debt for which the property of the lessee has been pledged as security is only contingent. It may arise at some time during the course of the lease, or it may never arise at all. Because there is no outstanding debt against the property pledged as security when the *horoi* are placed on it, there is not an amount of debt that can be inscribed on the *horoi*. That is the reason why the *horoi* affixed to property standing as security for the lease of an orphan's estate never record an amount of money in the way the *horoi* set up in connection with loans do. It is also the reason why the term ἀποτίμημα is employed to denote the security in leases instead of the phrases ὑποκειμένου (-ης, -ων) or πεπραμένου (-ης, -ων) ἐπὶ λύσει. The latter phrases imply that the property secures an existing obligation. The word ἀποτίμημα does not imply there is an existing obligation and is thus suitable to be inscribed on the *horoi* set up in connection with leases.

To understand why the word ἀποτίμημα was used to refer to real security in a dowry agreement, it is necessary to examine briefly the historical antecedents of the institution. The custom of giving a dowry had its roots in the practice of gift-giving in marriage during the Archaic period.[60] In fact, the Athenian term for

59 For the tendency of the creditor to describe a secured loan as a "sale," see Harris (1988b) [= Chapter II.2 of this volume] 362–75.

60 The two most important studies of gift-giving in marriage are Finley (1955) and Lacey (1966). Hom. *Il.* 9.144–8 implies that it was customary for gifts to be given to the husband of the bride. Morris (1986) 104–12 has mistaken notions about the difference between marriage in the Homeric world and marriage in Classical Athens. As a result, he fails to see the similarities and continuity between the two forms of marriage. Wolff (1944) was written before the works of Finley and Lacey and consequently does not understand the historical origins of the dowry. For brief but trenchant criticisms of Wolff's

dowry in the Classical period, προίξ, carries a trace of these roots, for the word appears to have meant "gift" in the Homeric poems (Hom. *Od.* 13.15). The right of the woman's relatives to the return of the dowry in the event of divorce had its origin in the Archaic custom of recompensing the woman's family with gifts if she was dismissed from her husband's household (Hom. *Od.* 2.112–13, 130–3 – ἀποτίνειν). As Greek society developed formal legal procedures, these gift-giving practices became formalized and subject to written regulations. The dowry was now assigned a monetary value and became part of the formal legal agreement called the ἐγγύη. The social pressure on the husband to allay the wrath of his wife's relatives in the event of divorce by recompensing them with gifts received formal expression in the law that gave the relatives of the divorced woman the legal right to bring an action for the return of the dowry.[61] At the same time, the husband was legally protected against exorbitant demands that could be exacted to the original value of the dowry (Is. 3.35). As a result of these historical antecedents, the Athenians tended for the most part to view the dowry in the same category as that given for the repayment of a loan. Insofar as the husband's obligation to return the dowry was only contingent, the dowry agreement was similar to a lease, which explains why in most cases the property given as security for a dowry is denoted by the same term, ἀποτίμημα, employed to refer to security in a lease agreement.

That, at any rate, was the majority view. There appears, however, to have been a dissenting faction, which held a minority view of the dowry. Three *horoi*, nos. 21A, 49, and 82, constitute our epigraphic evidence for the minority view.[62] On

view of the dowry, see Finley (1985) 243 note 53. Despite its many flaws, Wolff's article is still regarded as authoritative in recent treatments of marriage in Classical Athens. See, for example, Just (1989) 73, 284 note 8. The entire topic demands a fresh study.

[61] For the *dike proikos*, see [Arist.] *Ath. Pol.* 52.2 with Rhodes (1981) 584. I doubt this action could be used by a husband to force payment of part of a dowry promised to him, but not paid. As our analysis of Dem. 41.6–10 revealed, an outstanding amount of dowry was considered a debt and was thus subject to the laws concerning the repayment of loans.

[62] These *horoi* cannot have been put up on property pledged as security for the payment of dowry by a woman's relatives and are thus not comparable to the *horoi* set up by Polyeuctus (Dem. 41.6). In that case, the property was pledged to the husband, but on *horoi* nos. 49 and 82 we find the names of women, just as on the other *horoi* set up to secure the return of a dowry. *Horos* no. 21A is fragmentary, but Fine's restoration, which gives the names of a woman and her *kyrios*, is highly probable. *Horos* no. 93 is restored by Kirchner in *IG* ii^2 2683 to give a similar formula, but there are too few letters legible to guarantee certainty. The discussion of these *horoi* by Finley (1985) 51 is too brief and vague to be helpful; the criticism made by Finley (1985) 244 note 59 in regard to Kirchner's classification of *IG* ii^2 2681–3 is off the mark.

these *horoi* the term ἀποτίμημα is replaced by the phrase πεπραμένου (-ης, -ων) ἐπὶ λύσει, which is normally applied to security pledged for a loan and never to security in a lease agreement. One might dismiss these few exceptional cases as the products of carelessness in the use of legal terminology. Yet there is actually some legal justification for choosing the phrase πεπραμένου (-ης, -ων) ἐπὶ λύσει to describe property standing as security for the return of a dowry. One could argue that a dowry was in a way similar to a loan. Just as the lender gave the borrower a sum of money and received the right to repayment of an equivalent amount of cash, the man who gave a female relative in marriage and presented her husband with money or property as a dowry received the right to the repayment of an equivalent amount in the event of divorce. If the dowry was thought of in these terms, the husband's obligation to his wife's relative began as soon as he received the dowry. The repayment of the "loan" then fell due on the day the couple dissolved their union. Viewed in this manner, the dowry agreement contained the same asymmetry in its structure of legal obligation as did a loan. The husband "fell into debt" to his in-laws the moment they gave him the dowry. If the dowry was considered a debt, it created an immediate claim on the security furnished by the husband. Those who viewed the dowry in this way accordingly used the phrase πεπραμένου (-ης, ων) ἐπὶ λύσει, the terminology applied to the security in a loan, to describe the land or building provided as security by the husband.

Whether one conceived of the dowry as a loan or as a gift had no effect on the legal relationship between the husband and his wife's relatives. This difference of opinion created problems only when the husband had to calculate his total assets for liturgical purposes. The law granted the husband full rights over the dowry, which made it into an asset of his household ([Dem.] 42.67).[63] If the dowry was considered a gift, its value could not be counted as a debt against the husband's property. On the other hand, if the dowry was considered a loan, it created a debt and its value could be deducted from the total value of the husband's assets. As a matter of bookkeeping, the dowry posed something of a conundrum.

The difference of opinion led to the dispute we read about in the speech *Against Phaenippus* ([Dem.] 42.26–7). The speech was delivered at a trial arising

[63] Harrison (1968) 52–4 gives a short summary of the debate about the ownership of the dowry, but does not see the legal issue involved.

from an *antidosis*. As part of the *antidosis* procedure, each party was required to provide an inventory of all his holdings. When Phaenippus drew up the list of his possessions, he counted the dowry given for his mother Aristonoe as a debt and no doubt deducted its value from his total assets (ταύτῃ χρέως φησὶν ὀφειλεσθαι Φαίνιππος τὴν προῖκα). The speaker follows a different method of bookkeeping and does not list his own mother's dowry as a debt (οὐκ ἀπογράφω τήν προῖκα χρέως αὑτῇ). The speaker implicitly accuses Phaenippus of deceitful accounting practices when he declares that he himself has not attempted to mislead the court. As *horoi* nos. 21A, 49, and 82 demonstrate, however, Phaenippus' view of the dowry was shared by other Athenians. The speaker cites the law that gave the husband full rights over the dowry to support his view that the dowry should be counted as an unencumbered asset. The law may support the speaker's interpretation, but does not prove it correct, for the law addresses only the question of ownership. The law is silent about the way to treat the right to the return of the dowry held by the woman's relatives. If this right was similar to the right of the lender to repayment, then the dowry must be treated as creating an obligation. Despite the speaker's allegation of deceit, Phaenippus' view of the dowry had sound legal precedent in the procedures followed during the confiscation of property. When a man had his property seized by public officials as a result of conviction on a serious charge, his wife was put on the same footing as his creditors, and her dowry was treated as a debt that could be set apart from the rest of his assets.[64]

This conflict of opinion about the legal status of the dowry illustrates the kind of problems the Athenians encountered when attempting to translate a social custom rooted in the practice of gift-giving into the idiom of formal legal agreements. The existence of such an unresolved legal issue in Classical Athens is exactly what we would expect in a society whose law-code was relatively rudimentary and nowhere near as thorough and detailed as the system of Roman Law became under the Empire. As I have shown in an earlier article, a comparable conflict of views existed about the ownership of real security in loans.[65]

[64] Bekker, *Anecdota graeca*, 250: ἐνεπίσκημμα καὶ ἐνεπισκήψασθαι· προφώνησις γυναικὸς καὶ δανειστοῦ, δημευομένης οὐσίας, περὶ προικὸς καὶ χρέους, ὀφείλοντων αὐτὰ ἐξ αὐτῆς λαμβάνειν. The information presented in this passage is confirmed by the publication of a fragment of the *poletai* records for 367/66 (*Hesperia* 10 [1941] 14).

[65] Harris (1988b) [= Chapter II.2 in this volume] 362–76.

The chief advantage of this approach to the enigma of the term ἀποτίμημα is that it enables us to explain why each term is used in the context in which it is found. Neither Finley nor Wolff was able to explain, for example, the use of the term in loans or the fluctuations in terminology for the security pledged in a dowry agreement. This analysis of Athenian terminology for real security reveals that the Athenians were sophisticated enough in legal matters to recognize an important difference between the structures of obligation in leases and loans, respectively, and to understand the effect these differences had on the nature of the creditor's claim on the security. For instance, when Apollodorus ([Dem.] 49.11) describes the property of the general Timotheus and distinguishes between his land in the plain, which stood as ἀποτίμημα for the son of Eumelides, and the rest of his land, which ὑπέκειτο to several trierarchs for a loan, he was not using different terms for real security merely out of a desire to vary his style. The land in the plain had been pledged as security for the lease of an orphan's estate, the rest for a loan. Apollodorus knew that the structure of legal obligation was different in each arrangement and accordingly chose one term to refer to the security given for the lease and another expression for the security pledged in the loan. And he would not have troubled to make such a distinction unless the members of the court who heard the case shared his knowledge and expected Apollodorus to choose his words with care.[66]

III

We are now in a position to study the law on real security cited and discussed in Demosthenes' speech *Against Spudias* (Dem. 41.7–10).[67] The first thing to notice is that the statute uses the verb ἀποτιμᾶν. That is in accord with our conclusions so far. As we have seen, the verbs ὑποτιθέναι and ὑπόκεισθαι, as well as the verbs of sale πιπράσκειν and ἀποδίδοσθαι, are appropriate to describe the act of pledging security only in the context of loans. Unlike these verbs, ἀποτιμᾶν

[66] The legal knowledge of the average member of the Athenian court should not be underestimated. See Harris (1991a) 134–6.

[67] Previous attempts to interpret the law, such as those of Finley (1985) 52, 245 notes 61 and 62, and of Wolff (1954) 330–1, are based on erroneous views of ἀποτίμημα. For references to earlier treatments, see Wolff (1954) 330–1. My own view is closest to that of Pappulias (1909) 159–60, though his view of *apotimema* differs from mine, and he makes no attempt to place the law in the context of other Athenian laws about protecting ownership.

is suitable for describing a pledge of security in all three transactions where it is used. Since it is a general term, it was naturally chosen as the term employed in this general statute concerning real security.

To understand the meaning of the statute, our first task will be to examine the two paraphrases of its contents given by the speaker in *Against Spudias*. Our interpretation of the statute must then be tested to see whether it applies to the case described by the speaker. Our final job will be to place the law in the context of other Athenian laws about property and to search for the rationale behind its provisions.

After describing his dispute with Spudias over a house pledged to him as security by Polyeuctus, the speaker calls witnesses to corroborate his account of events. He next refers to the law that supports his claim to the house, then lists two unpaid loans made by Polyeuctus to Spudias (8–10). At the end of this part of his narrative, he calls more witnesses, cites documents, and has the law about real security read out by the clerk (10). As he instructs the clerk to read the law, he gives a short paraphrase of its contents, which ought to be accurate since the court would have been able immediately to catch any misrepresentation when it was read out to them by the clerk. According to the speaker, the law does not allow a suit to be brought (οὐκ ἐᾷ . . . ἔτι δίκην εἶναι) in regard to property pledged as security (τῶν ἀποτιμηθέντων) against those in possession (πρὸς τοὺς ἔχοντας). The participle is the standard term used of those who are in possession of a property at the time a dispute arises over its ownership.[68]

The question immediately emerges, who are those in possession? In a pledge of real security, there are two parties, the person who pledges the security for some obligation and the person who receives the pledge. If "those in possession" are the persons who pledged the property as security, the statute would deny those who received the pledge the right to bring an action in regard to the security. This cannot be the correct interpretation. If it were, the statute would bar the creditor who attempted to seize the security from a defaulting debtor from bringing an action to enforce his right to the debtor's property. That possibility is ruled out by the existence of the *dike exoules*, which did give the creditor the right to bring such a suit. Yet if "those in possession" are creditors who have seized a property pledged

[68] This was arbitrarily denied by Finley (1985) 245 note 61. The verb ἔχειν is used at [Dem.] 7.26 to denote possession in contrast to ownership. Many other passages show the word used in the same sense. See, for example, Dem. 24.13; [Dem.] 52.32; Is. 10.24.

as security after the debtor has defaulted, the statute bars the debtor and his heirs from bringing an action against the creditor in possession of the property. By denying the debtor's right to challenge the creditor's possession of the property, the statute in effect protects the creditor's right of ownership to property he has accepted as security and distrained upon in satisfaction of an unpaid debt.

This interpretation is confirmed by the speaker's first version of the law, which he claims sticks closely to its actual wording. According to the speaker, the law explicitly forbids (τὸν νόμον ὃς οὐκ ἐᾷ διαρρήδην) cases to be brought in regard to property that one has pledged as security (ὅσα τις ἀπετίμησεν εἶναι δίκας) by them and their heirs (οὔτε αὐτοῖς οὔτε κληρονόμοις). Who are "them" (αὐτοῖς)? The pronoun must refer to persons who pledge their property as security since there is no other noun in the sentence indicating who "them" might be. The difference in number between τις and αὐτοῖς need not trouble us. The word τις is a generalizing pronoun and the word αὐτοῖς is a generalizing plural.[69] The word αὐτοῖς cannot refer to persons who have accepted the security since they are nowhere mentioned in what precedes. The first version of the statute thus forbids whoever has pledged property as security and his heirs from bringing a suit in regard to this property. Both versions of the law are in perfect accord.

On this interpretation, the law directly applies to the dispute recounted by the speaker. Since we have already analyzed the case in detail in Section I, all that is necessary here is to recapitulate the relevant aspects of the case. Polyeuctus owed money to the speaker and shortly before his death pledged a house belonging to him as security for the debt. After Polyeuctus' death, the speaker appears to have considered himself the owner of the house, for he considered himself entitled to collect rent from the property. Spudias is attempting to prevent the speaker from collecting rent by bringing an action against him.[70] As the husband of Polyeuctus' daughter, Spudias has no doubt claimed that he has an equal right to the revenues

[69] For the generalizing plural, see Bers (1984) 24–7. For a comparable shift from singular to plural in a general statement, see Xen. *Hiero* 5.4. Cf. Smyth (1956) 271.

[70] The verb διακωλύει at Dem. 41.5 is a conative present – see Smyth (1956) 421. The verb refers to Spudias' suit, which was aimed in part at challenging the speaker's right to the property. It cannot refer to a physical attempt by Spudias to bar the speaker from entering the property, since the property was clearly occupied by those who were paying rent. It is also wrong to interpret this "lease" as a secured loan and to view the payment of rent as interest payments. There is no evidence from the speech that Polyeuctus ever agreed to pay the speaker interest on the unpaid portion of the dowry.

generated by the property. In response to Spudias' challenge to his ownership of the house, the speaker cites the law about real security. The law is directly relevant to the speaker's case. It forbids Spudias, who is acting on behalf of an heir of Polyeuctus, the person who pledged the house as security, to bring an action concerning the house. The speaker now considers himself to be in possession of the house and cites the law to protect himself against the claim made by Polyeuctus' heir.

Since the purpose of the law is to protect the creditor's right to retain property he has accepted as security and seized as the result of default, the law must be placed in the context of Athenian procedures for protecting ownership. When one Athenian challenged another Athenian's ownership of property, the person in possession was required to show that he had legally acquired the property. In a speech of Isaeus (10.24), we learn that the person in possession (τὸν ἔχοντα) of a disputed property (τῶν ἀμφισβητησίμων χωρίων) was compelled to bring forward either the person who pledged the property as security (θέτην) or the seller (πρατῆρα), or to demonstrate that the property had been awarded to him by a legal judgment (καταδεδικασμένον).[71] The procedure of appealing to the seller to warrant legitimate ownership is well attested in our sources and is referred to by the verb ἀνάγειν.[72] These procedures provided the person in possession with adequate proof of legitimate ownership in almost all cases. There is one significant exception: the situation where the creditor's right to the property pledged as security and seized after default was challenged by the debtor who pledged it to him. In this case the person whom the creditor would call on to warrant his ownership would be the very person who is contesting his ownership. The existing provisions about proving legitimate ownership thus failed to protect the creditor's title against the person from whom he had accepted the security. This defect in the law was remedied by the law about real security cited at Dem. 41.10. If a creditor seized property pledged to him as security, and the debtor from whom he had seized it brought an action against him in order to recover his property, the creditor could challenge the legality of his suit by bringing a countersuit, or παραγραφή.[73] The creditor would then show that the debtor

[71] For the correct interpretation of the passage, see Wyse (1904/1979) 668–9, who cited the relevant passages from Harpocration and Photius. Finley (1985) 232–3 note 51 arbitrarily rejects Wyse's interpretation.

[72] For the procedure, see Wyse (1904/1979) 436.

[73] For the *paragraphe* procedure, see Wolff (1966).

had pledged the property as security and defaulted on his obligation. Once he had established these facts, he would cite the law about real security to demonstrate that the debtor was not legally entitled to bring his suit. If he could convince the court of his version of the facts, the court would vote in his favor and bar the debtor from bringing his suit against the creditor.

Our discussion of the law cited at Dem. 41.10 decisively refutes Finley's contention that the Athenian law-code had no laws pertaining to real security. Though this law appears to have been the only one exclusively concerned with real security, the creditor who received property as security could resort to the *dike exoules* to enforce his rights against a defaulting debtor who refused to yield possession of the security. And there was evidently a general provision about methods of proving legitimate ownership that covered property obtained through a pledge of security.

The Athenian way of dealing with the legal issues surrounding real security stands in sharp contrast to the procedures of Roman Law. As I pointed out in the previous chapter, Roman Law differed from Athenian Law by providing formal modes of conveyance (*mancipatio* and *cessio in iure*) and separate procedures for asserting *iura in rem* (*vindicatio*) and *iura in personam* (*condictio*). Roman Law also drew a sharp distinction between the right of possession and the right of ownership by providing one remedy (the possessory interdict) to protect possession and another remedy (the *vindicatio*) to protect *dominium*. These formal procedures allowed the Romans to distinguish between *fiducia cum creditore*, where the ownership of the security passed to the creditor, *pignus*, where the creditor gained only *possessio*, and *hypotheca*, where the debtor retained both *dominium* and *possessio*. If the creditor received a pledge of security by *fiducia cum creditore*, he could protect his ownership of the security by means of *vindicatio* if the debtor defaulted and either refused to yield possession or challenged the creditor's right of ownership. In *pignus* the situation was different: the creditor could protect his possession of the security by means of a possessory interdict (Harris [1988] 358–61). The Athenians, unlike the Romans, had no such formal procedures that could be applied in a wide variety of situations to clarify legal issues in complex transactions like real security. Instead, they proceeded on an *ad hoc* basis. When they encountered a legal issue such as this one, they did not appeal to a specialized group of jurists whose task it was to apply their expert knowledge of broad legal principles to the solution of hard cases. Yet the absence of legal specialists in Classical Athens should not cause us to underestimate the legal knowledge of the men who staffed the Athenian courts.[74] As I hope to have shown, the terminology used by the Athenians to describe real security reveals a careful awareness of subtle legal differences. The rule of law was not an empty slogan in democratic Athens; it was an ideal that the average Athenian took very seriously.

Afterthoughts

Biscardi (1999) 173–98 shows that the principle of *prior tempore potior iure* was applied in private contracts in Athens and was recognized in several laws in the Hellenistic period. Biscardi shows also that in these laws the creditor obtained the right to sell the security only to recover the amount of his loan, but the debtor retained the right to the excess. This undermines Finley's view, which I accepted in this essay, that real security in Greece was substitutive, not collateral.

The study promised in note 25 was published as Harris (1994a) and is republished in this volume as Chapter IV.1.

[74] See note 66.

II.4 The Liability of Business Partners in Athenian Law: The Dispute between Lycon and Megacleides ([Dem.] 52.20–1)

One of the most striking features of Athenian laws regulating commercial activities is the absence of any concept akin to the modern legal notion of the partnership or corporation.[1] Despite the presence in Athenian society of numerous *koinoniai,* groups of individuals cooperating for some purpose, be it commercial or otherwise, Athenian Law concerned itself solely with individual persons and did not recognize the separate legal existence of collective entities.[2] And just as Athenian Law did not recognize the legal existence of partnerships or corporations, it also did not possess the notion of corporate liability. This meant that if someone entered into an agreement with a group of individuals and one of

I would like to thank the referee of *Classical Quarterly* for several intelligent suggestions that have significantly improved this chapter.

[1] For the absence of the legal notion of partnership or corporation in Athenian Law, see Finley (1951) 275 note 5. Harrison (1968) 242 note 1 questioned Finley's position, arguing that it rested merely on an inference from the fact that Attic documents do not differentiate consistently between the members of an association and the entity itself. But Finley's position is perfectly sound: see, for instance, Weber's discussion in Rheinstein and Shils (1954) 156–7: "The most rational actualization of the legal personality of organizations consists in the complete separation of the legal spheres of the members from the separately constituted legal sphere of the organization; while certain persons designated according to rules are regarded from the legal point of view as alone authorized to assume obligations and acquire rights from the organization, the legal relations thus created do not at all affect the individual members and their property and are not regarded as their contracts, but all these relations are imputed to a separate and distinct body of assets. Similarly, what the members as such may claim from or owe to the organization under its rules, belongs to or affects their own private assets, which are legally entirely separate from those of the organization."

[2] For the *koinonia* see Endenberg (1937).

those individuals violated the terms of the agreement, the plaintiff proceeded only against the individual who acted contrary to the agreement, not against the group as a whole.[3] If the plaintiff won his suit, he had a right to receive compensation only from the defendant's private property; he did not have a claim on all the funds held in common by the group.

An understanding of this aspect of Athenian Law helps to explain the puzzling features of the legal dispute between Lycon, a man from Heraclea, and Megacleides of Eleusis, mentioned by Apollodorus in his speech against Callippus ([Dem.] 52.20–1). Since his aim in the part of the speech where the dispute is described is to prove that Callippus and Lycon were not close friends and the details of the dispute are not relevant to this point, Apollodorus gives only a brief summary of the background of the case and of the nature of Lycon's charge against Megacleides. Yet, the brevity of his account notwithstanding, Apollodorus provides us with enough information to identify the legal issues in the case.[4] Besides illustrating the nature of liability in loans contracted by multiple borrowers, an analysis of the case will also shed light on an important aspect of security in maritime loans and enable us to resolve a textual problem in Apollodorus' speech.

The dispute concerns a loan of forty *mnai* that Lycon had made to Megacleides of Eleusis and his brother Thrasyllus for a voyage to Ace and back.[5] Apollodorus tells us that one of the men changed his mind and decided not to sail there nor to take the risk (μεταδόξαν αὐτῷ μὴ ἐκεῖσε πλεῖν μηδὲ κινδυνεύειν). The word αὐτῷ should refer to Megacleides in the same way that αὐτοῦ in the previous clause refers also to him. But Wolf was perplexed by the singular αὐτῷ.[6] Since the

[3] Lipsius (1905–15) 771 thought that the δίκαι κοινωνικαί mentioned at [Arist.] *Ath. Pol.* 52.2 were suits against or by corporations, but his view was rightly questioned by Harrison (1971) 22.

[4] One cannot argue that the case is not evidence about the principles of Athenian Law because it was decided by a private arbitrator and not by a law court. Private arbitrators were guided by the same legal principles as were the law courts. The parties in a suit might ask an arbitrator to ignore the legally stipulated penalties when making his judgment, but I am not concerned with the decision Archebiades might have reached. On this topic see Meyer-Laurin (1965) 41–5 with the bibliography cited there.

[5] Megacleides probably intended to return with a cargo of grain. For Ace as a major supplier of grain for Greece, see Herodas 2.16–17 with Headlam (1922) *ad loc.* For maritime loans in general, see the important articles of de Ste. Croix (1974) and Millett (1983).

[6] H. Wolf in Reiske (1774) 952: "Si subintelligas τοὺς δανεισαμένους [as the subject of πλεῖν], verte: cum mutata sententia non committendum esse putasset, ut illi cum periculo illuc navigarent. Sed durum hoc est, et parum consentaneum. Quare legere malim, μεταδόξαν αὐτοῖς." Wolf's emendation has been accepted by both the Loeb and Budé editors. Rennie's Oxford text retains αὐτῷ, but notes Wolf's proposal in the *apparatus criticus.*

loan was made to Megacleides and Thrasyllus for their voyage to Ace, he reasoned that both of them must have decided not to go there and therefore proposed to emend αὐτῷ to αὐτοῖς.

A consideration of the problems facing the maritime lender in antiquity reveals that the emendation is unnecessary. When a man lent money to a merchant for a trading voyage, it was customary for the merchant to pledge his ship or the cargo on it as security for the loan.[7] If the merchant defaulted on the loan, the lender could seize the ship or the cargo and sell it in lieu of repayment.[8] But what if the merchant decided to defraud the creditor by absconding with both cargo and ship? The lender would lose his money, and there would be no security for him to seize. Of course, the lender could accompany the merchant to keep an eye on him, but that would have been irksome. Indeed, we know of no case where a creditor chose to travel with the borrower for this purpose.[9] The solution to the problem was to have the lender make the loan to a pair of men, one of whom sailed with the ship while the other remained behind.[10] In the event that the borrower who sailed with the ship tried to defraud the lender by failing to return, the lender could then demand payment from the borrower who had remained behind, and if denied repayment, could initiate legal proceedings against him.

[7] Ship pledged as security: Dem. 32.14; 35.33; 56.3. Cargo pledged as security: Dem. 32.12; 34.6; 35.10, 52.

[8] For example, Dem. 33.6; 35.12.

[9] Hansen in Isager and Hansen (1975) 83 note 67 lists Lycon along with certain Massaliote citizens (Dem. 34.4–5, 12), Lampis and Theodorus (Dem. 34.6, 8, 22, 26, 40), as lenders who traveled with the ship. But there is no evidence in Dem. 32 that the Massaliote citizens sailed on the ship with their borrowers Zenothemis and Hegestratus, nor any in Dem. 34 that Theodorus traveled on Lampis' ship. Phormio claims that he repaid a loan to Lampis, but Chrysippus points out that his claim is implausible (Dem. 34.25–8). Besides, even if Lampis did lend money to Phormio, the former sailed with the ship not because he was a creditor, but because he was its *naukleros*.

[10] Thompson (1987) 601 suggests that this might have been the arrangement worked out between Lycon and the brothers, but does not pursue the possibility further. The passages he cites as referring to similar arrangements are not relevant to the question of maritime security: Dem. 34.8 concerns a letter sent by a creditor to his slave and a friend, both in Bosporus, requesting them to inspect the goods pledged to him as security. [Dem.] 49.31–2 deals with a deposit made by Timosthenes to Phormio. [Dem.] 52.3 and 7 describe how Lycon instructed Pasion to pay the money he owed to Cephisiades, who was at the time abroad on a trading voyage. Nor does he cite [Dem.] 56, the case that is actually relevant to his point. Finally, Thompson does not attempt to discover the rationale behind this arrangement. Previous scholars have not discussed this type of security arrangement in maritime loans. No treatment of it can be found in Isager and Hansen (1975), Cohen (1973), Vélissaropoulos (1980), and Carey and Reid (1985).

This was clearly the arrangement that was worked out between the lenders Dareius and Pamphilus and the borrowers Parmeniscus and Dionysodorus ([Dem.] 56.6).[11] Dareius and Pamphilus agreed to lend three thousand *drachmai* to Parmeniscus and Dionysodorus on the security of their ship for a voyage from the Piraeus to Egypt and back. Parmeniscus sailed the ship to Egypt while Dionysodorus stayed in Athens (7). According to Dionysodorus, the ship was damaged on its return voyage and was forced to put in at Rhodes, where Parmeniscus sold the grain he had bought with the loan (21). When Dareius and Pamphilus learned of this, they confronted Dionysodorus and demanded that he repay the loan with the interest already agreed on. Dionysodorus offered to repay the loan with the interest accumulated as far as Rhodes, but this proposal failed to satisfy the lenders, who then brought suit against him (11–18).[12] When the case came to trial, Parmeniscus was still plying the Mediterranean in the ship that had been pledged to Dareius and Pamphilus (4). In fact, the written agreement (συγγραφή) they had drawn up had provided for such an eventuality. In it the borrowers agreed that in the event that they defaulted and did not deliver up the ship, they would be liable to a penalty double the amount of the loan. They further agreed that the lenders could exact this penalty from either or both of them (45: τὴν δὲ πρᾶξιν εἶναι καὶ ἐξ ἑνὸς καὶ ἐξ ἀμφοῖν). Since Athenian Law did not consider that joint borrowers formed a single partnership and were thus jointly liable for any breach of the agreement, Dionysodorus would not normally have been held liable for anything Parmeniscus did contrary to the terms of the agreement. In the absence of anything corresponding to the modern legal notion of partnership or corporation, it was necessary to add this *praxis*-provision to enable Dareius and Pamphilus to proceed against Dionysodorus.[13]

[11] For a similar arrangement see Dem. 33.16–17: when Androcles lends money to Artemon and Apollodorus on the security of goods to be purchased in Chalcidice and sold in the Pontus, Lacritus, Artemon's brother, reassures him by stating that he is his brother's partner (κοινωνός) and by promising ποιήσειν . . . τὰ δίκαια ἅπαντα καὶ ἐπιδημήσειν Ἀθήνησι, τὸν ἀδελφὸν αὐτοῦ Ἀρτέμωνα πλεύσεσθαι ἐπὶ τοῖς χρήμασι. Androcles, however, was incautious and did not make sure that Lacritus was included in the *syngraphe*.

[12] For a discussion of the legal issue involved in the case and Dionysodorus' defense, see Meyer-Laurin (1965) 12–15. His analysis is superior to that of Carey and Reid (1985) 197–200, who mistakenly argue that Dionysodorus probably sought "some kind of 'equity' ruling."

[13] For a similar clause in a document in a maritime loan, see Dem. 35.12. For the purpose of the *praxis*-clause, see Wolff (1941) 428: "the primary purpose of the contractual *praxis*-provision" is to create "the

Applying what we have learned from the information found in [Dem.] 56 to the case described by Apollodorus, we can now see that the arrangement with Lycon must have called for Megacleides to sail to Ace while his brother remained in Athens. Since it was Megacleides who was supposed to sail to Ace, it was he alone who changed his mind and decided not to make the voyage there. That is why the text reads αὐτῷ, not αὐτοῖς.

Megacleides' change of mind appears to have been the cause of the dispute. He had promised Lycon that he would go to Ace, and Lycon had lent him money for the trip in the expectation that he would journey there and pay him interest upon his return to Athens. But when Megacleides changed his mind, a dispute arose about the payment of the interest (περὶ τῶν τόκων). Lycon, the lender, naturally claimed that the interest was still due since Megacleides had promised to pay it when the loan was made. By promising to pay it and then refusing to do so, Megacleides deceived him (ἐξηπατημένος). Megacleides probably defended himself by arguing that he did not owe the interest because he had never made the voyage.[14]

It is clear from Apollodorus' summary of the case that Lycon brought his suit against Megacleides alone, not Megacleides and Thrasyllus (ἐγκαλέσας τι τῷ Μεγακλείδῃ); note also that only Megacleides is brought forward as a witness to the dispute. One might argue that Lycon must have proceeded against both Megacleides and Thrasyllus since as joint borrowers they formed a partnership and were thus jointly liable. Such a view is mistaken, for it rests on the erroneous assumption that the Athenians possessed a notion of legal personality similar to our own. But, as we have seen, the Athenians, like the Romans, had no legal concept akin to our modern notion of partnership or corporation.[15] In Athenian Law each partner was individually responsible for his own actions. If one member of a group of borrowers or lenders breached the terms of the loan agreement, the

debtor's liability and subjection to a possible execution to be carried out by the person for whom the clause was made out, in cases not covered by any liability provided for by law." See also Simon (1964).

14 I follow the reconstruction offered by Thompson (1987) 601 note 4. It was probably disputes of this sort that led to the inclusion of phrases like σὺν ἡμιόλᾳ in the loan documents found on Greek papyri in Egypt. By adding this phrase, the debtor agreed beforehand to pay the stated interest on the loan even if he repaid the principal long before it was due. For the phrase and its meaning, see Lewis (1945).

15 For the absence of modern notions of juridical personality in Roman Law, see Nicholas (1962) 60–1. Cf. Taubenschlag (1944) 49: "there is no evidence of the existence of private bodies with a fully corporate personality in Greco-Roman private law in Egypt."

normal procedure was for the plaintiff to proceed against that one person, not the entire group.

The dispute between the borrower Pantaenetus and his creditors Evergus and Nicobulus provides a good illustration of this.[16] Nicobulus and Evergus lent Pantaenetus a sum of 105 *mnai* on the security of a workshop at Maroneia and the thirty slaves in it (Dem. 37.4). While Nicobulus was away on a business trip to the Pontus, Evergus took possession of the workshop on the grounds that Pantaenetus had failed to make interest payments and to fulfill his duties under the terms of their agreement (6–7). Unable to use the workshop, Pantaenetus fell behind in his payments on his mining lease from the state and was listed as a public debtor. The situation concerning the workshop was complicated by the fact that there was another set of creditors, the existence of whose claims Pantaenetus had previously hidden from Nicobulus and Evergus.[17] The dispute over the various claims to the workshop was settled by the three parties (7–16), but Pantaenetus was still angry about Evergus having caused him to miss his payments to the state and therefore brought a suit against him. After winning his suit against Evergus (2, 8, 46), Pantaenetus then decided to bring a separate action against Nicobulus. He charged Nicobulus with having plotted against him by instructing his slave Antigenes to seize his mine and the money his own slave was carrying as payment for the *katabole* to the state (22–9). In his speech against Pantaenetus, Nicobulus employs several lines of argument to prove that his opponent's suit is not actionable, but nowhere does he argue that Pantaenetus is legally required to bring one suit against both partners. And just as Pantaenetus was able to bring one suit against Evergus and then a separate suit against Nicobulus, Lycon brought a suit against Megacleides alone. After all, it had been Megacleides who had promised to sail to Ace and had then changed his mind. Since Thrasyllus had

[16] Carey and Reid (1985) 114–17 do not realize that the Athenians did not share our modern notion of juristic personality and consequently give a confused account of the relationship between Nicobulus and Evergus. For instance, they state that "the probability is that as partners in the loan both Nicobulus and Evergus could be held responsible for the acts committed by one of them." But if so, why doesn't the charge against Nicobulus drawn up by Pantaenetus (23–9) contain any mention of Evergus' actions?

[17] Previous analyses of the dispute are vitiated by their failure to understand the difference between the two proposals made by the other creditors at 12–13. For a discussion of the settlement worked out by the three parties and its implications for our understanding of real security in Classical Athens, see Harris (1988b) (= Chapter II.2 of this volume) 370–7.

apparently done nothing contrary to the terms of the agreement, he could not be charged with deceiving Lycon.[18]

We can now fill in the details omitted by Apollodorus. Lycon made a maritime loan to Megacleides and his brother Thrasyllus for a trading voyage to Ace. The loan was clearly interest-bearing, though we are not told what the rate was fixed at. According to the agreement, Megacleides was to travel to Ace while his brother remained in Athens. For some reason or other, Megacleides decided not to make the trip. Lycon then demanded repayment of the loan plus the interest promised to him. Megacleides offered to repay just the principal, but when his offer was refused, he apparently chose to keep the principal until an agreement could be reached.[19] Thereupon Lycon called on his friend Archebiades to settle the dispute. Thrasyllus never became involved in the dispute because he had done nothing contrary to the terms of the agreement with Lycon and because Lycon was not compelled by Athenian Law to proceed against both partners at the same time. The procedure followed in the case, though at first puzzling, makes perfect sense when we remember that the Athenians lacked the modern legal notion of partnership or corporation.

Afterthoughts

In the new Athenian Grain-Tax Law of 374/73 BCE there is a *praxis* clause similar to the one analyzed in this chapter that is also found in a clause concerning the liability of a group, in this case a *symmory* of men who have bought a contract to collect taxes. See lines 33–6 with the commentary in Stroud (1998) 66–7.

[18] Such an explanation of the procedure followed in the dispute is preferable to the suggestion of Thompson (1987) 601–2 that Apollodorus, though using the singular throughout the passage, considers the acts of Megacleides to be the work of both Megacleides and Thrasyllus. As we have seen, this assumption is unnecessary; the passage can easily be explained without resorting to any hypothesis about Apollodorus' linguistic habits. Moreover, the passage adduced by Thompson as a parallel, [Dem.] 35.6–7, is not really similar. Here the author employs the plural several times before switching to the singular. That is not the case in Apollodorus' account of Lycon's dispute. Apollodorus says only that the two men received the loan, but never states that both were involved in the ensuing dispute. Finally, if, as Thompson claims, both Megacleides and Thrasyllus participated in the arbitration, why was Megacleides alone called on to testify about Archebiades' role as arbitrator?

[19] Thompson (1987) 601 note 4 aptly compares the action of Dionysodorus at [Dem.] 56.12–16 and 32.

II.5 Did Solon Abolish Debt-Bondage?

THE *CONSTITUTION OF THE ATHENIANS* ATTRIBUTED TO ARISTOTLE INFORMS US IN several places that Solon abolished the practice of "lending on the [security of the] body" (δανείζειν ἐπὶ τοῖς σώμασι).[1] Several scholars have recently interpreted this to mean that Solon abolished the practice of debt-bondage. M. I. Finley believed that as a result of Solon's reforms "debt-bondage was abolished *tout court*."[2] Elsewhere Finley asserted "The Solonic revolution in Athens brought an end to debt-bondage" and also interpreted a major fragment of Solon's poetry (fr. 36 [West]) as a description of this reform. G. E. M. de Ste. Croix often disagreed with Finley, but on this point he did not differ: in his opinion, Solon "forbade for the future not merely enslavement for debt but also any kind of debt-bondage by the simple expedient of prohibiting the giving of the body as security."[3] This view has been accepted without question by several scholars such as Ober[4] and by Patterson.[5]

In this article I will argue that Solon did not abolish debt-bondage, but only enslavement for debt. Section I will analyze the difference between enslavement for debt and debt-bondage. Section II will examine the terminology used by Aristotle to describe Solon's reform and show that the law concerns enslavement for debt, not debt-bondage. Section III will provide evidence to show that debt-bondage continued to exist in Classical Athens long after Solon. Section IV will show that Solon's poetry reveals that the lawgiver was concerned about enslavement resulting

1 [Arist.] *Ath. Pol.* 2.2; 4.4; 6.1; 9.1. Cf. Plu. *Solon* 13.4; 15.2; *Moralia* 828f.

2 Finley (1981) 166. Cf. 157 ("freeing the debt-bondsmen of his day and abolishing the category from Athens henceforth"); 107 ("The Solonic revolution in Athens brought an end to debt-bondage"). Cf. 117–18, 122. Garlan (1988) 90–1 appears to follow Finley. Finley (1981) 117 believes that Solon fr. 36 (West) refers to this reform but this view is mistaken – see E. M. Harris (1997) and below.

3 De Ste. Croix (1981) 282 with note 27. Cf. 137 with note 2. See also Fisher (1993) 16: "both debt-bondage and slavery for debts were abolished."

4 Ober (1989) 59–63.

5 Patterson (1982) 125. Cf. Raaflaub (1993) 71. Shaw in Finley (1998) 27, 30 refers to Solon's abolition of debt-bondage as if it were an established fact.

from violence and raids for booty, not about debt-bondage that had come about because of a certain system of land tenure. Section V will place Solon's law in the context of class relations in Archaic and Classical Athens.

I

It is important to preface our discussion by drawing a clear distinction between enslavement for debt and debt-bondage.[6] In enslavement for debt the debtor becomes the slave of his creditor, who becomes his master and thus gains all the rights of ownership over the debtor. Different societies may place different restrictions on these rights, but the basic incidents of ownership remain constant from one society to the next. In all societies ownership is "the greatest possible interest in a thing which a mature system of law recognizes."[7] The Romans grouped the rights exercised by an owner under three main headings, the right to use (*ius utendi*), the right to enjoy the fruits (*ius fruendi*), and the right to "use up" (*ius abutendi*), that is, the right to consume or alienate. Modern legal theory breaks these into the following rights and duties: (i) right to possess, (ii) right to use, (iii) right to manage, (iv) right to income, (v) right to capital, (vi) right to security, (vii) transmissibility, (viii) absence of term, (ix) prohibition of harmful use, and (x) liability to execution. The Athenians and the citizens of other Greek *poleis* clearly recognized that owners exercised these powers over objects that belonged to them and that masters possessed all these rights over their slaves.[8] For instance, masters exercised complete physical control over their slaves: they could beat them, chain them up, starve them (Xen. *Mem.* 2.1.16), employ them as prostitutes ([Dem.] 59.18–23), or even castrate them (Hdt. 8.105). All money earned by slaves belonged to the master ([Dem.] 53.20), and likewise all contracts made by the slave were the

[6] Several scholars do not make a clear distinction between the two institutions, and it is therefore difficult to understand how they interpret Solon's law. For instance, Harrison (1968) 39 asserts "Since the time of Solon slavery for debt had disappeared from Athens," but it is not clear whether he is referring to debt-bondage or not. The same is true of Todd (1993) 172. Rhodes (1981) 125–6 believes Solon abolished "enslavement for debt," but then paradoxically states: "although it is generally true that after Solon's reforms debts were not incurred on the security of the body, there are signs that slavery for debt was not entirely impossible in later Athens." To make matters more confusing, Rhodes then cites passages referring to debt-bondage and outright slavery without clearly distinguishing between the two relationships.

[7] On the concept of ownership in general and the rights of owners, see Honoré (1961).

[8] For ownership as the right "to do whatever one wants" with an object, see Plato *Euthydemus* 301e–302a. For the rights of ownership in Athens and other Greek *poleis*, see Kränzlein (1963) 47–52.

responsibility of his master (Hyp. *Ath. passim*). If the master fell into debt, he could offer to hand over his slave to the creditor as compensation ([Dem.] 53.20–1), or if the master had his property confiscated by the *polis*, the *poletai* would seize his slaves and sell them.[9]

The most important rights for our purposes are the right to sell and the absence of term. As Aristotle (*Rh.*1.5.1361a21) observed, one of the main indications of ownership was the right to alienate by gift or sale. The master as owner had the right to sell his slave to whomever he pleased and take the price offered by the buyer without paying the slave anything. By the terms of the sale, the buyer acquired all the rights of ownership exercised by the former owner, and if he chose to sell, the next buyer acquired these same rights, and so on *ad infinitum*. This brings us to the incident called "absence of term." The owner does not exercise his rights for a fixed period of time ("term"); his rights are permanent.[10] When he dies, he has the right to transfer his possession to his heirs, whether by will or intestate succession. This incident is known as "transmissibility," and several wills preserved in the Attic orators reveal that masters in Athens enjoyed this right over their slaves (e.g., Dem. 27.9; Aeschin. 1.97). For the slave, this means that his subjection to his master or masters has no limit; he is a slave for life. There is no prospect of release from his status unless the master agrees to emancipate the slave. But nothing compels his master to free him.

Debt-bondage on the other hand is the "status or condition arising from a pledge by a debtor of his personal services or those of a third person under his control as security for a debt."[11] Unlike slavery, debt-bondage is not a permanent status: the debt-bondsman remains under the control of the creditor only until his debt is paid off. The creditor does not have all the rights exercised by an owner, just the right to his services for a certain period of time.[12] There is evidence for

9 See, for example, Meiggs and Lewis (1969) no. 79A (= *IG* i³ 421), lines 26–49.

10 On slavery as a perpetual relationship, see Patterson (1982) 9. Cf. Ballagh (1902) 28: "The distinguishing mark of the state of slavery is not the loss of liberty, political or civil, but the perpetuity and almost absolute character of that loss, whether voluntary or involuntary." Patterson (1982) 18–27 criticizes efforts to define slavery in terms of ownership, but his criticism rests on several misunderstandings of key legal concepts. Besides, his own definition of slavery is not incompatible with defining slavery in terms of ownership. I hope to discuss this issue in the future.

11 Article I of the Supplementary Convention on Slavery adopted by the United Nations in Geneva, 1956, quoted in de Ste. Croix (1981) 136.

12 Finley (1981) 151 claims that "'sale' into bondage and debt-bondage cannot be distinguished very sharply," but the ancient law codes make it clear that different rules applied to each status, making it easy to distinguish them.

debt-bondage in many ancient societies. In early Rome the Twelve Tables (VI.1) contained a clause about *nexum*, the Roman form of debt-bondage: *cum nexum faciet mancipiumve, uti lingua nuncupassit, ita ius est.*[13] Varro (*De Lingua Latina* 7.105) reports there was a dispute between the jurists Manilius and Mucius about how to classify *nexum*. Manilius believed *nexum* referred to all acts conducted by the formal procedure *per aes et libram*, including *mancipatio*. For Mucius *nexum* was different from *mancipatio*. Varro uses a dubious etymology to support Mucius' view: since *nexum* comes from *neque suum*, he reasons that the person subject to *nexum* did not become the property of the creditor, which made it unlike *mancipatio*, a procedure that transferred ownership. Whatever the value of Varro's etymology, his explanation reveals that the debtor in *nexum* did not fall into the position of a slave under the *dominium* of a master. In fact, Varro continues by defining the *nexus* as "a free man who [gives] his labor into servitude for money which he owes until he pays it off" (*liber qui suas operas in servitutem pro pecunia quam debebat dum solveret*). The status of the *nexus* was thus temporary and granted the creditor only a right to the debtor's labor. It was better than that of the *addictus* and the *iudicatus*, who could be put in chains and, if their obligation was not paid off, sold across the Tiber.[14] Since the *nexus* remained a free citizen, he was still eligible for military service (Livy 2.24.6). Though *nexum* contained several advantages for each party, it was subject to abuse by creditors and was finally abolished by the *lex Poetilia* in 313 BCE.[15]

Debt-bondage was not a Roman innovation: it was a common institution in many societies both before and after the Classical period in Greece. Several of the law collections from the Ancient Near East contain provisions about debt-bondage.[16] Section 117 of the laws of Hammurabi (reigned 1792–50 BCE) places a limit of three years for a person given in debt-bondage:

> If an obligation is outstanding against a man and he sells or gives into debt service his wife, his son or his daughter, they shall perform service in the

[13] The clause is found in Festus *s.v. numerata pecunia*. For an interesting suggestion about the combination of the terms *mancipium* and *nexum* in this clause, see Westbrooke (1989).

[14] See Aulus Gellius *Noctes Atticae* 20.1.45 with Watson (1975) 110–24.

[15] On this measure see MacCormack (1973).

[16] On debt-bondage in ancient Near Eastern Law, see Westbrook (1995), esp. 1656–60, and Dandamaev (1984) 178–9. For the laws from the ancient Near East, I have used the translations and system of reference found in Roth (1995). The distinction between slavery and debt-bondage is also found in the Middle Assyrian Laws dated to around 1076 BCE (compare the rule in A 48 with that in C 2–3).

> house of their buyer or of the one who holds them in debt service for three years; their release shall be secured in the fourth year.

The following provision, section 118, sets forth a different rule for slaves:

> If he should give a male or female slave into debt-service, the merchant may extend the term [beyond three years], he may sell him; there are no grounds for a claim.

Hammurabi makes a strict distinction between the treatment of free persons who are turned over for a debt and slaves in the same position: the latter can be sold, but the former can serve for only three years.

Debt-bondage is also well attested in the Hebrew Scriptures. Several laws guarantee that Hebrews can only fall into debt-bondage and must be released after a certain period. According to *Deuteronomy* 15.12–17 (cf. *Exodus* 21.2–11), if a Hebrew man or woman is "sold" to another, he or she can serve only for six years and must go free in the seventh year. *Leviticus* (25.25–55) states that the Hebrew who is sold must not serve as a slave but like a hired servant and should only serve until the Jubilee. Before the Jubilee, he can be redeemed by a relative or may redeem himself (48–9).

From the Greek world, there is evidence of the practice of debt-bondage in the laws of Gortyn. In an inscription dated to the early fifth century, there are several provisions about the *katakeimenos* or debt-bondsman (*Inscriptiones Creticae* 4.41.v.4–vi.16).[17] The first states that if the debt-bondsman causes damage on the orders of the person with whom he resides, he is not liable (lines 4–7: α[ἰ δέ] κα κελομένο ὅl̥ι κα παρῆι ϝεργάδδlηται ἢ πέρηι, ἄπατον l ἤμην). On the other hand, if his creditor denies the damage was done on his orders, the judge should decide on oath if there is no witness to support his denial (lines 7–11: αἰ δὲ πονίοι μlὴ κελομένο, τὸν δικlασστὰν ὀμνύντα κlρίνεν, αἰ μὴ ἀπονlιοι μαίτυρς). If a debt-bondsman damages another's property, he should pay the penalty himself (lines 11–14: ἀλλόlτριον δ' αἴ τί κ' ἀδικlέσει ὁ κατακείμενlος, αὐτὸν ἀτῆθαι). The protasis of the next clause and the subjects of the apodosis are preserved, but the rest of the clause is not preserved (lines 14–17: αἰl δέ κα μὲ ἔκηι ὀπὸ καταlστασεῖ, ὁ νικάσανςl κ' ὁ καταθέμενος). This clause dealt with the eventuality that the debt-bondsman caused damage but did not have

[17] For detailed analysis with references to earlier discussions, see Koerner (1993) 384–91.

enough money to pay the plaintiff. The preserved part of the stone mentions the successful plaintiff and the creditor, and Koerner was probably right to suggest that in such a case the law encouraged the two men to work out an agreement whereby the debt-bondsman could pay off both men either simultaneously or in succession.

The next column (vi) covers the case where someone harms the debt-bondsman (lines 2–12). In this case the creditor will bring the case and collect the payment of damages (αἰ δέ τις| [τ]ὸν κατακείμεν|ον ἀδικήσει ὁ κατ|αθέμενος μολησε|ῖ καὶ πρακσῆται τ|ὰς τιμὰνς ᾇι ἐλευθέ|ρο), half of which he will retain and half of which will go to the debt-bondsman (κ᾽ ὅτι ἐσπράκσ|εται τὰνν ἡμίναν ἔ|κεν τὸν κατακεί|μενον, τὰν δὲ τὸν καταθ|έμενον). If the creditor does not wish to bring an action against the defendant, the debt-bondsman may bring an action after he has paid off his debt (lines 12–6: αἰ δὲ κ᾽ ὁ κα|ταθέμενος μὴ λῆι| μολῆν, ῆ κ᾽ ἀποδôι τὸ ὀ|πήλομα αὐτὸς μολή|το). These provisions are valuable because they illustrate how the debt-bondsman held a status somewhere between slavery and freedom. The debt-bondsman was unlike a slave insofar as he could be held liable for any damage he caused and could possess his own funds from which he could pay damages. The slave had no money of his own; if he caused damage, his master was liable. But the debt-bondsman was similar to a slave to the extent that he could not bring an action on his own behalf until he paid off his debt. If his creditor brought the action, half of the award went to him and half to the debt-bondsman. If someone harmed a slave, the entire award went to the master; if someone harmed a free man, the victim collected the damages paid.

A provision from the lawcode of Gortyn (*Inscriptiones Creticae* 4.72.i, lines 2–3) also shows how the debt-bondsman was in a special position. The very first clause of the Great Code forbids a plaintiff who brings an action about a free man or a slave to seize him before the trial (ὄς κ᾽ ἐλευθέροι ἒ δόλοι μέλλει ἀν|πιμολêν, πρὸ δίκας μὲ ἄγεν).[18] The last clause in this section, however, provides an exception to this rule: it allows the creditor to seize the debt-bondsman and the successful plaintiff to seize the defendant, who has presumably failed to pay the amount awarded to the plaintiff (I, line 56–II, line 2: [τ]ὸν δὲ νενικαμένον κα[ὶ τὸν κα]|τακείμενον ἄγοντι ἄπατον | ἔμεν).

[18] For the interpretation of the first clause, see Maffi (1983) 3ff. and Gagarin (1988).

The term for debt-bondsman at Gortyn was κατακείμενος. Elsewhere in the Greek world, Pollux (3.82) informs us the term θῆτες was applied to "free men who because of poverty served for [the repayment of] money" (θῆτες ἐλευθέρων ἐστὶν ὀνόματα διὰ πενίαν ἐπ' ἀργυρίῳ δουλευόντων). Isocrates (14.48) also draws a careful distinction between debt-bondage (θητεία) and outright slavery when describing the fate of the children of the Plataean exiles after the Theban conquest of their city. He says many of their children had fallen into slavery because of small debts (πολλοὺς μὲν μικρῶν ἕνεκα συμβολαίων δουλεύοντας), while others were in a state of debt-bondage (θητεία). Since these exiles went to many different *poleis*, Isocrates clearly implies that debt-bondage was widespread in the Greek world, not a phenomenon confined to a few unusual communities.

II

In the previous section we analyzed the difference between outright slavery and debt-bondage. These two institutions existed side by side in many societies in the ancient Near East, in Classical Greece, and in Rome during the early Republic. And when Isocrates used the term in his *Plataicus*, he clearly expected his Athenian audience to be familiar with the institution of debt-bondage. But modern scholars believe that debt-bondage no longer existed in Athens at the time since Solon had abolished it over two centuries before. But did Solon really abolish debt-bondage?

The next task is to examine the meaning of the phrase "lending on [the security of] the body" (δανείζειν ἐπὶ τοῖς σώμασι). The expression δανείζειν ἐπί + a noun in the dative denotes a loan on real security as opposed to the procedure of *engye*, which was a form of personal security.[19] In this arrangement the debtor pledges an object in his possession as security for a loan. If the debtor defaults on the loan, the creditor has the right to seize the security, over which he thereby acquires the rights of ownership (see, e.g., [Dem.] 35.12; Dem. 37.4–6), which included the right to sell. In fact, the creditor in Athens regarded the pledge of security as a "sale with right of redemption." The rights of ownership acquired by the creditor were protected by the *dike exoules* and the law cited at

[19] Scholars such as Finley (1985) and Fine (1951), followed by Harrison (1968) 258 believed there were two or more forms of real security in Classical Athens. Chapter II.2 of this volume shows this view is incorrect, and this position has now been confirmed by Youni (1996) and endorsed by Todd (1993) 254–5.

Dem. 41.7–10.[20] Thus, a loan on the security of the body would grant the creditor the right to seize the debtor in the event of default, to make him his permanent slave, or, if he wished, to sell him to someone else. For the debtor, default would incur a permanent loss of status. Analysis of the phrase δανείζειν ἐπὶ τοῖς σώμασι reveals that Solon must have abolished enslavement for debt.[21] This appears to be the way Plutarch (*Solon* 13.4–5) interpreted the phrase: before Solon's reform men contracted debts on the security of their bodies (χρέα λαμβάνοντες ἐπὶ τοῖς σώμασι) and thus could be seized by their creditors (ἀγώγιμοι τοῖς δανείζουσιν ἦσαν). Some of these became slaves (δουλεύοντες), whereas others were sold abroad (οἱ δ᾽ ἐπὶ τὴν ξένην πιπρασκόμενοι). This is also consistent with our evidence from the fifth and fourth centuries, which indicates that enslavement of free persons, whether Athenian or non-Athenian, by private individuals was illegal ([Arist.] *Ath. Pol.* 52.1; Dem. 25.55; Din. 1.23). Imprisonment for debt was allowed in mercantile cases (Dem. 33.1; 35.47), but that is a different matter.

III

There are several pieces of evidence that show that debt-bondage continued to exist in Classical Athens, but the most extensive one comes from Menander's *Heros*. In this passage, the two slaves Daos (the slave of Laches and Myrrhine) and Getas are conversing. Daos tells Getas how he has fallen in love with a young girl named Plangon (18–19). Getas naturally asks if she is a slave (20: δούλη 'στιν;). Daos replies that yes, she is in a certain way (οὕτως ἡσυχῇ τρόπον τινά). He then

[20] Finley (1985) believed that the Athenians had no laws governing real security, but Harris (1993) (= Chapter II.3 in this volume) esp. 92–5, shows this view is mistaken.

[21] This is the way Westermann (1955) 4–5 interpreted Solon's reform. Westermann, however, did not discuss the continued existence of debt-bondage in Athens.

Isocr. 14.48 does not provide evidence for the existence of enslavement for debt in Athens. It deals with the fate of Plataean exiles, who found themselves in dire straits and thus unguarded by the legal protections enjoyed by those dwelling in Attica. Nor should one use Lys. 12.98 to show that children could be sold into slavery to pay off debts (οἱ δὲ παῖδες ὑμῶν, ὅσοι μὲν ἐνθάδε ἦσαν, ὑπὸ τούτων ἂν ὑβρίζοντο, οἱ δ᾽ ἐπὶ ξένης μικρῶν ἂν ἕνεκα συμβολαίων ἐδούλευον ἐρημίᾳ τῶν ἐπικουρησόντων.). In this passage Lysias is describing the abnormal conditions of Athens under the rule of the Thirty Tyrants. Adams (1905/1970) 128 suggested "Perhaps the term ἐδούλευον is used only for a strong expression as forced labor of a debtor unable to meet his note by money payment," but the fact that these children have been sold abroad indicates Lysias is referring to actual enslavement.

reveals that Plangon and her brother Gorgias are the children of a poor shepherd and freedman named Tibeios (21–5: ποιμὴν γὰρ ἦν Τίβειος οἰκῶν ἐνθαδὶ/ Πτελέασι, γεγονὼς οἰκέτης νέος ὤν ποτε./ ἐγένετο τούτῳ δίδυμα ταῦτα παιδία). Getas next asks if this Gorgias is the same man who is now looking after their cattle (26–7). Daos says he is and proceeds to explain why Gorgias is working on his master's estate. During a famine, Tibeios borrowed first one *mna,* later another, to feed his children but died before he could pay off the loan (26–30: ὁ Τίβειος ὁ πατὴρ εἰς τροφήν γε λαμβάνει/ τούτοις παρὰ τοὐμοῦ δεσπότου μνᾶν, καὶ πάλιν/ (λιμὸς γὰρ ἦν) μνᾶν, εἶτ' ἀπέσκλη). To pay for the expenses of his father's funeral, Gorgias borrowed another *mna.* Since he was unable to repay this loan and the debts he inherited from Tibeius, Gorgias took his sister and is now residing with Daos' master (ἐπιμένει) while working off the debt (36: τὸ χρέος ἀπεργαζόμενος). As part of the arrangement, Plangon too is working with Daos' mistress making wool and performing other menial tasks (37–8: ἐργάζεται ἔρια διακονεῖ τε).

Gorgias and his sister Plangon are clearly in a relationship of debt-bondage to Daos' master and mistress. They are not slaves in the full sense since they were not sold to Laches nor captured in war. Nor are they like hired laborers since they remain (ἐπιμένει) on Daos' property and are not free to come and go as they please. This is why in response to Getas' question about their status, Daos replies that Plangon is a slave only "in a certain way." Plangon and Gorgias are working to pay off their debt to Laches, who has a right to their labor only until the debt is paid off.[22]

[22] De Ste. Croix (1981) 163 argues that Solon's law was repealed by the oligarchy. This argument seeks to prove *ignotum per ignotius.* First, we do not know the date of Menander's *Heros,* so there is no reason to assume it was produced during one of the oligarchic regimes after 322. Second, there is no evidence that Solon's law was ever abolished after 322. Despite the devastating implications of this passage for his interpretation of Solon's reform, Finley (1981) 141 merely states "this particular story raises very difficult historical and legal problems. But they need not delay us." Finley never explains why these problems do not deserve analysis (one suspects this is a rhetorical bluff). On the other hand, if one rejects Finley's view of Solon's reform, the passage creates no problems at all. Like de Ste. Croix, Millett (1991) 78–9 also attempts to explain away this passage but with a different argument. Millett claims that Tibeius' children were "non-citizens, and presumably fell outside the scope of Solon's law." (There is a similar argument in Gomme and Sandbach [1973] 390–1 and Todd [1993] 181.) But the laws of Athens provided rights and protection to all free residents of Attica, foreigners, metics, and citizens alike, unless they specifically restricted their provisions to citizens. For noncitizens suing in Athenian courts see Dem. 21.176; [Dem.] 56 *passim;* [Dem.] 59.64–9, and the general statement of Dem. 7.13 with the discussion of de Ste. Croix (1961). For severe punishment of Athenians who violated the rights of

One might object that Menander does not depict real life or that Solon's law was abolished during the regime of Demetrius of Phaleron. But the word *apergasamenos* [working off] used to describe the relationship of debt-bondage is also found in a fragment of Isaeus preserved by Harpocration (*s.v.* ἀπεργασάμενος), who glosses the term as "paying back a loan from one's labor" (ἀπεργασάμενος. ἀντὶ τοῦ ἀποδοὺς ἐκ τῶν ἔργων ἐξ εἰργάσατο. οὕτως Ἰσαῖος ἐν τῷ Πρὸς Ἀπολλόδωρον), an explanation very close to Varro's definition of *nexum*. This indicates that the institution was familiar to the men who heard the case presented by Isaeus' client in the early fourth century BCE, that is, under the democracy.

Another example of debt-bondage comes from Terence's *Heautontimoroumenos*, which is based on Greek original (4–9) and set in Attica. In the play the slave Syrus tells Chremes how his mistress lent an old woman 1,000 drachmas (600–1). After the old woman died, her daughter was left as a pledge for the debt (603: *ea relicta huic arrabonist pro illo argento*) and cannot be released until the debt is paid (605–6: *Cliniam orat sibi uti id nunc det: illam illi tamen/post daturam: mille nummum poscit.* Cf. 790–6). The depiction of debt-bondage in the play cannot be the result of *contaminatio* since debt-bondage was abolished in Rome by the *lex Poetilia* in the late fourth century BCE.

In Attic tragedy there is an allusion to debt-bondage in Euripides' *Alcestis* (1–9). In the prologue to the play, Apollo explains how he came to work for Admetus. After Zeus killed his son Asklepius with his thunderbolt, Apollo grew angry and in retaliation killed the Cyclopes who forged the thunderbolt. In compensation for the murder, Zeus ordered Apollo to work in the house of Admetus (6–7: καί με θητεύειν πατὴρ/ θνητῷ παρ' ἀνδρὶ τῶνδ' ἄποιν' ἠνάγκασεν.). Apollo's relationship with Admetus is similar to that of Gorgias with Laches: the god is serving in the house of Admetus on a temporary basis as a means of repayment. Gorgias and his sister are paying off a loan incurred by their father and themselves; Apollo is working to pay off the debt incurred through blood-guilt.[23] The passage

noncitizens, see Dinarchus 1.23. Millett and Gomme and Sandbach also believe that Tibeius was the freedman of Laches and that this may have affected their status. Although Tibeius was formerly a slave (22), there is no evidence at all in the play that he ever belonged to Laches or that Laches freed him.

23 Finley (1981) 116–17, 150–1 believed that Heracles of Greek myth was in debt-bondage to Omphale for the murder of Iphitus, but all the versions of this story indicate that Heracles was sold into slavery to Omphale (Aeschylus *Agamemnon* 1040–1 [πραθέντα τλῆναι, δουλίας μάζης βίᾳ (?)], Sophocles *Trachiniai* 248–57 [ἐμπολητθείς, πραθείς], 274–6 [πρατόν]) and the price of the sale given to the children of Iphitus (D.S. 1.79.3–5: τὴν μὲν τιμὴν . . . τοῖς Ἰφίτου παισὶ ἀπέδωκε). This is very

from Pollux noted at the end of Section I confirms this interpretation of Apollo's status. In Euripides' play, Apollo refers to his relationship to Admetus with the verb θητεύειν (6. Cf. 2: θῆσσαν τράπεζαν). Pollux (3.82) informs us that the word θῆτες was used to refer to "free men who because of poverty served as slaves for [the repayment of] money" (θῆτες ἐλευθέρων ἐστὶν ὀνόματα διὰ πενίαν ἐπ' ἀργυρίῳ δουλευόντων). Although the passage in the *Alcestis* comes from a play about the mythical past, Euripides clearly assumed his Athenian audience was familiar with the institution of debt-bondage.

The form of servitude imposed on Apollo is similar to the institution of *kishshatum* attested in the Lawcode of Hammurabi. In Babylon in the fifteenth century BCE, any victim who suffered an injury had a right to revenge or to payment of ransom. As Westbrooke notes, "If the culprit could not pay the ransom (fixed or negotiated according to the circumstances of the case), the victim was entitled to take the culprit or members of his family or possibly one of his slaves into servitude." Those given for *kishshatum* had to be released after three years.[24]

Aristophanes appears to allude to debt-bondage at *Pl.* 147–8, where one of the characters says "I have become a slave because of a little bit of money since I am not rich" (ἔγωγέ τοι διὰ μικρὸν ἀργυρίδιον/δοῦλος γεγένημαι, διὰ τὸ μὴ πλουτεῖν ἴσως). But these words are spoken by Carion, who throughout the rest of the play is called a slave. In the prologue Carion refers to his master who has acquired him and bought him (4: τῷ κεκτημένῳ. 7: τὸν ἐωνημένον). He does not owe his master only his labor, but is under his complete control. When he irritates his master, the latter threatens to beat him (21–3). Later he calls him his most trusted slave and his most thievish (26–7). The name Carion also appears to be a foreign name; I have found no case where an Athenian citizen bears this name. The name appears thrice in the building accounts for Eleusis (*IG* ii^2 1672, lines 59, 67; 1673, line 22), but appears to identify someone who is not an Athenian citizen because he does not have a demotic, unlike other men recorded in the inscription. This would seem to indicate that Carion was a foreigner who fell into debt in his own country where there were no laws against enslaving debtors, then

different from the arrangement between Apollo and Admetus. Note also that Apollo is said to θητεύειν and is never called a slave, whereas Heracles is called a slave and is never said to θητεύειν. Finally, Omphale is said to have freed Heracles (ἐλεύθερον δ' ἀφεῖσα), an act that applies only to slaves.

[24] See Westbrook (1995) 1638. In this case, however, the obligation has arisen from a delict, not from a contract.

sold abroad to his master. Like many other slave names (e.g., Thrax, Thrassa, Skythes), it indicates the region from which the slave came. The Athenians and other Greeks no doubt thought that barbarians were capable of such behavior; Herodotus (5.6.1) believed the Thracians sold their children as slaves for export. The passage is thus not evidence for enslavement for debt in Attica, but a reflection of Athenian attitudes about the barbarian "Other."

There is better evidence for debt-bondage in Athens in Aristophanes' *Clouds* (240–1).[25] Strepsiades has borrowed large sums of money to support his son's passion for expensive horses. His debts have grown to the point where he cannot repay his creditors, who are threatening to take him to court and other measures. In one passage Strepsiades describes to Socrates the threat hanging over his head: he is worried about creditors not only distraining on his property (τὰ χρήματ' ἐνεχυράζομαι) but also seizing him physically and taking him away (ἄγομαι, φέρομαι). Strepsiades' use of the verb ἄγομαι is significant: in the Gortyn lawcode (I, line 56–II, line 2), the person who has won a judgment or has accepted a pledge of services in lieu of payment has the right to seize the debtor ([τ]ὸν δὲ νενικαμένον κα[ὶ τὸν κα]|τακείμενον *ἄγοντι* ἄπατονl ἔμεν) without going to court. One might argue that Strepsiades' creditors intended to drag him off to prison, not take him into debt-bondage. Imprisonment for debt appears to be connected only with the *dike emporike* or cases involving foreigners, who might try to evade their creditors by escaping abroad (Dem. 33.1; 35.47). But neither of these qualifications applies to Strepsiades, who is not a merchant and has not borrowed money for trade and thus does not fall under the terms of the *dike emporike*. Nor is Strepsiades a foreigner. The best way of explaining the source of Strepsiades' anxiety is that he is afraid his creditors are about to take him into custody as a debt-bondsman.[26]

A passage from Hyperides' speech *Against Athenogenes* also indicates that a creditor could seize a defaulting debtor. Epicrates, the plaintiff in the suit, has bought three slaves from Athenogenes and agreed to assume their debts on the understanding that they were not very large (5–9). When the creditors came forward and demanded payment, it turned out that the debts in fact amounted to five talents

[25] Dover (1968) 129 comments only on the meaning of the verbs ἄγειν and φέρειν but does not observe the connection with debt-bondage.

[26] For a parallel case, see Menander *Sicyonius* 133–40, where the son of a debtor who has lost a suit about a contract and then died can be seized by his father's creditor (ἀγώγιμόν) along with his property (τήν τ' οὐσίαν σου). Gomme and Sandbach (1973) *ad loc.* do not notice the parallel with Gortyn.

(9). Epicrates then confronted Athenogenes, who denied he had any knowledge of these debts (12). Several of the bystanders urged Epicrates to have Athenogenes arrested as an "enslaver" (ἀνδραποδιστήν. Cf. [Arist.] *Ath. Pol.* 52.1). Epicrates did not follow their advice, and these bystanders were obviously stretching the meaning of the term "enslaver," but their suggestion only makes sense if Epicrates could have been seized and reduced to debt-bondage, or "slavery in a way" to use Daos' expression.

Our final example of debt-bondage comes from Plato's *Euthyphro* (4c).[27] In the dialogue Euthyphro tells Socrates how a *pelates* of his, who was serving in debt-bondage (ἐθήτευεν), recently died. The *pelates* had become drunk and angry at one of their slaves and killed him. Note how Euthyphro carefully distinguishes between the status of the *pelates* and the slave, just as Isocrates (14.48) does. Euthyphro's father then bound the *pelates*' hands and feet and threw him in a ditch, where he left him while he waited to hear from the Exegetes how to proceed. While waiting for the answer, the *pelates* died of hunger, the cold, and his bonds.

The ambiguous status of the *pelates* between freedom and slavery would help to explain the bewilderment about how to proceed against him. Euthyphro's father treats him like a slave after the murder by having him bound, which was not appropriate for a free man (see Dem. 53.16, cf. Is. 8.41). Instead of going to the Archon Basileus and bringing a charge against him, the normal procedure against free men in homicide cases ([Arist.] *Ath. Pol.* 57.2–4), the father takes him into private custody. Yet he is genuinely uncertain about what to do since he sends a man to consult the Exegetes. And after the *pelates* dies, Euthyphro's father claims he should not be prosecuted because he acted justly. This explanation makes sense only if he regarded him as a slave. If the *pelates* had been a free man, Euthyphro's father would not have had the right to use self-help since his offense did not fit one of the categories of just killing (or killing according to the laws) listed in Dem. 23.53–61: he did not kill him as a result of ignorance in battle (55), in an athletic competition (54), attempting to steal or enslave another (60–1), or while raping or seducing a female relative (55–6).[28] On the other hand, masters had the right to kill their slaves without fear of prosecution (Antiphon 6.4). Yet Euthyphro

[27] My analysis of this passage owes much to Kidd (1990). Carawan (1998) 311–12 appears to be unaware of Kidd's essay and does not discuss the problems created by the status of the *pelates*. The analysis of Tulin (1996) 55–100 suffers from his assumption that debt-bondage did not exist in Classical Athens.

[28] This provision clearly covered cases of rape and seduction. See Harris (1990a) (= Chapter III.1 in this volume).

does not share his point of view and thinks he should prosecute his father for homicide by bringing a charge before the King-Archon as if the victim were a free man. This disagreement could have occurred only if there was some ambiguity about the status of the *pelates*. As a debt-bondsman, the *pelates*, like the *katekeimenos* at Gortyn, was somewhere between slavery and freedom, and this posed a problem for Euthyphro and his father about how to deal with the legal implications of his violent death.

Harrison argued that the law cited about the release of captives taken in war provided for enslavement for debt.[29] This law is known from Demosthenes' speech *Against Nicostratus* (53.11). Nicostratus was taken prisoner by a trireme while pursuing one of his own slaves who had run away. His captors brought him to Aegina and sold him there. Apollodorus, who delivered the speech, gave Deinon, Nicostratus' brother, money to travel to Aegina and recover his brother. Nicostratus was ransomed for twenty-six *mnai* and returned home. He then asked Apollodorus for money to pay those who had ransomed him. Apollodorus borrowed 1,000 *drachmai* on the security of some personal items and gave this to Nicostratus as a gift. When Nicostratus was unable to come up with the rest of the money, he made another appeal to Apollodorus. If he did not repay those who had ransomed him, he would be liable to seizure (ἀγώγιμος). At this point Nicostratus reminded him that the laws stipulate that the man who has been ransomed from the enemy shall belong to the person who ransomed him if he does not repay the ransom money (11: οἱ νόμοι κελεύουσι τοῦ λυσαμένου ἐκ τῶν πολεμίων εἶναι τὸν λυθέντα, ἐὰν μὴ ἀποδιδῷ τὰ λύτρα). There is a similar provision in the lawcode of Gortyn.[30]

The situation that the law deals with has nothing to do with enslavement for debt. The law pertains only to the prisoner who has been captured by the enemy or by pirates. It was generally recognized since the Homeric period that

[29] Harrison (1968) 165, followed by Todd (1993) 181 note 25. For the view that capture in war is equivalent to enslavement see Albertoni (1925) 507–8, who rightly draws attention to *IG* ii² 4357, where the terms λυτρωθὲς and ἐλευθερωθὲ[ς are used to describe a liberated captive. Note also that the law uses the genitive, which denotes ownership – see Kränzlein (1963) 20–1. Neither Harrison nor Todd appears to be aware of Albertoni's essay. The attempt of Bielman (1994) 315–19, esp. 317 note 337, to explain away this evidence is not convincing.

[30] *ICret.* IV 72 VI.46–51 (= Koerner [1993] #171 = van Effenterre and Ruzé [1994–95] #13) αἰ κ' ἐδδυσ[άμενον] πέ/ρα[νδε] ἐκς ἀλλοπολίας ὑπ' ἀν/άνκας ἐκόμενος κελομένο τι/ς λύσεται, ἐπὶ τôι ἀλλυσαμέν/οι ἔμεν, πρίν κ' ἀποδôι τὸ ἐπιβά/λλον.

anything captured in war belonged to the victor. In the *Iliad* (21.34–41, 76–9; 22.45; 24.751–3) Achilles has the right to sell men captured in war. The principle was still recognized in the fourth century: Plato (*R.* 5.468a–b) assumes that soldiers captured by the enemy in war were theirs to use as they pleased, and Aristotle (*Pol.* 1.6.1255a6–7) states there is general agreement that items captured in war belong to those who take them (ὁ γὰρ νόμος ὁμολογία τις ἐστιν, ἐν ᾗ τὰ κατὰ πόλεμον κρατούμενα τῶν κρατούντων εἶναί φασιν). Xenophon (*Cyr.* 7.5.73) says it is a universal law that when a city is captured, all the persons and the property in it belong to the conquerors (νόμος γὰρ ἐν πᾶσι ἀνθρώποις ἀίδιός ἐστιν, ὅταν πόλις ἁλῷ, τῶν ἑλόντων τὰ σώματα τῶν ἐν τῇ πόλει καὶ τὰ χρήματα). The person who was captured in war therefore became the slave of his captor. If someone paid ransom for the captive, he had two options: either he could release him for free or he could insist that the captive pay him back.[31] If the latter, the former captive remained a slave in the ownership of the man who paid ransom until the ransom was paid. The Athenian law about the repayment of ransom and its counterpart at Gortyn therefore do not relate to enslavement, but to release from slavery. In enslavement for debt, a free person becomes a slave through a failure to pay a debt. But Nicostratus became a slave when he was captured by the enemy. His enslavement was the result of warfare, not debt. The law states that he will remain in the power of those who paid his ransom until he repays the money they spent to buy him from his captors. In other words, it stipulates that the man who has become a slave through capture in war will remain a slave until a certain condition is fulfilled. The law does not authorize a creditor to enslave a free man for failure to pay a debt. It does not therefore form an exception to the rule forbidding loans made on the security of the body.

IV

So far we have found that the wording of Solon's law indicates he outlawed the enslavement of debtors and that the Athenians practiced debt-bondage long after Solon's legislation. A careful examination of the fragments of Solon's poetry confirms these conclusions. In his poetry Solon describes in general terms the

[31] The honorary decrees collected in Bielman (1994) were probably awarded to men who did not ask for repayment of ransom.

problems confronting Attica before his reforms, but he clearly pins the blame for contemporary troubles on violence and the breakdown of law and order. The cause of the crisis is *Dysnomia,* the chaos brought about by contempt for law (fr. 4.31 [West]: κακὰ πλεῖστα πόλει Δυσνομίη παρέχει). The remedy for the situation is *Eunomia,* respect for law and justice, which brings order, makes all things right, and punishes the unjust (fr. 4.32 [West] Εὐνομίη δ' εὔκοσμα καὶ ἄρτια πάντ' ἀποφαίνει). The men who have plunged Attica into strife do not honor Justice and steal the property belonging to the gods and to the people by their raids for booty (fr. 4.12–14 [West]: οὔθ' ἱερῶν κτεάνων οὔτε τι δημοσίων/ φειδόμενοι κλέπτουσιν ἐφ' ἁρπαγῇ ἄλλοθεν ἄλλος,/ οὐδὲ φυλάσσονται σεμνὰ Δίκης θέμεθλα).[32]

Many scholars have speculated that the main cause of the crisis confronting Solon was economic. For instance, Andrewes believed that the residents of Attica began to reclaim land abandoned in the Dark Age during the ninth century, but "the process was not evenly continued or rapidly completed" until the eighth century BCE when "the pattern of village settlement characteristic of Classical Athens" came into existence.[33] The wealthy retained control of the reclaimed land, which was worked by the poor who paid one-sixth of the produce to their lords. As overseas trade increased, the wealthy tried to extort a greater percentage from these dependent laborers or sold them abroad. A. French had a different view of the crisis: he argued that overpopulation in Attica led farmers to shift from cereal production to stockbreeding, to intensify cultivation, and to plant crops in marginal land.[34] All these factors led to declining fertility. Grain imports from abroad caused prices to slide and placed small farmers in a precarious position. "An economic situation resulting from soil exploitation, decreasing fertility, mounting shortages and rising prices would now be complicated by the strain of foreign competition."[35] As a result, the impoverished farmers fell into debt and became the serfs of the wealthy. Gallant claims to take an approach different from that of

[32] Rihll (1991) 104–10 assumes that κτεάνων . . . δημοσίων refers to communal land, which the wealthy were encroaching on, but this interpretation is impossible. Solon says that the wealthy steal these items as booty (κλέπτουσιν ἐφ' ἁρπαγῇ), which must refer to movables, not land. For other telling objections to Rihll's analysis of the Seisachtheia, see Foxhall (1997) 117. On the status of the *hektemoroi* and the nature of the Seisachtheia, see Harris (1997). The conclusions of this article, I believe, strengthen my analysis of Solon's legislation.

[33] Andrewes (1982).

[34] French (1956).

[35] French (1956).

French and Andrewes, but he shares some of their basic assumptions: there was population pressure in early Attica, which caused upper class farmers to extend their property into uncultivated land.[36] These élite farmers then allowed poor farmers to work in return for a one-sixth payment. When this system broke down, the tensions between rich and poor gave rise to conflict.

All these views of the crisis confronting Solon run into two serious objections. First, there is no evidence in Solon's poems that the leaders of the community were exploiting peasants tied to the soil by the peaceful means of laws about land tenure.[37] Second, the archaeological evidence does not support the view that overpopulation in Attica in particular or in Greece in general led to extensification of land as Andrewes, French, Gallant, and others have argued. The recent surveys conducted by Lohmann show that there was no expansion into less productive areas of Attica during the seventh or sixth centuries; this process occurred in the fifth and fourth centuries.[38] Evidence from field surveys in other parts of Greece reinforce this picture. As Foxhall observes, intensive archaeological surveys in the southern Argolid reveal "no evidence for dramatic changes in cultivation practices and most sites seem to be situated near areas of best agricultural land."[39] Surveys in Kea, Methana, and Boeotia have produced similar results. Foxhall rightly concludes: "This pattern hardly suggests over-population or a landscape approaching its carrying capacity in the Archaic period."[40] Neither the evidence of Solon's poetry nor the results of archaeological surveys support the view that economic factors brought on the *stasis* Solon sought to end.

What Solon (fr. 4.23–5 [West]) actually describes is a countryside torn by violence where powerful men seize poor men and sell them abroad.

> ταῦτα μὲν ἐν δήμῳ στρέφεται κακά. τῶν δὲ πενιχρῶν
> ἱκνέονται πολλοὶ γαῖαν ἐς ἀλλοδαπὴν
> *πραθέντες* δεσμοῖσι τ' ἀεικελίοισι δεθέντες.

[36] Gallant (1982). Morris (2002) 29–41 uncritically accepts Gallant's view of Solon's reforms, has nothing original to add, and ignores the decisive objections made by Foxhall (1997) and the evidence of archaeological surveys.

[37] One should not confuse Solon's abolition of enslavement for debt with the Seisachtheia. This was a different reform, which liberated the *hektemoroi* from the payments of "protection money" they had to pay to their lords. See Harris (1997).

[38] Lohmann (1993).

[39] Foxhall (1997) 127.

[40] Foxhall (1997) 127.

The fact that these men are sold abroad demonstrates that Solon is not referring to debt-bondage but outright enslavement. There is no need to invent some elaborate system of land tenure and dependent labor to understand these verses. Such a system is without parallel in contemporary sources for the Archaic period; to resort to this kind of hypothesis is to explain *ignotum per ignotius*. The threat to the poor resulted from the breakdown of law and order, which led to warfare and the kind of raids for slaves and booty one finds throughout the *Iliad* and the *Odyssey*. There are many examples in each poem. In the story he tells of his travels, Odysseus (*Od.* 9.39–43) recalls how he and his companions stopped on their way back from Troy to plunder the Ciconians, kill their men, and take their women as slaves. When Iasonides comes to sell the Achaians wine, they buy it with bronze, iron, hides, oxen, and the slaves they have taken in raids (*Il.* 7.470–5). Hecuba tells Hector how Achilles sacked her city of Thebe, killed her father, took their cattle, and took her mother – had she not been freed by payment of ransom, Achilles would have sold her. Her husband predicts that she too will become the slave of an Achaian once Troy falls and there will be no one to buy her out of slavery (*Il.* 6.414–65). When attempting to convince him to return to battle, Agamemnon promises to give Achilles seven Lesbian women whom he picked out for himself when Achilles captured their city (*Il.* 9.128–31, 270–3). Agamemnon promises another twenty women after they conquer Troy (9.135–40, 277–82). One of Achilles' slaves is called Iphis, whom he acquired during an attack on Skyros, the city of Euenous (*Il.* 9.663–8). In Nestor's household there is a slave named Hekamede, whom the old man received as a prize when Achilles sacked Tenedos (*Il.* 11.624–31, 636–41). In fact, one of the most effective ways of male bonding in epic is to join in raids to seize women and take them home: after Patroclus' death, the poet reminds us of happier days when Achilles and his companion went on raids for women together (*Il.* 18.28–31;18.338–42; happy for the men but not for the women 19.301–2). Achilles captured Briseis in an attack on Lyrnessus (*Il.* 19.56–60), where he slaughtered her husband and three brothers (*Il.* 19.282–302). Achilles captured Lycaon on the battlefield and sold him to Iason on Lemnos (21.35–44, cf. 23.746–9). Both Priam (*Il.* 22.44–5) and Hecuba (*Il.* 24.750–3) complain that Achilles has sold many of their children abroad. These raids for slaves and plunder remained a constant threat in the Greek world right through the Classical period. Thucydides (1.5) noted that the kind of raids that occur throughout the Homeric poems were still common in less settled parts of Greece during his own time. Apollodorus tells us that his neighbor Nicostratus was captured while abroad and would have remained a slave if he could not repay his ransom ([Dem.] 53.6–7). And Daos in Menander's *Shield* tells how his master Cleostratus went on a raid to capture barbarians and sell them (Men. *Aspis* 30–3 [Sandbach]).[41] Thus, there is no need to invent an economic crisis that led to increased numbers of poor Athenians falling into debt. The situation described by Solon was already familiar to the audience that heard the Homeric poems. It was a constant threat whenever *stasis* plagued a community and turned citizens (*politai*) into enemies (*polemioi*) who could be seized and sold into slavery.

The end of the *stasis* in Attica enabled Solon to free the poor who had been enslaved by violence, not by debt-bondage, during the breakdown of law and order. In fr. 36.8–15 [West], Solon lists his accomplishments.

> πολλοὺς δ' Ἀθήνας πατρίδ' ἐς θεόκτιτον
> ἀνηγαγον *πραθέντας*, ἄλλον ἐκδίκως,
> ἄλλον δικαίως, τοὺς δ' ἀναγκαίης ὕπο
> χρειοῦς φυγόντας, γλῶσσαν οὐκέτ' Ἀττικὴν
> ἱέντας, ὡς δὴ πολλαχῇ πλανωμένους·
> τοὺς δ ἐνθάδ' αὐτοῦ *δουλίην* ἀεικέα
> ἔχοντας, ἤθη *δεσποτέων* τρομεομένους,
> ἐλευθέρους ἔθηκα.

Besides bringing unity to Attica, he "has brought back to Athens, to the city founded by the gods, many men who have been sold, one unjustly, another justly, men who were in exile because of dire necessity, no longer speaking the Attic language, since they have wandered far and wide. Others, who suffered humiliating slavery here at home, trembling at their masters' whims, I have set free."[42] Solon must be referring to slaves in these lines, the same slaves whom he described as sold abroad in fr. 4.23–5 [West], as a result of raids for plunder. Finley thought that these lines referred to Solon's abolition of debt-bondage, but this is impossible because the many of those whom Solon brought back were sold abroad; as we saw before, creditors could not sell debt-bondsmen outside of Attica but only

[41] For the connection between piracy and the slave trade in the Hellenistic period, see de Souza (1999) 60–8.

[42] One should not translate "necessity of debt" but "dire necessity." Solon is using a Homeric expression (*Il.* 8.57), as is rightly pointed out by Campbell (1967) 252. Van Effenterre and Ruzé (1994) I: 66 rightly note the parallel with the phrase ὑπ' ἀν/ἄνκας ἐκόμενος used to describe someone captured and sold abroad in the the Gortyn Code (cited in note 30).

had a right to their labor until they paid back their loans. Second, Solon does not use the noun *thetes* or the verb *theteuein*, the words that denote debt-bondage, to describe their status. Third, he calls the men who have power over them *despotai* (line 14: δεσποτέων), the word for masters of slaves, not *katathemenos* (or some similar expression), the word that designates creditors who have accepted the labor of their debtors in lieu of repayment. Finally, these men have been set free – one releases (λύειν) debt-bondsmen from an obligation (Antiphon 5.63); one does not set them free because they are not completely slaves and have not lost all of their freedom. In short, everything one reads or can infer about the status of the men whom Solon rescued shows they are slaves seized and sold as a result of raids, not debt-bondsmen.[43] *Pace* Finley, Solon fr. 36 [West] has nothing to do with debt-bondage or its abolition.

V

The continued existence of debt-bondage in Classical Athens represented a compromise between two potentially conflicting principles in Athenian law and society.[44] The Athenians believed that their courts should enforce all contracts that parties entered into willingly provided they did not violate the law (Hyp. *Ath.* 13; Dem. 42.12; [Dem.] 56.2; Din. 3.4). Their belief in the sanctity of contracts and private property was so strong that they made it illegal to propose any redistribution of property ([Arist.] *Ath. Pol.* 56.2). That should come as no surprise in a

[43] In a comment on this argument, the anonymous referee from *Classical Quarterly* exclaims, "But it is POETRY!" The referee appears to assume that Greek poets did not use legal terms with the same accuracy and precision as prose authors did. This assumption is mistaken. For instance, Homer makes a strict distinction between the term ἄποινα, which designates payment to restore the liberty of someone captured in war, and ποινή, which refers to payment for damage or homicide – see the definitive treatment of Wilson (2002). For Euripides' use of the technical terminology of *apokeruxis*, see Cobetto Ghiggia (2001). For Aristophanes' use of the technical term *presbeis autokratores*, see Harris (2000b) 489–90, and for Aristophanes' use of legal terminology see Harris (2002b) [= *Envoi* in this volume]. Nor do poets and prose authors use the term ἀποκτείνειν, found in homicide statutes, in different ways – see Chapter IV.2 in this volume. Note also how Sophocles appears to draw a careful distinction in *Oedipus the King* between the status of the Corinthian Messenger (1029: ποιμὴν γὰρ ἦσθα κἀπὶ θητείᾳ πλάνης) and that of the Theban shepherd (1123: ἦ, δοῦλος οὐκ ὠνητός, ἀλλ' οἴκοι τραφείς). The list could be lengthened.

[44] Compare Watson (1975) 115 on the advantages of *nexum*. For a similar compromise about property ownership between the interests of the wealthy and those of the poor in Classical Athens, see Dem. 10.35–42 with Harris (1996) (= Chapter I.6 in this volume).

society where most citizens owned land (Lys. 34 *hypothesis*). On the other hand, the Athenians, although they practiced slavery without qualms, also recognized the need to protect the liberty of all free men, whether citizens or foreigners. They imposed harsh penalties for criminals who tried to enslave free men ([Arist.] *Ath. Pol.* 52.1). In fact, Dinarchus (1.23) refers to two cases where Athenian courts put citizens to death for attempting to hold foreigners as slaves.

Debt-bondage provided the Athenians with a crude way of reconciling the rights of creditors and debtors. The law granted creditors the right to seize borrowers who failed to repay their loans and to hold them until they were able to work off their debts. Yet at the same time, the law protected the freedom of debtors by denying creditors the ability to sell them into slavery as a way of recovering their loans. By providing lenders with a strong form of security, however, debt-bondage also made it easier for borrowers to gain credit. To citizens of modern democracies with liberal laws about bankruptcy, this solution may seem harsh. But the Athenians, like the rest of the Greeks, had very different notions about individual freedom, and their form of government had very little in common with modern democracy.[45]

Afterthoughts

After this essay was published, I came across Maffi (1999), who does not discuss debt-bondage, but interprets the phrase δανείζειν ἐπὶ τοῖς σώμασι in the same way that I do (the defaulting debtor "devient donc esclave du créancier, qui peut le garder à son service ou le vendre à l'étranger"). Maffi also has good criticisms of Bielman's analysis of the law cited at Dem. 53.11. For an excellent study of debt-bondage at Gortyn, see Kristensen (2004), who shows that this status was clearly differentiated from slavery in the Gortyn lawcode.

[45] I would like to thank Donna Wilson, Fred Naiden, and Raymond Westbrooke for reading over an earlier draft of this essay and for their help with the Near Eastern material. I have also profited from the detailed comments of the anonymous referee from *Classical Quarterly*, where this essay first appeared. None of these scholars should be held responsible for any remaining errors in the final version. Earlier versions of this essay were delivered to the American Philological Association at its Annual Meeting in Chicago during December 1997 and to the Association of Ancient Historians at its meeting in Madison, WI in April 1999. I would like to dedicate this essay to Alexandra Serman, who in our seventh year together delivered me, like the Hebrew slave, from debt-bondage.

II.6 Notes on a Lead Letter from the Athenian Agora

David R. Jordan has recently published a fascinating letter written on a lead tablet found in the Athenian *agora*.[1] The tablet was recovered during the excavations of 1972 from a well beside the orthostate shrine located near the Royal Stoa. The well contained other objects from the fourth century BCE, and the writing on the tablet appears to belong to the same period. Jordan provides a good photograph of the tablet with a transcription of the letters found on it and presents the following text:

1. Λῆσις {ις} ἐπιστέλλει Ξενοκλεῖ καὶ τῆι μητρὶ μηδαμῶς περιιδε̂ν
2. αὐτὸν ἀπολόμενον ἐν τῶι χαλκείωι, ἀλλὰ πρὸς τὸς δεσπότας αὐτô ἐλθε̂ν
3. καὶ ἐνευρέσθαι τι βέλτιον αὐτῶι. Ἀνθρώπωι γὰρ παραδέδομαι πάνυ πονηρῶι
4. μαστιγόμενος ἀπόλλυμαι δέδεμαι. προπηλακίζομαι· μᾶλλον μᾶλλον.

I give the following translation, which follows Jordan's rendering closely except for a few minor changes:

> Lesis is sending [a letter] to Xenocles and his mother [asking] that they by no means overlook that he is perishing in the foundry but that they come to his masters and that they have something better found for him. For I have been handed over to a thoroughly wicked man; I am perishing from being whipped; I am tied up; I am treated like dirt – more and more!

Jordan argues that Lesis was an apprentice and that the letter is evidence ("the only real testimonium" apart from *IG* II² 1553–78 and *SEG* XVIII 36) for "the institution of apprenticeship in 4th-century or earlier Athens." In Jordan's opinion, Lesis' mother has placed him under the supervision of the owner of the foundry

[1] Jordan (2000). The tablet is Agora Inv. IL 1702.

to learn the skill of metalwork. Since the owner is abusing him, he requests that she and Xenocles talk to the owner and find some better arrangement for him.

In this chapter, I will begin by examining the term δεσπότης and its implications for the status of Lesis. After showing that Lesis must be a slave, I will propose an alternative scenario for the situation that prompted Lesis to write his letter.

Jordan (98) notes "The word δεσπότης means 'master' usually in the sense of 'owner' according to the evidence assembled in *LSJ* and *DiccGE*" but claims "Here the word has a looser sense." Jordan never defines this looser sense nor cites any parallels for his proposed meaning of the term in this context. In fact, I have searched through the works of Aristophanes, Menander, and the Attic orators, the authors whose language is closest to everyday speech, and have found not a single example of the word δεσπότης with such a "looser sense" and certainly never with the meaning "master of a free apprentice."[2] On the contrary, these sources reveal that when someone calls a mortal a δεσπότης, the word normally means "master of slaves." And when someone calls a person his δεσπότης or someone is said to have a δεσπότης by a third party, that individual is *always* a slave. In oratory, the term is used sometimes as a metaphor to designate a tyrant or an imperial power, but that meaning is clearly not relevant in this context (see Appendix 1).

For instance, in Aristophanes' *Wasps* the slave Xanthias refers to Bdelycleon as his master (*Vesp.* 67, 87, 420, cf. 442). Carion, who refers to Chremylus as his master in Aristophanes' *Wealth* (*Pl.* 53, 67, 260, 262, 285, 319, 633, 819, cf. 1139), is obviously a slave (*Pl.* 1–7). The assistants who help Trygaeus in the *Peace* and call him their master are also slaves (*Pax* 54, 80, 90). Nicias, Demosthenes, and Cleon in the *Knights* refer to the People as their master because Aristophanes portrays them as slaves (*Eq.* 20, 40, 47, 53, 960). In the *Frogs*, the slave Xanthias refers to Dionysus as his master (*Ran.* 1, 272, 318, 739, cf. 750, 810).[3] In the *Clouds* Strepsiades talks to his slave Xanthias and asks him if he loves his master (*Nub.* 1488). The only other

[2] In the apprenticeship contracts from Ptolemaic and Roman Egypt, the master craftsman who takes on an apprentice is always called a διδάσκαλος (*BGU* IV 1021, line 12; *P.Oxy.* IV 725, line 14 [restored], 43; *P. Oxy.* XIV 1647, lines 19, 42–3) or ἐπιστάτης (*P. Oxy.* XXXI 2586, lines 7, 12, 14, 38). When these contracts contain the word δεσπότης, this person is always the master who is entrusting his slave to a craftsman (*BGU* IV 1021, line 7 [δοῦλον], lines 15 [τοῦ δεσπότου], *BGU* IV 1125, line 1 [τὸν δοῦλόν μου], line 7 [ὁ δεσπότης]). For a discussion of these contracts, see J. Hermann (1957–58) and Hengstl (1972).

[3] On the status of the doorman of Hades, see Dover (1993) 50.

context in Aristophanes where the term *despotes* is used is when characters address a god (*Av.* 835; *Pax* 385, 377, 389, 399, 648, 711; *Nub.* 264; *Vesp.* 389, 875; *Lys.* 940; *Pl.* 748), but that is obviously not relevant to the Agora letter. To my knowledge, the term is used only once in Menander when a mortal addresses a god (*Samia* 448); elsewhere in Menander the word always means "master of slaves" where the context allows us to determine its meaning (see Appendix II).

Instead of examining contemporary texts to understand the meaning of the term, Jordan makes the following argument:

> In deducing the relation between Lesis and Xenocles we should begin by asking if Lesis is a slave or free. If he is a slave, Xenocles must have contracted the apprenticeship as his owner or conceivably as his owner's representative, to whose compassion, in either case, the boy may, let us concede, be in a position to appeal. If he is a slave, though, his mother can have no legal part in the arrangement with the δεσπόται. Yet Lesis writes to her as well as to Xenokles, and, if the letter expresses his instructions accurately, asks them both to come to the δεσπόται and make a new arrangement.

I see no reason to assume that Lesis would not have asked his mother and Xenocles to intercede on his behalf even if they had no legal power over him. For instance, Achilles asks his mother Thetis to go to Zeus and request that he turn the tide of battle to restore his honor (*Iliad* 1.407–12). Thetis has no actual power in this situation, but Achilles clearly expects her to use her influence with the god. In his *Ephesian Tale*, Xenophon of Ephesus (2.6) recounts how Anthia begs Apsyrtus to stop torturing his slave Habrocomes. She too has no power, but still appeals to Apsyrtus in the hope of saving the innocent Habrocomes. To take an example from contemporary life, men on trial for serious crimes might ask their wives and children to appeal to the court for pity on their behalf (e.g., Dem. 21.99). Obviously, these women and children had no power to compel the court, but attempted to stir the judges' pity and sway their judgment.

To support his view of Lesis' status, Jordan (98) compares his plight to a story told by Lucian (*Somnium.* 3). Lucian's father, not a wealthy man, sent his son to learn the art of sculpture in the workshop of his wife's brother. When his uncle gave him a chisel and a slab of marble and told him to begin work, Lucian struck the marble with too much vigor and broke it. After his uncle beat him, Lucian fled to his home where he complained to his mother. But the editor notes that the similarity ends here: Lucian was able to leave, whereas Lesis was chained up and unable to flee. The difference in the response to the beating strongly suggests that Lesis did not enjoy the same status as Lucian did. As a free person, Lucian had the right to leave his uncle's workshop without fear. As a slave, Lesis could be chained up and beaten as a punishment (see Xen. *Mem.* 2.1.16: σκεψώμεθα δὲ καὶ τοῦτο, πῶς οἱ δεσπόται τοῖς τοιούτοις οἰκέταις χρῶνται· (. . .) τοῦ δὲ δραπετεύειν δεσμοῖς ἀπείργουσι; τὴν ἀργίαν δὲ πληγαῖς ἐξαναγκάζουσιν;). The best he could do was to write a letter and ask for someone to talk to his masters. If anything, the contrast between the situation of Lesis and the story about Lucian proves the very opposite of what Jordan is trying to argue.

One might object that the writer of this letter could not be a slave since slaves in ancient Athens were by and large illiterate. Though most slaves, in particular those working in the countryside, were probably illiterate, several texts from Classical Athens mention slaves who could read and write. In his speech *Against Aphobus*, Demosthenes (29.11, 21) refers to a slave who could read and write and who had taken a deposition. In *Against Apaturius* (Dem. 33.17), the plaintiff asserts that Parmeno had his own slave write down the terms of the agreement. The public slave who kept track of payments due to the public treasury obviously had to be literate ([Arist.] *Ath. Pol.* 47.5). In a dialogue of Plato, Euclides has a slave read from a book he has written about Socrates' conversation with Theaetetus (Pl. *Theaetetus.* 143c–d). And the slaves of the People in Aristophanes' *Knights* (109–45) are able to read the oracles they have stolen from the Paphlagonian slave.[4]

So far we have found that Lesis must be a slave: that is what the term δεσπότης indicates and everything about his situation compels us to conclude.[5] There is also no need to identify the owner of the forge (a single individual) with the masters of Lesis (two or more people) as Jordan does. Lesis' masters must have placed him in the hands of the owner of a foundry, possibly to learn the art of metal-working. Alternatively, his owners may have leased him to the owner of the

[4] On literacy among slaves in Classical Athens, see W. V. Harris (1989) 111.

[5] One of the referees of the journal where this essay first appeared puts forward the suggestion that "Lesis may be held in debt-bondage to repay debts contracted by his family." The language of the tablet does not support this proposal: the term used to designate the person who has seized a debtor and taken him into bondage is never δεσπότης, but καταθέμενος (*ICret* 4.41.vi.2–16). On debt-bondage and the terminology associated with it, see Harris (2002a) (= Chapter II.5 in this volume).

foundry in return for payment.[6] But if he is a slave, why does Lesis only ask his mother and Xenocles to appeal to his masters so that some better arrangement (presumably with another craftsman) be found for him? Why does he not ask them to have his masters take more serious steps?

Here it is necessary to examine Athenian rules about beating slaves. If someone caught a free person stealing or committing another offense, one had to follow the appropriate legal procedure for the offense. But if one caught a slave on his property stealing, one had the right to beat the slave even though the slave was not his property. One could not administer physical punishment to a free person. The distinction is well brought out in an anecdote found in a speech by Apollodorus ([Dem.] 53.16).[7] Apollodorus describes how his enemies tried to trick him by dressing as a slave a young citizen (*astos*) who was free and sending him onto his property to pluck roses.[8] His enemies expected that Apollodorus would catch the free boy and, thinking he was a slave, tie him up or beat him as a punishment (δήσαιμι ἢ πατάξαιμι ὡς δοῦλον ὄντα). If the plan worked, they would then prosecute him on a public charge of aggravated insult (γραφὴ ὕβρεως). In Aristophanes' *Acharnians* (271–6), Dicaeopolis catches a slave girl stealing fruit from his property and rapes her as a punishment.[9]

Since Lesis had been entrusted to the foundry owner, either to learn a craft or to provide him with labor, the foundry owner would have had the right to beat him if he failed to learn his lessons or carry out his duties, that is, as long as he had a good reason.[10] Jordan (99) rightly compares the opinion of Julian in

[6] For this kind of arrangement, see Dem. 53.20. This suggestion was also made by a reader of an early version of Jordan's article: see Jordan (2000) 97 note 19.

[7] Jordan (99) does not make a distinction between beating another's slaves for an offense and beating them for no reason at all. As a result, he finds the evidence about beating slaves contradictory. But the passage in the Old Oligarch ([Xen.] *Ath. Pol.* 1.10–11) must refer to beating slaves belonging to others without due cause. He is contrasting the rule in Athens, where one cannot beat a slave simply because he is a slave, with the custom in Sparta, where one can beat anyone's slaves regardless of wrongdoing (cf. Myron *FGrHist* 106 fr. 2).

[8] I do not find convincing the argument of E. Cohen (2000) 50–63 that *astoi* included *politai* and metics. See Whitehead (1977) 60–1.

[9] Cf. Doblhoffer (1994) 20: "Auch in den *Acharnen* des Aristophanes klingt diese Auffassung an, wenn es heisst, viel vergnüglicher als in den Krieg zu ziehen sei es, eine hübsche thrakische Sklavin beim Holzdiebstahl zu erwischen und zur Strafe zu vergewaltigen."

[10] Note also that in Menander's *Dyskolos,* when Pyrrhias reports Cnemon's attempts to hit him with various objects (110–21), Sostratus assumes that Pyrrhias must clearly have done something wrong to

Digest 9.2.5.3, who recognizes the right of masters to administer physical punishment to students (*levis dumtaxat castigatio concessa est docenti*). Lesis' only recourse was to have his mother and Xenocles appeal to his masters and ask them to place him under another craftsman, that is, "have a better position found for him."[11]

What is the status of Lesis' mother and their relationship to Xenocles? The mother could be either slave or free. The fact that Lesis is still a slave would indicate that his mother was a slave when he was born.[12] If she was later emancipated, her son would have remained a slave under the control of her former masters. If she was still a slave when Lesis wrote his letter, she might have been sold to another master. In many slave societies it was not unusual for masters to break up families by selling slaves to different people. The situation was familiar to the Athenians: in his *Trojan Women* (244–91), Euripides depicted the suffering endured by enslaved mothers separated from their children. In this case Xenocles might be the mother's new master.[13]

It is also possible that Lesis' mother might have received her freedom. In this case Xenocles could be a man she had begun to live with (for a similar case, see Dem. 47.72). Or she could have been sold to Xenocles, who then liberated her and became her *prostates*. Then again Xenocles could simply be a friend, who the mother thought might have some influence with Lesis' masters. Whatever Xenocles' relationship to Lesis and his mother, it is probably safe to rule out the possibility he is Lesis' father; if he were his father, Lesis certainly would have called him that in his letter, just as he calls his mother "mother."[14] The fact that Lesis

merit such treatment (141: [κακῶς ἐπό]εις τὸ χωρίον τι δηλαδή). When Pyrrhias defends himself by claiming he stole nothing ([οὐ μὰ Δί'] ἔκλεπτον), Sostratus remains incredulous: "do you mean someone was whipping you although you were doing nothing wrong?" (142–3: ἀλλ' ἐμαστίγου σέ τις οὐδὲν ἀδικοῦντα;).

11 Slaves could flee to the Theseum and make an appeal as suppliants (see Ar. *Eq.* 1311–12 with scholia *ad loc.*), but in the case of Lesis that was out of the question.

12 Although we do hear of cases where parents sold their children into slavery, this happened only in very unusual circumstances (Lys.12.98). Normally it was illegal to sell a family member into slavery (Dem. 25.55). For the harsh penalty imposed on enslavers, see [Arist.] *Ath. Pol.* 52.1.

13 Jordan (2000) 97 note 19 reports that a reader of an early version of his article suggested that Xenocles could be the master of Lesis and his mother, but that is unlikely since Lesis asks Xenocles to go to his masters, clearly indicating that Xenocles is not one of Lesis' masters.

14 One of the journal's referees claims that "the author is wrong to state that if Xenocles were Lesis' father, he would simply be called 'father' just as the mother is called mother." This objection has no force. As Dickey (1996) 230 has shown, fathers are addressed always as πάτερ in prose. E. Dickey

expects his mother to go and speak with his masters suggests that she has some freedom of movement, which would suggest that she has been emancipated. But we should not press this argument too far.

It is customary for ancient historians to observe that all our sources about slavery in Athens were written by the masters. In this letter we hear for the first time the voice of a slave. Demosthenes (21.49) imagines someone traveling to the barbarians and praising the Athenians for their humane treatment of their slaves. "They do not think it right," says the imaginary traveller, "for anyone to insult and abuse those whom they have paid a price for and acquired as their slaves. On the contrary, they have publicly established a law outlawing such treatment and have already punished with death those who have broken this law."[15] The letter written by Lesis tells a different story. Aristophanes and other comic writers made many jokes about masters beating slaves in their plays, but the reality was no laughing matter. Lesis was obviously suffering terrible abuse, and there was little he could do about it. Had he been alive during the Spartan occupation of Decelea and able to run away, Lesis might have joined the more than 20,000 Athenian slaves who voted with their feet to condemn their masters' cruelty (Th. 7.27.5). The letter also illustrates what the sociologist Orlando Patterson has called the "natal alienation" of the slave.[16] This means that slaves had no rights over their children, spouses, or other relatives, who were under the absolute control of their masters. From a legal point of view, the slave has no family rights. Although Lesis has a mother, she is helpless to do anything to save her son from beating without first going to his masters. Her ties of kinship with her son count for nothing compared to the rights of ownership exercised by his masters. It is they who have placed him with the foundry owner; it is they to whom his mother has to appeal for help; and it is they who will decide whether to remove him or not. The letter serves to remind us once again about the brutal reality of slavery in the world's first so-called "democracy" – which in many regards was not very democratic at all.

(personal communication 11/24/02) reports that having read through all the papyrus letters, she has found none in which a name without τῷ πατρί is used in the heading of a letter to a father.

[15] Cohen (2000) 146–8 takes this passage at face value.

[16] Patterson (1982) 7–9. Another indication of natal alienation in Attic inscriptions is the fact that slaves never carry a patronymic.

APPENDIX I. THE MEANING OF THE TERM δεσπότης IN ATTIC ORATORY

Aeschines – 3. 132 (political).

Antiphon – 2.3.2 (master of slaves); 2.3.4 (master of slaves); 5.48 (master of slaves); 5.69 (masters of slaves); 6.23 (master of slaves).

Demosthenes – 1.4 (political); 3.30 (political/figurative); 5.17 (political); 6.25 (political); 9.43 (political); 13.31 (political/ figurative); 15.27 (political); 18.47 (master of slaves), 235 (political/figurative), 296 (political); 19.69 (political); 20.16 (political), 107 (political/ figurative); 23.209 (political); 24.124 (master of slaves); 37.51 (master of slaves); 45.27 (master of slaves), 35 (master of slaves), 71 (master of slaves), 75 (master of slaves), 76 (master of slaves), 80 (master of slaves), 81 (master of slaves), 84 (master of slaves), 86 (master of slaves); 53.20 (master of slaves); 53.32 (master of slaves).

Hyperides – *Athenogenes* 22 (master of slaves); *Epitaphios* 20 (political).

Isocrates – *Antidosis* 40 (master of slaves/metaphor), 124 (owners of possessions), 233 (political); *Archidamus* 43 (political), 96 (master of slaves); *Areopagitikos* 65 (political); *Nicocles* 50 (owners of good things); *Panathenaicus* 59 (political), 106 (political), 255 (political); *Panegyricus* 80 (political), 90 (political), 117 (political), 121 (master of slaves in a metaphor about political subjection), 127 (political), 178 (political); *Philippus* 21 (political), 66 (political), 89 (political); *Plataicus* 61 (political); *On the Peace* 107 (political).

Lycurgus – *Leocrates* 30 (master of slaves), 104 (political).

Lysias – 5.5 (master of slaves); 7.16 (master of slaves/ metaphorical), 35 (master of slaves); 23.9 (master of slaves).

The term is not found in the works of Andocides, Dinarchus, and Isaeus.

APPENDIX II. THE MEANING OF THE TERM δεσπότης IN ARISTOPHANES AND MENANDER

For Menander I have used the edition of F. H. Sandbach (Oxford 1972). Aristophanes – *Acharnians* 247 (god); *Assemblywomen* 1125 (master of slaves), 1129 (master of slaves); *Birds* 60 (master of slaves), 71 (master of slaves), 80 (master of slaves),

835 (god); *Clouds* 264 (god), 1488 (master of slaves); *Frogs* 1 (master of slaves), 272 (master of slaves), 301 (master of slaves), 318 (master of slaves), 670 (master of slaves), 694 (master of slaves), 739 (master of slaves), 742 (master of slaves), 750 (master of slaves), 810 (master of slaves), 812 (master of slaves), 950 (master of slaves); *Knights* 20 (master of slaves), 40 (master of slaves), 47 (master of slaves), 53 (master of slaves), 58 (master of slaves), 960 (master of slaves); *Lysistrata* 940 (god); *Peace* 54 (master of slaves), 80 (master of slaves), 90 (master of slaves), 257 (master of slaves), 275 (master of slaves), 377 (god), 385 (god), 389 (god), 399 (god), 648 (god), 711 (god), 824 (master of slaves), 875 (master of slaves); *Thesmophoriazousai* 341 (master of slaves), 988 (god); *Wasps* 67 (master of slaves), 87 (master of slaves), 142 (master of slaves), 389 (god), 420 (master of slaves), 442 (master of slaves), 821 (god), 875 (god); *Wealth* 2 (master of slaves), 12 (master of slaves), 20 (master of slaves), 67 (master of slaves), 201 (master of slaves), 253 (master of slaves), 260 (master of slaves), 262 (master of slaves), 285 (master of slaves), 319 (master of slaves), 633 (master of slaves), 748 (god), 819 (master of slaves), 1103 (master of slaves), 1139 (master of slaves). Frs. 464 (?), 491 (?), 598 (?), 645b (master of slaves).

Menander – *Aspis* 214 (master of slaves), 240 (master of slaves); *Dyskolos* 300 (master of slaves), 577 (master of slaves), 589 (master of slaves), 625 (master of slaves), 637 (master of slaves); *Epitrepontes* 393 (master of slaves), 400 (master of slaves), 420 (master of slaves), 446 (master of slaves), 467 (master of slaves), 494 (master of slaves), 715 (master of slaves), 880 (master of slaves); *Heros* 16 (master of slaves), 29 (master of slaves), 31 (master of slaves), 42 (master of slaves); *Misoumenos* 172 (master of slaves?), 237 (master of slaves); *Perikeiromene* 359 (master of slaves), 364 (master of slaves); *Perinthia* 14 (master of slaves), 16 (master of slaves), fr. 3, line 1 (master of slaves); *Samia* 296 (master of slaves), 304 (master of slaves), 320 (master of slaves) 448 (god), 643 (master of slaves); *Sicyonius* 207 (master of slaves), 373 (master of slaves); *Fabula Incerta* fr. 336 (= Stobaeus *Eclogae* iv,32.42), line 6 (master of slaves?); fr. 722 (= *Papyrus Friburgensis* 12) line 6 (master of slaves).

III

Law and the Family

III.1 Did the Athenians Regard Seduction as a Worse Crime than Rape?

Λυσίας ὁ σοφιστής
– [Demosthenes] 59.21

ONE OF THE MOST INGENIOUS ARGUMENTS IN ALL OF ATTIC ORATORY IS TO BE FOUND in the speech Lysias wrote for Euphiletus to deliver at his trial for the murder of Eratosthenes (Lys. 1.30–5). In his speech Euphiletus first describes to the court how his wife was seduced by Eratosthenes, then recounts how he discovered the affair, caught the adulterer in the act, and despite an offer to pay compensation, slew him. Euphiletus defends his action by citing the law of the Areopagus that whoever kills an adulterer caught *in flagranti* with his wife cannot be convicted of murder. Euphiletus further points out that the same exemption applies to the man who catches someone seducing his *pallake.* If the lawgiver regarded the seduction of a *pallake* as so serious that it merited the death penalty, Euphiletus argues, he must have regarded the seduction of a wife as even more reprehensible, deserving a penalty worse than death.

Euphiletus then proceeds to claim that the lawgiver considered rape a far less serious crime than seduction. In support of his point, he had the clerk of the court read out a section from another law.[1] He singles out two provisions from this law, first, that the man who rapes (αἰσχύνῃ βίᾳ) a free man or a child shall pay only damages, and, second, that the man who rapes a woman shall be liable to the same penalty. From these provisions, he concludes that the lawgiver thought that rapists merited a less severe penalty than did seducers, for he punished the former merely with a fine, but the latter with death. Euphiletus' explanation for the difference

[1] It is uncertain what law Euphiletus cites in this passage. It may be the *dike blabes* (Dem. 21.43) or the *dike biaion* (Harp. *s.v.* βιαίων).

between the penalties for the two offenses is that whereas the rapist incurs the hatred of his victim, the seducer corrupts the very soul of the woman and gains greater control over her (οἰκειοτέρας αὐτοῖς ποιεῖν) than her husband has. The seducer thus gets the entire household under his control, making it impossible for the husband to know who is the father of his wife's children. The lawgiver obviously reasoned that such an atrocious crime deserves capital punishment.

We do not know if Euphiletus' argument convinced the court, but several modern scholars have judged it sound and have endorsed his conclusion that the law of Athens regarded seduction as a crime more heinous than rape.[2] Such a verdict is unwarranted. The argument presented by Euphiletus contains strong doses of both *suppressio veri* and *suggestio falsi*, and his conclusion is contradicted by several pieces of evidence.

Before examining the argument in detail, we ought to note the context in which it is found. Lysias did not write a legal textbook for his client; he wrote a speech for a man who was on trial for murder and had to convince the court of his innocence.[3] The best way to win the sympathy of the court was to argue that Eratosthenes had committed a crime so awful that he deserved nothing less than death. It was therefore in Euphiletus' interest to portray Eratosthenes' seduction of his wife as one of the worst crimes imaginable, an offense far more serious than rape because it posed a greater threat to a man's control over his household. The interpretation of Athenian statutes regarding rape and seduction presented in the speech is well suited to the purpose of strengthening Euphiletus' case, but it is

[2] For example, Harrison (1968) 34: "we can accept the broad point that paradoxically seduction was more severely dealt with than rape"; Pomeroy (1975) 86–7: "Seduction was considered a more heinous crime than rape"; MacDowell (1978) 124; Cole (1984) 103: "it was believed that *moicheia* could be punished more severely than sexual assault"); Salviat and Vatin (1971) 75: "la loi attique du IVe siècle était plus dure contre la μοιχεία que contre le viol"); Carey (1989) 80. Several of these authors detect flaws in Euphiletus' argument, but none questions his overall conclusion. Cf. Lipsius (1905–15) 432–3. Beauchet (1897) I: 239 and Cohen (1984a) 153 note Euphiletus' conclusion without explicitly endorsing or rejecting it. Bateman (1958) 278 observes "Lysias' argument ignores the existence of various legal courses and penalties that could be taken against an adulterer, and also the fact that a rapist could be punished by death." However, Bateman does not analyze the argument in detail and his observation has been ignored in recent scholarship. Plu. *Solon* 23 states that the law of Athens treated seduction with greater severity than rape, but his view may be derived from Lysias' speech. Whatever his source, his view is vulnerable to the same objections that can be brought against Euphiletus' argument. Note, however, that Plutarch found this state of affairs paradoxical.

[3] Euphiletus' case was probably tried by the court at the Delphinium (Dem. 23.74; [Arist.] *Ath. Pol.* 57.3). For a discussion of the identity of the *ephetai* who sat in this court, see Rhodes (1981) 646–8.

obviously the slanted interpretation of an advocate, not the impartial analysis of a legal scholar.[4]

The first piece of sophistry in Euphiletus' argument is his misrepresentation of the import of the law about the competence of the Areopagus. The law is not primarily concerned with seduction and does not lay down penalties for that crime. Rather, it deals with lawful homicide, enumerating the circumstances in which a man kills someone but cannot be condemned for murder.[5] This is clear from Dem. 23.53–4, where the law is more fully discussed. There we learn that the provision pertaining to the man who kills someone caught having intercourse with his wife is only one of several in the law. Other provisions exempt from condemnation those who kill someone during an athletic contest and those who in ignorance kill another Athenian during battle. Although Euphiletus claims that the law imposes the death penalty on an adulterer caught in the act (Lys. 1.33, 47–50), it is obvious that this was not the intent of the law. All the law states is that the man who catches someone having intercourse with his wife and kills him cannot be condemned for murder. The law about the Areopagus does not inflict the death penalty on adulterers; it only specifies what constitutes lawful homicide.[6]

Second, Euphiletus suppresses the fact that the law about the Areopagus also exempted from condemnation for murder the man who killed someone caught in the act of raping his wife, daughter, mother, or *pallake*. Euphiletus gives the impression that the law applied only to the murder of adulterers caught *in flagranti*, but such a narrow interpretation of the statute of the statute is unlikely to be correct. For, as Harrison observes, if it were permissible to kill the adulterer caught in the act, but not the rapist, "it would clearly have been impossible for the husband exercising his right of immediate self-help to establish to his own satisfaction and in such a way as to be able to prove it subsequently that his wife had been seduced, not raped."[7] In fact, Demosthenes' discussion of the law

[4] For a general treatment of the problems involved in using the Attic orators as sources for Athenian Law, see Wolff (1974). One should note that Euphiletus' case rests on the statute about lawful homicide. The strained interpretation of the law and the misrepresentation of the penalties for rape in 30–5 serve only to blacken Eratosthenes' deed, not to establish Euphiletus' innocence.

[5] For the categories of murder in Athenian law, see Gagarin (1981a) 3–4. I have borrowed the term "lawful homicide" from Gagarin.

[6] Well argued by Cohen (1984a) 149–50 with references to earlier literature.

[7] Harrison (1968) 34.

(23.54) indicates that it applied to anyone caught "on top of" (ἐπὶ) a wife, mother, sister, daughter, or *pallake* kept for the purpose of bearing free children. Contrary to what Euphiletus implies, the exemption granted by the law was not restricted to those who killed seducers. It obviously covered the killing of all those, both rapists and seducers, who were caught having intercourse with a female relative of the killer.[8] That this broader interpretation of the statute is correct is proven by the myth of Ares' trial before the Areopagus. According to the myth, Ares caught Halirrhothius raping his daughter and killed him. When Halirrhothius' father Poseidon prosecuted Ares before the Areopagus, the court acquitted him.[9] The myth is clearly designed to illustrate how the provisions of the statute about lawful homicide worked in practice, and thus confirms our point that the statute applied to the murder of men caught raping a wife, daughter, mother, sister, or *pallake*.[10]

Yet despite these indications that Lysias' client is being less than truthful, S. G. Cole has come to the defense of Euphiletus' interpretation of the law about the Areopagus. Her argument needs to be quoted in full:

> I would like to suggest that the original law on intentional (*sic*) homicide was stated almost exactly as it stands in Demosthenes' text (23.53), that its intention was not to distinguish between rape and *moicheia*, but simply, as it states, to exonerate a *kyrios* who killed someone caught in intercourse with a woman under his protection. At some time between this law and the speech of Lysias, another law, one on sexual assault, was introduced, whether by Solon, as Plutarch says, or by someone else. This new law encouraged distinction between rape as an act of violence, and *moicheia* as an act of choice. Because of this distinction, the original law came to be thought of as a law on *moicheia*, and when later writers such as Lysias, Aristotle, and Plutarch refer to it, they describe it as a law on *moicheia*.[11]

[8] Cohen (1984a) 151–2. Unlike Euphiletus, whose argument is dictated by the rhetorical strategy of his speech, Demosthenes had no reason to distort the provisions of the law about lawful homicide since the question of rape as opposed to seduction was not relevant to his case against Aristocrates. [Arist.] *Ath. Pol.* 57.3 is not evidence that the law applied only to those who killed *moichoi*: see Cohen (1984a) 152 note 13.

[9] Apollodorus 3.14.2 (βιαζόμενος); Paus. 1.21.4 (αἰσχύνοντα). Cf. Hellanicus *FGrHist* 323a fr. 22 and Din. 1.86.

[10] Cf. Cole (1984) 100–1.

[11] Cole (1984) 103.

This argument is as flawed as that of Euphiletus. To start off, there is no evidence that the "original law," that is, the law about the Areopagus, "came to be known as a law on *moicheia*." Aristotle (*Ath. Pol.* 57.3) does not refer to it as a law on *moicheia*. All he does is to list some of the cases that come before the Areopagus sitting in the Delphinium. Plutarch (*Solon* 23) states only that Solon allowed the man who caught a *moichos* in the act to kill him. Furthermore, it is not clear how the new law brought about a reinterpretation of the law about the Areopagus. If the law about the Areopagus originally covered the murder of both seducers and rapists, it would have continued to do so unless it was amended or superseded by new legislation. But there is no indication in our sources that this ever happened, and Cole does not explain how else such a change might have come about.[12] And if Cole really believes that the law about the Areopagus received a narrower interpretation sometime before Euphiletus delivered his speech, how does she circumvent Harrison's objection to such an interpretation of the law? But the most serious objection to her view, indeed the fatal one, is that it clashes with the evidence of Dem. 23.54, a text from the same period as, if not later than, Lys. 1. Nothing in the discussion of the law found in that passage suggests that the law was at the time known "as a law about *moicheia*" and applied only to seducers caught in the act. Cole's plea on behalf of Euphiletus' fallacious interpretation of the law must be rejected.[13]

Euphiletus' third rhetorical misdemeanour involves *suppressio veri*. Euphiletus implies that the only legal remedy in cases of rape was a procedure that provided merely for the payment of damages. What he does not say is that rape qualified as an act of *hybris*.[14] Aristotle (*Rhet.* 1373b28–1374a17) informs us that *hybris* was an

[12] Cole's claim that the law about the Areopagus "came to be thought of as a law on *moicheia*" conceals a fundamental misconception about Athenian Law. In the absence of jurisprudence and a law of precedent, there could be no development of statutory intepretation of the sort she appears to suggest. All the Athenian courts did was to judge; they did not "make law" by their decisions. In the Athenian legal system, there was nothing similar to the *ius honorarium* of Roman Law.

[13] Dem. 23 was delivered in 352/51 (D. H. *Amm.* 1.4). If the work of Lysias himself, Euphiletus' speech must have been composed several years before that. For a convenient summary of what is known about Lysias' life, see Carey (1989) 1–3. We might also point out that if, as Cole plausibly maintains, the myth of Ares' trial illustrates the provisions of the statute about lawful homicide, then the broader interpretation of the statute was current in the late fifth century, when Hellanicus recounted it, and also late in the fourth century, when Dinarchus alluded to it.

[14] For rape as an act of *hybris*, see Eur. *Hipp.* 1073; Hdt. 6.137; Pl. *Lg.* 874c; Aeschin. 1.15–17 (the law about *hybris* cited in the context of a discussion of sexual offences). Cf. Fisher (1976) 193 note 44. Dover

act of violence that brought dishonor on the victim.[15] The act of rape is in several places referred to by the verbs αἰσχύνειν and ἀτιμᾶν.[16] Since rape was an act of *hybris*, it could be prosecuted by means of a *graphe hybreos*.[17] We know that this action was an *agon timetos*, in other words, an action where the successful prosecutor could propose any penalty he wished, including capital punishment, for the convicted criminal.[18] Of course, the prosecutor might propose a milder penalty, and the procedure also allowed the defendant to put forward an alternative penalty that would presumably be less severe than the one demanded by his opponent. But that is beside the point. The fact remains that the prosecutor could propose the death penalty for the convicted rapist, and the court could vote to impose it.[19] Here again, we have found Euphiletus guilty on another count of *suppressio veri*. His failure to mention the possibility of prosecuting the rapist by means of a *graphe hybreos*, a procedure that allowed for the death penalty, gives the false impression that the only penalty available in cases of rape was a fine.

On the other hand, we have no certain knowledge about the penalty for conviction on the *graphe moicheias*. Since many *graphai* were *agones timetoi*, it is possible that the successful prosecutor on this charge could ask for the death penalty. This inference gains support from a passage in another speech of Lysias (13.68) where it is stated that the penalty for *moicheia* is death. Harrison, however, holds that this passage does not allude to the *graphe moicheias* but to "the right of the husband to kill when he caught the offender in the act."[20]

(1978) 36 claims that the rapist could not necessarily be prosecuted for *hybris*, but his argument is rightly questioned by Cole (1984) 99 note 14.

15 On this aspect of *hybris*, see Fisher (1979) 32–47.

16 αἰσχύνειν referring to an act of rape: Lys. 1.32; Paus. 1.21.4. ἀτιμάζειν referring to an act of rape: Eur. *Hipp*. 885–6.

17 One cannot argue that although rape was called *hybris* in ordinary language, the crime may have fallen outside the legal definition of the term. The Athenians never formulated such technical juristic definitions: see D. Cohen (1983) 5–7. For a discussion of the nature of the offence subject to the *graphê hybreôs*, see Gagarin (1979a). One should note that rape certainly fits the definition of *hybris* provided by Aristotle in his *Rhetoric*, a work written in part for those composing speeches to be delivered in court.

18 *Graphe hybreos* as an *agon timetos*: Dem. 21.47. On the *agon timetos* see Harrison (1971) 80–2. Death as a possible penalty for *hybris*: Lys. fr. 44 (Thalheim); Din. 1. 23.

19 Harrison (1968) 35 recognizes that rape could be prosecuted by means of a *graphe hybreos*, but claims that the prosecutor in such a case could not demand the death penalty. He cites no evidence for his view, which apparently rests on nothing more than an inference drawn from Euphiletus' assertion that seduction was punished more severely than rape. Cole (1984) 99 is unaware of the possible penalties for *hybris* and consequently does not see their implication for Euphiletus' argument.

20 Harrison (1968) 34–5. Harrison nevertheless thinks that the penalty for conviction on the *graphe moicheias* was death.

On the basis of what is known about the *graphe* for unjust imprisonment of an alleged seducer, Cole has suggested that capital punishment was not available for those convicted on a *graphe moicheias*.[21] If a man accused of seduction brought a *graphe* for unjust imprisonment against the *kyrios* of the woman whom he had allegedly seduced and lost his case, the law allowed the vindicated *kyrios* to do anything he wished to the *moichos*, provided he did not use a knife ([Dem.]59.66). Cole argues that this meant that the seducer could not be killed in this circumstance and has therefrom drawn the conclusion that the *graphe moicheias* is unlikely to have permitted a stiffer punishment. I am not certain that the phrase ἄνευ ἐγχειριδίου in the law about unjust imprisonment of an alleged seducer was inserted to prevent the killing of the adulterer. We should bear in mind that the punishment was to take place ἐπὶ . . . τοῦ δικαστηρίου. The phrase may have been aimed at preventing the shedding of blood in the court and thereby incurring pollution.[22] Or it may have been aimed at prohibiting castration of the *moichos*, an act the Athenians considered inhuman and barbaric.[23] But even if the man who brought a suit on this *graphe* and lost could not be punished with death, the inference drawn from this statute about the *graphe moicheias* may not be correct. In sum, we have no reason to rule out the possibility that the man convicted on the *graphe moicheias* might be condemned to death. In fact, the little evidence there is appears to point in the other direction.

We can now present a summation of our case against Euphiletus' view that the laws of Athens treated seduction with greater severity than rape. Euphiletus attempts to mislead the court by claiming that the law of the Areopagus punished adultery with death, but this is not true. This law pertained only to lawful homicide and did not create an action against seducers that provided for the death penalty for convicted *moichoi*. Euphiletus also neglects to mention that this law accorded the same exemption from condemnation to the husband who caught a man raping his wife. Finally, Euphiletus passes over in silence the possibility of prosecuting a rapist on a *graphe hybreos*, a procedure that permitted the successful prosecutor to demand the death penalty. Contrary to Euphiletus' assertion, the laws of Athens punished rape with no less severity than they did seduction, and possibly more.

[21] Cole (1984) 104.

[22] For concern about avoiding pollution in the courts, see Antiphon 5.11.

[23] Hdt. 8.105–6. This idea was suggested to me independently by Professor R. Billows and Professor W. Greenwalt. For a discussion of other punishments inflicted on the adulterer, see D. Cohen (1984b) 385–7.

A similar attitude toward rape and seduction is evident in the lawcode of Gortyn.[24] That code imposes a penalty of one hundred staters on the free man who rapes a free person and double the amount on the slave who rapes a free person (column II, 2–7). The penalty for a slave who rapes another slave is five staters (column II, 9–10). The penalties for seduction are the same. If a free man seduces a free woman in the house of her father, brother, or husband, the penalty is one hundred staters (column II, 20–3). For the slave who seduces a free woman, the penalty is double, and for the slave who seduces another slave, five staters (column II, 25–8). The only exception is for the free man who is caught seducing a free woman in a house not belonging to father, brother, or husband; in this case the penalty is only fifty staters (column II, 23–4). The fines for these penalties may have been less at Athens: Plutarch (*Solon* 23) reports that the penalty in Athens for the rape of a free woman was only one hundred drachmas.[25] Despite the difference in the amount of the fine for rape, both communities appear to have considered rape and seduction equally serious crimes. The evidence from Gortyn thus provides comparative support for the conclusions we have reached about the penalties for rape and seduction in Athens.

The exposure of the fallacies in Euphiletus' argument has methodological implications for the study of Athenian social history. Although scholars have long recognized that the Attic orators are often unreliable sources for contemporary events, they have generally trusted their statements as evidence for popular morality. Yet here too caution is required. Euphiletus' presentation of the Athenian statutes regarding rape and seduction is dictated by the rhetorical constraints of his case. It is not a reflection of widely held social attitudes.

One final question remains: why did Lysias think that Euphiletus could get away with this specious argument? From a woman's point of view, the argument is especially repulsive, for it claims that the victim of rape, the woman who against her will is forced to have sexual intercourse, suffers less than the woman who is seduced. But the court that heard Euphiletus' case did not include any women among its members. On the other hand, the men who decided the case may have found his argument compelling. They, like Euphiletus, were the masters of their

[24] I cite from Willetts (1967). However, I follow M. I. Finley (1981) 135–7 in seeing no distinction between the terms ϝοικεύς and δοῦλος and translate both as "slave."

[25] For a discussion of the various attempts to reconcile Plutarch's information with that found in Lys. 1.30–5, see Cole (1984) 102–3.

respective households and were concerned with maintaining control over their wives and children. From their point of view, Euphiletus had a point of sorts: the *moichos* did in a way pose a greater threat to their authority in the household, and thereby to their honor, than did a rapist. Whereas the rapist exercised power over a woman's body for just a short time, the *moichos* could win a long-lasting mastery over her soul. To the men who heard Euphiletus' case, this argument may have been quite seductive.

APPENDIX

D. Cohen, following the lead of M. H. Hansen, has recently argued that *moichoi* were subject to *apagoge* to the Eleven, a procedure that might result in the death penalty for the offender.[26] Cohen also claims to find an allusion to this procedure in Euphiletus' speech (Lys. 1.29).[27]

The *apagoge* procedure is described in the *Constitution of the Athenians* ([Arist.] *Ath. Pol.* 52.1):

> καθιστᾶσι δὲ καὶ τοὺς ἕνδεκα κλήρῳ, τοὺς ἐπιμελησομένους τῶν ἐν τῷ δεσμωτρίῳ, καὶ τοὺς ἀπαγομένους κλέπτας καὶ τοὺς ἀνδραποδιστὰς καὶ τοὺς λωποδύτας ἂν μὲν [ὁμολογῶ]σι, θανάτῳ ζημιώσαντας, ἂν δ' ἀμφισβητῶσιν, εἰσάξοντας εἰς τὸ δικαστήριον, κἂν μὲν ἀποφύγωσι, ἀφήσοντας, εἰ δὲ μή, τότε θανατώσοντας.

An entry in Photius (*s.v.* οἱ ἕνδεκα) adds the qualification that only those caught in the act (ἐπ' αὐτοφώρῳ) were subject to this procedure.[28] Contemporary evidence

[26] Cohen (1984a) 156–7; Hansen (1976a) 44–5. Hansen's views about *apagoge* have been criticized by Gagarin (1979b) 317–22. Hansen responded in Hansen (1981). Cohen's article exhibits no awareness of Gagarin's criticisms nor of Hansen's reply. The view that a *moichos* was a *kakourgos* and was thus subject to *apagoge* was earlier put forward by Paoli (1950) 152 and rejected by Harrison (1968) 35 note 1.

[27] Cohen's attempt in D. Cohen (1984a) 156–62, esp. 157, to detect an allusion to the *apagoge* procedure in Lys. 1.26–9 must be rejected. Cohen notes the use of the verbs ἀμφισβητεῖν and ὁμολογεῖν in this passage and at [Arist.] *Ath. Pol.* 52.1, but this proves nothing. In the former passage the criminal Eratosthenes admits his offense to Euphiletus, a private citizen, whereas in the latter the criminal confesses to a board of magistrates. Eratosthenes' admission of guilt at Lys. 1.26–9 is a preliminary step in his attempt to convince Euphiletus to accept his offer of compensation. For the use of the verb ὁμολογεῖν in a similar situation, see Ar. *Vesp.* 1417–25. Cohen's reconstruction of the law of adultery is likewise fanciful.

[28] Hansen (1976a) 48–52 attempted to formulate a new definition of the phrase ἐπ' αὐτωφώρῳ, but this has been refuted by D. Cohen (1983) 52–7.

also links this qualification with the procedure (Is. 4.28; Dem. 45.81). Not all types of criminals are subject to *apagoge* to the Eleven, but only those classified as *kakourgoi*. The passages that explicitly provide information about this procedure list only three types of criminals under this unsavory rubric: κλέπται, ἀνδραποδισταί, λωποδῦται.[29]

But Hansen has drawn attention to Aeschin. 1.90–1 and has claimed that it shows that *moichoi* were also characterized as *kakourgoi* and thus subject to *apagoge* to the Eleven. We need to have the passage in front of us:

> δέδεικται φανερὰ ὁδός, δι' ἧς οἱ τὰ μέγιστα κακουργοῦντες ἀποφεύξονται. τίς γὰρ ἢ τῶν λωποδυτῶν ἢ τῶν κλεπτῶν ἢ τῶν μοιχῶν ἢ τῶν ἀνδροφόνων ἢ τῶν τὰ μέγιστα μὲν ἀδικοῦντων, λάθρᾳ πραττόντων, δώσει δίκην; καὶ γὰρ τούτων οἱ μὲν ἐπ' αὐτοφώρῳ ἁλόντες, ἐὰν ὁμολογῶσι, παραχρῆμα θανάτῳ ζημιοῦνται, οἱ δὲ λαθόντες καὶ ἔξαρνοι γενόμενοι κρίνονται ἐν τοῖς δικαστηρίοις, εὑρίσκεται δὲ ἡ ἀλήθεια ἐκ τῶν εἰκότων.

Hansen claims that in this passage "the procedure ἀπαγωγή . . . is lucidly discussed by Aeschines" and that Aeschines categorizes *moichoi* and *andrapodistai* as *kakourgoi*.[30] But nowhere in the passage does Aeschines "say explicitly or even imply that adulterers, killers and οἱ τὰ μέγιστα ἀδικοῦντες are all legally classified as *kakourgoi*."[31] The passage hardly qualifies as a "lucid" discussion of *apagoge*. Indeed, neither the noun *apagoge* nor the cognate verb *apagein* occurs in the passage. The technical term *kakourgoi* is likewise absent.[32] The role of the Eleven in the procedure is passed over in silence. And Aeschines omits *andrapodistai* from the list of those subject to the procedure, and does not mention the possibility of submitting a case initiated by *apagoge* to a court in the event that the defendant denies his guilt. Aeschines' aim in this passage is not to discuss a particular legal procedure, but to make a more general point about the punishment of all types of serious criminals. The language he uses makes this certain: οἱ τὰ μέγιστα κακουργοῦντες,

[29] Antiphon 5.9; [Arist.] *Ath. Pol.* 52.1; Lys. 10.7–10; Dem. 24.113; Dem. 54.24; Isoc. 15.90.

[30] Hansen (1981) 22–3. The following discussion shows that Hansen's claim "It is apparent that Aeschin. 1.90–1 and Arist. *Ath. Pol.* 52.1 are interdependent sources" is implausible.

[31] Gagarin (1979b) 322 note 60.

[32] While the noun κακοῦργοι could have a general meaning ("wrongdoers") as well as a narrower one (those subject to *apagoge* to the Eleven), there is no evidence to show that the participle κακουργοῦντες ever had such a restricted meaning.

τῶν τὰ μέγιστα μὲν ἀδικοῦντων. Although the phrase οἱ μὲν ἐπ' αὐτοφώρῳ ἁλόντες, ἐὰν ὁμολογῶσι, παραχρῆμα θανάτῳ ζημιοῦνται might appear to allude to one of the features of the *apagoge* procedure, the next clause (οἱ δὲ λαθόντες καὶ ἔξαρνοι γενόμενοι κρίνονται ἐν τοῖς δικαστηρίοις) cannot since those who avoid being caught in the act are not subject to the procedure. If Aeschines were a student taking an examination on Athenian Law and submitted 1.90–1 as an answer to a question about *apagoge* to the Eleven, I doubt his examiner would give him even partial credit. Yet what is most striking is that in none of the passages where the procedure is explicitly discussed, sometimes with the accompaniment of the actual text of the law read out by the clerk, are *moichoi* listed as *kakourgoi*. Hansen's argument, resting as it does on no solid foundation of ancient evidence, topples, dragging down with it Cohen's interpretation of Lys. 1.29.

Afterthoughts

The main points of this essay appear to have generally been accepted: see, for example, Lefkowitz (1993) 20; Ogden (1997) 33; Pierce (1997) 183; Foxhall (1991) (though with some minor differences), Sommerstein (1998) 111, and especially Brown (1991), who draws attention to Menander *Dyskolos* 289–93, where the character Gorgias obviously considers sexual violence and seduction equally serious offenses. On the studies of rape in New Comedy in Lape (2001), Scafuro (1997), and Rosivach (1998), see the next chapter in this volume.

The most extensive reply to this essay has been Carey (1995). Carey accepts most of my conclusions: we agree that the law on just homicide covered both rape and seduction on the basis of Dem. 23.53–4, that the rapist could be prosecuted by a *graphe hybreos*, that the law cited at Lys. 1.28 is not the law concerning *apagoge kakourgon*, and that Aeschin. 1.90–2 is not a discussion of the *apagoge* procedure. (Cf. Fisher [2001] 224–6 and Manuwald (1995) 149 note 3, both of whom also accept this last point.) He also makes a strong argument against the view of Cohen (1991a) 168 that "*moicheia* was an area in which the Greek competitive spirit came to the fore." Carey then argues persuasively that the law cited at Lys. 1.28 is probably the law that permitted the killing of a *moichos* caught in the act, which is mentioned at Plu. *Solon* 23. Carey contrasts this with the law on *hybris*, which only granted the possibility of execution after a trial. This may be so, but the law on just homicide still permitted the killing of a rapist caught in the act. Carey admits that "Probably the right to kill the rapist was still available under the letter of the homicide law of Drakon" but then asks "But was this a realistic option in the classical period?" Carey then argues on the basis of Euphiletus' argument in Lys. 1 that "a defence based on homicide law, together with a claim that the dead man committed rape, would be unlikely to succeed in practice. Even in the case of *moicheia,* the killer may have found the jury lukewarm in its sympathy, since it would appear that by the classical period the use of ransom had become the most common remedy against *moichoi.*" But Carey presents no evidence to support any of these points, and one might also point out that Dem. 23. 53–4 strongly suggests that someone who killed a person committing sexual violence would stand a very good chance of being acquitted if he appealed to the law on just homicide. Carey then claims that "the impact of the post-Drakonian legislation dealing with *moicheia* and rape was probably to narrow the definition of the phrase ἐπὶ δάμαρτι." But this idea is virtually similar to that of Cole (1984) and is vulnerable to the same objections to her view that I made in my essay. As an alternative, Carey suggests that "the code of Drakon acknowledged no distinction between adultery and rape, and that this distinction begins with the code of Solon. At any rate the letter of the law would still allow a defense on the generic ground that a man was caught 'at/with' one's wife etc. But in the Athenian context a defence based on the letter of the law was not necessarily a strong defence." I see no reason to accept this last point, which is also not supported by evidence. Even if one accepted this point (which I do not), the argument cuts both ways: one could argue that if a defense based on the letter of the law was not strong, then one based on the letter of the law about *moicheia* was also not strong. Carey goes on to point out correctly that the woman who consented to have relations with a *moichos* was punished, whereas the victim of rape was not. This is true but not relevant to the question of the respective penalties for the rapist and the *moichos.* Carey is also right to stress the serious threat that *moicheia* posed to the husband and to his control over his household. But that still does not affect the question of the actual legal penalties for the two offenses. On the question of the legal penalties for seduction and sexual violence, my basic conclusion appears secure: both crimes could be punished with death.

Omitowoju (1997) accepts my main points, but claims that one could not bring a *graphe hybreos* unless the woman were respectable. Her argument is contradicted by the sources: the law on *hybris* at Dem. 21.48 explicitly states that a charge can be brought for acts of *hybris* committed against slaves, and Din. 1.23 alludes to a case where a man was put to death for committing *hybris* against a woman of low status. For a more extensive critique of her arguments, see Harris (1998). Omitowoju (2002) repeats many of the questionable points made in Omitowoju (1997) but does not take account of the criticisms of Harris (1998).

On punishments for the *moichos*, see now Carey (1993).

On the meaning of the term *ep' autophoro*, see now Harris (1994c) = Chapter IV.I.[33]

[33] An earlier version of this chapter was presented to the NEH Seminar on the Family in ancient Greece held at the Graduate Center of the City University of New York in the summer of 1989. I would like to thank Professor S. Pomeroy, who led the seminar, for inviting me to speak, and all the members of the seminar for a lively discussion. Gratitude is also due to Dr. S. C. Todd, whose comments on an earlier draft removed various errors and suggested many good points, several of which I have incorporated. He should not be held responsible for any gaffes, blunders, or howlers that remain.

III.2 Did Rape Exist in Classical Athens? Further Reflections on the Laws about Sexual Violence

I

When studying the evidence for sexual violence in Classical Athens, one is immediately struck by a curious fact: the ancient Greeks had no word that is the precise equivalent of our word "rape." This, of course, does not mean that acts that we would call acts of rape did not occur in Classical Athens or in other Greek *poleis*. On the contrary, our sources make it abundantly clear that such acts did occur. For instance, Pausanias (9.13.5; cf. Xen. *Hell.* 6.4.7) tells the story of two young Boeotian women who were the victims of sexual violence (βιάζονται) at the hands of two Spartan soldiers. In shame at their dishonor (ὕβρεως), both women killed themselves. When their father was unable to obtain justice for his daughters from the Spartan authorities, he too committed suicide. For us there is no doubt that this was an act of rape; in fact that is the way translators render the term. In the prologue to Euripides' *Ion,* the god Hermes tells us that Apollo "married by force" (10–11) the young Creusa, who became pregnant and bore a son, whom she exposed. The language of tragedy is more delicate, but still makes clear that Apollo had sex with Creusa against her will. We would not hesitate to call what Apollo did to Creusa an act of rape.

But in each of these passages the author does not use a word that is equivalent to our term "rape." Pausanias uses the term *hybris* when he refers to the rape of the two young Boeotian women, but this term has a broader semantic range than the word "rape" in English. For instance, when Meidias harassed Demosthenes and finally punched him in the head at the festival of Dionysus in 348, Demosthenes charged him with the crime of *hybris* (Dem. 21.13–19). When Harmodius' sister was selected to serve as a basket-bearer at a religious festival, but Hipparchus took away this honor, Thucydides (6.57.3) says that the tyrant treated her brother Harmodius with *hybris*. In Sophocles' *Antigone* (309, 482), Creon calls Antigone's refusal to obey his order not to bury Polynices an act of *hybris*. Herodotus (2.32.3) relates that the sons of the leaders among the Nasamones once crossed the desert and went farther than anyone had before. The historian calls these young men *hybristai*, men who commit acts of *hybris*. The word *hybris* therefore had a very wide range of meaning. It sometimes refers to an act of rape, but it can also refer to any act that "damages the sexual honour or reputation of a person or a family, such as the seduction of a wife (Lys. 1.4, 16, 25)."[1] And the noun *bia* ("force" or "violence") and the verb *biazein* ("to force" or "to use violence") can refer to any action where someone uses violence or threatens to use it.

If the Athenians and other Greeks did not have a single term for an act of sexual violence, can we assume that they had one single attitude toward all acts of sexual violence? We have a single term "rape" because we do not think one can make any distinction between different kinds of sexual violence. In our eyes, the act of forcing someone to have sex against his or her will or without his or her consent is a serious crime that is punishable by severe penalties.[2] Even though the legal definition of rape in the United States in particular has been modified in the past thirty years, absence of consent on the part of the victim has always been one of the constant features in the definition of the crime.[3] Even in the Middle Ages, Bracton assumed that rape was an offense where a man has sexual relations

[1] See, for instance, Cohen (1991b) 177: "Violence or coercion are not necessary components of *hybris* in ordinary language." Doblhofer (1994) 5–7 notes that there is no exact equivalent for the German word *Vergewaltigung* in Greek or Latin, but does not explore the implications of this fact.

[2] For the definition of rape in modern criminal codes in the United States, see the Appendix to this chapter.

[3] Take, for instance, the objection of Brownmiller (1975) 428–9 to the view of Sir Matthew Hale that a man cannot rape his own wife. Hale thought that "A husband cannot be guilty of rape upon his wife for by their mutual matrimonial consent and contract the wife hath given up herself in this kind to her husband, which she cannot retract." Brownmiller argues that "consent is better arrived at each time for if women are to be what we believe we are – equal partners – then intercourse must be construed as an act of desire and not as a wifely duty, enforced by the permissible threat of bodily harm or of economic sanctions." Despite their differences, both writers implicitly agree that the absence of consent is a major element in the definition of rape. Where they disagree is about the nature of consent. Lape (2001) 84 therefore exaggerates when she claims that "definitions of rape vary widely in ordinary discourse, dictionary entries, and statutory designations."

with a woman against her will.[4] As we will see, however, the Greeks referred to some acts of sexual violence as *hybris,* a serious crime, but viewed other acts of sexual violence more leniently. This would suggest that the Greeks did not have a single standard for evaluating acts of sexual violence. Instead of grouping all kinds of sexual violence into one category and giving it one single label ("rape"), the Athenians and other Greeks made distinctions among such acts that we do not make. Therefore, when one uses the word "rape" when analyzing the ancient sources, one may be imposing an anachronistic concept on the evidence, a concept that may prove to be an obstacle to our understanding of ancient attitudes.

Not surprisingly, attempts to answer the question "What was *the* attitude to rape in Classical Athens?" have produced some very strange results. In an otherwise valuable study of women in New Comedy, Fantham shows that she is well aware that the laws of Athens punished rape, but claims that ancient audiences "seem to have found rape a human error, when mitigated by darkness, drink, and youthful desire."[5] Scafuro notes that "the rapists of New Comedy frequently plead in their defense that they did not intend their deed; they acted out of love, or drunkenness or youthful impetuosity." She compares these arguments to those found in forensic oratory where according to her "speakers use various arguments such as intoxication to prove the absence of intention." She reaches the paradoxical conclusion that in New Comedy "The rape is thus an admitted fact, but the young man is not a 'rapist.'"[6] Rosivach too knows that there were laws against sexual assault and recognizes that "Rape, it should be stressed, is never commended or even approved in New Comedy, and it is sometimes even criticized. It is unacceptable, anti-social behavior." Yet he hastens to add that "the plays also regularly make the point that the rapist's rational capacities were diminished by drink and/or youthful passion and the seductive effects of the night." So while ancient audiences hated rape, they loved the rapist: "if the act of rape is to be censured, the agent is less so, especially since no one ever asks

[4] This is implicit in Bracton's list of possible defenses against a charge of rape: "that he had her as his concubine and *amica* before the day and the year mentioned in the appeal (...) of that he had her and defiled her with her consent and not against her will, and that if she now appeals it is in hatred of another woman whom he has as his concubine, or whom he has married, or that it is at the instigation of one of her kinsmen" (Thorne [1968] II: 417–17 quoted in Brownmiller [1975] 18).

[5] Fantham (1975) 54–5.

[6] Scafuro (1997) 246–54.

why he allowed himself to get drunk in the first place." The playwrights therefore seem to have sent a rather contradictory message about rape to their audiences: New Comedy "even while censuring the fact of rape, nonetheless welcomes the rapist. (. . .) Every happy ending inevitably sends a message to its audience that self-serving violence of the powerful against the vulnerable, especially violence of male against female, is permissible despite any public protestations to the contrary."[7] In a study of rape in Menander, S. Lape takes a similar approach and claims that "The nocturnal setting" of the rape "usually lends the act the cover of anonymity" and notes that wine and passion often supply the motive for the assault.[8] "This conventional stylization," she argues, "is calculated specifically to decriminalize rape. The anonymity of the act obscures the social identities of the victim and assailant while the rapist's diminished capacity supplies a crucial explanatory factor leading to the conventional wisdom that New Comic rapists cannot be held accountable for their actions because they act without thinking." She thus arrives at the conclusion that "New Comedy divests rape of a social context." It strips "coerced sexual intercourse of the features that could make it actionable as *hubris* in Athenian law."[9]

There are two main objections to these attempts to explain away the treatment of sexual violence in New Comedy. It is true that in several plays the young men attempt to obtain pardon by saying that they were drunk or carried away by passion. But in other plays this excuse is not given. In Menander's *Samia* (38–49), Moschion tells how upon returning from the fields one day, he came upon some women celebrating the Adonia. He stayed to watch, and besides their noise made it impossible to sleep. Moschion tactfully skips over the details of what happened

[7] Rosivach (1998) 39–42.

[8] Lape (2001) 93.

[9] Lape (2001) 94. How rape is stripped of a "social context" is not clearly explained by Lape. One might point out that both the aggressor and the victim in New Comedy are members of society when the offense occurs and thus subject to all the norms of their society, and this does not change afterwards. To "divest rape of a social context" one would have to place the action on a desert island, in a location removed from any human society. Certainly the characters that threaten to go to court in the plays of Plautus and Terence do not consider that these factors divest sexual violence of a legal context. In general, I do not find convincing Lape's attempt to interpret the rape-plot in New Comedy in terms of democratic ideology. As Euphiletus says (Lys. 1.1), the penalties for *moicheia* are not peculiar to Athens, but found in all constitutions, both in democracies and oligarchies. There is no reason to doubt his statement: the lawcode of Gortyn, hardly a democratic community, contains several provisions on rape and seduction that are similar to those found in Athenian Law. See the previous chapter.

next and says only that the girl became pregnant. Since he blames himself, the girl was obviously not at fault (47–51). Here there is no indication that Moschion was drinking; in fact, he was returning from work in the fields. In Menander's *Georgos* (30) an old woman named Philinna reminds Myrrhine how a young man has wronged her daughter. Nothing in the remaining fragments of the play would allow us to decide whether the young man was drunk at the time or not. And in Terence's *Eunuchus* Chaerea disguises himself as a eunuch and enters the house of Thais, who has him look after Pamphila. When he is alone with Pamphila, he makes love to her despite her protests. Chaerea is quite sober as he carries out his plot, and he achieves his aim by careful planning. Though he later claims his motive was love and not insult, there is no question of "diminished capacity" in his case.[10]

But were drunkenness, youthful enthusiasm, and passion really considered to be legitimate excuses in Athenian Law and society? In the *Politics* (2.9.1274b) Aristotle mentions a law of Pittacus imposing a larger fine on men who commit an offense when drunk. He noticed that men who are drunk are more prone to commit outrage (ὑβρίζειν) than men who are sober. In the *Nicomachean Ethics* (3.5.1113b) the philosopher observes that several legislators inflict double penalties on offenders who are drunk. Their reasoning is that the offender could have avoided getting drunk. If his drunkenness causes him to do something in ignorance, he has only himself to blame for his own ignorance. Far from considering drunkenness an excuse, these legislators held that people who committed crimes when intoxicated should still be held responsible for their actions.

Two cases described by Demosthenes in *Against Meidias* reveal that the Athenian courts did not consider drunkenness, darkness, and passion as legitimate excuses. In one case, a man named Ctesicles was carrying a whip while marching in a religious procession (Dem. 21.180–1). While drunk, he struck someone who happened to be a personal enemy. Demosthenes reports that "he appeared to strike with intent to insult and not because of the wine. On the contrary, he appeared to commit the offense of treating free men like slaves and used the procession and his drunken state as an excuse." Since the court judged that his intent was to insult his enemy, the court condemned him to death, and he was executed. In the other case, a man hit one of the Thesmothetai, an important official, who was defending the freedom of a female musician (Dem. 21.36). The assailant "had three excuses:

[10] Rosivach (1998) 46 realizes that the *Eunuchus* poses problems for his analysis of rape in New Comedy.

drunkenness, passion, and ignorance because the action took place in darkness and at night" (Dem. 21.38).[11] The Thesmothete did not prosecute the assailant but agreed to settle the case out of court for a sum of money (Dem. 21.39). But even though the case did not go to trial, Demosthenes implies that it could have. Indeed, if the man was actually innocent and confident that these excuses would secure his acquittal, why did he agree to pay his victim a sum of money? This is not the way innocent men act. Drunkenness, passion, and ignorance clearly did not exculpate his conduct and as a result he found it necessary to reach a settlement so as to avoid an inevitable conviction in court.[12]

In the speech *Against Conon,* the plaintiff Ariston, who claims to be the victim of drunken violence, goes so far as to argue that there is no excuse whatsoever for committing outrage (*hybris*). If a young man commits outrage, his age may justify mitigating his penalty, but it is not a reason to acquit him of his crime (Dem. 54.21). And if drunkenness were an exculpatory factor, an accuser who was attempting to prove that a defendant was guilty certainly would not say that his opponent was drunk when he committed his offense. Yet Ariston makes a point of mentioning that his assailants had been drinking and that Conon's son was acting drunk (Dem. 54.7), and so does the speaker in Lysias' speech *Against Simon* (Lys. 3.12, 18, 19). In these speeches the accuser appears to mention the defendant's drunkenness in support of their charges, not in extenuation of his conduct. In Aristophanes' *Wasps* when Philocleon gets drunk and starts beating people up, one of his victims does not think his intoxication renders him innocent (Ar. *Vesp.* 1299–300). Instead, he goes ahead and summons him on a charge of *hybris* (1415–18). His son Bdelycleon is so worried that his father will be convicted that he offers to reach an out-of-court settlement (1418–20). In Plautus' *Aulularia* (747–51), Euclio firmly rejects love and

[11] The darkness in this case only made the assailant unaware of the status of the person whom he struck, not the nature of his offense. His ignorance of his victim's official position would have made it difficult to prosecute him for striking a magistrate (Dem. 21.32–3), but would not have protected him from a private action for assault and battery (*dike aeikeias*) or a public action for outrage (*graphe hybreos*).

[12] Scafuro (1997) 249 claims that "Demosthenes represents the private settlements" of the cases mentioned in this section "as flagrant breaches of the court system" and "insinuates that bribery was involved." I see nothing in Demosthenes' language that suggests this, and there was certainly nothing illegal about these out-of-court settlements – see Harris (1999) [= Chapter IV.3 in this volume]. Scafuro cites these two cases to show "The absence of the intention to insult might be claimed on the basis of a disturbed state of mind brought about by love, drunkenness, anger, and ignorance arising out of external factors such as the darkness of night" but does not note that in both cases these excuses did not exculpate the defendant.

drunkenness as excuses: "If the law is such that you can use this kind of an excuse, let's go and rip gold jewelry from matrons openly and in broad daylight. If we should be caught, we would excuse our conduct by saying that we were drunk or did it out of love. Wine and love are much too inexpensive if drunken lovers have the right to do whatever they want without fear of punishment."[13] And when Xenophon is accused of beating soldiers during the March of the Ten Thousand and charged with *hybris*, he does not try to defend himself by claiming he was drunk at the time. Quite the opposite: through questioning one of his accusers, Xenophon proves that he was justified in striking him and not acting out of *hybris* by establishing that he was *not* intoxicated or in love (*Anabasis* 5.8.1–5). So one cannot claim that drunkenness, youth, and passion were regarded as legitimate excuses in Athenian Law and society. This way of explaining (or perhaps explaining away) the rapes in New Comedy does not work.

A second approach has been to claim that the rapes that occur in New Comedy were not really rapes. D. Cohen appears to have been the first to suggest this way of disposing of the evidence from Menander, Plautus, and Terence: "Rape of young, unmarried women at festivals plays a prominent role in the plots of several comedies of Menander, but it is often not clear whether the sexual transaction really was based upon force or it simply was referred to as such in order to help preserve the reputation of the girl."[14] Sommerstein takes this idea one step farther and suggests that the rape-plot represents "a real-life strategy for dealing with the embarrassing situation of a pregnant daughter." In his view what has *really* happened is that the young man has actually only seduced his *inamorata*, but to save her reputation everyone covers up the facts "by explaining that the young man was overpowered by passion into committing a rash act of violence but has repented and been forgiven by his victim." This was a clever strategy "for young people of either sex who wished to marry according to their inclinations rather than according to the interests of their elders."[15] But as Rosivach rightly observes, "there is absolutely no evidence in the texts to support the speculation that any were really consensual sex referred to as rape to protect the reputation of the young

[13] For a similar statement that there is no excuse for committing *hybris*, see Philippides fr. 27 K-A (also noted by Scafuro [1997] 251) and Plautus *Truculentus* 829–33.

[14] Cohen (1990) 148 note 3. Cf. Brown (1993) 197 who notes, however, that no woman in New Comedy is ever said to have actually been a willing partner since this would have lowered her moral stature in the eyes of the audience.

[15] Sommerstein (1998) 112.

women." True, women raised to be courtesans or prostitutes may have consensual sex with young men in New Comedy, but the women in these plays who are victims of rape "are all respectable, and respectable women do not willingly have sex outside of marriage."[16] Cohen commits the fallacy of treating New Comedy as if it were a historical source that reports actual events. Although the texts do not say that the women were *actually* seduced as opposed to raped, Cohen appears to think that there was some real event behind the text, which he knows *must have happened* based on his assumptions about Athenian society – and despite the absence of any evidence whatsoever. There might have existed a strategy such as the one Sommerstein describes, but without any source stating it did exist, there is also the possibility that it might not have existed at all.

A third approach has been to remove the obstacle created by the evidence of New Comedy by arguing that the plays of Menander, Plautus, and Terence belong to a fictional world that bore little or no relationship to contemporary reality. Leisner-Jensen believes that the rape-plot is merely a matter of literary convention: "The conventional ingredients occurring in the rape-stories, down to details, all of them undoubtedly based on reality, make it unlikely that this is a frequent or commonplace feature fetched from everyday life in Athens. The universe of comedy is as conventional as that of all other literary genres."[17] Such a thing could never have happened in Classical Athens because Leisner-Jensen finds it much too horrible: "But how is it that a consummated rape could at all appear in Greek plays meant for a laughter-provoking pastime? A rape is a tragical and fatal experience to the victim and a serious criminal offence. Could it be different to the citizens of fourth-century Athens?"[18] The consequences of assuming that New Comedy might reflect reality are simply too staggering for this scholar: "I can hardly believe that a corresponding proportion of marriages in Athens should have been based on a consummated rape." As a result, they "cannot be explained and understood by reference to actual social and legal conditions in fourteenth-century (*sic*) Athens and Hellas." Pierce is less certain than Leisner-Jensen, but is still skeptical: "rapists might well have married their victims in real life as well as in drama. But this is really no more than supposition (...) Rape in these plays may, then, in the majority of cases, be just a means to an end,

[16] Rosivach (1998) 14.
[17] Leisner-Jensen (2002) 95.
[18] Leisner-Jensen (2002) 195–6.

and as a comic convention or plot device it would have borne no relation to real life."[19]

There are several implicit assumptions in these views. First, Leisner-Jensen appears to think that the Athenians must have shared our views of sexual violence; since we find rape so offensive, the Athenians must also have found it offensive. But there is no reason to make such an assumption: the Athenians held very different views from ours about a wide range of topics such as war, slavery, and infanticide. Is it not also possible that they held a different view of sexual violence? Second, both scholars seem to assume that literary conventions may bear no relation at all to real life. This is true in the case of science fiction and other genres, but Menander was renowned in antiquity for his realism. His depiction of marriage practices, the rules about the *epikleros*, and other legal procedures is generally judged to be reliable; why would he have invented this kind of solution to the problem of sexual violence?[20]

But the strongest argument against the view that the rape-plot was just a matter of literary convention and corresponded to nothing in daily life is the comparative evidence found in several Central and South American countries. For instance, in Peru as recently as 1997 the penal code exonerated a rapist if he offered to marry the victim, and she accepted his offer. Similar laws were on the books in Costa Rica, Argentina, Brazil, Chile, Columbia, Ecuador, Guatemala, Honduras, Nicaragua, Panama, Paraguay, the Dominican Republic, and Venezuela. Violeta Bermúdez, director of Manuela Ramos, a leading women's rights group in Peru, estimated in 1997 that 25,000 women a year were being raped and that a large percentage of these cases were resolved by offers of marriage. Mrs. Bermúdez reported at the time that "in many poor and rural areas of Peru, relatives put pressure on rape victims to accept a rapist's offer, which the relative believe will restore honor to the victim and her family."[21] If such a practice is well attested in modern societies, there is no reason to disbelieve sources attesting to its existence in Classical Athens.

A new approach is clearly needed if we are going to make progress in understanding ancient attitudes to sexual violence. The first step in this new approach

[19] Pierce (1997) 177–8.

[20] See, for example, MacDowell (1982). Brown (1983) is not quite as confident as MacDowell about the possibility of using Menander as a reliable source for details of the law that are not attested elsewhere, but still believes that "His plays certainly provide important evidence on legal matters," although he was "sometimes indifferent to detail."

[21] *New York Times*, March 12, 1997, A1 and A12.

should be to avoid modern and anachronistic concepts when analyzing the ancient evidence. Above all, we should stop using the word "rape" and looking for "the Athenian attitude toward rape" or "the Greek concept of rape." The Greeks did not have a word for "rape," and therefore the search for the Greek concept of rape is a quest to find something that did not exist. What we should examine are Greek attitudes toward sexual violence: why were some acts of sexual violence condemned and punished severely and why were other acts of sexual violence treated more leniently? The second step is to examine a broader range of evidence than previous scholars have studied. Fantham, Scafuro, and Rosivach look primarily at New Comedy with some attention to forensic oratory, but they do not examine myth, tragedy, history, or Old Comedy.[22] Cohen by contrast concentrates on forensic oratory but avoids myth and New Comedy. Each literary genre tends to select and privilege certain aspects of social reality; a tendency to concentrate on one genre to the exclusion of others will result in a distorted view of ancient views. If we are going to understand Athenian and Greek attitudes to sexual violence, we should look at as many different kinds of evidence as possible, not arbitrarily select some evidence and ignore the rest. My survey of the evidence is not exhaustive, but I have tried to cover a wider range of sources than previous scholars have.

I will proceed by grouping the evidence into two categories. In Section II, I will examine cases where sexual violence against women is portrayed as wrong and/or subject to punishment. This punishment may be inflicted at the hands of her husband, father or other relative, or by the legal authorities. In many of these cases sexual violence is denoted by the term *hybris* ("outrage" or "aggravated insult"). I will begin with stories from myth and tragedy, then move to history, and finally examine a statement condemning sexual violence in Menander's *Dyskolos*. In each example, it is important to study not only the narrative of events, but also the way the author presents these events and the reasons why he considers the act of sexual violence wrong and deserving punishment. After having discovered

[22] There is no extensive discussion of sexual violence against women in Foucault (1984), nor in the essays found in Halperin, Winkler, Zeitlin (1990), Larmour, Miller, and Platter (1998), and Nussbaum and Sihvola (2002). Omitowoju (2002) discusses Menander's plays but does not treat the plays of Terence and Plautus that are based on Menandrian originals. She devotes a few paragraphs (185–6) to Euripides' *Ion*, which, as she notes, contradicts her main thesis that Athenian authors did not pay attention to women's lack of consent in acts of sexual violence.

Ideally, a study of sexual violence in ancient Greece would include an analysis of its depiction in vase painting and sculpture. Arafat (1997) and Kilmer (1997) analyze some Late Archaic and Early Classical vases, but a complete study still remains a *desideratum*.

the reasons why the Athenians found sexual violence a crime, we will be in a better position to understand the legal procedures that they created to prosecute this offense in certain circumstances. In Section III, I will study cases where sexual violence against women is either condoned or treated leniently, starting again with Euripides' *Ion* and other myths, next looking at New Comedy, then considering some other cases in different genres. Here we need to observe carefully how these cases differ from those in the group studied in Section II. Are there elements lacking in the second group present in the first? Is there a uniform attitude toward sexual violence, or do attitudes toward it vary according to context?

II

We begin with Attic tragedy.[23] In Sophocles' *Women of Trachis* (555–77), Deianeira recalls how she and her husband Heracles came to the river Evenus and asked the centaur Nessus to carry them across. Nessus took Deianeira first, but in midstream began to touch her with "vain hands" (565: ψαύει ματαίαις χερσίν). Heracles, seeing what was happening from the river-bank, took his bow and killed Nessus with an arrow. Tragedy maintains a certain decorum about the description of Nessus' crime, but Diodorus (4.36.3–5) is more explicit: the historian says that Nessus felt desire for Deianeira and tried to use force against her (βιάσασθαι). When she called out to her husband, Heracles killed the centaur with an arrow while he was having intercourse (μεταξὺ μισγόμενος).[24] No version of the myth

[23] In Aeschylus' *Suppliant Women*, the Danaids repeatedly state that they are unwilling to marry their cousins and call their attempt to force them into marriage an act of *hybris* (29–30, 81, 104, 426, 487, 528, 817–18, 845, 880, 881). However, I have not included this play in my survey because the legal issue in the play is complicated by the fact that the Danaids are Egyptian and thus subject to an Egyptian law that gives their cousins rights over them (Aesch. *Suppl.* 387–91, 933, 984). For a discussion of the legal issue in the play, see Friis Johansen and Whittle (1980) 29–40.

In the prologue to Euripides' *Trojan Women* (69–70), the goddess Athena complains about the *hybris* done to her and her temple when the Locrian Ajax dragged away Cassandra by force. But Athena punishes the Greeks not for the violence done to Cassandra per se, but for violating her temple and not respecting the rights of asylum – see Nilsson (1955–61) 66–9 and Touchefeu in *LIMC* 1.1.336–7.

The earliest example of punishment for attempted sexual violence is found in Odysseus' account of the underworld, where he describes how he saw Tityos being punished for dragging Leto (*Od.* 11.576–81).

[24] Cf. Apollodorus 2.7.6; Hyginus *Fabula* 34. The killing of Nessus for his attempt on Deianeira was popular in vase painting – see *LIMC* 6.1.838–46. On several vases the painter indicates Deianeira's lack of consent by her gestures of protest or her appeal to Heracles for help.

says that Heracles had to atone for this murder the way he did after the murder of Eurystheus. The hero's killing of Nessus is portrayed as a just punishment of an attempted rape.

In Euripides' *Hippolytus* there is an accusation of sexual violence, which turns out to be false, but Theseus' reaction to the charge is very revealing about his attitude toward the crime. After the nurse discloses to Hippolytus Phaedra's love for him, Phaedra decides to kill herself, but first extracts a promise from her stepson not to tell anyone about her passion. Before hanging herself, she writes a note and leaves it attached to her wrist accusing Hippolytus of having used force to enter her bed. When her husband Theseus returns and reads the note, he shouts:

> Hippolytus has dared to put his hand by force (βίᾳ)
> To my marriage-bed, dishonoring (ἀτιμάσας) the eye of Zeus.
> (885–6, trans. Kovacs)

Theseus says the action took place by force, but the way that he expresses himself is telling: the offense was against *his* marriage bed. In other words, Hippolytus' crime was directed not so much at Phaedra as against his father. When Hippolytus enters and tries to defend himself, Theseus repeats his point: his son has brought shame on his marriage bed (943–4: ᾔσχυνε τἀμὰ λέκτρα). His attack is not on Phaedra, but on his father's marriage to her. Even after Hippolytus attempts to prove his innocence and swears an oath denying his guilt, Theseus remains certain that his son "has dishonored his father" (1040: τὸν τέκοντ' ἀτιμάσας). Although Hippolytus is his own son, Theseus banishes him (1045–54) and calls down a curse on his head (887–90), which causes his death. Though it is obvious that Hippolytus has been accused of sexual violence, Theseus always stresses the wrong that is done to him; he never approaches the crime from Phaedra's point of view or emphasizes her lack of consent.

An act of sexual violence leads to revenge and tragedy in Sophocles' *Tereus*. Only fragments remain from the play, but summaries of the tragedy in later sources make it possible to recover the basic features of the plot.[25] Pandion, the king of Athens, married Zeuxippe and had two sons, Erectheus and Butes, and two daughters, Procne and Philomela. When Pandion needed help in his war against Labdacus, he called on Tereus, the king of Thrace, for help. After winning the war, Pandion gave his daughter Procne to Tereus in marriage (Apollodorus 3.14.8).

[25] For summaries in later sources and the fragments of Sophocles' *Tereus*, see Radt (1977) 435–45.

The versions of the story differ at this point, but Sophocles followed the version reported by Tzetzes.[26] In this version Procne requested to see her sister, so Tereus went to Athens to escort Philomela to Thrace. On their way back, Tereus used violence to deflower her and cut out her tongue to prevent her from reporting his crime to her sister. After joining her sister, Philomela wove a robe with figures depicting what had happened to her and showed it to Procne. To take revenge on Tereus, Procne killed their son Itys and served him as a meal to his father. When he discovered what she had done, he pursued both sisters, who had fled. To evade capture, they asked the gods to transform them into birds; Procne became a nightingale, Philomela a swallow. The sisters appear to have been criticized in Sophocles' play for taking their vengeance too far,[27] but in Demosthenes' *Funeral Oration* (60.28) they are held up as an example, which the soldiers of the tribe Pandionis followed when they fought against Philip II at Chaeronea. Like Procne and Philomela, who punished Tereus for his *hybris* toward them, the men of Pandionis also showed courage when they saw all of Greece as the victim of Macedonian *hybris*. Here again, sexual violence is clearly condemned as *hybris* and merits serious punishment.

Turning to history, we find a series of abductions in the very first chapters of Herodotus' account of the *Persian War* (Hdt. 1.1–5).[28] According to Persian storytellers, the Phoenicians once came to Argos on a trading voyage. On the fifth or sixth day after their arrival, the king's daughter Io came to the shore with many Argive women to go shopping. The Phoenicians rushed at them and took away Io and several other women. The Greeks retaliated by taking Europa, the daughter of the king of Tyre. According to Herodotus, "this evened the score." In the next round, the Greeks went to Colchis and abducted Medea, the daughter of the king. When the king sent a herald to demand her back, the Greeks replied that since they had received no justice for the abduction of Io, they would not make amends for Medea. In the third round, Alexander (Paris), the son of Priam, after hearing these stories, wished to abduct a woman from Greece, thinking that he would not be punished for it. After he took Helen, the Greeks sent messengers to ask for

[26] The summary found in *P. Oxy.* 3013 is probably the hypothesis of Sophocles' *Tereus* and is similar to the version found in Tzetzes. See Haslam (1975) 150 note 3. Apollodorus (3.14.8) implies that Tereus deceived Philomela by telling her that Procne was dead, but Hyginus *Fabula* 45 reports that Tereus used force (*compressit*).

[27] See Stobaeus 3.20.32 = Sophocles *Tereus* fr. 589 (Radt).

[28] Sexual violence in Herodotus is studied in a perceptive essay by Harrison (1997).

her back and for compensation for the abduction. They received the reply that since there was no compensation for Medea, there would be none for Helen. Not content with this answer, the Greeks raised an expedition and destroyed the power of Priam "on account of a single woman."

In his account of Egypt in Book 2, Herodotus (2.113–15) returns to the story of Paris and Helen.[29] When Paris was sailing back to Troy from Sparta, he was blown off course and forced to land in Egypt at the mouth of the Nile. There some of his slaves deserted and sought refuge as suppliants in the temple of Heracles. Wishing to do some harm to their former master, they told the priests and Thonis, the official in charge of the area, about what happened to Helen and "the wrong committed against Menelaus" (2.113.3). Thonis sent a messenger to report the news of Paris' crime to King Proteus and how he had tricked the wife of his host and stolen his property. Proteus ordered Thonis to seize Paris and to take him along with Helen and the stolen goods to his palace at Memphis. When he started to ask Paris how he took Helen, Paris tried to avoid answering, but his slaves told the king the truth. At this point Proteus expressed his shock at the way Paris treated his Spartan host, then declared he would keep Helen in Egypt until her husband came to get her.

Two features of these stories are significant for understanding Greek attitudes toward sexual violence. First, abduction by one group is seen as a legitimate response to an abduction committed by another group. In our eyes, no woman should be removed from her community against her will. The Geneva Convention protects women of all countries against rape and abduction by the enemies of their country, no matter how wrong the policies of their own country may be. The Greeks appear to have viewed the matter differently: when the Greeks respond to Io's capture by taking Europa, Herodotus does not condemn both sides equally, but regards the Greek action as justifiable revenge. The fact that Europa is innocent of wrongdoing is immaterial. Second, Paris' abduction of Helen through deceit is not seen as an offense against her but as a violation of the guest–host relationship and a wrong done to Menelaus (Hdt. 2.115.4). Helen's own role in the abduction is a little vague. On the one hand, Paris is said to have abducted her (2.113.1: ἁρπάσαντα), which suggests her abduction was against her will, but he is also

[29] Even though Herodotus appears to have drawn on local sources for his account of Egypt, it is generally agreed that the story of Helen is based on Greek myth and mirrors Greek attitudes. On the sources for Book 2 of Herodotus, see Lloyd (1988) esp. 33, 45.

said to have aroused her emotions (we might translate ἀναπτερώσας at 2.115.4 as "set her heart aflutter"), which seems to imply seduction. But Herodotus places her abduction on the same level as that of Io, who was clearly seized against her will. What counts for him is not her consent or lack of consent, but Paris' violation of Menelaus' rights as husband and host.[30]

Moving from Egypt of the Pharaohs to Greece just before the Persian Wars, we encounter a story about rape that concerns the Macedonians (Hdt. 5.18–21). Before the Persian Wars, Darius sent Persian envoys to ask for earth and water from the Macedonians, the tokens of political subjection. Amyntas, the king of Macedon, agreed and invited the envoys to dinner. They had a great deal to drink, then insisted that the Macedonians bring their wives to drink with them. When Amyntas says that this is not the Greek custom for women to join in drinking, the Persians insist. Here we should bear in mind that the only women who joined men at *symposia* were courtesans;[31] for the Persians to request that Macedonian women sit with them as they drank is to treat them as if they were prostitutes, an insult to their honor. To prevent trouble, Amyntas had the women sit opposite his guests, but the Persians complained that they should not have come at all if they are to remain at a distance. Under pressure Amyntas ordered them to sit next to their guests. The Persians, who were quite drunk, began to fondle their breasts and tried to kiss them (Herodotus is quite explicit on this point). Amyntas, though horrified, held his tongue, but his son Alexander could not bear the situation and asked his father to let him entertain the guests. Amyntas yielded to his son, and Alexander told the Persians they could go to bed with any of the women they wanted and ordered the women back to their quarters. He then dressed some young men in their clothes, and when the Persians came to sleep with the women, the young men killed them.

The striking feature about this story is that Herodotus does not say whether the women were willing or not, even though it is hard to imagine they welcomed the fondling by the Persians. What Herodotus stresses is the reaction of Amyntas and Alexander. There is no indication that Alexander asked the women how they felt before he went ahead with his plot. As far as he was concerned, the Persians had insulted the women by insisting that they sit with them as they drank, then

[30] Cf. Harrison (1997) 190: "his crime, an infringement of the obligations of guest-friendship, is perceived as being committed against Menelaus rather than Helen herself."

[31] Is. 3.14 with Wyse (1904/79) *ad loc.*

fondling them and trying to kiss them. For this insult to their honor, and his own, they deserved to die.

In his account of the battle of Leuctra, Xenophon (*Hell.* 6.4.7) mentions the monument of two virgins who were said to have committed suicide because they had been "forced" (i.e., to have sex) by two Spartans. Pausanias (9.13.5) gives more details: a Boeotian named Scedasus lived near Leuctra and had two daughters, Molpia and Hippo. When these girls reached adolescence, two Spartans Phrourarichidas and Parthenius, "used force on them contrary to what is right (βιάζονται παρὰ θέμιδα)." The girls could not bear the insult to their honor (ὕβρεως) and hanged themselves. When their father Scedasus went to Sparta and could not obtain justice for this crime, he too killed himself. The version given by Plutarch (*Pelopidas* 20) is similar, but he omits the names of the girls and adds that the father called down curses on the Spartans before killing himself before his daughters' tomb.[32] Two points are worth noting here. First, Pausanius says that the Spartans used force contrary to *themis* or "what is right," which would seem to suggest that in other cases it was not contrary to justice to use force against a woman. Second, the shame felt by the victims is shared by their father, who has not been able to protect women who are in his household. When he cannot avenge their suffering, he cannot bear the dishonor and also kills himself.

The tragedy of Scedasus' daughters was repeated on a massive scale during the raid of the Gauls on the Kallieans in 279/78.[33] In Pausanias' account (10.22.2) of the raid, women threatened with rape killed themselves or died after being raped. The Gauls "butchered every human male of that entire race, the old men and the children at the breast; and the Gauls drank the blood and ate the flesh of those slaughtered babies that were fattest with milk. Any women and mature virgins with a spark of pride killed themselves as soon as the city fell; those who lived were subjected with wanton violence to every form of outrage (*hybris*) by men as remote from mercy as they were remote from love (ἴσον μὲν ἐλέου, ἴσον δὲ τὰς φύσεις καὶ ἔρωτος ἀπέχοντες). Women who came upon a Gaulish sword committed

[32] Diodorus (15.54) gives a slightly different version: he says that some Spartans also committed the same crime against the daughters of Leuctrus and does not mention the suicide of Scedasus.

[33] There is no reason to be skeptical of Pausanias' account of this atrocity. Excavations at Kallipolis have confirmed the destruction of the city in this period. See Habicht (1985) 32–5 with the references cited there. For sexual violence against women taken in war, see the evidence collected by Pritchett (1991) 238–41.

suicide with their own hands; it was not long before the others were to die by famishing hunger and sleeplessness, outraged in an endless succession by pitiless and barbarous men; they mated with the dying; they mated with those already dead" (trans. Levi). The news of this atrocity was so alarming to the women in nearby towns that they joined their husbands in attacking the Gauls.

What is curious about Pausanias' account, however, is the way he describes the actions of the Gauls. He remarks that they were as removed from mercy as they were removed from love. The implication seems to be that their violence would not have been so awful if their motive was love instead of humiliation. In other words, when Pausanias condemns the actions of the Gauls, he views it more from the point of view of the intention of the aggressor and does not focus on the absence of consent on the part of the victim. This is a point to which we will return.

When we turn to New Comedy, we find that in the vast majority of cases where a young man commits sexual violence, he is treated leniently and allowed to marry the victim – if he is not married to her already. We will look at these in Section III. But in a passage from Menander's *Dyskolos* (289–98), we encounter a less indulgent attitude. Gorgias, a hard-working farmer, has seen Sostratus, a rich young man from the city, lurking around his father's farm and suspects that he may have designs on his sister.

> Gorgias: You seem to be keen on some foul deed,
> intending to persuade a free-born virgin
> or watching for an opportunity to accomplish
> a deed that deserves many deaths.

As Brown has rightly noted, Gorgias suggests that Sostratus is planning to make love to the girl either by persuading her or by achieving his goal against her will.[34] Yet though he considers the latter possibility a terrible crime, he considers both offenses more of a crime against himself than against the girl, an insult to his own honor as much as to hers.

> It is certainly not right for your leisure to cause
> trouble for us who never have any leisure.
> Keep in mind that a poor man, when wronged,

[34] Brown (1991).

> is the most difficult thing in the world.
> At first he is pitiable, but then he considers
> everything that he has suffered not merely
> an injustice but an insult to his honor (*hybrin*).

It makes little difference to Gorgias how Sostratus succeeds in making love to his sister; either way, the wrong is one that is done to him.[35]

Several key themes emerge from this survey of passages depicting sexual violence. The main one is that the wrong is always done to the husband, father, or other male relative. The offense is generally seen in terms of damage done to their honor. Second, in several passages the emphasis is less on the absence of the woman's consent than on the intent of the aggressor. What seems to makes his action wrong is not so much his use of force – whether Sostratus intends to use force or persuasion does not make much difference to Gorgias – as his motive for using force. Third, the main concern is with honor, not with the issue of consent. Sexual violence is not a unique crime, but one of many possible threats to the honor of men and the women under their control.

An understanding of Greek attitudes toward sexual violence helps us to explain certain salient features of the legal procedures that were employed to punish this crime. First to note is the absence of a specific statute outlawing rape per se or directed only at acts of sexual violence toward women. There were legal procedures that someone could employ against a person who had committed sexual violence, but their main aim was not to protect a woman's autonomy and her right to choose who her sexual partners would be. This makes sense in a society where women were under the control of their fathers before marriage and subject to the will of their husbands after marriage. When a woman was given to a man, it was her father who concluded the agreement with her husband and determined the nature of the union, either one based on a pledge (*engye*) or a form of concubinage (*pallake*), which in turn determined the status of her children (*gnesioi* or *nothoi*).[36] A

[35] A fragment of Menander (*Fabula Incerta* 13–17, 23–5, 27–8) that is not attributed to a specific play also concerns sexual violence. A young man, Chaireas, claims that the daughter of Cleainetus has been pledged to him in marriage and says that Moschion has assaulted and thus forced her into marriage. Although his claim is part of a ruse, it is significant that he says the wrong done by Moschion was done to him, not the girl. For the plot and analysis of the fragments, see Gomme and Sandbach (1973) 683–9.

[36] On marriage as a legal act, see Vérilhac and Vial (1998) 229–65 with the conclusion at 265: "le marriage grec n'a jamais été un acte par lequel deux conjoints s'unissaient l'un à l'autre sur un pied d'égalité.

marriage did not require a woman's consent to become valid. The father was also the one who set the amount of the dowry and handed it over to the husband; if there was a divorce, the father initiated the action to recover the dowry if it was not returned.[37] The father also appears to have had the power to terminate the marriage, and in some cases we read that husbands in their wills determined who would marry their widows.[38] That is not to say that the Athenians did not think that a woman was incapable of giving or withholding her consent. The Athenians were quite capable of distinguishing between sexual acts where the woman gave her consent and where she did not. The woman who allowed herself to be seduced was punished by a certain loss of rights; no evidence suggests that the victims of sexual violence were subject to similar treatment.[39] But protecting a woman against sexual violence was not the law's main concern. What was more important was protecting men's control over their wives, daughters and other female relatives.[40] For instance, when Euphiletus compares men who have sex with other men's wives against their will with those who seduce them, he evaluates the two types of men not in terms of the effect they have on the woman but on her husband's control over his household (Lys. 1.32–6). A threat to this control could come either through force (sexual violence) or through persuasion (seduction). These two alternatives were not viewed as fundamentally different, but as two sides of a single threat.

Un marriage impliquait nécessairement trois personnes: le marié, la mariée, et l'auteur de la dation. Non seulement la presence d'un tiers était indispensable, mais c'était lui qui avait le role principal et l'initiative dans l'acte juridique. Le role actif revenait aux deux hommes, le marié et le père de la mariée. Cette dernière, sauf exception rarissime, avait un role passif."

37 On practices for the dowry, see Vérilhac and Vial (1998) 125–208.

38 For the father's right to terminate his daughter's marriage (*aphaeresis*), see Dem. 41.6 with Cohn-Haft (1995). For men giving their wives to new husbands, see Dem. 36.28–9.

39 For the punishment of women who allow themselves to be seduced, see Aeschin. 1.183 and Dem. 59.86 with Fisher (2001) 336–7 and Kapparis (1999) 354–7. This evidence undermines the view of Omitowoju (2002) that Athenian Law paid no attention to women's consent.

40 Cf. Foxhall (1991) 299: "Rape, seduction, and *moikheia* are therefore not so much offenses against women or 'the husband-wife relationship' as they are offenses against men's authority over their households and against their power to control the sexual activities of household members." Cf. Porter (1986) 217: "From Old Testament Jewish codes up to feudalism, rape was treated primarily as theft, as a property offense, but one perpetrated against *men*. The crime was principally that of stealing or abducting a woman from her rightful proprietors, normally her father or husband. Moreover, in the case of a maiden, rape destroyed her property value on the marriage market, and because defloration polluted, heaped shame on her family."

This would explain why in the statute concerning just homicide or homicide according to the laws, nothing is said about the woman's absence of consent and no distinction is made between cases of sexual violence and acts of seduction.[41] The statute listed various situations where a man could not be convicted for homicide. It is therefore concerned with the cases where the law allowed a man to use lethal force or did not hold him responsible for murder if he caused death (Dem. 23.53; [Arist.] *Ath. Pol.* 57.3).[42] If he were accused of homicide and alleged that the killing took place in one of the situations enumerated in the law, his case would go to the Delphinion, not the Areopagus. In other words, the law is about what men can or cannot do – its primary concern is not with what men cannot or cannot do to women. One of the situations covered by the law was the one where a man caught someone "with" or "on top of" or "in intercourse with" his wife, mother, sister, daughter, or concubine (*pallake*) kept for the purpose of free children. By exempting him from conviction in this case, the law recognizes the man's right to use violence against those who challenge his authority over the women under his control. It is not aimed at protecting just his authority over his partner in an *engye* union, who would produce the *gnesioi* children who will inherit his property.[43] The law covers every woman that might live in his household, including a concubine living with him and kept for the purpose of free children who will be *nothoi* and thus ineligible to receive a share of his estate. It obviously did not cover prostitutes kept in a brothel ([Dem.] 59.66). Since it protects male control and not female autonomy, it grants a male the right to use force against all threats to his control and makes no distinction between consensual acts and those committed by force.

The second legal procedure that could be used in cases of sexual violence is the *graphe hybreos*, the public action for *hybris*.[44] *Hybris* is a complex offense, which

[41] See Harris (1990) [= Chapter III.1].

[42] On the category of just homicide or homicide according to the laws, see MacDowell (1963) 70–81.

[43] *Pace* Cohen (1984a), who thinks that the punishment of *moicheia* was aimed primarily at protecting the marriage bond, and Doblhofer (1994) 106–11, who believes that the penalties against rape mainly protected the legitimacy of offspring – see Harris (1996b).

[44] On the *graphe hybreos* as a procedure for punishing sexual violence, see Harris (1990) [= the previous essay]. For successful prosecution of sexual violence on this procedure, see Din. 1.23 with Doblhofer (1994) 52, rightly rejecting Cole (1984) 104. There is no need to think, as does MacDowell (1976a) 28–9, that prosecutions for *hybris* were difficult to prove and thus rare. On the contrary, the Old Oligarch ([Xen.] *Ath. Pol.* 3.5), when explaining the large number of cases in Athenian courts, lists cases of *hybris* as one reason. For an argument that Demosthenes' case against Meidias was a charge of *hybris*, see Harris

covers a wide range of actions. As with all offenses, there are two aspects to *hybris*, a subjective side and an objective side.[45] As a state of mind, *hybris* is a disposition that causes a person to act in a certain way and is characterized by certain forms of behavior (subjective side).[46] MacDowell has described *hybris* as a state "of having energy or power and misusing it self-indulgently." As a wrongful action, *hybris* is a deed that affects another person and inflicts harm and suffering (objective side). When the verb *hybrizein* is used without an object in the active voice, the emphasis is clearly on the state of mind of the person who commits *hybris* (e.g., Hom. *Od.* 1.227). When the verb is used in the passive, the emphasis shifts to the effects of *hybris* inflicted on the victim (e.g., Dem. 21.1,75).

As a legal offense, *hybris* always involves a victim who suffers dishonor or shame as a result of the defendant's actions. To prove a charge of *hybris*, therefore, one had to show, first, that the offender acted in a certain state of mind, and second, that the victim incurred shame or dishonor. As Aristotle (*Rhet.* 1374a14) states, "if someone strikes another person, he does not in each case commit an act of *hybris*, but only if he does so for a certain reason such as to dishonor him or for his own pleasure." Aristotle stresses this aspect of *hybris* in Book 2 of the *Rhetoric* (1378b23–35):

> The *hybrizon* also demeans: for *hybris* is doing and saying things which cause shame for the victim, not for the purpose of gaining anything beyond the action itself, but simply to experience pleasure. For those who act in retaliation do not commit *hybris* but take revenge. The reason why people who commit *hybris* feel pleasure is that they think that they are far superior by treating other people badly. Dishonor is the result of *hybris*, and one who

(1989) 130–1. Omitowoju (1997) believes that one could bring a charge of *hybris* in cases of sexual assault only if the victim were respectable, but see Harris (1998).

Pace Fisher (1992) 36 the text of the law about *hybris* preserved at Dem. 21.47 is a forgery – see Harris (1992c) 75–8.

[45] In what follows I draw heavily on the valuable work of MacDowell (1976a) and Fisher (1992). The views of the two scholars, though clashing on several points, are not incompatible. Their differences stem mainly from the fact that each emphasizes a separate side of *hybris*: MacDowell tends to stress the subjective aspect, whereas Fisher concentrates on the objective aspect. As a result, both scholars argue to some extent at cross-purposes.

[46] Fisher (1992) 130, 133, 148, 173, 402 understands that *hybris* is in many cases a disposition but limits the subjective aspect of the offense to the intent to dishonor someone. But Fisher cannot explain away passages where the verb *hybrizein* is used without an object or where there is an act of *hybris* with no victim involved – see MacDowell (1990) 21 and Cairns (1996).

> dishonors demeans someone since what has no value has no honor either for good or for bad. That is why Achilles in his anger said:
> he dishonored me since he has taken my prize and keeps it. [*Il.* 1.356]
> and
> he treated me as if I were some vagabond without respect [*Il.* 9.948 = 17.59]
> since he was angry for these reasons.

In Isocrates' speech *Against Lochites* (5–6), the plaintiff accuses the defendant not only of beating him but also committing *hybris* because he humiliated him:

> If there was no *hybris* present in his actions, I would never have come before you. But as it is, I am here in front of you to obtain justice from him not for the other damage incurred from his blows, but for the mistreatment and the dishonor. These are the things that are most likely to cause men to grow angry and seek the greatest revenge.

Demosthenes (21.72) describes the devastating effects of *hybris* and the sense of humiliation felt by the victim in a passage from his *Against Meidias*:

> It is not the fact of being beaten which is terrible for free men, but when it is done with the intent to insult. There are many things which a man who strikes might do, men of Athens, but the victim might not be able to describe to someone else even one of these things: the way he stands, the way he looks, his tone of voice, when he strikes to insult, or when he acts like an enemy, or when he punches, or when he hits him on the jaw. When men are not used to being insulted, this is what stirs them up, this is what drives them to distraction. No one, men of Athens, would by reporting these actions be able to convey to his audience the terrible effect of outrage in the exact way that it really and truly appears to the victim and those who witness it.

What made *hybris* different from merely hitting someone was in part the intent to cause dishonor. When Ariston tries to prove that he suffered *hybris* at the hands of Conon, he lays stress on his opponent's behavior after striking him:

> This man Conon here, his son and the son of Andromenes fell on and first pulled my cloak off, then tripped me and pushed me into the mud. They jumped on me and beat me so violently that they split my lip open and my eyes were closed shut. They left me in such an awful state that I could not get up nor make a sound. Lying there, I heard them say many terrible things, most of which was quite abusive (I would be reluctant to go into the details

> in front of you), but I will tell you about the thing that is a sign of his *hybris* and proof that the whole business was his responsibility. He started to crow, imitating a fighting cock that has won a victory; his friends asked him to beat his elbows against his sides like wings.
>
> (Dem. 54.9)

The violence is an act of *hybris* not so much because of the physical injury but because of the assailant's attitude. Conon beats his victim for no apparent reason other than to enjoy his own sense of superiority over him. The emphasis is on his intent to humiliate and to rob his victim of his self-respect.

As this brief discussion should make clear, the crime of *hybris* in Classical Athens is far different from the crime of rape in modern law. In rape the emphasis is on the victim's lack of consent – the crime violates the person's right to make decisions about his or her sexuality.[47] But in Classical Athens it was men who determined by and large when and with whom women could have sexual relations. In contrast to rape, *hybris* is an offense that looks partly at the intention of the aggressor, partly at the effect on the honor of the victim and her relatives. In the modern crime of rape the intent of the aggressor is irrelevant: if a man forces a woman to have sexual relations against her will, it makes no difference whether he was in love with her or not. And in a modern courtroom a defendant could not try to avoid conviction on a charge of rape by claiming that he acted out of love and did not intend to humiliate his victim. One must also bear in mind that the charge of *hybris* committed against a woman would be brought by a man and was therefore as much a way of vindicating his own honor as that of the woman. As we saw in the case of Scedasus, men found it imperative to avenge the dishonor done to their daughters. When Scedasus could not do this, the sense of humiliation was too much for him to bear, so he killed himself. And it was the man who decided whether to bring the charge or not. In other words, it was his conception of her honor that counted, not hers. This is consistent with what we have discerned in the passages from literature where sexual violence is described.

An understanding of the differences between the ancient idea of *hybris* and the modern concept of rape helps explain some of the distinctive features that we have noticed in the accounts of sexual violence studied in this section. First is the emphasis on the dishonor inflicted not only on the woman but also on her husband and male relatives. For Theseus Hippolytus' assault on Phaedra was an

[47] For definitions of rape in modern statutes, see the Appendix.

attack on his honor more than a crime against her person. The abduction of Helen was a wrong against Menelaus, not an offense against Helen. Second is the relative lack of interest in the victim's point of view. When the Persians start to fondle the Macedonian women, the story is told from the point of view of their male relatives, who feel themselves insulted. When the Gauls attack the Kallieans, the narrative looks at their intent, which had nothing to do with love, not with the absence of consent on the part of the women. When Gorgias suspects Sostratus of plotting against his sister, it makes little difference to him how he accomplishes his goal, with or without her consent.

Now that it is clear why the Athenians and other Greeks condemned some types of sexual violence, it will be possible to find out why they took different attitudes toward other forms of it.

III

This section will examine cases of sexual violence where the assailant is either treated leniently or not punished at all. In all these cases the act of sexual violence is not called *hybris*. Here it is crucial to analyze the particular features of each case to discover how it differs from the cases where sexual violence is condemned as *hybris*. This in turn will help us to understand why these cases are treated differently from those studied in Section II.

We start again with tragedy. In Euripides' *Ion* an act of sexual violence is the driving force behind the entire plot. The play begins with the prologue where the god Hermes relates how Apollo "placed the yoke of marriage on Creusa, the daughter of Erechtheus, by force" (10–11; cf. 891–901, 941: *akousa*).[48] Creusa became pregnant and gave birth to a child, whom she exposed in the same cave where she was assaulted by Apollo (15–21). Although she expected him to die, she left certain tokens with him (26–7). Apollo ordered his brother Hermes to take the child to the steps of his temple at Delphi, where it was discovered by a priestess there (28–42). Even though the priestess assumed that the child was left there by some local girl, she did not cast it out of the precinct, but kept the child and raised him (43–51).

Years later, Creusa comes to Delphi with her husband Xuthus, the king of Athens. The couple cannot have children and have come to consult Apollo in

[48] I do not understand how Lefkowitz (1993) 27 can state that Apollo "did not use force."

hopes of finding a solution to their problem. Creusa arrives at the temple first and meets Ion, who now serves as a slave protecting the shrine (236–51). Not knowing that he is her son, Creusa tells him that she has come to consult with Apollo on behalf of a friend whose situation is similar to her own (329–80). She claims that her friend wishes to know what has become of her child, but in reality she has come to find her own son. After telling her story, Creusa reproaches Apollo not for using force against her friend, but only because Apollo did not keep the child for her so that she could bury him, if dead, or see him again, if alive (384–9; cf. 252–4, 425–6). Ion too finds fault with the god, but his criticism is similar to Creusa's: the god is wrong not for making love to her against her will, but for doing so and then abandoning his child (436–9). He goes so far as to accuse Apollo, Poseidon, and Zeus of hypocrisy because they set down laws for men, then break the laws that impose penalties for using violence (440–51). Ion here alludes to the *dike biaion*, a private action for damages that could be brought in cases of sexual violence.[49] In the ode that follows this scene, the chorus refers to the child born from Apollo and Creusa's friend as the "*hybris* of a bitter marriage" (506). Here the stress appears to be on the humiliation of bearing a child out of wedlock, which the mother exposed so as to avoid shame in the eyes of her parents and of society. Finally, when Creusa tells her slave what Apollo did to her, he calls the god evil (952: *kakos*. cf. 961) for not protecting the child (951–66). None of these characters is reluctant to criticize the god's conduct, but his use of force is not what causes their disapproval.

When Xuthus arrives to consult the god, he is told that the first person whom he meets on leaving the temple is his son. This turns out to be Ion, who is understandably skeptical at first that Xuthus is his father, but gradually allows himself to be convinced (517–675). Creusa, still unaware that Ion is her son, becomes jealous of her husband's child by another woman and with the aid of her slave plots to kill him (747–1047). When her attempt to poison him is thwarted and exposed, she is tried and condemned to death by the Delphian authorities (1106–228). To escape punishment, Creusa flees to the altar of Apollo and becomes the god's suppliant (1250–60). Ion enters and tells Creusa that she should leave

[49] Scafuro (1997) 211 believes that the money paid to the victim in a *dike biaion* was used to increase the amount of the victim's dowry, but her idea is rightly rejected by Omitowoju (2002) 69–70 on the grounds that a court case would have drawn attention to the victim's loss of virginity and would only have diminished her chances of finding a husband.

the altar because she is guilty of murder (1261–319). At this point, the priestess emerges from the temple and reveals the cradle that was left with Ion when he was abandoned (1320–68). This enables Creusa to realize that Ion is her son, and mother and child are finally reunited (1369–509). But when Creusa tells him that Apollo is his true father, Ion is skeptical until the goddess Athena appears, reveals the truth, and predicts a glorious future for the boy as the ancestor of the Ionian race (1512–619).

The final scene of the play is very significant for our understanding of Athenian attitudes toward sexual violence. When Athena tells Ion and Creusa how Apollo has contrived to place Ion in the line of succession for the kingship of Athens, she states that "Apollo has done all things well" (1595). Then Creusa praises the god:

> Hear now what I have to say. I praise Phoebus, though before I did not praise him, because he has given me back the son I did not take care of. Lovely now in my eyes are the gates of the god's oracular shrine, which I once hated. Now my hands cling with pleasure to the door knocker as I bid the gates farewell.
>
> (1609–13 [trans. Kovacs])

Her language is revealing. She does not see the return of Ion and his glorious future as compensation for the wrong done to her by Apollo's rape. A modern woman might have replied, "Well, Apollo, you bastard, that is the least you could do after raping me and abandoning me and my child." Creusa does not pardon Apollo, but praises him, and her praise is unqualified. What is more, she implicitly admits to being wrong for failing to praise him before (252–4). Now one might be tempted to discount this evidence since Apollo is a god and Creusa is a mortal – surely, one might object, different rules apply. But earlier in the play, Ion says that gods ought to be held to the same standard of justice as mortals (440–51). Previously, all that Creusa and the other characters have criticized Apollo for is abandoning his child. Now that it is clear that Apollo did not allow his child to die, he is seen as wise and just, his conduct above reproach. Once Creusa sees that the consequences of Apollo's violence are beneficial to herself and her child, she has no grounds for charging him with *hybris* because the god's intent was not to bring shame on her, but to glorify her and her descendants. This strikes a modern audience as strange: for us all sexual violence is wrong and is condemned as rape. But for the Athenians, as well as the other Greeks, attitudes toward sexual violence vary according to context. If the intent of the aggressor is to shame and humiliate his victim, to take his pleasure without a thought for her offspring, he is condemned for committing *hybris* and punished. But if the aggressor acts with good intentions and seeks to enhance the status of his child, he cannot be blamed and may even be praised.

This pattern – a god falls in love with a mortal woman and makes love to her against her will, followed by the birth of illustrious offspring – is found in several Greek myths. In the *Homeric Hymn to the Dioscuri* (17.4), Leda is said to have been subdued by Zeus (ὑποδμηθεῖσα) and gives birth to Castor and Pollux. Apollodorus (3.12.6) reports that Aeacus pursued Psamathe, the daughter of Nereus, who changed herself into a seal to avoid contact with him. Her trick seems to have failed since she gave birth to Phocus, who was the ancestor of the Phocians. One of the most famous examples of the pattern is the myth of Zeus and Europa. The most elaborate version of the myth is the one told by the Hellenistic poet Moschus.[50] His poem tells the story of Zeus' passion for Europa when he sees her playing in a meadow with several other young women and how he changes himself into a handsome bull (Moschus 2.74–88). Thus transformed, Zeus approaches the girls, who are attracted by his beauty and immortal fragrance and begin to touch him (89–101). Finding him mild and gentle, Europa innocently places herself on his back to go for a ride (102–9). At this point the bull dashes toward the sea and rushes out into the waves (109–14). When the bull is so far out in the water that the shore is no longer visible, Europa starts to sense that something is amiss and grows worried (115–51). To calm her fears, Zeus speaks these words to her:

> Have courage, young maid; do not fear the waves of the sea. Even though I appear close up to be a bull, I am actually Zeus himself, since I can take any shape that I like. It was desire for you that made me take on the appearance of a bull and go so long a distance out to sea. Crete, the land that bore me, will soon welcome you when your wedding will take place. From me you will bear famous sons, who will rule as scepter-bearing kings among mortals.
>
> (153–61)

[50] For sources and representations on vases, see Robertson in *LIMC* 4.1: 76–92.

Zeus neglects the fact that he has lured Europa into a position where she is powerless to resist and never asks for her consent. What counts for him is that he is acting out of love and that she will have the distinction of bearing remarkable offspring.[51] Since his intent is not to dishonor her and the result of his action will bring her fame and glory, not shame, there is no *hybris* involved, and he is therefore doing nothing wrong. This is what distinguishes him (at least in his own eyes and those of the audience) from Nessus when he laid his hands on Deianeira and the Persians who fondled the Macedonian women; Zeus may be committing sexual violence, but he is not culpable as long as he does it for the right reasons – or what he thinks are the right reasons.

In the *Homeric Hymn to Demeter,* Persephone is abducted by Hades and also receives honor even though there are no offspring of hers mentioned. Several passages in the poem stress the lack of consent on her part. In the opening verses, Hades is said to have seized her (ἥρπαξεν). When she is snatched away against her will, she cries out and calls on Zeus to witness the injustice (19–20 [ἀέκουσαν]; cf. 30, 56, 405–33). But when Demeter tells Helios that her daughter has been taken away by force and without her consent (64–73), he advises her to stop lamenting and says that she should not be angry for no good reason (μάψ). After all, Hades is a quite respectable son-in-law; in fact, he is her own brother! As for honors, he has the kingdom that was allotted to him in the original threefold division of the universe. Far from causing her any shame, the abduction has elevated her to the position of the wife of the man who rules among the dead. Thus, Helios implicitly argues that Demeter has no grounds for complaint because the consequences of the abduction have proved to be so advantageous for her daughter.[52]

One finds a similar attitude toward sexual violence in the plays of New Comedy.[53] There are two basic kinds of plots involving sexual violence. In the first, a young man assaults a young virgin, who becomes pregnant. Later, unaware of her

[51] In Hom. *Il.* 14.321–2 her offspring are Minos and Rhadamnathys. In a fragment of Aeschylus' *Carians or Europa* she bears Minos, Rhadamanthys, and Sarpedon. See Radt (1977) 217–21.

[52] What causes Demeter to grieve is not so much the violence done to her daughter as the loss of her company. Once she is promised that her daughter will dwell with her for two-thirds of the year (*Homeric Hymn to Demeter* 445–7), she consents to the arrangement and makes no further protest.

[53] Rosivach (1998) 13–50 analyzes plots in New Comedy that contain acts of sexual violence. Even though I do not agree with some of his analysis and conclusions, I have found his collection of the evidence more valuable than that of Omitowoju (2002) 169–203, whose treatment is selective and superficial.

identity, the young man marries his victim. In most cases the husband believes that the father of the child is someone else, and this leads to various complications in the plot. After many twists and turns, the plot ends happily when the husband realizes his wife's child is his after all.[54] In the second type of plot, a young man has sex with a young virgin against her will, then is allowed to marry her.[55] There are several examples of the second kind of plot, but the most valuable ones for helping us to understand ancient attitudes toward sexual violence are two plays of Terence based on plays of Menander, *The Brothers* and *The Eunuch*.[56]

In *The Brothers* a young man named Aeschinus has forced himself on Pamphila, the daughter of Sostrata, and made her pregnant. By the beginning of the play, Pamphila is about to give birth, but Sostrata's slave, the nurse Canthara, assures her that "In the circumstances, things couldn't have turned out better than they have, mistress. I mean, given she's been the victim of an offense, that he's the person involved, such a nice young man of such good birth and from such a fine family" (295–97). And Sostrata agrees: "You're right. May the gods keep him safe for us!" (298) (trans. adapted from Barsby). The fact that her daughter's sexual initiation took place in less than romantic circumstances does not seem to bother her very much. The violence done to her is less important than the prospect of a marriage with a good family. When Sostrata hears from her slave Geta that Aeschinus is in love with someone else, the two worry about Sostrata's reputation (340: *tua fama*) as well as her daughter's future (330–42). Even though Aeschinus was drunk when he made her daughter pregnant, this does not stop Sostrata from thinking about taking him to court (344–50). When Demea informs his brother Micio that his adoptive son Aeschinus has debauched (467: *vitiavit*) Sostrata's daughter, he says that this is not what is most serious about her situation (468–9). The act of violence was "only human" since done under the influence of the night, love, wine, and youth (470–1). What is most shocking is that after promising to marry her, Aeschinus has taken up with a woman of lower status and has forgotten about Pamphila (471–7). Micio too feels that what makes his son's

[54] For this kind of plot see Rosivach (1998) 27–35.

[55] For this kind of plot see Rosivach (1998) 14–23.

[56] On Menander's *Adelphoe* as the source for Terence's *Adelphoe*, see Martin (1976) 19–21. On Menander's *Eunouchos* and *Kolax* as the sources for Terence's *Eunuchus*, see Ludwig (1959) and Lowe (1983). For Athenian laws and legal procedures alluded to in Terence's *Eunuchus*, see lines 957 and 960–1 with Barsby (1999) 262–3.

conduct reprehensible is not so much the violence done to Pamphila but his actions afterwards:

> In what country, may I ask, do you think you are living? You ruined a girl you had no right to touch. That was your first wrongdoing and serious enough, but it was human. Many respectable men have done the same. But after the event, tell me, did you give the matter any thought? Did you think of the future: what needed to be done and how? If you were ashamed to tell me about this yourself, how was I to find out? While you sat around doing nothing, ten months have passed. You've betrayed yourself and the poor girl and the child: you couldn't have behaved worse.
>
> 685–92 (trans. adapted from Barsby)

What is striking here is the similarity with the criticism made of Apollo in Euripides' *Ion*: Aeschinus is faulted not so much for acting against the will of his victim as for neglecting his responsibilities as father. As long as he is willing to look after his child, there is nothing wrong with his conduct.

In Terence's *Eunuch* the victim is a young girl named Pamphila, who was stolen from Attica as a child by pirates. These pirates sold her to a merchant, who in turn gave her to a woman living in Samos (107–10, 114–15). The woman realized that the girl was freeborn and raised her as her own daughter (116–17). This woman also had a daughter of her own named Thais, who became a courtesan. After the woman died, her brother sold Pamphila to the soldier Thraso (130–5). The play takes places in Athens, where Thais now resides and has Phaedria as her lover. As the play begins, Thais has become the lover of Thraso in the hope of getting him to give her Pamphila as a present so she can restore her to her parents and win their friendship (137–49). To give Thraso the impression that she no longer cares for Phaedria, she asks the latter to leave for two days until he gives her Pamphila. Phaedria is naturally jealous, but consents to stay away (180–96). But not to be outdone by Thraso's generosity, Phaedria gives Thais a slave-girl from Ethiopia and a eunuch, each worth twenty *mnai* (163–9). A little later Phaedria's brother Chaerea tells his slave Parmeno that he has seen Pamphila and fallen in love with her (292–319). At Parmeno's suggestion, Chaerea dresses up in the clothes of the eunuch that his brother has given Thais and takes his place in her household. When Chaerea is left alone with Pamphila, he locks the door and takes advantage of the opportunity (*occasionem*) to have sex with her (369–90, 564–606). There can be no question about Chaerea's use of violence: Thais' slave Pythias describes how he ripped her dress and tore her hair (645–6).

The key passage in the play for attitudes toward sexual violence is the scene where Thais confronts Chaerea.[57] When she asks him what he has done, he says he did "something trivial" (*paullum quidem*). Thais responds with the indignant question: "Does it seem trivial to you to dishonor (*vitiare*) a girl who is a citizen?" Chaerea offers the excuse that he thought she was a slave like himself. But what causes Thais to worry is not the harm done to Pamphila, but the effect that it may have on her attempt to forge a social connection with her family (867–71). To console her, Chaerea offers his own friendship (872–5) and assures her that when he assaulted Pamphila, he did it not to insult but out of love (877–8: *unum hoc scito, contumeliae non me fecisse causa, sed amoris*). To our way of thinking this is irrelevant: what makes sexual violence wrong is the absence of the victim's consent. But by claiming that he acted out of love, Chaerea avoids the charge of *hybris*, which alone would have made his conduct reprehensible. To show that his words are sincere, he then offers to marry her (885–8). It is important to note that the claim to have acted out of love is not sufficient to get Chaerea out of the trouble he has caused. Even if Chaerea's motive is not completely dishonorable, the objective damage to Pamphila's reputation still remains. The only way to remove the dishonor of becoming pregnant out of wedlock is for Chaerea to marry Pamphila and restore to her the honor she otherwise would have lost. Thus, the motive of love is not an "excuse" as claimed by certain scholars. The shame caused by sexual violence to a woman and her family cannot be explained away by citing excuses; the claims of honor must be respected by an act of marriage.

This attitude toward solving the "problem" of sexual violence finds a depressing parallel in modern Peru, where as noted earlier, a law in the penal code written in 1920, but still in effect in 1997, absolved a defendant in a rape case if he consents to marry his victim.[58] Despite attempts to change the law in 1997, many Peruvians

[57] Konstan (1986) 387 sees Chaerea as "an engaging scamp witty, frank and ebullient" and believes "An untroubled empathy with the youth is licensed by the holiday mood of the comedy, as well as by the custom of the genre, which will require that he accept as wife the citizen whom he has violated." See, however, Smith (1994), who rightly questions Konstan's view that the audience would have completely sympathized with Chaerea. What may have made the audience less inclined to judge Chaerea harshly was his ignorance of Pamphila's true status. For attitudes toward the use of sexual violence as a punishment for slaves and Chaerea's motivation, see note 63.

[58] See note 21.

thought the law should remain in place. "'Marriage is the right and proper thing to do after a rape,' said Jaime Baquero, a taxi driver. 'A raped woman is a used item. No one wants her. At least with this law the woman will get a husband.'" Even though the victims are often reluctant to accept these offers, it is reported that "in many poor and rural areas of Peru, relatives put pressure on rape victims to accept a rapist's offer, which the relatives believe will restore honor to the victim and her family. When the victim does not want to marry, her family often tells her incorrectly that the law requires her to do so or to withdraw the charges." One should note that in Terence's *Eunuchus* it is Thais who decides to accept Chaerea's offer and that Pamphila is apparently not consulted, and that in other plays such as Terence's *The Brothers* the victim is not asked whether the solution accepted by her relatives is acceptable to her. And when Thais ponders what to do, it is her own interests that guide her (865–71), not those of Pamphila, just as in modern Peru it is often the parents who decide for the victim what course of action to take.

Our analysis so far has shown that there was no single standard for judging acts of sexual violence. Attitudes toward these acts varied according to the context and to the intent of the aggressor. If the man using violence aimed at causing dishonor, he was guilty of *hybris* and deserved punishment. Absent this intent to humiliate, an aggressor would be judged more leniently provided he was willing to do something to remove the shame caused by his act of violence. But were there other situations where sexual assault was not considered a serious offense?

In the cases examined in Section II, the victims were not under the control of the aggressor, who was usually an outsider. But what about the man who used force to compel sex with his own wife? Here there was no threat to the husband's control over his spouse. Besides, one would assume that no husband would intend to dishonor a woman living under his own protection. In fact, Aristophanes alludes to this kind of situation in the *Lysistrata* (160–6). When Lysistrata proposes that the women of Athens go on a sex-strike, one asks what they should do if their husbands take them into the bedroom by force (βίᾳ). Lysistrata advises that they grab a hold of the door. "But what if they strike us?" the woman continues. Lysistrata then proposes: "You should submit in the grudgingest way – there's no pleasure in it when it's done by force – and you should vex them generally, and have no fear, they'll tire of it very quickly. For no man is ever going to get any gratification unless it suits the woman that he should." When the women swear an oath not to sleep with their husbands, they pledge "And if he force me by force against my will (ἄκουσαν βιάζηται βίᾳ)(...) I will submit grudgingly and will not thrust back" (225–7) (trans. Sommerstein). As Sommerstein rightly observes, "In a play which is often, and rightly, cited as evidence that the marital relationship was more important to the Athenian male than has sometimes been claimed, this is an uncomfortable indication that that relationship could include, as apparently quite a normal incident, forced sex accompanied by physical violence."[59] What is significant in the way the violence is described is that the women do not call it *hybris*. Nor could they, since the man was acting out of desire for a woman who was under his control and given to him by her relatives "for the purpose of bearing legitimate children" (Men. *Perikeiromene* 1013). It would thus be no dishonor for a woman to become pregnant after having sex with her own husband – even if against her will.[60]

Finally, sexual violence could be used as a form of punishment and not be considered *hybris*.[61] Aristotle in the *Rhetoric* (1378b) observes that one who acts in retaliation for some wrong does not commit *hybris* but takes revenge. Thus, when the Phoenicians took Io, Herodotus (1.1) reports that the Greeks considered themselves justified in abducting Europa. In Aristophanes' *Acharnians* (271–5), Dicaeopolis catches a Thracian slave girl stealing wood and has forcible sex with her as a punishment. In these cases, however, the violence is inflicted on a foreigner and a slave, both outsiders. The abduction of Europa in retaliation is in keeping with the Greek practice of reprisals (*sulan*) in inter-state relations.[62] And the slave girl is not entitled to the same protections as a free person. Had she been free, Dicaeopolis would not have been able to act the same way (Dem. 53.15–16).[63]

59 Sommerstein (1998) 107. Sommerstein goes on to note that "if it were not an obvious and safe thing for the frustrated husband to attempt, it would not have been mentioned, since it has no comic point; rather it is a genuine weakness in Lysistrata's plan and has to be disposed of if that plan is to be effective."

60 One should perhaps compare the thoughts of Soames in the *Forsyte Saga* on the morning after he has raped his wife: "The incident was really of no great moment; women made a fuss about it in books; but in the cool judgment of right-thinking men, of men of the world, such as he recollected often received praise in the Divorce Court, he had but done his best to sustain the sanctity of marriage, to prevent her from abandoning her duty" (quoted in Brownmiller [1975] 427). At the time when Brownmiller wrote, men could not be convicted of raping their wives in many jurisdictions in the United States.

61 Doblhofer (1994) 45–6 collects the evidence for the use of rape as a punishment, but does not offer much in the way of analysis and does not discuss the abduction of Europa in Herodotus. This use of sexual violence as punishment is not discussed by Cohen (1991b) and (1993).

62 On the practice of reprisals (*sulan*), see Bravo (1980).

63 Note that Chaerea in the *Eunuchus* (382) regards his plot to have sex with Pamphila (who he thinks is a slave) as justifiable revenge on the courtesan Thais for arousing the desires of young men. As Barsby

The different standard for citizens can be seen in a story from the Macedonian court. Diodorus (16.93.3–95.4) relates that there was a Pausanias who was the favorite of King Philip II. When Philip began to transfer his affections to another Pausanias, he insulted his rival by calling him a hermaphrodite and accused him of being promiscuous. This caused the other Pausanias to seek death in battle. To punish the first Pausanias, Attalus invited him to dinner, made him drunk, then handed him over to his muledrivers for *hybris*, to be sexually assaulted. When Pausanias sobered up, he did not consider this justified and accused Attalus in front of the king. The king voiced his disapproval but took no steps against Attalus since he needed his services. This was too much for Pausanias, who later assassinated Philip for his failure to avenge the insult. What therefore may have been appropriate for a slave or a foreigner was not appropriate for a free citizen.

To sum up, in the modern United States and Europe as well as many other countries, women are recognized as full citizens with equal rights. The laws of these countries recognize that women have the right to make decisions about all aspects of their lives and that any attempt to infringe these rights is illegal, if not a crime. Since rape violates a woman's right to make decisions about the most intimate aspect of her life and can also have devastating psychological effects, it is therefore severely punished.

In Classical Athens, women did not enjoy these rights. Decisions about women's lives lay largely (though not completely) in the hands of men, who monopolized all basic legal and political rights. Sexual violence against women was therefore evaluated not so much for its impact on the victim (though poets and artists were not indifferent to their suffering) as for its effects on men's power and honor. If sexual violence threatened a man's authority in his household, it might incur harsh penalties. If such violence served a "useful" purpose, such as fathering demigods or intimidating slaves and foreigners, the Greeks did not object to its use. And if a young man claimed that he had sexually assaulted a young woman out of

(1999) 247 observes, Thais at lines 864–5 "admits the possibility that as a courtesan she has deserved such treatment." In other words, the violence done to her slave was just retaliation for the suffering caused by her seductive charms.

Earlier versions of this essay were presented to the Brooklyn College Classics Club, December, 1994; to the Classics Department, Drew University, October 1995; Department of Classics, Fordham University, April 1997; to the Graduate Program in Classics, CUNY Graduate School, February 2000; and to the Department of Classics, University of Pennsylvania, November 2000.

desire and without intent to insult her, he was treated leniently as long as he was willing to eradicate through marriage the shame and embarrassment caused by his actions.

IV

If there is a larger lesson to be learned from the study of laws of Classical Athens regarding sexual violence, it is that one should not study Athenian legal procedures in isolation. If we are to understand why the Athenians dealt with sexual violence in the way that they did, one must also look at the substantive aspects of these procedures and pay close attention to the terms used to denote various offenses. And these terms cannot be fully analyzed without placing them in the context of the social relations of the society that created these laws. Sexual violence has not had one meaning throughout time; different societies have devised different responses to the problems posed by this type of aggression, and those responses have been shaped by the interests of those holding positions of power and authority. We may not like the way that Athenians dealt with the issue of sexual violence, but we will never make progress in our understanding of their attitudes if we are not willing to think away our own assumptions about the issue and to approach the Athenians on their own terms.

APPENDIX. THE DEFINITION OF RAPE IN CONTEMPORARY AMERICAN CRIMINAL CODES

VIRGINIA CRIMINAL CODE §18.2–61. RAPE.

A. If any person has sexual intercourse with a complaining witness who is not his or her spouse or causes a complaining witness, whether or not his or her spouse, to engage in sexual intercourse with any other person and such act is accomplished (i) against the complaining witness's will, by force, threat or intimidation of or against the complaining witness or another person, or (ii) through the use of the complaining witness's mental incapacity or physical helplessness, or (iii) with a child under age thirteen as the victim, he or she shall be guilty of rape.

B. If any person has sexual intercourse with his or her spouse and such act is accomplished against the spouse's will by force, threat or intimidation of or against the spouse or another, he or she shall be guilty of rape.

South Dakota Criminal Code 22–22–1.

Rape defined – Degrees – Felony. Rape is an act of sexual penetration accomplished with any person under any of the following circumstances:

(1) If the victim is less than ten years of age; or
(2) Through the use of force, coercion, or threats of immediate and great bodily harm against the victim or other persons within the victim's presence, accompanied by apparent power of execution; or
(3) If the victim is incapable, because of physical or mental incapacity, of giving consent to such act; or
(4) If the victim is incapable of giving consent because of any intoxicating, narcotic, or anesthetic agent or hypnosis; or
(5) If the victim is ten years of age, but less than sixteen years of age, and the perpetrator is at least three years older than the victim; or
(6) If persons who are not legally married and who are within degrees of consanguinity within which marriages are by the laws of this state declared void pursuant to § 25–1–6, which is also defined as incest; or
(7) If the victim is ten years of age but less than eighteen years of age and is the child of a spouse or former spouse of the perpetrator.

United States Code Title 10 (Armed Forces), Section 920 (rape and carnal knowledge).

(a) Any person subject to this chapter who commits an act of sexual intercourse, by force and without consent, is guilty of rape and shall be punished by death or such other punishment as a court-martial may direct.

III.3A Women and Lending in Athenian Society: A *Horos* Re-Examined

πάντα γὰρ δι' ἀρσένων
γυναιξὶ πράσσειν εἰκός, αἵτινες σοφαί
– Euripides *Suppliant Women* 40–1

The laws of Athens granted women few privileges and placed several restrictions on their conduct. Women did not hold public office, vote in the Assembly, serve as members of a court, or bring lawsuits.[1] In financial matters, women were limited to transactions that involved less than the value of a *medimnus* of barley, an amount just large enough to feed a family for only a week.[2] One might get the impression from this law that women in Athens had very little to do with financial matters and played virtually no role in activities like large-scale lending. But the impression would be a false one. Laws can only prescribe or proscribe certain actions. They do not describe what life was actually like. Of course, the letter of the law, if vigorously enforced, must be observed. Human beings, however, are always capable or finding devices that enable them to subvert the spirit of the law. For instance, the law barring women from transactions involving more than a *medimnus* of barley was clearly aimed at discouraging women from handling large sums of money. By denying loans made by women the protection of the law, this statute attempted to prevent women from participating in important financial

[1] For the lack of political and legal rights for women, see Just (1989) 13–39. Just's discussion of legal evidence is flawed by his mistaken view that "the actual giving of evidence to an Athenian court" constituted a "privilege" (34; cf. 39). Giving evidence was a duty that litigants could compel witnesses to perform (Aeschin. 1.46; 2.68; [Dem.] 59.28). This mistake is repeated by Trevett (1991) 21–7, and seriously undermines his arguments.

[2] Is. 10.10. For a careful discussion of the law and its implications, see Kuenen-Janssens (1941). On the absence of property rights for women, see de Ste. Croix (1970).

matters, an area that was supposed to remain under the control of husbands and male relatives. Yet we know of several cases where women exerted influence in important decisions concerning money. Though the laws might deprive them of the formal means of exercising power, women could always find informal methods of influencing events.[3] This evidence should cause us to question the view that women were merely passive participants in social and economic life, incapable of taking the initiative in matters that affected them.[4] On the contrary, resourceful women could find ways of taking an active role in financial business.

My purpose in this chapter is to study a *horos* that provides valuable evidence about the role of women in lending at Athens. The *horos* I will examine here was discovered in the Athenian Agora during January of 1939 and was published by J. V. A. Fine in his *Horoi: Studies in Mortgage, Real Security, and Land Tenure in Athens* (16–22). The *horos* is undated, but like other Attic *horoi* must belong to the fourth or third century BCE.[5] Fine provided a drawing of the fragmentary *horos*, a photograph, a restored text, and a detailed commentary. Shortly thereafter, M. I. Finley reprinted Fine's restored text of the *horos* and included it as no. 114A in the collection of *horoi* contained in his *Studies in Land and Credit in Ancient Athens, 500–200 B.C.* (188). Finley criticized some of Fine's restorations, but offered no general discussion of the inscription, which, despite its importance, has not received further treatment.[6] The *horos* is unusual in several regards. First, it was set up in connection with an *eranos* loan. Second, the transaction recorded on the stone involved both personal and real security. Third and most significant for our purposes, the person who collected the *eranos* was a woman. A fresh study of the *horos* will not only enable us to make some progress with the restoration of the text, but also cast some light on the role of women in the economic sphere. If the restored text proposed

[3] Hunter (1989).

[4] For a forceful challenge to the view that Athenian women were largely passive, see Foxhall (1989). Foxhall (22) draws a distinction between "individual ownership" that was legally in the hands of men and the ways that "in everyday life, property was used by households" where women played a considerable role. My position is close to hers, but I would refrain from speaking of rights enjoyed by women as Foxhall (38) does. Rights *stricto sensu* must be enforceable by the person who holds them, and Athenian women did not enjoy this formal type of rights. I prefer to approach the issue in terms of a more clear-cut distinction between legal statutes and social conventions. For the distinction see Weber (1947) 127–9. My own position is closer to that of Hunter (1989) 44–5, though I think she presses the implications of the word *kyria* in certain passages too far.

[5] For the dates of the *horoi*, see Millett in Finley (1985) ix–x.

[6] Schaps (1979) 66, 130 note 51 notes the relevance of this *horos* for the economic position of women in ancient Athens, but does not discuss it in detail.

here is correct, this *horos* demonstrates that women's role in financial matters was potentially much more extensive than the evidence of Athenian Law would lead us to assume.

A few words first about the nature of the *eranos* loan. The Greeks originally used the term *eranos* to refer to a common meal that was held either for conviviality or as part of a religious celebration.[7] The distinctive feature of this kind of meal was that each of the participants recompensed the host for his generosity either by bringing a contribution to the meal or by later taking his turn in offering a meal to the group. This practice gave rise to clubs called ἔρανοι, whose members were called ἐρανισταί.[8] The word ἔρανος was also applied to the contribution each member brought to the repast.[9] As early as the fifth century BCE, however, the term ἔρανος acquired another meaning. In addition to its traditional meaning, the word was now used to refer to a loan of money collected from several individuals, usually relatives and friends, or from a group of people such as an *eranos*-club.[10] If the loan was collected from several individuals, the contributions might be solicited either by the borrower himself or by a third party called a πληρωτής. After "collecting the *eranos*" (ἔρανον συλλέγειν), the *plerotes* handed over the money to the borrower and was responsible for administering the terms of the loan.[11] An *eranos*-loan appears to have generally been given to friends and relatives in

[7] Hom. *Od.* 1.226 with scholia *ad loc.*; 11.415; Pindar *Olympian* 1.38; *Pythian* 5.77. See also Maier (1969) 14–15.

[8] Arist. *NE* 1160a19; *IG* ii² 1265; 1291; 1369, lines 24–44. For the *eranos*-club, see San Nicolò (1913–15) 1:212–25.

[9] Apollodorus 23.36; Diogenes Laertius 6.63; Theophrastus *Characters* 15.7. Cf. Maier (1969) 19. The word also came to be used for any type of contribution: Dem. 10.40; 25.21; Th. 2.43.1–2.

[10] Maier (1969) 25–8. *Eranos*-loan collected from friends: Antiphon *Tetr.* 1.2.9; [Dem.] 59.31; Diogenes Laertius 8.87; Pl. *Lg.* 915e; Theophrastus *Characters* 15.17; 17.9; Nepos *Epaminondas* 3.4–6. It is often difficult to tell in any particular case whether the *eranistai* who contribute to the loan constitute a society ("Verein" in German; see Maier [1969] 75–104) or are simply a group of lenders brought together for the temporary purpose of making the loan. For a discussion of the *eranos*-clubs mentioned in *IG* ii² 1553, lines 20–3; 1556, lines 27–9; 1557B, lines 105–7; 1558A, lines 37–43; 1559, lines 26–31; 1568, lines 18–23; 1569A, lines 18–21; 1570, lines 24–6, 57–62, 82–4; 1571, lines 8–13; 1572, lines 8–11, see Finley (1985) 104–5. The term *eranos* is often found alongside words for debt: Ar. *Ach.* 615; Dem. 27.25; Hyp. *Ath.* 9, 19; Lycurgus *Leocr.* 22.

[11] *Eranos*-loan collected by the borrower: Antiphon *Tetralogy* 1.2.9; [Dem.] 53.11; 59.31. For the term *plerotes* and his duties, see Dem. 21.101, 184; 25.21; Harpocration *s.v.* πληρωτής; Hyp. *Ath.* 9. The person who collected the contributions might also be called the ἐρανάρχης: Harpocration *loc. cit.*; Diogenes Laertius 6.63. Lipsius (1905–15) 732 note 205; T. Reinach, "Eranos" in C. Daremberg and E. Saglio (1877–1919) vol. 2.1, 806; Fine (1951) 19; and Finley (1985) 101 all mistakenly thought that the word *plerotes* meant "contributor," but see J. Vondeling (1961) 37 and 229 note 1 and Maier (1969) 34–5.

need.[12] That is probably the reason why we never find interest being charged for an *eranos*-loan.[13]

We now proceed to the *horos* in question. In his publication of the inscription, Fine offered the following text with restorations:

[ὅρο]ς οἰκίας π[ε]-
[πρα]ένης Δι[ο]-
[τίμ?]οι Μελιτεῖ
[τιμ]ῆς ἧς ἐνεγύη[σε]
[ἀραβ]ῶνα τοῦ ἐράν[ου]
[τοῦ π]εντακοσιοδρ[άχ]-
[μου] πληρώτρια Δη-
[μὼ? ἕ]ως ἂν διεξ-
[έλθηι]

The restoration of the formula [ὅρο]ς οἰκίας π[ε]|[πρα]ένης (lines 1–2) is undoubtedly correct.[14] The formula and the demotic Μελιτεῖ (line 3) both demand the name of a man in the dative case after the perfect passive participle π[ε]|[πρα]ένης (lines 1–2), and that is consistent with the omicron and the iota read by Fine.[15] Fine suggested *exempli gratia* the restoration Δι[ο]|[τίμ]οι, which I will retain for the sake of convenience.[16] The restoration of ἐράν[ου] in line 6

[12] *Eranos*-loan given to a friend in need: Antiphon *Tetralogy*. 1.2.9; Dem. 53.11; Pliny *Epistles* 10.93; Theophrastus *Characters* 17.9. Despite the charitable nature of the *eranos*-loan, the borrower was still expected to repay: Maier (1969) 43–8. The *dikai eranikai* mentioned at [Arist.] *Ath. Pol.* 52.2 probably involve *eranos*-loans: see Maier (1969) 137–9. Plato (*Lg.* 915e) wished to ban such suits from Magnesia: see Finley (1985) 292 note 81.

[13] *Eranos*-loan is interest-free: Maier (1969) 120–5. LSJ *s.v. eranos* states that *BGU* 1165, line 16 refers to interest on an *eranos*-loan, but the passage more likely refers to interest on arrears. See San Nicolò (1913–15) 2:221–2.

[14] For another example of this formula, see *horos* no. 114, lines 1–3. The formula customarily includes the phrase ἐπὶ λύσει (e.g., *horoi* nos. 69, 71–80). For omission of the phrase see *infra*.

[15] I have checked Fine's readings against a squeeze of the *horos* in the Epigraphical Library at the Institute for Advanced Study at Princeton. There is a space after the final iota in the demotic in line 3 and no trace of a letter on the right hand edge of this line. Fine's other readings are likewise consistent with what I was able to read on the squeeze. I would like to thank Professor Habicht for discussing the squeeze with me.

[16] For the spelling of the dative, see Threatte (1980) 334–5. Other possibilities for the name are Diodoros and Diphilos. One might argue that these names are preferable to Diotimos since they are attested for the deme of Melite (Diodoros, [Dem.] 59.58; Diphilos, *IG* ii[2] 1011, lines 113 [*anno* 106/05], whereas Diotimos is not. But such an argument should not be pressed: see Thompson (1974).

cannot be bettered and receives confirmation from the word πληρώτρια in line 8, a *hapax legomenon*, but obviously "the female form of the masculine πληρωτής" (Fine), the person who collects the *eranos* loan. The restoration of the adjective [π]εντακοσιοδρ[άχ]l[μου] is unavoidable and certainly fits the context, which requires an adjective modifying the noun ἐράν[ου] and expressing the monetary value of the loan.[17] Fine's restorations for lines 8–9 are attractive, but speculative. His supplements for line 4 and the left edge of line 5 are questionable. Although the restoration of lines 8–9 does not affect our interpretation of the *horos*, lines 4–5 appear to contain important information about the nature of the transaction described by the inscription. We must postpone for the moment our analysis of lines 4–5 until after we have discussed lines 1–3, which can be restored with a high degree of certainty.

Fine drew attention to the absence of the phrase ἐπὶ λύσει after the participle πεπραμένης, from which he concluded that the *horos* "publicized not a mortgage, but a sale" and ruled out the possibility that the house mentioned in line 1 had been pledged as security to the man from Melite named in lines 2–3. Fine held that Diotimos "had agreed to buy the house and presumably had taken possession. Since he had not yet paid the price, and consequently had not acquired ownership, the *horos* stone was set up to notify any third party that the vendor still retained ownership and would continue to retain ownership until Diotimos, after recovering the 500 drachmas which he had contributed to an eranos loan, paid the price in full." This explanation makes little sense. If the vendor retained ownership, why was the house described as "sold to Diotimos" (πεπραμένης)? There are two *horoi*, nos. 3 and 12A, which publicize the fact that part of the price to be paid for the property is still owing, but the formulae on these two *horoi* are utterly dissimilar from the wording found on *horos* 114A. Besides, if the vendor wanted to publicize the fact that he still owned the property, why did he not put his name on the *horos* as creditors normally did?[18] Finally, the *horoi* never state where the borrower intends to find the money with which to repay the loan, a fact that is irrelevant to their purpose. When a sum of money is recorded, it is always the amount of the loan for which the property, where the *horos* has been placed, has been

[17] Cf. *SIG*³ 1215, lines 5–6.

[18] Name of the creditor on *horos*: *horoi* nos. 3, 5, 6, 8, 11, 13–15, 17, 19, etc. Apart from the possible exception of *horos* no. 39, the only *horoi* that record the name of the debtor come from Amorgos: *horoi* nos. 9, 102. For a discussion for these *horoi*, see Finley (1985) 11.

pledged as security. The *horoi* never record the amounts of other debts owed to the borrower.[19]

Fine's main error was his mistaken assumption that the absence of the phrase ἐπὶ λύσει excluded the possibility that the text of the stone indicated a pledge of security. Fine apparently disregarded the Athenian habit of using the language of sale without the addition of this phrase to express the notion of real security.[20] In general, the use of the language of sale in contexts relating to real security reflects the view of the creditor that the property pledged as security had been "sold" to him, or, in other words, belonged to him until the loan was repaid.[21] In contexts where the circumstances of the "sale" are described and where it is therefore obvious that the "sale" is a pledge of security that forms part of a loan agreement, it is not necessary to differentiate this "sale" from a normal sale by appending the phrase ἐπὶ λύσει. On the other hand, most of the *horoi* do not give any hint about the nature of the transactions that lay behind the "sales" that they publicize. As a result, it was necessary to place the phrase ἐπὶ λύσει after the word πεπραμένου (-ης, -ων) in the formula found on the *horoi* for the purpose for indicating clearly the conditions on which the lender and borrower had made the "sale."[22] On the *horoi* that mentioned *eranistai* or an *eranos*, however, that was not necessary. Anyone who read that the "sale" had been made in the context of an *eranos*-loan would have immediately recognized that this "sale" had taken place as part of a loan agreement and was thus a pledge of security and not a regular sale. It is certainly no coincidence that all the Attic *horoi* that employ the language of sale without the phrase ἐπὶ λύσει involve transactions with *eranistai*.[23] We ought, therefore, to reject Fine's view that this *horos* publicizes a sale, a function that the *horoi* never appear to have had.[24] Instead, the *horos* shows that the house had been "sold" to Diotimos to secure the *eranos*-loan mentioned in line 5.

19 For example, *horoi* nos. 3, 8, 12A, 13, 14.

20 For the use of the language of sale without the addition of the phrase ἐπὶ λύσει to indicate a pledge of real security, see Dem. 37.4–17 with discussion in Harris (1988) 370–6 (= Chapter II.2 in this volume); Pollux *Onomasticon* 8.142 (= Hyp. fr. 193 [Blass]); Crosby (1941) 14–27, no. 1, lines 16–25.

21 Harris (1988) 361–77. Cf. [Dem.] 33.8.

22 Harris (1988) 377–9. Cf. Finley (1985) 103–4.

23 *Horoi* nos. 112, 113, 114. Pringsheim (1950) 165 thought that these *horoi* publicized sale, but his view was rightly questioned by Finley (1985) 290 note 70. Pringsheim presented his view in a fuller form in Pringsheim (1953a). (His discussion of *horos* no. 114A in this article adds nothing to Fine's analysis.) For trenchant criticisms of this article, see Millett in Finley (1985) xv–xviii.

24 There are several texts indicating that the *horoi* were used to publicize real security (e.g., Dem. 41.6; [Dem.] 49.11; *IG* ii² 1183, lines 28–9; see also the entries in the lexica cited by Finley [1985] 211 note 27). No ancient evidence states that they were ever used to publicize sale.

We can now turn to lines 4–6. Fine proposed the following restorations:

4 [τιμ]ῆς ἧς ἐνεγύη[σε]
5 [ἀραβ]ῶνα τοῦ ἐράν[ου]
6 [τοῦ π]εντακοσιοδρ[άχ]-

Fine (18) gave this translation of his restored text: "for the price of which he has pledged his deposit (payment, contribution) in the five hundred drachma *eranos* loan." Finley (188) demonstrated that "both the restoration and interpretation are impossible." First, ἐγγύη was a pledge of personal security "whereby someone guaranteed the performance of an obligation by a second party, not self-performance." It was not the pledge of an object. Second, Fine can cite no parallel for the use of the word ἀραβών carrying the meaning "deposit, payment, or contribution," and the word is certainly never used to mean "contribution to an *eranos*-loan."[25] Fine's restorations are unacceptable. Another solution must be found.

A comparison with the wording found on a *horos* from Arkesine on the island of Amorgos (*horos* no. 8) reveals interesting parallels and enables us to make some progress with the restoration of lines 4–5 on *horos* no. 114A. Fine correctly noted that in line 4 there appears to be a form of the verb ἐγγυάω, which indicates that this *horos* publicized not only a pledge of real security, but also a pledge of personal security.[26] We find the same combination of real and personal security on *horos* no. 8, the relevant portions of which are given below:

1 ὅρος χωρίων [τῶν ἐν . . .]
ρει καὶ οἰκίας καὶ κ[ήπων]
τῶν Ξενοκλέος καὶ τῶ[ν κει]-
μένων ἐμ Φυλινχείαι καὶ τῶν
5 ἐπικυρβίων ἐνεχέρων ὑποκει-
6 μένων . . .
8 . . . τῶ[ι] ἐράν[ωι]
καὶ Ἀρισταγόραι τῶι ἀρχεράνωι

[25] The words for contribution to an *eranos*-loan are φορά (Dem. 25.21) and ἔρανος (Theophrastus *Characters* 15.7 with Vondeling [1961] 57). The inscription published by Lejeune and Pouilloux (1988) may indicate that an ἀρραβών could be a valuable object instead of a monetary payment (cf. Chadwick [1990]). But this does not alter Finley's basic point, which is that an ἀρραβών is "an earnest of a future action by the person making the payment" (188). It is therefore dissimilar from a contribution to an *eranos*-loan "in which the person receiving the money assumes an obligation for the future, namely, repayment" (*ibid*).

[26] For personal security in an *eranos*-loan, see Lys. fr. 16 with Maier (1969) 129–32. For the combination of personal security and real security, see Partsch (1909) 256–71.

καὶ τῆι γυναικὶ αὐ[τοῦ] Ἐχε[νίκηι]
πρὸς τὴν ἐγγύαν ἣν ἐγ[...]
το Ξενοκλῆν τοῦ ἐρά[νου ὃν]
συνέλεξεν Ἀρισταγόρα[ς]

The text of this *horos* indicates that Aristagoras had collected an *eranos*-loan for an unnamed borrower (τοῦ ἐρά[νου ὃν] | συνέλεξεν Ἀρισταγόρα[ς]). Xenocles agreed to become suretor for the loan (τὴν ἐγγύαν ἣν ἐγ[...] |το Ξενοκλῆν τοῦ ἐρά[νου]) and pledged certain properties of his own (χωρίων ... καὶ οἰκίας καὶ κ[ήπων] | τῶν Ξενοκλέος) as security to the group of lenders, Aristagoras and his wife Echenike (τῶ[ι] ἐράν[ωι] | καὶ Ἀρισταγόραι τῶι ἀρχεράνωι | καὶ τῆι γυναικὶ αὐ[τοῦ] Ἐχε[νίκηι]).[27] The similarities in wording shared by the two *horoi* are noteworthy:

1) The word *horos* followed by word(s) for property in the genitive	8 ὅρος χωρίων ... καὶ οἰκίας καὶ κ[ήπων] (lines 1–2) 114A [ὅρο]ς οἰκίας (line 1)
2) Passive participle in the genitive for word denoting pledge of real security	8 ὑποκεμείνων (lines 5–6) 114A πεπραμένης (lines 1–2)
3) Name of person(s) to whom property has been pledged in the dative	8 τῶ[ι] ἐράν[ωι] καὶ Ἀριστ-αγόραι ... καὶ ... Ἐχε[νίκηι] (lines 9–10) 114A Δι[οτίμ?]οι (lines 2–3)
4) Relative pronoun followed by verb	8 ἣν ἐγ[...]το (lines 10–11) 114A ἧς ἐνεγυη[...] (line 4)
5) Name in the accusative	8 Ξενοκλῆν (line 12) 114A [Δι?]ῶνα [28] (line 5)
6) The word *eranos* in the genitive	8 τοῦ ἐρά[νου] (line 12) 114A τοῦ ἐράν[ου] (line 5)
7) Name of the person who collected the *eranos* loan	8 συνέλεξεν Ἀρισταγόρα[ς] (line 13) 114A πληρώτρια Δη[...] (line 7)

[27] Cf. Finley (1985) 101–2.

[28] Other names, such as Neon, are also possible. Since we cannot calculate the precise number of spaces available for the name due to the absence of the left hand side of the stone, the actual name may have been even longer. I would like to thank two of the referees from *Phoenix* for pointing this out. Fine himself suggested [Κίμ]ωνα.

Fine (1951) 18 noticed that "Epigraphically the restoration of a proper name (...) is most suitable," but put forward three objections. His first objection was that there is no demotic following the name. But the *horoi* often omit the demotic (e.g., *horos* no. 18, lines 5–6; *horos* no. 32, lines 6–7; *horos* no. 40,

On the basis of these similarities, I propose the following restored text for lines 4–5 of *horos* no. 114A:

[ἐγγύ]ης ἧς ἐνεγυή[σα]-
[το Δι?]ῶνα το ἐράν[ου]

I offer this translation: "In regard to the pledge of personal security that he [i.e., Diotimos] received from Dion for the *eranos*-loan."[29]

There are, to be sure, some minor differences between the texts of the two *horoi*. The wording of *horos* no. 8 is fuller than that of *horos* no. 114A, but that is consistent with the characteristic style of the *horoi* from Amorgos, which tend to be more explicit than those from Attica, which are generally more abbreviated.[30] On *horos* no. 114A we find the word ἐγγύης, the genitive of connection ("in regard to the pledge of personal security") in place of the phrase πρὸς τὴν ἐγγύαν.[31] The relative pronoun ἣν in the accusative on *horos* no. 8 has become genitive ἧς on *horos* no. 114A by attraction with its antecedent ἐγγύης.[32] And the verb συνέλεξεν on *horos* no. 8 is replaced by the noun πληρώτρια on *horos* no. 114A. But the basic structure of the formulae on both *horoi* is the same, and the parts within correspond exactly.

We can now offer a revised text and translation of *horos* no. 114A:

[ὅρο]ς οἰκίας π[ε]-
[πρα]ένης Δι̣[ο]-
[τίμ]οι Μελιτεῖ
[ἐγγύ]ης ἧς ἐνεγυή[σα]-
[το Δι?]ῶνα τοῦ ἐράν[ου]
[τοῦ π]εντακοσιοδρ[άχ]-
[μου]πληρώτρια Δη-
[μώ? ἕ]ως ἂν διεξ-

line 3; *horos* no. 73, lines 4–5). Fine's other two objections rest on a misunderstanding of the nature of the transaction described in lines 4–5.

[29] For the expression ἐγγύην ἐγγυᾶσθαί τινα, see Pl. *Phaedrus* 115d; *Lg.* 953e. On the basis of the indisputable similarities between the two *horoi*, I would tentatively suggest the restoration ἐγ[γυήσατ]ο in lines 11–12 of *horos* no. 6. For the omission of the augment, see Smyth (1956) no. 438.

[30] Cf. Finley (1985) 11. "We find in the Amorgian *horoi* a tendency to spell out the transaction in some detail."

[31] For the genitive of connection, see Smyth (1956) nos. 1380–1. A similar use of the genitive can be found on *horos* 12A, lines 6–7 ("for the price owing").

[32] For attraction of the relative, see Smyth (1956) no. 2522.

9 [ἐλθηι]

> Horos of a house "sold" [i.e., pledged as security] to Diotimos (?) of Melite in regard to the pledge of personal security he received from Dion (?) for the *eranos*-loan of five hundred drachmas. Demo (?) was the one who collected the *eranos*-loan.

This interpretation of the text found on the *horos* indicates the following scenario: Demo collected an *eranos*-loan for an unnamed borrower. Dion promised to act as surety for this loan and pledged his house as security to ensure repayment.

There is one major point of difference between *horos* no. 8 and *horos* no. 114A. On *horos* no. 8 the property has been pledged as security to the man who collected the *eranos*-loan along with his wife and the other contributors who formed the *eranos*. On *horos* no. 114A, however, the house has been pledged as security to a man from the deme of Melite; his precise name may be beyond recovery, but his gender is not. And his gender is different from that of the person who collected the loan, that is, the *plerotria* of line 7. Why was the *eranos*-loan mentioned on *horos* no. 114A collected by one person, a woman, but the property pledged as security to another person, this one male? The formula found on *horos* no. 114A differs not only from that found on *horos* no. 8 from Amorgos, but also from those found on other Attic *horoi*. For instance, on the only *horos* where we find the word *plerotes*, the masculine form of the noun *plerotria*, the property is pledged to Leochares, the *plerotes*, and his fellow *eranistai* (*horos* no. 40: [ὅρ]ος χωρίο πε|[π]ραμένου... ἐπὶ λύσει | Λεωχάρει πληρωτεῖ | [κ]αὶ συνερανισταῖς ΙΧΧΧ). The remaining *horoi* that concern *eranos*-loans have a slightly different formula. On these *horoi*, the property is pledged as security to the *eranistai* with (μετά) some person, presumably the leader of the *eranos* or the *plerotes*.[33]

The reason for the departure on *horos* no. 114A from the standard arrangement must be connected to the fact that the person who collected the *eranos*-loan was a woman. As we noted before, women were forbidden by Athenian Law from lending more than the value of a *medimnus* of barley. The effect of this legal prohibition would have been that a woman who lent money to someone could not have legal proceedings initiated against him if he refused to repay (Schaps [1979] 52–8). The statute may have discouraged women from lending money, but

[33] *Horoi* nos. 30, 31, 31A-B, 32, 42, 70, 112, 114, 163A. For the use of the preposition μετά to indicate the leader of a group, compare Th. 1.60.2; 62.1. See also Finley (1985) 277.

it did not stop the woman named in lines 7–8 of *horos* no. 114A from soliciting contributions for a five-hundred drachma *eranos*-loan and thereby becoming the *plerotria* for the loan. Yet since she could not initiate legal proceedings in the event that the borrower defaulted, she had to enlist the assistance of a man, presumably a relative, to cooperate with her. Though she could not seize the property of the surety, the man named in lines 2–3 could. That is why the house of the surety was "sold" to him and not the *plerotria*.

The problem encountered by the *plerotria* on *horos* no. 114A was similar to that faced by the metic Phormio when Pasion leased him his bank (Dem. 36.6). As a metic, Phormio could not own land in Attica.[34] In consequence, he could not seize any land that had been pledged as security for a loan. When Phormio took over the bank, he found that most of the loans were unsecured, but, to his embarrassment, several were secured by real estate in Attica. The former category posed no problem, for if the borrowers refused to repay, he could prosecute them before the Polemarch.[35] But if those who had borrowed on real security defaulted, Phormio was barred from foreclosing on their property, for that would make him the owner of land in Attica. To overcome this legal hurdle, Pasion had all the secured loans transferred to his account. Phormio could thus go ahead and administer the loans, that is, collect interest payments and recover the principal, but if one of the debtors were to default, Pasion could step in and seize the property pledged as security. The position of the *plerotria* was similar to that of Phormio: she could administer the *eranos*-loans, but could not seize the property of the suretor were the borrower to default and the suretor to renege on his pledge. Both Phormio and the *plerotria* found themselves up against legal barriers, but that did not prevent them from administering loans and thus taking an active role in the world of Athenian business. Through the cooperation of Pasion, Phormio was able to maneuver around the legal disabilities of his metic status. With the help of the man who received the pledge of security on *horos* no. 114A, the *plerotria* managed to evade the legal restrictions placed on Athenian women.

Horos no. 114A affords a revealing glimpse into the role of women in the Athenian economy. We can now see that there existed a gap between the behavior that the laws of Athens prescribed for women and the way they might act in real

[34] On the legal position of metics, see Whitehead (1977) 70–2.

[35] [Arist.] *Ath. Pol.* 58.2–3 with Whitehead (1977) 92–3.

life.[36] *De iure* the *plerotria* was powerless. She could not lend more than a paltry sum, nor own property. In the eyes of the law she was almost completely passive. *De facto,* the Athenian woman was quite capable of taking the initiative in collecting the *eranos*-loan.

This insight helps us explain another loan involving a woman, which has so far perplexed modern scholars. Our source for the loan is a speech delivered concerning the estate of Polyeuctus (Dem. 41). The speaker is married to one of the daughters of Polyeuctus and is trying to recover from his father-in-law's estate money he claims is owed to him, but which is now in the hands of Spoudias, who is married to Polyeuctus' other daughter. One of the sums in dispute is a loan of 1,800 drachmas, which Spoudias borrowed from his mother-in-law, the wife of Polyeuctus (Dem. 41.9: ἣν μὲν γὰρ τὸ ἀργύριον παρὰ τῆς Πολυεύκτου δεδανεισμένος γυναικός). Evidence for this loan consisted in part of papers left behind by Polyeuctus' wife at her death. The speaker's statement appears to be quite straightforward. Yet the loan appears to be in violation of the law barring women from dealing in transactions larger than the value of a *medimnus* of barley. But the text is not quite straightforward. In the previous sentence (Dem. 41.8), the speaker summarizes the deposition of Aristogenes, who was present as Polyeuctus, shortly before his death, declared what money was owed to him by various people. Among these loans were two made to Spoudias. The first was a sum of two *mnai* with interest for a slave that Spoudias had bought from him on credit. The second was the loan of 1,800 drachmas (ὀκτακοσίας δὲ καὶ χιλίας, which agrees with ὀφειλομένας αὑτῷ earlier in the sentence and is also the object of the verb ἐγκαλεῖν).[37] In the following sentence, the speaker explains that this sum was lent to Spoudias by Polyeuctus' wife. The money is loaned by Polyeuctus' wife, but is owed to her husband Polyeuctus and is part of his estate. There is no contradiction between the two statements. Each represents one side of a complex reality. *De facto* the loan was made by Polyeuctus' wife. It was she who obviously

[36] For an interesting discussion of the gap between ideology and reality in respect to the restrictions on women, see Cohen (1989).

[37] Recent scholars who have commented on Dem. 41.9 have not paid attention to the information contained in the previous sentence. Hunter (1989) 301 ("1,800 *drachmai* which the widow herself loaned to Spudias"), 302 ("older women carry out financial transactions far in excess of the limit specified in Isaeus 10.10"); Foxhall (1989) 42, note 104 ("Polyeuktos' wife loaned her son-in-law a large amount of money" and "she seems to have left behind at her death carefully prepared accounts of her financial affairs, apparently separate from those of Polyeuktos"); Schaps (1979) 65.

handed over the money and recorded the transaction in her papers. *De iure* the loan was made from Polyeuctus' property and upon his death was owed to his estate. This reveals that even though the money in a household legally belonged to the husband, the wife might still administer the household's finances and make important decisions about how to manage larger sums of money.

These two examples should cause us to rethink any assumptions we might make about the position of women on the basis of the evidence drawn from the Athenian lawcode. Despite the legal restrictions imposed on her, the resourceful *plerotria* of *horos* no. 114A was able to solicit contributions totaling 500 drachmas, a considerable amount of money. This sum was as much as a laborer working for a drachma a day would be able to earn in two years.[38] For an estate worth four talents, large enough to shoulder liturgical burdens, 500 drachmas represented two months of revenues at a 10 percent annual rate of return.[39] The wife of Polyeuctus made a loan to her son-in-law that was more than three times this amount. When the loan became the subject of a legal dispute, her son-in-law relied in part on her papers as evidence for the transaction.[40] And collecting an *eranos*-loan or making loans to relatives was by no means dishonorable. In fact, the Athenians viewed collecting *eranos*-loans for friends in need a very commendable action, a demonstration of *philotimia*. It was the sort of thing one boasted in court to prove one's noble character and good citizenship.[41]

Of course, we should not exaggerate the range of possibilities open to a woman in ancient Athens. The laws placing restrictions on her activities were a considerable barrier, and her ability to act depended on the consent of a man who could always change his fickle mind. What we ought to question is the traditional picture of the passive Athenian woman who kept to the house and spent her days

[38] For the wages of workmen, see Randall (1953).

[39] For the size of liturgical estates, see Davies (1971) xxiii–xxiv.

[40] The testimony of Aristogenes is also submitted to prove the existence of the loan to Spoudias.

[41] Antiphon *Tetralogy* 1.2.12. Fine (1951) 20 believed that the *plerotria* "presumably (...) was not an Athenian citizen" since "there is no reference to Demo's κύριος." He further suggests she may have been a *hetaira*. Nothing compels us to accept either suggestion. The absence of information about her *kyrios* on the *horos* is of little significance since the Attic *horoi* often are very abbreviated, giving only the bare essentials of the transactions they publicize. In addition, we have seen that respectable married women such as the wife of Polyeuctus were capable of lending large sums of money. Finally, there is no reason to believe that female metics would be allowed to act without the consent of their *kyrios* when Athenian women required their approval. It would have been perverse for the Athenians to grant to female metics a privilege they denied to citizen women.

obediently raising children, preparing meals, and weaving at her loom. Inside the household, she might take an active role in the management of family finances. And with the cooperation of her husband or a male relative, she might take the initiative in a limited but significant way outside the home. Although the Athenian woman had little or nor power in the legal sphere, that did not stop her from playing an active role in economic life.[42]

[42] I would like to thank the referees of *Phoenix*, where this essay first appeared, for much helpful advice and several good suggestions for improvement. Thanks are also due to my colleague Sarah Pomeroy for reading over an earlier draft of this article and offering encouraging comments.

III.3B Notes on a *Horos* from the Athenian Agora

Edward M. Harris and Kenneth Tuite

IN 1951 J. V. A. FINE PUBLISHED A *HOROS* THAT HAD BEEN DISCOVERED IN THE Athenian Agora during January of 1939.[1] The *horos* is undated, but like the other Attic *horoi* must belong to the fourth or third century BCE. Shortly thereafter, M. I. Finley reprinted Fine's text of the inscription with his restorations as no. 114A in his collection of *horoi* appended to his study of land and credit in Athens.[2] Finley criticized some of Fine's restorations, but neither discussed the inscription in detail nor offered any restorations of his own. Several years ago, Harris examined a squeeze of the inscription at the Institute for Advanced Study in Princeton. In a recent article he proposed new restorations in lines 4 and 5 on the basis of similarities in phraseology with the text of a *horos* found on Amorgos.[3]

During the Winter of 1997, Tuite examined the *horos* at the American excavations in the Athenian Agora with the permission of Professor John Camp and Professor Ronald Stroud. During his examination of the *horos,* he found traces of letters in line 2 and line 4. Since the publication of his article, Harris found an Attic parallel for the phrase he restored in lines 4–5, which is closer in similarity than the phrase found on the *horos* from Amorgos. In this article we present Tuite's findings (Part I) and Harris' revised analysis of the restoration of lines 4–5 (Part II).

I

A few years ago, I had the opportunity to re-examine the stone and observed some features previously overlooked. The stone is of bluish-whitish marble

[1] Agora Inv. no 5639; Fine (1951) 16–22.

[2] Finley (1985) 188. In this article we refer to the *horoi* with the numbers assigned to them by Finley and Millett. The *horos* has recently been reprinted by Lalonde in Lalonde, Langdon, and Walbank (1991) 49–50 with Fine's restorations (cf. the perceptive review of Chaniotis [1994]). Lalonde notes Finley's criticisms of Fine's restorations but does not propose any alternative restorations.

[3] Harris (1992b) [= Chapter III.3A of this volume].

(height: 16.8 cm; width 15.7 cm; thickness 3.1 cm) with a worked face and rough surfaces on all other sides. The three *vacats* at the end of lines 2, 3, and 8 suggest that the slanting upper right edge of the stone marks its original edge. While one might argue that the cutter began a new line after Μελιτεῖ simply because he did not wish to divide words between lines, he did not face that choice when he left the *vacat* after the final E on line 2. Enough of the stone survives for another letter, but he chose to leave the area blank. An addition of a letter would have crowded the current edge, which, if the stone did indeed end here in antiquity, may have caused the cutter to begin a new line. Due to the irregularity of the stone, however, one cannot make this determination with any certainty. The letters are quite irregular and rudely cut, ranging in height from 0.6 cm to 1.5 cm. The interlinear spacing ranges from practically zero to 0.2 cm. There is a *vacat* beneath line 8 of the text that stretches 1.4 cm to the end of the stone.

Text of Agora no. 5639

[ὅρο]ς οἰκίας π[ε]-
[πρα]ένης Δε- vacat
[? ξιθέ]οι Μελιτεῖ vacat
[ἐγ]ύης ἧς ἐνεγύη[σα]-
[το Δι]ῶνα τοῦ ἐράν[ου]
[τοῦ π]εντακοσιοδρ[άχ]-
[μου] πλ̣ηρώτρια Δη-
[μὼ? ἕ]ως ἂν διεξ-
[έλθηι] *vacat*

Lines 2–3 Δι[ο]|[τιμ]οι Fine; Δε[ᵛ|ξιθέ]οι Tuite
Line 4 [τιμ]ῆς Fine; [ἐγγ]ύης Harris
Lines 4–5 ἐνεγύη[σε | ἀραβ]ῶνα Fine; ἐνεγυή[σα]|[το Δι]ῶνα Harris
Date: between ca. 360–180 BCE.[4]
Translation: *Horos* of a house sold [i.e., pledged as security] to De[xithe]us of Melite in regard to the pledge of personal security which he [i.e., De[xithe]us] received from Dion for the *eranos* loan of 500 drachmas. The person who collected the loan was Demo. Until it expires . . .
Line 2: Of the dotted N all but the top of an unattached vertical stroke survives. Given the context, Fine has restored a N, and I observed that nothing would prohibit such a reading.

[4] For the dates of the security *horoi*, see Millett in Finley (1985) ix–x.

Of the dotted second Ε the top half of a vertical stroke and a short horizontal crossbar emerging from the bottom of the former survives. A small, unattached horizontal stroke, which may or may not belong to this letter, also survives. The lower crossbar (actually the middle crossbar) is clear, despite the chip, rendering Fine's proposed Ι impossible. Enough of the surface is preserved to the right of this letter to rule out the possibility of an Η unless the right vertical stroke began at the lower (middle) crossbar, something that the other examples of this letter in this inscription do not have. One could, if one discounts the small, unattached stroke, read a one drachma symbol, but given the context a house sold for eleven drachmas as security for a five hundred drachma *eranos* loan borders on the absurd. When John Traill graciously looked at the stone with me, he suggested an epsilon with an unattached top cross stroke. Despite the lack of a similar letter in the inscription, I tentatively suggest an Ε since no other reading seems possible.

This renders Fine's proposal to restore the name Διοτίμοι untenable. I therefore tentatively suggest the name Δεξιθέοι; a Δεξίθεος Μελιτεύς (PA 3218) is attested at Demo. 57.37. In the absence of the patronymic and any indication of the date of the *horos*, it is impossible to know whether this Dexitheus (if the restoration is correct) is identical with the man named in the speech of Demosthenes.

Line 4: Of the dotted first Υ, the bottom quarter of an unattached, vertical stroke survives. The stone above and to the right of this also breaks along a diagonal line consistent with the right diagonal stroke of an Υ of the same type found at the end of the same line. Given the many irregularities of the letter shapes, one could posit other alternatives. The lack of a slant in this stroke, however, suggests the reading of an Υ (as Harris proposes) rather than a Μ (as Fine maintains) since the stroke of the other examples of this letter in this inscription all slant.

Line 7: Of the dotted A the bottom third of an unattached diagonal stroke beginning in the lower left survives.

Line 8: While Fine dots this ω, close examination of the stone reveals a series of strokes that present a mirror image of the ω in line 5. Of the dotted Ξ only the left third of an unattached, horizontal stroke along the top of the letter space survives. There is no reason to question Fine's reading here.

II

The *horos* is of particular interest for several reasons. First, it combines pledges of personal security and real security; second, it involves an *eranos* loan; and third, the person who collected the *eranos* loan appears to have been a woman.

Fine believed that the *horos* was set up to publicize a sale, not a pledge of real security, but the Athenians do not appear to have used *horoi* for this purpose.[5] The standard formula found on the *horoi* for a pledge of real security for a loan is πεπραμένου (-ης, ων) ἐπὶ λύσει. The use of language of sale to express the transaction reflects the view of the creditor that the property pledged to him as security has been "sold" to him, or, in other words, that he is the owner of the security until it is redeemed (or "bought back") by repayment of the loan.[6] In cases where the circumstances surrounding the "sale" are described and it is therefore clear that the "sale" is a pledge of security, it was not necessary to add the phrase to distinguish this type of sale from an outright sale where the seller retained no right to reclaim the property.[7] Since the sale referred to on this *horos* took place in relation to a pledge of personal security and an *eranos* loan, anyone who read the *horos* would have understood the nature of the "sale." As a result, the phrase ἐπὶ λύσει is not found on this *horos* and on several other *horoi* that state they were set up in connection with an *eranos* loan.[8] On most of the *horoi*, however, nothing is said about the circumstances of the sale. This made it necessary to add the phrase ἐπὶ λύσει to show that the "sale" was a pledge of security and that the seller retained the right to "buy back" the property by paying off his creditor(s).

Pledges of security were normally made for loans and rent due on leases,[9] but in this case the property has been sold to a certain De[xithe]us in exchange for a pledge of personal security. We find an exact parallel for this combination of real security and personal security on *horos* no. 18 (ὅρος χωρίου | καὶ οἰκίας πεπραμέν[ω]|ν ἐπὶ λύσει | Ἁγνοδήμ[ω]ι καὶ συνεν|γυηταῖς | XXX). On this *horos* an unnamed individual has pledged his land and house as security to Hagnodemos and others who are acting as his sureties for another transaction, which the *horos* does not tell us about. In the *horos* examined here, however, the

[5] For other criticisms of Fine's view, see Harris (1992b) 313–14 [= Chapter III.3A of this volume].

[6] For an analysis of the terminology and its legal implications, see Harris (1988) [= Chapter II.2 of this volume]. The conclusions of this article are accepted by Todd (1993) 254–5 and Youni (1996) but have escaped the notice of Lambert (1996).

[7] When the orators wish to make it clear that a conveyance is an outright sale and not a pledge of security, they add the word καθάπαξ. See Dem. 37.31, 50; [Dem.] 59.29.

[8] See Harris (1992b) 313–15 [= Chapter III.3A of this volume]. To the list of *horoi* cited there in note 23, now add *SEG* 43 (1993) 55 = Petrakos (1992 [1995]) 38, no. 8 inv. 1105.

[9] For the terminology employed in security for leases and dowries, see Harris (1993) [= Chapter II.3 of this volume].

name of the person (Dion?) to whom De[xithe]us of Melite has given a pledge of personal security appears to have been recorded.

The formula used here to indicate that De[xithe]us is acting as surety for this person is without parallel on the other Attic *horoi*,[10] but we find the same formula in the records of the *poletai* for the years 342/41–339/38.[11] These records show that Meixidemus of Myrrhinous had agreed to act as surety for three people. First, he had agreed to act as surety for Philistides, the son of Philistides, of Aixone (469–70: ἐγγύην ἣν ἐl νεγυήσατο Φιλιστίδην Φιλιστίδου Αἰξ.), for his payments to the treasury for his right to collect the tax on metics in the archonship of Pythodorus (343/42) (470–1: μετlασχόντα τέλους μετοικίου ἐπὶ Πυθοδότου) and also for a five-drachma fee (474–75: ἑτέραν ἐγγύην ἐν τοῖς ἔργlοις τὴν πεντεδραχμίαν). Second, he had agreed to act as surety for Telemachus, son of Hermolochus, a metic living in the Piraeus (477–8: ἑτέραν ἐγγύην ἣν ἐνεγlυήσατο Τηλέμαχον ᾿Ερμολόχου ἐμ Π· οἰκ·), for his payments for the right in the five-drachma fee for the hero Theseus (478–9: μετασχlόντα τέλος τῆς πεντεδραχμίας τῆς τῶι Θησεlῖ), and for a contract to quarry stone in the Piraeus (483–4: ἑτέ[ρα]ν ἐγγύην λιθοτομίαν ἐν Πεlιραεῖ). Third, he had agreed to act as surety for Callicrates, the son of Callicrates, a metic living in Besa (485–7: ἑτέ[ραν ἐγγύl η]ν ἣν ἐνεγυήσατο Καλλικράτην Κα[λλικράτο]lς Βησῃ· οἰκ·), for his payments to the treasury in exchange for the right to collect a one-drachma fee for the god Asclepius (487–8: μετασχόντα τέλους τῆς [δραχμῆς τ]lῶι ᾿Ασκληπιῶι). When the three men failed to make their payments, the sums were doubled (490–1: τούτων [διπλῶν γε]lγενημένων).[12] After they did not make the additional payments (491: οὐκ ἐκτεισάντων τεῖ [πόλει]), and Meixidemus failed to make good on his pledges (493–4: οὔτε Μειξιδήμου τὰς ἐγ[γύας ἃς ἤγ]γυήσατο πρὸς τὴν πόλιν), he

[10] Fine (1951) 18 believed that the phrase should be restored [τιμ]ῆς ἧς and translated "for the price of which he has pledged his deposit (payment, contribution) in the five hundred drachma eranos loan" but could cite no parallel for this phrase in either inscriptions or the literary sources. Finley (1985) 188 rightly pointed out that ἐγγύη "is a transaction "whereby someone guaranteed the performance of an obligation by a second party, not self-performance," and that the word never appears to have meant "deposit, payment of contribution." Cf. Harris (1992b) 315.

[11] For the text see Lalonde, Langdon, Walbank (1991) P26, lines 462–98. In Harris (1992b) I made my restoration of lines 4–5 on the basis of a parallel with a phrase found on a *horos* from Amorgos, for which I was criticized by Maffi (1993) 649–50. The exact parallel for the phrase in the records of the *poletai* shows that Maffi was wrong to question my restoration.

[12] Cf. [Arist.] *Ath. Pol.* 48.1.

was listed as a public debtor (494–5: ἐκγε[γραμμένο ἐ]ν ἀκροπόλει)[13] and his property was subject to confiscation. A lodging house in the Piraeus was reported to the authorities by Euthycles, the son of Eucles, from the deme of Koile, and sold to satisfy his debts to the treasury (495–8).

What is important for our purposes is the formula for the three pledges of personal security. In all three cases we find:

1. The word ἐγγύη in the accusative – ἐγγύην (469, 477, 485–6).
2. Relative pronoun – ἣν (469, 477, 486).
3. Verb in the Aorist Middle – ἐνεγυήσατο (469–70, 473–4, 486)
4. Name of the Person for whom the Pledge was given in the Accusative – Φιλιστίδην (470), Τηλέμαχον (478), Καλλικράτην (486).
5. Name of the Obligation which the pledge secures – τέλους μετοικίου (471), τὴν πεντεδραχμίαν (475), τέλος πεντεδραχμίας τῆς τῶι Θησεῖ (479–80), λιθοτομίαν (483), τέλους τῆς δραχμῆς τῶι Ἀσκληπιῶι (487–8).

These parallels confirm the restoration I proposed for lines 4–8 several years ago: (1) [ἐγγ]ύης (2) ἧς (3) ἐνεγύη[σα]|[το (4) Δι]ῶνα (5) τοῦ ἐράν[ου] | [τοῦ π]εντακοσιοδρ[άχ]|[μου]. The only difference is unimportant: the accusative ἣν has become the genitive ἧς by attraction to the antecedent [ἐγγ]ύης in the genitive. The phrase should be translated: "in regard to the pledge of personal security that he (De[xithe]us) gave to Dion (?) [for repayment] of the five-hundred drachma *eranos* loan."[14]

The *horos* not only tells us that the pledge was given for an *eranos* loan but also gives the name of Demo, who acted as πληρώτρια (7–8). As Fine rightly saw, the word πληρώτρια, a *hapax legomenon,* is clearly the feminine form of the word πληρωτής.[15] The word πληρωτής designates the person who collected the

[13] The reading ἐκγεγ[γραμένο in Lalonde, Langon, Walbank (1991) P26 line 494 appears to be a mistake.

[14] In Harris (1992b) I mistakenly translated the phrase "in regard to the pledge of personal security that he [i.e., Diotimus] received from Dion (?) for the *eranos*-loan."

[15] The pair of terms πληρωτής/πληρώτρια is similar to other pairs such as ψάλτης /ψαλτρία, κιθαριστής/κιθαριστρία, etc. For the form see Smythe (1956) no. 839.b.2. Maffi (1993) needlessly questions Fine's view that πληρώτρια is the feminine form of πληρωτής. Maffi suggests the word is a neuter plural and similar to the term ἐγγυητήριον found in the lead tablet from Pech-Maho (*SEG* 38 [1988] 1036, line 5). Maffi's suggestion is morphologically implausible since the suffix in ἐγγυητήριον is -ήριον, -ήρια not -τρία. For the parallel to be convincing, the form would have to be πληροτήρια.

contributions to the *eranos* loan, handed over money to the borrower, and administered the terms of the loan.[16] This word appears on *horos* no. 40: [ὅρ]ος χωρίο πεl[π]ραμένου{ι} ἐπὶ λύσει | Λεωχάρει πληρωτεῖ | [κ]αὶ συνερανισταῖς | XXX.

It is crucial to note how the formula of *horos* no. 40 differs from that found on *horos* no. 114A. In the former the property is pledged as security to the man who collected the *eranos* loan and the others who contributed to it. In the latter (as I noted in my previous article), this probably has to do with the fact that the person who collected the loan was a woman. As a woman (let us call her Demo), she was unable to initiate legal proceedings. This meant that if the borrower defaulted on his payments, she could not proceed against him in court or seize his property. For this reason De[xithe]us intervened and pledged to repay the loan in case the borrower defaulted. In exchange for this pledge, De[xithe]us obtained from the borrower the right to claim his property in the event that the latter could not repay.

If this analysis is correct, the *horos* is valuable for illustrating both the extent of women's involvement in lending and the limits on that involvement. As a woman, Demo could collect the contributions for the *eranos* loan and give them to the borrower. She could also ask for repayment and distribute this money to contributors. But in the event of default, she was powerless since she could not bring a legal action.[17] This necessitated the cooperation of Dexitheus, who could pledge to the lenders that they would be repaid one way or another. If legal action were necessary, Dexitheus could proceed against the borrower to compensate himself for any payments he had to make to the lenders. Although without legal

[16] Maffi (1993) 649–50 is skeptical of this translation, which he claimed was "en contradiction avec Dem. 21.101 et 184, l'un des principaux témoignages en la matière." Maffi does not note, however, that in these two passages Demosthenes explicitly states that the πληρωτής "collects (συλλέγειν) the loan," a role that is different from "contributing to an *eranos* loan," an action that is expressed by the verb εἰσφέρειν ([Dem.] 59.32). Cf. Hesychius *s.v.* πληρωτής (ἐράνου συναγωγός). Fine (1951) 19; Finley (1985) 101, Millett (1991) 153, and MacDowell (1990) 149, 197 all erroneously translate as "contributor." For the correct translation see Vondeling (1961) 37 and 229 note 1, and Maier (1969) 34–5. Cf. Harris (1992b) 312 note 11.

[17] On women's lack of power in this sphere, de Ste. Croix (1970) and Schaps (1979) still remain fundamental. Hunter (1994) shows that women were active in managing property but does not succeed in showing that women enjoyed rights to property on the basis of passages such as Dem. 41.9. See Harris (1992) 319–20 with note 37. Cohen (1998) 53–7 has nothing original to add to the discussion.

capacity, a woman in Athens could play a role in financial transactions, but to do so she required the assistance of a man.

Afterthoughts

For an interesting study of the effect that the limitations on women's rights to property had on their affective relationships, see Johnstone (2003).

On the wages of workers, see now Loomis (1998).

III.4 The Date of Apollodorus' Speech against Timotheus and Its Implications for Athenian History and Legal Procedure

THE DATE OF APOLLODORUS' SPEECH AGAINST THE ATHENIAN GENERAL TIMOTHEUS ([Dem.] 49) has not been a matter of dispute since Arnold Schaefer over a century ago assigned it to the archonship of Molon (362/61).[1] His dating of the speech has been followed by almost all scholars and appears in several standard works of reference.[2] After such a long period of virtually unquestioned acceptance, the time has come to challenge this dating, which, as we will soon see, rests on an assumption for which there is no evidence at all.

We need to begin by examining Schaefer's method of determining the *terminus post quem* for the delivery of the speech. Schaefer noted that Pasicles, the younger brother of Apollodorus, gave testimony as a witness at the trial of Timotheus ([Dem.] 49.42). On the grounds that Pasicles could not have appeared as a witness until he had reached the age of majority, Schaefer argued that the speech

[1] Schaefer (1858) 137–43. Schaefer refuted the proposal of Rehdantz (1845) 195ff. to date the speech between 360 and 356.

[2] To my knowledge, the only skeptic has been Klee (1937). Klee dated the speech to 368/67, but did not state his reasons in this article. I suspect that they are to be found in his Jena dissertation of 1925 (*non vidi*). Klee's position was noted by Finley (1952) 273 note 60 and Kallet (1983) 239–40. Finley took no position on the matter, whereas Kallet arbitrarily preferred Schaefer's dating without putting forward any reasons for doing so. Others who have followed Schaefer include Blass (1887–98) 3:522–3; Kirchner (1903/1966) #7737 (Iphicrates); #9988 (Menestheus); #13700 (Timotheus); Murray (1939) 375; Davies (1971) 250–1, 429, 510; Gernet (1959) 11.

could not have been delivered before the archonship of Molon (362/61), the year in which Pasicles turned eighteen.[3]

Whereas there can be no question that a youth in Athens attained the age of majority on reaching his eighteenth birthday,[4] there is no evidence that would allow us to say whether or not those younger than eighteen were forbidden to testify in Athenian courts. The only text which deals with the issue is from Plato's *Laws* (937a–b), where we find a discussion about laws relating to evidence at trials and a recommendation that only in homicide cases should children and slaves be allowed to give testimony. Needless to say, this passage is of no assistance; in his *Laws* Plato was legislating for an ideal state, not describing actual legal practice in Classical Athens. Although the code presented in the *Laws* does owe much to Athenian statutes, it does not follow them in detail and in several regards diverges significantly from Athenian practices. Consequently, it cannot be used as a source for Athenian legislation.[5] On the other hand, it is true that the rest of the speeches of the Attic orators that have been preserved do not appear to provide us with a single example of a minor giving testimony. Yet this need not be due to the existence of a law that prohibited them from doing so. The Athenians were certainly not averse to allowing children and their mothers to appear in court – on the contrary, we know that it was customary for a defendant to introduce his mourning family into court to win the sympathy of the judges.[6] If we have

[3] Schaefer (1858) 140. When Pasicles reached the age of majority, the lease of the bank and shield factory to Phormion, which had lasted for eight years, was terminated (Dem. 36.4–10, 37). This lease began before the death of Pasion in 370/69 ([Dem.] 46.13), but sometime after the archonship of Alcisthenes (372/71), for at that time Phormion is described as ἐπικαθήμενον ἐπὶ τῇ τραπέζῃ, not τὸν μισθούμενον ([Dem.] 49.17, 60). Schaefer assumed that the lease began shortly after Pasion's death. He may well have been correct, but we cannot rule out any date between 372/71 and 370/69 for the beginning of the lease. For the sake of argument, I will adopt Schaefer's date for the beginning of the lease when discussing his attempt to date [Dem.] 49.

[4] [Arist.] *Ath. Pol.* 42.1 with Rhodes (1981) 498. Sealey (1957) and Golden (1979) have argued on the basis of Dem. 27 that in some cases youths could be enrolled before their eighteenth birthday. I plan to argue elsewhere that there is no reason to trust this evidence.

[5] See Morrow (1939) 124: "But Plato does not uniformly adhere to Athenian law and practice of his day. We have noticed in the preceding pages many points on which Platonic law departs from its Athenian model, some of them trivial, but others of considerable importance affecting the status of the slave." See also Cohen (1983) 128: "it might be wise to hesitate before summarily concluding, as some scholars have done, that Plato narrowly defined *hierosulia* as actual theft from temples and thus based his law closely upon an Athenian model (. . .) in a variety of particulars Plato's law of *hierosulia* clearly differs from Athens'."

[6] For example, Aeschin. 2.179; Hyperides *Eux.* 41; Lys. 20.34; Dem. 21.99, 186–8; Pl. *Ap.* 34c.

no examples in other speeches of a minor giving evidence at a trial, it is quite possibly attributable to the fact that those under eighteen spent almost all their time at home, in school, or at the gymnasium and were thus never witnesses to business transactions nor took part in public affairs.[7] Yet, if the only witness to an event that later became the subject of a legal dispute happened to be a minor, it is hard to believe that the Athenians would not have permitted him to testify. We know that the testimony of a woman, if given under oath, was acceptable as evidence[8] and that foreigners, who were not even Athenian citizens, were not barred from appearing as witnesses in court.[9] The testimony of slaves obtained under torture was also considered admissible as evidence in Athens.[10] If their evidence was deemed acceptable, what reasons would the Athenians have had to reject the testimony of a minor, both of whose parents were Athenian citizens?

At this point, we cannot give a definitive answer to this question. All that we can say is that the absence of any known example of a minor giving testimony in an Athenian court need not betoken the existence of a statute prohibiting one from doing so. In short, we have no *a priori* grounds for ruling out the possibility that Pasicles could have given testimony at the trial of Timotheus before he reached the age of eighteen. And that in turn means that Schaefer's argument that Apollodorus could not have delivered his speech against Timotheus before the archonship of Molon (362/61), the year in which Pasicles came of age, rests on no firm foundation. To date the speech using this approach would be to determine *ignotum per ignotius*.

There are additional reasons for questioning Schaefer's dating of the speech. By placing the trial in 362/61, Schaefer was forced to argue that Timotheus, who was sent in 364/63 to relieve Iphicrates in the continuing campaign to retake Amphipolis, was recalled from his campaign there before the middle of 362, returned to Athens where he was brought to court by Apollodorus before the late

7 For the close supervision of children, see Pl. *Lysis* 208c–e.

8 Harrison (1971) 152. Leisi (1907) 12–18 notes that none of our sources actually state that women could not testify. He concludes that they were not allowed to testify from the absence of any testimony given by a woman in the speeches of the Attic orators. However, he realized that [Dem.] 47.70 might be an exception to this and also observed that "Da die beschworene Aussage gleich einem Zeugnisse niedergeschrieben und zu den Akten gegeben wurde, so unterscheidet sie sich fast gar nicht vom Zeugnisse." The assertion of MacDowell (1978) 243 ("Women [...] seem never to have given evidence"] is a misleading oversimplification.

9 For foreigners giving evidence, see [Dem.] 49.22; Aeschin. 2.143.

10 For the testimony of slaves, see Thür (1977).

summer of that year, and then was later reappointed to lead the campaign against Amphipolis in 360/59.[11] Such a reconstruction of events creates several problems. First of all, it gives Timotheus an initial command of only two years against Amphipolis. Two years is a surprisingly short tenure for a man who, despite his ultimate failure to capture Amphipolis, was by all indications remarkably successful during his campaigns in Northern Greece. By contrast, Iphicrates, who appears to have won no significant victories during his attempt to regain the former Athenian colony, was given a command of four years.[12] If Timotheus' efforts met with such stunning success, why was he terminated so soon? Second, it is difficult to believe that Timotheus could have achieved all that he did in the area in only two years. Dinarchus (1.14 = 3.17) and Isocrates (15.113ff.) speak of him taking more than twenty cities, including Methone, Pydna, and Potidaea. Not only did Timotheus conduct campaigns in this area during his time there, but he also had to sail off to the Hellespont to lift the siege of Cyzicus.[13] That is quite a lot of activity to squeeze into two years. Third, it is improbable that Timotheus would have been relieved in 362/61 when he appears to have still enjoyed a high degree of popularity in Athens. Proof of his continuing popularity can be found in an inscription (*IG* ii^2 110) that records a decree of praise for Menelaus, a Pelagonian, passed in the sixth prytany of the archonship of Charicleides (363/62), that is, early in 362. This decree was moved and passed on the recommendation of Timotheus (line 6). The willingness of the Assembly to award such honors to a candidate put forward by Timotheus surely indicates that he must have still been held in high esteem in Athens at the time and makes recall shortly afterwards extremely unlikely. Nevertheless, it is possible that Timotheus suffered a serious defeat and that this setback caused the Athenians to relieve him of his command sometime before the middle of 362. Yet, if Timotheus did lose an important battle that is not reported to us by our sources and was subsequently deprived of his command, why did the Athenians reappoint him to the same command in 360/59? Such a failure would certainly have discouraged the Athenians from entrusting him a second time with the task of retaking Amphipolis. In the face of these objections,

[11] Schaefer (1885) 1:101–2, 155. For the date of the initial appointment, see D. S. 15.81.6. For the date of Timotheus' final failure, see the scholia to Aeschin. 2.31.

[12] Iphicrates arrived in Northern Greece around the time of the death of Alexander II of Macedon in 368/67 (D. S. 15.71.1; Aeschin. 2.28–9). He spent more than three years trying to take Amphipolis (Dem. 23.149).

[13] D. S. 15.81.6; Cornelius Nepos *Timotheus* 1.3.

we should reject Schaefer's hypothesis that Timotheus was recalled in late 363/62 and returned to Athens where he was brought to trial by Apollodorus in the following archon-year. It is much more likely that Timotheus' campaign against Amphipolis lasted uninterruptedly from 364/63 to 360/59, during which time he could not have been prosecuted by Apollodorus.[14]

So far we have found that Schaefer's method of dating the speech rested on an unjustified assumption and that his proposed date compelled him to posit an extremely implausible hypothesis about Timotheus' recall. It is now necessary to find a better means of dating the speech. This will require a short account of Phormion's lease of Pasion's bank. Sometime between 372/71 and his death in 370/69, Pasion leased his bank to his former slave Phormion.[15] After Pasion passed away, the bank was inherited by his sons, Apollodorus and Pasicles, who jointly received the revenues from the lease. The lease of the bank to Phormion came to an end when Pasicles came of age and lasted for a total of eight years, that is, until sometime between 364/63 and 362/61. At this juncture, Apollodorus was given a choice between the bank and the shield factory, which had also been leased to Phormion during the preceding years. Apollodorus chose the shield factory, which, though less lucrative, represented the safer investment, and signed a release, thereby renouncing any claims on the bank, which passed into the hands of Pasicles (Dem. 36.11, 37–8).[16] If the debts owed to the bank by Timotheus were

[14] If Apollodorus had attempted to bring his suit against Timotheus to court in the latter's absence, his relatives and associates would have sworn an oath that he was away on public business. The court would then have voted on whether or not to grant a postponement (see Dem. 48.25–6 with Harrison [1971] 155). It is hardly conceivable that the court would not have accepted Timotheus' excuse.

[15] See note 3.

[16] At Dem. 36.12–13 it is claimed by the speaker that after Phormion's lease had been terminated, Apollodorus leased the bank to other men at the same rate charged to Phormion. This claim is made to demonstrate that Apollodorus did not in this period consider that the bank had lost assets during the time that it was leased to Phormion. This is one of several arguments put forward to show that Phormion never embezzled funds from the bank. Evidence is subsequently produced to confirm this allegation. This charge is, however, irreconcilable with the fact that immediately (εὐθὺς) after the termination of the lease to Phormion, the bank was turned over to Pasicles, who, as sole owner of the bank, should have been the one who subsequently leased it to Xenon and his associates. Furthermore, we are later told that after the end of the lease of the shield factory and bank to Phormion, Apollodorus received the payment of one talent a year (Dem. 36.37); this was the amount paid by the shield factory (Dem. 36.11). That Apollodorus received the revenue of the shield factory alone after the end of the lease to Phormion is supported by the testimony of witnesses (Dem. 36.40).

The solution to this conundrum is probably that the speaker is not telling the truth when he claims that Apollodorus leased the bank to Xenon and his associates. It is clear that these men testified

still outstanding after this time, it was up to Pasicles to prosecute Timotheus for failure to repay them. Of course, we know that it was Apollodorus, not Pasicles, who brought the action against Timotheus and delivered the speech at the trial.[17] Our knowledge of the history of the bank would therefore lead us to conclude that the trial must have taken place in 362/61 at the very latest, for after that year Apollodorus no longer possessed a share of the bank and was in no position to prosecute Timotheus for his failure to repay the money still owed to the bank. Paradoxically enough, the year that Schaefer believed to be the *terminus post quem* turns out to be the *terminus ante quem*. The real *terminus post quem* is the death of Pasion in the year 370/69.

We can narrow these rather wide limits of 370/69 and 362/61 somewhat when we take into account the fact that Timotheus was abroad serving as general from 366/65 onwards.[18] Most of 368/67 can also be ruled out since during that year Apollodorus was performing a trierarchy that took him around the Peloponnese and as far away as Sicily.[19] This leaves 369/68 and 367/66. Allowing for the possibility that Pasion may have died early in 370/69 and that Timotheus may

that they had leased the two properties from Pasicles and Apollodorus. Given our knowledge of the division, this should mean that Pasicles leased the bank to them, and Apollodorus leased to them the shield factory, with each one receiving the rent from the property that he owned. However, by claiming that Apollodorus was the one who leased the bank, the speaker gives the impression that what is meant by the testimony of these men is that they leased both properties as a single unit from Apollodorus and Pasicles together, who held these properties jointly.

17 For Apollodorus as the prosecutor in this suit, see [Dem.] 49 *hyp.* and Plu. *Dem.* 15. Apollodorus claims that the loans to Timotheus were part of his share of the inheritance ([Dem.] 49.43: γίγνεται ἐμὸν τὸ μέρος) and claims that his brother testified to this. But it is clear that the loans were made from the bank ([Dem.] 49.4: ἀπὸ τῆς τραπέζης; cf. 7, 17, 29, 33) and that by the terms of Pasion's will the bank was inherited jointly by Apollodorus and Pasicles. Although Apollodorus gives the impression that his brother's testimony supported his claim, it is clear from the preceding section that Pasicles testified only that their father indicated to them the debts that were owed to him and did not say anything about them forming part of his brother's share. Two other facts confirm our suspicion that Apollodorus was lying when he claimed that Timotheus' debts were part of his portion. First, there is Apollodorus' failure to cite Pasion's will at this point (for the will see Dem. 36.7). Second, there is the charge made at Dem. 36.36 that Apollodorus collected twenty talents from debtors listed in the account books left behind by his father and kept more than half of this amount, thus depriving his brother of his fair share – the sums collected from Timotheus were obviously part of these debts. This charge is supported by documents and witnesses (Dem. 36.40).

18 For Timotheus as general in 366/65, see *IG* ii^2 108, lines 9–10. The campaign against Samos probably took place in the following year and immediately preceded Timotheus' appointment to the campaign against Amphipolis (D. S. 18.8.9).

19 Dem. 45.3; [Dem.] 46.20–1; 53.5 with Davies (1971) 440.

have returned to Athens soon afterwards, we should not exclude the last months of that year either. If we knew the date of Timotheus' return to Athens after his service with the king of Persia, we might be able to choose among these three years, but our sources provide us with no information that might help us to answer this question.[20]

An earlier dating of the speech brings with it one immediate benefit: it allows us to make better sense of Apollodorus' actions in the case. According to Apollodorus, Pasion took considerable risk in lending Timotheus large sums of money since the latter had no property to offer as security for these loans ([Dem.] 49.2, 11, 61), but did so out of friendship and with the assurance that Timotheus would be able to repay him after his lucrative service with the king of Persia ([Dem.] 49.3, 64). If we accept Schaefer's date of 362/61, we would have to assume that Apollodorus did not try to recover his money from Timotheus as soon as the latter returned to Athens (sometime before 366/65) the very way his father had expected to, but waited four years or longer to try to collect these debts. Alternatively, we would be forced to conclude that Apollodorus did ask for the money immediately upon Timotheus' return, but, after failing to obtain repayment, waited four or more years to start legal proceedings against the defaulting general. Considering that Timotheus must have been quite a wealthy man after fighting for the Great King[21] and that the loans given to him were not interest-bearing, it is hard to understand why Apollodorus – who was never one to let slip any opportunity to lay his hands on cold cash – would have delayed in his attempts to recover the sums owed to the bank. On the other hand, if we accept the earlier dating proposed here, this problem does not arise, and nothing prevents us from concluding that Apollodorus did ask Timotheus to repay the borrowed sums soon after the

[20] If we follow Cawkwell (1973) 759–61 and date *IG* ii² 1609 to 370/69, we could confidently assert that Timotheus, who is listed as trierarch in that inscription (line 100), had returned to Athens by then. But the date of this inscription is controversial – Davies (1969) has argued for 366/65. I myself find it difficult to accept a dating of 370/69, for that would mean that Apollodorus, who is also listed as a trierarch in the inscription (line 89), would not have had enough money of his own to qualify for inclusion on the list of those eligible for this liturgy before he inherited his share of his father's estate.

[21] In 367/66 Timotheus' fortune was a matter of public knowledge and official record (Dem. 27.7). Apollodorus' claims about his wealth are thus more credible than Timotheus' denials ([Dem.] 49.67). Timotheus' newly acquired fortune enabled him to repay his other creditors and to remove the *horoi* from his property ([Dem.] 49.12). Such an explanation for the disappearance of the *horoi* is far more plausible than the malicious one offered by Apollodorus.

latter's return to Athens, and that soon after being refused payment, Apollodorus began legal proceedings.

Our redating of Apollodorus' speech against Timotheus is not without some consequences. These are:

1) The marriage of Iphicrates' son Menestheus to the daughter of Timotheus, mentioned in this speech ([Dem.] 49.66), can now be dated to sometime between late 370/69 (the earliest Timotheus could have returned to Athens) and the end of 367/66 (the latest possible date for [Dem.] 49).[22] The redating of their marriage reveals that the reconciliation between Timotheus and Iphicrates occurred much sooner than was previously thought. It is now clear that not long after returning from Egypt, Timotheus decided to end his quarrel with his old enemy. The money he earned from his service with the Great King no doubt enabled him to provide his daughter with a handsome dowry, making her all the more attractive to Menestheus. This matrimonial investment soon produced political dividends, for Timotheus was elected general by 366/65, if not sooner. Timotheus' speedy return to favor in Athens must have owed much to the influential backing of Iphicrates and his son.
2) Since we know that Apollodorus' prosecution must have occurred before 366/65 and that his brother did not come of age until after 364/63, the latter must have been a minor when he testified in support of his older brother at the trial of Timotheus.[23] We now have a clear-cut example of a minor appearing as a witness in an Athenian court, which confirms our earlier impression that Schaefer was wrong to assume that such a thing was not possible. As a result, we can assert with some confidence that minors were permitted to give testimony in Athenian courts. If we do not have more examples of them doing so, it is because they were normally confined to

[22] For Schaefer's dating of the marriage, see Schaefer (1885) I:122 and Schaefer (1858) 139, 142. Kirchner (1903/1966) #9988 (Menestheus), #13700 (Timotheus), and Davies (1971) 250–1 both accept Schaefer's date for the marriage. Kallet (1983) 239–41 has argued that the marriage could not have taken place in 362 since "Iphikrates was still in Thrace" and the reconciliation between him and Timotheus "would strongly suggest, if not require, Iphikrates' presence in Athens." She preferred to place it between 371 and 368 when both men were in Athens. (She arbitrarily accepts Cawkwell's dating of *IG* ii² 1609 and passes over in silence Davies' case for putting it in 366/65.) Her argument is hardly compelling; Menestheus did not need his father's presence to marry the daughter of Timotheus, and the reconciliation of the two men could easily have been established through intermediaries.

[23] For Pasicles' coming of age, see note 3.

home, school, or the gymnasium and were thus rarely if ever witnesses to the kinds of events that might become the subject of legal action.

3) We have uncovered another case where the legislation presented by Plato in his *Laws* differed from that of Athens. In that work Plato proposed that minors be barred from testifying in all cases save those involving homicide – our redating of [Dem.] 49 has revealed that no such prohibition existed in Athens, where males under the age of eighteen could appear as witnesses in other kinds of suits. This should serve as an additional warning to those who would quarry Plato's *Laws* for evidence about Athenian statutes.

Afterthoughts

Trevett (1991) argues for a return to Schaefer's dating of the speech to 362/61. Trevett criticizes several of my arguments, but still cannot show that there was any law barring minors from giving evidence. Instead, he resorts to mere assertion: "I see nothing at all implausible in the idea that women and children were barred from giving evidence in court." He rejects my method of dating the speech by claiming that the loans were part of Apollodorus' share of the inheritance. He ignores, however, the evidence that the loans were made from the bank (see the evidence provided in note 17); the loans could only form part of Apollodorus' share of the inheritance while he retained an interest in the bank, which he did not after Pasicles came of age.

Trevett's argument is rejected by Rowe (2000) 288 note 37: "I agree with Harris (46) that 'the absence of any known example of a minor giving evidence in an Athenian court need not betoken the existence of a statute prohibiting one from doing so.' Trevett's (1991, 21–7) attempt to refute Harris is not in my judgment successful." Rowe then rightly observes that neither I nor Trevett appear to have read Klee's dissertation, which provides strong arguments for the earlier date. According to Rowe, Klee notes that "two passages (6 and 8) refer to Timotheus' second strategia as his 'last' (ὕστερον), and, second, Apollodorus appears to know nothing about Timotheus' subsequent campaign in the Hellespont and Thrace, which he might have exploited to Timotheus' embarrassment. These two reasons, combined with those supplied by Harris, make the earlier dates, especially 368/7, preferable to the later date."

I would slightly alter my argument in note 16. Instead of claiming that the speaker is not telling the truth at Dem. 36.12–13, I would say that he is using the verb ἐμίσθωσεν in the loose sense of "arranging the terms of the lease." For a similar use of the verb, see [Arist.] *Ath. Pol.* 56.7 where the Archon arranges the terms of leases for property of orphans and heiresses (μισθοῖ δὲ καὶ τοὺς οἴκους τῶν ὀρφανῶν καὶ τῶν ἐπικλήρων). The Archon is obviously not the owner of the property, which belongs to the orphans and the heiresses.

The study promised in note 4 has been published in Harris (1989).

III.5 A Note on Adoption and Deme Registration

The Athenian law of adoption allowed a man who had no γνήσιοι children to adopt a son to serve as his κληρονόμος.[1] As part of the process of adoption, the adopted son was entered on the deme register of his adoptive father.[2] After the process was completed, the adopted son lost all rights of inheritance in his natural family.[3] The adopted son might return to his natural family on one condition – that he left a son in the household of his adoptive father to serve as κληρονόμος.[4]

L. Rubinstein has recently claimed on the basis of [Dem.] 44 that an "adopted son ceased to be a member of the deme of his adoptive father when he returned to the family of his natural father."[5] Yet she admits that "there is no information as to whether there was any procedure of readmission when he returned to the deme of his natural father." I will argue that the evidence found in [Dem.] 44 indicates on the contrary that the adopted son who chose to return to the household of his natural father retained his membership in the deme of his adoptive father. This interpretation of the evidence found in the speech will enable us to understand how Clearchus, the son and κληρονόμος of the general Nausicles, came to have a different demotic from that of his father.

[1] Is. 2.13; 3.68; 6.28; Dem. 46.14. The text of the law inserted into the text at Dem. 46.14 is probably a fake – I hope to discuss this matter elsewhere. I prefer not to translate the word κληρονόμος with the English word "heir" since the Athenians, like the Romans, employed the principle of universal succession. For this principle and its differences from modern practices, see Nicholas (1962) 235–6. I would like to thank L. Rubinstein for reading over an earlier draft of this essay and helping me to improve it. She should not be held responsible for the views expressed herein or for any remaining errors. My disagreement with her on this one point does not in any way diminish my admiration for her splendid study of adoption in Athens. I would also like to thank Professor Angelos Chaniotis for reading over this essay and offering helpful suggestions.

[2] Is. 7.28 with Rubinstein (1993) 37–9.

[3] Is. 7.23; 9.2; 9.33; 10.4 with Rubinstein (1993) 45.

[4] Is. 6.44; 9.33; 10.11; [Dem.] 44.64 and 68; Antiphon fr. IV (Baiter and Sauppe) = Harp. 228.

[5] Rubinstein (1993) 58.

When analyzing the statements of the speaker in [Dem.] 44, it is necessary to keep several considerations in mind. First, the speaker presents only one side of the case – the speeches delivered by his opponents Leostratus and Leochares have not been preserved. The speaker naturally stresses the legitimacy of his own claims to the property of Archiades and casts doubts on the claims made by his adversaries. Second, it is important to distinguish between what the speaker asserts and what he is actually able to prove by means of documents and witnesses. Finally, one needs to be on the watch for the speaker's attempts to mislead the court by using ambiguous language.[6]

The basic facts of the case are simple and straightforward. Archiades had two brothers named Meidylides and Archippus and a sister called Archedice. Archiades and his brothers gave Archedice in marriage to Leostratus of Eleusis ([Dem.] 44.9, 17). This marriage led to the birth of a daughter, who was later married to another man from Eleusis.[7] This couple had a child whom they named Leocrates (who will be called Leocrates I to distinguish him from his homonymous grandson) (17). Archiades chose not to marry and during his lifetime (ζῶντος) adopted Leocrates I as his κληρονόμος. As part of the adoption procedure, Leocrates would have been enrolled as a member of Archiades' deme Otryne. The speaker attempts to arouse suspicions about the validity of the adoption by claiming it took place while Meidylides was abroad and that Meidylides intended to challenge the claims of Leocrates I after Archiades died (19–20). But there is no reason to question the adoption. Indeed, the speaker himself provides evidence for the adoption later in the speech (30). Furthermore, he admits that Meidylides never actually brought a suit against Leocrates I during the entire time he remained in possession of Archiades' estate (20).[8]

Sometime later, Leocrates "returned to the Eleusinians from whence he had originally come" (ἐπανῆλθεν αὐτὸς εἰς τοὺς Ἐλευσινίους, ὅθεν ἦν

[6] For a general discussion of the problems involved in using the speeches of the Attic orators as historical sources, see Harris (1995) 7–16.

[7] μετὰ δὲ ταῦτα ἐκ θυγατρὸς τῆς ἐκδοθείσης ἀδελφῆς ταύτης αὐτῶν γίγνεται Λεωκράτης ὁ πατὴρ Λεωστράτου τουτουί. This phrase is mistranslated by A. T. Murray in his Loeb edition of the speech as "and after a time from this sister of theirs, thus given in marriage, there was born Leocrates." Murray takes no notice of the word θυγατρὸς.

[8] The speaker claims that Meidylides refrained from bringing a suit only because he was swayed by the pleas of his relatives. But if there was truly something amiss with the adoption, why did he not pursue his case? It is also noteworthy that Meidylides died before the trial (20) and that the speaker produces no evidence to prove that Meidylides contemplated challenging the claims of Leocrates I.

τὸ ἐξ ἀρχῆς), "leaving behind this man Leostratus as a γνήσιος son in the house" of his adoptive father (ἐγκαταλιπὼν τουτονὶ Λεώστρατον ἐν τῷ οἴκῳ υἱὸν γνήσιον, 21). One thing is clear – Leocrates I took advantage of the law that allowed an adopted son to return to the house of his father if he left behind a γνήσιος son in the house of his adoptive father.[9] Like his father, Leostratus also took advantage of the law, for he subsequently "returned to the Eleusinians as his father had done" (ἐπανέρχεται, ὥσπερ ὁ πατὴρ αὐτοῦ, ἐπὶ τοὺς Ἐλευσινίους), "leaving behind a γνήσιος son" (ἐγκαταλιπὼν υἱὸν γνήσιον) in the house of Archiades.[10] This son was named Leocrates after his grandfather and later died without issue (24).

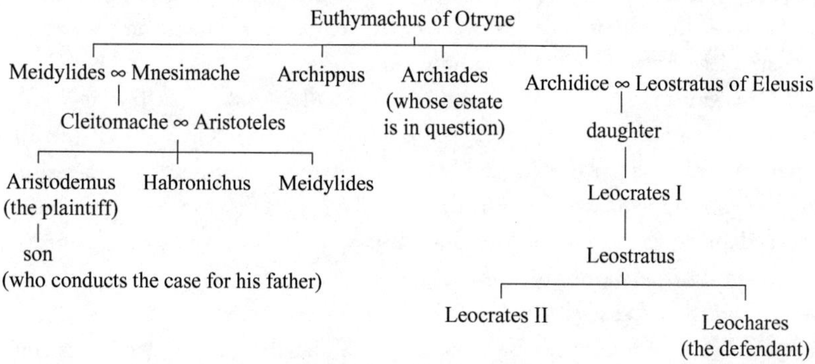

What does the speaker mean by the phrase "returned to the Eleusinians"? Does it merely mean that Leocrates I and Leostratus simply changed their residence from Otryne to Eleusis, where their family's property was probably located? Or does it mean that they changed both their residence and their official deme registration at the same time? The speaker deliberately leaves it unclear since it is to his advantage to stress the ties of Leocrates I and Leostratus to Eleusis as a way of undercutting their ties to Otryne, the deme of their adoptive father, thereby undermining his

9 The speaker expresses himself more clearly when referring to Leostratus' return at 33: ἀπεληλυθὼς γ' εἰς τὸν πατρῷον οἶκον.

10 The speaker uses similar language at 26, 28, 34, 35, 44, 46. At 39 the speaker describes Leostratus as ἐν Ἐλευσινίοις δημοτευόμενος. For the meaning of the verb δημοτεύεσθαι, see Whitehead (1986) 68–9. This phrase need only imply that Leostratus was somehow active in the deme, but need not imply official registration. There is no reason to question the speaker's account of these actions since he later provides evidence to show that Leocrates and Leostratus returned to Eleusis (44).

claim to the property of Archiades.[11] Yet although the speaker may wish to give the impression Leocrates I and Leostratus were enrolled on the official deme list of Eleusis, he never says this explicitly nor provides any evidence to that effect. In fact, the speaker admits Leostratus was enrolled on the assembly list of the deme Otryne at the time of the trial (35).[12] He also states that Leostratus listed himself as a member of Otryne on the affidavit he submitted to the archon (39).[13] The speaker nevertheless claims that Leostratus was unsuccessful in his attempt to have his name placed on the official deme register of Otryne. He further alleges that he stopped Leostratus from collecting his distribution from the Theoric Fund as a member of Otryne on the grounds that he was not yet enrolled on the deme's official list (35–40). Failing to secure his own admission, Leostratus succeeded in getting his son Leochares enrolled as a son of Archiades on the deme register of Otryne and later introduced to the phratry of Archiades (41–3).

Here it is crucial to separate what the speaker alleges and what he can prove by producing evidence. The speaker has to admit that Leostratus at the time of the trial was enrolled on the Assembly list of Otryne. He gives the impression that the registration took place only after he filed his affidavit in response to the speaker's claim to the estate of Archiades. But he provides no evidence to prove his assertion. Furthermore, the speaker admits that Leocrates I was adopted by Archiades and that Leostratus was left in the house of Archiades as his adopted son. But if both were adopted by Archiades – a fact that the speaker does not dispute – they both would have been registered as members of Archiades' deme of Otryne at the time of their adoption, not later just before the trial. When the speaker brings forward witnesses to corroborate his account, all they testify to is that 1) Leostratus "returned to the Eleusinians" after leaving a *gnesios* son in the house of Archiades, 2) Leostratus' father had earlier done the same thing, and 3) Leochares was enrolled on the official deme list of Otryne before he was enrolled in the phratry of Archiades (44: ὡς ὁ νῦν διαμεμαρτυρηκὼς

[11] Later in the speech he tries to exploit this: τὸ μετὰ ταῦτα τοίνυν πῶς οὐκ ἄτοπον καὶ δεινόν ἐστι, ἅμα παρακαταβεβληκέναι τοῦ κλήρου πρὸς τῷ ἄρχοντι ὡς ὄντα αὐτὸν Ἀρχιάδου Λεώστρατον τουτονί, *τὸν Ἐλευσίνιον τοῦ Ὀτρυνέως* (52). The speaker is misleading since Eleusis was only Leostratus' deme of residence, not the deme where he was registered (see below), whereas Archiades was registered as a member of the deme of Otryne.

[12] For the relationship between the official deme list and the assembly list, see Whitehead (1986) 104.

[13] The speaker attempts to maneuver around this awkward fact by claiming that Leostratus deceived the archon, but there is no reason to take his unproven charge seriously. Moreover we know the archons and other magistrates normally paid careful attention to the precise wording of applications submitted to them – see Is. 6.12; 10.2; Lys. 13.86.

πρότερον εἰς τοὺς δημότας ἢ εἰς τοὺς φράτερας ἐνεγράφη, τούτων ὑμῖν τὰς τῶν φρατέρων καὶ τὰς τῶν δημοτῶν μαρτυρίας ἀναγνώσεται).[14] In other words, the speaker provides no evidence that Leostratus was not enrolled on the official deme register of Otryne.

To sum up our points so far: the speaker nowhere states explicitly that Leocrates I and Leostratus changed their official deme registration when they returned to the family of their natural father, which resided in Eleusis. Second, the speaker admits that Leostratus was at one time the adopted son of Archiades and thus would have been registered as a member of the deme of their adoptive father. Third, the speaker admits that at the time of the speech Leostratus was enrolled on the Assembly list of Otryne. Fourth, the speaker admits that Leostratus listed himself as a member of the deme of Otryne on the affidavit that he submitted to the archon, who accepted it in that form. Thus, the speaker makes several statements indicating Leostratus was a member of Otryne and never proves he was not. Contrary to Rubinstein's claim, the evidence of [Dem.] 44 indicates that after an adopted son returned to the household of his natural family, he could remain registered on the official register of his adoptive father's deme.

The evidence from [Dem.] 44 enables us to explain why Clearchus, the son and κληρονόμος of the politician Nausicles, had a different demotic from that of his father.[15] Nausicles was the son of a man named Clearchus and a member of the deme of Oe (*IG* ii² 1496, lines 40–2, 49–51; 1623, lines 329–33).[16] Nausicles named his son Clearchus after his own father. The younger Clearchus was also active in politics and served on an embassy to Nicanor with his father's old associate Phocion in 318 (D. S. 18.64.5).

Father and son served as joint trierarchs in 332/31 (*IG* ii² 1628, lines 100–2).[17] In an inscription dated to 326/25, we learn that Clearchus returned naval equipment in 325/24 (*IG* ii² 1629, lines 707–14). In this inscription Clearchus is described as Ναυσικλέους Ὀῆθεν /κληρονόμου, yet Clearchus' deme is Aigilia (Αἰγιλιῶς),

[14] The normal procedure was for a man to be introduced to the phratry soon after birth, then enrolled on the deme register once he reached the age of majority at 18. See Lambert (1993) 161–78. But Leochares was posthumously adopted only after the death of his brother Leocrates II (24). It is also necessary to bear in mind that phratry membership was not a necessary prerequisite for membership in a deme, which merely required the candidate to prove that both his parents were Athenians – see [Arist.] *Ath. Pol.* 42.1. This of course meant that νόθοι, who were not members of a phratry, could be Athenian citizens. See MacDowell (1976b).

[15] For the career of his father Nausicles, see E. M. Harris (1994b).

[16] For Nausicles' deme, see also *IG* ii² 1496, lines 40–1; 1623, lines 329–30.

[17] [τριήραρχο]ς Ναυσικλῆς Ὀῆθε,/[συντριήραρχ]ος Κλέαρχος [Ναυσικ]λέους Αἰγιλι.

whereas his father's deme is Oe.[18] The example of Leostratus in [Dem.] 44 enables us to understand how this came about. Clearchus was adopted by someone in the deme of Aigilia. As a result, he was entered on the official deme register of Aigilia as all adopted sons were. At some later time, Clearchus left a son to serve as κληρονόμος in the household of his adoptive father in Aigilia and returned to the household of his natural father Nausicles.[19] This enabled Clearchus to become Nausicles' κληρονόμος upon the latter's death. He was thus similar to Leostratus, who returned to the household of his natural father and left his son Leocrates II in the household of his adoptive father Archiades. Yet despite his return to his father's household, Clearchus remained registered in Aigilia, the deme of his adoptive father, just as Leostratus remained a member of Otryne, the deme of his adoptive father Archiades.

Afterthoughts

On adoption in Athens, see now Cobetto Ghiggia (1999). In his analysis of [Dem.] 44, Cobetto Ghiggia follows Rubinstein on the question of deme registration, but does not take account of my essay, which may have appeared too late for him to see. He also does not treat the question of Clearchus' demotic.

[18] For Clearchus' deme, see also *IG* ii[2] 1628, lines 71–2. Kirchner (1903/1966) #10552 attempted to explain the different demotics of father and son by assuming that Nausicles was adopted by a citizen of Agilia and left his son Clearchus in his household, then returned to the household of his natural father: "Nemper Nausicles per adoptionem transierat in domum civis Agiliensis cuiusdam; iam cum in hac Agiliensium domo reliquisset Clearchum filium, rursus rediit in pristinam familiam quae erat Ὀῆθεν." Kirchner's solution is accepted by Davies (1971) 397. But if Clearchus remained in his adoptive family after his father Nausicles returned to the family of his natural father, he could not have become Nausicles' κληρονόμος upon his death. See note 3.

[19] Rubinstein *per litteras* suggests that it may have been possible for an adopted son in certain cases to inherit the property of his natural father without returning to his household. She draws to my attention the case of Cyronides, who was adopted by Xenaenetus, but was allegedly able to gain control of the property of his natural father Aristarchus (Is. 10.5). But the speaker never actually proves that Cyronides took over Aristarchus' property (the witnesses at 7 do not testify to this). Furthermore, the speaker cites the law to demonstrate that Cyronides' alleged usurpation of the property was illegal (Is. 10.4, 10–11). She also observes that Phaenippus is said to have enjoyed the income of two estates, both that of his natural father Callippus and that of his adoptive father Philostratus (Dem. 42.21). But Phaenippus could have inherited both estates without breaking the law if his adoption by Philostratus occurred after the death of Callippus.

IV

Aspects of Procedure

IV.1 "In the Act" or "Red-Handed"? *Apagoge* to the Eleven and *Furtum Manifestum*

WHEN DEALING WITH CERTAIN TYPES OF COMMON CRIMINALS, THE LAWS OF ATHENS meted out harsh punishments. One of the most expeditious procedures for punishing criminals was called *apagoge* ("leading away" or arrest) to the Eleven, a board of magistrates selected by lot each year to run the prison in Athens. The *Constitution of the Athenians* (52.1) describes the procedure: "the Eleven punish with death those who are arrested as thieves (*kleptas*), enslavers (*andrapodistas*) and robbers (*lopodutas*) if they confess, while if they dispute the charge, they bring them before the court. If they are acquitted, the Eleven release them, and, if not, execute them." The arrest could be made by any Athenian provided one essential condition was met: the offender had to be taken ἐπ' αὐτοφώρῳ. For instance, when Dionysius, a private citizen, employed the *apagoge* procedure to arrest Agoratus, the Eleven insisted that Dionysius add the words *ep'autophoro* on the indictment presented to them (Lys. 13.85–7). In a speech of Isaeus (4.28), we are told Chariades was arrested as a thief *ep'autophoro* and thrown into prison. According to the speaker, the Eleven, who should have put him to death, were derelict in their duty and released him. For this failure to inflict the standard punishment, all the Eleven were executed that year. The story may be courtroom slander, but it nevertheless shows that the thief had to be taken *ep'autophoro* for the Eleven to execute him. Apollodorus ([Dem.] 45.81) alludes to the procedure when accusing Phormion of embezzling money from his father's bank. Apollodorus asks Phormion how he would have defended himself if he had been arrested and taken away as a thief caught *ep'autophoro*. Since Phormion was subject to this procedure, he should have been executed for his misdeed. Apollodorus presents us with a hypothetical argument, but takes for granted that the thief caught *ep'autophoro* was subject to capital punishment.

Scholars and translators have generally taken the phrase *ep'autophoro* to mean "in the act" or "*in flagrante delicto*."[1] A scholion on Aristophanes *Plutus* 455 appears to support this view: "obviously, in the very act." Yet the Suda (*s.v. ep'autophoro*) provides a different gloss: "self-evident, before one's eyes, caught with the stolen item itself." Did the felon have to be caught committing the crime or only with the stolen object in his possession? The second possibility would incline us to translate the phrase as "red-handed," which the *Oxford English Dictionary* defines as "having the evidences of guilt still upon the person." And was it necessary in *apagoge* to the Eleven for the criminal to be physically seized while committing the crime or in possession of the stolen object, or only that he be witnessed in those circumstances? A related question is, why were only three types of *kakourgoi*, namely thieves, enslavers, and robbers, explicitly listed as subject to this procedure? These are the questions this chapter will try to answer.

In regard to the main question, we find a fascinating clue in the *Institutes* of Justinian (4.1.3). This work equates the phrase *ep'autophoro* with the term *manifestus fur* in Roman Law. Justinian's *Institutes* were promulgated in 533 AD, but the same comparison of terms is found in a passage of Ulpian preserved in the *Digest* (47.2.3). I hasten to point out that Ulpian was murdered by his troops in 223 AD and thus wrote roughly five and a half centuries after the composition of the Aristotelian *Constitution of the Athenians*.[2] Yet it would be ill advised to dismiss Justinian's *Institutes* and Ulpian from the witness box without interrogating them further. After all, Justinian's *Institutes* and Ulpian drew on a long tradition of Roman jurisprudence reaching back to the Late Republic. Their sources were still not contemporary with Classical Athens, but the *iuris prudentes* of the Late Republic were typical members of the Roman upper classes and thus no doubt familiar with the Attic orators, who provided models for the forensic speeches delivered by the advocates they

[1] This is the translation endorsed by Cohen (1983) 52. Harrison (1971) 224 adopts the same translation. Cf. Gernet (1968) 129–30. Hansen (1976a) 48–53 believes that *ep'autophoro* originally meant "to catch the offender while the offense is being committed" or "during pursuit" and compares the third definition of *furtum manifestum* given by Gaius *Institutes* 3.184, but ignores the rest of Gaius' discussion. The term was later extended because it could also apply "if stolen goods were found during a house-search." For criticisms of Hansen's analysis, see Cohen (1983) 52–7. Hansen's view is followed by Rhodes (1981) 580–1. Latte (1968) 269–70 believes the term was later applied to "Entdeckung auf frischer, 'handhafter' Tat," but originally meant "auf Grund eigener Entdeckung."

[2] For the date of the *Constitution of the Athenians*, see Rhodes (1981) 51–8.

advised. Writers like Dionysius of Halicarnassus catered to this elite audience, producing literary essays on Demosthenes, Lysias, and others in the canon of the orators.[3] It would therefore be wrong to discard the statements found in Ulpian and Justinian as mere guesswork. The jurists whose works they consulted are quite likely to have read the works of Lysias and Demosthenes and to have come upon the phrase *ep'autophoro*. They may also have consulted commentaries on the orators by Alexandrian scholars like Didymus. Yet there is no guarantee that the sources of Ulpian and Justinian understood the phrase correctly when they read their Isaeus or Dinarchus. We should therefore treat their statement that *ep'autophoro* was similar in meaning to the term *fur manifestus* not as evidence of comparable value to the contemporary evidence of the Attic orators, but rather as a hypothesis that offers an approach to the study of the phrase. Like all hypotheses, their statements must be tested against the evidence found in the Classical period to determine whether it is valid or not.

Before proceeding to test this explanation against the evidence found in the orators, however, it is first necessary to understand precisely what the term *fur manifestus* means. Both Justinian and Gaius indicate there was some controversy about the criteria to be used when determining whether a thief was a *fur manifestus* or not. As we will see, there was general agreement about the basic sense of the term and its distinction from the *fur nec manifestus*. To understand the meaning of the term, therefore, we should look for the common element underlying the various positions taken by the jurists and examine the reasons for their divergent views. This will help us to understand exactly what the clue offered by Ulpian and Justinian tells us. What we should not do is to select arbitrarily one of these different views and label it the "correct" view, all others being rejected as erroneous, then use that view alone to interpret the phrase *ep'autophoro*.[4]

We need to preface our discussion with some general remarks about the nature of theft and how it differed from the other major offense against property in Roman Law, the delict of *damnum iniuria datum*, or "loss wrongfully inflicted." This delict was punishable under the *lex Aquilia* and applied to anyone who killed a slave or four-footed herd animal belonging to another person (*Digest* 9.2.2.pr) or who caused loss wrongfully by burning, breaking, or rending (*Digest* 9.2.27.5).

[3] Note that Dionysius dedicated his essay on Thucydides to Aelius Tubero, who is probably to be identified with the historian and jurist of the same name. See Bowersock (1965) 129–30.

[4] This mistake is made by Hansen (1976a) 49.

The act that created liability under the statute occurred at a given moment in time. Before that moment, the animal or slave was alive, or the object still intact. After that moment, the slave or animal is no longer alive, or the object is damaged and rendered less valuable or worthless to its owner. As a result, the offender normally does not abscond with the *corpus delicti*. Indeed, it would make little sense to drag away the slave's corpse or to collect the broken fragments of a shattered vase and wrap them in one's toga since they are no longer of any value. This is of some consequence when it comes to identifying the person who committed the *damnum*. If the person is not seen wreaking the damage by the owner or other witnesses, it is impossible to track him down. Any effort to convict the person who caused the damage and avoided detection would have to be convicted solely on circumstantial evidence. If not caught in the act of breaking a vase or slaying an ox, it would be difficult to prove that the offender was actually guilty of causing the damage. To borrow the language of the *kakourgoi* in the Reagan administration, the person who causes damage and avoids detection would enjoy "plausible deniability."

The job of tracking down a thief is potentially much easier. Unlike the delict of *damnum*, where the defendant does not retain possession of the *corpus delicti*, the essence of theft is that the defendant not only takes the stolen object, but also retains possession of it until he disposes of it. Even if the thief is not caught in the act of taking the stolen object, it is still possible to find him in possession of it at some later time. The person who is discovered with the stolen object may not be the actual thief – he may have bought the object unaware that it was stolen – but there is nonetheless a strong *prima facie* case against him. The burden of proof is on him to show that he obtained the object by some means other than removing it from the owner's possession. Whatever the manner by which he gained possession of the stolen object, he still cannot deny that he fulfills one of the major objective elements of wrongdoing. To establish his innocence he must produce the actual thief or in some other way show that he did not take the object from the owner's possession.

This brings us to Gaius' discussion of *furtum manifestum* (*Institutes*. 3.183–94), a passage that Justinian's *Institutes* draws on. Gaius' treatment of the term indicates that the jurists realized that the longer the period between the commission of the theft and the time when the stolen object was discovered in someone's possession, the greater the likelihood that the person in possession of the stolen object was not the person who removed it from the owner's possession (i.e., was not the actual thief). A thief knows that he will be caught if the object is found in his hands, so he normally tries to dispose of the object by trading it with someone. Or he may hide it in the woods or a cave where it might be found by some unsuspecting bypasser. This naturally led to a debate about the length of time beyond which a *furtum* was no longer *manifestum*.

Gaius enumerates four positions the jurists took on the issue. The narrowest definition is that the theft is manifest when the thief is taken in the act (184: *dum fit, deprehenditur*). Almost as restrictive is the next view, which holds that manifest theft occurs when the thief is taken in the place where the theft is committed (*eo loco deprehenditur, ubi fit*). Gaius gives three examples of cases covered by this definition. First, there is the man who steals olives from a grove of olive trees and is caught in the grove, second the man who steals grapes from a vineyard and is caught in the vineyard, and third, the man who steals objects from a house and is caught in the house. This helps to explain *eo loco*, which must refer to a piece of property. More inclusive is the view that *furtum* is *manifestum* when the thief is caught carrying the stolen object before he reaches the place where he planned to take it. To borrow the example cited above, this definition would cover the thief caught with stolen grapes after he left the vineyard. The final and most expansive definition is that the *furtum* is *manifestum* whenever the thief is seen carrying the stolen object.

Evidently all four views had their advocates, but Gaius says the widest definition did not gain widespread approval. Gaius also criticizes the third view that the *furtum* was *manifestum* as long as the thief was caught before he reached the place where he planned to bring the stolen object.[5] His objection is that those who held this view did not specify how long this criterion was to apply. He further notes that thieves often attempt to carry goods from one city to another. His implicit argument appears to be that it might be difficult to tell several days after the theft was committed whether the person caught taking the stolen object from one city to another was the actual thief. Hence his argument for a time-limit. Despite Gaius' objections, the *lanx et licium* procedure found in the Twelve Tables provides evidence for a broader definition of *furtum manifestum*. Gaius (*Institutes*. 3.192–4) himself says that the Twelve Tables allowed for the search through the house of a suspected thief provided one entered naked except for a dish (*lanx*) and a loin-cloth (*licium*).[6] If the stolen object was found on the premises, the suspect was judged

[5] This view was held by Ulpian (*Digest* 47.2.3.5) and Paul (*Digest* 47.2.4).

[6] The procedure disappeared as a result of the *lex Aebutia* of ca. 150 BCE (Aulus Gellius 16.10.8).

to have committed *furtum manifestum*. This points to a more expansive conception of *furtum manifestum* since here the thief has already deposited the stolen object in the place where he had planned to bring it.[7]

Gaius claims the second view had the most supporters, but Justinian's *Institutes* (4.1.1–3), which reports only the first three views and omits the fourth, appears to endorse the third view. There is also some difference of opinion as to whether the thief must be physically seized (*deprehenditur*) with the stolen object or only seen with it in his possession. Gaius appears to endorse the interpretation that the thief must be physically seized while holding the goods. The only place he uses the phrase *tenens visus* is when describing the fourth view, which he rejects. Justinian's *Institutes,* on the other hand, is more inclusive on this score: this work seems to side with the view that the *furtum* is *manifestum* when the thief is only seen with the stolen item (*quamdiu eam rem fur tenens visus vel deprehensus fuerit sive in publico sive in privato vel a domino vel ab alio antequam eo pervenit quo perferre ac deponere rem destinassit*).

What emerges from this debate is that what distinguished *furtum manifestum* from *furtum nec manifestum* is the nature of the evidence for the delict. The *fur manifestus* is the thief who has clearly or manifestly removed an object from the owner's possession. *Furtum nec manifestum* thus covered cases where it was not absolutely clear whether the person caught or observed in possession of the stolen object was the actual thief. *Furtum nec manifestum* could thus cover cases involving finders who made no attempt to locate an owner who had lost the object unwillingly and those who had received stolen goods.[8] The difference in evidence was accompanied by a major substantive difference. In *furtum manifestum* all the elements of the standard case were unquestionably present: it was clear (*manifestum*) that the offender had removed someone else's property (*rem alienam amovit*) in order to appropriate it (*intercipiendi causa*), then continued to "handle" it (*contrectat*) against the owner's will (*invito domino*) with fraudulent intention (*contrectatio fraudulosa*) to make a profit (*lucri*

[7] The *lanx et licium* procedure reveals that the jurists did not expand the limits of *furtum manifestum* implicit in the Twelve Tables, but may in fact have narrowed them. Thus de Zulueta (1953) 199, following de Visscher (1931) 137, is unlikely to be correct when he asserts that the third view listed by Gaius was "the primitive test."

[8] For finders liable for *furtum*, see *Digest* 47.2.43.4 and in general Powell (1959) 509–24. Note that Gaius *Institutes* 3.194 states that the *fur manifestus* must be the actual thief, but those who were not actual *fures* could still be held legally liable for *furtum* even if they had not committed the offense (*at illud sane lex facere potest, ut proinde aliquis poena teneatur atque si furtum . . . admississet, quamvis nihil eorum admiserit*).

faciendi gratia).[9] In *furtum nec manifestum* all the elements are definitely present except for one: it is uncertain whether the offender actually removed the object from the owner's possession.

The substantive difference provides the explanation for the difference between the penalties for the two kinds of *furtum*. Under the Twelve Tables, the penalty for *furtum manfestum* was capital: a free man was flogged, then made the *servus addictus* of the plaintiff. A slave found guilty on this charge was flogged and put to death (Gaius *Institutes* 3.189). Later, the Praetor reduced the penalty to a fourfold payment of the stolen object's value, but the possibility of harsher punishment remained if the plaintiff brought the thief before the *tresviri capitales* or other magistrates.[10] Since an important substantive element was missing in *furtum nec manifestum*, the penalty was only twice the value of the stolen object (Gaius *Institutes* 3.190; Justinian *Institutes* 4.1.5).[11]

Since "handling" (*contrectatio*) was the common element shared by both forms of theft in Roman Law, we can now understand why the Roman jurists considered this the key element in *furtum* and did not consider asportation necessary (Gaius *Institutes* 3.195: *furtum autem fit non solum cum quis intercipiendi causa rem alienam amovit*). *Furtum* was thus radically different from larceny in the Common Law, the key element of which is a trespassory taking.[12] This conclusion has major implications for our understanding of the way the jurists treated *furtum*, but my topic here is Athenian Law so I reserve that discussion for another occasion.

[9] Gaius *Institutes* 3.195. Cf. *Digest* 47.2.1.3 (Paul): *furtum est contrectatio rei fraudulosa lucri faciendi gratia vel ipsius rei vel etiam usus eius possessionisve*. See also Justinian *Institutes* 4.1.1.

[10] For the jurisdiction of the *tresviri capitales*, see W. Kunkel (1962) Chapter 12. For punishment *extra ordinem*, see *Digest* 47.2.57.1; 47.2.92.

[11] My analysis thus differs considerably from the traditional explanation of the distinction between *furtum manifestum* and *furtum nec manifestum*. The earliest example of the traditional view I have found is Maine (1861/1986) 315: "The ancient lawgiver doubtless considered that the injured proprietor, if left to himself, would inflict a very different punishment when his blood was hot from that with which he would be satisfied when the Thief was detected after a considerable interval; and to this calculation the legal scale of penalties was adjusted." A similar explanation is given by de Zulueta (1953) 199: "That by the basic *Twelve Tables* a thief caught in the act should have been dealt with more severely than one detected later requires no special Roman explanation. The explanation of this common primitive phenomenon is that in the case of flagrant theft the sufferer's indignation is hotter and also that the delinquent's guilt is certain."

[12] See the British Larceny Act of 1916: "A person steals who without consent of the owner, fraudulently and without a claim of right made in good faith, takes and carries away anything capable of being stolen with intent, at the time of such taking, permanently to deprive the owner thereof" (quoted in Powell [1959] 509).

For our purposes, the important thing to notice is the similarity between the law of the Twelve Tables and Athenian Law in regard to the penalties for theft. For *furtum manifestum* the penalty is *capitalis*; slaves are punished with execution, and free men with "social death," that is, enslavement.[13] The thief taken *ep'autophoro* and brought before the Eleven by *apagoge* is also punished with death. For *furtum nec manifestum* the penalty is double the value of the stolen object. The penalty on the *dike klopes* is the same (Dem. 24.105, 114). But was the substantive difference between the two procedures for theft in Athenian Law similar to the substantive difference between the two delicts in Roman Law? That depends on the meaning of *ep'autophoro*, the question we began this essay with. Now that we understand the meaning of the term *furtum manifestum*, we are in a position to compare it with the Greek phrase *ep'autophoro*. If the comparison of *furtum manifestum* with the phrase *ep'autophoro* made by Ulpian and repeated in Justinian's *Institutes* is correct, we should find that the phrase has the meaning of "clear," "obvious," or "manifest" in the passages where it is used. It should thus be found in passages describing situations where the evidence for the crime makes the offender's guilt "obvious." Conversely, it should emerge that the translation "in the act" is not an appropriate rendering for *ep'autophoro* in every passage where the phrase is used.

It is best to begin at the beginning of the term's history in Greek literature. The earliest attested uses of the phrase occur in two passages from Herodotus. The first is found in Herodotus' account of the downfall suffered by the Spartan king Leotychidas (6.72). During his campaign in Thessaly, Leotychidas had the opportunity of subduing the entire region, but instead accepted a large bribe of silver coins (ἐδωροδόκησε ἀργύριον πολλόν). He was caught *ep'autophoro* in his camp seated on a glove or, more likely, a long sleeve of a garment (χειρίδι) full of coins.[14] As a result, he was brought to trial and condemned to exile. Leotychidas was not caught in the act of taking the bribe since the discovery of his crime took place in the Spartan camp, and the money was found where Leotychidas had concealed it. The mere presence of silver coins in a garment does not appear incriminating to us, but we must bear in mind that the Spartans did not

[13] For this view of slavery, see Patterson (1982) 35–76.

[14] For the meaning of *cheiris*, see *Od.* 24.230; Xen. *Cyr.* 8.8.17; Xen. *Hell.* 2.1.8. The *cheiris* seems to have been larger than a glove and designed to cover both the hand and part of the arm.

mint silver coins in this period and banned or restricted the possession of gold and silver (Xen. *Lac. Pol.* 7.4–6).[15] For the Spartans, therefore, the mere possession of silver coins was strong *prima facie* evidence of wrongdoing. Coupled with his failure to conquer Thessaly when the opportunity presented itself, the money found in his garment was strong evidence that he had been bribed. The phrase *ep'autophoro* must mean that his *dorodokia* (bribery) was clear, not that he had been caught in the act of receiving money from the Thessalians in exchange for breaking off his campaign.

The other passage in Herodotus is his account of Onomarchus' departure from Athens. According to Herodotus (7.6.3), Onomarchus was dismissed by the tyrant Hipparchus after he was caught *ep'autophoro* by Lasus of Hermione in an act of forgery. Lasus accused Onomarchus of slipping into an oracle of Musaeus a verse of his own composition about the islands around Lemnos disappearing into the sea. It is improbable that Lasus secretly entered the room where Onomarchus was composing his forgery and watched as he placed the spurious verse in his edition of Musaeus. It is far more likely that Lasus detected the forgery by comparing a reliable copy of Musaeus' oracles with the bogus edition fabricated by Onomarchus. In other words, Lasus did not catch Onomarchus in the act, but rather had incontrovertible evidence that he had committed forgery. Once again, the best translation is "clearly" or "manifestly."[16]

Moving on to the Attic orators, we come upon the term in the account given by Aeschines (3.9–10) of the way in which corrupt politicians formerly avoided convictions for embezzlement of public funds. Aeschines uses the term in regard to magistrates who at their *euthynai* (rendering of accounts) are proven to have embezzled money (ἐπ᾽ αὐτοφώρῳ κλεπταὶ τῶν δημοσίων χρημάτων ἐξελεγχόμενοι). Under the *euthynai* procedure, every magistrate was required to submit an account of all the funds he had received and disbursed during his term of office (Aeschin. 3.14–24; [Arist.] *Ath. Pol.* 48.3–4). These sums were checked against the amount of money he handed on to his successor in office. If the sums did not tally, the magistrate

[15] Cf. Plb. 6.49.

[16] A de Sélincourt translates the phrase containing *ep'autophoro* thus: "Lasus of Hermione had caught him in the very act of the forgery." Yet in the story of Leotychidas he translates the phrase as "red-handed." Herodotus also uses the phrase at 6.137.3, but the context does not help to determine its meaning. The passages in Herodotus, being the earliest attested uses of the phrase, undermine any theory of development from a narrow meaning of the phrase to a broader one.

was "clearly" guilty of embezzlement.[17] Aeschines is not referring to magistrates who are caught in the act of taking public funds during their terms of office. He is talking about the *euthynai,* which took place after the magistrate left office and placed the funds under his control in the hands of his successor. Besides, a magistrate caught in the act of pilfering money entrusted to him would have been immediately deposed and would never have made it to his *euthynai.* We must again translate the phrase *ep'autophoro* as "clearly" or "obviously."

Dinarchus uses the phrase three times in his speech against Demosthenes and once in his speech against Aristogeiton, both delivered at trials arising out of the Harpalus affair. Harpalus was appointed Alexander's treasurer, but in 324 fled from Babylon with 5,000 talents and an army of 6,000 soldiers (D. S. 17.108.6). When he tried to obtain asylum with his troops in Athens, he was at first rebuffed, then later returned with only three ships and a large sum of money and allowed to enter the city ([Plu.] *Mor.* 846a). Soon afterwards, envoys came from Antipater and Olympias and demanded his surrender (D. S. 17.108.7). Demosthenes argued that the Athenians should surrender Harpalus only to ambassadors sent by Alexander (Hyp. *Dem.* col. 8), yet at the same time passed a motion to have Harpalus arrested and his money deposited on the Acropolis (Din. 1.89). Harpalus declared the entire sum to amount to 700 talents, but the total amount was later discovered to be only 350 talents (Hyp. *Dem.* cols. 9–11). Harpalus was later allowed to escape, collected the troops he had left at Taenarum, and fled to Crete where he was murdered (Hyp. *Dem.*, col. 12; D. S. 17.108.7–8). Suspicion of bribery fell on Demosthenes, who declared his innocence and proposed that Areopagus investigate the matter (Hyp. *Dem.* col. 2; Din. 1.61). The Areopagus was either very thorough or very leisurely in its work, for it took six months to complete its report (Din. 1.45). The final report listed the names of those who had taken money and the amounts they had received (Hyp. *Dem.* cols. 5–6). Demosthenes and Aristogeiton were among those named. Ten prosecutors were appointed by the Assembly (Din. 2.6), and the accused were tried in court.

Dinarchus wrote speeches for the men who prosecuted Demosthenes and Aristogeiton. In the speech *Against Demosthenes* (1.29), the prosecutor urges the court

[17] For other passages where *kleptes, kleptein,* and *klope* are used in the context of embezzlement, see Aeschin. 1.110–11, 113; [Arist.] *Ath. Pol.* 54.2; Ar. *Eq.* 436, 444, 1224, 1226; Dem. 22.65; 24.112; 27.29, 40, 48; 58.15; Din. 1.70; Lys. 27.11. Cohen (1983) 30–3 attempts to explain this evidence away, but his arguments are not convincing.

not to acquit Demosthenes, who was caught *ep'autophoro* holding gifts against the interest of the city. From what we know of the Harpalus affair, Demosthenes was not caught in the act of receiving gifts from the Macedonian. The investigation into the whereabouts of the money took place after Harpalus left Athens. The prosecutor is referring to the conclusion of the report delivered by the Areopagus, which declared that Demosthenes had received money from Harpalus (Hyp. *Dem.* cols. 5–6). As the speaker says, the evidence they had was the money that was in his possession (δῶρα ἔχοντα). We do not know whether the Areopagus actually entered Demosthenes' house and came upon the money or relied on the testimony of witnesses. Whatever their evidence, the Areopagus could not have arrested Demosthenes caught in the act of taking gifts. Later on in the speech (53–4), the prosecutor states that in the view of the entire Areopagus Demosthenes was caught taking money *ep'autophoro*. Still further on in the speech (77), Demosthenes is called an *ep'autophoro* thief and traitor. In a similar fashion, Aristogeiton is also said to have been caught *ep'autophoro* holding gifts contrary to the interests of the city (Din. 2.6). In all four passages, the best translation is "clearly" or "obviously."

Not surprisingly, the phrase lent itself to some rhetorical abuse at the hands of overzealous prosecutors. Like scholars, prosecutors often buttress a frail argument by claiming weak evidence "clearly" or "obviously" proves their point. When prosecuting Aeschines in 343 for treason, Demosthenes had a notoriously weak case and had to prove his charge by circumstantial evidence.[18] That does not prevent him from asserting that the evidence reveals Aeschines to be a traitor *ep'autophoro*. Demosthenes (19.121–3) recounts how Aeschines tried to avoid going on the Third Embassy to Philip after Demosthenes, who had been a member of the First and Second Embassies to Philip, declined to participate on this occasion. Demosthenes nowhere accuses Aeschines of receiving a bribe during the Third Embassy – that allegedly took place during the Second Embassy (Dem. 19.166–8). The reason Demosthenes brings up Aeschines' initial refusal to go on the Third Embassy is that it reveals Aeschines was afraid his opponent would expose his plot and persuade the Athenians to thwart Philip's plans while he was away. For Demosthenes this anxiety constitutes "clear" proof (*ep'autophoro* – ἐξελέγξει) that Aeschines had taken bribes (δεδωροδοκηκότ'). The translation "in the act" does not fit the context.

[18] For the weakness of Demosthenes' charge, see Harris (1995) Chapter 5.

The phrase *ep'autophoro* is found also in the speech Apollodorus delivered against Stephanus ([Dem.] 45.81). In the passage in question, Apollodorus addresses Phormion and accuses him of embezzling money from his father Pasion. Phormion had been the manager of Pasion's bank (49.17, 60) and continued to run it under a leasing agreement (Dem. 36.4–10, 37).[19] Apollodorus describes a hypothetical situation: what if I were to put all the property you stole from my father's bank on your back and led you away as an *ep'autophoro* thief? Where would you say you received the money from? Apollodorus is not describing the possibility of catching Phormion in the act of embezzling funds.[20] That was no longer possible since Phormion had ceased to be manager of the bank many years ago. Apollodorus claims that Phormion is still in possession of the embezzled funds and threatens to pile them on his back and drag him to the Eleven. This money allegedly taken from the bank would then serve as incriminating evidence. To defend himself, Phormion would have to produce another person willing to state that he gave Phormion the money (*anagoge*).[21] The threat is imaginary, but the hypothetical arrest is to be made on the grounds that Phormion's guilt is made "obvious" by his possession of the money. Were Phormion to be seized, he would be just like the *fur manifestus* caught with stolen goods.

These texts make it manifest, clear, and obvious that *ep'autophoro* should be translated "manifest," "clear," or "obvious." In fact, Lysias (1.21) appears to gloss the phrase with the word *phaneron* – "obvious." "In the act" does not work as a translation in the passages we have examined.[22] The next question to be answered is whether being caught *ep'autophoro* means being physically seized with incriminating evidence or only witnessed in highly incriminating circumstances. The most illuminating passage for this question is in the speech Aeschines delivered against Timarchus in late 346.[23] As is widely recognized, Aeschines' case against Timarchus was quite weak.[24] In the absence of any witnesses to Timarchus' alleged prostitution, Aeschines had to convict his opponent by resorting to the court's

[19] On Pasion's bank, see Harris (1988a) (= Chapter III.4 in this volume).

[20] Cohen (1983) 57 has not read the passage carefully and thinks that Apollodorus is addressing Stephanus.

[21] On the *anagoge* procedure, see Wyse (1904/1979) 436.

[22] For other passages where the translation "in the act" is inappropriate, see Aeschin. 2.88; Dem. 19.132; 23.157; 39.26; Lys. 7.42. Note the phrase is often used with the verb ἐλέγχειν: Aeschin. 3.10; Dem. 19.121, 293; 23.157; Lys. 7.42; 13.30 (cf. Aeschin. 2.88 [δείξαιμι]; Dem. 39.26 [ἐπιδεικνύει]). One "clearly" or "obviously" shows or proves something – once again, the translation "in the act" does not fit the context.

[23] For the date of the speech, see Harris (1985).

[24] See Harris (1995) Chapter 5.4.

knowledge of rumors and innuendo. Aeschines tries to get the court to believe that Timarchus' entire lifestyle bears witness against him, so there is no need of witnesses to prove his guilt. Aeschines complains that it is unfair to demand him to call witnesses. He argues that if only those crimes that can be proven by the testimony of witnesses are punished, those who commit misdeeds without being detected will never be brought to justice. Aeschines gives the examples of robbers (*lopoduton*), seducers (*moichon*), thieves (*klepton*), and murderers (*androphonon*).[25] Those who are *halontes*, which can mean both "physically seized" or "detected" (the Greek verb has the same ambiguity as the English verb "caught"), and confess, are executed. Those who avoid detection and deny their guilt are tried in court and the truth is established ἐκ τῶν εἰκότων – "from the probabilities" (C. D. Adams in the Loeb translation translates this "from circumstantial evidence"). The *ep'autophoro* criminal is thus contrasted with the one who escapes detection and is convicted not by the testimony of those who witnessed him committing the crime, but by what is generally known about his character and conduct. Since the *ep'autophoro* criminal is set opposite this kind of criminal, he must be one whose guilt is clearly established by eyewitness testimony.

Where the Athenians drew the line between *ep'autophoro* or manifest guilt and guilt determined *ek ton eikoton* is not altogether clear. Indeed, there may have been some debate about where to draw the line, just as there existed differences of opinion in Roman Law about how to define *furtum manifestum*. That does not imply that the Athenians did not understand the term *ep'autophoro* or that the Romans did not understand the term *furtum manifestum*. All this reveals is that Athenian Law and Roman Law, like all legal systems, possessed what H. L. A. Hart calls an "open texture."[26] Although the basic idea expressed by each term was essentially well understood by those who used them, some debate might inevitably arise about how to apply them in particular circumstances. These were the "hard cases" where some might argue that the evidence was incontrovertible and clear, yet others might disagree.

Our examination of the term *ep'autophoro* shows that the statement of Ulpian is basically correct: the term is equivalent to the word *manifestum* in *furtum manifestum*.

[25] One should not use this passage as evidence for the kinds of offenders subject to *apagoge* to the Eleven – see the Appendix to Chapter 3.1. Cohen (1991a) 111–12 repeats this mistake, which invalidates much of his analysis of the punishment of adultery at Athens.

[26] Hart (1961) 120–32. The term "open texture" is misunderstood by Osborne (1985).

The next question to answer is whether the contrast between *furtum manifestum* and *furtum nec manifestum* in Roman Law is similar to the contrast between the type of theft punished by *apagoge* to the Eleven (κλοπὴ ἐπ' αὐτοφώρῳ) and that punished by the *dike klopes*. As we noted earlier, in *furtum manifestum* there must be strong evidence that the defendant actually removed the stolen object from the plaintiff's possession, whereas in *furtum nec manifestum* it was necessary to prove only that the plaintiff owned the stolen object and that the defendant held it contrary to the plaintiff's will (*cum quis alienam rem invito domino contrectat*). In similar fashion, the *kleptes ep'autophoro* in Athenian Law was the one who has manifestly removed the stolen object from the owner's possession. But for conviction on the *dike klopes*, it appears that the plaintiff was required to show only that he had lost possession of the object and that the defendant had it in his possession. This follows from the wording of the statute for the *dike klopes* (Dem. 24.105): the procedure is available for whatever someone loses (ὅ τι ἂν τις ἀπολέσῃ).[27]

Just as there existed a major substantive difference between *furtum manifestum* and *furtum nec manfestum*, there was also a similar difference between the type of theft punished by *apagoge* to the Eleven and that punished by the *dike klopes*. This in turn explains the difference in penalties between the two offenses: for conviction in the *apagoge* procedure the penalty is death, in the *dike klopes* only double the amount of the stolen object, the same as the penalty in *furtum nec manifestum*. Since in both the *dike klopes* and *furtum nec manifestum* asportation is either not present or cannot be proven, the penalty is less.[28]

So far we have only considered the type of thief (*kleptes*) subject to *apagoge* to the Eleven. In addition to thieves, however, one could punish two other categories of offender by this procedure: *andrapodistai* and *lopodutai* ([Arist.] *Ath. Pol.* 52.1). What did these three categories have in common? Before looking for the answer to this question, it is necessary to determine the meaning of the two other terms. The meaning of *andrapodistes* poses no problem: the word refers to the person who

[27] Cf. Cohen (1983) 62–8.

[28] Cohen (1983) 52–61 is incorrect when he considers *klope ep'autophoro* to be "aggravated theft." Aggravation requires violence or the threat of violence. But just as violence was not a required element in the *Tatbestand* of *furtum manifestum*, there is no evidence showing that the *kleptes ep'autophoro* was necessarily one who employed violence. In fact, the passages where the phrase is used to describe embezzlers prove the contrary. In both Roman Law (Gaius *Institutes* 3.209) and Athenian Law (Dem. 21.44), aggravated theft was dealt with under a separate statute. One of the major flaws in Cohen's analysis is his tendency to confuse the concept of "flagrance" and "aggravation." Cf. MacDowell (1985) 230.

makes a free person into a slave. But what is the difference between *kleptai* and *lopodutai*, which I have translated above as "robbers" for the sake of convenience? It is unlikely that the two terms denote the same type of offender, or that one term refers to a general class of offender, while the other refers to a subset of the general class. If that were the case, only one of the two terms would stand in the law.

The difference between the two terms appears to relate to the manner of acquiring the stolen object. In his definition of theft in the *Rhetoric* (1374a), Aristotle includes stealth (λάθρᾳ) as one of the elements of the offense. The passages where the verb *kleptein* and the nouns *klope* and *kleptes* are used tend to bear him out (Ar. *Eq.* 109–11 [while the owner sleeps], *Vesp.* 237–9 [λαθόντ'], *Ec.* 26–7 [λαθεῖν]; Dem. 24.114 [ὑφέλοιτο used as variant of κλέπτοι]). The frequent use of these verbs in cases of embezzlement provides further support for Aristotle's definition. Finally, one should note that the verb can also mean "deceive" (Hom. *Il.* 1.132; 14.217; Pindar *Pythian* 3.29; 4.29; Hesiod *Theogony* 613; Aeschin. 3.35, 142, 200) and is used to describe cases of fraud (Aeschin. 3.146; Ar. *Pax* 1232–34 with the *scholion ad loc.*; Sophocles *Philoctetes* 75–8, 1271–2).

Lopodusia, the crime of the *lopodutes,* is an open taking. The basic meaning of the noun *lopodutes* is one who strips off someone's clothing. The meaning is well illustrated in the case described in Demosthenes' speech *Against Conon* (Dem. 54.1, 8, 24), where Ariston describes how the defendant knocked him down and yanked his clothes from him (8: ἐξέδυσαν). A passage from Aristophanes *Birds* (496–8) describes a similar situation and labels the offender a *lopodutes.*

The element common to all three offenses is that in each case the offender absconds with the *corpus delicti* and can thus be caught after the commission of his offense "red-handed," that is, with the *corpus delicti* in his possession. The *kleptes* can be caught after the theft with the stolen object on his person or in his house. The *andrapodistes* can be found with the free person whom he has enslaved chained up on his property.[29] And the *lopodutes* can be arrested with the clothing he has snatched from his victim. It is therefore not surprising that *moichoi,* those who have consensual sexual relations with women without the approval of their *kyrios,* are not included in the list of *kakourgoi* subject to *apagoge* to the Eleven. Unlike the other

[29] Two of the cases mentioned in Din. 1.23 are probably punishments for enslavement. Menon, a miller, was put to death for placing a free youth from Pallene in his mill. Work in a mill was considered a punishment fit for slaves (Lys. 1.18; Eur. *Cyclops* 240; Dem. 45.33; Men. *Heros* 3). Euthymachus was executed for putting an Olynthian girl in a brothel (*ep'oikematos*). This too was an activity associated with slaves – see [Dem.] 59.18–23.

offenses, there is no "clear" or "manifest" evidence for *moicheia* after the offense has been committed.[30]

Two important methodological points emerge from this study of theft in Athenian Law. First, it is better to seek parallels for Athenian legal practices and ideas in the law of the early Roman Republic than in the Common Law of the late Medieval and Early Modern England. The social and economic environment of Rome at the time of the Twelve Tables was much more similar to that of Classical Athens than England at the time of Bracton or in the period when the Carrier's Case was decided. The development of commerce in Early Medieval England led to the creation of possessorial immunity in the Common Law. This in turn led to strict distinction between larceny, which required a trespassory taking, and embezzlement.[31] D. Cohen has tried to read this distinction into the Athenian evidence, but, as our study has shown, *klope* extended far beyond larceny to include embezzlement and fraud.[32] The absence of such a distinction and of the concept of possessorial immunity in Athenian Law is not surprising given the level of social and economic organization.

Second, one should use analogies from Roman Law only as hypotheses. A concept in Roman Law may help us to understand some aspect of Athenian Law or it may not. The only way to find out is to treat the Roman concept as a hypothesis, which is then tested against the evidence with the same philological rigor that one needs to apply whenever one reads an ancient Greek text. What one should not do is to assume that an idea drawn from Roman Law provides "the key" to solving a problem in Athenian Law simply on the basis of some superficial similarity in vocabulary. For instance, the use of the term *hypotheca* in the *Digest* has led many scholars to assume that this form of security was similar to the Athenian *hypotheke* and to infer that the Athenians, like the Romans, possessed two or more different forms of real security. In this case, the analogy drawn from Roman Law turns out to be seriously misleading and has caused scholars like M. I. Finley and J. V. A. Fine to search for distinctions between different forms of real security

[30] For this reason, different rules applied for *moichoi*. The *kyrios* of the woman could kill the *moichos*, but had to discover him "on top of" the woman – see Lys. 1.30. This argument strengthens the case for rejecting the idea of Cohen (1991a) 111–12 that the law about *apagoge* to the Eleven made *moichoi* subject to the procedure. I owe this point to Professor Alberto Maffi.

[31] On the importance of possessorial immuity in Common Law, see Fletcher (1978) 81–3.

[32] Cohen (1983) 10–33.

in Athenian Law that did not exist. But in regard to theft, the analogy between the *fur manifestus* and the *kleptes ep'autophoro* is very fruitful and helps us understand why certain types of offenders were subject to *apagoge* to the Eleven, and others were not.

Finally, our analysis of theft in Athenian Law demonstrates the value of examining substantive issues when studying different types of Athenian legal procedures. It was not social factors that account for the variety of legal procedures in Athenian Law. The procedure was made to fit the crime, not the social status of the plaintiff.[33]

Afterthoughts

The conclusions of this essay are accepted by Kapparis (1996) 72 note 19, MacDowell (2000) 254, Fisher (2001) 225–6, and Carey (2004). Carey develops at greater length the general point made in the final paragraph of this essay that there were major substantive differences between various procedures in Athenian Law. On Cohen (1983) compare the criticisms of Bauman (1996) 55: "Cohen's full-length study dots too many i's, crosses too many t's, devotes too little space to conceptualization, and rigorously avoids any comparison with Roman law, although comparing English law with misguided enthusiasm."

Pepe (no date) argues for the traditional translation of *ep'autophoro* ("in the act") on the basis of passages like Men. *Misoumenos* 218 (where the phrase can be translated as "in the act" but has also been translated as "red-handed" by Arnott in his Loeb edition), but does not examine the use of the term in passages like Eur. *Ion* 1214; Hdt. 6.72, Aeschin. 3.9–10; Din. 1.29, 77; 2.9; Dem. 19.121–3, and [Dem.] 45.81, where it is impossible to use the translation that she proposes. In fact, I can find no reference to any of these passages in her *Indice delle fonti*. She also claims that at Antiphon 1.3, where the speaker says that the stepmother was caught *ep'autophoro* several times plotting the death of her husband, "la donna, si specifica, era stata sorpresa dal padre dell'accusatore proprio sul fatto di preparare delle pozioni, con le quali, verosimilimente, mirava ad avvelenarlo." She then refers to Antiphon 1.9, where it appears that the father had indeed caught the stepmother trying to give

[33] Osborne (1985) argues on the basis of Dem. 22.26–7 that the Athenians created different types of procedures to suit the different social positions of potential litigants and that substantive differences were not important. This study has, I hope, shown how mistaken such an approach is. On the issue of real security in Athenian Law, see Harris (1988b) (= Chapter II.2 in this volume) and Harris (1993) (= Chapter II.3 in this volume).

him a love potion. But she does not discuss the rest of the speech, especially the section (14–20) where the accuser says that the stepmother instructed a slave to pour a potion, allegedly containing poison, into some wine and to give it to Philoneus and her husband. Philoneus died immediately, and the husband twenty days later. The slave was then tortured and, presumably after confessing, put to death. In this case the stepmother was not caught in the act of giving the poison to her husband nor in the act of giving orders to the slave. Her guilt only became "obvious" after the deaths of Philoneus and her husband (for a similar case of "obvious" guilt in a case of poisoning see Eur. *Ion* 1214, which is discussed in the next chapter). Pepe (no date) 102–3 note 146 also claims that I have not discussed Aeschines 1.90–1 but appears to have overlooked my analysis of the passage in this essay as well as the discussion in Harris (1990a) 376–7. In general, Pepe tends to examine only those passages that support her thesis and to ignore the evidence that contradicts it.

IV.2 How to Kill in Attic Greek: The Semantics of the Verb (ἀπο)κτείνειν and Their Implications for Athenian Homicide Law

RECENTLY THERE HAS BEEN CONSIDERABLE DEBATE AMONG SCHOLARS ABOUT THE jurisdiction of the different courts that tried cases of homicide in Classical Athens. Much of the debate has focused on the distinction between homicide committed by one's own hand (αὐτοχείρ) and homicide accomplished by plotting or planning (βουλεύσας). For instance, Gagarin (1990) argues that it made little or no difference whether the accused had brought about the death of his victim by his own hand or merely by plotting. Thür (1991) and MacDowell (1963), on the other hand, claim that cases where the defendant was accused only of plotting to kill were tried at the Palladion, not at the Areopagus. This chapter will reexamine these issues but will approach the evidence from a different angle. In the past scholars have treated the issue of jurisdiction as essentially a question of procedure.[1] This chapter will begin instead by examining a substantive issue, namely, the semantics of the Attic verb (ἀπο)κτείνειν. A better understanding of the meaning of this word will help to resolve some of the controversies about the jurisdiction of the Areopagus and the Palladion.

The verb (ἀπο)κτείνειν appears to present no problems with translation; as any standard lexicon states, the verb means "to kill" in English, "tuer" in French,

[1] This is a result of the traditional assumption that Athenian Law was mostly concerned with procedural matters. For the traditional view, see, for example, Hansen (1975) 10; Todd (1993) 64f; Cohen (1995) 190. Carey (1998) rightly questions the traditional assumption that "Athenian law was primarily procedural in its orientation." If the arguments in this chapter are convincing, they lend additional support to Carey's criticism of the *communis opinio*.

"uccidere" in Italian, and "töten" in German. But the verb "to kill" in English is an unusual one. For all transitive verbs such as "to hit," "to see," or "to break" there is normally an agent and an object. If John hits Frank, that is, strikes him with his hand, we can immediately say "John hit Frank." We do not have to wait to discover whether Frank has been hit by that person or not. If John hits a vase, it either shatters immediately or it does not, so we can tell very quickly whether he is responsible for breaking the vase. But it is not so easy with the verb "to kill." If John stabs Frank now and then as a result of his wound Frank immediately dies, there can be no doubt that John has killed Frank. But what if John stabs Frank now, and then as a result of his wound he dies next Thursday? Next Thursday we will be able to assert confidently that John killed Frank. But what are we to say about John between now and Thursday?

The reason why we are uncertain about how to describe John's stabbing of Frank between now and next Thursday is because the verb "to kill" involves essentially three elements: an action by the agent (striking in this case), a change of state in the victim (from life to death), and a causal relationship between the agent's action and the change of state in the victim (the blow brought about massive bleeding, which led to the victim's death).[2] This change of state in the victim can occur immediately – Frank dies immediately – or at some subsequent point in time – Frank dies next Thursday, or next month. This makes the verb "to kill" very different from the verbs "to break" or "to hit." If John strikes a vase, it either breaks when he strikes it or it does not. We do not have to wait until next week until we can say John has broken the vase. But if John strikes Frank, we may have to be patient and wait until the necessary change of state occurs in Frank to declare "John has killed Frank."

This has major consequences. It means that the verb "to kill" in English means essentially "to be responsible for the death of some other person or animal." Normally, we employ the verb in cases where there is direct physical causality. It is also permissible to use the verb in cases where the action of the agent is more remotely related to the death of the victim. A person who gives a victim poison, which that person believes to be a harmless drug, can be said to have killed. Or we say that "Stalin killed the kulaks." Obviously, the General Secretary of the Communist Party did not get his hands dirty liquidating thousands of peasants,

[2] For these three elements in homicide, see Fletcher (1978) 355.

but had the work performed by his agents. We say "Stalin killed the kulaks" because we believe Stalin was responsible for the deaths of these kulaks by issuing orders that resulted in their deaths.

This is not merely a *façon de parler*. The German courts recently found Egon Krenz, the former leader of East Germany, guilty of manslaughter for the shooting deaths of people trying to cross the Berlin Wall (*The New York Times*, August 26, 1997, page A6). Krenz had no direct role in the shootings and "prosecutors presented no evidence that Mr. Krenz or his associates had ordered any shootings or that they had directly supervised activities of the border patrols." Krenz and two associates, Günther Shabowski and Günther Kleiber, were found guilty simply because "they were in charge of overall government policy." The main evidence the prosecutors brought forward proved only "that Politburo members were always informed about shootings at the borders." Beyond that, the prosecutors pointed to "Politburo documents containing praise for the border patrols." Even though Krenz and his associates were responsible only for formulating a policy that led to fatal shootings, they were nevertheless held responsible for these killings and convicted of manslaughter.

What about the verb ἀποκτείνειν? Did it encompass killings only by direct physical causality, or did it cover all cases of causing death? Should it be translated by the English verb "to slay," usually employed in contexts where the agent uses direct physical force to bring about the death of the victim? Or should we translate the Attic verb with the English verb "to kill"? This may seem like a fine point of philology, but it has far-reaching consequences, as we will soon see.

Let us begin with an example from tragedy. In the prologue of Euripides' *Hippolytus*, the vindictive Aphrodite predicts that Hippolytus' father Theseus will kill (κτενεῖ) the young man by means of curses (ἀραῖσιν) that Poseidon has granted to him (43–6). As the plot unfolds, we find that Theseus, upon reading Phaedra's note that Hippolytus has raped her, calls down curses on his son, who immediately leaves in a horse-drawn chariot. A few miles out of Troezen a monster rises from the sea, frightening the horses, who bolt and drag Hippolytus until he is fatally injured (1211–46). Theseus never lays a hand on Hippolytus, yet at the end of the play Artemis declares that he has killed his son (1287: ἀποκτείνας; 1320–4: παῖδ' οὐχ ὁσίως σὸν ἀπέκτεινας/ κατέκανες. Cf. Hippolytus' words at 1413). Theseus certainly believes he is guilty of murder since he asks Hippolytus to absolve him and thus release him from the pollution that would ensue if he were to remain unforgiven (1448–50):

Theseus: Will you die leaving my hand unclean?
(ἦ τὴν ἐμὴν ἄναγνον ἐκλιπὼν χέρα;)
Hippolytus: No indeed, since I will free you of [responsibility for] murder.
(οὐ δῆτ', ἐπεί σε τοῦδ' ἐλευθερῶ φόνου.)[3]
Theseus: What are you saying? Do you release me from the taint of blood?
(τί φῄς; ἀφίης αἵματός μ' ἐλεύθερον;)

In Aeschylus' *Agamemnon* we find the verb used to describe the action of a person who brings about death by plotting. Aegisthus plots with his lover Clytemnestra to kill Agamemnon, but Clytemnestra alone carries out the murder, whereas Aegisthus is outside the house (1608: θυραῖος ὢν. Cf. 1635: δρᾶσαι τόδ' ἔργον *οὐκ* ἔτλης *αὐτοκτόνως* and 1644: *οὐκ αὐτὸς* ἠνάριζες). Despite his absence, Aegisthus boasts to the chorus that he plotted the entire murder. The chorus is shocked at his boastful arrogance and cannot believe their ears. They ask him if he really claims to have willingly killed Agamemnon and to have been solely responsible for plotting his death (1613–14: σὺ δ' ἄνδρα τόνδε φῂς ἑκὼν *κατακτανεῖν*/ μόνος δ' ἔποικτον τόνδε *βουλεῦσαι* φόνον). Aegisthus disagrees with the chorus on several matters but does not differ with them on this point. In this passage the man who plots successfully is also said to have killed despite the fact that he did not touch the victim.[4]

One might argue that this is an extended use of the verb κτείνειν only used in poetry, but this usage is also well attested in prose. Aeschines (1.173) addresses the Athenians, saying "you killed Socrates the sophist," yet we know from Plato's *Phaedo* that Socrates drank hemlock. The members of the court were responsible for the death of Socrates by passing a sentence of death on him. Aeschines (2.77) says the Thirty Tyrants killed (ἀπέκτειναν) 1,500 citizens. The Thirty obviously did not slay all these citizens with their own hands, but sentenced them to death. Aeschines (3.224) says Demosthenes killed (ἀπέκτεινας) the alleged spy

[3] The use of the word φόνος in this passage undermines the view of Thür (1991) 55 that "both offenses, *phonos* as well as *trauma*, could have one element in common: the direct use of one's own hands." Note also Antiphon 6.9, 36, where the speaker is accused of *phonos* although he did not touch the victim with his own hands. For discussion of the charge in this case, see below.

[4] Gagarin (1990) 94 notes that "there are parallels in ordinary (non-legal, non-rhetorical) Greek for the designation of the planner as the killer" and cites Euripides *Medea* 486–7.

Anaxinus: Demosthenes (18.137) admits that he was responsible for having him executed because he arrested him and accused him of spying. Aeschines (3.243) says Iphicrates killed a unit of Lacedaemonian soldiers. Iphicrates is unlikely to have dispatched each enemy soldier by himself; he obviously led the troops that defeated the Lacedaemonian troops. In other words, his leadership was responsible for their deaths. Andocides (1.66) addresses the Athenians and says "you killed" (ἀπεκτείνατε) Diocleides by handing him over to a court. In this case the Athenian people were responsible for the death of Diocleides by having him brought to trial. Andocides (2.7) describes the position he found himself in after being denounced for profanation of the Mysteries. If he refused to name those actually guilty, he would kill (ἀποκτεῖναι) his own father. On the other hand, if he were to denounce them, he would avoid becoming the killer (φονέα γένεσθαι) of his own father. This extended meaning of the verb occurs not only in everyday prose but also in legal texts. Andocides (1.95–8) cites an Athenian law against tyranny containing an oath sworn by all Athenians: I will kill both by word and by deed and by vote and by my own hand (κτενῶ καὶ λόγῳ καὶ ἔργῳ καὶ ψήφῳ καὶ τῇ ἐμαυτοῦ χειρὶ) all tyrants. One cannot therefore argue that the verb had one meaning in everyday speech, but a more narrow, technical meaning in Athenian statutes.

Two passages show that the Athenians were well aware of the substantive implications of the meaning of the verb. First, Andocides (1.94) states that the man who planned murder is liable to the same treatment as the man who accomplished the deed with his own hand (τὸν βουλεύσαντα ἐν τῷ αὐτῷ ἐνέχεσθαι καὶ τὸν τῇ χειρὶ ἐργασάμενον). As Gagarin (1990) 93 points out, this means not merely that both were "liable to the same penalty" (MacDowell [1963] 66), but liable to the same treatment in all respects. Second, Draco's homicide law (*IG* i³ 104.11–13) begins with the phrase καὶ ἐὰμ [μ]ὲ 'κ [π]ρονο[ία]ς [κ]τ[ένει τίς τινα . . .], then glosses the verb with the phrase αἴτ[ι]ον φό[νο] in exactly the way Andocides (2.7) explained the verb. According to Stroud's widely accepted supplement, the law goes on to state that its provisions apply to "the man who did the deed or plotted" [. . . τὸν ἐργασάμενον] ἒ [β]ολεύσαντα (Wolff suggested ἢ τὸν αὐτόχειρα ἢ τὸν] βολεύσαντα).[5] This indicates that the Athenians already

[5] For a clear and sensible discussion of the text, see Gagarin (1981a) 37–41. This clause is alluded to at Antiphon 4.2.6: ἀπολύει δέ με καὶ ὁ νόμος καθ' ὃν διώκομαι. Τὸν γὰρ ἐπιβουλεύσαντα κελεύει φονέα εἶναι. Gagarin (1981a) 17 perceptively notes "the fact that Orestes takes revenge on both Klytaimnestra and Aigisthos" at *Od.* 11.422–30 "seems to indicate that an accomplice or conspirator in a homicide case was considered equally liable" already in the period of the Homeric epics.

understood the substantive implications of the verb (ἀπο)κτείνειν in the Archaic period. Contrary to the assumptions of some scholars, this phrase reveals that the early Greek lawgivers were not just interested in procedural questions, but also appreciated the importance of substantive issues when formulating their statutes.

Plato also recognized the implications of the verb in his *Laws* (872a–d). In his lawcode for Magnesia, the one who plots death against another and is responsible for bringing about death as a result of his planning (τῇ βουλήσει τε καὶ ἐπιβουλεύσει ἀποκτείνας) is also considered polluted (μὴ καθαρὸς τὴν ψυχὴν τοῦ φόνου). The same procedures apply against the man who planned homicide as against the man who kills with his own hand except in regard to personal security. The person who plans a murder is also subject to the same penalties as the man who kills with his own hand except in regard to burial. Plato obviously bases this provision on the principle of Athenian Law stated by Andocides: the man who kills with his own hand and the one who plans murder are both subject to the same treatment. Since Plato makes both kinds of offenders subject to the same procedures and the same penalties and since he clearly bases this provision on Athenian Law, this supports Gagarin's interpretation of the Andocides' passage as applying both to procedure and to penalty.[6]

The Athenians carefully distinguished between killing brought about by direct physical action and killing that could be referred to by the verbs κτείνειν and ἀποκτείνειν. The best example is from Plato's *Euthyphro* (4b7–e1). Euthyphro describes how a dependent of his father became drunk and slew (ἀποσφάττει) one of their slaves. His father bound the killer and threw him in a ditch, then sent a man off to the Exegetes to find out what to do. The killer in the meantime died of hunger, cold, and his shackles. Euthyphro consequently brought a charge against his father "since he killed" (ὅτι ἀπέκτεινεν). What is interesting is that Euthyphro appears to distinguish between the act of the dependent, who slew, that is, killed by direct physical violence, and the action of his father, who caused the death of the dependent. Although his father did not bring about the dependent's death by bloodshed, Euthyphro still considers his father guilty of homicide and brings a formal charge against him.

A passage from Lysias' *Against Agoratus* shows that Athenians might allow the causal chain to be stretched a good distance when it came to accepting homicide cases. According to the speaker, Agoratus denounced to the Council several

[6] Gagarin (1990) 93f.

men who were later executed. Among these men was the speaker's brother-in-law Dionysodorus (Lys. 13.41–2; note how the speaker uses the expressions αἴτιος ἦν τοῦ θανάτου and τὸν πατέρα αὐτοῦ Ἀγόρατος ἀπέκτεινε interchangeably). When the speaker accused Agoratus of murder before the Eleven, his charge was accepted. In his speech to the court (Lys. 13.87), the speaker replies to the objection that Agoratus did not "clearly" (ἐπ' αὐτοφώρῳ) kill his brother.[7] "For it is not only a clear case of killing if someone strikes and fells with a club or a knife since on your argument nobody will be found to have killed (ἀποκτείνας) the men whom you denounced. For no one struck them, no one slew them (ἀπέσφαξεν), but they died being forced by your denunciation. Is not this person responsible for death (αἴτιος τοῦ θανάτου)? Is not this person clearly guilty? Who else is responsible (αἴτιος)? So then how did you not kill him (ἀποκτείνας)?" Here the speaker makes a distinction between killing accomplished by direct physical causality (ἀπέσφαξεν) and being responsible for another's death (αἴτιος τοῦ θανάτου). He clearly interprets the verb (ἀπο)κτείνειν in the latter sense.[8] What is significant is that the Eleven agreed with the speaker's interpretation of the verb, for otherwise they would not have accepted his case and brought it to trial.

We do not know whether the court sided with the accuser's interpretation of the law, but there is another case where the Areopagus appears to have condemned a man for murder although he did not touch the victim but only encouraged his assailant. In Dem. 54.25 the plaintiff Ariston states that his attacker Conon would have been condemned for murder if he had died as a result of his wounds even though he might not have even touched the plaintiff. Ariston cites the precedent of a case tried before the Areopagus and uses an *a fortiori* argument: he tells how the father of the priestess of Brauron did not touch his victim but only encouraged his

[7] For the meaning of the phrase, see the previous chapter.

[8] This helps to explain the wording of the special provision for the prosecution of homicide committed before the amnesty of 403 ([Arist.] *Ath. Pol.* 39.5: τὰς δὲ δίκας τοῦ φόνου εἶναι κατὰ τὰ πάτρια εἴ τίς τινα αὐτόχειρ ἀπέκτεινεν ἢ ἔτρωσεν). As Rhodes (1981) *ad loc.* notes, "There would be no special point in stipulating that for homicide trials traditional procedure was to be followed, and presumably the purpose of this sequence is to state an exception to the rule laid down in the following sentence, μηδενὶ πρὸς μηδένα μνησικακεῖν, the amnesty is not to apply to cases of homicide or of wounding covered in the homicide law (cf. 57.iii with commentary) in which a man is accused mot merely of arresting or of procuring a condemnation (that is, of helping to implement the policies of the Thirty) but of doing the deed in person." If the verb only referred to killing brought about by direct physical causality, there would have been no need to add the adjective αὐτόχειρ.

attacker to strike (τῷ πατάξαντι τύπτειν παρεκελεύσατο). The charge must be "intentional homicide" (φόνος ἐκ προνοίας) since 1) the case was tried at the Areopagus, 2) the penalty was exile, which was an alternative penalty on this charge (Dem. 23.70), and 3) the previous sentence compares the father's case to a hypothetical case of φόνος ἐκ προνοίας.[9]

This case reveals that the Athenian courts allowed the causal chain to be stretched back rather far. Euthyphro brought an accusation against his father for tying up the *pelates* and leaving him exposed to the elements. In the Agoratus case the Eleven accepted a case where a man caused death by his denunciation. In this case the Areopagus convicted a man for causing his death by encouraging his attacker to strike.

Our analysis of the verb (ἀπο)κτείνειν enables us to resolve the controversy between MacDowell and Gagarin over the nature of the charges in Antiphon 1 and Antiphon 6. Gagarin (1990) 94–5 has argued that the speaker in Antiphon 1 has brought a charge of φόνος ἐκ προνοίας against his stepmother. MacDowell (1963) 62–3 thinks the charge was only plotting (βούλευσις).[10] The facts of the case are as follows: the speaker accuses his stepmother of having given a drug to the slave concubine of Philoneos and instructing her to pour it into the drinks of her master and her husband, the speaker's father. The stepmother told the concubine that the drug was a love potion that would enable her to regain the love of her master Philoneos (5–10). The speaker claims that the stepmother knew the drug was in fact poison when she gave it to the concubine, but the stepmother later denied the charge (9). Philoneos died immediately after drinking the potion, but the speaker's father fell ill and passed away twenty days later (18–20). As our analysis has shown,

[9] Cf. Gagarin (1990) 97; Gagarin (1981a) 111–15. MacDowell (1963) 67–8 objects to this view because in cases for *phonos ek pronoias* the defendant could go into exile voluntarily, but the court could not sentence him to exile, whereas the verb ἐξέβαλεν found in the text "cannot mean that he went into exile voluntarily." MacDowell has not taken into account the use of the same verb at Din. 1.28: οὗτος Φιλοκράτει συναπολογεῖτο τῷ γράψαντι πρὸς Φίλιππον εἰρήνην, δι' ἣν ὑμεῖς ἐκεῖνον ἐξεβάλετε. Here Dinarchus says "you [i.e., the Athenian court] banished him," yet we know from Aeschin. 2.6 and Dem. 19.116 (cf. *Hesperia* 5 (1936) 399–400, lines 111–15) that Philocrates fled from Athens before his case came to trial. The Dinarchus passage confirms the suggestion of Carey and Reid (1985) 93 (cf. Lewis [1990] 358) that at Dem. 54.25 " ἐξέβαλεν is a succinct way of saying that the defendant fled after his first speech." Wallace (1989) 101–2 does not understand the semantics of the verb and thus cannot understand why this case was tried at the Areopagus. Thür (1991) 58–9 has similar difficulties in explaining the case, which, as Wallace (1991) 78 points out, contradicts his view that the Areopagus tried only cases of murder committed by the accused's own hands.

[10] Wallace (1989) 101 and Thür (1991) 65 follow MacDowell.

the stepmother could be described as "killing" her husband because she brought about his death. Thus, the speaker states that his stepmother killed her husband by sending the drug and by ordering the concubine to put it into her drink (26: ἡ δὲ πέμψασα τὸ φάρμακον καὶ κελεύσασα ἐκείνῳ δοῦναι πιεῖν *ἀπέκτεινεν* ἡμῶν τὸν πατέρα.) He accordingly charges his stepmother with the murder of her husband. As he states at the outset of his speech, "I will show their mother was the killer of my father" (3: ἀποδείξω . . . τὴν τούτων μητέρα φονέα οὖσαν τοῦ ἡμετέρου πατρός). Moreover, he refers to her as one "who killed willingly and deliberately" (5: τῆς δὲ ἑκουσίως ἐκ προνοίας *ἀποκτεινάσης*). He describes his half-brothers who are defending their mother as men who are pleading on behalf of one who killed (22: τῆς ἀποκτεινάσης. Cf. 25: τὴν ἀποκτείνασαν). As the language of the speech indicates, the stepmother is charged with killing, not merely with planning. Since she is alleged to have intended to kill the victim, the formal charge must have been φόνος ἐκ προνοίας, which would have been tried at the Areopagus. Our analysis of the verb shows that the speaker's charge is consistent with the way the Athenians understood the term and applied the law of homicide.

A similar controversy exists about the nature of the charge in Antiphon 6. Gagarin (1990) 95 holds that the charge is φόνος ἀκούσιος, whereas MacDowell (1963) 63–4 believes it is plotting (βούλευσις). In this case both the accusers and the defendant agree that the death of the victim did not occur as the result of a deliberate act (19: αὐτοὶ οἱ κατήγοροι ὁμολογοῦσι μὴ ἐκ προνοίας μηδ' ἐκ παρασκευῆς γενέσθαι τὸν θάνατον), which indicates that the charge was not φόνος ἐκ προνοίας. The case concerns a chorus boy who was given a potion to improve his voice and died after drinking it. The accusers state that the defendant killed the boy by forcing him to drink the potion (21: *ἀποκτείναιμι* ἐγὼ ἐν τῷ χορῷ, φάρμακον ἀναγκάσας πιεῖν). The speaker asserts (15) that he "did not compel the boy to drink the potion nor gave it to him nor was present when he drank it." His accusers have sworn that he killed the boy by planning his death (διωμόσαντο . . . *ἀποκτεῖναί* με Διόδοτον βουλεύσαντα τὸν θάνατον). The speaker denies that he killed either with his own hand or by planning (ἐγὼ δὲ μὴ *ἀποκτεῖναι*, μήτε χειρὶ ἐργασάμενος μήτε βουλεύσας). The charge is clearly that the speaker "killed" and the charge is homicide (9: φόνου διώκοντες; 36: φόνου δίκην), not planning. Since the accusers admit the boy died against the defendant's will, he must have been charged with φόνος ἀκούσιος, for which the penalty was exile (4). The case is thus parallel to the case of the stepmother: in both cases the defendant is accused of giving a potion to someone who in turn gave it to the victim. In the first case, however, the defendant is accused of acting deliberately, in the second, the death took place against the will of the defendant. Yet in both cases the defendant, although not giving the drug directly to the victim, is still considered responsible for the death of the victim and is therefore accused of killing him and charged with homicide.

If the person who plotted a murder that was successfully carried out by someone else could be charged with φόνος, what was the charge of βούλευσις found at [Arist.] *Ath. Pol.* 57.3? This must have been used against one who merely plotted a murder. One would normally have brought this charge against a person who plotted to kill, when the murder was not actually carried out. Technically speaking, however, one might also bring this charge against a person who plotted to kill when someone else carried out the murder, although normally in this case one would bring a charge of φόνος ἐκ προνοίας.[11] Thus, one could bring a charge of βούλευσις against a person who plotted to kill whether the victim died or not. That is how Harpocration (*s. v.* βουλεύσεως) interpreted the charge: ἐγκλήματος ὄνομα ἐπὶ δυοῖν ταττόμενον πραγμάτοιν. τὸ μὲν γάρ ἐστιν ὅταν ἐξ ἐπιβουλῆς τίς τινι κατασκευάσῃ θάνατον, ἐάν τε ἀποθάνῃ ὁ ἐπιβουλευθεὶς ἐάν τε μή. There is no reason to doubt Harpocration since he bases his view not on his own conjecture but on the evidence of a lost speech of Isaeus (τοῦ μὲν οὖν προτέρου μάρτυς Ἰσαῖος ἐν τῷ πρὸς Εὐκλείδην). Harpocration's interpretation of the charge also finds confirmation in a declamation of Libanius (50.12–14), who was well read in the Attic orators.[12]

Gagarin has argued, however, that we should not trust Harpocration's testimony for the charge of βούλευσις. Gagarin (83–7) notes that the Athenians also used this word to refer to "the wrongful inscription as a state debtor." He then assumes that "Once the Athenians had designated this action by the name βούλευσις, they would naturally be unlikely to use the same name for a completely unrelated action." I see no need to commit the nominalist fallacy, that is, the mistaken

[11] This kind of overlap of procedures is a well-attested feature of Athenian Law and other legal systems. See, for example, Dem. 54.1–2, where the accuser states that he could have proceeded against the defendant by *apagoge* to the Eleven or by a *graphe hybreos* instead of a *dike aikeias*. This procedural flexibility should not be confused with "open texture," which relates to the substantive aspect of law – on this see Harris (1994a) 150 note 16.

[12] Despite his knowledge of the orators, Libanius can often be an unreliable source for Athenian Law. See Harris (1996a) 57–65 (= I.6).

assumption that every name must refer to only one separate and distinct object or class of objects. In reality, however, there were two different names, one for each type of charge: βούλευσις was the name of the charge for the wrongful inscription of a state debtor, whereas βούλευσις φόνου was the name of the charge for plotting a homicide.

To support his assumption, Gagarin must argue that the term βούλευσις is used in a nontechnical sense at [Arist.] *Ath. Pol.* 57.3, but his arguments are inconsistent. Gagarin (86) argues that "In 59.3 βουλεύσεως must be used in a technical sense, just like every other action on that list." The logic underlying Gagarin's argument appears to be that if the other terms in the list at *Ath. Pol.* 59.3 are technical, that is, refer to a separate and distinct type of legal action, then the term βουλεύσεως must also refer to a separate and distinct type of legal action. To be consistent, Gagarin ought to apply the same reasoning to 57.3 and likewise conclude that "in 57.3 βουλεύσεως must be used in a technical sense just like every other action on that list." Instead, Gagarin (86) arbitrarily declares that "here [i.e., at 57.3], however, βουλεύσεως need not be a technical term since it is immediately apparent that it stands for βουλεύσεως τοῦ φόνου or perhaps βουλεύσεως τοῦ ἀκουσίου φόνου just as ἀκουσίων clearly represents ἀκουσίων φόνων." The logic of this argument escapes me. If Gagarin means that βουλεύσεως is not a technical term since it is an abbreviation for βουλεύσεως τοῦ φόνου or βουλεύσεως τοῦ ἀκουσίου φόνου, we would also be forced to conclude that since ἀκουσίων at 57.3 is an abbreviation for ἀκουσίων φόνων, it too is not a technical term. I doubt Gagarin or any other scholar would accept that conclusion. There is thus no reason to believe βουλεύσεως at *Ath. Pol.* 57.3. is not a term for a separate action for planning a homicide and is thus distinct from φόνος ἐκ προνοίας and φόνος ἀκούσιος.

Gagarin (91) tries to dispose of Harpocration by suggesting he "may have been misled in his thinking about βουλεύσεως by the presence in the *Ath. Pol.* of two different uses of the term, both apparently technical. Without any direct evidence about the substance of the action of βουλεύσεως in homicide cases, Harpocration derived a plausible definition from the general non-technical meaning of βούλευσις as plot or conspiracy." This misrepresents the matter: Harpocration did not rely solely on the *Ath. Pol.* but also drew on Isaeus' speech *Against Eucleides* and thus found independent confirmation for his reading of *Ath. Pol.* 57.3.

The only difficulty with my interpretation might appear to be that Harpocration in the same entry refers to a speech of Dinarchus and reports that the speaker says that cases of plotting were tried at the Areopagos (Δείναρχος δὲ ἐν τῷ κατὰ

Πιστίου ἐν Ἀρείῳ πάγῳ). We do not have any other fragments or testimonia for these speeches, but it is possible to provide an explanation for the apparent conflict between Isaeus and the *Constitution of the Athenians* on the one hand and Dinarchus on the other. In both speeches the defendant was charged with plotting a homicide. In Dinarchus' *Against Pistias*, the plot devised by the defendant was carried out, so he was αἴτιος φόνου and was accordingly charged with φόνος ἐκ προνοίας, which was tried at the Areopagus. In Isaeus' *Against Eucleides*, however, the defendant's plot to kill was either not carried out or not carried out successfully. His accusers could therefore charge him only with plotting homicide (βουλεύσεως φόνου), not with killing (φόνος or ἀποκτείνειν), and he was tried at the Palladion.

If this is the correct explanation, Harpocration read in each speech that the defendant was charged with plotting, but did not realize that it made a difference whether the victim of the plot died or not. Unaware that the man who plotted a homicide that was carried out could be charged with φόνος ἐκ προνοίας, he mistakenly thought that both defendants were brought to court on the same formal charge (βουλεύσεως φόνου), but was perplexed by the fact that each case was tried in a different court. Had he realized that plotting a successful homicide could be tried as φόνος ἐκ προνοίας, he would have realized that there was no real discrepancy. Such an explanation is superior to that of Gagarin, which would require us to discard evidence whose reliability we have no good reason to question.

The evidence of tragedy shows that the Athenians considered planning a homicide a serious offense that deserved severe punishment and lends support to the testimony of Harpocration. Ajax in Sophocles' play named after him grows enraged when the Achaean leaders do not award him the arms of Achilles and plots their deaths. To protect them from harm, Athena drives Ajax temporarily insane. In his madness Ajax slaughters the herds of the Achaeans. When he recovers his sanity, Ajax decides to commit suicide to avoid punishment at the hands of his intended victims. Even after his death, Menelaus accuses Ajax of having plotted to bring death to the entire army (1055–6: ὅστις στρατῷ ξύμπαντι *βουλεύσας φόνον*/νύκτωρ ἐπεστράτευσεν, ὡς ἕλοι δορί). If one of the gods had not foiled his attempt, he and his brother would have died a most shameful death (1057–9: κεἰ μὴ θεῶν τις τήνδε πεῖραν ἔσβεσεν, ἡμεῖς.../θανόντες ἂν προὐκείμεθ' αἰσχίστῳ μόρῳ). Menelaus tells his half-brother Teucer that Ajax deserves harsh punishment for this crime (1062–5). Even though Ajax is not brought to trial, it is clear that had he lived, he would have been subject to a serious penalty for plotting to kill the Achaean leaders despite his failure to attain his bloody goal.

In Euripides' *Ion,* however, the person who plots to kill and does not succeed is caught, tried for her offense, and sentenced to death. Creusa plots to kill Ion because she is angry at Apollo for giving her husband Xuthus a son when the god has shown no concern for the child she bore to him after he raped her. Her old slave suggests that she take her revenge by killing Ion (978). The Old Man suggests arming slaves with swords. Creusa rejects this suggestion since the murder would be obvious and slaves are weak (983). He then invites her to plan something (984: σὺ νῦν *βούλευέ* τι). Creusa tells him how she possesses two drops of blood from the Gorgon killed by Athena: one of the drops is life-giving, the other fatal (1001–13). She instructs the Old Man to pour the fatal drop into Ion's cup before he drinks, and the slave promises to do it (1040). At a feast given by Xuthus to celebrate his "reunion" with his son, the old slave follows his mistress' orders and puts the poison in Ion's cup. Before the young man drinks, however, he pours out a libation. At this point a flock of doves flies in, and one drinks the libation poured out by Ion. The dove immediately goes into convulsions and dies (1207). Ion shouts out "Who intended to kill me?" (1210: τίς ἀνθρώπων μ' ἔμελλεν *κτενεῖν*) and grabs the old slave, since he is clearly guilty (1214: ἐπ' αὐτφώρῳ πρέσβυν ὡς ἔχονθ' ἕλοι).[13] The old slave is tortured and confesses the entire plot (1215–16). Ion then goes to the Delphian authorities and accuses Creusa of attempting to kill him with poison (1217–21). The authorities vote to condemn her to death by stoning for attempting to kill him and bring about death in the holy precinct (1222–5: Δελφῶν δ' ἄνακτες ὥρισαν πετρορριφῆ/θανεῖν ἐμὴν δέσποιναν οὐ ψήφῳ μιᾷ,/τὸν ἱερὸν ὡς *κτείνουσαν* ἔν τ' ἀνακτόροις/*φόνον* τιθεῖσαν).[14] True, the scene is set in Delphi, but it is more significant that Euripides wrote the play for an Athenian audience. We should not go so far as to conclude from this evidence that the penalty for planning a murder was capital punishment in Athenian Law.[15] But

[13] This passage lends additional support to my argument that the phrase should be translated "clearly" or "manifestly" since the old slave is not caught in the act of putting the poison into Ion's cup but is arrested because his guilt is manifest or clear.

[14] For the conative use of the present to convey the sense of attempting, see Smyth (1956) #1878. In the beginning of the next scene, Creusa tells the chorus how she was condemned by the court's vote for murder (1250–1, 1256).

[15] The circumstances surrounding the attempted murder of Ion (the status of Ion as a temple slave and the location of the deed in a sacred precinct) may account for the harshness of the penalty. It is more likely that the penalty for attempted murder in Athenian Law was the same as that for ἀκούσιος φόνος, the other homicide charge that was tried at the Palladion, but this is only speculation.

Euripides and Sophocles would not have portrayed the punishment of attempted homicide in a way that would have been strange or unfamiliar to their audience. Both authors clearly expected their audience to find attempted homicide a serious crime that deserved a severe penalty.

The conclusions of this chapter can be briefly summarized. The verb (ἀπο)κτείνειν in Attic Greek is used to denote the act of causing death. It describes the action of one who brings about death by direct physical causality (e.g., stabbing, strangling, beating) or by indirect means (plotting, giving orders to magistrates, or encouraging an assailant to strike). This means that the person who plotted a homicide that was carried out by someone else could be charged with murder (φόνος), not merely planning. The charge of planning a murder (βούλευσις), on the other hand, was brought against a man accused of plotting to kill whether or not the victim died. This is how Harpocration interpreted the charge, and there is no reason to question his testimony. If there is a larger lesson to be learned, it is that we need to pay closer attention to substantive issues when examining questions of Athenian Law and legal procedure. And we can understand the substantive provisions of Athenian laws only by studying Attic Greek. Analogies from other legal systems may help or they may hinder our efforts to understand Athenian Law. But they are no substitute for studying the Athenian statutes in the original language in which they were written.

Afterthoughts

The main argument of this essay is accepted by Carey (2004), who develops the general point made in the last paragraph at greater length.

IV.3 The Penalty for Frivolous Prosecution in Athenian Law

THE ATHENIANS INTENDED THEIR COURTS TO ENFORCE THE LAWS AND TO RENDER justice. Lycurgus (*Leocr.* 4) succinctly describes the aims of the legal system: "It is the function of the law to indicate what must not be done, the task of the accuser to denounce those who are subject to the penalties set forth in the laws, and the duty of the judge to punish those whom both of these have brought before him." In his speech against Aristogeiton, Demosthenes (25.6) reminds the court that it is their duty to show their anger by punishing crime and urges them to fulfill their role as guardians of the law (φύλακες τῶν νόμων. Cf. Dem. 24.36; Din. 3.16). The courts were not designed to be just another arena for citizens to pursue private feuds or to harass their enemies with suits lacking any legal merit.

In *graphai* and other public suits, the aim of the courts was to punish those who had broken the law. As Lycurgus (*Leocr.* 6) puts it, "it is the duty of the just citizen therefore not to bring to public trial for the sake of private quarrels people who have done the city no wrong, but to regard those who have broken the law as his own enemies and to view crimes that affect the common welfare as providing public grounds for his enmity against them."[1] Demosthenes (18.123) takes it for granted that "our ancestors set up these courts not for us to have you meet here to listen to us pour foul insults on each other for personal reasons, but for us to examine whether someone has done the city an injustice." The charge an accuser brings should be directed at the wrongs for which the laws provide penalties (ἀδικήματα ... ὧν ἐν τοῖς νόμοις εἰσὶν αἱ τιμωρίαι). The kinds of slanders that personal enemies make against each other have no place in court.

[1] Compare Lys. 31.2: ποιήσομαι κατηγορίαν, οὐ μέντοι γε ἰδίαν ἔχθραν οὐδεμίαν μεταπορευόμενος and Dem. 23.1: νομίσῃ μήτ' ἰδίας ἔχθρας ἐμὲ μηδεμιᾶς ἕνεκα ἥκειν Ἀριστοκράτους κατηγορήσαντα τουτουί. Cf. Dem. 23.190 and Lys. 26.15. When accusers admit that they have previously quarreled with the defendant, they are careful to justify their charges by claiming that their case follows the laws and serves the public good. See especially Aeschin. 1.1–2 (αἱ γὰρ ἴδιαι ἔχθραι πολλὰ πάνυ τῶν κοινῶν ἐπανορθοῦσι). Cohen (1995) 83 states that litigants "advance vengeance as a respectable motivation for litigation," but the passages cited here show that Cohen's generalization is simplistic and misleading.

Demosthenes (18.278) says "the respectable citizen should not ask judges who meet to decide public cases to lend their support to his grudge or personal feud."[2]

The Athenians enacted several measures to prevent litigants from abusing the legal system for personal gain.[3] To prevent litigants from prolonging disputes and tying up the courts with endless wrangling, the Athenians recognized the principle of *res iudicata* and made it illegal to bring a case to court once a verdict had been rendered.[4] The laws of Athens also encouraged out-of-court settlements by recognizing such agreements as legally binding (Dem. 36.25; 37.1). If a litigant brought a case that had already been judged by a court or settled by private agreement, the defendant could bring a *paragraphe* action to stop the case from going to trial.[5] For many types of private cases, there existed a statute of limitations requiring that the accuser bring his charge before a certain date (e.g., Dem. 36.26–7; Dem. 38.17).[6] Demosthenes (36.27) interprets this measure as a means for forcing litigants to make their charges without a long delay to ensure that there will be witnesses to the relevant facts of the case. And litigants could not bring a case without legal justification. If the plaint submitted by an accuser did not conform to the terms of the law under which it was brought, the magistrate to whom it was presented might reject it.[7] For instance, when Dionysodorus charged Agoratus with murder before the Eleven, these magistrates refused to accept the case until he expressed his charge with the correct language so that his case fell under their jurisdiction (Lys. 13.85–7).[8] The ultimate deterrent to frivolous prosecution is found in the *diapsephisis* procedure: if a deme voted to revoke the citizenship of one

[2] See also Dem. 18.283–4, 290–3, 306–9. Demosthenes (18.281) claims that he himself pursues only the public interest, not his own.

[3] The account of measures against legal abuse found in Christ (1998) 28–32 is incomplete and unreliable.

[4] The only way to overturn a verdict was for a litigant to bring an action for false testimony against one of his opponent's witnesses. Cohen (1995) 92 claims that in Demosthenes' litigation with his guardians "legal judgments are by no means binding, nor do they serve to terminate or resolve the conflict," but fails to draw a distinction between "dispute" and "conflict." The Athenian courts, like most legal systems, aimed at resolving disputes by their verdicts, but could only regulate conflict. For the distinction between conflict and dispute, see Nader and Todd (1978) 6, 14–15.

[5] Harrison (1971) 106–24.

[6] Harrison (1971) 116–20. There was no statute of limitations for cases of homicide: Lys. 13.83.

[7] Bonner and Smith (1938) 75 note 2.

[8] The Eleven required him to add the phrase ἐπ' αὐτοφώρῳ. For the meaning of this phrase, see Chapter IV.1 in this volume. For the power of the magistrate to reject a case that contravened the laws, see also Antiphon 6.37, 42.

of its members, and that person appealed the decision to a court in Athens, then lost his case, he was sold into slavery ([Arist.] *Ath. Pol.* 42.1).

The courts also required payment of fees called *prytaneia* by the plaintiff and defendant to discourage frivolous litigation in private cases. If the amount in dispute was more than 1,000 drachmas, each litigant paid thirty drachmas each. If the amount was less than 1,000 drachmas, but more than 100, each paid three drachmas. After the trial the loser reimbursed the winner for his fee.[9] In some private suits the unsuccessful plaintiff had to pay a fine of one-sixth of the amount claimed.[10] In cases where someone claimed that a person being held as a slave was actually free but failed to prove his case, he had to pay the owner of the slave five hundred drachmas and in addition pay a fine of an equal amount to the treasury ([Dem.] 58.19–20).

With a few exceptions, Athenian Law did not require the citizen who brought a public case to pay court fees.[11] But there were severe penalties for the prosecutor who brought a charge that was so weak that it failed to gain at least one-fifth of the votes cast by the court. According to Theophrastus (fr. 4b Szegedy-Maszak):

> Ἀθήνησι οὖν ἐν τοῖς δημοσίοις ἀγῶσιν, ἐὰν μὴ μεταλάβῃ τις τὸ πέμπτον μέρος, χιλίας ἀποτίνει καὶ ἔτι πρόσεστί τις ἀτιμία οἷον τὸ ἐξεῖναι μήτε γράψασθαι παρανόμον μήτε φαίνειν μήτε ἐφηγεῖσθαι.[12]
>
> At Athens in public cases, if someone does not gain a share of one-fifth [of the votes], he owes a fine of 1,000 drachmas and in addition he loses certain rights such as the ability to bring a *graphe* or a *phasis* or an *ephegesis* against an illegal action.

The evidence of Theophrastus is confirmed by several passages in the orators. Many texts refer to the penalty of 1,000 drachmas,[13] and several mention the loss

[9] For the *prytaneia*, see Pollux 8.38 with Harrison (1971) 92–4. The fee was waived in cases involving less than 100 drachmas.

[10] On the *epobolia*, see Harrison (1971) 181–3.

[11] For the exceptions, see [Arist.] *Ath. Pol.* 59.3 with Harrison (1971) 94.

[12] Similar information can be found in Pollux 8. 52–3. Reiske proposed emending παρανόμον to παρανόμων and was followed by Harrison (1971) 83 note 2 and MacDowell (1990) 327. But the emendation is unnecessary and vulnerable to several objections. See Harris (1992c) 79. The conclusion reached in that article is accepted by Wallace (1998) 66 note 5.

[13] [And.] 4.18; Dem. 23.80; 24.7; [Dem.] 58.6.

of the right to prosecute.[14] Demosthenes (26.9) states that when the prosecutor fails to gain one-fifth of the votes, he permanently loses the right to bring a *graphe* or use the *apagoge* or *ephegesis* procedures (τὸ λοιπὸν μὴ γράφεσθαι μηδ᾽ ἀπάγειν μηδ᾽ ἐφηγεῖσθαι). When bringing his *apographe* against Nicostratus, Apollodorus ([Dem.] 53.1) states that if he loses the case, he risks a fine of 1,000 drachmas and loss of the right to bring public charges again.[15] Hyperides (*Eux.* 34) says that the court did not give Tisis of Agryle one-fifth of the votes when he brought his *apographe* against Euthycrates and penalized him with *atimia* (ἠτίμωσαν). In his speech for Ctesiphon, Demosthenes (18.266; cf. 82) says that Aeschines is in danger of losing the right to prosecute if he receives less than one-fifth of the votes.[16] These penalties also applied when a prosecutor brought a public charge, then failed to bring the case to trial. Demosthenes (58.6) states explicitly that if a prosecutor initiates a *graphe*, *phasis*, or another public charge and does not follow through with his case (μὴ ἐπεξίῃ), he will pay a fine of 1,000 drachmas. Demosthenes (21.103) tells the court how Euctemon brought a charge of desertion against him (Εὐκτήμων Λουσιεὺς ἐγράψατο Δημοσθένην Παιανιέα λιποταξίου). When Euctemon failed to follow through on his prosecution, he suffered *atimia*, that is, he lost his right to prosecute (ἠτίμωκεν αὑτὸν οὐκ ἐπεξελθών). The evidence of Theophrastus and the orators is clear: the accuser who brought a public charge, then failed to follow through his prosecution or to win at least one-fifth of the votes at the trial had to pay a fine of 1,000 drachmas and lost his right to bring all public charges in the future.[17]

Despite the ancient evidence, M. H. Hansen has argued that the prosecutor subject to the penalty lost only his right to bring a case of the same type in the future, not his entire right to prosecute on public charges.[18] He points first to

[14] Cohen (1995) 102–3, 117 appears to believe there was only a fine for not receiving one-fifth of the votes; he does not mention the *atimia* even though he discusses [Dem.] 53.1–2, where this penalty is explicitly mentioned.

[15] Apollodorus exaggerates for rhetorical purposes by neglecting to add that these penalties would apply only if he failed to gain one-fifth of the votes.

[16] Cf. And. 1.33; Dem. 26.9.

[17] According to Pollux 8.52–3 there was only a penalty of 1,000 drachmas and no *atimia* for the prosecutor who did not gain one-fifth of the votes in an *eisangelia*. Hansen (1975) 29–31 argues that this penalty was introduced between 333 and 330 and that there was no penalty at all in an *eisangelia* before this.

[18] Hansen (1976a) 63–5. For references to the opinions of earlier scholars, see Wankel (1976) 562. Hansen is followed by Todd (1993) 143 and MacDowell (1990) 327–8. MacDowell rightly rejects the proposal of Paoli (1930) 322–3, followed by Harrison (1971) 83, that the only kind of *atimia* suffered by frivolous

Demosthenes' *Against Eubulides* (57) "where the defendant Euxitheos relates that Euboulides once, as prosecutor in a γραφὴ ἀσεβείας, had obtained less than one-fifth of the votes of the jurors. In the trial of Euxitheos Euboulides nevertheless appears before the jurors as one of the prosecutors appointed by the deme." There are three objections to Hansen's use of this evidence. First, the speaker provides no evidence to prove his charge. One might just as easily argue that the allegation must be false because Euboulides later appeared as prosecutor. Second, there is no indication that the trial that resulted when a candidate rejected at a *diapsephisis* appealed the deme's decision to a court in Athens was one of those covered by the law. In this procedure there was no formal accusation made by an accuser. Third, the person who was in danger of losing his citizenship was appealing the decision of the deme, not defending himself against a charge brought by an individual. Although the advocates who spoke in favor of the deme were called accusers (κατήγοροι), they are not the ones who bring a charge against the defendant. They were appointed by the deme to argue its case against the rejected candidate.[19] They are thus not like accusers in a *graphe, endeixis,* or *ephegesis,* but similar to the prosecutors whom the *polis* elected in certain important cases.[20]

Hansen next points to Dem. 21.103 and 139, where he claims "Demosthenes refers to a γραφὴ λιποταξίου which Euctemon had brought against him but withdrawn before the trial."[21] Euctemon incurred *atimia,* but a few paragraphs later Demosthenes refers to him once more as a sycophant who habitually gave evidence in court for pay. These passages do not support Hansen's argument either. Demosthenes (21.139) says that Meidias is protected (προβέβληται) by Polyeuctus, Timocrates, and Euctemon, but does not describe what kind of protection they afford him. Demosthenes adds that there is another group (πρὸς ἔτι

prosecutors was the same one that applied to all citizens condemned to pay a fine, that is, total disenfranchisement that ended when the fine was paid.

[19] For appeal against a deme's decision about citizenship, see [Arist.]*Ath. Pol.* 42.1 with Rhodes (1981) 501; "The κατήγοροι are accusers, who in opposition to the candidate will state the deme's case for rejecting him." Note that *Ath. Pol.* 59.4 does not group these cases with *dikai* and *graphai,* but with *dokimasiai* for magistrates and appeals from verdicts of the Council.

[20] For prosecutors elected or appointed by the *polis,* see Dem. 20.146; Aeschin. 1.19 and Harrison (1971) 34–5 with note 2. There is no indication they were subject to the penalties for frivolous prosecution. Indeed, it would be unfair for them to suffer for losing a case that the *polis* had brought against the defendants.

[21] To be precise, Euctemon did not withdraw the *graphe* but failed to follow through on his prosecution. For the distinction, see below.

ἕτεροι τούτοις), a cabal composed of witnesses (. . .) who easily nod in silent assent at his lies." Demosthenes' language clearly indicates that this is a second group, distinct from the one containing Euctemon. Even if Euctemon were in this group, Demosthenes never says that they brought public charges against Meidias' opponents.

MacDowell has observed that Diodorus in the speech Demosthenes (24.7, 14) wrote for him to deliver against Timocrates alleges that Androtion brought a *graphe asebeias* against him but failed to gain one-fifth of the votes at the trial and was fined 1,000 drachmas.[22] Later in the same speech, Diodorus (Dem. 24.14) reports that Androtion brought a *graphe paranomon* against Euctemon. But Diodorus presents no evidence to support his allegation, and his testimony is suspect since Diodorus had every reason to exaggerate the extent of Androtion's defeat. One can just as easily argue that Diodorus misrepresented the court's vote in an attempt to portray his opponent as a sycophant. That is why he mentions only the fine of 1,000 drachmas and not the *atimia*. If he had mentioned the *atimia*, the court would have easily been able to detect the inconsistency in his account of Androtion's actions.[23] A careful examination of the evidence cited by Hansen and MacDowell reveals that there is no reason to doubt Theophrastus and the orators when they say that the prosecutor who failed to gain one-fifth of the votes at the trial or to follow through his case lost the right to bring public charges in the future.

Hansen has also argued that the ban on those subject to these penalties was not strictly enforced: "a blind eye was often turned to *atimoi* who behaved as *epitimoi*." He points to "at least fifteen cases where the prosecutor withdrew a public action with impunity, as against only four examples of the prosecutor being fined and punished with partial *atimia*."[24] If this is true, it has major implications for our view of Athenian Law, for it would give the impression that the Athenians did not take the enforcement of the penalties for frivolous prosecution very seriously.

Several of the passages cited by Hansen, however, are so vague or give so little information that it would be unsafe to conclude that the prosecutors in these cases

22 MacDowell (1990) 327–8.

23 Wallace (1998) 68 suggests that in cases of impiety "failed prosecutors were subject only to a fine, not partial *atimia*," but cites no evidence to support his argument. We should also question Aeschines' charge (2.93) that Demosthenes did not follow through on his *graphe* against Demomeles before the Areopagus, which imposed a fine on him (ἐπιβολήν). Moreover, it is not certain that the charge was actually a *graphe*: see Hansen (1983b).

24 Hansen (1976) 59–60, followed by Christ (1998) 29.

actually violated the law. Hansen draws attention to Plato's *Crito* (45e), where Crito says that he is afraid that the fact that Socrates' case came to court when it was possible to avoid a trial will make people think that he and his friends failed because of their cowardice and poor character. But Crito does not specify what means he would have used to prevent the case from coming to trial. In any event, Meletus did not withdraw his charge, and the case went to trial. Hansen claims that Demosthenes (21.36–9) describes a case where "a *proedros* withdraws a public action against Polyzelos for having assaulted a public official," but Demosthenes does not say that the official ever summoned Polyzelus or lodged a formal complaint against him before a magistrate. On the contrary, Demosthenes states that the official agreed to a private settlement (ἰδίᾳ διαλυσάμενος) and did not bring Polyzelus to court (οὐδ' εἰσήγαγε τὸν Πολύζηλον).[25]

In another case listed by Hansen the prosecutor did not withdraw the charge, but actually brought the case to trial. Hansen believes that at And. 1.122 we find a case "where the prosecutor probably withdrew a public action with impunity." The incident described by Andocides took place as part of his feud with Callias. Andocides (1.120–1) says he put in a claim to marry his cousin, the daughter of Epilycus, who had become an *epikleros* after the death of her father. Callias also wanted her and put in a claim under his son's name. To thwart Andocides, he paid Cephisius 1,000 drachmas to bring an *endeixis* against him. When Callias saw that Andocides was not about to desist, he told three of his friends that he was prepared to convince Cephisius to come to an agreement. Andocides does not specify the form of the agreement, but since Andocides says that he refused to settle and invited him to proceed with his prosecution (εἶπον αὐτῷ... κατηγορεῖν), it appears that Callias intended to persuade Cephisius to drop his suit. Andocides did not come to an agreement, and Cephisius therefore was forced to bring his case to court. Since Cephisius did not actually withdraw the suit, he was not subject to the penalties for frivolous prosecution.

Hansen also claims that Timarchus violated the law regarding frivolous prosecutions during the *diapsephisis* of 346. Aeschines (1.114) relates that Timarchus claimed that Philotades was a former slave of his and persuaded the members of his deme to revoke his citizenship (ἀποψηφίσασθαι). Philotades then appealed his case to a court. Timarchus was one of the five accusers appointed by the

[25] The phrase ἐρρῶσθαι πολλὰ τοῖς νόμοις εἰπών also implies that the official chose not to have recourse to a legal procedure.

deme to conduct the case (ἐπιστὰς τῇ κατηγορίᾳ) and swore an oath that he would not take a bribe, but accepted twenty *mnai* from Leuconides the brother of Philotades and betrayed the case (προὔδωκεν). First of all, the trial took place as part of a *diapsephisis*, not one of the procedures covered under the law that penalized those who brought a *graphe, phasis, apographe*, or *ephegesis*. Second, it is not clear what Aeschines means by "betrayed." There is no indication that this latter type of prosecution was subject to the same penalties that applied to volunteer prosecutors. Second, when Aeschines criticizes Timarchus' conduct in the case, he blames him for violating his oath not to accept gifts, not for violating the law about frivolous prosecution (114–15: ὀμόσας μὴ λαβεῖν δῶρα μηδὲ λήψεσθαι ... τὸν ὅρκον ἐπιώρκησεν). Third, there is no reason to think that Timarchus was in a position to have the suit dropped, because the deme had passed the vote against Philotades, and Philotades was the one who initiated the appeal. Finally, if Philotades agreed to have the case dropped, the vote to exclude him from citizenship would have remained in effect. For him to regain his citizenship, Philotades had to have the case go forward. As a result, Philotades would therefore not have paid Timarchus to make sure the case did not go to trial. It is more likely that what Aeschines means by "betrayed" was that Timarchus presented a weak case at the appeal and persuaded his fellow prosecutors to do the same so that the court would vote in Philotades' favor.[26]

In several other cases Hansen believes the prosecutor withdrew a public action with impunity. In these cases, however, which we will examine below, the speaker never says that the prosecutor did not "follow through" (ἐπεξελθεῖν) or that the prosecutor suffered any penalty for withdrawing his action. Hansen's interpretation of these cases depends on his implicit assumption that the verb ἐπεξελθεῖν, "to follow through," must have a narrow meaning and can refer only to the action of bringing a case to trial. The verb certainly does cover this action: for instance, the speaker at Antiphon 6.37 says that he could not follow through his case and

[26] Aristophanes *Wasps* 691–5 provides an example of this kind of scheme. See MacDowell (1971) 227. Hansen, followed by Cohen (1995) 99–100, interprets Aeschin. 3.52 to mean that Demosthenes withdrew his *graphe hybreos* against Meidias, but it is more likely that Aeschines alludes to the kind of scheme mentioned by Aristophanes. I owe this point to Lene Rubinstein. There is no reason to accept the interpretation made by Plutarch (*Dem.* 12) of Aeschines' charge. Plutarch's idea that Demosthenes never brought the case to court has led several scholars to look for signs of incompleteness in Dem. 21, but there is no reason to believe that Aeschines' charge is reliable as evidence or that the speech is an unfinished draft – see Harris (1989) and Harris (1992c) 74–5. The arguments in these articles are ignored by Cohen, who uncritically accepts Aeschines' story and Plutarch's interpretation of it.

denounce his opponent's crime to the court (μηδὲ . . . οἷός τε γενοίμην ἐπεξελθεῖν μηδ' ἐνδεῖξαι τῷ δικαστηρίῳ) after they brought a charge of homicide against him. In this passage the speaker cannot follow through (ἐπεξελθεῖν) because he cannot bring his case to court (ἐνδεῖξαι τῷ δικαστηρίῳ). On the other hand, Hansen rules out the possibility that the verb could have a broader meaning and that bringing a case to court was only one way of "following through." This means that the law could have allowed the prosecutor to "follow through" either by bringing the case to court or by formally withdrawing the charge at the *anakrisis*. What was illegal was to summon a defendant and present a formal charge against him before the magistrate, then fail to follow through on the charge by not appearing at the *anakrisis* or failing to prosecute the case in court after attending the *anakrisis*.

Two passages confirm this inference. Demosthenes (21.103) reports that Meidias convinced Euctemon to accuse Demosthenes of desertion (Εὐκτήμων Λουσιεὺς ἐγράψατο Δημοσθένην Παιανιέα λιποταξίου). But after bringing the charge, Euctemon did not attend the *anakrisis* (οὔτ' ἀνεκρίνετο). As a result, he suffered *atimia,* that is, lost his right to bring public cases (ἠτίμωκεν αὑτὸν) because he did not follow through his prosecution (οὐκ ἐπεξελθών). Epichares (Dem. 58.8) states that Theocrines brought a *phasis* against Micon and summoned him to appear (ταύτην τὴν φάσιν . . . ἔδωκε μὲν οὗτος προσκαλεσάμενος Μίκωνα). He presented the charge to the secretary of the Market Supervisors, who displayed it in front of their office. When the magistrates summoned Theocrines to the *anakrisis* (εἰς τὴν ἀνακρίσιν καλούμενος. Cf.8 : καλούντων αὐτὸν εἰς τὴν ἀνακρίσιν τῶν ἀρχόντων), however, he did not obey their orders nor "follow through" (οὐκ ὑπήκουσεν οὐδ' ἐπεξῆλθεν).[27] Because of his failure to show up at the *anakrisis,* Theocrines is subject to the penalty of 1,000 drachmas (ταῖς χιλίαις . . . ἔνοχός ἐστιν), which is the penalty for violating the law about bringing frivolous charges.[28] In both these cases failure to follow through a prosecution is equated with failure to appear at the *anakrisis*.

These two cases are markedly different from several other cases cited by Hansen. In these other cases, the prosecutor came to an agreement with his opponent

[27] The speaker claims that Theocrines bribed the secretary of the Supervisors of the Port to cancel the charge. This would indicate that if one were to withdraw the charge, one had to do it at the *anakrisis*. One could not try to withdraw the charge before appearing at the *anakrisis*.

[28] The speaker says that Theocrines is also subject to arrest for bringing baseless charges against merchants, but this is a separate charge.

and formally withdrew his indictment, an action that must have taken place at the *anakrisis*. Two of these cases occur in Apollodorus' speech *Against Neaira* ([Dem.] 59). Apollodorus ([Dem.] 59.64–70) relates how Stephanus plotted with Neaira against Epaenetus, who had been her lover in the past. Stephanus lured Epaenetus to the countryside, caught him having sex with Neaira's daughter, and charged him with *moicheia*.[29] Epaenetus promised to pay him thirty *mnai* and name two men as sureties. After Stephanus released him, Epaenetus brought a charge of wrongful confinement against him before the Thesmothetae (69: γράφεται πρὸς τοὺς θεσμοθέτας γραφὴν Στέφανον τουτονὶ ἀδίκως εἱρχθῆναι ὑπ' αὐτοῦ). Before the case went any further, Stephanus, fearing conviction, invited Epaenetus to settle the dispute by arbitration. Epaenetus consented and withdrew his charges (69: ἀνελομένου τὴν γραφὴν ἣν ἐδίωκε Στέφανον).[30] There is no reason to question Apollodorus' account since he provides both the sureties and the arbitrators as witnesses (70–1).[31] Here the accuser appears to have dropped the charge immediately after presenting it to the magistrate and before the case proceeded to trial. For this reason, Apollodorus does not criticize Epaenetus for his decision and never says his withdrawing the charges made him subject to punishment.

Apollodorus ([Dem.] 59.52–4) also recounts how Phrastor brought a *graphe* against Stephanus before the Thesmothetai charging him with pledging the daughter of a foreigner in marriage as if she were the daughter of a citizen. Stephanus and Phrastor came to a settlement by which each agreed to drop his suit against the other (τὴν δίκην τοῦ σίτου ἀνείλετο, καὶ ὁ Φράστωρ τὴν γραφὴν παρὰ τῶν θεσμοθετῶν [*scil.* ἀνείλετο]).[32] Once again, Apollodorus does not say Phrastor did anything illegal or was subject to a fine or *atimia*. It is also striking that in each case the prosecutor who withdrew the case was willing to testify that he did so. If withdrawing a case were illegal, it is hard to believe that Epaenetus and Phrastor would have admitted that they had broken the law in front of the court.

[29] The view advanced by Cohen (1984a) that *moicheia* is equivalent to the modern concept of adultery is anachronistic and is disproved by this passage, as has now been recognized by many scholars, beginning with Cantarella (1991).

[30] Kapparis (1999) 314 does not comment on Epaenetus' withdrawal of his charge.

[31] For guidelines to evaluating the reliability of statements found in the orators, see E. M. Harris (1995) 7–16.

[32] Kapparis (1999) 275 does not comment on Phrastor's withdrawal of his charge.

There are several other similar cases. Epichares (Dem. 58.32) reports that Theocrines summoned Polyeuctus and brought a *graphe* for maltreatment of an orphan against him before the Archon (προσκαλεσάμενος τὸν Πολύευκτον ἀποφέρει γραφὴν κατ' αὐτοῦ κακώσεως πρὸς τὸν ἄρχοντα). After he received two hundred drachmas from Polyeuctus, he withdrew his charge (τὴν γραφὴν ἀνείλετο). Epichares criticizes Theocrines for abandoning the orphan (προδοὺς τὸν ὀρφανόν) but not for violating the law about frivolous prosecutions. Earlier in the speech, Epichares states that Theocrines has summoned and indicted several others on the *graphe paranomon* (24: προσκαλεσάμενος καὶ γραψάμενος), then settled with the defendants in return for money (μικρὸν ἀργύριον λαμβάνων ἀπαλλάττεται). The speaker attacks the practice of using the *graphe paranomon* for this purpose, calling it detrimental to the democracy, yet never says it is illegal or that Theocrines should have suffered a penalty for withdrawing these indictments. Epichares says also that Theocrines would have withdrawn (ἂν ἀνείλετο) his *graphe paranomon* against his father if he had been willing to pay him a thousand drachmas (Dem. 58.33–4). Although the speaker is quick to accuse Theocrines of every imaginable crime, he does not say that his proposal was illegal.

Dinarchus (1.94) provides another example of a prosecutor withdrawing an indictment. The speaker accuses Demosthenes of inconsistency (μεταβαλλόμενος) and gives three examples of how Demosthenes changed his mind. First, he proposed that no one should worship any but the traditional gods, then declared that the people should not dispute the divine honors granted to Alexander. Second, he indicted Callimedon by *eisangelia* for conspiring with exiles in Megara to overthrow the democracy, then withdrew the indictment (τὴν εἰσαγγελίαν ... ἀναιρούμενος). Third, he claimed there was a plot against the dockyards, then made no proposal to deal with the threat. The speaker does not criticize Demosthenes for breaking the law in the first and third examples; his complaint is that Demosthenes says one thing, then does something else. This indicates that there was also nothing illegal about withdrawing his indictment against Callimedon. Moreover, the speaker never says that it was illegal for Demosthenes to withdraw his indictment or that he incurred a penalty for doing so.[33]

[33] One could also explain the absence of any penalty in this case by arguing that there was no penalty for withdrawing an *eisangelia* before trial. See Hansen (1975) 30–1.

Demosthenes (20.145) mentions three *graphai* brought against Leptines. The first never went to trial because the prosecutor died, and the third was somehow compromised (παρασκευάσθη), though Demosthenes is rather vague about the details. In the second case, however, Demosthenes says the prosecutor came to an agreement and withdrew the case (πεισθεὶς ὑπὸ σοῦ διαγράψατο). Once again, there is no indication that the prosecutor broke the terms of the law against frivolous prosecutions or was subject to a fine.[34]

These cases are very different from those involving Theocrines' *phasis* and Euctemon's *graphe lipotaxiou*. Neither Theocrines nor Euctemon showed up for the *anakrisis* and formally withdrew his case; Theocrines was brought to trial for violating the law, and Euctemon was punished with *atimia*. In each of these cases, by contrast, the speaker never says the person who dropped the suit violated the terms of the law (that is, never uses the phrase οὐκ ἐπεξελθεῖν), did anything illegal, or was subject to a fine or loss of rights. Epichares (58.32) does criticize Theocrines for betraying the orphan, but not for breaking the law about frivolous prosecutions. What is important to note is that in all these examples, the speaker says that the charge was formally withdrawn (Din. 1.94: ἀναιρούμενος; [Dem.] 59.53: ἀνείλετο; 69: ἀνελομένου; Dem. 58.32: ἀνείλετο; 34: ἀνείλετο, ἀναιρεθῶσιν; Dem. 20.145: διεγράψατο). This must mean that when the parties met at the *anakrisis*, the prosecutor informed the magistrate that he wished to cancel his indictment, thus formally ending the procedure. This in turn indicates that the prosecutor could "follow through" (ἐπεξελθεῖν) on his charge by either of two means: he could bring the case to trial, or alternatively he could withdraw his charge at the *anakrisis*. What the prosecutor could not do was simply to let the case drop after making his initial indictment as Theocrines and Euctemon did. He had to "follow through" in one way or another. If he did not, he was in violation of the law and subject to a fine and loss of the right to prosecute.[35]

This analysis of the law against frivolous prosecutions allows us to explain several cases where an agreement was reached between the litigants and as a result their dispute never went to trial. The first example is described in Lys. *Against*

[34] Demosthenes reports that Leptines claims these three prosecutors broke the law (οὐκ ἐπεξῆλθον), but Demosthenes obviously disagrees with him and puts forward his own account of what happened to contradict his claim.

[35] A prosecutor who attended the *anakrisis*, then did not show up at the trial, was probably also subject to the penalties imposed by the law.

Andocides 6.11–12. The speaker claims that Andocides, soon after returning to Athens from exile, summoned Archippus before the Archon Basileus on a charge of impiety (προσεκαλέσατο δίκην ἀσεβείας πρὸς τὸν βασιλέα).[36] When they met before the magistrate, Andocides claimed Archippus committed sacrilege against his ancestral Herm and applied for an *anakrisis* (ἔλαχεν . . . φάσκων τὸν Ἀρχιππον ἀσεβεῖν περὶ τὸν Ἑρμῆν τὸν αὐτοῦ πατρῷον). Archippus denied the charge, but preferred to settle by offering payment. The settlement evidently included a promise on the part of Andocides to withdraw his charge at the *anakrisis*, which had not yet taken place. This would explain why the speaker never says Andocides broke the law or was subject to a fine of 1,000 drachmas and loss of the right to bring public charges.[37] A similar type of agreement may have also taken place between the Thesmothete and the man who beat him mentioned at Dem. 21.36–9. Demosthenes says that the Thesmothete settled the dispute in return for payment (ἰδίᾳ πεισθεὶς ὁπόσῳ δήποτ᾽ ἀργυρίῳ). Although Demosthenes does not explicitly say whether the Thesmothete had already initiated proceedings or not, the phrase καθυφεὶς τὸν ἀγῶνα, "dropping the case," appears to indicate that he had. If this is the case, it is important to observe that Demosthenes criticizes him only for failing to use the remedies provided by the legal system and does not say the settlement violated the law. Apollodorus ([Dem.] 45.4–5) may also allude to this kind of agreement. Apollodorus says he brought a *graphe hybreos* against Phormion for marrying his mother. At first, the case did not go to court because no trials were taking place. Apollodorus then skips over what follows (ἵνα συμτέμω), saying only that Phormion did not think he had to do what he had agreed to (ὡμολόγησε). This implies there was an

[36] The charge must be a *graphe asebeias* because it was brought before the Archon Basileus. See [Arist.] *Ath. Pol.* 57.2; Hyp. 4.6; Dem. 35.48. The fact that the speaker uses the term *dike* does not mean that this must have been a private suit – see Pollux 8.41 (ἐκαλοῦντο αἱ γραφαὶ δίκαι, οὐ μέντοι αἱ δίκαι καὶ γραφαί). There is no reason to think Andocides brought a *dike asebeias* on the basis of Dem. 22.27, which mentions the possibility of making a charge of *asebeia* by δικάζεσθαι πρὸς Εὐμολπίδας. We know too little about the judicial competence of the Eumolpidai to know what this means. For a suggestion, see Parker (1996) 296 ("this tribunal doubtless adjudicated on offences against the Mysteries alone, and could perhaps only impose such penalties as exclusion from a shrine"). On the other hand, even if one could bring a *dike asebeias* before the Eumolpidai, the speaker in Lys. 6 says Andocides brought his case before the Archon Basileus, not the Eumolpidai.

[37] The speaker criticizes Andocides not for breaking the law but for his hypocrisy in accusing someone else of the very crime he is now on trial for. He adds that if Andocides thought it right to punish someone else for impiety, the judges should now punish him for the same crime. This argument appears to take for granted the legality of Andocides' actions against Archippus.

agreement, in which Apollodorus probably agreed to withdraw his case against Phormio.[38]

The message conveyed by the penalties for frivolous prosecution should be clear: the Athenians did not want litigants to view the procedures created to prosecute public cases as just another means of pursuing private vendettas. The right to bring *graphai* and other public charges was a valuable privilege, one so important that the Athenians considered just one serious abuse of the right as grounds for permanently revoking it. And there is no reason to think that the Athenians did not enforce the *atimia* that was imposed as a penalty for frivolous prosecution or that "a blind eye was often turned to *atimoi* who behaved as *epitimoi*." The procedures for public cases were created to protect the community's interest. If someone used these procedures merely to pursue his own vendetta, the Athenians believed he could not be trusted to use the courts to look after the public interest. When Aeschines brought a *graphe paranomon* without legal merit just to slander Demosthenes, the court put an end to his career as prosecutor.[39]

It is interesting to compare the Athenian approach to the problem of frivolous prosecutions with the approach taken by English Law in the eighteenth and nineteenth centuries. During this period, most prosecutions on criminal charges were made by private individuals or corporations.[40] The English courts recognized that litigants might use the system to harass opponents with baseless accusations, but did not penalize prosecutors who failed to win their cases by a wide margin. By the early eighteenth century, the courts created a tort of malicious prosecution. To recover damages, the victim had to prove that there was no reasonable cause for the accusation. There were also criminal charges for perjury or conspiracy to prefer a malicious indictment, but these could not be used in capital cases out of fear they would discourage prosecution. As Douglas Hay has observed,

[38] Aeschines (2.148) alleges that Nicodemus of Aphidna indicted Demosthenes for desertion (ἐγράφης λιποταξίου), but Demosthenes was "saved" (ἐσώθης) by paying off Nicodemus (τὸν γραψάμενον Νικόδημον τὸν Ἀφιδναῖον χρήμασιν πείσας). Aeschines does not say that Nicodemus withdrew the case, and it is possible that Aeschines may allude to the kind of arrangement discussed in note 26. Dem. 25.47 may also allude to this kind of arrangement between Aristogeiton and Demades (τὰς κατὰ Δημάδου γραφὰς . . . ἐξέλιπεν).

[39] For discussion of the trial and Aeschines' motives, see Harris (1995) 139–48, 173–4 and Harris (1994a) 140–8. Note that a certain Lycinus, who brought a *graphe paranomon* against Philocrates and failed to gain one-fifth of the votes (Aeschin. 2.14; cf. 3.62), is never again attested in our sources, presumably because the resulting *atimia* put an end to his political career.

[40] My account relies on Hay (1989).

however, "a prosecution for perjury was both expensive and difficult, as it entailed the technicalities and costs associated with trials for serious misdemeanour, and perhaps also required (as a criminal proceeding) a higher standard of proof."[41] This meant that the best way for a victim to proceed was the action for malicious prosecution, but litigants often found it difficult to recover damages with this action. Hay notes that "the records of lawsuits in the courts at Westminster suggest that few victims of malicious prosecutions began actions. The rolls of the three common law courts for four sample years between 1740 and 1815, covering over 3,000 civil cases, do not identify a single case for malicious prosecution. The fuller information extant for one court, Common Pleas, shows one case out of 710 actions in six sample years between the interregnum and 1840."[42] By contrast, the punishment for frivolous prosecution in Athens was automatic and far more severe. The victim did not have to prove that the prosecution lacked reasonable cause or knowingly made false statements. All he had to do was to gain acquittal by a wide margin.

At the same time, the Athenians wished to encourage out-of-court settlements by allowing a prosecutor to withdraw his charge after indicting the defendant without suffering a penalty. By allowing litigants to end a dispute by private settlement, the Athenians helped to reduce the caseload of the courts and to prevent their legal system from becoming overburdened. If they did not permit a prosecutor to withdraw an indictment after lodging it, this would have meant that every time a magistrate received a public charge, the case would have to be tried in court. We do not know how many public charges were made every month, but our sources inform us that a public case took up an entire day and required at least 501 judges, each of whom had to be paid three obols.[43] Although convictions were often very lucrative for the *polis*, acquittals brought no money into the treasury.[44]

[41] Hay (1989) 350.

[42] Hay (1989) 353.

[43] For the trial of a *graphe* taking an entire day, see Aeschin. 3.197–8 with Rhodes (1981) 723–8. For the size of courts in a public suit, see [Arist.] *Ath. Pol.* 68.1; Dem. 24.9 and the scholia *ad loc.* With Rhodes (1981) 729.

[44] If the prosecutor failed to gain one-fifth of the votes cast, the *polis* would collect the fine of 1,000 drachmas. The most profitable case we know about was Lycurgus' conviction of Diphilus, which brought in 160 talents (Plu. *Mor.* 843d). Christ (1998) 29 claims "Athenians were lax about the collection of state debts," but ignores the fine paid by Diphilus, passages like 20.63 (Satyrus collects 34 talents), and the abundant records of the *poletai* (see *IG* i^3 421–30; Lalonde, Langdon, and Walbank [1991] 53–144). Christ cites Dem.25.85–91, where Aristogeiton is reported to claim there are many men in debt to the treasury. He appears not to have observed that the speaker agrees with Aristogeiton only if one considers two debtors "many."

Requiring prosecutors to try every case they brought would not only have been time-consuming, but also expensive.

This approach certainly had advantages and permitted litigants to use the threat of a public charge to force their opponents to agree to private settlements in cases where the victim had suffered a serious violation of his rights. This is what happened in the two cases described by Apollodorus in his speech *Against Neaira* ([Dem.] 59.50–4, 64–70). Phrastor claimed that Stephanus had betrothed Phano to him under false pretenses and divorced her without returning her dowry. When Stephanus brought a suit to recover the dowry, Phrastor replied by bringing a *graphe* against him on the grounds that he had given in marriage the daughter of a foreigner. The threat of prosecution encouraged Stephanus to withdraw his claim against Phrastor in return for having the case against him dropped. Epaenetus thought Stephanus had extorted money from him by claiming he had seduced his daughter and used the threat of a *graphe* to compel him to submit their dispute to arbitration.[45]

But the approach also had its disadvantages. In cases where the defendant had committed an offense not against an individual, but against the entire community, it permitted the defendant to buy off his prosecutor and avoid paying a fine to the *polis*. For example, when Theocrines brought his *phasis* against Micon, if he had convicted him, half of the price of the goods confiscated would have been sold by the state.[46] By withdrawing the charge in exchange for payment by the defendant, Theocrines might have deprived the *polis* of a considerable sum of money. For this reason, the law about frivolous prosecutions appears to have forbidden some kinds of settlements, especially those designed to cheat the treasury of fines or other payments ([Dem.] 58.5: τὸν νόμον . . . τὸν περὶ τῶν φαινόντων καὶ οὐκ ἐπεξιόντων, ἀλλὰ διαλυομένων παρὰ τοὺς νόμους).[47] According to Epicrates, the rule was that in private matters litigants could make whatever agreement they could persuade each other to accept, but in matters involving the treasury, the settlement could not violate the law ([Dem.] 58.20: προσήκει τοὺς ἀντιδίκους ὑπὲρ μὲν τῶν ἰδίων, ὅπως αὐτοὺς πείθωσι, διοικεῖσθαι πρὸς ἀλλήλους, ὑπὲρ δὲ τῶν πρὸς τὸ δημόσιον, ὅπως οἱ νόμοι κελεύωσιν). For instance, Theocrines had claimed that the slave woman of Cephisodorus was a free person

[45] This strategy is forbidden in the American legal system, where it is illegal to use a criminal charge, or the threat of one, to force a settlement in a civil case.

[46] On the procedure of *phasis*, see MacDowell (1991).

[47] The law clearly did not forbid all settlements, but only those that violated the laws.

([Dem.] 58.19–20). If the prosecutor in such a case did not prove his charge, he had to pay the owner of the slave 500 drachmas and in addition pay a fine of an equal amount to the treasury. The speechwriter Ctesicles, however, brokered a settlement between the two opponents, which allowed Theocrines to avoid paying the fine to the treasury, a settlement Epicrates says was illegal. By requiring the prosecutor who came to an agreement with the defendant to withdraw formally his charge at the *anakrisis*, the law made it possible for a magistrate to question the litigants and to ensure that they had not conspired to deprive the *polis* of a fine.

Another drawback in allowing settlements for public charges was the possibility that a skilled speaker, who enjoyed influence with the courts, could bring a specious charge against an average citizen, who would prefer to pay off his prosecutor rather than risk conviction in court. This is not a theoretical possibility; our sources reveal that it was a common problem.[48] The Athenians could have prevented this abuse by requiring that all public charges had to go to trial, but this would have brought the disadvantages we noted above. To solve this problem, the Athenians created the *graphe sycophantias*.[49] This charge was made not against men who withdrew public suits, but sycophants who brought false charges for the sole purpose of extorting money from defendants.[50] In these ways, the Athenians were able to retain the advantages of allowing prosecutors to withdraw a case after making an indictment while at the same time providing a means of punishing those who abused the right of withdrawing a case.

Afterthoughts

Wallace (forthcoming) accepts most of the points in this essay. First, he agrees with my reasons for retaining the reading of A for the scholion on Dem. 22.3. Second,

[48] Harvey (1990) 111 note 27 lists thirty-four examples of this practice. Todd (1993) 93 note 18 claims that accusations of blackmail were rare and calls the numerous examples cited by Harvey "the few exceptions"!

[49] For the *graphe sykophantias*, see Harvey (1990) 106–7, who argues the procedure applied in cases where "the prosecutor could provide no proper evidence, witnesses or proofs, so that it became clear that he had either hoped that his victim would pay him not to go to law, or that he was bringing his case solely in order to obtain the prosecutor's share of the fine." Todd (1993) 93, followed by Christ (1998) 238, note 14, believes that Harvey claims "the word must have been legally defined," but Harvey makes no such claim. He merely attempts to provide a definition of the term that accounts for the way it is used in our sources.

[50] Epichares (Dem. 58.12–13) makes a distinction between bringing a serious charge, then making an illegal settlement with the defendant out of court, and bringing a false charge. Only the latter is considered *sycophantia*.

he follows my view that the penalty for failing to obtain one-fifth of the votes cast in a public action was partial *atimia,* whereby the accuser lost the right to bring any kind of public action in the future. Third, Wallace accepts my argument that it was permissible to withdraw a public charge without penalty at the *anakrisis.* Wallace, however, argues that the penalty for failing to follow through on a public charge was only a fine of 1,000 drachmas and did not include partial *atimia.* His view on this issue is contradicted by the evidence of the *Lexicon Cantabrigiense s.v.* πρόστιμον (for the text, see Harrison [1971] 83 note 2), which is confirmed by Dem. 21.103. For a detailed refutation of Wallace's argument, see Harris (forthcoming d).

For more criticisms of Cohen (1995) that the Athenians viewed their courts merely as an arena to pursue private feuds with little regard for the law, see now Rubinstein (2000) *passim,* Kurihara (2003), and Harris (forthcoming a). The last essay shows how the measures against frivolous prosecution worked in practice to reduce litigiousness and to discourage litigants from using the courts to pursue private vendettas.

V

Envoi

V.1 Pheidippides the Legislator: A Note on Aristophanes' *Clouds*

In Aristophanes' *Clouds* Strepsiades sends his son Pheidippides to the Thinkery of Socrates to learn the Weaker Argument (1107–10). Before he enters the Thinkery, Stronger Argument tells the young man what he will acquire under the tutelage of Weaker Argument: a sallow complexion, a terrible physique, a large tongue, and a long decree (1015–19). After he returns from the Thinkery, he shows off his newly acquired legal knowledge by showing his father how to twist the law and evade his creditors (1178–200).[1]

Pheidippides again demonstrates how much he has learned about law when he beats his father (1420–6). Strepsiades objects that it is a law (νομίζεται) that a father should not suffer such treatment. Pheidippides points out that there was someone who originally established this law (οὔκουν ἀνὴρ ὁ τὸν νόμον θεὶς τοῦτον ἦν τὸ πρῶτον) and persuaded the men of old to accept it. Cannot he too make a new law (ἔξεστι κἀμοὶ καινὸν ... θεῖναι νόμον)? This law would order that henceforth (τὸ λοιπόν) sons should beat their fathers back, that is, for the blows they received as children (cf. 1408–15). He then adds an exemption clause: so many blows (ὅσας δὲ πληγὰς) as we children received before the law was established are granted a release (ἀφίεμεν).

Pheidippides' humorous proposal reveals his detailed knowledge of the language of Athenian laws and decrees.[2] When the Athenians passed a measure in the Assembly, they often indicated that its provisions would take effect "henceforth" (τὸ λοιπόν). This meant that the provisions would not apply before the

[1] In this passage Pheidippides interprets that law by analyzing the intent of the lawgiver, a type of argument often found in the orators (e.g., Aeschin. 1.17, 24; 3.11, 44; Hyp. *Ath.* 21). See Hillgruber (1988) 115–16.

[2] Dover (1968) 260 notes that the word ἀφίεμεν "sounds a formal, legal note," but does not comment on the other legal terminology in the passage.

date the measure was passed.[3] There are several examples in decrees preserved in fifth-century inscriptions. For instance, a decree dated to around 448 establishes Overseers for the Goddesses Demeter and Kore (*IG* i³ 32). The decree calls for the Overseers to serve for a year after swearing an oath (line 17), and "*henceforth* men are to be elected in the same way every year to oversee the annual income received by the Two Goddesses" (lines 18–20: *τὸ λοιπὸν* κατὰ ταὐτα hαιρε͂σθαι κ[α]τ' ἐνιαῦτον τὸς ἄνδ[ρ]ας). The same decree instructs these officials "*henceforth* to spend whatever is necessary in consultation with the Priests and with the Council" (lines 28–30: ἀναλίσκειν δὲ ὅ τι ἂν [μ]άλιστα δέει μετὰ τõν hιερέον καὶ τε͂ς β[ολ]ε͂ς βολευομένος *τὸ λοιπόν*). One finds the same expression in the decree passed by Callias (probably in 434/33) about the Treasurers of the Other Gods (*IG* i³ 52). The Assembly gives these treasurers the following order: "*Henceforth* let the successive treasurers write up on a stele and give to the *logistai* an account of the money present [at the start of their term] and the revenues for the gods and if anything is spent during the year and let them submit to scrutiny" (lines A 24–7: καὶ *τὸ λοιπὸν* ἀναγραφόντον hοι αἰεὶ ταμίαι ἐς στέλεν καὶ λόγον διδόντον τõν τε ὄντον χρεμάτον καὶ τõν προσιόντον τοῖς θεοῖς καὶ ἐάν τι ἀ[π]αναλίσεται κατὰ τὸν ἐνιαυτόν, πρὸς τὸς λογιστάς, καὶ εὐθύνας διδόντον). The Interim Constitution of 411 also employs the expression. This document orders the Council to conduct an election of the generals and other officials for the present, then states that "henceforth" the Council will conduct the election according to "what is written" ([Arist.] *Ath. Pol.* 31.3: *τὸ δὲ λοιπὸν* τὴν αἵρεσιν ποιεῖσθαι τούτων τὴν βουλὴν κατὰ τὰ γεγραμμένα).[4]

A decree from Erythrai dated to the 450s, which sets up a new constitution for the city, probably imitates this feature of Athenian decrees since the measure was drawn up under Athenian supervision (*IG* i³ 14.13–15).[5] The decree calls for the Overseers and Garrison-Commander to select a Council by lot, but henceforth the Council and the Garrison-Commander will conduct the lot (*τὸ δὲ λοιπὸν* τὲν βολὲν καὶ τὸν [φρόρ]αρχον). We find the same expression in a law from Lindos dated to the late fifth century about booty.[6] The decree calls for all who serve as soldiers on public expeditions or as mercenaries to contribute one-sixtieth of their

3 For the rationale behind this feature of Athenian laws, see Dem. 24.41–4.

4 For the relationship between this clause and what precedes, see Rhodes (1981) 402–3.

5 For the date, see Meiggs and Lewis (1969) 92–3.

6 I have used the text found in Koerner (1993) #56.

wages to the god Enyalius (lines 5–10). "Henceforth," however, the individuals are to turn the money over to the priest (lines 13–16: *τὸ δὲ λοιπὸν* τὸ ἀπὸ λαῶν τ[οὶ] α[ὐτοὶ] ἰδιῶται πα[ρδ]ι[δ]ό[ντlω] τῶι ἰαρῆι). The decree also calls for the Overseers to write down what the generals have, and "henceforth" what those who serve as soldiers have (lines 23–4: τὸ λοιπόν, οἵ κα στρατεύωνται). Since the beginning of the decree appears to imitate the language of Athenian decrees, the people of Lindos may also have borrowed the expression from the same source.[7]

It was also not unusual for Athenian laws and decrees to add clauses providing some special treatment for a certain class of individuals or objects. These clauses often began with some form of the relative pronoun ὅσος. For instance, the decree that established the Athenian colony at Brea, probably in the 440s, contains a clause ordering as many soldiers as are registered as colonists to go to the colony within thirty days after they come to Athens (*IG* i³ 46, lines 26–9: hόσοι δ ἂν γράφσοντα[ι ἐποικέσεν τõ]ν στρατιοτõν, ἐπειδὰν hέκοσ[ι Ἀθέναζε, τριά]κοντα ἑμερõν ἐμ Βρέαι ἒναι ἐπ[οικέσοντας...]).[8] In a decree probably from 446/45, the Assembly sets forth regulations for Athenian relations with Chalcis (*IG* i³ 40). In the section on taxes, the decree marks out a special category of foreigners, "as many as" live in Chalcis but do not pay taxes to Athens (even if they have been granted an exemption by the Athenian people), and orders them to pay taxes to Chalcis, just as the other Chalcideans do (lines 52–7: τὸς δὲ χσένος τὸς ἐν Χαλκίδι, *h*όσοι οἰκõντες μὲ τελõσιν Ἀθέναζε, καὶ εἴ τοι δέδοται *h*υπὸ τõ δέμο τõ Ἀθεναίον ἀτέλεια, τὸς δὲ ἄλλος τελε͂ν ἐς Χαλκίδα, καθάπερ *h*οι ἄλλοι Χαλκιδέες). A law of Solon quoted in a speech of Demosthenes (44.67–8) grants the right to make a will in any way they wish to "as many men who" were not adopted when Solon entered office ("ὅσοι μὴ ἐπεποίηντο" φησίν "ὅτε Σόλων εἰσῄει εἰς τὴν ἀρχήν, ἐξεῖναι αὐτοῖς διαθέσθαι ὅπως ἂν ἐθέλωσιν"). The law from Lindos examined above threatens the general who does not collect money for the god Enyalius from the soldiers with a charge of impiety and punishment, then states the same will apply to "as many men as" go on expeditions as private

[7] Lines 1–5 appear to contain an Athenian-style prescript with the standard enactment formula (ἔδοξε τᾶι βωλᾶι καὶ τῶ]ι δάμωι), the name of the Epistates (Οι[.... ἐ]πεστάτει), the name of the secretary (Σ[......] ἐγραμμάτευε), and the name of the proposer followed by the verb εἶπε (Ἀγ[άθ]αρχος εἶπε).

[8] There appears to be a similar kind of clause in *IG* i³ 34, lines 58–60: [...*h*]όσοι δὲ τôν ἀπα[γόντον Ἀθέναζε ἐς τὸ πινάκιον ἀν]αγεγράφαται ὀφέλοντες...].

individuals, that is, serve as mercenaries (lines 46–7: κατὰ ταῦτα δὲ καὶ ὅσσ[οι] ἰδίαι στρατεύωνται).

In some laws and decrees, we find both the expression τὸ λοιπόν together with a ὅσος clause. Perhaps the best example is the final clause in the recently discovered Grain-Tax Law passed in 375/74.[9] The law changes the method of collecting two taxes, the one-twentieth tax from the islands and the one-fiftieth tax on grain imported to Athens.[10] The men who buy the contract to collect the tax are to make their payments in grain, and the grain given to the *polis* is to be sold with the proceeds paid into the Military Fund (lines 36–55). The amount of money "as much as" had been handed over as a down-payment in the last year (lines 57–9: ὅσο[ν]περ πέρυσιν <η>ῦρεν ἐκ τοῖν δυοῖν δεκά[.]ιν) for the present contract is to be paid into the general budget (line 59: τὸ μὲν νῦν εἶναι εἰς τὴν διοίκησι[ν . . .]). "Henceforth," however, this amount is not to be subtracted from the payments made, that is, from the money paid to the Military Fund (lines 60–1: τὸ λοιπὸν μὴ <ἀ>φαιρεῖν τὼ δύο δεκά[.] ἐκ τῶν κατ<α>βαλλομένων χρημάτων).[11] The two features are also combined in a fifth-century law about the honor of dining in the Prytaneion dated to the 430s (*IG* i^{3} 131 = Koerner [1993] #13). The law grants this honor to "as many as" have won certain horse races at the major Panhellenic festivals (lines 15–17: ho[π]όσο[ι δὲ hάρματι τελείοι ἒ hίπποι κ]έλετι νενι[κ]έκασι Ὀ[λ]υμπ[ίασι ἒ Πυθοῖ ἒ hισθμοῖ ἒ Νεμέαι.]) or may henceforth win these contests (lines 17–18: [. . . ἒ] νικέσοσι τὸ λοιπό[ν], ἖ναι [καὶ αὐτοῖσι σίτεσιν]). One finds a similar pairing in a fifth-century decree from Erythrai about the office of secretary (Koerner [1993] #74, lines 1–9 = *I Erythrai* 1, lines 1–9). None of those "as many as" have served as secretary in the magistracy of Chalcides onwards (lines 1–3: ὅσοι ἤδη ἐγραμμάτευσαν ἀπὸ Χαλκίδευ ἔκαθεν τούτων . . . μηδενὶ) are permitted to serve as secretary to any office (lines 3–5: μὴ ἐξεῖναι γραμματεῦσαι ἔτι μηδενὶ μηδεμιῆι ἀρχῆι) and "henceforth" no one may serve as secretary to the same office more than once (lines 5–7: μηδὲ τὸ λοιπὸν γραμματεύεν ἐξεῖναι μηδενὶ πλέον ἢ ἅπαξ τῆι αὐτῆι ἀρχῆι) nor to more than one treasurer nor can the same person serve as secretary to two offices (lines 7–9: μηδὲ ταμίαι πλέον ἢ ἑνί, μηδὲ δύο τιμαῖς τὸν αὐτόν).[12]

[9] For the text, see Stroud (1998). For an explanation of the bidding procedure see Osborne (2000).

[10] For the nature of the two taxes, see Harris (1999b) 270–2.

[11] For the meaning of the final clause, see Harris (1999b) 269–70.

[12] Engelmann and Merkelbach (1972) compare this provision with [Arist.] *Ath. Pol.* 62.3, which forbids anyone from holding the same office twice, but this law only prohibits secretaries from serving the

Although his father Strepsiades is not too pleased with the result, it is clear that Pheidippides has received a first-rate education about laws and decrees at the Thinkery. Like a good legislator, Pheidippides states that the law he enacts is to apply "henceforth" (τὸ λοιπόν) and appends a special exemption clause beginning with ὅσας. This study not only makes a small contribution to our understanding of Aristophanes' comic genius, but also reveals something about the audience that watched his plays. Aristophanes would not have imitated the language of Athenian laws and decrees so carefully unless he thought his audience was knowledgeable enough to appreciate the joke.[13] His use of legal language clearly indicates that he expected the Athenian to be familiar with the expressions commonly found in laws and decrees. But that should come as no surprise when one considers that most Athenians must have had a considerable knowledge of their laws; they often listened to debates in the Assembly about legislation, served at least once on the Council where they helped prepare motions for the Assembly, and might act as judges in the popular courts for a year or more.[14] One should never underestimate the legal expertise of the average Athenian.[15]

Afterthoughts

On legal language in Aristophanes, see now Willi (2003) 72–9, especially the conclusion: "it is clear that large proportions of the legal vocabulary even in such a topical play as *Wasps* did not belong to an exclusive specialists' discourse. This appears to be a consequence of the Athenian legal system, in which a large part of the citizens over thirty could and did serve as jurors. As a consequence, a

same magistrate twice. A closer parallel is the law found at Lys. 30.29 for undersecretaries in Athens (ὑπογραμματεῦσαι μὲν οὐκ ἔξεστι δὶς τὸν αὐτὸν τῇ ἀρχῇ τῇ αὐτῇ).

[13] For another example of Aristophanes' use of the language of laws and decrees, see *Av.* 1040–1 (χρῆσθαι... τοῖς μέτροισι καὶ σταθμοῖς καὶ ψηφίσμασι καθάπερ Ὀλοφύξιοι) with *IG* i³ 1453, clause 10 (μὴ χρῆται νομ[ίσμασι τοῖς Ἀθηνα]ίων ἢ σταθμοῖς ἢ μέτ[ροις . .]) with Dunbar (1995) 568–72. Or compare the use of the term καθάπερ in *Ec.* 61 (καθάπερ ἦν ξυγκείμενον) with *IG* i³ 127, lines 16–17 (καθάπερ ξύνκειται Ἀθηναίοις καὶ Σαμίοις) and in *Ec.* 75 (καθάπερ εἴπομεν) with *IG* i³ 46, lines 38–9 (καθάπερ Δεμοκλ[ε]ίδες εἶπεν). Finally note the use of the term ἔδοξε at *Ec.* 18 and 59.

[14] For the legal knowledge of the average Athenian, see Harris (1994a) 135–6.

[15] See, for instance, Christ (1998) 203–8, who argues unconvincingly that the Athenians prided themselves on being amateurs in legal matters. Cf. Cohen (1995) 180: "in an Athenian trial all the untutored (*sic*) judges knew about (...) the applicable laws, was what the two contesting litigants chose to tell them." For a litigant assuming that the judges knew the law without him having to tell them what it is, see Dem. 37.18.

I would like to thank my colleague Donna Wilson for reading over a draft of this note.

comparatively advanced mastery of legal vocabulary was recognized as the cultural standard. Of course Aristophanes may have preferred not to use many words exactly because they were too technical. But even that would point in the same direction: if Aristophanes, in a play centred on legal matters, did not make fun of legal vocabulary, this vocabulary was probably not regarded as technical. The democratic organization of the lawcourts prevented not only the creation of an inaccessible legal language, but also the folk-linguistic idea that legal language is hard to understand and employ."

Bibliography

Abbreviations used in the Bibliography

AC = *Antiquité classique*
AHR = *American Historical Review*
AJA = *American Journal of Archaeology*
AJP = *American Journal of Philology*
Arch. Delt. = *Archaiologikon Deltion*
BCH = *Bulletin de Correspondence Hellénique*
BSA = *Annual of the British School at Athens*
CA = *Classical Antiquity*
CIM = *Classica et Medievalia*
CJ = *Classical Journal*
CP = *Classical Philology*
CR = *Classical Review*
CQ = *Classical Quarterly*
EMC/CV = *Échos du monde classique/Classical Views*
EtCl = *Études classiques*
G&R = *Greece and Rome*
GRBS = *Greek, Roman and Byzantine Studies*
HSCP= *Harvard Studies in Classical Philology*
HThR = *Harvard Theological Review*
JHS = *Journal of Hellenic Studies*
JJP = *Journal of Juristic Papyrology*
LCM = *Liverpool Classical Monthly*
MusB = *Musée Belge*
NC = *Numismatic Chronicle*
RE = *Real Enzyklopädie der klassischen Altertumswissenschaft*, ed. G. Pauly and A. Wissowa
REG = *Revue des études grecques*
RHDFE = *Revue historique de droit français et étranger*
RFIC = *Rivista di filologia e di istruzione classica*
RIDA = *Revue internationale des droits de l'antiquité*
RHist = *Revue Historique*
RhM = *Rheinisches Museum*
Riv. dir. int. = *Rivista di diritto internazionale*
SymbOslo = *Symbolae Osloenses*
TAPA = *Transactions of the American Philological Association*

ZPE = *Zeitschrift für Papyrologie und Epigraphik*
ZSS = *Zeitschrift für Savigny Stiftung: Romanistische Abteilung*

Works Cited

Adams, C. D. (1905/1970). Reprint of *Lysias: Selected Speeches.* Norman, OK.

Aerts, W. J. (1965). *Periphrastica.* Amsterdam.

Albertoni, A. (1925). "*Redemptus ab hostibus.*" *Riv. dir. int.* 17: 358–78, 500–27.

Andrewes, A. (1982). "The growth of the Athenian state," in *The Cambridge Ancient History*[2] III. 3: 360–91.

Arafat, K. W. (1997). "State of the art – art of the state: Sexual violence and politics in Late Archaic and Early Classical vase-painting," in Deacy and Pierce (1997): 97–21.

Astin, A. E. (1957). "The Lex Annalis before Sulla," *Latomus* 16: 588–613.

Astin, A. E. (1958). "The Lex Annalis before Sulla," *Latomus* 17: 49–64.

Austin, J. L. (1961). *Philosophical Papers.* Oxford.

Badian, E. (1980). "Philip II and Thrace," *Pulpudeva* 4: 51–71.

Ballagh, J. C. (1902). *History of Slavery in Virginia.* Baltimore.

Barsby, J., ed. (1999). *Terence: Eunuchus.* Cambridge.

Bateman, J. J. (1958). "Lysias and the law," *TAPA* 89: 276–85.

Bauman, R. A. (1996). "The interface of Greek and Roman Law," *RIDA*[3] 43: 39–62.

Beauchet, L. (1897). *Histoire du droit privé de la république athénienne.* Paris.

Behrend, D. (1979). *Attische Pachturkunden: Ein Beitrag zur Beschreibung der μίσθωσις nach der griechischen Inschriften.* Munich.

Benardete, S. (1975). "A reading of Sophocles' *Antigone,*" *Interpretation* 4: 148–96, 5: 1–55, 148–84.

Bennett, L. J. and W. Blake Tyrrell. (1990). "Sophocles' *Antigone* and Funeral Oratory," *AJP* 111: 441–56.

Bers, V. (1984). *Greek Poetic Syntax in the Classical Age.* New Haven.

Bertrand-Dagenbach, C., A. Chauvot, M. Matter, and J.-M. Salamito, eds. (1999). *Carcer: Prison et privation de liberté dans l'antiquité classique.* Paris.

Bielman, A. (1994). *Retour à la liberté. Libération et sauvetage des prisonniers en Grèce ancienne* (= *Études Épigraphiques* 1). Athens and Lausanne.

Biscardi, A. (1999). *Scritti di diritto Greco.* Milan.

Blaise, F. (1994). "Solon. Fragment 36 W. Pratique et fondation des normes politiques," *REG* 108: 24–37.

Blass, F. (1887–98). *Die attische Beredsamkeit.* Leipzig.

de Blois, L. (forthcoming). "Plutarch's *Solon*: Commonplace or historical reality?" in Blok and Lardinois (forthcoming).

Blok, J. (forthcoming). "Solon's funeral laws: Questions of authenticity and function," in Blok and Lardinois (forthcoming).

Blok, J. and A. Lardinois, eds. (forthcoming). *Solon of Athens: New Historical and Philological Approaches.* Leiden.

Boegehold, A. (1996). "Resistance to change in the law at Athens," in Ober and Hedrick (1996): 203–14.

Bonner, R. J. and G. Smith. (1938). *The Administration of Justice from Homer to Aristotle.* Chicago.
Bottéro, J. (1992). *Mesopotamia: Writing, Reasoning, and the Gods.* Trans. by Z. Bahrani and M. Van de Mieroop. Chicago.
Bourriot, F. (1976). *Recherches sur la nature du genos: Étude d'histoire sociale athénienne dans les périodes archaïque et classique.* Lille.
Bowersock, G. W. (1965). *Augustus and the Greek World.* Oxford.
Bowra, M. (1944). *Sophoclean Tragedy.* Oxford.
Bradeen, D. W. and M. F. MacGregor, eds. (1974). *Phoros, Tribute to Benjamin Dean Meritt.* Locut Valley, NY.
Bravo, B. (1980). "Sulân," *Annali della scuola normale di Pisa,* series 3, 10.3: 675–987.
Bresson, A. (2000). *La cité marchande.* Bordeaux.
Briant, P. (2002). *From Cyrus to Alexander: A History of the Persian Empire.* Winona Lake, IL.
Brown, P. G. McG. (1983). "Menander's dramatic technique and the law of Athens," *CQ* 33: 412–20.
Brown, P. G. McG. (1991). "Athenian attitudes to rape and seduction: The evidence of Menander's *Dyskolos,*" *CQ* 41: 533–4.
Brown, P. G. McG. (1993). "Love and marriage in Greek New Comedy," *CQ* 43: 189-205.
Brownmiller, S. (1975). *Against Our Will: Men, Women, and Rape.* New York.
Brun, P. (1983). *Eisphora-Syntaxis-Stratiotika: Recherches sur les finances militaires d'Athènes au IVe siècle.* Paris.
Buchanan, J. (1962). *Theorika.* New York.
Burchfiel, K. (1994). "The myth of 'prelaw' in early Greece," in Thür (1994): 79–104.
Burkert, W. (1985). *Greek Religion: Archaic and Classical.* Trans. J. Raffan. Oxford.
Busolt, G. (1893–4). *Griechische Geschichte.* Gotha.
Busolt, G. and H. Swoboda. (1920–26). *Griechische Staatskunde.* Munich.
Cahn, H. (1977). "Asiut. Kritische Bemerkungen zu einer Schatzfundpublikation," *Revue Suisse de numismatique* 56: 279–87.
Cairns, D. (1996). "*Hybris,* dishonour, and thinking big," *JHS* 116: 1–32.
Campbell, D. A. (1967). *Greek Lyric Poetry: A Selection of Early Greek Lyric, Elegiac and Iambic Poetry.* London.
Cantarella, E. (1991). "*Moicheia*: Reconsidering a problem," in Gagarin (1991): 289–304.
Cantarella, E. and G. Thür, eds. (2001). *Symposion 1997: Vorträge zur griechischen und hellenistischen Rechtsgeschichte.* Cologne, Weimar, and Vienna.
Carawan, E. (1984). "*Akriton Apokteinein*: Execution without trial in fourth-century Athens," *GRBS* 25: 111–22.
Carawan, E. (1998). *Rhetoric and the Law of Draco.* Oxford.
Carey, C. (1989). *Lysias: Selected Speeches.* Cambridge.
Carey, C. (1992). *Apollodorus: Against Neaira [Demosthenes] 59.* Warminster.
Carey, C. (1993). "Return of the radish or just when you thought it safe to go back into the kitchen," *LCM* 18.4: 53–5.
Carey, C. (1995). "Rape and adultery in Athenian Law," *CQ* 45: 407–17.
Carey, C. (1996). "*Nomos* in Attic rhetoric and oratory," *JHS* 116: 33–46.
Carey, C. (1998). "The shape of Athenian laws," *CQ* 48: 93–109.
Carey, C. (2004). "Offence and procedure in Athenian Law," in Harris and Rubinstein (2004): 111–36.

Carey, C. and R. Reid. (1985). *Demosthenes: Selected Private Speeches*. Cambridge.
Cartledge, P., P. Millett, and S. Todd, eds. (1990). *Nomos: Essays in Athenian Law, Politics, and Society*. Cambridge.
Cartledge, P., P. Millett, and S. von Reden, eds. (1998). *Essays in Order, Conflict and Community in Classical Athens*. Cambridge.
Cartledge, P., E. Cohen, and L. Foxhall, eds. (2002). *Money, Labour and Land: Approaches to the Economy of Ancient Greece*. London and New York.
Cawkwell, G. L. (1962). "Demosthenes and the Stratiotic Fund," *Mnemosyne* 15: 377–83.
Cawkwell, G. L. (1963). "Eubulus," *JHS* 83: 47–67.
Cawkwell, G. (1973). "The date of *IG* ii^2 1609 again," *Historia* 22: 759–61.
Chadwick, J. (1990). "The Pech-Maho lead," *ZPE* 82: 161–6.
Chaniotis, A. (1994). Review of Lalonde, Langdon, and Walbank (1991).
Chaniotis, A. (2004). "Justifying territorial claims in Classical and Hellenistic Greece: The beginnings of international law," in Harris and Rubinstein (2004): 185–213.
Christ, M. (1998). *The Litigious Athenian*. Baltimore and London.
Classen, J. and J. Steup. (1963). *Thukidides*.[6] Berlin.
Clinton, K. (1980). "A law in the city Eleusinion concerning the Mysteries," *Hesperia* 49: 258–88.
Cohen, D. (1983). *Theft in Athenian Law*. Munich.
Cohen, D. (1984a). "The Athenian law of adultery," *RIDA* 31: 147–65.
Cohen, D. (1984b). "A note on Aristophanes and the punishment of adultery in Athenian Law," *ZSS* 102: 385–87.
Cohen, D. (1989). "Seclusion, separation, and the status of women in Classical Athens," *G&R* 36: 3–15.
Cohen, D. (1991a). *Law, Sexuality, and Society: The Enforcement of Morals in Classical Athens*. Cambridge.
Cohen, D. (1991b). "Sexuality, violence, and the Athenian law of *Hybris*," *G&R* 28: 171–88.
Cohen, D. (1993). "Consent and sexual relations in Classical Athens," in Laiou (1993): 5–16.
Cohen, D. (1995). *Law, Violence, and Community in Classical Athens*. Cambridge.
Cohen, D. (1998). "Women, property and status in Demosthenes 41 and 57," *DIKE* 1: 53–62.
Cohen, D., ed. (2002). *Demokratie, Recht und soziale Kontrolle im klassischen Athen* (= *Schriften des Historischen Kollegs Kolloquien* 49). Munich.
Cohen, E. E. (1973). *Ancient Athenian Maritime Courts*. Princeton.
Cohen, E. E. (2000). *The Athenian Nation*. Princeton.
Cohn-Haft, L. (1995). "Divorce in Classical Athens," *JHS* 115: 1–15.
Cole, S. G. (1984). "Greek sanctions against sexual assault," *CP* 79: 97–113.
Conomis, N. (1961). "Notes on the Fragments of Lycurgus," *Klio* 39: 72–152.
Cook, R. M. (1946). "Ionia and Greece in the eighth and seventh centuries B.C.," *JHS* 66: 67–98.
Crawley, R. (1874/1910). Reissue of *Thucydides: The Peloponnesian War*. London.
Crook, J. A. (1967). *Law and Life of Rome, 90 BC–AD 212*. London.
Crosby, M. (1941). "Greek inscriptions," *Hesperia* 10: 14–27.
Dandamaev, M. A. (1984). *Slavery in Babylonia*. Dekalb, IL.
Daremberg, C. and E. Saglio, eds. (1877–1919). *Dictionnaire des antiquités grecques et romaines*. Paris.

Dareste, R., B. Haussoullier, and T. Reinach. (1891–1904). *Recueil des inscriptions juridiques grecques.* Paris.

David, E. (1985). "The trial of Spartan kings," *RIDA*[3] 32: 131–40.

Davies, J. K. (1969). "The date of *IG* ii[2] 1609," *Historia* 18: 309–33.

Davies, J. K. (1971). *Athenian Propertied Families 600–300 B.C.* Oxford.

Deacy, S. and K. F. Pierce, eds. (1997). *Rape in Antiquity: Sexual Violence in the Greek and Roman Worlds.* London.

Denniston, J. D. (1954). *The Greek Particles*[2]. Oxford.

Develin, R. (1989). *Athenian Officials 684–321 B.C.* Cambridge.

Dickey, E. (1996). *Greek Forms of Address.* Oxford.

Dilts, M. R. (1983–86). *Scholia Demosthenica.* Vols. I–II. Leipzig.

Dilts, M. R. (1985). "Palaeologian scholia on the orations of Demosthenes," *CIM* 36: 257–9.

Dinsmoor, W. B. (1931). *The Archons of Athens in the Hellenistic Period.* Cambridge, MA.

Doblhofer, G. (1994). *Vergewaltigung in der Antike.* Stuttgart and Leipzig.

Dodds, E. R. (1960). *Euripides: Bacchae*[2]. Oxford.

Dover, K. J. (1968). *Aristophanes: Clouds.* Oxford.

Dover, K. J. (1974). *Greek Popular Morality.* Oxford.

Dover, K. J. (1978). *Greek Homosexuality.* Cambridge, MA.

Dover, K. J. (1993). *Aristophanes: Frogs.* Oxford.

Dow, S. and A. H. Travis. (1943). "Demetrios of Phaleron and his lawgiving," *Hesperia* 12: 144–65.

Drerup, E. (1898). "Über die bei den attischen Rednern eingelegten Urkunden," *Jahrbuch für Classische Philologie* Supplementband 24: 221–366.

Duchêne, H. (1992). *La stèle du port* (= *Études thasiennes* XIV). Athens and Paris.

Dunbar, N. (1995). *Aristophanes: Birds.* Oxford.

van Effenterre, H. and F. Ruzé. (1994–95). *Nomima: Recueil d'inscriptions politiques et juridiques de l'archaïsme grec.* Two volumes. Paris. (= *Nomima* I and *Nomima* II).

Ehrenberg, V. (1965). *Der Staat der Griechen.* Stuttgart.

Endenburg, P. J. T. (1937). *Koinonia: En Gemeenschap von Zaken bij de Griken in den klassieken Tijd.* Amsterdam.

Engelmann, H. and R. Merkelbach. (1972). *Die Inschriften von Erythrai und Klazomenai.* Bonn.

Erbse, H. (1956). "Über die Midiana des Demosthenes," *Hermes* 84: 135–51.

Errington, R. M. (1994). "Ἐκκλησία κυρία in Athens," *Chiron* 24: 135–60.

Fantham, E. (1975). "Sex, status and survival in Hellenistic Athens: A study of women in New Comedy," *Phoenix* 26: 44–74.

Faraguna, M. (1997). "Registrazioni catastali nel mondo Greco: Il caso di Atene," *Athenaeum* 85: 1–33.

Faraguna, M. (2000). "A proposito degli archivi nel mondo Greco: terra e registrazioni fondiarie," *Chiron* 30: 65–115.

Ferguson, W. S. (1944). "The Attic Orgeones," *HThR* 37: 61–140.

Figueira, T. (1986). "*Sitopolai* and *sitophylakes* in Lysias' 'Against the Graindealers': Governmental intervention in the Athenian economy," *Phoenix* 40: 14–71.

Figueira, T. (2003). "*Xenelasia* and social control in Classical Sparta," *CQ* 53: 44–74.

Fine, J. V. A. (1951). *Horoi: Studies in Mortgage, Real Security and Land Tenure in Ancient Athens* [= *Hesperia* Suppl. 9]. Princeton.

Finkelstein, J. J. (1961). "Ammiaduqa' edict and the Babylonian lawcodes," *Journal of Cuneiform Studies* 15: 91–104.

Finley, M. I. (1951). "Some problems of Greek Law: A consideration of Pringsheim on sale," *Seminar* 9: 72–91.

Finley, M. I. (1952). *Studies in Land and Credit in Ancient Athens, 500–200 B.C.* New Brunswick.

Finley, M. I. (1953). "Multiple charges on real property in Athenian Law: New evidence from an Agora inscription," in *Studi in onore di Vincenzo Arangio-Ruiz*. Naples: 473–91.

Finley, M. I. (1955). "Marriage, gift, and sale in the Homeric world," *RIDA* 2: 167–94.

Finley, M. I. (1957). "Homer and Mycenae: Property and tenure," *Historia* 6: 133–59.

Finley, M. I. (1966). "The problem of the unity of Greek Law," in *Atti del 1° Congresso Internazionale della Società del Diritto*. Florence: 129–44.

Finley, M. I. (1968). "The alienability of land in ancient Greece," *Eirene* 7: 25–32.

Finley, M. I. (1975). *The Use and Abuse of History*. London.

Finley, M. I. (1978). *The World of Odysseus*^{2}. London.

Finley, M. I. (1981). *Economy and Society in Ancient Greece*. Ed. B. D. Shaw and R. P. Saller. London.

Finley, M. I. (1985). *Studies in Land and Credit in Ancient Athens, 500–200 B.C.* Rev. by P. Millett. New Brunswick.

Finley, M. I. (1998). *Ancient Slavery and Modern Ideology*. Expanded Edition. Ed. B. D. Shaw. Princeton.

Fisher, N. R. E. (1976). "*Hybris* and Dishonour I," *G&R* 23: 177–93.

Fisher, N. R. E. (1979). "*Hybris* and Dishonour II," *G&R* 26: 32–47.

Fisher, N. R. E. (1992). *Hybris*. Warminster.

Fisher, N. R. E. (1993). *Slavery in Classical Greece*. London.

Fisher, N. R. E. (2001). *Aeschines: Against Timarchus*. Oxford.

Flensted-Jensen, P., T. H. Nielsen, and L. Rubinstein, eds. (2000). *Polis & Politics: Studies in Ancient Greek History*. Copenhagen.

Fletcher, G. (1978). *Rethinking Criminal Law*. Boston and Toronto.

Foley, H. (1995). "Tragedy and democratic ideology: The case of Sophocles' Antigone," in B. Goff, ed. *History, Tragedy, Theory: Dialogues on Athenian Drama*. Austin, TX: 131–50.

Forster, E. S. (1927). *Isaeus*. Cambridge, MA.

Foucault, M. (1984). *Histoire de la sexualité II: L'usage des plaisirs*. Paris.

Foxhall, L. (1989). "Household, gender, and property in Classical Athens," *CQ* 39: 22–4.

Foxhall, L. (1991). "Response to Eva Cantarella," in Gagarin (1991): 297–304.

Foxhall, L. (1997). "A View from the top: Evaluating the Solonian property classes," in Mitchell and Rhodes (1997): 113–36.

Foxhall, L. and A. D. E. Lewis, eds. (1996). *Greek Law in its Political Setting*. Oxford.

Foxhall, L. and J. Salmon, eds. (1998). *Thinking Men: Masculinity and its Self-Representation in the Classical Tradition*. London and New York.

Francotte, H. (1913). "Études sur Démosthène: Démosthène et le théorique," *MusB* 17: 69–71.

French, A. (1956). "The economic background to Solon's reforms," CQ 50: 11–25.

Friis Johansen, H. and E. W. Whittle. (1980). *Aeschylus: The Suppliants*. Copenhagen.

Fuks, A. (1951). "Kolonos misthios: Labour exchange in Classical Athens," *Eranos* 49: 171–3.

Gagarin, M. (1979a). "The Athenian law against *Hybris,*" in G. W. Bowersock *et al.*, eds. *Arktouros.* Berlin and New York: 229–36.
Gagarin, M. (1979b). "The prosecution of homicide in Athens," *GRBS* 20: 301–23.
Gagarin, M. (1981). *Drakon and Early Athenian Homicide Law.* New Haven.
Gagarin, M. (1986). *Early Greek Law.* Berkeley and Los Angeles.
Gagarin, M. (1988). "The First Law of the Gortyn Code," *GRBS* 29: 335–43.
Gagarin, M. (1990). "*Bouleusis* in Athenian homicide law," in Nenci and Thür (1990): 81–99.
Gagarin, M., ed. (1991). *Symposion 1990.* Cologne and Vienna.
Gagarin, M. (2000). "The *Basileus* in Athenian homicide law," in Flensted-Jensen, Nielsen, and Rubinstein (2000): 569–79.
Gagarin, M. (forthcoming). "Legal procedure in Solon's laws," in Blok and Lardinois (forthcoming).
Gagarin, M. and R. W. Wallace, eds. (2005). *Symposion 2001: Vorträge zur griechischen und hellenistischen Rechtsgeschichte.* Cologne and Vienna.
Gallant, T. W. (1982). "Agricultural systems, land tenure, and the reforms of Solon," *BSA* 77: 111–24.
Garlan, Y. (1988). *Slavery in Ancient Greece.* Trans. Janet Lloyd. Ithaca.
Garnsey, P. (1988). *Famine and Food Supply in the Graeco-Roman World.* Cambridge.
Garnsey, P., K. Hopkins, and C. R. Whittaker, eds. (1983). *Trade in the Ancient Economy.* Cambridge.
Gauthier, P. (1972). *Symbola. Les étrangers et la justice dans les cités grecques.* Paris.
Gauthier, P. (1981). "De Lysias à Aristote (*Ath. Pol.* 51.4): le commerce du grain à Athènes et les fonctions des sitophylaques," *RHDFE* 59: 5–28.
Gauthier, P. (1987). "Bulletin épigraphique: Institutions," *REG* 100: 308–37.
Gauthier, P. (1989). "Bulletin épigraphique: Institutions," *REG* 102: 390–408.
Germain, L. R. F. (1968). *La publicité des sûretés foncières dans la Grèce classique et hellénistique.* Dissertation. Paris.
Germain, L. R. F. (1975). "Les *horoi*: exposé de la méthode littérale et des resultats obtenus," in Wolff (1975): 333–46.
Germain, L. R. F. (1982–84). "Une sûreté mal connue: l'*apotimema* attique. Étude de la troisième famille d'*apotimema,*" in *Studi in onore di Arnaldo Biscardi.* Vol. 3: 445–57. Milan.
Gernet, L. (1951). "Le droit de la vente et la notion du contrat en Grèce d'après M. Pringsheim," *RHDFE* 29: 560–84.
Gernet, L. (1955). "Horoi," in *Studi in onore di Ugo Enrico Paoli.* Florence: 345–53.
Gernet, L. (1959). *Démosthène: plaidoyers civils.* III. Paris.
Gernet, L. (1968). *Droit et société en grèce antique.* Paris.
Ghiggia, P. Cobetto. (1999). *L' adozione ad Atene in epoca classica.* Alessandria.
Ghiggia, P. Cobetto. (2001). "Una testimonianza sull'*apokeryxis* nell'*Alcesti* di Euripide," in Cantarella and Thür (2001): 53–60.
Glotz, G. (1928). *La cité grecque.* Paris.
Glotz, G. (1932). "Démosthène et les finances athéniennes de 346 à 339," *RHist* 170: 385–97.
Golden, M. (1979). "Demosthenes and the age of majority in Athens," *Phoenix* 33: 25–38.
Goldhill, S. (1986). *Reading Greek Tragedy.* Cambridge.
Gomme, A. W. (1956). *A Historical Commentary on Thucydides.* Volume 2. Oxford.

Gomme, A. W., A. Andrewes, and K. J. Dover. (1981). *A Historical Commentary on Thucydides*. Volume 5. Oxford.

Gomme, A. W. and F. H. Sandbach. (1973). *Menander: A Commentary*. Oxford.

Goody, J. (1986). *The Logic of Writing and the Organization of Society*. Cambridge.

Grant, J. R. (1971). "Thucydides 2.37.1," *Phoenix* 25: 104–7.

Griffith, M. (1983). *Aeschylus: Prometheus Bound*. Cambridge.

Griffith, M. (1999). *Sophocles: Antigone*. Cambridge.

Guarducci, M. (1935–50). *Inscriptiones Creticae*. 4 vols. Rome (= *ICret*).

Guest, A. G., ed. (1961). *Oxford Essays in Jurisprudence*. Oxford.

Günter, E. (1914). *Die Sicherungsübereignung im griechischem Recht*. Dissertation Königsberg.

Habicht, C. (1979). *Untersuchungen zur politischen Geschichte Athens* (= *Vestigia* 30). Munich.

Habicht, C. (1982). *Studien zur Geschichte Athens in hellenistischer Zeit* (= *Hypomnemata* 73). Gottingen.

Habicht, C. (1985). *Pausanias' Guide to Ancient Greece*. Berkeley and Los Angeles.

Habicht, C. (1988). "The eponymous archons of Athens from 159/58 to 141/40," *Hesperia* 57: 237–47.

Hajdu, I. (2002). *Kommentar zur 4. Philippischen Rede des Demosthenes*. Berlin and New York.

Hall, E. (1989). *Inventing the Barbarian*. Oxford.

Hall, J. (2002). *Hellenicity: Between Ethnicity and Culture*. Cambridge.

Halperin, D. M., J. J. Winkler, and F. I. Zeitlin, eds. (1990). *Before Sexuality: The Construction of Erotic Experience in the Ancient Greek World*. Princeton.

Hansen, M. H. (1974). *The Sovereignty of the People's Court in the Fourth Century B.C. and the Public Action against Unconstitutional Proposals*. Odense.

Hansen, M. H. (1975). *Eisangelia: The Sovereignty of the People's Court in Athens in the Fourth Century B.C. and the Impeachment of Generals and Politicians*. Odense.

Hansen. M. H. (1976a). *Apagoge, Endeixis, and Ephegesis against Kakourgoi, Atimoi, and Pheugontes*. Odense.

Hansen, M. H. (1976b). "The Theoric Fund and the *graphe paranomon* against Apollodoros," *GRBS* 17: 235–46.

Hansen, M. H. (1977). "How often did the *Ecclesia* meet?" *GRBS* 18: 43–70.

Hansen, M. H. (1978). "*Nomos* and *Psephisma* in fourth-century Athens," *GRBS* 19: 315–30.

Hansen, M. H. (1979a). "Did the Athenian *Ecclesia* legislate after 403/2?" *GRBS* 20: 27–53.

Hansen, M. H. (1979b). "Ἐκκλησία Σύγκλητος in Hellenistic Athens," *GRBS* 20: 149–56.

Hansen, M. H. (1981). "The prosecution of homicide: A reply," *GRBS* 22: 21–30.

Hansen, M. H. (1982). "When did the Athenian *Ecclesia* meet?" *GRBS* 23: 331–50.

Hansen, M. H. (1983a). *The Athenian Ecclesia: A Collection of Articles* (= *Opuscula Graecolatina* 26). Odense.

Hansen, M. H. (1983b). "*Graphe* or *dike traumatos*?" *GRBS* 24: 307–20.

Hansen, M. H. (1987a). "How often did the Athenian Assembly meet? A reply," *GRBS* 28: 35–50.

Hansen, M. H. (1987b). *The Athenian Assembly in the Age of Demosthenes*. Oxford and New York.

Hansen, M. H. (1991). *The Athenian Democracy in the Age of Demosthenes*. Oxford.

Hansen, M. H. (1993). "Was the Athenian Ekklesia convened according to the Festival Calendar or the Bouleutic Calendar?" *AJP* 114: 99–113.

Hansen, M. H. (1998). *Polis and City-State: An Ancient Concept and Its Modern Equivalent*. Copenhagen.

Hansen, M. H. and F. W. Mitchel. (1984). "The number of *ecclesiai* in forth-century Athens," *SymbOslo* 59: 13–19.

Harris, E. M. (1985). "The date of the trial of Timarchus," *Hermes* 113: 376–80.

Harris, E. M. (1986). "How often did the Athenian Assembly meet?" *CQ* 36: 363–77.

Harris, E. M. (1988a). "The date of Apollodorus' speech against Timotheus and its implications for Athenian history and legal procedure," *AJP* 109: 44–52.

Harris, E. M. (1988b). "When is a sale not a sale? The riddle of Athenian terminology for real security revisited," *CQ* 38: 351–81.

Harris, E. M. (1989). "Demosthenes' speech *Against Meidias*," *HSCP* 92: 117–36.

Harris, E. M. (1990a). "Did the Athenians consider seduction a worse crime than rape?" *CQ* 40: 370–7.

Harris, E. M. (1990b). "The Constitution of the Five Thousand," *HSCP* 93: 243–80.

Harris, E. M. (1991a). "Response to Trevor Saunders," in Gagarin (1991): 134–6.

Harris, E. M. (1991b). "When did the Athenian Assembly meet? Some new evidence," *AJP* 112: 329–45.

Harris, E. M. (1992a). "Pericles' praise of Athenian democracy," *HSCP* 94: 57–67.

Harris, E. M. (1992b). "Women and lending in Classical Athens: A *horos* re–Examined," *Phoenix* 4: 309–21.

Harris, E. M. (1992c). Review of MacDowell (1990). *CP* 87: 71–80.

Harris, E. M. (1993). "*Apotimema.* Athenian terminology for real security in leases and dowry arrangements," *CQ* 43: 73–95.

Harris, E. M. (1994a). "Law and oratory," in Worthington (1994): 130–50.

Harris, E. M. (1994b). "Demosthenes loses a friend and Nausicles gains a position: A prosopographical note on Athenian politics after Chaeronea," *Historia* 43: 378–84.

Harris, E. M. (1994c). "'In the act' or 'red-handed'? *Furtum Manifestum* and *Apagoge* to the Eleven," in Thür (1994): 129–46.

Harris, E. M. (1995). *Aeschines and Athenian Politics.* Oxford.

Harris, E. M. (1996a). "Demosthenes and the Theoric Fund," in Wallace and Harris (1996): 57–76.

Harris, E. M. (1996b). Review of Doblhofer (1994). *CR* 46: 327–9.

Harris, E. M. (1997). "Solon and the Seisachtheia," in Mitchell and Rhodes (1997): 103–12.

Harris, E. M. (1998). Review-Discussion of Deacy and Peirce (1997). *EMC/CV* 40 (16): 483–96.

Harris. E. M. (1999a). "The penalties for frivolous prosecution in Athenian Law," *DIKE* 2: 123–42.

Harris, E. M. (1999b). "Notes on the new grain-tax law," *ZPE* 128:

Harris, E. M. (2000a). "Open texture in Athenian Law,"*DIKE* 3: 27–79.

Harris, E. M. (2000b). "The authenticity of Andocides' *De Pace*: A subversive essay," in *Polis and Politics: Studies in Ancient Greek History*, P. Flensted-Jensen, T. Nielsen, and L. Rubinstein, eds. Copenhagen: 479–506.

Harris, E. M. (2001a). "How to kill in Attic Greek: The semantics of the Verb (ἀπο)κτείνειν and their implications for Athenian homicide law," in Cantarella and Thür (2001): 75–88.

Harris, E. M. (2001b). Review of Bresson (2001). *Bryn Mawr Classical Review* 2001.09.40.

Harris, E. M. (2002a). "Did Solon abolish debt-bondage?" *CQ* 52: 415–30.

Harris, E. M. (2002b). "Pheidippides the legislator: A note on Aristophanes' *Clouds*," *ZPE* 140: 3–5.

Harris, E. M. (2002c). "Workshop, household and marketplace," in Cartledge, Cohen, and Foxhall (2002): 67–99.

Harris, E. M. (2004a). "Antigone the lawyer, or The ambiguities of *Nomos*," in Harris and Rubinstein (2004): 19–56.

Harris, E. M. (2004b). "Le rôle de *l'epieikeia* dans les tribunaux athéniens," *RHDFE* 82: 1–13.

Harris, E. M. (2004c). "More thoughts on open texture in Athenian Law," in *Nomos – estudos sobre direito antigo*, ed. D. Leao, D. Rosetti, and M. Fialho. Coimbra: 241–63.

Harris, E. M. (2005). "Feuding or the rule of law? The nature of litigation in Classical Athens: An essay in legal sociology," in Gagarin and Wallace (2005): 125–41.

Harris, E. M. (forthcoming a). "Notes on a lead letter from the Athenian Agora," forthcoming in *HSCP* 102.

Harris, E. M. (forthcoming b). "Solon and the spirit of Early Greek Law," in Blok and A. Lardinois (forthcoming).

Harris, E. M. (forthcoming c). "Did the Athenian courts attempt to achieve consistency? Oral tradition and written records in the Athenian administration of Justice," forthcoming in C. Cooper, ed. *The Politics of Orality*. Leiden.

Harris, E. M. (forthcoming d). "Reply to Robert Wallace," in Rupprecht (forthcoming).

Harris, E. M. and L. Rubinstein, eds. (2004). *The Law and the Courts in Ancient Greece*. London.

Harris, W. V. (1989). *Ancient Literacy*. Cambridge, MA.

Harrison, A. R. W. (1968). *The Law of Athens: Family and Property*. Oxford.

Harrison, A. R. W. (1971). *The Law of Athens: Procedure*. Oxford.

Harrison, T. (1997). "Herodotus and the ancient Greek idea of rape," in Deacy and Pierce (1997): 185–208.

Hart, H. L. A. (1961). *The Concept of Law*. Oxford.

Harvey, D. (1966). "Literacy in the Athenian democracy," *REG* 79: 585–635.

Harvey, D. (1990). "The sycophant and sycophancy: Vexatious redefinition?" in Cartledge, Millett, and Todd (1990): 103–21.

Haslam, M. W. (1975). "The authenticity of Euripides' *Phoenissae* 1–2 and Sophocles' *Electra* 1," *GRBS* 16: 149–74.

Haubold, J. (2000). *Homer's People: Epic Poetry and Social Formation*. Cambridge.

Hay, D. (1989). "Prosecution and power: Malicious prosecution in the English courts 1750–1850," in Hay and Snyder (1989): 343–95.

Hay, D. and F. Snyder, eds. (1989). *Policing and Prosecution in Britain 1758–1850*. Oxford.

Headlam, W. (1922). *Herodas: The Mimes and Fragments*. Cambridge.

Heinen, H. (1972). *Untersuchungen zur hellenistischen Geschichte des 3. Jahrhunderts v. Chr.* Weisbaden.

Hengstl, J. (1972). *Private Arbeitsverhältnisse freier Personen in den hellenistischen Papyri bis Diokletian*. Bonn.

Henry, A. (1977). *The Prescripts of Athenian Decrees* (= *Mnemosyne* Suppl. 44). Leiden.

Herman, G. (1980–81). "The friends of the Early Hellenistic rulers: Servants or officials?" *Talanta* 12–13: 103–49.

Hermann, J. (1957–58). "Vertragsinhalt und Rechtsnatur der DIDASKALIKAI," *JJP* 11–12: 119–38.

Hester, D. A. (1971). "Sophocles the unphilosophical," *Mnemosyne* 24: 11–59.

Hignett, C. (1952). *A History of the Athenian Constitution*. Oxford.

Hillgruber, M. (1988). *Die zehnte Rede des Lysias: Einleitung, Text, und Kommentar mit einem Anhang über die Gesetzinterpretationen bei den attischen Rednern* (= *Untersuchungen zur antiken Literatur und Geschichte*). Berlin.

Hitzig, H. F. (1895). *Das griechische Pfandrecht.* Munich.

Hölkeskamp, K.-J. (1992). "Written law in Archaic Greece," *Proceedings of the Cambridge Philological Society* 38: 87–117.

Hölkeskamp, K.-J. (1999). *Scheidsrichter, Gesetzgeber, und Gesetzgebung im archaischen Griechenland.* Wiesbaden.

Hölkeskamp, K.-J. (2002). "Nomos, Thesmos, und Verwandtes. Vergleichende Überlegungen zur Konzeptualisierung geschriebenen Rechts im klassischen Griechenland," in Cohen (2002): 115–46.

Honoré, A. M. (1961). "Ownership," in Guest (1961): 107–21.

Hornblower, S. (1987). *Thucydides.* Baltimore.

Hornblower, S. (1991). *A Commentary on Thucydides.* Volume I. Oxford.

Hunter, V. (1989). "The Athenian widow and her kin," *Journal of Family History* 14: 291–311.

Hunter, V. J. (1994). *Policing Athens: Social Control in the Attic Lawsuits, 420–320 B.C.* Princeton.

Isager, S. and M. H. Hansen. (1975). *Aspects of Athenian Society in the Fourth Century B.C.* Odense.

Jeffery, L. (1961). *The Local Scripts of Archaic Greece.* Oxford.

Johnstone, S. (2003). "Women, property, and surveillance in Classical Athens," *CA* 22: 247–74.

Jones, A. H. M. (1960). *Athenian Democracy.* Oxford.

Jordan, David R. (2000). "A personal letter found in the Athenian Agora," *Hesperia* 69: 91–103.

Just, R. (1989). *Women in Athenian Law and Life.* London.

Kagan, D. (1982). "The dates of the earliest coins," *AJA* 86: 343–60.

Kagan, D. (1987). *The Fall of the Athenian Empire.* Ithaca.

Kahrstedt, U. (1929). "Demosthenes und die Theorika," *Nachrichten von der Gesellschaft der Wissenschaften und der Georg-Augusts- Universität zu Göttingen* 36: 156–63.

Kallet, L. (1983). "Iphikrates, Timotheos, and Athens, 371–360 B.C.," *GRBS* 24: 239–52.

Kapparis, K. (1996). "Humiliating the adulterer: The law and the practice in Classical Athens," *RIDA*[3] 43: 63–77.

Kapparis, K. A. (1999). *Apollodorus "Against Neaira."* Berlin and New York.

Karapa, (1974). "The Attic Decress from the Epigraphical Museum,"*Arch. Delt.* 29A: 159–63.

Kaser, M. (1944). "Das altgriechische Eigentumsschutz," *ZSS* 64: 134–205.

Kidd, I. G. (1990). "The case of homicide in Plato's *Euthyphro*," in E. M. Craik, ed. *Owls to Athens: Essays on Classical Subjects presented to Sir Kenneth Dover* Oxford: 213–21.

Kilmer, M. (1997). "Rape in early red-figure pottery: Violence and the threat of violence in homoerotic and hetero-erotic contexts," in Deacy and Pierce (1997): 123–41.

Kirchner, J. (1903/1966). Reprint of *Prosopographia Attica.* Berlin.

Klee, K. (1937). "Timotheus," *RE*[2] 6A: 1327.

Knox, B. M. W. (1964). *The Heroic Temper.* Berkeley and Los Angeles.

Koerner, R. (1993). *Inschriftliche Gesetztexte der Frühen Griechischen Polis,* ed. K. Hallof. Cologne, Weimar, and Vienna.

Konstan, D. (1986). "Love in Terence's *Eunuchus*: The origins of erotic subjectivity," *AJP* 107: 369–93.

Kraay, C. M. (1964). "Hoards, small change, and the origin of coinage," *JHS* 84: 76–91.

Kränzlein, A. (1963). *Eigentum und Besitz im griechischen Recht.* Berlin.

Kristensen, K. R. (2004). "Gortynian debt bondage: Some new considerations on IC IV 41 IV–VII, 47 and 72 I.56–II.2, X.25–32," *ZPE* 149: 73–9.

Kroll, J. H. (2000). Review of L. Kurke, *Coins, Bodies, Games and Gold: The Politics of Meaning in Archaic Greece*. *CJ* 96: 85–90.

Kroll, J. H. and N. Waggoner. (1984). "Dating the earliest coins of Athens, Corinth and Aegina," *AJA* 88: 325–40.

Kuenen-Janssens, L. J. (1941). "Some notes on the competence of the Athenian woman to conduct a transaction," *Mnemosyne* 9 (1941): 199–214.

Kunkel, W. (1962). *Untersuchungen zur Entwicklung des römischen Kriminalverfahrens*. Munich.

Kurihara, A. (2003). "Personal enmity as a motivation in forensic speeches," *CQ* 53: 464–77.

Kußmaul, R. (1969). *Synthekai: Beiträge zur Geschichte des attischen Obligationenrechts*. Dissertation. Basel.

Lacey, W. K. C. (1966). "Homeric *Hedna* and Penelope's *Kyrios*," *JHS* 86: 55–68.

Lafont, S. (2000). "Codification et subsidiarité dans les droits du proche-orient," in Lévy (2000): 49–64.

Laiou, A. (1993). *Consent and Coercion to Sex and Marriage in Ancient and Medieval Societies*. Washington, DC.

Lalonde, G. V., M. K. Langdon, and M. B. Walbank (1991). *The Athenian Agora XIX: Inscriptions*. Princeton.

Lambert, S. D. (1993). *The Phratries of Attica*. Ann Arbor.

Lambert, S. D. (1996). "Two notes on Attic Horoi," *ZPE* 110: 77–83.

Lane Fox, R. (1994). "Aeschines and Athenian democracy," in Osborne and Hornblower (1994): 135–57.

Lape, S. (2001). "Democratic ideology and the poetics of rape in Menandrian comedy," *CA* 20.1: 79–119.

Lardinois, A. P. M. H. (forthcoming). "Have we Solon's verses?" in Blok and Lardinois (forthcoming).

Larmour, D. H. J., P. A. Miller, and C. Platter, eds. (1998). *Rethinking Sexuality: Foucault and Classical Antiquity*. Princeton.

Larsen, J. A. O. (1955). "The Boeotian Confederacy," *TAPA* 86: 40–50.

Latte, K. (1968). *Kleine Schriften*. Munich.

Lattimore, S., trans. (1998). *Thucydides: The Peloponnesian War*. Indianapolis.

Lefkowitz, M. (1993). "Seduction and rape in Greek myth," in Laiou (1993): 17–37.

Leisi, E. (1907). *Der Zeuge im attischen Recht*. Frauenfeld.

Lejeune, M. and J. Pouilloux (1988). "Une transaction commerciale ionienne au ve siècle av. n. è. à Pech Maho," *Comptes rendus de l' académie des inscriptions*: 526–36.

Leissner-Jensen, M. (2002). "*Vis comica*: Consummated Rape in Greek and Roman New Comedy" *CIM* 53: 173–96.

Leppin, H. (1999). *Thukydides und die Verfassung der Polis*. Berlin.

Lévy, E. (2000). *La codification des lois dans l'antiquité*. Paris.

Lewis, D. M. (1954). "Notes on Attic inscriptions," *BSA* 49: 17–20.

Lewis, D. M. (1988). "The Archon Charikles," *Horos* 6: 19–20.

Lewis, D. M. (1990). Review of Carey and Reid (1986). *CR* 40: 358.

Lewis, D. M. (1997). *Selected Papers in Greek and Near Eastern History*. Cambridge.

Lewis, N. (1945). "The meaning of σὺν ἡμιολίᾳ and kindred expressions in loan contracts," *TAPA* 76: 126–39.
Linders, T. (1974). *Studies in the Treasure Records of Artemis Brauronia found in Athens.* Meisenheim am Glan.
Lipsius, J. H. (1905–15). *Das attische Recht und Rechtsverfahren.* Leipzig.
Lloyd, A. B. (1988). "Herodotus' account of Pharaonic history," *Historia* 37: 22–53.
Lohmann, H. (1993). *Atene. Forschungen zur Siedlungs- und Wirtschaftsstruktur des klassischen Attika.* Two volumes. Cologne.
Loomis, W. T. (1998). *Wages, Welfare Costs, and Inflation in Classical Athens.* Ann Arbor.
Loraux, N. (1986). *The Invention of Athens.* Cambridge, MA.
Lowe, J. C. B. (1983). "The *Eunuchus*: Terence and Menander," *CQ* 33: 428–44.
Ludwig, W. (1959). "Von Terenz zu Menander," *Philologus* 103: 1–38.
Lyons, J. (1977). *Semantics.* Two volumes. Cambridge.
MacCormack, G. (1973). "The lex Poetilia," *Labeo* 19: 306ff.
MacDowell, D. M. (1963). *Athenian Homicide Law in the Age of the Orators.* Manchester.
MacDowell, D. M. (1971). *Aristophanes' Wasps.* Oxford.
MacDowell, D. M. (1976a). "*Hybris* in Athens," *G&R* 23: 14–30.
MacDowell, D. M. (1976b). "Bastards as Athenian citizens," *CQ* 26: 88–91.
MacDowell, D. M. (1978). *The Law in Classical Athens.* London.
MacDowell, D. M. (1982). "Love versus the law: An essay on Menander's *Aspis*," *G&R* 29: 42–52.
MacDowell, D. M. (1985). Review of Cohen (1983). *CR* 35: 230.
MacDowell, D. M. (1986). *Spartan Law.* Edinburgh.
MacDowell, D. M. (1989a). "The *Oikos* in Athenian Law," *CQ* 39: 10–21.
MacDowell, D. M. (1989b). "Athenian laws about choruses," in Nieto (1989): 10–31.
MacDowell, D. M. (1989c). "The authenticity of Demosthenes 29 (Against Aphobos III) as a source of information about Athenian Law," in Thür (1989): 253–62.
MacDowell, D. M. (1990). *Demosthenes: Against Meidias.* Oxford.
MacDowell, D. M. (1991). "The Athenian procedure of phasis," in Gagarin (1991): 187–98.
MacDowell, D. M. (2000). *Demosthenes: On the False Embassy (Oration 19).* Oxford.
Maffi, A. (1983). *Studi di epigraphia giuridica.* Milan.
Maffi, A. (1993). "Chronique." *RHDFE* 71: 425–53.
Maffi, A. (1999). "Emprisonnement pour dettes dans le monde grec," in Bertrand-Dagenbach, Chauvot, Matter, and Salamito (1999): 7–18.
Maffi, A. (2002). "Studi recenti sulla Grande Rhetra," *DIKE* 5 (2002): 195–236.
Maier, G. (1969). *Eranos als Kreditinstitut.* Dissertation. Erlangen.
Maine, H. S. (1861/1986). Reprint of *Ancient Law.* London.
Manigk, A. (1914). Review of Pappulias (1909). *Berliner philologische Wochenschrift* 34: 205–13.
Manigk, A. (1916). "Hyperocha," *RE* 9: cols 292–321.
Manuwald, B. (1995). "Zur rechtlichen Problematik von Antiphon, or. 5," *RhM* 138: 41–59.
Marchant, E. C. (1891/1966). Reprint of *Thucydides, Book II.* London.
Martin, R. H., ed. (1976). *Terence: Adelphoe.* Cambridge.
McCabe, D. F. (1981). *The Prose Rhythm of Demosthenes.* New York.
Meier, C. (1990). *The Greek Discovery of Politics.* Trans. D. McLintock. Cambridge, MA.

Meiggs, R. and D. Lewis (1969). *A Selection of Greek Historical Inscriptions.* Oxford.

Meikle, S. (1978). "Aristotle and the political economy of the *polis,*" *JHS* 98: 57–73.

Meritt, B. D. (1961). *The Athenian Year.* Berkeley and Los Angeles.

Meritt, B. D. (1977). "Athenian archons 347/6–48/7 B.C.," *Historia* 26: 161–91.

Meyer, E. (1899). *Forschungen zur alten Geschichte.* Vol. 2. Halle.

Meyer-Laurin, H. (1965). *Gesetz und Billigkeit im attischen Prozeß.* Weimar.

Migeotte, L. (2002). *L'économie des cites grecques de l'archaîsme au Haut-Empire romain.* Paris.

Migeotte, L. (2005). "Les pouvoirs des agoranomes dans les cités grecques," in Gagarin and Wallace (2005): 287–301.

Mikalson, J (1975). *The Sacred and Civil Calendar of the Athenian Year.* Princeton.

Miller, I. (1990). *Bloodtaking and Peacemaking: Feud, Law, and Society in Saga Iceland.* Chicago and London.

Millett, P. C. (1983). "Maritime loans and the structure of credit in fourth-century Athens," in Garnsey, Hopkins, and Whittaker (1983): 36–52.

Millett, P. C. (1990). "Sale, credit, and exchange in Athenian law and society," in Cartledge, Millett, and Todd (1990): 167–94.

Millett, P. C. (1991). *Lending and Borrowing in Ancient Athens.* Cambridge.

Milns, R. D. (1989). "Hermias of Atarneus and the Fourth Philippic," in *Filologia e Forme letterarie: Studi offerti a Francesco della Corte. Urbino:* 285–95.

Mirhady, D. (1991). "The oath-challenge in Athens," *CQ* 41: 78–83.

Mitchel, F. W. (1962). "Demades of Paiania and *IG* II^2 1493, 1494, 1495," *TAPA* 93: 213–29.

Mitchell, L. and P. J. Rhodes, eds. (1997). *The Development of the Polis in the Archaic Period.* London and New York.

Mitsos, M. Th. (1983). "Une inscription d'Argos," *BCH* 107: 243–49.

Moore, J. M. (1975). *Aristotle and Xenophon on Democracy and Oligarchy.* Berkeley and Los Angeles.

Morris, I. (1986). "The use and abuse of Homer," *CA* 5: 81–138.

Morris, I. (2002). "Hard surfaces," in Cartledge, Cohen, and Foxhall (2002): 8–43.

Morrow, G. (1939). *Plato's Law of Slavery and its Relation to Greek Law.* Urbana, IL.

Mülke, C. (2002). *Solons politische Elegien und Iamben (Fr. 1–13; 32–7 West): Einleitung, Text, Übersetzung, Kommentar.* Munich.

Müller, G. (1967). *Sophokles Antigone.* Heidelberg.

Murray, A. T. (1939). *Demosthenes V: Private Orations.* Cambridge, MA.

Nader, L. and H. F. Todd (1978). *The Disputing Process: Law in Ten Societies.* New York.

Naiden, F. (2004). "Supplication and the law," in Harris and Rubinstein (2004): 71–91.

Nenci, G. and G. Thür, eds. (1990). *Symposion 1988. Vorträge zur griechischen und hellenistischen Rechtsgeschichte.* Cologne and Vienna.

Nicholas, B. (1962). *An Introduction to Roman Law.* Oxford.

Nieto, F., ed. (1989). *Symposion 1989: Vorträge zur griechischen und hellenistischen Rechtsgeschichte.* Cologne and Vienna.

Nilsson, M. P. (1955–61). *Geschichte der griechischen Religion^2.* Munich.

Nussbaum, M. (1986). *The Fragility of Goodness.* Cambridge.

Nussbaum, M. C. and J. Sihvola, eds. (2002). *The Sleep of Reason: Erotic Experience and Sexual Ethics in Ancient Greece and Rome.* Chicago and London.

Ober, J. (1989). *Mass and Elite in Democratic Athens.* Princeton.
Ober, J. (forthcoming). "Solon and the *Horoi*: Facts on the ground in Archaic Athens," in Blok and Lardinois (forthcoming).
Ober, J. and C. Hedrick, eds. (1996). *Demokratia: A Conversation on Democracies, Ancient and Modern.* Princeton.
Ogden, D. (1997). "Rape, adultery, and protection of bloodlines in Classical Athens," in Deacy and Pierce (1997): 25–41.
Oliver, J. H. (1935). "Greek inscriptions," *Hesperia* 4: 1–70.
Oliver, J. H. (1955). "Praise of Periclean Athens as a mixed constitution," *RhM* 109: 37–40.
Omitowoju, R. (1997). "Regulating rape: Soap operas and self-interest in the Athenian courts," in Deacy and Pierce (1997): 1–24.
Omitowoju, R. (2002). *Rape and the Politics of Consent in Classical Athens.* Cambridge.
van Oooteghem, J. (1932). "Démosthène et le Théôrikon," *EtCl* 1: 388–407.
Osborne, M. J. (1989). "The chronology of Athens in the mid-third century B.C.," *ZPE* 18: 209–42.
Osborne, R. G. (1985). "Law in action in Classical Athens," *JHS* 105: 40–58.
Osborne, R. (2000). Review of Stroud (1998). *CR* 50: 172–3.
Osborne, R. and S. Hornblower. (1994). *Ritual, Finance, Politics: Democratic Accounts Presented to David Lewis.* Oxford.
Ostwald, M. (1969). *Nomos and the Beginnings of Athenian Democracy.* Oxford.
Ostwald, M. (1973). "Was there a concept of ἄγραφος νόμος in Classical Greece?" in E. N. Lee, A. P. D. Mourelatos, and R. M. Rorty, eds. *Exegesis and Argument: Studies in Greek Philosophy Presented to Gregory Vlastos.* Assen: 70–104.
Ostwald, M. (1986). *From Popular Sovereignty to the Sovereignty of Law.* Berkeley and Los Angeles.
Oudemans, Th. C. W. and A. P. M. H. Lardinois. (1987). *Tragic Ambiguity: Anthropology, Philosophy, and Sophocles' Antigone.* Leiden.
Paoli, U. E. (1930). *Studi di diritto attico.* Florence.
Paoli, U. E. (1932). "Il processo di Agorato," *RFIC* 10: 289–308.
Paoli, U. E. (1950). "Il reato di adulterio in diritto attico," *Studia et documenta historiae et iuris.* 16: 123–70.
Pappulias, D. P. (1909). Ἡ ἐμπράγματος ἀσφάλεια κατὰ τὸ ἑλληνικὸν καὶ τὸ ῥωμαικὸν νόμον. Leipzig.
Parker, R. (1983). *Miasma: Pollution and Purification in Early Greek Religion.* Oxford.
Parker, R. (1996). *Athenian Religion.* Oxford.
Parker, R. (2004). "What are sacred laws?" in Harris and Rubinstein (2004): 57–70.
Partsch, J. (1909). *Griechische Burgschaftsrecht.* Leipzig and Berlin.
Patterson, O. (1982). *Slavery and Social Death.* Cambridge, MA.
Peçirka, J. (1966). *The Formula for the Grant of Enktesis in Attic Inscriptions.* Prague.
Pelliccia, H. (1991). "Anacreon 13 (358 PMG)," *CP* 86: 35.
Pepe, L. (no date). *Ricerche sul furto nelle XII Tavole e nel diritto attico.* Milan.
Petrakos, P. (1992). "Anaskaphe Rhamnountos (in Modern Greek)," *Praktika tes en Athenais Archaiologikes Hetaireias* 38: 1–31.
Picirilli, L. (1981). "'Nomoi' cantati e 'nomoi' scritti," *Civiltà classica e christiana* 2: 7–11.

Piérart, M. (2000). "Argos. Une autre démocratie," in Flensted-Jensen, Nielsen, Rubinstein (2000): 296–314.
Pierce, K. F. (1997). "The portrayal of rape in New Comedy," in Deacy and Pierce (1997): 163–84.
Pomeroy, S. (1975). *Goddesses, Whores, Wives, and Slaves: Women in Classical Antiquity*. New York.
Porter, R. (1986). "Rape – does it have a historical meaning?" in Tomaselli and Porter (1986): 216–37.
Pospisil, L. (1971). *Anthropology of Law: A Comparative Theory*. New York.
Powell, R. (1959). "*Furtum* by a finder," *Tulane Law Review* 33: 509–24.
Price, M. J. (1976). Review or Weidauer (1975). *NC* 136: 273–5.
Pringsheim, F. (1950). *Greek Law of Sale*. Weimar.
Pringsheim, F. (1953a). "Griechische Kauf-Horoi," in *Festschrift Hans Lewald*. Basel: 143–60.
Pringsheim, F. (1953b). Review of Finley (1952). *Gnomon* 25: 223–31.
Pritchett, W. K. (1952). Review or Fine (1951). *AHR* 38: 338.
Pritchett, W. K. (1985). *The Greek State at War. Part IV*. Berkeley and Los Angeles.
Pritchett, W. K. (1991). *The Greek State at War. Part V*. Berkeley and Los Angeles.
Pritchett, W. K. (2001). *Athenian Calendars and Ekklesias*. Amsterdam.
Pritchett, W. K. and B. D. Meritt. (1940). *The Chronology of Hellenistic Athens*. Cambridge, MA.
Pritchett, W. K. and Neugebauer, O. (1947). *The Calendars of Athens*. Cambridge, MA.
Raaflaub, K. (1985). *Die Entdeckung der Freiheit*. Munich.
Raaflaub, K. (1990). "Perceptions of democracy in fifth-century Athens," in *Aspects of Athenian Democracy* (= *Classica et Mediaevalia Dissertationes* 11). Copenhagen.
Raaflaub, K. A. (1993). "Homer to Solon. The rise of the polis. The written sources," in M. H. Hansen, ed. *The Ancient Greek City State* (= *Historisk-filofiske Meddelelser* 67). Copenhagen.
Raape, L. (1912). *Der Verfall des griechischen Pfandes*. Halle.
Race, W. H. (1982). *The Classical Priamel from Homer to Boethius*. Leiden.
Rackham, H., trans. (1935). *Aristotle: The Athenian Constitution, the Eudemian Ethics, on Virtues and Vices*. Cambridge, MA.
Radt, S., ed. (1977). *Tragicorum Graecorum Fragmenta*. Vol. 4: *Sophocles*. Göttingen.
Randall, J. H. (1953). "The Erectheum workmen," *AJA* 57: 199–210.
Raubitschek, A. E. (1958). "Theophrastus on ostracism," *Classica et Mediaevalia* 19: 79–109.
Rehdantz, M. (1845). *Vitae Chabriae, Iphicratis, Timothei Atheniensium*. Dissertation. Berlin.
Reinach, T. (1877–1919). "Eranos," in C. Daremberg and E. Saglio, eds. *Dictionnaire des antiquités grecques et romaines*. Paris. vol. 2.1: 806.
Reiske, J. J. (1774). *Oratorum Graecorum* X. Leipzig.
Renehan, R. (1976). *Studies in Greek Texts*. Gottingen.
Rheinstein, M. and E. Shils. (1954). *Max Weber on Law and Society*. New York.
Rhodes, P. J. (1972). *The Athenian Boule*. Oxford.
Rhodes, P. J. (1980). "Athenian democracy after 403 B.C.," *CJ* 75: 305–23.
Rhodes, P. J. (1981). *A Commentary on the Aristotelian Athenaion Politeia*. Oxford.
Rhodes, P. J. (1985). "Nomothesia in the fourth-century Athens," *CQ* 35: 55–60.
Rhodes, P. J. (1988a). *Thucydides: History II*. Warminster.
Rhodes, P. J. (1988b). Review of Hansen (1987b). *CR* 38: 310–11.
Rhodes, P. J. (2003). *Ancient Democracy and Modern Ideology*. London.

Rhodes, P. J. (forthcoming). "The reforms of Solon: An optimistic view," in Blok and Lardinois (forthcoming).

Rhodes, P. J. with D. M. Lewis (1997). *The Decrees of the Greek States.* Oxford.

Rhodes, P. J. and R. Osborne (2003). *Greek Historical Inscriptions 404–323 BC.* Oxford.

Richer, N. (1998). *Les éphores: Études sur l'histoire et sur l'image de Sparte (VIIIe–IIIe siècles avant Jésus-Christ).* Paris.

Rihll, T. (1991). "Partners in crime?" *JHS* 111: 100–20.

Robinson, E. S. G. (1951). "The coins from the Ephesian Artemision reconsidered," *JHS* 71: 156–67.

Robinson, R. (1953). *Plato's Earlier Dialectic²*. Oxford.

de Romilly, J. (1962). *Thucydide: La guerre du Péloponèse, Livre II.* Paris.

Rosivach, V. (1998). *When a Young Man Falls in Love: The Sexual Exploitation of Women in New Comedy.* New York.

Roth, M. T. (1995). *Law Collections from Mesopotamia and Asia Minor.* Atlanta, GA.

Roussel, P. (1922). *Isée: Discours.* Paris.

Roussel, P. and M. Launey. (1937). *Inscriptions de Délos.* Paris.

Rowe, G. (2000). "Anti-Isocratean sentiment in Demosthenes' *Against Androtion,*" *Historia* 49: 278–302.

Rubinstein, L. (1993). *Adoption in IV. Century Athens.* Copenhagen.

Rubinstein, L. (1998). "The political perception of the *idiots,*" in Cartledge, Millett, and von Reden (1998): 125–43.

Rubinstein, L. (2000). *Litigation and Cooperation: Supporting Speakers in the Courts of Classical Athens.* Stuttgart.

Rupprecht, H.-A., ed. (forthcoming). *Symposion 2003: Vorträge zur griechischen und hellenistischen Rechtsgeschichte.* Cologne and Vienna.

Ruschenbusch, E. (1966). *SOLONOS NOMOI. Die Fragmente des Solonischen Gesetzwerkes mit einer Text- und Überlieferungsgeschichte.* Weisbaden.

Rusten, J. (1989). *Thucydides: The Peloponnesian War, Book II.* Cambridge.

de Ste. Croix, G. E. M. (1956). "The Constitution of the Five Thousand," *Historia* 5: 1–23.

de Ste. Croix, G. E. M. (1961). "Notes on jurisdiction in the Athenian Empire," *CQ* 11: 94–112, 268–80.

de Ste. Croix, G. E. M. (1964). Review of Buchanan (1962). *CR* 14: 190–2.

de Ste. Croix, G. E. M. (1970). "Some observations on the property rights of Athenian women," *CR* 84 (1970) 273–8.

de Ste. Croix, G. E. M. (1972). *The Origins of the Peloponnesian War.* London.

de Ste. Croix, G. E. M. (1974). "Ancient Greek and Roman maritime loans," in H. Edey and B. S. Yamey, eds. *Essays in Honour of W. T. Baxter.* London.

de Ste. Croix, G. E. M. (1981). *The Class Struggle in the Ancient Greek World.* London.

Salviat, F. and Vatin, C. (1971). *Inscriptions de Grèce centrale.* Paris.

San Nicolò, M. (1913–15). *Agyptisches Vereinswesen zur Zeit der Ptolemaer und Römer* (= *Münchener Beiträge zur Papyrusforschung und antiken Rechtsgeshichte* 2). Munich.

Savalli-Lestrade, I. (1998). *Les philoi royaux dans l'Asie mineure hellénistique.* Paris.

Scafuro, A. (1997). *The Forensic Stage: Settling Disputes in Greco-Roman New Comedy.* Cambridge.

Scafuro, A. (forthcoming). "Identifying Solon's laws," in Blok and Lardinois (forthcoming).

Schaefer, A. (1858). *Demosthenes und seine Zeit: Beilagen.* Leipzig.

Schaefer, A. (1885). *Demosthenes und seine Zeit*². Leipzig.
Schaps, D. (1979). *Economic Rights of Women in Ancient Greece.* Edinburgh.
Schaps, D. (2004). *The Invention of Coinage and the Monetization of Ancient Greece.* Ann Arbor.
Schlatter R., ed. (1975). *Hobbes' Thucydides.* New Brunswick.
Schulz, F. (1951). *Classical Roman Law.* Oxford.
Schwan, W. (1934). "Theorikon," *RE* 5A: 2233–7.
Schwenk, C. (1985). *Athens in the Age of Alexander the Great: The Dated Laws and Decrees of the Lykourgan Era, 338–322 BC.* Chicago.
Seaford, R. (2004). *Money and the Early Greek Mind: Homer, Philosophy, Tragedy.* Cambridge.
Sealey, R. (1957). "On coming of age in Athens," *CR* 71:195–7.
Sealey, R. (1987). *The Athenian Republic: Democracy or Rule of Law?* University Park, PA and London.
Sealey, R. (1994). *The Justice of the Greeks.* Ann Arbor.
Siewert, P. (1977). "The Ephebic Oath in fifth-century Athens," *JHS* 97: 102–11.
Simon, D. (1964). *Studien zur Praxis der Stipulationklausel.* Munich.
Smith, L. P. (1994). "Audience response to rape," *Helios* 21: 21–38.
Smyth, H. W. (1890). *Syntax of the Moods and Tenses of the Greek Verb.* Boston.
Smyth, H. W. (1956). *Greek Grammar.* Rev. by G. Messing. Cambridge, MA.
Sommerstein, A. H. (1998). "Rape and young manhood in Athenian comedy," in Foxhall and Salmon (1998): 100–14.
Sourvinou-Inwood, C. (1989). "Assumptions and the creation of meaning: Reading Sophocles' *Antigone*," *JHS* 109: 134–48.
Sourvinou-Inwood, C. (1990). "What is *polis* religion?" in Murray and Price, eds. *The Greek City.* Oxford: 295–322.
de Souza, P. (1999). *Piracy in the Greco-Roman World.* Cambridge.
Stafford, E. (1997). "Themis: Religion and order in the archaic polis," in Mitchell and Rhodes (1997): 158–67.
Stanley, P. V. (1976). "Ancient Greek market regulations and controls." Dissertation. Berkeley.
Staveley, E. S. (1972). *Greek and Roman Voting and Elections.* London.
Stevenson, G. (1936). "The Constitution of Theramenes," *JHS* 56: 48–57.
Stockton, D. (1990). *The Classical Athenian Democracy.* Oxford.
Stroud, R. S. (1998). *The Athenian Grain-Tax Law of 374/3 B.C.* (= *Hesperia* Supplement 29). Princeton.
Szanto, E. (1897). "Hypothek und Scheinkauf im griechischem Recht," *Wiener Studien* 9: 279–96.
Szegedy-Maszak, A. (1978). "Legends of the Greek lawgivers," *GRBS* 19: 199–209.
Taubenschlag, R. (1944). *The Law of Greco-Roman Egypt in the Light of the Papryi.* New York.
Thomas, R. (1994). "Law and the lawgiver in the Athenian democracy," in R. Osborne and S. Hornblower, eds. *Ritual, Finance, Politics: Athenian Democratic Accounts Presented to David Lewis.* Oxford: 9–31.
Thomas, R. (1996). "Written in stone? Liberty, equality, orality and the codification of law," in Foxhall and Lewis (1996): 19–31.
Thompson, W. E. (1974). "*Tot Atheniensibus idem nomen erat*," in Bradeen and MacGregor (1974): 144–9.
Thompson, W. E. (1982). "The Athenian entrepreneur," *AC* 51: 53–85.
Thompson, W. E. (1987). "The commercial dispute at D. 52.20," *AJP* 108: 600–2.
Thorne, Samuel. E., trans. and ed. (1968). *Bracton on the Laws and Customs of England.* Cambridge, MA.

Threatte, L. (1980). *The Grammar of Attic Inscriptions 1: Phonology*. Berlin.
Thür, G. (1977). *Beweisführung vor Schwurgerichtshöfen Athens: Die Proklesis zur Basanos*. Vienna.
Thür, G., ed. (1989). *Symposion 1985: Vorträge zur griechischen und hellenistischen Rechtsgeschichte*. Cologne and Vienna.
Thür, G. (1991). "The jurisdiction of the Areopagos in homicide cases," in Gagarin (1991): 53–72.
Thür, G., ed. (1994). *Symposion 1993: Vorträge zur griechischen und hellenistischen Rechtsgeschichte*. Cologne, Weimar, and Vienna: 129–46.
Tod, M. N. (1948). *A Selection of Greek Historical Inscriptions II: From 403 to 323 BC*^{2}.Oxford.
Todd, S. C. (1993). *The Shape of Athenian Law*. Oxford.
Todd, S. C. and P. C. Millett. (1990). "Law, society, and Athens," in Cartledge, Millett, and Todd (1990): 1–18.
Tomaselli, S. and R. Porter, eds. (1986). *Rape*. Oxford.
Tracy, S. V. (1978). "Five letter-cutters of Hellenistic Athens," *Hesperia* 57: 244–68.
Tracy, S. V. (1984). "The date of the Athenian Archon Achaios," *American Journal of Ancient History* 9: 43–7.
Trevett, J. C. (1991). "The date of [Demosthenes] 49: A re-examination," *Phoenix* 45: 21–7.
Trevett, J. (1992). *Apollodorus the Son of Pasion*. Oxford.
Tulin, A. (1996). *Dike Phonou: The Right of Prosecution and Attic Homicide Procedure*. Stuttgart and Leipzig.
van Effenterre, H. and F. Ruzé. (1994–95). *Nomima: Recueil d'inscriptions politiques et juridiques de l'archaisme grec*. Paris and Rome. (= *Nomima* I and *Nomima* II).
van Ooteghem, J. (1932). "Démosthène et le Théôrikon," *EtCl* 1: 388–407.
Vélissaropoulos, J. (1980). *Les nauclères grecs. Recherches sur les institutions maritime en Grèce et dans l'Orient hellenisé*. Geneva.
Vélissaropoulos, J. (1994). "Altgriechische πίστις und Vertrauenshaftung," in Thür (1994): 185–90.
Vérilhac, A.-M., and C. Vial. (1998). *Le marriage grec du vi^e siècle av. J.-C. à l'époque d'Auguste*. Paris.
Vince, J. H. (1930). *Demosthenes*. Cambridge, MA.
de Visscher, F. (1931). *Études de droit romain*. Paris.
Vlastos, G. (1964). "Isonomia Politike," in J. Mau and E. G. Schmidt, eds. *Isonomia: Studien zur Gleichheitsvorstellung im griechischen Denken*. Berlin.
Vlastos, G. (1973). *Platonic Studies*. Princeton.
Vondeling, J. (1961). *Eranos*. Dissertation. Groningen.
Vretska, H. (1966). "Pericles und die Herrschaft des Würdigsten," *RhM* 109: 108–20.
Wallace, R. W. (1987). "The origin of electrum coinage," *AJA* 91: 385–97.
Wallace, R. W. (1989). *The Areopagos Council, to 307 B.C.* Baltimore and London.
Wallace, R. W. (1991). "Response to Gerhard Thür," in Gagarin (1991): 73–9.
Wallace, R. W. (1998). "Unconvicted or potential 'Atimoi' in Ancient Athens," *DIKE* 1: 63–78.
Wallace, R. W. (forthcoming). "The penalties for frivolous prosecution," in Rupprecht (forthcoming).
Wallace, R. W. and E. M. Harris., eds. (1996). *Transitions to Empire: Essays in Greco-Roman History, 360–146 B.C. in Honor of E. Badian*. Norman, OK and London.
Wankel, H. (1976). *Demosthenes: Rede für Ktesiphon über den Kranz*. Heidelberg.
Warner, R. (1954/1982). Reprint of *Thucydides: History of the Peloponnesian War*. London.
Watkins, C. (1967). "An Indo-European construction in Greek and Latin," *HSCP* 71: 115–19.

Watson, A. (1975). *Rome of the XII Tables: Persons and Property*. Princeton.

Weber, M. (1947). *The Theory of Social and Economic Organization*. Trans. A. M. Henderson and T. Parsons. New York.

Weidauer, L. (1975). *Probleme der frühen Elektronprägung*. Freiburg.

Westbrooke, R. (1989). "Restrictions on alienation of property in Early Roman Law," in P. Birks, ed. *New Perspectives in the Roman Law of Property: Essays for Barry Nicholas*. Oxford: 207–13.

Westbrook, R. (1995). "Slave and master in Ancient Near Eastern law," *Chicago Kent Law Review* 70.4: 1631–76.

Westbrook, R. (2000). "Codification and canonization," in Lévy (2000): 33–47.

Westbrook, R., ed. (2003). *A History of Near Eastern Law*. Leiden.

Westermann, W. L. (1955). *The Slave Systems of Greek and Roman Antiquity*. Philadephia.

Whitehead, D. (1977). *The Ideology of the Athenian Metic* (= *Proceedings of the Cambridge Philological Society* Suppl. vol. 4). Cambridge.

Whitehead, D. (1986). *The Demes of Attica*. Princeton.

Whitman, C. H. (1951). *Sophocles: A Study in Heroic Humanism*. Cambridge, MA.

Wilamowitz-Möllendorf, U. (1893). *Aristoteles und Athen*. Berlin.

Wilhelm, A. (1914). "Demosthenes und die Theorika," *Mitteilungen des deutschen archaeologischen Instituts. Athenische Abteilung* 39: 156–63.

Willetts, R. F. (1967). *The Lawcode of Gortyn*. Berlin.

Willi, A. (2003). *The Languages of Aristophanes: Aspects of Linguistic Variation in Classical Attic Greek*. Oxford.

Wilson, D. (2002). *Ransom, Revenge, and Heroic Identity*. Cambridge.

Wolf, E. (1952). *Griechisches Rechtsdenken* II: *Rechtsphilosophie und Rechtsdichtung im Zeitalter der Sophistik*. Frankfurt.

Wolff, H. J. (1941). "The praxis-provision in papyri contracts," *TAPA* 72: 418–38.

Wolff, H. J. (1944). "Marriage law and family organization in Ancient Athens," *Traditio* 2: 53–65.

Wolff, H. J. (1954). "Das attische *apotimema*," in *Festschrift für Ernst Rabel*. Tubingen. 2.293–333.

Wolff, H. J. (1957). "Die Grundlagen des griechischen Vertragsrecht," *ZSS* 74: 26–72.

Wolff, H. J. (1966). *Die attische Paragraphe*. Weimar.

Wolff, H. J. (1974). *Opuscula diversa*. Amsterdam.

Wolff, H. J., ed. (1975). *Symposion 1971: Vorträge zur griechischen und hellenistischen Rechtsgeschichte*. Cologne and Vienna.

Wörrle, M. (1964). *Untersuchungen zur Verfassungsgeschichte von Argos im 5. Jahrhundert vor Christus*. Dissertation. Erlangen-Nürnberg.

Worthington, I. (1992). *A Historical Commentary on Dinarchus: Rhetoric and Conspiracy in Later Fourth-Century Athens*. Ann Arbor.

Worthington, I. (1994). *Persuasion: Greek Rhetoric in Action*. London and New York.

Wycherley, R. E. (1957). *The Athenian Agora III: Literary and Epigraphical Testimonia*. Princeton.

Wyse, W. (1904/1979). Reprint of *The Speeches of Isaeus*. New York.

Youni, M. (1996). "À propos de quatre inscriptions olynthiennes," *Tekmeria* 2: 135–53.

Ziolkowski, J. E. (1981). *Thucydides and the Tradition of Funeral Speeches at Athens*. New York.

de Zulueta, F. (1953). *The Institutes of Gaius* II. Oxford.

Index Locorum

Inscriptions and Papyri

Subject Index